Marketing Management and the Decision Sciences:

Theory and Applications

Contributors

Lee Adler
Harry Allison
Melvin Anshen
Richard H. Brien
Simon Broadbent
John J. Cardwell
Gwyn Collins
Donald F. Cox
William R. Darden
Ralph L. Day
James F. Engel
Peter T. FitzRoy
Ronald E. Frank
Robert E. Good
Paul E. Green
Michael H. Halbert
Virgil E. Harder
J. L. Heskett
Charles L. Hinkle

Ronald A. Howard
James N. Kennedy
Philip Kotler
Alfred A. Kuehn
Jack B. Landis
Frank R. Lindell
Bruce Mallen
William F. Massy
Belden Menkus
Gordon E. Miracle
Harry V. Roberts
Thomas S. Robertson
Donald P. Robin
Patrick J. Robinson
James E. Stafford
Jean Stoetzel
Arleigh W. Walker
Martin R. Warshaw
Frederick E. Webster, Jr.

Harold Weitz

Marketing Management and the Decision Sciences:
Theory and Applications

WILLIAM R. DARDEN
The University of Georgia

RUDOLPH P. LAMONE
The University of Maryland

ALLYN AND BACON
BOSTON

To Donna and Linda—

Truly the decision makers and driving forces.

Contents

Preface

Like the pilot who "flies by the seat of his pants," the marketing executive frequently finds that his problems are ill-structured and that his decisions are too often based on intuition and experience. Yet the aviators of yesterday have found that technology and knowledge have changed the environment for flying: Instrumentation, flight control, and other factors have both increased the knowledge and sophistication required of the pilot and, at the same time, decreased the role of experience and intuition allowed. Similarly, the marketing manager who plans and makes decisions solely on the basis of experience and spur-of-the-moment intuitions may become the last relic of a bygone era or management.

The above analogy provides an insight into the present paradox of marketers. On the one hand, the complexities of segmented markets, conglomerate business organizations, governmental restrictions, technical and psychological product requirements, and large-scale competition provide an environment which is both confusing and frustrating. On the other hand, marketers are hearing about an increasing array of tools, techniques, and quantitative approaches which purportedly are "guaranteed" to bring order out of chaos, to provide decision rules (algorithms and heuristics) for problem-solving, and to generate orderly business programming to replace much of the present uncertainty.

This trend toward an increasing emphasis on the scientific approach to management problems goes under a number of names—operations research, management science, systems analysis. Since all these disciplines are concerned with the very core of a manager's job—decision-making—we may refer to them collectively as the *decision sciences*. Today's marketing executive, if only in self-defense, must have some basic understanding of the capabilities and limitations of the decision sciences in order to aid him in seeking out not only solutions to new problems, but also new and refined solutions to old problems.

This book is designed to introduce classes in marketing to readings in the theory and applications of the decision sciences to marketing. The reader, whether an executive or an undergraduate, is exposed to

operations research in marketing, marketing systems, decision techniques in marketing, statistical tools useful for market research, the applications of marketing games, and the promise of the computer in marketing.

The purpose of this book is in part to close the gap between analyst and marketing manager. It attempts to describe the decision sciences —what they are, how they are used, where they have been applied, and the problems of acceptance and implementation both now and in the future. While some overlapping of content in the readings is expected, it should be helpful in reinforcing central concepts as well as presenting them in another advantageous perspective.

The editors feel that the decision sciences have much to offer the field of marketing. It is hoped that this book of readings will help to propagate many of the worthwhile ideas developed by leading scholars and practitioners of marketing. The editors would also like to extend their thanks to those authors who have agreed to the reprinting of their works in this book. Specific credits appear with the articles.

WILLIAM R. DARDEN
RUDOLPH P. LAMONE

PART I | Content and Scope of the Decision Sciences in Marketing

In recent years, managers have made some strides in the application of the decision sciences to marketing problems. Linear programming has helped in the location of plants and warehouses; it has also been successfully used to allocate the advertising budget optimally among media. Simulation, with the help of the computer, is successfully attacking a wide array of marketing problems, ranging from industry-wide demand simulation to determining the optimum number of cash registers within a supermarket.

The role of the new systems philosophy in marketing has not been completely settled. However, flows of information, materials, and energy (both human and otherwise) are being arranged into *pervasive systems* for planning and control purposes.

Functional systems (such as advertising, sales, etc.) are described as having specific goals and having some elements in common with information, materials (products), and energy systems. The goal of systems analysis is to define the system in terms of the problem to be solved, making sure that all interactive elements of importance to the solution of the problem are contained within the new system. The objective of such analysis is always the optimization of the goals of the firm. To accomplish this goal, marketing management has to consider its interface with the other functional areas of the enterprise (such as production and purchasing) and its interface with its external environment (consumers, government, etc.).

Management Science and Marketing

> *Every great scientific truth goes through three*
> *stages. First people say it conflicts with the Bible.*
> *Next, they say it has been discovered before.*
> *Lastly, they say they have always believed it.*
> *—Louis Agassiz*

> *Science is not a sacred cow. Science is a horse.*
> *Don't worship it. Feed it.*
> *—Aubrey Eben*

In "Marketing and Management Science—A Marriage on the Rocks?"
John J. Cardwell suggests that "marketing applications of management sciences are an evolutionary development rather than a radical
new departure." Melvin Anshen agrees with Cardwell in "Management Science: Status and Prospects;" he goes on to point out the
many reasons for this "lag" in the adoption of scientific methods in
marketing. Anshen emphasizes that the area of "Marketing Costs"
employs the tenets of management science to a greater degree than
any other marketing area; here measurement is possible and management control standards can be imposed with some success.

Philip Kotler reviews the current use of operations research to
solve marketing problems in industry. He shows that business has
substantially accepted formal methods of decision making in such
areas as transportation, plant and warehouse location, production
scheduling, and inventory control.

Management Science in Marketing: Status and Prospects

Melvin Anshen

BACKGROUND

The practice of administration in marketing has been handicapped by a type of cultural lag. In every phase of marketing operations the application of systematic methodology to the management task has trailed by approximately one generation the experience in the field of production. Recognition of the causes of this lag helps to explain the current state of management science in marketing and will contribute to an understanding of future prospects and opportunities. This understanding has relevance for advances in the science and its application, on one hand, and in management's willingness and ability to use a scientific approach to making marketing decisions, on the other.

The existence and dimensions of the relatively backward state of management science in marketing were clearly delineated in the first issue of the Institute's journal. In the Smiddy-Naum paper, "Evolution of a 'Science of Managing' in America," with one minor exception the pattern of historical development of a scientific approach was documented by either (1) progress specifically grounded in production experience and applications, or (2) advances in general administrative practices with a strong orientation toward production. The work of Taylor and his associates began with the machine and the workflow. The Gilbreths were also production-based in their studies of combinations of worker skills and machine operations. Progress in the construction of an organized methodology of management tech-

Reprinted with permission from *Management Science,* vol. 2, no. 3 (April, 1956), pp. 222–231.

I wish to acknowledge the stimulation provided by the constructive criticism of Professor W. W. Cooper of Carnegie Institute of Technology. The opinions and conclusions expressed in this paper are my responsibility, however.

niques and in the generalization of conclusions from observation and experiment in the decades between the two great wars was generally oriented in the factory or used the production process as a take-off point for reaching the general management level. Only in recent years have the tasks of marketing management been approached with the tools of a systematic methodology.

Many of the causes of this historical pattern can be readily identified. The Industrial Revolution was organized around a power-machine-workflow-worker complex. The primary opportunities for realizing its initial potentials were in production where repetitive activities were carried on in concentrated work areas, inviting observation, adaptation, experiment, measurement, and control. A good share of production managers came to their jobs from engineering backgrounds. They were systems-minded, products of a rationalistic philosophy, accustomed to think in terms of predictability, measurement, and control. Moreover, the problems they faced were sufficiently stimulating to provoke an imaginative response.

This intellectual set provided a favorable environment for looking at the tasks of production management in terms of productivity and efficiency, and for assessing performance in terms of (1) physical inputs and outputs, and (2) dollar costs and revenues. As a natural result, the science of cost accounting was developed initially in the production area. The information produced by systematized cost records was a further incentive for rationalizing management. It identified opportunities for improvement of performance, and it yielded more or less precise measures of results. The entire line of development helped to create in recent years a favorable environment for the application of more powerful tools of analysis, drawn principally from mathematics and statistics, leading to a pronounced trend toward rationalizing many types of decision making.

Against this brief over-view, the contrasts in marketing stand out clearly. There has been no revolutionary force in marketing comparable to the introduction of the power-driven machine in production. Many marketing activities are carried on over extended geographic areas. They lack the simple repetitive characteristics of factory production. They are not easily measured and controlled. To a much greater extent than in production they involve people dealing with people (and it is worth reminding ourselves that even the more limited human element in production has been a continually frustrating factor for management). The managers of marketing activities generally have not come to their assignments from educational and business experiences of an engineering rationalistic cast. One domi-

nant influence in the marketing process—the consumer—is outside of management's direct control and is only partially, and until now usually unpredictably, susceptible to manipulation and influence. Cost accounting was not introduced into marketing at an early stage. When it did begin to make its way it encountered serious application difficulties because of (1) nonstandardization of operations, and (2) the presence of overhead and joint costs to a degree seldom discovered in production situations. Finally, the influence of the salesman and the possibility of escaping from profit-squeeze situations by price manipulation and product differentiation have tended to divert attention from efforts to improve management's performance by the development and application of systematic methodology to decision making.

STATUS

The status of scientifically-determined management practice is not uniform throughout the field of marketing. It will be useful, therefore, to consider individually the more important operating and functional areas. For purposes of this review, the range can be surveyed from what is generally regarded as the most advanced sector—marketing research (conceived as focusing on problems of market measurement) —through marketing costs and price policies to the relatively backward area of sales promotion programs, still largely dominated by cut-and-try and inspiration.

Throughout this discussion the concept of "management science" or "scientifically determined management practice" will be treated without definitional rigor. At the current stage of management practice in marketing little is gained from precise conceptual demarcation. The frame of reference adopted here is simple and broad: what progress has been made toward defining and applying a methodological approach to management problems, thereby laying a foundation for (1) defining alternative management strategies; (2) formulating techniques for maximizing and minimizing, or optimum seeking; and (3) controlled experimentation leading to generalization and predictability?

Marketing Research

Scientific management in marketing is most advanced in marketing research—the description and measurement of markets for products and services. The advanced status can be identified in (1) the method-

ology of research, both quantitative and qualitative; and (2) the use of research findings in management decision making. The state of current achievement is impressive when one recognizes that marketing research as an organized activity is not more than forty-five years old and that the first year for which we possess a Census of Distribution is 1929.

The field has recognizable sub-categories with different achievement indices.

(1) *Generalized fact collection.* This area is bulwarked by the activities of the federal government, but is supported also by research programs of state and local governments, trade associations, foundations, educational institutions, and a number of private companies (notably in the publishing and advertising industries). In retail distribution there is a well-developed institutional taxonomy: types of business firms, volume of business (including historical trends and market shares), operating costs, productivity. Wholesale distribution has not attained the same descriptive status, while manufacturers' marketing operations are largely unknown territory. There is also a growing documentation of product ows [sic]. It is worth observing that in addition to the impressive quantity of data collected, the many deficiencies in quality have been recognized (in scope, purity, and consistency over time) and work is under way to remove them.

As might be expected from the nature of the information yielded by these generalized fact-collecting activities, management uses it less as a direct guide in decision making than to establish benchmarks from which specific market measurements can provide extensions for determining policies and evaluating performance.

Two research opportunities of critical importance can be identified, as well as others somewhat less urgent. The first major opportunity grows out of the time-lags (between the period to which data apply and the date of their publication when they become available as raw material for decision making) that characterize practically all generalized fact-collecting programs. These lags vary from weeks (in the case of some sample-based data on business activity) to years (in the case of the Census of Business). One obvious result is that a substantial proportion of management decisions in marketing is made on the basis of grossly fragmentary or stale information. The quality of decision making could be improved if mathematical and related technicalities could contribute to the development of short-cuts that would sharply reduce time-lags between collection and publication. Somewhat more subtle is the possibility that the availability of current data would invite management's attention to a field for decision making

which is now substantially ignored because market phenomena are not promptly quantified through established reporting channels.

The second major research opportunity is in the improvement and extension of techniques for reporting and interpreting consumer and business plans and expectations. We are on the threshold of discovery with respect to ascertaining consumer purchase plans for durable goods and business investment plans for plant and equipment. Unresolved problems of theory and technique hamper rapid progress and stand as a challenge to management scientists. We need better reporting. We need better understanding of what is reported. We need a more sophisticated grasp of the linkage between plans and actions, including understanding and measurement of the factors that cause changes in plans and expectations.

(2) *Measurement of specific markets.* A large number of complementary techniques have been developed in the last two decades for measuring past and current purchase performance of customers. Some of these proceed from economic aggregates (gross national product, national income, disposable income, etc.) to product markets to brand share-of-market calculations. Others are constructs from single-firm data. Sampling techniques have been applied to the movement of certain classes of merchandise through retail channels (as in the well-established Nielsen surveys of grocery and drug outlets, and, more recently, in efforts to devise comparable methods for some hard goods categories). These produce data on retailers' sales and inventories by time periods, in geographic-area, type-of-store, product-class, and individual-brand detail. Sampling has also been used to explore consumer purchasing, through direct interviews and pantry inventories, relying on both continuous panel and one-time survey groups.

Other aspects of customer behavior related to market activity have been measured: radio and television listening patterns; brand familiarity; advertising readership; institutional attitudes (toward brand names, toward retail stores, toward shopping services).

Management has introduced these data into a broad range of marketing decisions, thereby effecting a partial substitution of scientifically-determined choice of policy and strategy for the improvisation of the business "artist." This gain in the rationality of decision making has been particularly marked in the distribution of consumers' goods, and within this genus, most notably in the species of convenience goods, distinguished for high frequency of purchase at low prices. The range of decisions so influenced includes those dealing with: (1) product policy (introduction, change, and abandonment of products;

packaging innovations; and, to a limited extent, price determination);
(2) channels of distribution; (3) intensity of distribution (number
and types of sales outlets); (4) amount and character of advertising;
(5) composition of the sales promotion "mix" (advertising, sales
efforts directed at dealers, display, etc.); (6) adjustments of sales
promotion efforts to seasonal purchase patterns; and (7) management
of inventory through the distribution stream.

The methodological foundation is strongest in the area related to
the physical distribution of merchandise. It retains weaknesses or
unresolved technological disputes in the exploration of cause-effect
relationships in multi-factored market situations, such as the definition
and prediction of consumers' responses to changes in sales promotion
programs in market settings indeterminately influenced by activities
of competitors. It is least satisfactory, as a basis for management
decision, when applied to non-purchase activities (such as reading
or listening to advertising) in an effort to relate them to either
promotional budgets or sales experience. Individual and social psychology have significant contributions to make in this area.

(3) *Forecasting market potentials.* The greatest interest in recent
market research activity has centered on the problems involved in
forecasting. Techniques of statistical extrapolation have been explored
rather thoroughly, and their inherent deficiencies for other than
steady-state situations are well understood. The experimental frontier
is the introduction of techniques of psychological exploration—the
entry into the foggy world of attitudes, plans, and expectations.
Objective appraisal of the current status of management science in
this area might perhaps conclude that (a) the major possibilities of
achievement have been generally defined, (b) some of the more obvious problems of methodology have been brought to experimental
test, and (c) the ratio of potential to achievement is still very high.
We see the first flow of a fascinating literature touching on such topics
as habit as a governing factor in consumer purchase decisions, the
measurement of attitudes and their influence on purchase patterns, the
time horizons of purchase planning, the relation of purchase plans to
their execution, the influence of expectation on behavior, and others.

The products of statistical extrapolation—including long-range and
mid-range economic forecasting—are an important element in management decision making, particularly in capital budgeting. In the
area of plans, expectations, and attitudes, however, management has
not passed beyond a stage of awareness that a tool is being forged of
great potential significance in the future. In view of the complex
technological difficulties still to be resolved, particularly those in-

volved in time series analysis under relatively uncontrolled conditions, one can assess this management attitude as sound. The time for application is still ahead.

Marketing Costs

Considerable progress toward scientifically-determined management has been made in some parts of the general area staked out by the phrase "marketing costs." It will be useful to consider the extent and significance of the achievement under three headings: (1) cost determination, (2) cost control, and (3) cost as a factor in decision making.

(1) *Cost determination.* All who have wrestled with cost issues recognize that in complex organizations cost determination is never definitive and is always arbitrary. To achieve a reasonable level of descriptive uniformity, a willingness to accept standards is required. There can be no doubt that marketing has lagged behind production on this count. Again in this area, as was noted with respect to the field of institutional taxonomy, the retailing sector has taken the lead. The cooperation of the larger department stores with such academic institutions as the Harvard Business School, as well as with the department store trade group, the National Retail Dry Goods Association, has resulted in a valuable uniform chart of expense accounts and an accumulating historical record of cost performance over an extended period of time. For many specialized types of retailing, trade associations, Dun & Bradstreet, and certain supplying wholesalers and manufacturers have helped to establish a comparable record of considerably shorter duration. For some types of wholesaling—the drug trade is probably the outstanding example—a comparable body of cost data is available. But for distribution by manufacturers, considered as a whole and for individual commodity classes, we have still to accomplish the initial step of securing agreement on (a) a comprehensive range of activities to be included as marketing operations, and (b) a classification of accounts among which costs can be distributed.

(2) *Cost control.* Curiously enough, in view of the retarded stage of development, marketing management, particularly in wholesaling and manufacturing, generally places greater emphasis on cost control than on cost determination (in the sense of agreement on a generally applicable chart of accounts and the collection of consistent cost data over sustained periods of time). As might be anticipated, this attitude often results in a pattern of expense-oriented decisions that are back-

ward- rather than forward-looking, designed rather more to seek the maintenance of existing cost levels than to relate expenses to revenues marginally or as part of comprehensive product distribution plans. An even more critical issue is suggested by the thesis that a servo-mechanism approach—self-influencing correction fluctuating around a predetermined standard—is neither the optimum nor the practical working target. It is more important to develop cost data and to house them within a cost control system that exerts continuing pressure toward lower cost levels than to determine standards that provide base lines from which to measure variances. In the existing circumstances, realistic flexible budgeting procedures are not frequently encountered. Nor are many managements in a position to stipulate levels at which costs shall be controlled that reflect considerations of characteristic performance of standard functions either in the same industry or in distribution generally. The management issues are further complicated by the absence of techniques for measuring the benefits of cost-supported actions. The prime target remains the confrontation of gains and costs at the margin. In this context, perhaps the most devastating criticism of the state of management science in marketing is that administrators are supplied with information on neither marginal costs nor marginal revenues. Finally, the absence of standards as a foundation for controlling and reducing costs creates exceedingly difficult problems in pricing intrafirm transfers of products. Management's control of operations within vertically-integrated business structures can rarely be described as scientifically-determined, as Joel Dean observed in his recent *Harvard Business Review* article ("Decentralization and Intracompany Pricing," July–August, 1955).

(3) *Cost in decision making*. A simple summation of these comments on cost determination and control suggests that marketing management is not in a position to make broad use of cost information for rational decision making. No more striking illustration of the truth of this conclusion, particularly in the administration of manufacturers' marketing activities, can be found than in the recent history of manufacturers' operations under the pricing strictures of the Robinson-Patman Act. The records of Federal Trade Commission investigations of alleged discriminatory pricing practices (among other provisions, the act places on manufacturers the burden of proving that quantity discount schedules can be justified by realized economies in manufacturing and distribution expenses) and informal comments of marketing administrators agree in suggesting the rarity of the company that has established cost data related to scale of operations. Almost equally rare is the seller who has determined and analyzed selling

costs by type of customer, size of order, frequency of sales contact and order placement, and comparable expense-influencing factors. In the absence of this type of cost information, rational selection of customers, management of salesforce activities, and pricing of optional sales services are virtually impossible.

Formulating Price Policies

Many observers of marketing will agree in the judgment that the area of price policy is in a period of transition from limited to extensive reliance on scientifically-determined decision making. The substantial price literature originating in economic theory, coupled with the high visibility of price phenomena and the growing availability of published price data, has encouraged fundamental research. The principal gap—which is now beginning to be bridged—lies between the formulation of internally consistent and logical theory on one side and empirical exploration on the other. The target of research is increased information, not on the shape of the static demand curve of economic theory—a grossly simplified and misleading concept in terms of realistic price-making—but rather of the multi-layered and time-phased demand structure knowledge of which is the essential foundation for dynamic price-making in imperfectly-competitive and uncertain markets. The principal problem is the establishment of statistical control of multiple determinants of demand that obscure systematic analysis of price-sales relationships extending over time.

A variety of techniques have been brought to bear on this central problem: (1) controlled experiment (as in local area testing); (2) determination of buyers' alternate costs (particularly applicable for producers' equipment where engineering estimates of potential savings are feasible); and (3) multiple correlation analysis (applicable where historical records provide a base for studying multi-variable factor relationships over extended time periods). All have clearly-defined fields for relevant application. The principal requirements in the period ahead are an attitude of empiricism on the part of marketing management and, on the part of economic analysts, an imaginative grasp of the practical limitations imposed by market pressures.

Managing Sales Promotion Programs

The backward state of management science in the administration of sales promotion programs is pointedly demonstrated by the fact that nowhere in the literature of marketing can one discover rules of general applicability or a research methodology that will provide

answers to such common questions as the following (which can be visualized as addressed to his sales and advertising managers by the president of a company manufacturing a line of consumers' hard goods sold through wholesale and retail channels):

How much money should we spend on advertising next year?

What is the best division of the total advertising budget among the various available media?

How can we make rational decisions with respect to complementary budgets for advertising and other sales activities in local areas?

The existing array of popular decision rules for setting advertising budgets is self-revealing: (1) a fixed percentage of last year's sales (or this year's sales forecast), the percentage usually determined by historical precedent or industry pattern; (2) a fixed number of dollars per unit sold last year, or forecast to be sold this year; (3) "what we can afford"—which in practice usually turns out to be the fixed-percentage rule modified by recent profit performance and short-term profit forecasts. No marketing manager seriously defends these procedures. There simply is no better practice available.

The underlying cause is no mystery. With the prime exception of organizations that sell direct-by-mail and use no other promotional or distribution channel, and the partial exception of manufacturers of grocery and drug products who purchase sales performance reporting services, manufacturers do not know how to establish direct cause-effect relationships between sales promotion outlays and sales to ultimate consumers. A panoramic variety of measures of indirect relationships are available. These include measures of magazine and newspaper readership of advertising; measures of radio and television audiences; and measures of consumer familiarity with brands, slogans, and copy themes. There is also, of course, the raw information on what was spent and what was sold, with such a gossamer bridge between the two as the interested parties may be willing to construct. But the problems introduced by questions of more or less in total, or alternate allocations of the total among different media, are not answerable through existing methodology.

The over-all effect on the character of decision making is clear. First, past experience exerts a dominating influence on current decisions. There is a tendency to go on doing what has been done as long as the results are generally favorable. Second, in the absence of successful experience there is a disposition to ape the performance of competitors. Third, if neither of these seems to work well, a new advertising agency is engaged. Any management scientist can make his own calculation of the extent to which optimizing is practiced in such a setting.

PROSPECTS AND OPPORTUNITIES

Considered against the background of the progress in management science in the direction of production and in the organization of general management activities, this review of marketing is not an impressive story. But the reverse of the coin is a picture of opportunity. Nor are interest and incentive lacking among executives responsible for distribution. They have two spurs: (1) however imprecise they may be, all measures of marketing costs agree that they represent in the aggregate from fifty to fifty-five percent of total costs paid for commodities by consumers; (2) crude research suggests that "labor" productivity in marketing is low and is not recording gains comparable to those secured in production. The opportunity for scientific management is further increased by the dynamism that has distinguished marketing operations in recent years. Changes in marketing institutions and market structures have occurred at a rate unequalled in earlier periods, and with these changes has come an experimental attitude on the part of management, a disposition to question established practices.

Predicting the specific gains that will be achieved in establishing a scientifically-determined administration of marketing is much more difficult than identifying opportunities. Reference can be made to only a few obvious areas in which the prospects are unusually good for advances in the application of the scientific management way of approaching administrative problems.

We are witnessing an upheaval in marketing structures and institutions. This revolution is most visible to observers in retailing, where it is allied to the development of metropolitan areas, to almost universal ownership of the automobile, to the high cost of personal service, and to increased leisure time, to name only a few of the influences. But it is also occurring deeper in the organization of commodity distribution. Here its effects are being felt, with less spectacular impact so far as the public is concerned, in wholesaling and in manufacturers' sales operations. Channels of distribution, horizontal and vertical integration, product diversification, and linkages of the production-inventory-sales stream are all experiencing dynamic change. The earlier discussion in this paper concludes that many of the elements essential to a rational administration of this change are lacking. There is a challenging opportunity for (1) the definition of costs connected with alternate strategies (including opportunity costs), and (2) the use of cost information in decision making. In this area, merely bringing marketing management to the position

already secured in production management would be a gain of great significance and value.

In the measurement of markets, quantitative techniques have made considerable progress both in theoretical development and in practical application. Study of the motivational foundation of spending patterns (plans, attitudes, expectations) is just getting under way. It needs imaginative interdisciplinary support to establish valid propositions and a theory of influence and prediction. More than parenthetically, it also needs guardians of tact and wisdom to protect this infant sphere of knowledge from premature and uninformed exploitation by advertising executives and sales managers, an unfortunate development that now threatens. Again, the opportunity is substantial for a significant gain in the application of scientific management practices.

The field of sales management viewed in its broadest terms—including the direction of personal sales activities and the integration of advertising with other sales functions—presents a third major opportunity for management science. Primarily what are needed are methods for grappling with multivariable situations as they occur in the world rather than the single-variable methods of classic laboratory science. Hopefully, it should be possible to start with qualitative or rough quantitative approaches and gradually develop tools of greater precision. This suggests the use of mathematical models in both their qualitative and quantitative aspects. Techniques grounded in mathematics, notably including linear programming, search theory, and game theory (particularly non-zero sum multi-person games) have outstanding potential contributions. Marketing budgets involve commitments on too large a scale to permit executives to continue to accept historical patterns in a management world in which rational exploration of alternative strategies and planned optimizing are becoming standard operating procedures. This suggests a potentially welcome cooperative attitude from management. The embryonic studies now in progress and the techniques now being developed may foster still further scientific advances which will lead to a fruitful marriage between practical necessity and opportunity for research.

Marketing and Management Science— A Marriage on the Rocks?

John J. Cardwell

> We have a good-sized OR group, and we've been in computers ever since 1960, so we're certainly not fighting progress. But if you know of anybody who's solved a major marketing problem with operations research or computers, I'd like to hear about it. We never have.

This remark, made recently by the chief executive of a half-billion-dollar packaged goods company, underlines a serious question of many senior executives: Can management sciences be practically and profitably employed in marketing? Many top marketing men are frankly skeptical about the possibilities. They have heard plenty of promises, but except for the area of marketing logistics—inventory control and the like—they have yet to see much in the way of performance.

Their attitude is an understandable one, for marketing success hinges on logistics less often than on the critically important strategic decisions. And here, to date, management sciences have provided little real help.

To explore the reasons for this poor record and possibly to develop some insights of practical value to top management, McKinsey & Company recently undertook a research study into the experiences of fourteen companies, with annual sales ranging from $300 million to more than $2 billion, who were reputedly among the leaders in their efforts to apply the management sciences to marketing.

From extensive interviewing in these highly diverse companies, balanced with analysis of the existing literature, some findings have emerged that have implications for every marketing manager. Most importantly, the evidence makes it clear that no key marketing execu-

Reprinted with permission from the *California Management Review*, vol. X, no. 4 (Summer, 1968), pp. 3–12. Copyright 1968 by the Regents of the University of California.

tive in any sizable company can afford to ignore or belittle the computer's potential—any more than he can afford to take the more overblown claims of management science enthusiasts without a healthy pinch of salt. Our study indicates that management sciences, *realistically applied,* can offer unique, yet economic, solutions to certain kinds of marketing strategy problems.

EVOLUTIONARY PROCESS

Marketing applications of management sciences are an evolutionary development rather than a radical new departure. For at least the past decade, the main thrust of progress in marketing management has been toward fact-founded, research-oriented decision making and the replacement of intuition or "hunch" by a serious effort to quantify marketing variables. First, marketers learned to make heavy use of consumer and market research. Next came computer applications in inventory forecasting and control and other aspects of marketing logistics. In these projects, typically, not marketers, but manufacturing engineers or other staff groups provided the leadership; nonetheless, marketers adapted to the new systems and learned to use them effectively.

Currently, we are witnessing the first, frequently painful, efforts to extend the application of the management sciences to sensitive and critically important issues of marketing strategy. These applications are really at an embryonic stage. No one can predict with assurance what will happen over the next few years. But there is already evidence to suggest that, at least under certain conditions, management sciences can play an important role in planning marketing strategy.

Figure 1   The marketing spectrum

In fact, our study shows that a few companies have already achieved substantial payoffs by applying management sciences to certain problems in these areas.

Before discussing strategic applications further, however, a brief review of some of the more commonplace computer contributions to marketing systems may be useful.

EXAMPLES OF CURRENT ROLE

MANAGEMENT SCIENCES AND MARKETING SYSTEMS. From a managerial point of view, it is useful to view marketing as comprising a spectrum of activities ranging from broad over-all strategic decision making to more or less mechanical administration. By looking at marketing in this way instead of viewing it as a collection of separate functional categories (distribution, advertising, pricing, etc.), one may see the entire function, in all its complexity, as a single orderly decision-making process. (See Fig. 1.)

This concept of a marketing spectrum is helpful in enabling us to position the current role of the management sciences. For it becomes immediately obvious that the principal contribution of management science to date has been made on the mechanical, systems side of marketing, that is, to the activities grouped in Figure 1 under "Administrative Systems" and "Information Systems."

Most of the large and well-regarded companies participating in our study had successfully computerized at least some of these systems (Fig. 2), in some cases with striking success. Consider these two examples:

One company with an immense product line and a total finished goods inventory of over $100 million, characterized by a complex pattern of withdrawals, found that by carefully analyzing fluctuations in inventory levels and reorder times with the aid of management science techniques it could rather easily construct a set of "decision rules" that actually decreased stockouts while significantly lowering the safety stock requirements. It thereby achieved over-all inventory reductions of more than 20 percent, along with improved balance among products and sizes. Assuming it cost only 10 cents to carry each dollar's worth of inventory—including the cost of capital, warehouse overhead, obsolescence, and pilferage—this meant annual savings of more than $2 million.

By improving its sales forecasting methods by the application of management science techniques, another manufacturer sharply reduced outages and achieved tangible improvement in customer service levels and

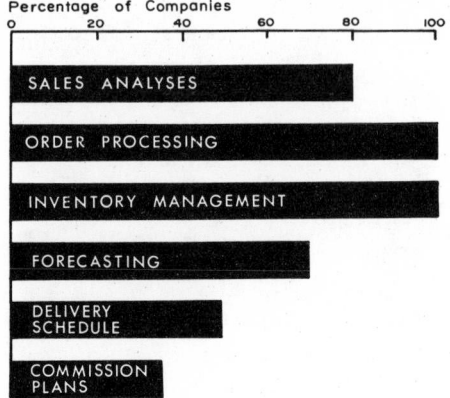

Figure 2   Type and extent of applications in survey companies

sales effectiveness. This company's delivery performance had deteriorated as its sales had grown—a not uncommon problem. Reliability of delivery was far more important to its customers, however, than elapsed time from order to receipt. By applying relatively straightforward statistical analyses, management succeeded in sharpening the reliability of its forecasts. The results: far more accurate production and delivery scheduling.

A CONTINUING TREND

Despite some disappointments and difficulties, therefore, it seems inevitable that more and more companies will seek to apply management science concepts and techniques to a growing range of problems at the systems end of the marketing spectrum. The cost-reduction potential, improved accuracy, and increased machine capabilities all argue strongly for a continuation of the trend. And the techniques, fortunately, are known and tested.

From the viewpoint of the marketing executive, then, it will become increasingly necessary to computerize systems activities in marketing. His competitors have done so or soon will, and his customers will expect it. More immediately, the opportunity to save money is too evident to be ignored.

MARKETING SUCCESS

THE PAYOFF IN MARKETING STRATEGY. Despite the impressive contributions of the management sciences in marketing systems, however, success or failure in the market place is more often determined by

activities at the opposite end of the marketing spectrum. Miles Laboratories, for example, reportedly gives a new advertising campaign—not superior information or administration—most of the credit for the recent increase in Alka-Seltzer's sales volume and market share. Similarly, Pet Milk management is said to believe that Sego's success stems from a strategic decision to distribute mainly through food chains rather than through the traditional drug outlets preferred by its chief competitor. In most businesses, decisions such as these are the key to marketing success and often even to survival, while the downstream systems activities merely determine how efficiently these strategy decisions are carried out.

Why have management science applications in the administrative and informational support systems been so much more successful than applications at the strategy end of the spectrum? The evidence of our study suggests that the answer lies in the nature of the applications themselves—specifically, in the contrasting nature of the inputs, the relationships, and the outputs involved. Let us consider the systems and strategy applications in turn.

SYSTEMS APPLICATIONS

MARKETING SYSTEMS. Systems applications such as inventory control and scheduling of delivery fleets are a direct and logical extension of the traditional engineering-oriented systems from which the management sciences grew. A linear program developed to aid in managing a petroleum refinery, for example, is not really very different from a linear program designed to allocate a delivery truck fleet to best meet customer demands.

More generally, traditional techniques of the management sciences exhibit three key characteristics, all of which are typically present in marketing systems applications:

> *Accurate inputs.* The necessary input data—such as current inventory status, cost of storing inventory, cost of a new order, lead time, and patterns of inventory withdrawals—either are known precisely or can be estimated with a high degree of accuracy.
>
> *Well-defined relationships.* For example, this relationship between a beginning inventory, the rate of inventory withdrawal, and the ending inventory can be precisely stated in mathematical terms.
>
> *A measurable (optimum) end product.* The desired result can also be stated quite specifically. For example, the objective might be least total

cost at some given level of customer service, defined in terms of the number of outages or back orders management regards as tolerable. (The higher the specified customer service level, the higher the required inventory minimum and consequently the cost.)

THE STRATEGIC END

STRATEGIC APPLICATIONS. Problems at the strategic end of the marketing spectrum, however, rarely display these characteristics. Input data—e.g., on competitor promotional plans or consumer buying intentions—are usually imprecise, if they are not missing altogether. Relationships are too numerous or too complex for useful definition; e.g., print media and television are likely to have quite different impacts on sales results in any given market, and the difference cannot be explicitly and exhaustively defined. The end product rarely lends itself to definition in conventional management science terms; for example, how would a grocery executive go about specifying an "optimum" pricing policy? In fact, the whole concept of mathematical optimality seems dubious in the strategy area, precisely because of the nature of the data and the almost overpowering variety and complexity of relationships.

In sum, because strategic marketing problems differ fundamentally from the more traditional problems of marketing operations, management science techniques developed to deal with systems problems are largely inappropriate for marketing strategy.

NEW ORIENTATION NECESSARY

This means that a different approach is necessary. The evidence of our study suggests that the key lies in *substituting a problem orientation for the technique orientation* that has proved so successful in the systems area. Instead of seeking solutions from the application of the techniques at hand, which may not be appropriate to the problem, marketers should start from the nature of the given problem and try to shape the techniques to fit.

One company learned the hard way. Determined to capitalize on the occult computer arts, this company charged its OR staff with developing a workable system for selecting advertising media. The result was a mathematically elegant linear program which, to the best of my knowledge, has never been used. Finding too many holes in

the input assumptions, the product management group refused to even try the new system. Instead of turning immediately to the computer, this company should have allowed its marketing people to analyze the problem and call in computer expertise at their discretion.

Failure to understand and practice this problem orientation largely explains marketing executives' prevailing disenchantment with the management sciences. It lies, I believe, at the root of what are frequently referred to as communications problems, fear of new technology, or the other administrative reasons cited to account for the fact that the management sciences have not yet made substantial inroads into marketing strategy. Some of these administrative problems, of course, are real and pressing. But there are many instances where the "fear of new technology," to take one frequently mentioned difficulty, ought to be interpreted not as an indictment of marketing managers but as an indication of the inadequacy of the technology.

TWO EXAMPLES

A handful of companies have already applied a problem orientation to strategic management science applications with considerable success. I cite two examples from among the fourteen companies surveyed.

The first, a major oil company, is now making far more profitable service station location decisions as a result of a management science application.

The second, a food retailing chain, has built a better image and improved its profits through a new approach to pricing.

Each of these applications had some limitations, but each represented a substantial success. And in each case the key point to that success was the problem orientation.

EXAMPLE: EXPANSION OF RETAIL LOCATIONS. Three years ago a major petroleum refiner and marketer faced a serious problem: A $20 million expenditure on new service station locations wasn't paying off. The new stations were failing at a rate of 15 percent a year; even in the successful units, the gallonage sold was barely at the industry average. Further analysis showed that actual gallonage in the 588 newest units that had been in operation at least a year was averaging only 70 percent of preconstruction estimates, but the discrepancies between estimate and performance varied so widely from

one station to the next that the possible causes could only be guessed at.

THE MOST CRITICAL FACTOR

As almost any gasoline marketer or other retailer will agree, the selection of new sites (i.e., locations for service stations) is the single most critical factor for success in the business. Not only do new stations account for a considerable current cash outlay, but their number and location are the principal determinants of future profits and, often, of future survival. Little wonder, then, that the management of this company was deeply concerned.

Against this background, management launched an intensive study with the single purpose of devising a feasible and practical approach to upgrading the entire expansion effort. Although this project ultimately resulted in a reasonably sophisticated computerized model, the study team's original charter did not even mention the management sciences—the sole objective was to solve a real and immediate business problem. And *the problem was solved*. Today, failures have been reduced to under 3 percent, and the average gallonage sold has doubled.

The study team began by attempting to work out possible correlations between actual gallonage sold and any factor or combination of factors that could be ascertained before purchase of the site. If such correlations could be found, the team reasoned, then future site selection decisions could obviously be built around them.

Two hundred and thirty-nine widely dispersed service stations were used in the analysis. Traffic counts, number of nearby competitors, visibility measures, required land investment, and other conventional measures taken from the company's own "reconnaissance reports" were among the factors considered for possible correlation with gallonage sold.

Surprisingly, no significant relationships were discovered between actual gallonage and any of the factors considered. Except on interstate highways and other major thoroughfares, for example, traffic volume past a site showed little direct relation to gallonage. In fact, all the factors in combination accounted for less than half the variations in volume.

The total impact of all factors on ultimate gallonage varied widely from market to market and from area to area within markets. More-

over, the potential of a given site seemed to depend on whose gas was being sold.

INTENSIVE ANALYSIS

Accordingly, several metropolitan markets were selected for intensive analysis by marketing teams to test the impact of demographic characteristics (e.g., income level and population density) and competitive characteristics (e.g., market share and share of outlets). The most significant of the new factors uncovered by these analyses was the relationship between market share and a unit's gallonage performance.

It would normally be expected that as a company's share of outlets increased, its share of market would increase proportionately (the dotted line in Figure 3). Analysis showed, however, that below a

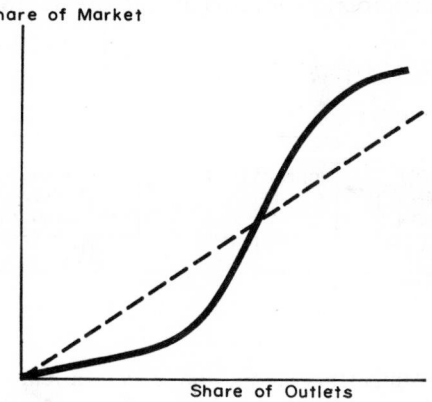

Figure 3   Relationship of outlets to market share

certain share of market, incremental new outlets were substantially below average in gallonage, while above this point their performance rapidly climbed. Above the critical share of market, in effect, each new station located in an area not only added its own volume to the company's total but apparently increased the average of all units in the area as well.

Other factors than market share, of course, must be considered in allocating market expansion money profitably. Such factors include profit contribution per gallon, average investment requirements (involving a series of management assumptions on site availability, costs, available capital, price stability, etc.), assumed growth potential, and

competitors' assumed expansion intentions. These factors were first developed and tabulated in the study to serve as a basis for ranking the attractiveness of each market area. The resulting priority listing, however, failed to take into account many complex interrelationships —for example, what growth rate is adequate to offset a low netback (gross margin for the product, area by area) in a market where the company controls only an 8 percent share? Nor did it suggest the level of investment likely to yield the optimum over-all return on investment in each of the selected expansion areas.

EXPANSION MODEL

Here it was necessary to turn to management sciences to develop a computerized "expansion model" by means of which management could quickly compute and compare all the various alternatives in order to determine the most appropriate investment allocations. (See Fig. 4.)

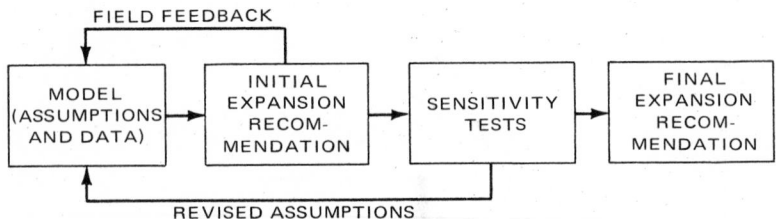

Figure 4   Expansion model

The model incorporates statements about the effect of current market share, netback, and population growth, together with corporate policies on available expansion money and desired return and assumptions about expected volume and costs. These factors are run through the computer to generate an "initial expansion recommendation," which may then be tempered by field feedback on such factors as site availability, as well as by the results of sensitivity testing (determining the responsiveness of the results to changes in any one or a combination of the input factors). From all of this, the computer then generates a "final expansion recommendation." The real value of this model lies in three related capabilities:

1. It allows management to test a wide variety of alternative assumptions and strategies and to approximate the effect of each, before committing funds.

2. Through sensitivity testing it helps management to assess the risks attendant on various expansion alternatives.

3. Recognizing that no mechanical system can cope by itself with the bewildering array of variables in a typical marketing strategy problem, it provides for managerial input at several points along the way.

RESTRUCTURING THE APPROACH

Notable in this success story was the "problem orientation" displayed by management. The marketing vice-president had no preconceptions about the value of the management sciences in his site selection decisions; he was interested only in a workable solution. But when that solution turned out to require mathematical sophistication and computing capacity beyond what a clerical staff could offer, he did not hesitate to add the appropriate skills to his study team.

Even then, however, he and his immediate subordinates stayed with the problem. Together with the technicians, they restructured the traditional approach in three ways:

They used assumptions and probability estimates to allow for imprecise input data and uncertain relationships.

They verified their estimates, where needed, by simulation and experimentation (sensitivity tests).

Instead of "answers" in the form of mathematical optimums, they sought to develop feedback systems that could provide for: manipulation of more data than could have been handled manually; continuous automatic surveillance of results against plan—a kind of mechanical "management by exception" to spotlight potential problems and opportunities more quickly; and storing of "experience" so that each new decision could be as good as the last, or better.

PATTERN REPEATED

Every successful application of the management sciences to marketing strategy analyzed in our study has exhibited this same pattern. Perhaps more important, we have found no practical successes built on the more conventional approach. The problem-oriented approach—simple enough in principle but nonetheless a dramatic departure from traditional practices—can be seen again in the second example.

EXAMPLE: SETTING PRICING POLICY. To maintain its price image and control its margins, a large food chain had to review literally thousands of items almost weekly. Like most of its competitors, this chain was struggling through a difficult profit squeeze, aggravated by customer and government pressures to reduce its "unreasonably high" prices—which routine price surveys of its seven major competitors showed were higher than average.

In the markets it served, however, pricing conditions were chaotic. Arbitrarily assigning an index value of 100 to its own prices, the company found that its competitors' indexes ranged from 98 to 102. However, trying to meet the lowest competitive price on every product would have brought the company's index down to 90—a sure way to go out of business in an already low-margin industry. (The corresponding highest-price index would have been 108).

PRICING CHAOS

How could the company price to ensure an equitable return and at the same time stay competitive? It was clear that prices on 6,500 to 7,000 items would need to be reviewed, and so many supplier cost changes and competitor price changes occurred each week that no manual system could do the job. Obviously, a computer would have to be part of the solution.

The company listed all the factors bearing on price, including manufacturer's cost, direct handling and selling costs, competitor prices, and movement of the product. They then developed a set of rules to govern pricing decisions for each major mechandise category. (For instance: "Nationally branded canned peas must generate a gross profit of 25 percent, provided the resulting retail price does not exceed the local average price of the three lowest competitors.") At the same time, "exception criteria" were specified to guard against undesirable consequences. (For instance: "Single out for judgmental review items on which the machine-computed price reduced movement by 5 percent or more during the previous reporting period.")

EARLY RESULTS PROMISING

The model thus developed proved to be a powerful pricing and management information tool. Each week the computer generates a series of suggested prices and an exception list that is passed to buyers and

merchandisers for review. Product movement, new competitor prices, and supplier cost changes are entered into the system weekly, together with any indicated changes in pricing rules or exception criteria, and the cycle is repeated.

Although this system is too new for conclusive evaluation, the early results have been highly promising. In addition to a mechanism for setting and implementing pricing policy, the system provides a simulation capability for pretesting new pricing strategies, as well as data collection files for evaluating advertisements, promotions, and other price decisions. It constitutes, in short, a highly useful management-oriented (and largely management-defined) information system with considerable potential future expansion in such areas as monitoring performance on features and displays.

CONCLUSIONS AND FORECAST

IMPLICATIONS FOR THE FUTURE. What does all this add up to for marketing executives? Obviously, the management sciences can make a highly profitable and sometimes unique contribution to the solution of certain kinds of marketing strategy problems. Beyond this, as the examples suggest, one condition of success is the active involvement of the marketing executives themselves. In neither of the two cases cited did the management sciences enter into consideration until well along in the process.

In short, the place to start is not with the operations research or computer capability but with business itself: the competitive and economic environment in which it operates, its own strengths and weaknesses, and the opportunities and problems they engender. More specifically, *five management guidelines* can be drawn from our study:

FOCUS ON SPECIFIC KEY MARKETING PROBLEMS, NOT GLOBAL ISSUES OR PURE RESEARCH. Efforts by management scientists in universities (and to a lesser extent in corporations) to construct computer-based "total marketing models" that simulate the entire complex marketing decision process have not yet, to my knowledge, produced very useful results. Unsupported claims for such systems have probably contributed, in fact, to business skepticism about the management sciences in general, particularly in the light of corporate experience with some of these sweeping systems revisions.

Almost five years ago, for example, a large and successful manufacturer embarked on an effort to computerize most of his marketing

process, from order entry to stock replenishment. As management envisioned the system, an order filed by a salesman anywhere in the world would be sourced automatically at the most profitable manufacturing location or warehouse and scheduled for delivery. With each transaction, inventory levels, sales statistics, and accounting records would be automatically updated. Any executive would routinely be able to interrogate the central processing unit and be informed of current sales and profitability by customer and by product, plant operating rates, and so on. Today, more than $2 million down the road, the project has yet to produce a workable set of computer programs to implement this concept. Understandably, the entire management sciences effort is less than well regarded by top management.

For the next several years, it seems clear, the real opportunity for management sciences lies in selective strategic uses, where the nature of the problem dictates the tools to be used.

SEEK OUT RECURRING PROBLEM SITUATIONS, NOT ISOLATED DECISIONS. To date, successful strategic applications of the management sciences have been almost wholly confined to recurrent problems, not one-time decisions such as whether or not to enter a particular business or make a major change in distribution channels. Assumptions, simulation and experimentation, and feedback systems are most appropriate and can offer the most significant improvement over raw judgment where the decision is one that recurs periodically in a reasonably stable environment, so that experience can be accumulated and used to improve future decisions. Food store pricing, for example, exhibits all these characteristics: pricing decisions must be made weekly; they are affected by manufacturer's cost, competitive prices, movement, and the company's own desired "image." All these elements can be stated, measured, programmed, and periodically fed back through the system to update decisions. Advertising spending levels similarly meet most of these tests in a number of businesses. The problem of predicting next year's fashions, on the other hand, meets none of them.

SELECT ONLY AREAS WHERE THE COMPANY IS WILLING TO MAKE AGGRESSIVE CHANGES IN STRATEGY. In both of the successful applications discussed, the company was deliberately acting on its environment, not reacting to it. Successful strategic applications of the management sciences inevitably result in change, extending more often than not beyond the area of immediate application. The service sta-

tion site selection project, for example, changed not only the headquarters budgeting and planning operation but also the jobs of field real estate people, territory managers, and even division managers who had previously been responsible for allocating expansion money.

Such changes are often felt in functional areas outside the marketing organization. They can require modifications in manufacturing practices or financial policy. The problem singled out for study, therefore, ought to be one about which management is actively unhappy and willing to endure the pangs of change in return for a solution.

Precisely because the desired end products cannot be rigidly defined, a considerable measure of risk inevitably attends most new applications. This risk has at least three dimensions: the chance that no adequate technology can be devised for economic solution of the problem; the possibility that sufficiently accurate data cannot be made available at reasonable cost; and the possibility that the solutions, even when they can be economically developed, will not be implemented—perhaps because the price of change is too high.

Even unqualified success, it should be noted, can be uncomfortably long in coming. The site selection model described above, for example, was nearly two years in development. And since some failures—perhaps a good many at first—are bound to be mixed in with the successes, the profit return requirement should probably be set quite high: three or four to one, or even higher, depending on management's own assessment of the likelihood of success.

A corollary point that warrants mention, although its significance is far from clear, is that none of the companies that have had real success in marketing strategy applications of the management sciences is among the generally recognized leaders in American industry. The companies most frequently noted as "most advanced," "best managed," and the like are notably absent from the management sciences honor roll. This is a curious finding, for which we have no ready explanation. The answer may be simply that the leader companies feel they are performing so well that they need not rush into largely uncharted fields. In any event, this finding does tend to underscore the vital importance of an active desire for change.

BE ALERT TO OPPORTUNITIES TO EXPAND AN INITIAL APPLICATION TO BROADER MARKETING USES. The food pricing system described earlier appears to have considerable potential for expansion into a comprehensive marketing data system. Its capacity to remember costs, competitor prices, and movement is now being used in various ways—as a framework for collection of these data on an ongoing

basis, a simulator to evaluate new pricing decision rules and explore alternative promotional and feature policies, a mechanism to ensure that pricing policies are implemented, and a device for the conduct of experiments. In short, the basic system seems capable of performing far more than was realized at first. The same is generally true of other successful applications we have seen.

Although it is too early to generalize very usefully about this feature of successful strategic applications, one clear rule does emerge: *Seek opportunities to install uniform coding and programming standards and to capture available marketing information on a disaggregated basis.*

One fairly large company, generally regarded (with some justice) as a leader in computer technology, recently had to embark on a massive project to accomplish precisely this. The company is multi-divisional, but the product codes vary from division to division, as do customer codes, destination codes, and programming languages. There is even variation of this kind within some of the larger divisions. Thus, for example, computer programs written for inventory management are not compatible with those written for marketing forecasts. The company has spent a considerable amount of money in recent years to collect data. Yet the data collected are, in a very real sense, neither available nor useful except for the special purposes for which they were collected—purposes too often dictated by accountants, not managers.

Evidence indicates, moreover, that many other companies are in much the same predicament. And the problems they confront are far from trivial. In addition to the excessive cost of incompatible data systems, valuable information is frequently lost. Had the project teams in the site selection application or the pricing application been hampered by this problem, it might have taken them another year to accumulate the data and perform the analyses necessary to design and implement the model.

This is not to suggest that every company should immediately start building a massive data bank before reasonably precise uses for the data are known or payoffs have been estimated. But it does suggest the wisdom of making sure that the routine data normally collected are processed and stored in an orderly way, so that they will be available for other uses in the future.

RECOGNIZE THAT MUCH OF THE LEADERSHIP BURDEN WILL INEVITABLY FALL ON MARKETING MEN, NOT MANAGEMENT SCIENTISTS. A few companies have already achieved substantial payoffs by applying

the management sciences to certain problems of marketing strategy. But the methods by which they have achieved success are neither easy nor obvious. They involve a dramatic shift from much of what has gone on in the past. Most importantly, they show that the key to future success lies less with the management scientists than with the marketers. Only marketing executives have the judgment and managerial "feel" necessary to ensure the successful application of computers to marketing. Only they are in a position to focus efforts on the real "make-or-break" payoff opportunities, provide the necessary judgments and market knowledge needed to define the relationships, and make the application work by using and improving it over time.

However, since marketers will need to rely on computer specialists and operations researchers for technical assistance, it makes good sense to begin building management science capabilities into the marketing operation early, even in the absence of specific problems. In the considerable period of mutual education that lies ahead, the management scientist himself can provide useful advice on how his skills can be best employed. But it is marketing men who must supply the real leadership.

One knowledgeable executive summarized the situation, perhaps a little too neatly, by saying: "The computer isn't going to take over marketing; in fact, nothing much is going to happen until marketing men take over the computer." Probably a better answer lies in a cooperative effort between management scientists and marketing personnel. Such a joint effort could lead to an earlier fulfillment of the promise that some of us see in the application of computers to marketing programs.

Operations Research in Marketing

Philip Kotler

Businessmen have readily accepted the increasing formalization of decision making in many business areas: inventory control, production scheduling, warehouse location, transportation routing, and financial planning. The application of higher mathematics to the solution of problems in these areas—often called operations research —is no longer exceptional. In fact, it seems to be the rule.

The same cannot be said for marketing decisions. Over 99% of all marketing decisions in this country are still made on the basis of intuitive judgment unaided by any advanced mathematical analysis.

To many, this seems natural. Marketing decisions are often more complex than decisions in the other areas; the information is never adequate, competition is unfathomable, customers are unpredictable, and the marketing effects typically are lagged and highly conditional. How can operations research make any headway in such a context?

Yet headway is being made. In a relatively few, but determined, companies the time-honored and simple marketing approaches are taking a backseat to more sophisticated patterns for marketing decision making. In these companies, the very complexity of marketing processes is treated as an argument for the development of more, not less, theory and analysis.

For the businessman who has *not* sensed this development, the question is: What is going on? And for the businessman who *has* sensed it, the question is: What is being achieved? In fact, the intent of this article is to answer not just these two broad questions, but four specific queries:

1. What indications are there of mathematical ferment in marketing?
2. What specific practical applications have occurred?

Reprinted with permission from *Harvard Business Review,* vol. 45, no. 1 (January–February, 1967), pp. 30–46. © 1967 by the President and Fellows of Harvard College; all rights reserved.

3. What further developments are on the horizon?
4. What organizational strictures are there in marketing operations research, and what payout can a company expect?

EVIDENCE OF FERMENT

Although business operations research is over 20 years old—dating from some highly successful inventory and production breakthroughs right after World War II—marketing operations research is only a fledgling. The first published marketing decision models appeared in the middle 1950s and were quite primitive. They dealt with such perennial problems as optimal budgeting of advertising, allocation of sales resources, and pricing of products. Each model found its critics who proceeded to offer a more complex treatment; these in turn became the simple models next under attack.

By the early 1960s, some highly original marketing decision models had been developed. And, today, the published literature has grown to include a bibliography listing over 200 marketing articles of a mathematical nature and several collections of readings.[1] A number of journals such as *Management Science, Journal of Marketing Research,* and the *Journal of Advertising Research* increasingly feature sophisticated mathematical marketing articles.

One of the first companies to lay money on the line for extensive research into improved marketing decision models was Du Pont. The company put over $1 million dollars in the hands of a specific group of company operations researchers to discover and quantify how advertising works.[2] Other Du Pont operations researchers made some early applications of modern decision theory to problems in product pricing and new product introduction.

Also making early appearances in marketing operations research were such companies as Scott Paper which conducted sophisticated

[1] Robert D. Buzzell, *A Basic Bibliography on Mathematical Methods in Marketing* (Chicago: American Marketing Association, 1962); *Mathematical Methods and Models in Marketing,* edited by Frank M. Bass, et al. (Homewood, Illinois: Richard D. Irwin, Inc., 1961); *Quantitative Techniques in Marketing Analysis,* edited by Ronald Frank, et al. (Homewood, Illinois: Richard D. Irwin, Inc., 1962); *Marketing and the Computer,* edited by Wroe Alderson and Stanley Shapiro (Englewood Cliffs, New Jersey: Prentice-Hall, Inc., 1962); and *Marketing Models, Quantitative and Behavioral,* edited by Ralph L. Day (Scranton, Pennsylvania: International Textbook Company, 1964).

[2] "A Profit Yardstick for Advertising," *Business Week,* November 22, 1958.

field advertising experiments, and Monsanto which developed a large number of computer programs to help its executives analyze a variety of marketing problems;[3] General Electric which has worked for many years on the construction of simulators of specific markets, and Ford which is carrying out advanced marketing systems analysis through simulation.

These organizations have since been joined in the pursuit of new answers to old marketing riddles by such companies as Pillsbury, Union Carbide, Anheuser-Busch, Lever Brothers, and Westinghouse Electric.

In addition, advertising agencies such as Batten, Barton, Durstine & Osborn and Young & Rubicam have reported the development of sophisticated models in the areas of media selection and new product development.

A variety of other indicators exist to show the ferment in this field. An increasing number of universities are sponsoring special short summer sessions on marketing operations research. Business response has exceeded expectations, and usually the programs have to turn down qualified applicants for lack of space. Marketing teachers themselves are going back to school to learn about these new mathematical techniques and their practical applications.

In still another development, The Diebold Group, Inc. sent out in 1966 an elaborate questionnaire to companies and academics doing marketing operations research in order to find out what is being done. Their summary report indicates among other things that the marketing areas of greatest application (in descending order) seem to be: internal profit analysis, market analysis, competitive strategy, sales effort effectiveness, and pricing. Similarly, the most promising techniques (also in descending order) appear to be: simulation, modeling, Monte Carlo methods, linear programming, and critical path analysis.

SPECIFIC APPLICATIONS

Clearly, this is an area of great ferment. But the question must be asked whether any hardheaded models, patterns, or techniques have actually emerged. Are any executives making their decisions in the light of results from a complicated mathematical marketing model?

[3] William A. Clarke, "Monsanto Chemical Company: A Total Systems Approach to Marketing," in *Total Systems*, edited by Alan D. Meacham and Van B. Thompson (Detroit: American Data Processing, Inc., 1962), pp. 130–142.

The answer is *yes.* Today, after one decade of work in this area, techniques of operations research have scored some successes in marketing. Viable models have been developed and are being used in such marketing decision-making areas as (1) new products, (2) pricing, (3) physical distribution, (4) advertising, and (5) sales force management. Let us look at each of these specific practical applications.

1. New Products

Two different types of evaluation take place in the course of considering a new product. The first, a compatibility evaluation, usually comes before the second, a profit evaluation.

Compatibility evaluation questions whether or not the product proposal is possible and desirable considering the various company objectives and resources. A good product proposal, for example, may have to be stopped or dropped if it is recognized that the company cannot gain access to the needed distribution channels or lacks the financial resources, or that the proposal is incompatible with the company image. Many factors have to be looked at in this connection. The major device for formally considering and weighing these factors was suggested over a decade ago and has been modified several times since then.[4] It consists of listing the important company and marketing factors, assigning weights to reflect their relative importance, and scoring each factor according to the degree to which it is favorable in the total picture. By multiplying the factor scores by the factor weights, a single number is derived which reflects the desirability of developing the product.

If a firm finds it can logically undertake development of a new product in terms of company objectives and resources, it must determine whether it would in fact be worthwhile to do so. The question is answered by a *profit evaluation.*

The earliest profit evaluation model proposed a straightforward break-even analysis of a new product proposal in terms of its total expected sales and costs. Sometimes the payout period was made the deciding factor. More recent models have introduced additional factors, such as product life cycle considerations, cash flow discount-

---

[4] See Charles H. Kline, "The Strategy of Product Policy," *Harvard Business Review,* July–August 1955, pp. 91–100; John T. O'Meara, Jr., "Selecting Profitable Products," *Harvard Business Review,* January–February 1961, pp. 83–89; and Barry Richman, "A Rating Scale for Product Innovation," *Business Horizons,* Summer 1962, pp. 37–42.

ing, sales effect of marketing mix variations, explicit consideration of uncertainty, and so forth. A few of the more recent models are described briefly:

One of the early refinements of profit evaluation was the *future earnings discounting* method outlined by Disman at Abbott Laboratories.[5] This approach is used in a number of companies. Instead of estimating whether the company can expect to sell enough in a reasonably short time to break even, Disman makes a direct calculation of the present value of the project. This involves estimating probable revenues and costs each year from the time of product introduction to some number of years later, the period known as the planning horizon. The expected income stream is discounted at the company's opportunity cost of capital to yield the expected present value (V) of the product proposal at the date of its commercial introduction.

Disman also recommends that this present value be scaled down by the subjective probability (P) of the company's actually achieving technical and commercial success. He calls the result the proposal's maximum economic justification (MEJ = PV), which represents the maximum amount the company is willing to invest in developing the new product. The proposal's MEJ is compared to the estimated development cost (I). A go-decision is indicated whenever MEJ $\geqq$ I. If several product proposals are being compared and not all can be developed, their relative attractiveness is indicated by the ratio MEJ/I.

A different approach to profit evaluation has been developed by BBD&O and is known by the name of DEMON (*DE*cision *M*apping via *O*ptimum Go-No *N*etworks).[6] The model is set up to indicate whether to go national (Go), drop the product (No), or collect further information on the product's chance of success (On). The decision is made on the basis of which alternative promises the highest expected return. When the answer is *On*, the model indicates which particular marketing research study is the best to carry out—that is, best in the sense that it would probably do the most to reduce the uncertainty clouding the *Go-No* alternatives. After this study is made, the results lead to a revision in the proposed marketing strategy, and a new evaluation is then made of the *Go-No-On* alternatives.

This approach requires that top management state its constraints regarding the planning period, payout period, minimal acceptable profit return, profits required to go national, marketing research budget, and the

---

[5] Solomon Disman, "Selecting R & D Projects for Profit," *Chemical Engineering,* December 24, 1962, pp. 87–90.

[6] David B. Learner, "DEMON New Product Planning: A Case History," in *New Directions in Marketing,* edited by Frederick E. Webster, Jr. (Chicago: American Marketing Association, 1965).

degree of confidence needed. Furthermore, management must state its marketing program for introducing the product. The proposed advertising, sales promotion, distribution, and pricing plans are critical in making an estimate of product sales. Given demand, costs, and management objectives and constraints, the model leads to an estimate of the probable return and risk of the commercialization decision and indicates the desirable action.

The model is being used by a number of BBD&O's client companies. One large drug firm found that DEMON recommended a radically different marketing strategy than the intuitive approach to back a new product. The company proceeded to implement the DEMON strategy in one set of matched territories and the intuitive strategy in another. At last report, the DEMON strategy was proving to be the superior approach.

A complex simulation model recently developed by Urban has all the characteristics of previous models plus one additional factor too often omitted: product interdependence.[7] When a new product is related on the demand and/or cost side to other company products, the deciding factor should not be the new product's absolute profits but the differential profits on the whole product line with and without the new product. The estimated profits for the new product must be adjusted downward if it reduces the profits on the company's other products.

Urban's model, which is called SPRINTER (*S*pecification of *PR*ofits with *IN*teraction under *T*rial and *E*rror *R*esponse), specifically incorporates executive estimates of demand and cost interrelationships between the new product and all other products in the line. The model was tested on a new product in a large chemical company with such good results that the company is thinking of implementing SPRINTER on a large scale.

2. Pricing Models

Though there is much talk about the growing role of nonprice factors in the marketing process, pricing remains a very complex issue for many companies. Pricing is a problem when a new product is being introduced, when a price change is contemplated in the face of uncertain customer and competitor reactions, and when a company must react to a competitor who has just changed his price. Pricing is also a problem in industries when companies submit sealed bids for jobs. And it is a problem when the company's product line is characterized by substantial demand and cost interdependencies.

In each of these areas, work is progressing in the development of

---

[7] Glen Lee Urban, *A Quantitative Model of Product Planning with Special Emphasis on Product Interdependence* (an unpublished doctoral dissertation, Northwestern University, 1966).

useful mathematical models. Two examples—the first on price modification and the other on competitive bidding—are cited to illustrate
the practicality of such operations research techniques:

An increasing number of companies are using Bayesian decision theory
for formal analysis of the likely response of customers and competitors to
a contemplated company *price modification* decision. Green recently described a specific application by a large chemical manufacturer.[8] The
company had been selling a plastic substance to industrial users for several years and had captured 40% of that market. Top management
became concerned as to whether or not its current price of $1 per pound
could be maintained much longer because of a developing oversupply.
Management saw that the solution to its problem lay in penetrating a
certain market segment which was closely held by a substitute plastic
product produced by six companies. Therefore, it was decided to evaluate
the following four alternatives: maintaining the price at $1, or reducing
the price to 93¢, 85¢, and 80¢, respectively.

Among the chief uncertainties top management considered were: How
much penetration in the key segment would take place without a price
reduction? How would the six companies producing the substitute plastic
react to each possible price reduction? How much penetration in the key
segment would take place for every possible price reaction by the suppliers of the substitute plastic? How much would penetration into the key
segment speed up penetration in other segments? If the key segment was
not penetrated, what would be the probability that the company's competitors would initiate price reductions soon? What would be the impact
of a price reduction on the decision of existing competitors to expand
their capacity and/or potential competitors to enter the industry?

The data-gathering phase consisted mainly of asking key sales personnel
to place subjective probabilities on the various possible states of the key
uncertainties.

The next step was to estimate the likely payoffs of different courses of
action. A decision tree analysis revealed that there were over 400 possible
outcomes. For this reason, the estimation of expected payoffs was programmed on a computer. The results indicated that in all cases a price
reduction had a higher expected payoff than status quo pricing; in fact, a
price reduction to 80¢ had the highest expected payoff.

Finally, to check the sensitivity of these results to the original assump-

---

[8] See Paul E. Green, "Bayesian Decision Theory in Pricing Strategy," *Journal
of Marketing,* January 1963, pp. 5–14. The Bayesian approach calls for executives to carefully define the company's objective(s), possible alternatives, major
events affecting each alternative, and probabilities of these events. These data
allow a calculation to be made of the expected value of each alternative along
with the value of gathering more information before acting.

tions, the results were recomputed for alternative assumptions on the rate of market growth and on the appropriate cost of capital. It was found that the ranking of the strategies was unaffected by the change in the assumptions.

The theory of *competitive bidding* has received considerable refinement in the hands of applied mathematicians.[9] The objective of a company in a bidding situation is to get the contract, and this means setting a lower price than the competition. The lower the company sets its bid, the lower its potential profits but the higher its probability of getting the contract award. As is readily apparent, the chief hurdle is that of estimating the probability of getting the contract at various bidding levels. This requires estimating the bids of various competitors.

A large drug supply company has developed a method of deriving estimates through a regression analysis of the recent bidding history. While the company's final bid is based on a consideration of many factors, the formal analysis has proved increasingly useful in clarifying the implications of alternative bidding tactics.

3. Physical Distribution

Recently, a number of developments have renewed management's interest in the logistics problems and have led managers to wonder whether they are overlooking many opportunities, not only for cost saving but also for improved demand creation. Among these factors are the rising costs of physical distribution, the importance of service as a competitive marketing weapon, and the characteristic lack of coordination of company physical distribution decisions.

The transportation area has proved one of the ripest for the application of advanced mathematical techniques. One well-publicized early application concerned the mathematical determination of the optimal shipping schedules for the H. J. Heinz Company.[10] Consider:

In 1953 Heinz ketchup was manufactured in 6 plants and distributed from about 70 warehouses that were scattered throughout the country. The company's plant capacity on the West Coast exceeded that region's market requirements, while the reverse was true in the East. Therefore, the total freight bill could not be minimized by simply shipping output

[9] See C. W. Churchman, Russell L. Ackoff, and E. Leonard Arnoff, *Introduction to Operations Research* (New York: John Wiley & Sons, Inc., 1957), pp. 559–573.

[10] See Alexander Henderson and Robert Schlaifer, "Mathematical Programming: Better Information for Better Decision Making," *Harvard Business Review*, May–June 1954, pp. 73–100.

from each plant to the warehouse nearest to it. The problem of finding a shipping schedule to minimize the total freight cost was translated into programming terms, and the computer was able to deliver a better schedule at a faster speed than experienced company personnel could do. Linear programming saved the company thousands of dollars on a single scheduling problem and allowed the company to schedule on a monthly rather than a quarterly basis to take advantage of new information as soon as it became available.

Since the early application of linear programming to the problem of finding the best shipping schedule, the technique has been extended to solve the total system problem of the best warehouse locations, inventory levels, and transportation methods. However, the total system problem is so complex that linear programming is usable only with a great many simplifications. Some investigators have preferred to take the route of modeling the physical distribution problem in all its complexity and trying to find a satisfactory solution through the technique of simulation.[11]

One of the most widely used simulation programs, developed by Shycon and Maffei, is capable of simulating a system of up to 40 warehouses, 4,000 customers, and 10 factories.[12] Another program, developed by Kuehn and Hamburger and employed by a number of large companies, uses a technique midway between mathematical programming and simulation, which is called heuristic programming.[13] In this application, the physical distribution system is modeled flexibly, and certain arbitrary but plausible rules (called heuristics) are introduced to lead to quick and satisfactory solutions. Still another simulation has been reported by a General Electric subsidiary with $50 million in sales.[14] GE found that through simulation it could save $2.9 million a year by some specific changes in its physical distribution system.

Altogether, the value of mathematical analysis in the physical distribution area has been established almost beyond a doubt.

[11] Linear programming, Markov processes, simulation, and other mathematical techniques applicable to marketing operations research are explained and illustrated in my article, "The Use of Mathematical Models in Marketing," *Journal of Marketing,* October 1963, pp. 31–41.

[12] Harvey N. Shycon and Richard M. Maffei, "Simulation: Tool for Better Distribution," *Harvard Business Review,* November–December 1960, pp. 65–75.

[13] Alfred A. Kuehn and Michael J. Hamburger, "A Heuristic Program for Locating Warehouses," *Management Science,* July 1963, pp. 643–666.

[14] "The Case for 90% Satisfaction," *Business Week,* January 14, 1961.

4. Advertising Expenditures

A number of thorny problems confront companies in connection with the wise use of advertising monies. They would like to have better ways to analyze whether they are *spending* too little or too much on advertising; whether they are *timing* their advertising expenditures optimally through the year; whether their agency is choosing the best *media;* and so forth. Some of the recent mathematical work has shed light on these and other important problems in advertising.

One of the earliest and still most interesting *spending level* studies on advertising was developed by Vidale and Wolfe at Arthur D. Little, Inc.[15] These men worked with a number of cases on file and formulated a mathematical model for the effect of advertising on sales. The effect, they discovered, depends heavily on four factors:

1. The level of advertising expenditure.
2. The response constant, which shows how many dollars of sales would be generated per dollar of advertising at a zero sales level.
3. The market saturation level.
4. The sales decay constant, or percentage decline in sales per period that would take place in the absence of advertising.

These factors are related in an equation, and the job facing any particular company is to estimate the parameters (i.e., response constant, saturation level, and sales decay constant) for its brand. Given the parameters, the company can solve the equation for the level of advertising necessary to achieve a particular level of sales or profits. The equation shows that the company wishing to achieve a higher level of sales must spend more on advertising (a) the higher the ratio of the decay constant to the response constant, (b) the higher the absolute level of sales, and (c) the closer sales are to the saturation level.

More elaborate models of the advertising-sales relationship have been developed since then. A model by Kuehn deserves special mention in this connection because it was tested against some actual industry situations and incorporates a more complete set of marketing factors.[16] In Kuehn's model, company sales are a function of:

[15] M. L. Vidale and H. B. Wolfe, "An Operations-Research Study of Sales Response to Advertising," *Operations Research,* June 1957, pp. 370–381.

[16] See Alfred A. Kuehn, "A Model for Budgeting Advertising," in *Mathematical Models and Methods in Marketing,* edited by Frank M. Bass, et al. (Homewood, Illinois: Richard D. Irwin, Inc., 1961), pp. 302–353.

The percentage of customers with brand loyalty and the rate of decay in this brand loyalty.

The percentage of customers not committed to this firm or its main competitors.

The size and rate of growth of the total market.

The relative influence of price and distribution in the marketing process.

The relative influence of the interaction of product characteristics and advertising in the marketing process.

The relative share and effectiveness of the advertising expenditure.

Given the variables and the information required as inputs to this model, it is possible for a company to derive a theoretically optimal advertising expenditure level.

Kuehn's model also permits a determination to be made of the optimal *timing pattern* of advertising expenditures through the year. Given seasonal sales movements, Kuehn shows that the appropriate timing pattern depends on many factors, two important ones of which are the degree of advertising carryover and the amount of habitual brand choice. Thus, under specific assumptions, the only time such expenditures should be varied to coincide in phasing and amplitude with seasonal sales movements is when advertising has no carryover effect and when buyers have no habitual behavior. (If either of these conditions are violated, advertising expenditures should peak before sales peak.) Accordingly, the greater the amount of the advertising carryover effect, the greater the lead time should be; and the smaller the amount of habitual purchasing behavior, the more the advertising curve should vary in amplitude than the sales curve. These and other conclusions were drawn from his elaborate model of the advertising influence process.[17]

A somewhat different approach to the timing question has been developed by Forrester of M.I.T.[18] His technique, called Industrial Dynamics, involves modeling the company and its environment as a closed loop information feedback system. Through the company flow men, material, machines, orders, and information at varying rates guided by decisions on objectives and current information as to their degree of attainment. In one of his company applications Forrester showed how the poor timing of advertising expenditure was responsi-

[17] Alfred A. Kuehn, "How Advertising Performance Depends on Other Marketing Factors," *Journal of Advertising Research,* March 1962, pp. 2–10.

[18] Jay W. Forrester, *Industrial Dynamics* (Cambridge: The Massachusetts Institute of Technology Press, 1961).

ble for accentuating production and inventory fluctuations.[19] This stemmed from the fact that advertising has a lagged impact on customer behavior; customer buying decisions at retail have a lagged impact on factory sales; and factory sales have a lagged impact on production scheduling and new advertising scheduling. By setting up a simulation of the process of information and decision delays, Forrester is able to investigate systematically the effect of different timing patterns of advertising expenditures on production and inventory stability.

A third area of advertising decision making that has benefited from advanced mathematical analysis is *media selection.* On October 1, 1962, *Advertising Age* carried the headline "Y&R, BBD&O Unleash Media Computerization," and later BBD&O sponsored full-page newspaper and magazine advertisements reading "Linear Programming showed one BBD&O client how to get $1.67 worth of effective advertising for every dollar in his budget."

The model developed at BBD&O uses a linear programming approach.[20] The problem is stated as one of selecting the media mix which would maximize the number of effective exposures subject to (a) the size of the total advertising budget, (b) specified minimum and maximum usage rates of various media, and (c) specified exposure rates to different market segments.

In the meantime, the Young & Rubicam agency has developed a different approach that they have dubbed the high assay model.[21] This model, although it is also an optimizing type, is designed to get around the simplifications—such as assuming constant effects of repeated exposures, constant media costs, no allowance for audience overlaps among media, and no indication of the best scheduling for the chosen media—necessitated by a linear programming statement of the problem. (Some of these simplifications, of course, are remediable through more complex programming statements of the problem.)

The Y&R model uses a sequential rather than a simultaneous decision process. The basic idea is to start with the media available

---

[19] Jay W. Forrester, "Advertising: A Problem in Industrial Dynamics," *Harvard Business Review,* March–April 1959, pp. 100–110.

[20] See Robert D. Buzzell, "Batten, Barton, Durstine & Osborne, Inc.: Use of Linear Programming Methods in the Selection of Advertising Media," *Mathematical Models and Marketing Management* (Boston: Division of Research, Harvard Business School, 1964), pp. 77–111. Buzzell's book is an excellent introduction to the problems and prospects of marketing operations research.

[21] See William T. Moran, "Practical Media Decisions and the Computer," *Journal of Marketing,* July 1963, pp. 26–30.

in the first week and select the single "best buy." After this selection is made, all the remaining media choices are reevaluated to take into account audience duplication and potential media discounts. Then, if the achieved exposure for the week is below the optimal rate, a second selection is made for the same week. The optimal rate is a complex function of several marketing and media variables. The cycling process continues until the optimal exposure rate for the week is reached, at which point new media choices are considered for the next week.

A simulation model has been developed by the Simulmatics Corporation which does not profess to find the "best" media plan, but rather to estimate the exposure value of any given media plan.[22] The model consists of a sample universe of 2,944 make-believe media users representing a cross section of the U.S. population by sex, age, type of community, employment status, and education. Each individual's media choices are determined probabilistically as a function of his socioeconomic characteristics and location in one of 98 U.S. communities. A particular client media schedule is exposed to all the persons in this hypothetical population. As the simulation of the year's schedule progresses, the computer tabulates the number and types of people being exposed.

Summary graphs and tables are automatically prepared at the end of the hypothetical year's run, and they supply a multidimensional picture of the schedule's probable impact. The advertiser examines these tabulations and then decides whether the audience profile, and the reach and frequency characteristics of the proposed media schedule, are satisfactory. Simulation complements the two previous models in that it is a means of developing the dynamic reach, and/or frequency characteristics, of a given schedule over 52 weeks.

5. Sales Force

In spite of the great cost and importance of personal selling in the marketing mix, surprisingly little operations research has been reported in this area. Much more analysis has been conducted on the optimal use of advertising funds, which in many ways is a less tangible problem than the optimal use of sales resources. Nevertheless, the few studies that have been conducted are significant for sales force management.

---

[22] See *Simulmatics Media-Mix: Technical Description* (New York: The Simulmatics Corporation, October 1962).

A problem which has received a great amount of attention from operations researchers is *salesman routing*. Suppose a salesman must make calls in *n* cities. This means that there are *n* factorial possible routes. Specifically, given 5 cities, there are 120 possible routes; 10 cities, over 3,000,000 possible routes. The problem is to find the one route through these cities that minimizes either the total travel time or travel cost. A number of different models have been developed.[23] The real challenge is to find a program which can solve the large *n* case without requiring too much computer time or cost. Research is currently being conducted in this area both in companies and in universities.

Markov process analysis has been used by a large insurance company to aid in the analysis of its sales force *manpower needs*.[24] Each year the company loses a fraction of its sales force through resignation, retirement, and death. The exiting salesmen have different levels of experience, education, and ability. The company has to hire new men to replace those who leave and additional men to meet the company's growth requirements. Top management's problem is to estimate future manpower needs by class of service and age in the light of the turnover characteristics and planned sales growth.

The first step is to calculate "survival" rates for agents in various service and age classes. These estimated rates are then used in a Markov analysis to project future characteristics of the sales force if no new men are hired. Different alternative recruitment patterns are analyzed for their effect on the composition of the future sales force and probable level of sales. For a given sales target, the operations researchers are able to recommend to top management the minimum number and types of agents to recruit each year.

The best level and allocation of sales effort depends on the correct assessment of customer response to variations in the *number of calls*. There are at least two published descriptions of attempts to derive the sales response curve empirically. One relies on a multiple regression performed on past sales data; the other depends on a planned experiment to generate information about the relationship.

---

[23] See Little, John D. C., Murty, Katta G., Sweeney, Dura W., and Karel, Caroline, "An Algorithm for the Traveling Salesman Problem," *Operations Research,* November–December 1963, pp. 972–989; and Robert L. Karg and Gerald L. Thompson, "A Heuristic Approach to Solving Traveling Salesman Problems," *Management Science,* January 1964, pp. 225–248.

[24] Joe Midler, *A Simulation Model of Sales Force Development with Application to Manpower Replacement, Sales Forecasting, and Corporate Growth* (unpublished paper. Northwestern Mutual Life Insurance Co., Milwaukee, 1961).

The first investigation was made by the Operations Research Group at Case Institute for the General Electric Company.[25] Customers were sorted into classes on the basis of similar characteristics. The accounts in each class were sorted again into subclasses on the basis of the call time spent with each customer. Then the average dollar volume was computed for each subclass. Finally, a curve was drawn through the scatter of points to show the relationship between average dollar volume and sales-call time.

The scatter for each class of account lay in a basically positive direction, but unfortunately was too diffused to permit the fitting of a statistically significant curve. The operations researchers, after trying other approaches that fared no better, concluded that the lack of a clear relationship could be explained by one of three hypotheses:

1. Uniform sales response curves do not exist for similar accounts.
2. Uniform response curves exist, but are difficult to measure because of imperfections in the classification of accounts and basic data.
3. Uniform response curves exist, but the data in this particular study revealed only the upper plateaus of the curves.

The researchers rejected the first hypothesis because it would remove the major justification for call norms and also would go against intuition. They rejected the second hypothesis because experienced salesmen reported that they thought the classification of accounts was quite discriminating. This left the third hypothesis, which they tentatively accepted but could not prove. It implied that salesmen typically spent more time with accounts than was necessary.

On the basis of this hypothesis, the research group recommended that the number of calls be cut back. They felt strongly that some diversion of calls from present accounts to new accounts was warranted and would also result in a substantial net increase in business. This recommendation was followed, and company sales remained high.

In a different effort, Magee described an experiment where salesmen were asked to vary their call pattern in a particular way to determine what effect this would have on sales.[26] His experiment called for

[25] Clark Waid, Donald F. Clark, and Russell L. Ackoff, "Allocation of Sales Effort in the Lamp Division of the General Electric Company," *Operations Research,* December 1956, pp. 629–647.

[26] See John F. Magee, "Determining the Optimum Allocation of Expenditures for Promotional Effort with Operations Research Methods," *The Frontiers of Marketing Thought and Science,* edited by Frank M. Bass (Chicago: American

first sorting accounts into major classes. Each account class was then randomly split into three sets. The respective salesmen were asked to spend less than five hours a month with accounts in the first set, five to nine hours a month with the second set, and a minimum of ten hours a month with the third set for a specified period of time. The results indicated that call time had a definite effect on sales volume, with the most profitable call norm in this particular situation appearing to be five to nine hours a month.

FUTURE DEVELOPMENTS

Although a number of models are now being used as an aid to marketing decision making, a much larger number are still in the R & D stage. They need to undergo further development and testing before they are ready for practical application. Two novel developments— *market simulators* and *rote marketing*—are particularly intriguing, and when they finally achieve operational status, they will raise marketing decision making to an entirely new plane of performance.

Market Simulators

Companies are showing an increased interest in developing total marketing decision models rather than separate ones for pricing, advertising, distribution, and so forth. In fact, the essential problem facing top marketing management is to define the proper level, mix, allocation, and timing of diverse marketing efforts and instruments. To this end, some companies are developing computerized models of their markets to serve as a creditable basis for testing and predicting response to alternative marketing programs and to important exogenous events.

The most advanced market simulators are microbehavioral. They include (a) a representative set of final customers who are distributed geographically, (b) a representative set of marketing channel members, such as retailers and wholesalers, and (c) specific competitors.[27]

Marketing Association, 1958), pp. 140–156; see also Arthur A. Brown, Frank I. Hulswit, and John D. Kettelle, "A Study of Sales Operations," *Operations Research*, June 1956, pp. 296–308.

[27] For a pioneering effort, see Arnold E. Amstutz, *Management Use of Computerized Micro-Analytic Behavioral Simulations*, Working Paper 169–66 (Cambridge: Alfred P. Sloan School of Management, M.I.T., March 1966); see also Philip Kotler, "The Competitive Marketing Simulator: A New Management Tool," *California Management Review*. Spring 1965, pp. 49–60.

The market simulator embodies the company's best understanding of the structure, character, and behavior of any market in which it sells. Much of the mathematical formulation is based on hard facts derived through statistical surveys and analysis; the rest, on management's reported feel for the nature of response. The use of the simulator comes into play when management is hammering out or searching for a new marketing strategy. Alternative strategies are tried out on the simulator, along with expected events and responses, to yield a picture over time of probable sales and costs to the organization.

Among the companies which have simulators in some stage of development are Pillsbury (cake market),[28] Lever Brothers (detergent market),[29] and General Electric (flashbulb market). In addition, a large drug company has a simulator of the proprietary drug market, and a large rubber company has one for the rubber tire market.

General Electric's simulator was built in order to determine why certain standard promotions yielded quite different sales results at different times. The erratic behavior became understandable when the response interaction of various entities in the marketing channel was simulated. Moreover, the simulator was also credited with improving promotion planning and sales results.

Lever Brothers' simulator grew out of a simple marketing game which got more complex with each edition until the executives began to comment that the game almost resembled the real world. At that point, the research potentialities of the business simulation were clearly recognized.

Rote Marketing

Ever since inventory systems became partially automatized, with the computer assuming the responsibility of determining order points and issuing reorders, some marketing operations researchers have been searching for similar semiroutine decisions in the marketing area which might be turned over to a rote marketer—the computer. An intelligent computer program could process the incoming data, interpret it carefully, and make the decisions or flash a red light when human judgment is required.

One area of possible opportunity is department store merchan-

---

[28] "Pillsbury Finds a New Mix That Pays," *Business Week,* June 25, 1966, p. 178.

[29] Alfred A. Kuehn and Doyle L. Weiss, "Marketing Analysis Training Exercise," *Behavioral Science,* January 1965, pp. 51–67.

dising. A large department store is currently experimenting with a computer program which can make ordering, pricing, and markdown decisions on some staple items and thus free buyers' time for less routine decisions. Another area is in order processing. The central computer at a large paper company is being programmed to receive order inquiries, determine whether the orders can be filled, and schedule the delivery date or schedule production in the event of stockout.

Work is being undertaken in some academic circles to automatize the higher level marketing decisions. The objective is to develop a total information feedback control program for adjusting marketing mix variables to ongoing changes in sales and profits. Thus a drop in sales will lead to specific changes in price, advertising, and distribution effort, all calculated to restore sales or profits to previous levels. The optimality of any such rote program can be tested on a market simulator or against real world experience.[30]

ORGANIZATIONAL STRICTURES

Lest a company be carried away with too much enthusiasm for sophisticated decision models, it should be noted that there are some organizational cautions in the proper use of marketing operations research. The company interested in starting a model-building program should observe these three strictures:

(1) The man (or men) hired to organize this work should have a familiarity and strong interest in marketing. Operations researchers who have worked strictly on inventory or queuing problems often lack the temperament necessary to work with marketing processes that are typically loose-ended, stochastic, lagged, non-linear, interactive, and downright difficult. They tend to over-simplify the marketing problem for the sake of using a ready-made technique instead of creating the techniques needed to meet the problem.

(2) At the outset, a plan of attack should be developed. What marketing decisions pose the biggest problems? Which have the greatest hope of benefiting from more formalization? In what order should they be attacked? What accomplishments are expected? The old dilemma will arise about whether to start work on small problems

---

[30] See George H. Haines, Jr., "The Rote Marketer," *Behavioral Science,* October 1961, pp. 357–365; and Philip Kotler, "Competitive Strategies for New Product Marketing Over the Life Cycle," *Management Science,* December 1965, pp. 104–119.

with a high probability of early success, or on large problems that will most likely take more years to conquer but which are vastly more important. For the demonstration effect, the former are probably best tackled first.

(3) The marketing operations researcher should not be set up in a little department by himself. He needs the stimulus of others. It is not desirable to locate him in the operations research department, because this is too distracting from his real task. To sense the full aroma of live marketing decision making, it is best that he be in daily contact with line and staff marketing men.

If these strictures are observed, chances are that the company will derive substantial benefits from marketing operations research.

There will be the direct benefit, hopefully, of making distinctly better decisions through the aid of sophisticated models. To this must be added all the indirect benefits of the model-building process: enrichment of executive understanding; explication of conflicts in assumptions held by different executives; and serendipity, the pleasant discovery of unexpected byproducts.

CONCLUDING NOTE

The payout potential of investment in marketing operations research can be documented in some specific instances, such as Du Pont's ability to predict the sales response to a new advertising campaign within a few percentage points of the actual results; or General Electric's reported savings as a result of adopting a new market logistics strategy suggested by a physical distribution simulation. But specific instances are not as telling as another and surer sign—namely, that of the persistent and growing investment made in marketing operations research by companies which have been pioneering in it.

Increasingly, the cost of doing business is the cost of marketing. Billions of dollars have to be spent in almost a blind way to protect and enhance market franchises. Any development that sheds some light on where the money should go, and what is being achieved, will be a boon to management. Marketing operations research is a major ray of hope in this connection.

Marketing Systems

Lee Adler views marketing from a systems perspective in Chapter 2. Adler's approach is "managerial and philosophical" in nature and contributes the view of marketing as a subsystem of the total firm system.

Harry Allison portrays marketing management as planners and strategists—not mere technicians performing routine tasks for which decision rules can be programmed on computers. Allison goes even further: he proposes that the "job of the marketing staff is that of identifying all relevant marketing alternatives confronting the firm, of choosing from among these alternatives the particular alternative at each output level which best satisfies the goals of the firms. . . ." Allison emphasizes that even poor alternatives can provide "balance" and proceeds to provide a conceptual framework for use in such "balancing."

Systems Approach to Marketing

Lee Adler

More and more businessmen today recognize that corporate success is, in most cases, synonymous with marketing success and with the coming of age of a new breed of professional managers. They find it increasingly important not only to pay lip service to the marketing concept but to do something about it in terms of (a) customer orientation, rather than navel-gazing in the factory, (b) organizational revisions to implement the marketing concept, and (c) a more orderly approach to problem solving.

In an increasing number of companies we see more conscious and formal efforts to apply rational, fact-based methods for solving marketing problems, and greater recognition of the benefits these methods offer. While these benefits may be newly realized, there is nothing new about the underlying philosophy; in the parlance of military men and engineers, it is the systems approach. For, whether we like it or not, marketing is, by definition, a system, if we accept Webster's definition of system as "an assemblage of objects united by some form of regular interaction or interdependence." Certainly, the interaction of such "objects" as product, pricing, promotion, sales calls, distribution, and so on fits the definition.

There is an expanding list of sophisticated applications of systems theory—and not in one but in many sectors of the marketing front. The construction of mathematical and/or logical models to describe, quantify, and evaluate alternate marketing strategies and mixes is an obvious case in point. So, too, is the formulation of management information systems[1] and of marketing plans with built-in performance

[1] See, for example, Donald F. Cox and Robert E. Good, "How to Build a Marketing Information System," *Harvard Business Review,* May–June, 1967.

measurements of predetermined goals. But no less vital is the role of the systems approach in the design and sale of products and services. When J. P. Stevens Company color-harmonizes linens and bed-spreads, and towels and bath mats, it is creating a product system. And when Avco Corporation sells systems management to the space exploration field, involving the marriage of many scientific disciplines as well as adherence to budgetary constraints, on-time performance, and quality control, it is creating a *service* system.

In this article I shall discuss the utilization of the systems concept in marketing in both quantitative and qualitative ways with case his-tories drawn from various industries. In doing so, my focus will be more managerial and philosophical than technical, and I will seek to dissipate some of the hocus-pocus, glamor, mystery, and fear which pervade the field. The systems concept is not esoteric or "science fic-tion" in nature (although it sometimes *sounds* that way in promo-tional descriptions). Its advantages are not subtle or indirect; as we shall see, they are as real and immediate as decision making itself. The limitations are also real, and these, too, will be discussed.

(Readers interested in a brief summary of the background and the conceptual development of the systems approach may wish to turn to the box on page 62.)

PROMISING APPLICATIONS

Now let us look at some examples of corporate application of the systems approach. Here we will deal with specific parts or "sub-systems" of the total marketing system. Exhibit 1 is a schematic por-trayal of these relationships.

Products and Services

The objective of the systems approach in product management is to provide a complete "offering" to the market rather than merely a product. If the purpose of business is to create a customer at a profit, then the needs of the customer must be carefully attended to; we must, in short, study what the customer is buying or wants to buy, rather than what we are trying to sell.

In the consumer products field we have forged ahead in under-standing that the customer buys nutrition (not bread), beauty (not

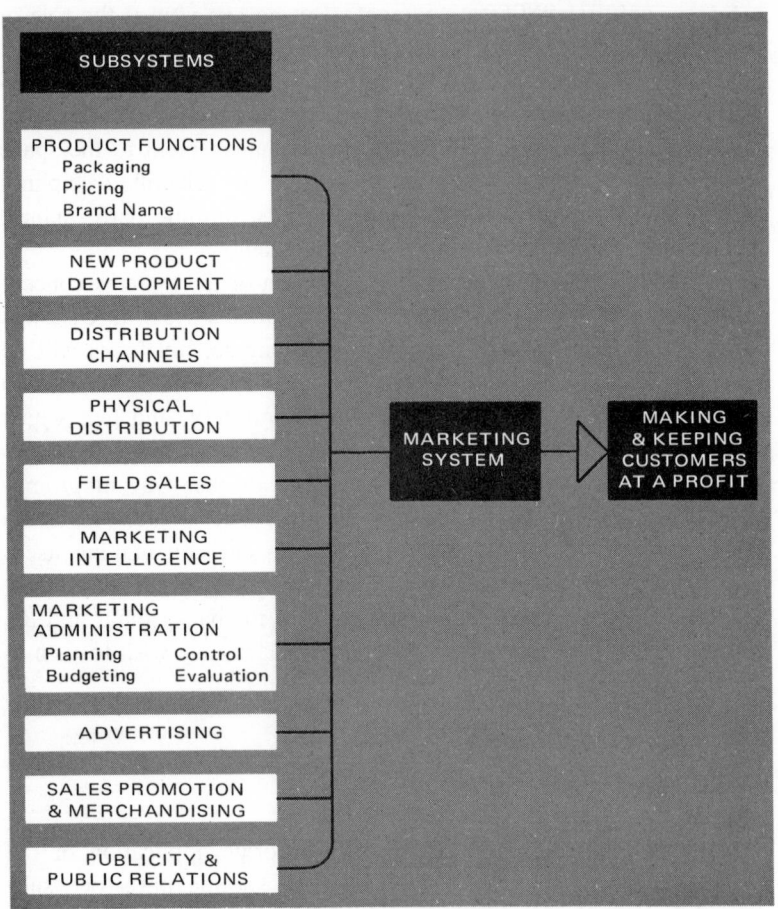

Exhibit 1   Marketing subsystems and the total system

cosmetics), warmth (not fuel oil). But in industrial products this concept has been slower in gaining a foothold. Where it has gained a foothold, it expresses itself in two ways: the creation of a complete product system sold (1) as a unit, or (2) as a component or components which are part of a larger consumption system.

Perhaps the most eloquent testimony to the workability and value of the systems approach comes from companies that have actually used it. For a good example let us turn to the case of The Carborundum Company. This experience is especially noteworthy because it comes from industrial marketing, where, as just indicated, progress with the systems concept has generally been slow.

BIRTH OF THE CONCEPT. Founded in 1894, the company was content for many years to sell abrasives. It offered an extremely broad line of grinding wheels, coated abrasives, and abrasive grain, with a reputed capacity for 200,000 different products of varying type, grade, and formulation. But the focus was on the product.

In the mid-1950s, Carborundum perceived that the market for abrasives could be broadened considerably if—looking at abrasives through customers' eyes—it would see the product as fitting into *metal polishing, cleaning,* or *removal systems.* Now Carborundum is concerned with all aspects of abrading—the machine, the contact wheel, the workpiece, the labor cost, the overhead rate, the abrasive, and, above all, the customer's objective. In the words of Carborundum's president, W. H. Wendel:

> That objective is never the abrasive per se, but rather the creation of a certain dimension, a type of finish, or a required shape, always related to a minimum cost. Since there are many variables to consider, just one can be misleading. To render maximum service, Carborundum (must offer) a complete system.[2]

ORGANIZATIONAL OVERHAUL. To offer such a system, management had to overhaul important parts of the organization:

(1) The company needed to enhance its knowledge of the total system. As Wendel explains:

> We felt we had excellent knowledge of coated abrasive products, but that we didn't have the application and machine know-how in depth. To be really successful in the business, we had to know as much about the machine tools as we did the abrasives.[3]

To fill this need, Carborundum made three acquisitions—The Tysaman Machine Company, which builds heavy-duty snagging, billet grinding, and abrasive cut-off machines; Curtis Machine Company, a maker of belt sanders; and Pangborn Corporation, which supplied systems capability in abrasive blast cleaning and finishing.

(2) The company's abrasive divisions were reorganized, and the management of them was realigned to accommodate the new philoso-

---

[2] "Abrasive Maker's Systems Approach Opens New Markets," *Steel,* December 27, 1965, p. 38.

[3] Ibid.

phy and its application. The company found that *centering responsibility for the full system in one profit center* proved to be the most effective method of coordinating approaches in application engineering, choice of distribution channels, brand identification, field sales operations, and so forth. This method was particularly valuable for integrating the acquisitions into the new program.

(3) An Abrasives Systems Center was established to handle development work and to solve customer problems.

(4) Technical conferences and seminars were held to educate customers on the new developments.

(5) Salesmen were trained in machine and application knowledge.

PLANNING. A key tool in the systems approach is planning—in particular, the use of what I like to call "total business plans." (This term emphasizes the contrast with company plans that cover only limited functions.) At Carborundum, total business plans are developed with extreme care by the operating companies and divisions. Very specific objectives are established, and then detailed action programs are outlined to achieve these objectives. The action programs extend throughout the organization, including the manufacturing and development branches of the operating unit. Management sets specific dates for the completion of action steps and defines who is responsible for them. Also, it carefully measures results against established objectives. This is done both in the financial reporting system and in various marketing committees.

QUANTITATIVE METHODS. Carborundum has utilized various operations research techniques, like decision tree analysis and PERT, to aid in molding plans and strategies. For example, one analysis, which concerned itself with determining the necessity for plant expansion, was based on different possible levels of success for the marketing plan. In addition, the computer has been used for inventory management, evaluation of alternate pricing strategies for systems selling, and the measurement of marketing achievements against goals.

It should be noted, though, that these quantitative techniques are management tools only and that much of the application of systems thinking to the redeployment of Carborundum's business is qualitative in nature.

GAINS ACHIEVED. As a consequence of these developments, the company has opened up vast new markets. To quote Carborundum's president again:

Customers don't want a grinding wheel, they want metal removed. . . . The U.S. and Canadian market for abrasives amounts to $700 million a year. But what companies spend on stock removal—to bore, grind, cut, shape, and finish metal—amounts to $30 billion a year.[4]

Illustrating this market expansion in the steel industry is Corborundum's commercial success with three new developments—hot grinding, an arborless wheel to speed metal removal and cut grinding costs, and high-speed conditioning of carbon steel billets. All represent conversions from nonabrasive methods. Carborundum now also finds that the close relationship with customers gives it a competitive edge, opens top customer management doors, gains entree for salesmen with prospects they had never been able to "crack" before. Perhaps the ultimate accolade is the company's report that customers even come to the organization itself, regarding it as a consultant as well as a supplier.

Profitable Innovation

The intense pressure to originate successful new products cannot be met without methodologies calculated to enhance the probabilities of profitable innovation. The systems approach has a bearing here, too. Exhibit 2 shows a model for "tracking" products through the many stages of ideation, development, and testing to ultimate full-scale commercialization. This diagram is in effect a larger version of the "New Product Development" box in Exhibit 1.

Observe that this is a logical (specifically, sequential), rather than numerical, model. While some elements of the total system (e.g., alternate distribution channels and various media mixes) can be analyzed by means of operations research techniques, the model has not been cast in mathematical terms. Rather, the flow diagram as a whole is used as a checklist to make sure "all bases are covered" and to help organize the chronological sequence of steps in new product development. It also serves as a conceptual foundation for formal PERT application, should management desire such a step, and for the gradual development of a series of equations linking together elements in the diagrams, should it seem useful to experiment with mathematical models.

[4] "Carborundum Grinds at Faster Clip," *Business Week,* July 23, 1966, pp. 58, 60.

Exhibit 2 Work flow and systems chart for management of new products. This flow diagram was developed by Paul E. Funk, President, and his staff at McCann/TISM, Inc.

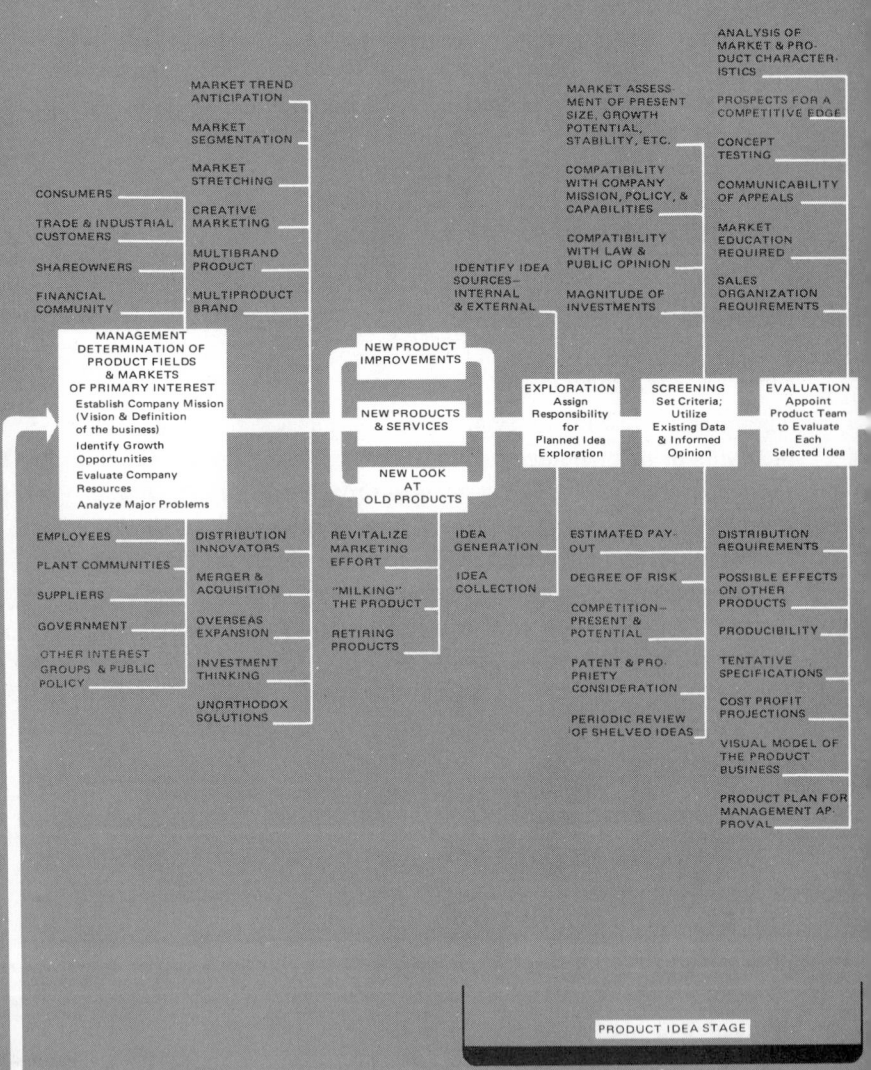

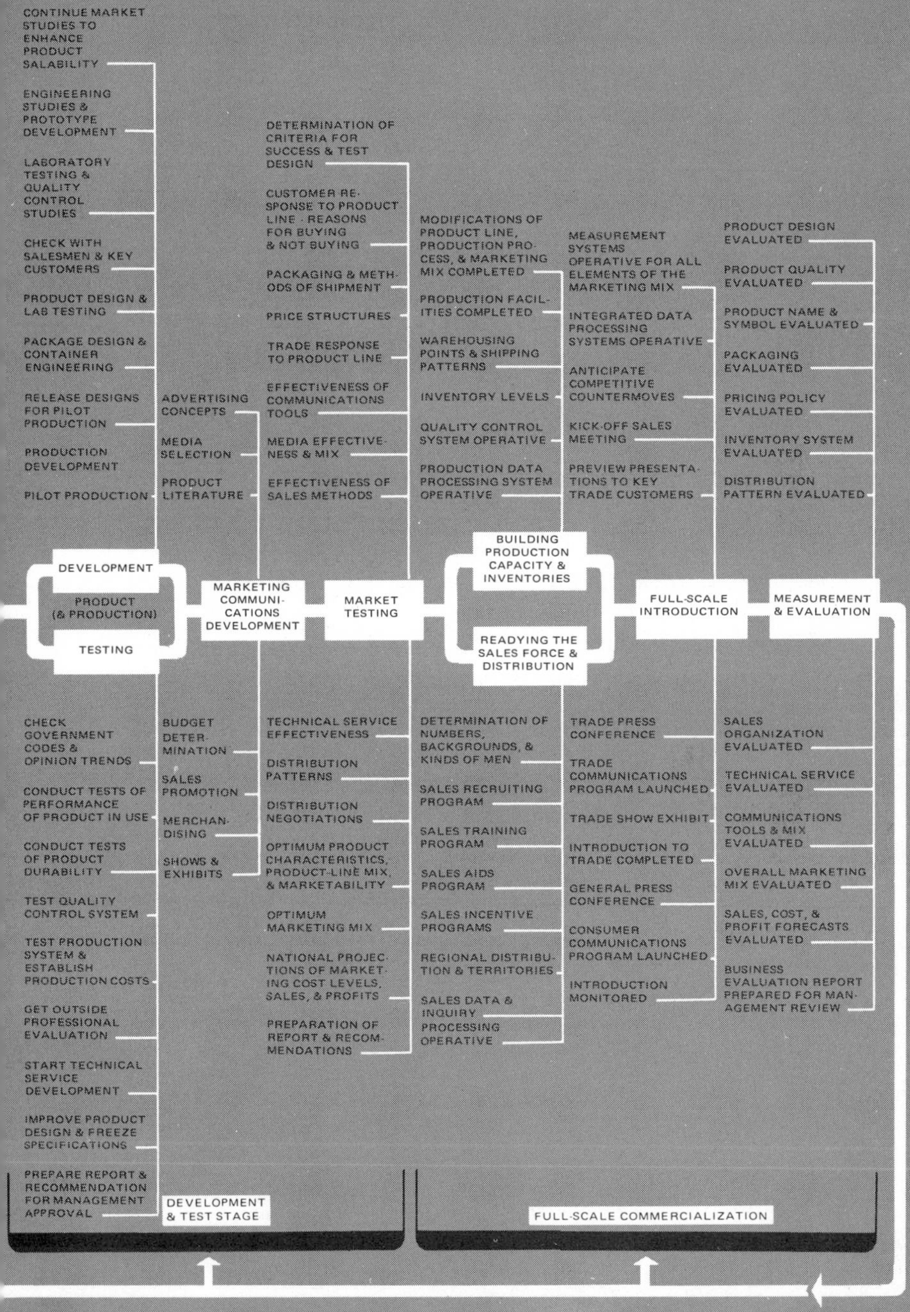
CONTINUE MARKET STUDIES TO ENHANCE PRODUCT SALABILITY
ENGINEERING STUDIES & PROTOTYPE DEVELOPMENT
LABORATORY TESTING & QUALITY CONTROL STUDIES
CHECK WITH SALESMEN & KEY CUSTOMERS
PRODUCT DESIGN & LAB TESTING
PACKAGE DESIGN & CONTAINER ENGINEERING
RELEASE DESIGNS FOR PILOT PRODUCTION
PRODUCTION DEVELOPMENT
PILOT PRODUCTION
ADVERTISING CONCEPTS
MEDIA SELECTION
PRODUCT LITERATURE
DETERMINATION OF CRITERIA FOR SUCCESS & TEST DESIGN
CUSTOMER RESPONSE TO PRODUCT LINE - REASONS FOR BUYING & NOT BUYING
PACKAGING & METHODS OF SHIPMENT
PRICE STRUCTURES
TRADE RESPONSE TO PRODUCT LINE
EFFECTIVENESS OF COMMUNICATIONS TOOLS
MEDIA EFFECTIVENESS & MIX
EFFECTIVENESS OF SALES METHODS
MODIFICATIONS OF PRODUCT LINE, PRODUCTION PROCESS, & MARKETING MIX COMPLETED
PRODUCTION FACILITIES COMPLETED
WAREHOUSING POINTS & SHIPPING PATTERNS
INVENTORY LEVELS
QUALITY CONTROL SYSTEM OPERATIVE
PRODUCTION DATA PROCESSING SYSTEM OPERATIVE
MEASUREMENT SYSTEMS OPERATIVE FOR ALL ELEMENTS OF THE MARKETING MIX
INTEGRATED DATA PROCESSING SYSTEMS OPERATIVE
ANTICIPATE COMPETITIVE COUNTERMOVES
KICK-OFF SALES MEETING
PREVIEW PRESENTATIONS TO KEY TRADE CUSTOMERS
PRODUCT DESIGN EVALUATED
PRODUCT QUALITY EVALUATED
PRODUCT NAME & SYMBOL EVALUATED
PACKAGING EVALUATED
PRICING POLICY EVALUATED
INVENTORY SYSTEM EVALUATED
DISTRIBUTION PATTERN EVALUATED
PRODUCT DEVELOPMENT (& PRODUCTION) TESTING
MARKETING COMMUNICATIONS DEVELOPMENT
MARKET TESTING
BUILDING PRODUCTION CAPACITY & INVENTORIES
READYING THE SALES FORCE & DISTRIBUTION
FULL-SCALE INTRODUCTION
MEASUREMENT & EVALUATION
CHECK GOVERNMENT CODES & OPINION TRENDS
CONDUCT TESTS OF PERFORMANCE OF PRODUCT IN USE
CONDUCT TESTS OF PRODUCT DURABILITY
TEST QUALITY CONTROL SYSTEM
TEST PRODUCTION SYSTEM & ESTABLISH PRODUCTION COSTS
GET OUTSIDE PROFESSIONAL EVALUATION
START TECHNICAL SERVICE DEVELOPMENT
IMPROVE PRODUCT DESIGN & FREEZE SPECIFICATIONS
PREPARE REPORT & RECOMMENDATION FOR MANAGEMENT APPROVAL
BUDGET DETERMINATION
SALES PROMOTION
MERCHANDISING
SHOWS & EXHIBITS
TECHNICAL SERVICE EFFECTIVENESS
DISTRIBUTION PATTERNS
DISTRIBUTION NEGOTIATIONS
OPTIMUM PRODUCT CHARACTERISTICS, PRODUCT-LINE MIX, & MARKETABILITY
OPTIMUM MARKETING MIX
NATIONAL PROJECTIONS OF MARKETING COST LEVELS, SALES, & PROFITS
PREPARATION OF REPORT & RECOMMENDATIONS
DETERMINATION OF NUMBERS, BACKGROUNDS, & KINDS OF MEN
SALES RECRUITING PROGRAM
SALES TRAINING PROGRAM
SALES AIDS PROGRAM
SALES INCENTIVE PROGRAMS
REGIONAL DISTRIBUTION & TERRITORIES
SALES DATA & INQUIRY PROCESSING OPERATIVE
TRADE PRESS CONFERENCE
TRADE COMMUNICATIONS PROGRAM LAUNCHED
TRADE SHOW EXHIBIT
INTRODUCTION TO TRADE COMPLETED
GENERAL PRESS CONFERENCE
CONSUMER COMMUNICATIONS PROGRAM LAUNCHED
INTRODUCTION MONITORED
SALES ORGANIZATION EVALUATED
TECHNICAL SERVICE EVALUATED
COMMUNICATIONS TOOLS & MIX EVALUATED
OVERALL MARKETING MIX EVALUATED
SALES, COST, & PROFIT FORECASTS EVALUATED
BUSINESS EVALUATION REPORT PREPARED FOR MANAGEMENT REVIEW
DEVELOPMENT & TEST STAGE
FULL-SCALE COMMERCIALIZATION

Marketing Intelligence

The traditional notion of marketing research is fast becoming antiquated. For it leads to dreary chronicles of the past rather than focusing on the present and shedding light on the future. It is particularistic, tending to concentrate on the study of tiny fractions of a marketing problem rather than on the problem as a whole. It lends itself to assuaging the curiosity of the moment, to fire-fighting, to resolving internecine disputes. It is a slave to technique. I shall not, therefore, relate the term *marketing research* to the systems approach —although I recognize, of course, that some leading businessmen and writers are breathing new life and scope into the ideas referred to by that term.

The role of the systems approach is to help evolve a *marketing intelligence* system tailored to the needs of each marketer. Such a system would serve as the ever-alert nerve center of the marketing operation. It would have these major characteristics:

Continuous surveillance of the market.

A team of research techniques used in tandem.

A network of data sources.

Integrated analysis of data from the various sources.

Effective utilization of automatic data-processing equipment to distill mountains of raw information speedily.

Strong concentration not just on reporting findings but also on practical, action-oriented recommendations.

CONCEPT IN USE. A practical instance of the use of such an intelligence system is supplied by Mead Johnson Nutritionals (division of Mead Johnson & Company), manufacturers of Metrecal, Pablum, Bib, Nutrament, and other nutritional specialties. As Exhibit 3 shows, the company's Marketing Intelligence Department has provided information from these sources:

A continuing large-scale consumer market study covering attitudinal and behavioral data dealing with weight control.

Nielsen store audit data, on a bimonthly basis.

A monthly sales audit conducted among a panel of 100 high-volume food stores in 20 markets to provide advance indications of brand share shifts.

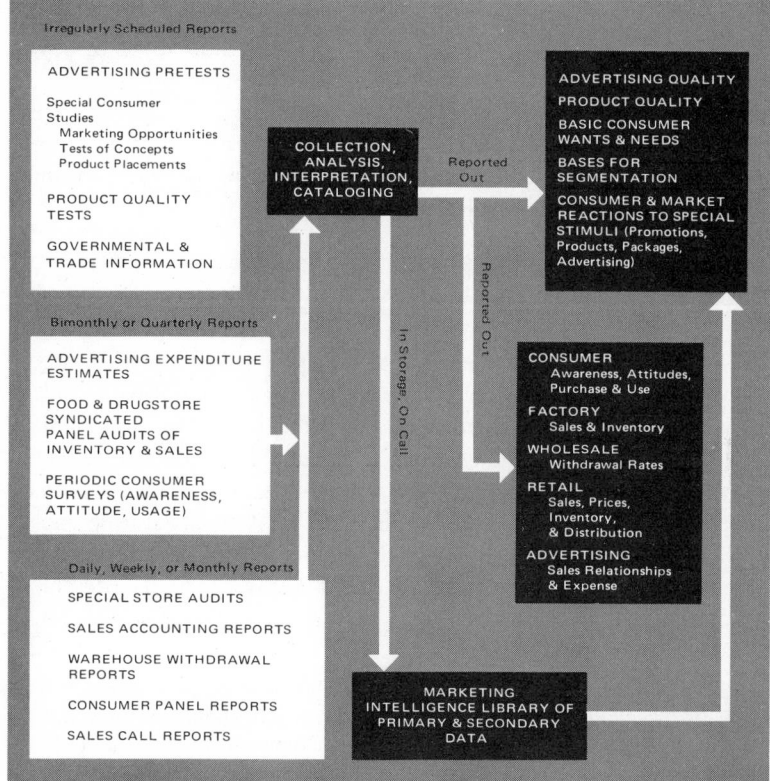

Exhibit 3   Mead Johnson's marketing intelligence system

Supermarket warehouse withdrawal figures from Time, Inc.'s new service, Selling Areas-Marketing, Inc.

Salesmen's weekly reports (which, in addition to serving the purposes of sales management control, call for reconnaissance on competitive promotions, new product launches, price changes, and so forth).

Advertising expenditure data, by media class, from the company's accounting department.

Figures on sales and related topics from company factories.

Competitive advertising expenditure and exposure data, supplied by the division's advertising agencies at periodic intervals.

A panel of weight-conscious women.

To exemplify the type of outputs possible from this system, Mead Johnson will be able, with the help of analyses of factory sales data, warehouse withdrawal information, and consumer purchases from

Nielsen, to monitor transactions at each stage of the flow of goods through the distribution channel and to detect accumulations or developing shortages. Management will also be able to spot sources of potential problems in time to deal with them effectively. For example, if factory sales exceed consumer purchases, more promotional pressure is required. By contrast, if factory sales lag behind consumer purchases, sales effort must be further stimulated.

WHAT IS THE SYSTEMS APPROACH?

There seems to be agreement that the systems approach sprang to life as a semantically identifiable term sometime during World War II. It was associated with the problem of how to bomb targets deep in Germany more effectively from British bases, with the Manhattan Project, and with studies of optimum search patterns for destroyers to use in locating U-boats during the Battle of the North Atlantic.* Subsequently, it was utilized in the defeat of the Berlin blockade. It has reached its present culmination in the success of great military systems such as Polaris and Minuteman.

Not surprisingly, the parallels between military and marketing strategies being what they are, the definition of the systems approach propounded by The RAND Corporation for the U.S. Air Force is perfectly apt for marketers:

An inquiry to aid a decision-maker choose a course of action by systematically investigating his proper objectives, comparing quantitatively where possible the costs, effectiveness, and risks associated with the alternative policies or strategies for achieving them, and *formulating additional alternatives if those examined are found wanting.*†

The systems approach is thus an orderly, "architectural" discipline for dealing with complex problems of choice under uncertainty.

Typically, in such problems, multiple and possibly conflicting objectives exist. The task of the systems analyst is to specify a

---

* See Glen McDaniel, "The Meaning of The Systems Movement to the Acceleration and Direction of the American Economy," in *Proceedings of the 1964 Systems Engineering Conference* (New York: Clapp & Poliak, Inc., 1964), p. 1; see also E. S. Quade, editor, *Analysis for Military Decisions* (Santa Monica, California: The RAND Corporation, 1964), p. 6.

† Quade, op. cit., p. 4.

closed operating network in which the components will work together so as to yield the optimum balance of economy, efficiency, and risk minimization. Put more broadly, the systems approach attempts to apply the "scientific method" to complex marketing problems studied *as a whole;* it seeks to discipline marketing.

But disciplining marketing is no easy matter. Marketing must be perceived as a *process* rather than as a series of isolated, discrete actions; competitors must be viewed as components of each marketer's own system. The process must also be comprehended as involving a flow and counterflow of information and behavior between marketers and customers. Some years ago, Marion Harper, Jr., now chairman of The Interpublic Group of Companies, Inc., referred to the flow of information in marketing communications as the cycle of "listen (i.e., marketing research), publish (messages, media), listen (more marketing research), revise, publish, listen. . . ." More recently, Raymond A. Bauer referred to the "transactional" nature of communications as a factor in the motivations, frames of reference, needs, and so forth of recipients of messages. The desires of the communicator alone are but part of the picture.‡

Pushing this new awareness of the intricacies of marketing communications still further, Theodore Levitt identified the interactions between five different forces—source effect (i.e., the reputation or credibility of the sponsor of the message), sleeper effect (the declining influence of source credibility with the passage of time), message effect (the character and quality of the message), communicator effect (the impact of the transmitter—e.g., a salesman), and audience effect (the competence and responsibility of the audience).§ Casting a still broader net are efforts to model the entire purchasing process, and perhaps the ultimate application of the systems concept is attempts to make mathematical models of the entire marketing process.

Mounting recognition of the almost countless elements involved in marketing and of the mind-boggling complexity of their interactions is a wholesome (though painful) experience. Nevertheless, I believe we must not ignore other ramifications of the systems approach which are qualitative in nature. For the

‡ "Communications as a Transaction," *Public Opinion Quarterly,* Spring 1963, p. 83.

§ See Theodore Levitt, *Industrial Purchasing Behavior* (Boston: Division of Research, Harvard Business School, 1965), p. 25ff.

world of marketing offers a vast panorama of non- or part-mathematical systems and opportunities to apply systems thinking. We must not become so bedazzled by the brouhaha of the operations research experts as to lose sight of the larger picture.

Similarly, the company has been able to devise a practical measurement of advertising's effectiveness in stimulating sales—a measurement that is particularly appropriate to fast-moving packaged goods. By relating advertising outlays and exposure data to the number of prospects trying out a product during a campaign (the number is obtained from the continuing consumer survey), it is possible to calculate the advertising cost of recruiting such a prospect. By persisting in such analyses during several campaigns, the relative value of alternative advertising approaches can be weighed. Since measurement of the sales, as opposed to the communications, effects of promotion is a horrendously difficult, costly, and chancy process, the full significance of this achievement is difficult to exaggerate.

BENEFITS REALIZED. Mead Johnson's marketing intelligence system has been helpful to management in a number of ways. In addition to giving executives early warning of new trends and problems, and valuable insights into future conditions, it is leading to a systematic *body* of knowledge about company markets rather than to isolated scraps of information. This knowledge in turn should lead ultimately to a theory of marketing in each field that will explain the mysteries that baffle marketers today. What is more, the company expects that the system will help to free its marketing intelligence people from fire-fighting projects so that they can concentrate on long-term factors and eventually be more consistently creative.

Despite these gains, it is important to note that Mead Johnson feels it has a long road still to travel. More work is needed in linking individual data banks. Conceptual schemes must be proved out in practice; ways must still be found to reduce an awesome volume of data, swelled periodically by new information from improved sources, so as to make intelligence more immediately accessible to decision makers. And perhaps the biggest problem of the moment, one underlying some of the others, is the difficulty in finding qualified marketing-oriented programmers.

Physical Distribution

A veritable revolution is now taking place in physical distribution. Total systems are being evolved out of the former hodgepodge of

separate responsibilities, which were typically scattered among different departments of the same company. These systems include traffic and transportation, warehousing, materials handling, protective packaging, order processing, production planning, inventory control, customer service, market forecasting, and plant and warehouse site selection. Motivating this revolution are the computer, company drives to reduce distribution costs, and innovations in transportation, such as jet air freight, container ships, the interstate highway network, and larger and more versatile freight cars.

Distribution is one area of marketing where the "bread-and-butter" uses of the computer are relatively easily deployed for such functions as order processing, real-time inventory level reports, and tracking the movements of goods. Further into the future lie mathematical models which will include every factor bearing on distribution. Not only will packaging, materials handling, transportation and warehouse, order processing, and related costs be considered in such models; also included will be sales forecasts by product, production rates by factory, warehouse locations and capacities, speeds of different carriers, etc. In short, a complete picture will be developed for management.

PROGRAM IN ACTION. The experiences of the Norge Division of Borg-Warner Corporation point up the values of the systems approach in physical distribution. The firm was confronted externally with complaints from its dealers and distributors, who were trying to cope with swollen inventories and the pressures of "loading deals." Internally, because coordination of effort between the six departments involved in distribution was at a minimum, distribution costs and accounts receivable were mounting persistently.

To grapple with this situation, Norge undertook a comprehensive analysis of its distribution system. Out of this grew a new philosophy. A company executive has described the philosophy to me as follows:

An effective system of physical distribution cannot begin at the end of the production line. It must also apply at the very beginning of the production process—at the planning, scheduling, and forecasting stages. Logistics, in short, is part of a larger marketing system, not just an evaluation of freight rates. We must worry not only about finished refrigerators, but also about the motors coming from another manufacturer, and even about where the copper that goes into those motors will come from. We must be concerned with *total flow.*

To implement this philosophy, the appliance manufacturer took the following steps:

(1) It reorganized the forecasting, production scheduling, warehousing, order processing, and shipping functions into *one* department headed by a director of physical distribution.

(2) The management information system was improved with the help of EDP equipment tied into the communications network. This step made it possible to process and report data more speedily on orders received, inventory levels, and the actual movement of goods.

(3) Management used a combination of computer and manual techniques to weigh trade-offs among increased costs of multiple warehousing, reduced long-haul freight and local drayage costs, reduced inventory pipeline, and the sales value of an improved "total" product offering. Also assessed were trade-offs between shorter production runs and higher inventory levels, thereby challenging the traditional "wisdom" of production-oriented managers that the longer the run, the better.

(4) The company is setting up new regional warehouses.

As a result of these moves, Norge has been able to lower inventories throughout its sales channels and to reduce accounts receivable. These gains have led, in turn, to a reduction of the company's overall investment and a concomitant increase in profitability.

It is essential to note that even though Norge has used operations research as part of its systems approach, many aspects of the program are qualitative. Thus far, the company has found that the development of an all-encompassing model is not warranted because of (a) the time and cost involved, (b) the probability that the situation will change before the model is completed, (c) a concern that such a model would be so complex as to be unworkable, and (d) the difficulty of testing many of the assumptions used. In addition, management has not tried to quantify the impact of its actions on distributor and retailer attitudes and behavior, possible competitive countermoves, and numerous other factors contributing to results.

Toward Total Integration

The integration of systems developed for product management, product innovation, marketing intelligence, physical distribution, and the other functions or "subsystems" embraced by the term *marketing* creates a total marketing system. Thus, marketing plans composed according to a step-by-step outline, ranging from enunciation of objectives and implementational steps to audit and adjustment to environmental changes, constitute a complete application of systems

theory. Further, as the various subsystems of the overall system are linked quantitatively, so that the effect of modifications in one element can be detected in other elements, and as the influences of competitive moves on each element are analyzed numerically, then the total scheme becomes truly sophisticated.

PLUSES AND MINUSES

Two elements underlie the use and benefits of systems theory—order and knowledge. The first is a homely virtue, the second a lofty goal. Marketing is obviously not alone among all human pursuits in needing them; but, compared with its business neighbors, production and finance, marketing's need is acute indeed. The application of the systems concept can bring considerable advantages. It offers:

A methodical problem-solving orientation—with a broader frame of reference so that all aspects of a problem are examined.

Coordinated deployment of all appropriate tools of marketing.

Greater efficiency and economy of marketing operations.

Quicker recognition of impending problems made possible by better understanding of the complex interplay of many trends and forces.

A stimulus to innovation.

A means of quantitatively verifying results.

These functional benefits in turn yield rich rewards in the marketplace. The most important gains are:

A deeper penetration of existing markets. As an illustration, the Advanced Data Division of Litton Industries has become a leader in the automatic revenue control business by designing systems meshing together "hardware" and "software."

A broadening of markets. For example, the tourist industry has attracted millions of additional travelers by creating packaged tours that are really product-service systems. These systems are far more convenient and economical than anything the consumer could assemble himself.

An extension of product lines. Systems management makes it more feasible to seek out compatibilities among independently developed systems. Evidence of this idea is the work of automatic control system specialists since the early 1950s.[5] Now similar signs are apparent in

[5] See *Automatic and Manual Control: Papers Contributed to the Conference at Cranford, 1951,* edited by A. Tustin (London: Butterworth's Scientific Publications, 1952).

marketing. For example, Acme Visible Records is currently dovetailing the design and sale of its record-keeping systems with data-processing machines and forms.

A lessening of competition or a strengthened capacity to cope with competition. The systems approach tends to make a company's product line more unique and attractive. Carborundum's innovation in metal-removal systems is a perfect illustration of this.

Problems in Practice

Having just enumerated in glowing terms the benefits of the systems approach, realism demands that I give "equal time" to the awesome difficulties its utilization presents. There is no better evidence of this than the gulf between the elegant and sophisticated models with which recent marketing literature abounds and the actual number of situations in which those models really work. For the truth of the matter is that we are still in the foothills of this development, despite the advances of a few leaders. Let us consider some of the obstacles.

TIME AND MANPOWER COSTS. First of all, the systems approach requires considerable time to implement; it took one company over a year to portray its physical distribution system in a mathematical model before it could even begin to solve its problems. RCA's Electronic Data Processing Division reports models taking three to five years to build, after which holes in the data network have to be filled and the model tested against history. Add to this the need for manpower of exceptional intellectual ability, conceptual skills, and specialized education—manpower that is in exceedingly short supply. Because the problems are complex and involve all elements of the business, one man alone cannot solve them. He lacks the knowledge, tools, and controls. And so many people must be involved. It follows that the activation of systems theory can be very costly.

ABSENCE OF "CANNED" SOLUTIONS. Unlike other business functions where standardized approaches to problem solving are available, systems must be tailored to the individual situation of each firm. Even the same problem in different companies in the same industry will frequently lead to different solutions because of the impact of other inputs, unique perceptions of the environment, and varying corporate missions. These factors, too, compound time and expense demands.

"NET UNCERTAINTIES." Even after exhaustive analysis, full optimization of a total problem cannot be obtained. Some uncertainty

will always remain and must be dealt with on the basis of judgment and experience.

LACK OF HARD DATA. In the world of engineering, the systems evolved to date have consisted all or mostly of machines. Systems engineers have been wise enough to avoid the irrationalities of man until they master control of machines. Marketing model-builders, however, have not been able to choose, for the distributor, salesman, customer, and competitor are central to marketing. We must, there-fore, incorporate not only quantitative measures of the dimensions of things and processes (e.g., market potential, media outlays, and shipping rates), but also psychological measures of comprehension, attitudes, motivations, intentions, needs—yes, even psychological measures of physical behavior. What is needed is a marriage of the physical and behavioral sciences—and we are about as advanced in this blending of disciplines as astronomy was in the Middle Ages.

Consider the advertising media fields as an instance of the problem:

A number of advertising agencies have evolved linear programming or simulation techniques to assess alternate media schedules. One of the key sets of data used covers the probabilities of exposure to all or part of the audience of a TV program, magazine, or radio station. But what is exposure, and how do you measure it? What is optimum frequency of exposure, and how do you measure it? How does advertising prevail on the predispositions and perceptions of a potential customer? Is it better to judge advertising effects on the basis of exposure opportunity, "impact" (whatever that is), messages retained, message comprehension, or attitude shifts or uptrends in purchase intentions? We do not have these answers yet.

Even assuming precise knowledge of market dimensions, product performance, competitive standing, weights of marketing pressure exerted by direct selling, advertising and promotion, and so on, most marketers do not yet know, except in isolated cases, how one force will affect another. For instance, how does a company "image" affect the setting in which its salesmen work? How does a company's reputa-tion for service affect customer buying behavior?

NATURE OF MARKETING MEN. Man is an actor on this stage in another role. A good many marketing executives, in the deepest recesses of their psyches, are artists, not analysts. For them, marketing is an art form, and, in my opinion, they really do not want it to be any other way. Their temperament is antipathetic to system, order, knowl-edge. They enjoy flying by the seat of their pants—though you will

never get them to admit it. They revel in chaos, abhor facts, and fear research. They hate to be trammeled by written plans. And they love to spend, but are loathe to assess the results of their spending.

Obviously, such men cannot be sold readily on the value and practicality of the systems approach! It takes time, experience, and many facts to influence their thinking.

Surmounting the Barriers

All is not gloom, however. The barriers described are being overcome in various ways. While operations research techniques have not yet made much headway in evolving total marketing systems and in areas where man is emotionally engaged, their accomplishments in solving inventory control problems, in sales analysis, in site selection, and in other areas have made many businessmen more sympathetic and open-minded to them.

Also, mathematical models—even the ones that do not work well yet—serve to bolster comprehension of the need for system as well as to clarify the intricacies among subsystems. Many models are in this sense learning models; they teach us how to ask more insightful questions. Moreover, they pinpoint data gaps and invite a more systematized method for reaching judgments where complete information does not exist. Because the computer abhors vague generalities, it forces managers to analyze their roles, objectives, and criteria more concretely. Paradoxically, it demands more, not less, of its human masters.

Of course, resistance to mathematical models by no means makes resistance to the systems approach necessary. There are many cases where no need may ever arise to use mathematics or computers. For the essence of the systems approach is not its techniques, but the enumeration of options and their implications. A simple checklist may be the only tool needed. I would even argue that some hard thinking in a quiet room may be enough. This being the case, the whole trend to more analysis and logic in management thinking, as reflected in business periodicals, business schools, and the practices of many companies, will work in favor of the development of the systems approach.

It is important to note at this juncture that not all marketers need the systems approach in its formal, elaborate sense. The success of some companies is rooted in other than marketing talents; their expertise may lie in finance, technology, administration, or even in personnel—as in the case of holding companies having an almost uncanny ability to hire brilliant operating managers and the self-control

to leave them alone. In addition, a very simple marketing operation—for example, a company marketing one product through one distribution channel—may have no use for the systems concept.

APPLYING THE APPROACH

Not illogically, there is a system for applying the systems approach. It may be outlined as a sequence of steps:

1. *Define the problem and clarify objectives.* Care must be exercised not to accept the view of the propounder of the problem lest the analyst be defeated at the outset.

2. *Test the definition of the problem.* Expand its parameters to the limit. For example, to solve physical distribution problems it is necessary to study the marketplace (customer preferences, usage rates, market size, and so forth), as well as the production process (which plants produce which items most efficiently, what the interplant movements of raw materials are, and so forth). Delineate the extremes of these factors, their changeability, and the limitations on management's ability to work with them.

3. *Build a model.* Portray all factors graphically, indicating logical and chronological sequences—the dynamic flow of information, decisions, and events. "Closed circuits" should be used where there is information feedback or go, no-go and recycle signals (see Exhibit 2).

4. *Set concrete objectives.* For example, if a firm wants to make daily deliveries to every customer, prohibitive as the cost may be, manipulation of the model will yield one set of answers. But if the desire is to optimize service at lowest cost, then another set of answers will be needed. The more crisply and precisely targets are stated, the more specific the results will be.

5. *Develop alternative solutions.* It is crucial to be as open-minded as possible at this stage. The analyst must seek to expand the list of options rather than merely assess those given to him, then reduce the list to a smaller number of practical or relevant ones.

6. *Set up criteria or tests of relative value.*

7. *Quantify some or all of the factors or "variables."* The extent to which this is done depends, of course, on management's inclinations and the "state of the art."

8. *Manipulate the model.* That is, weigh the costs, effectiveness, profitability, and risks of each alternative.

9. *Interpret the results, and choose one or more courses of action.*

10. *Verify the results.* Do they make sense when viewed against the world as executives know it? Can their validity be tested by experiments and investigations?

Forethought and Perspective

Successful systems do not blossom overnight. From primitive beginnings, they evolve over a period of time as managers and systems specialists learn to understand each other better, and learn how to structure problems and how to push out the frontiers of the "universe" with which they are dealing. Companies must be prepared to invest time, money, and energy in making systems management feasible. This entails a solid foundation of historical data even before the conceptual framework for the system can be constructed. Accordingly, considerable time should be invested at the outset in *thinking* about the problem, its appropriate scope, options, and criteria of choice before plunging into analysis.

Not only technicians, but most of us have a way of falling in love with techniques. We hail each one that comes along—*deus ex machina*. Historically, commercial research has wallowed in several such passions (e.g., probability sampling, motivation research, and semantic scaling), and now operations research appears to be doing the same thing. Significantly, each technique has come, in the fullness of time, to take its place as one, but only one, instrument in the research tool chest. We must therefore have a broad and dispassionate perspective on the systems approach at this juncture. We must recognize that the computer does not possess greater magical properties than the abacus. It, too, is a tool, albeit a brilliant one.

Put another way, executives must continue to exercise their judgment and experience. Systems analysis is no substitute for common sense. The computer must adapt itself to their styles, personalities, and modes of problem solving. It is an aid to management, not a surrogate. Businessmen may be slow, but the good ones are bright; the electronic monster, by contrast, is a speedy idiot. It demands great acuity of wit from its human managers lest they be deluged in an avalanche of useless paper. (The story is told of a sales manager who had just found out about the impressive capabilities of his company's computer and called for a detailed sales analysis of all products. The report was duly prepared and wheeled into his office on a dolly.)

Systems users must be prepared to revise continually. There are two reasons for this. First, the boundaries of systems keep changing;

constraints are modified; competition makes fresh incursions; variables, being what they are, vary, and new ones crop up. Second, the analytical process is iterative. Usually, one "pass" at problem formulation and searches for solutions will not suffice, and it will be necessary to "recycle" as early hypotheses are challenged and new, more fruitful insights are stimulated by the inquiry. Moreover, it is impossible to select objectives without knowledge of their effects and costs. That knowledge can come only from analysis, and it frequently requires review and revision.

Despite all the efforts at quantification, systems analysis is still largely an art. It relies frequently on inputs based on human judgment; even when the inputs are numerical, they are determined, at least in part, by judgment. Similarly, the outputs must pass through the sieve of human interpretation. Hence, there is a positive correlation between the pay-off from a system and the managerial level involved in its design. The higher the level, the more rewarding the results.

Finally, let me observe that marketing people merit their own access to computers as well as programmers who understand marketing. Left in the hands of accountants, the timing, content, and format of output are often out of phase with marketing needs.

CONCLUSION

Nearly 800 years ago a monk wrote the following about St. Godric, a merchant later turned hermit:

He laboured not only as a merchant but also as a shipman . . . to Denmark, Flanders, and Scotland; in which lands he found certain rare, and therefore more precious, wares, which he carried to other parts wherein he knew them to be least familiar, and coveted by the inhabitants beyond the price of gold itself, wherefore he exchanged these wares for others coveted by men of other lands. . . .[6]

How St. Godric "knew" about his markets we are not told, marketing having been in a primitive state in 1170. How some of us marketers today "know" is, in my opinion, sometimes no less mysterious than it was eight centuries ago. But we are trying to change that, and I will hazard the not very venturesome forecast that the era of "by

[6] *Life of St. Godric,* by Reginald, a monk of Durham, c. 1170.

guess and by gosh" marketing is drawing to a close. One evidence of this trend is marketers' intensified search for knowledge that will improve their command over their destinies. This search is being spurred on by a number of powerful developments. To describe them briefly:

The growing complexity of technology and the accelerating pace of technological innovation.

The advent of the computer, inspiring and making possible analysis of the relationships between systems components.

The intensification of competition, lent impetus by the extraordinary velocity of new product development and the tendency of diversification to thrust everybody into everybody else's business.

The preference of buyers for purchasing from as few sources as possible, thereby avoiding the problems of assembling bits and pieces themselves and achieving greater reliability, economy, and administrative convenience. (Mrs. Jones would rather buy a complete vacuum cleaner from one source than the housing from one manufacturer, the hose from another, and the attachments from still another. And industrial buyers are not much different from Mrs. Jones. They would rather buy an automated machine tool from one manufacturer than design and assemble the components themselves. Not to be overlooked, in this connection, is the tremendous influence of the U.S. government in buying systems for its military and aerospace programs.)

The further development and application of the systems approach to marketing represents, in my judgment, the leading edge in both marketing theory and practice. At the moment, we are still much closer to St. Godric than to the millenium, and the road will be rocky and tortuous. But if we are ever to convert marketing into a more scientific pursuit, this is the road we must travel. The systems concept can teach us how our businesses really behave in the marketing arena, thereby extending managerial leverage and control. It can help us to confront more intelligently the awesome complexity of marketing, to deal with the hazards and opportunities of technological change, and to cope with the intensification of competition. And in the process, the concept will help us to feed the hungry maws of our expensive computers with more satisfying fare.

Framework for Marketing Strategy

Harry Allison

The purpose of this paper is to accent both the need for a systematic approach to marketing management decision-making and the need—in each decision-making situation—for a complete consideration of the many variables involved. The emphasis is on how marketing decisions should be made rather than on how they are, in fact, made; yet, it is hoped that the former is kept parallel enough with the latter so that the marketing practitioner does not feel uncomfortable.

The ideas presented are not particularly new. The writer has drawn heavily from an article by P. J. Verdoorn[1] and also from writings by Wroe Alderson,[2] Albert W. Frey,[3] Alfred R. Oxenfeldt,[4] D. M. Phelps, and John A. Howard.[5] Comments of colleagues and students have also contributed to all sections of this article.

Briefly, the framework views the job of the marketing staff as that of identifying all relevant marketing alternatives confronting the firm, of choosing from among these alternatives the particular alternative at each output level which best satisfies the goals of the firm, and of carrying out the marketing side of the firm's final plan of action as efficiently and effectively as possible.

The process of choosing among the relevant alternatives involves the marketing staff in an attempt to maximize long-run total revenue net of selling costs at particular output levels, given the outside-imposed and firm-imposed restrictions on the marketing staff's actions.[6] This requires that optimum use be made of those factors which both affect total revenue net of selling costs and are under the control of the firm.

To achieve optimum use of these firm-controlled factors, the marketing staff must take into account not only the effect of the firm-controlled factors on each other, but also the impact of those

Reprinted with permission from the *California Management Review,* vol. IV, no. 1 (Fall, 1961), pp. 75–95. Copyright 1961 by the Regents of the University of California.

factors which affect total revenue net of selling costs and are in some way influenced, but not controlled, by the firm and the effect of those factors which affect total revenue net of selling costs but are neither controlled nor influenced by the firm.

Optimum use of each firm-controlled factor which affects total revenue net of selling costs implies that—within the outside-imposed and firm-imposed restrictions—the marketing staff allocates the firm's marketing efforts in such a way that all expenditures on marketing are put to the best possible use. This, in turn, requires that the marginal effort expended on each controlled factor returns the same marginal revenue net of selling costs per dollar spent and that no better obtainable combined use for the controlled factors exists at the particular levels of output.

The optimum output level for the firm is determined by equating marginal revenue net of selling costs to marginal cost of production. When there are no effective restrictions on the actions of the marketing and production staffs and when the above equalities are realized, each controlled factor in marketing and production is exploited to the point where the marginal contribution net of all costs—marketing and production costs, including the cost of the factor itself—of the last dollar expended on each factor is zero.

IDENTIFYING ALTERNATIVES

Selected marketing plans can, of course, be no better than the best of the identified alternatives. Whether the specific group of alternatives under consideration for a particular output level includes the optimum marketing plan for that level depends on the marketing intuition and imaginative reasoning of the individuals involved; on their own past experience; on their observation of current and former practices of the firm, competitors, and firms in other industries; and on the time and resources devoted to devising plans. The availability of both time and resources for use in determining alternatives is frequently limited. Even if not, at some point, the benefits anticipated from any further search for alternatives will no longer justify the cost.

RESTRICTIONS IMPOSED BY THE FIRM

Firm-imposed restrictions on the marketing staff's freedom to choose among the alternatives it does identify may arise from goals or objectives established for the firm by top management, restrictions set by

top management on the manipulation of the firm-controlled factors affecting total revenue net of selling costs, or the past activities of the firm.

THE FIRM'S GOALS. The goals or objectives of the firm may range from unqualified short- or long-run profit maximization to goals which by no means need result in either maximum short-run or maximum long-run profits.[7]

Where non-profit-maximizing goals are involved, the marketing staff must first sort the identified marketing alternatives to remove those which do not meet the requirements of the non-profit goals of the firm. Alternatives satisfying the non-profit goals are then sorted by their long-run profit contribution with the marketing staff selecting the plan—for each output level—which seems likely to yield the largest total revenue net of selling costs over the long run.[8]

This view sees the goal of the firm not as maximum long-run profits per se, but rather as long-run profits that are as large as possible, given the restricting effect of any and all non-profit goals instituted by the firm's top management. In such context the non-profit goals become simply a part of firm-imposed restrictions on the actions of the marketing and/or production staff. Should the marketing staff find certain non-profit goals too restrictive, it can always appeal to top management to relax the restrictions. However, the marketing staff does not control the final decision on the goals. Therefore, at some point, it must accept the goals established by top management whether it likes them or not.

LIMITS ON THE MANIPULATION OF FIRM-CONTROLLED FACTORS. The dictates of top management with regard to manipulation of firm-controlled factors which affect total revenue net of selling costs may be another restriction on the marketing staff. Such restrictions could be applied through any of the controlled factors cited later in this paper. A few examples of restriction by top management are (1) setting maximum or minimum prices beyond which the marketing staff cannot go, (2) prescribing or proscribing certain channels of distribution, or (3) insisting that advertising and/or personal selling expenditures not go beyond a certain level.

PAST ACTIVITIES OF THE FIRM. Further firm-imposed restrictions on the actions of the marketing staff arise from past activities of the firm. First, there may be a positive or negative prepossession toward an identified alternative as a result of the firm's previous experience with that alternative or a parallel version of it.

If the firm is reasonably prosperous, its existing marketing policies

create a resistance to change simply through their past acceptance and current performance. These existing policies are tried and proven and, as such, hold a degree of attractiveness over the uncertainty of even the most promising of the other alternatives. Likewise, marketing policies which have failed in the past carry a stigma which heavily discounts their current and future consideration, regardless of a change in the conditions involved in their failure.

Secondly, past activities have brought the firm into the current period with a number of commitments which are binding for the present and carry an actual or implied obligation for the future.[9] Such commitments can be changed if there is sufficient time. However, the change may involve absorbing losses on some sunk costs, buying the firm out of certain long term obligations, and/or accepting some loss of goodwill from those who feel that implied obligations are being disregarded. The situation parallels the production problem of obsolescence in which case the firm finds itself with existing plant and equipment that falls short of the ideal.

OUTSIDE-IMPOSED RESTRICTIONS

The marketing staff finds its range of choice among alternatives limited by forces outside the firm as well as by its own top management. Outside-imposed restrictions may take the form of insufficient time, government regulation, industry environment, and rationing of inputs.

INSUFFICIENT TIME. The time restriction has its first impact through limiting the amount of effort the marketing staff can expend in searching for, and in evaluating, alternatives. The result is that fewer alternatives are identified, fewer receive detailed evaluation, and less extensive analyses are given to those that are evaluated.

The other effect of the time restriction is to make some of the identified alternatives unobtainable simply because it is impossible to complete at least one necessary element of those alternatives within the time available. Such situations can best be described by the term *short-run*.

GOVERNMENT REGULATION. Various types of local, state, federal, and foreign government regulations restrict the actions of the marketing staff in many and varied ways. Licensing requirements, pricing restrictions, foreign exchange regulations, control of advertising appeals, and restraints on relationships with customers, agents, and

competitors, are just a few of the many examples that could be cited here.

INDUSTRY ENVIRONMENT. Various industry practices growing out of the market structure and historical experience of the industry may have acquired sanction through strength of usage, or been adopted through informal or formal agreement. Trade discount structures and channels of distribution often fall into the first category, frequency of model changes and pricing into the second, and advertising copy into the third. While in these cases the firm can adopt marketing alternatives which take it outside the industry pattern, the demands of customers, pressure of competition, and the threat of actual chastisement by industry leaders heavily discount such alternatives.

RATIONING OF INPUTS. At times the marketing staff may have to set aside otherwise desirable alternatives because the firm, through no fault of its own, is unable to secure the particular inputs needed—such as financing, materials, or personnel, to carry them out.

Some outside-imposed restrictions classed as rationing of inputs might also be viewed as arising from time restrictions. For example, if enough time were available, additional salesmen could be trained to meet the requirements of any proposal. Also, in some cases of material shortages, additional time may be all that is needed for suppliers to expand their plants and equipment to fill the firm's orders for materials without unreasonable delay.

Most outside-imposed restrictions are beyond the control or the influence of the firm's top management, and must, therefore, be accepted by the marketing staff as unmodifiable. The nature of certain industry practices and certain government regulations—particularly those designed specifically for the industry of which the firm is a part—can, however, frequently be influenced by the firm itself. If the firm is in a dominant position within its own industry, it may even control industry acceptance or rejection of particular practices. If nothing else, it is certainly the firm's top management who must decide how closely the firm will adhere to specific industry practices.

REVENUE NET OF SELLING COSTS

As indicated earlier, the identified alternatives satisfying both firm-imposed and outside-imposed restrictions must be evaluated at each output level in terms of their expected total revenue net of selling costs. Such evaluation requires extensive consideration of all factors

affecting total sales and any of the selling costs. This is no small task, as the range of such factors is extremely broad. It seems particularly useful in marketing decision-making to group the many and varied factors affecting revenue and selling costs on the basis of the degree of control held over them by the firm. Such a classification results in the following categories: (1) factors controlled by the firm, (2) factors influenced but not controlled by the firm, and (3) factors neither influenced nor controlled by the firm.

It will be noted that these groupings of factors affecting total revenue net of selling costs include many of the considerations brought up earlier in discussing firm-imposed and outside-imposed restrictions. There, these factors entered only when they were fixed values set by internal or external forces and, as such, were given conditions within the bounds of which the marketing staff had to operate. The present section includes these considerations when they do not have fixed, predetermined values but rather are variables whose value is either under the control of the marketing staff or whose value must be assessed or predicted by the marketing staff as a part of the process of evaluating the impact of alternative marketing programs.

FIRM-CONTROLLED FACTORS

The firm-controlled factors affecting total revenue net of selling costs are of primary interest because these are factors that the marketing staff can, and does, manipulate in trying to evolve optimum marketing programs for specific levels of output.

They include advertising, assortment, channel(s) of distribution, geographic outreach, group(s) of customers to whom the firm tries to appeal, location(s) for the firm, marketing research, organizational structure and administrative framework for the marketing functions, personal selling, physical distribution, pricing, product design features, quality level, sales promotion including miscellaneous devices, and services.

This list of controlled factors is not intended to be exhaustive or to cite only areas of equivalent importance. Rather, it is intended to point up the primary areas of marketing decision. The controlled factors—and also the factors in the two groupings which follow—have been listed alphabetically in order to avoid the almost impossible task of assigning a ranking of relative importance to each factor.

Each category has a number of subparts. For example, advertising would involve decisions about such things as the total amount to be spent on advertising; copy content; media selection; timing of campaigns; use to be made of cooperative advertisements and promotional allowances; allocation of the advertising budget according to type of final customer, channel agency, and geographic area.

There are many opportunities for disagreement concerning the most appropriate assignment of the subparts. In the case of advertising, the aspect of the geographic allocation might just as well be included under the category of geographic outreach, allocation by type of final customer with the category of the group(s) of customers to whom the firm tries to appeal, and the allocation by channel agency and the use to be made of cooperative advertisements and promotional allowances with the category of channel(s) of distribution. The essential thing is that all subparts are recognized and accounted for, regardless of the category under which they are listed.

Objections may also arise because some readers prefer to take some of the aspects given only sub-category status in the above classification and elevate them to full-category status. Other readers may want to drop certain factors from the listing presented and relegate them to sub-category status. For example, the group of customers to whom the firm tries to appeal could be viewed as the result of decisions on services, quality level, product design features, pricing. Or a decision with regard to customer groups could be viewed as largely predetermining the services, quality level, product design features, pricing, etc.

The position taken here is that none of the listed controlled factors should be relegated to such a subordinate position that its use in a particular marketing program is arrived at without direct consideration. All the cited controlled factors should be recognized as specific areas of decision involved in designing marketing programs, and as such each should be dealt with directly and not piecemeal through the summation of decisions on other controlled factors.

For the purpose of manipulating the firm-controlled factors, it is essential, however, that the interdependence of the controlled factors be recognized—what the marketing staff does with one of these factors affects the performance of the effort expended on the others. Likewise, it needs to be recognized that most of the controlled factors are to some degree a substitute for each other, e.g., a price reduction may be used instead of an increase in advertising or personal selling expenditures or a higher cost location in place of some of the advertising outlays.

FIRM-INFLUENCED FACTORS

The influenced-but-not-controlled factors encompass all those areas in which the firm's own actions may well create reactions that in turn have an impact on the firm's total sales and its selling costs. Factors influenced but not controlled include such categories as:

Actions of producers of substitute and complementary goods
Cooperation of the independent channel agencies selling the firm's products
Number of competitors
Performance of the firm's employees
Reactions of buyers
Technology affecting use of the firm's products

The most sensitive factor in the above grouping is that of the actions of producers of substitute and complementary goods, in particular the actions of competitors. No marketing alternative can be evaluated without making allowance for the impact of the counterstrategy that the alternative is likely to elicit from competitors. The simplest counterstrategy for competitors frequently is to try to parallel the firm's own actions; however, competitive marketing staffs have at their disposal all the firm-controlled factors mentioned earlier, and may choose to manipulate any one, or any combination, of them in trying to hit upon the most effective counterstrategy.

The category of cooperation of the independent channel agancies selling the firm's products includes such things as compliance with pricing recommendations, participation in promotional campaigns, stocking of minimum inventory, and providing repair service and repair parts. The number of competitors is influenced primarily through the firm's pricing and advertising policies although any of the controlled factors might be manipulated in such a manner as to close out—or make unattractive—opportunities to potential competitors.

The performance of the firm's employees involves such considerations as morale; competence—a result of recruiting policies, training programs, and experience; stimulation of the sales force through leadership and appropriate compensation; proper control and coordination procedures; and lack of disruptions such as strikes.

In regard to the reactions of buyers, the firm, of course, hopes to influence buyers in a positive way toward itself and in a negative way

toward competitors. Advertising and personal selling are the most direct factors for realizing this, but actually all the controlled factors are manipulated with the goal of influencing buyer reactions in a manner favorable to the firm.

Technology affecting use of the firm's products is influenced through the firm's own research on additional uses and through what encouragement or discouragement the firm's marketing program creates in regard to research by others either to find additional uses for the product or to create substitute products.

OUTSIDE FACTORS

A number of factors outside both the influence and the control of the firm have an impact on the absolute and the relative effectiveness of given levels of the firm-controlled factors. These same factors also affect the manner in which the influenced-but-not-controlled factors react to various manipulations of the firm-controlled factors.

Changes in these reactions, in turn, have a secondary impact on the effectiveness of the firm-controlled factors. Thus, in evaluating alternatives, allowance must be made for both primary and secondary effects of the anticipated levels of the neither-influenced-nor-controlled factors. This group includes acts of God, buyer expectations with regard to the future level of economic activity, demand for complementary items and items of which the firm's product is a part, general level of economic activity, government action in foreign policy and in domestic monetary and tax matters, population characteristics including distribution by age, education, ethnic background, geographic area, income, etc., population size, and standard of living.

Droughts, hail storms, or unseasonal frosts may destroy or damage certain crops so that sellers of packing and canning supplies find little market response regardless of how firm-controlled factors are manipulated in the marketing program. Furthermore, under these conditions, the relative effectiveness of increased personal selling versus a price concession may be somewhat different than in a normal crop year.

In addition, the bleak prospects for sales may have a negative impact on the morale of the sales force and, through this, a secondary negative reaction on the effectiveness of the personal selling factor. Likewise, different buyer expectations, such as optimistic versus pessimistic outlooks of industrial, commercial, or household buyers with regard to the future level of economic activity, generally call for

different marketing approaches, if a firm's marketing staff is to achieve the maximum feasible total revenue net of selling costs for a given output level.

An example of the impact of the demand for an item of which the firm's product is a part would be the impact of the demand for new housing on the sales of a firm manufacturing bathroom fixtures. The absolute and relative responses to alternative manipulations of the controlled factors might vary considerably with the demand for new housing. Also, changes in the standard of living might progressively shift a firm's product from the category of a luxury toward that of a necessity. Such a change would have repercussions on the effectiveness of the different firm-controlled factors.

CONDITIONS TO BE MET

In choosing from the various alternative manipulations of firm-controlled marketing factors at a given level of output, the marketing staff should not seek the plan with the lowest selling costs as such a plan usually produces relatively little total revenue; nor should it seek the plan with the highest total revenue as such a plan usually has exceptionally high selling costs. The goal, rather, is to sort the feasible alternatives at each output level to determine which alternative yields the maximum total revenue net of selling costs for that output level.

If no one plan satisfies both the lowest selling costs and the highest total revenue criteria for a particular output, it becomes very probable that the plan chosen on the basis of maximum total revenue net of selling costs will be neither the minimum selling costs plan nor the maximum total revenue plan for that output. Of course, once a plan is chosen as the best of the feasible alternatives at a given output level, the marketing staff should be prepared to execute that plan at the lowest possible cost and in a manner which would maximize the total revenue realized from that plan. In short, the marketing staff is responsible for carrying out chosen plans as efficiently and as effectively as possible.

MARGINAL REVENUE NET

In manipulating the levels of the firm-controlled factors for any particular marketing alternative, the marketing staff should equalize the net return over selling costs to the marginal effort expended on

all of the firm-controlled marketing factors. This net return to the marginal effort can be referred to as the marginal revenue net of selling costs and is defined as the change in total revenue minus the change in all selling costs—including changes in the cost of the marketing factor being manipulated—associated with the increasing sales by one unit. If all controlled marketing factors except one are held constant in securing the one unit increase in sales, the marginal revenue net of selling costs from the additional unit of sales can be viewed as the return to the marginal effort expended on a particular controlled marketing factor. Unless the marginal revenues net of selling costs are equal for the last dollars spent on advertising, location, personal selling, services, etc., at a particular level of output, the firm's total revenue net of selling costs—and, therefore, the firm's profits—for that output level can be increased by transferring marginal dollars from the controlled factors yielding the lower marginal return into the controlled factors yielding the higher marginal return.

For example, if the last dollar spent on advertising has a marginal revenue net of selling costs of 50 cents, while the last dollar spent on personal selling returns only 25 cents, total revenue net of selling costs can be increased by taking marginal dollars out of personal selling and applying them to advertising where the net return is higher. As the amount spent on advertising is increased, the marginal revenue net of selling costs of dollars spent on advertising will decline (presumably the richer return areas have already been exploited so that additional expenditures are confronted with declining returns). Conversely as the amount spent on personal selling is reduced, the marginal revenue net of selling costs of dollars spent on personal selling will increase (the marginal dollars are removed from the least lucrative areas so that the marginal revenue net of selling costs for the remaining dollars is higher).

Conceptually, this transfer of effort from the low-return variables to the high-return variables would pay dividends as long as inequalities remained among the marginal revenues net of selling costs. In actual practice, of course, expenditures on advertising, rent, personal selling, services, etc., would not be made in dollar increments even at the margin but rather would be varied in chunks of lump sum amounts. Thus, at best, the equality condition for marginal revenues net of selling costs could only be approximated.

SPREADING COSTS AND REVENUES

It should be noted that the period of time used in the calculation of the marginal revenue net of selling costs associated with a specific change should be sufficiently long to give a reasonable spreading out of any one-time marketing costs that may be involved in the change, or else only a realistic part—rather than all—of the one-time costs should be charged against the change.

This same consideration would hold for the revenue data as well. The initial impact on revenue of a specific change may be either extremely light or extremely heavy relative to the longer run impact. In such situations again, the period of time used in the calculation of the marginal revenue net of selling costs should be long enough to give a reasonable leveling out of the initial reaction, or else the original impact data should be adjusted for the failure to do so.

BALANCED PROGRAM

While the condition of balanced effort as reflected in the equality of the marginal revenues net of selling costs for all of the firm-controlled factors is a necessary condition for maximizing total revenue net of selling costs at any output level, it is not in itself sufficient to assure that the desired maximum is achieved. Poor marketing programs can be balanced so that the marginal revenues net of selling costs are equal just as in the case of good marketing programs.

Thus, not only should a balanced program be achieved at each output level, but it should be the best possible balanced program for that level of output. In order to maximize total revenue net of selling costs for a particular output level, not only must the condition of equal marginal revenues net of selling costs be attained for all controlled marketing factors, but also it must not be possible to increase the total revenue net of selling costs for that output level by altering the nature of the marketing program through changing any one controlled factor or combination of controlled factors.

SALES ENGINEERS

From the perspective of what is to follow, the marketing staff is looked upon as a group of sales engineers working with a sales function to produce dollars of revenue net of selling costs just as produc-

tion engineers are traditionally viewed as working with a production function to produce units of product. The sales inputs are the firm-controlled marketing factors.

These have a cost to the firm just as have production inputs.[10] The marketing staff's performance is measured in dollars of total revenue net of selling costs. It is charged with manipulating the firm-controlled marketing inputs within the context of known marketing techniques in a manner that realizes the maximum long run revenue net of selling costs at each output level within the restrictions, if any, which are imposed by the outside forces or by the firm itself.

While the task of the marketing staff and its approach to that task seem to parallel the production situation, the marketing side of the firm is not nearly as neat conceptually as the production side. Factors outside the direct control of the firm have a much greater significance for marketing. Furthermore, the impact of the many revenue affecting factors—including the firm-controlled factors—on total revenue net of selling costs can be assessed much less accurately than can the impact of production factors on output and production costs.

THE SALES FUNCTION

In Chart I a number of equal-sales contours representing progressively larger sales have been determined, and the equal-cost lines tangent to each have been inserted thereby identifying the economically efficient way to sell each of the indicated levels of output.[11] It should be noted that for any one set of contours, such as that given in Chart I, a number of things are taken as being constant at particular levels. They are (1) all firm-controlled marketing factors, other than the two being manipulated, (2) all of the neither-influenced-nor-controlled marketing factors, and (3) the initial level of all of the influenced-but-not-controlled marketing factors. The impact of any changes induced in the level of the influenced-but-not-controlled factors through manipulating the two controlled factors is incorporated into the estimated values for the sales level contours.

For low levels of sales the equal-sales contours would intersect both of the illustrated axes, as these lower levels could be attained either with relatively large amounts of advertising and no personal selling or with relatively large amounts of personal selling and no advertising.

At high levels of sales where large amounts of advertising and personal selling are being used, the equal-sales contours may begin to turn back on themselves as either extreme of the contour is ap-

CHART I

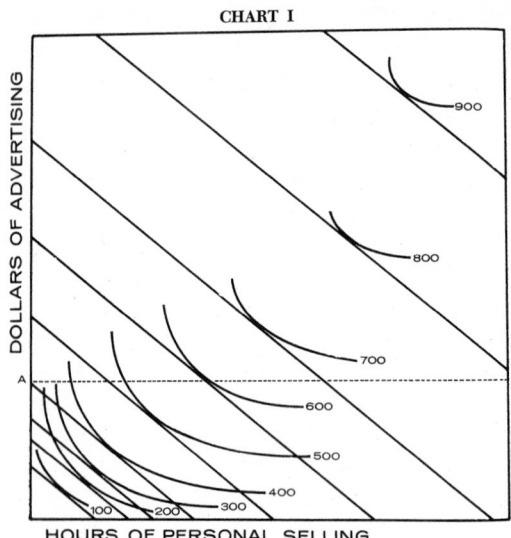

HOURS OF PERSONAL SELLING

proached. For example, the firm's marketing staff might find it had so saturated the market in which it was working with personal selling that it was realizing a negative unit-of-sales return to marginal increases in personal selling effort. Therefore, it would be forced to increase advertising outlays along with increases in the personal selling outlay in order to remain on a given equal-sales contour, that is, in order to overcome the negative impact from the increased calls of the sales force.

Naturally, the marketing staff would not be interested in pushing any controlled marketing factor into the area where marginal increments had a negative return unless it was required to do so by firm-imposed restrictions—for instance, using a certain size of sales force in order to give employment to all of the relatives of top management.

A change in the value of any of the factors assumed to be constant changes the illustrated sales surface. Thus, given the many variables taken to be constant, the realistic range of values they might have, and the resulting numerous possible combinations that might arise, there is literally a multitude of the illustrated advertising and personal selling relationships.

The proportion of such relationships having significance for a particular decision-making situation is usually relatively small, since the marketing staff is only interested in the more promising of the feasible levels for the controlled factors and in the more probable

of the possible levels for the influenced-but-not-controlled and the neither-influenced-nor-controlled factors. Taking a relatively small proportion of a multitude of relationships, however, still yields a sizable number of relationships that are relevant to any one particular decision-making situation.

There is some further help in that, even within a particular relationship, ranges of the two observed variables are eliminated from consideration either because such levels are not feasible or because they hold little or no promise.

Furthermore, while the equal-sales contours are drawn as continuous relationships in the theoretical cases, the marketing staff generally finds it sufficient—even within the more promising ranges of the variables—to evaluate a series of discrete points. The latter occurs either because finer gradations are not feasible owing to the imperfect divisibility of one or more of the inputs or because it is sufficiently accurate to use these points as benchmarks and interpolate between them in order to get the continuous curve.

TOTAL CURVE

The series of tangency points between the equal-sales contours and the equal-cost lines in Chart I supply the data for deriving the total-revenue-net-of-selling-costs curve. Each tangency point represents a particular level of sales achieved at some indicated selling cost to the firm. The sales level multiplied by the price per unit—taken as fixed in this example—minus the sum of the cost indicated by the appropriate equal-cost line and the cost of the other selling factors taken as fixed for the two-variable analysis yields the total revenue net of selling costs for that level of output. Repeating the process over the range of sales levels and plotting the resulting dollar data against output produces a curve similar to that shown in Chart II.

The total-revenue-net-of-selling-costs curve may initially rise at an increasing or decreasing rate depending upon whether increasing returns occur.[12] However, as the sales level increases, the curve eventually begins to rise at a decreasing rate, reaches a peak, and then falls toward—and finally through—zero. Unless firm-imposed restrictions force the marketing staff to do so, it is not going to be interested in plans carrying sales beyond the peak point of this curve, since in the falling range the marginal revenues net of selling costs for the manipulated factors are negative.

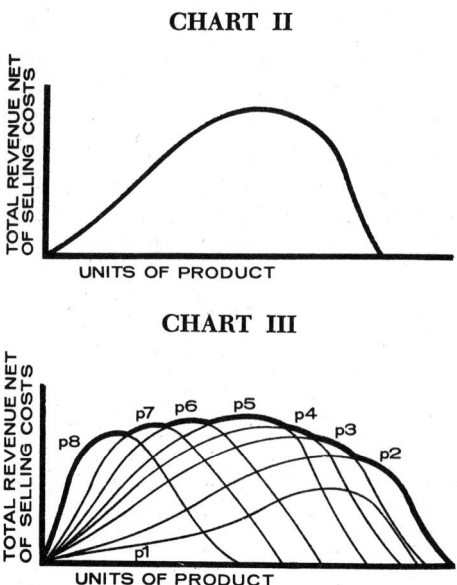

CHART II

TOTAL REVENUE NET OF SELLING COSTS

UNITS OF PRODUCT

CHART III

TOTAL REVENUE NET OF SELLING COSTS

p8 p7 p6 p5 p4 p3 p2 p1

UNITS OF PRODUCT

INCORPORATING ADDITIONAL INPUTS

A third firm-controlled marketing input can be graphically accounted for by developing a sales function—like that in Chart I—for each of the relevant levels of the third input. The tangency points on each of these sales functions can then be reduced to individual total-revenue-net-of-selling-costs curves by the process described above.

These curves can, in turn, all be plotted on the same set of total dollars versus output axes as shown in Chart III. The highest sections of the resulting family of curves then trace the appropriate total-revenue-net-of-selling-costs curve for the three-input relationship. If fine enough gradations of the third variable are used, the high points of the individual curves should trace a smooth, continuous curve. Otherwise, the curve derived from the high points would have a scalloped effect as shown in Chart III.

This approach is especially useful with those variables that are particularly difficult or clumsy to treat as one of two manipulated variables generating a sales function such as was done earlier in the example dealing with advertising and personal selling. Price is one of the several variables that fall into this category. Thus, in Chart III, each total revenue-net-of-selling-costs curve can be viewed as repre-

senting the optimum combinations of advertising and personal selling for selling various quantities of the product at a particular price level.[13]

A fourth firm-controlled marketing factor can be incorporated by constructing a family of curves such as that shown in Chart III for alternative levels of the fourth factor. These several families of total-revenue-net-of-selling-costs curves can then all be plotted on the same diagram with the highest sections of these curves being taken to make up the total-revenue-net-of-selling-costs curve for the four-input case.

An example could be developed using the four inputs, advertising, personal selling, price, and channel of distribution. For each alternative channel a family of total-revenue-net-of-selling-costs curves reflecting varying combinations of advertising, personal selling, and price could be derived as discussed in the three-variable case cited. In most situations the channels of interest are restricted to two or three possibilities so that the task would not be so formidable as it might seem at first thought.

It is just a short step from the above four-variable example to the multi-variable case where, rather than develop the complete sales functions and the resulting families of total-revenue-net-of-selling-costs curves, the marketing staff intensively evaluates only what appear to be the most relevant alternative combinations of the firm-controlled marketing factors.

The total-revenue-net-of-selling-costs curve is then represented by a disconnected series of points, each of which identifies the maximum total-revenue-net-of-selling-costs plan for a specific output level. The basic reasoning patterns of a sales function and its companion total-revenue-net-of-selling-costs curve still apply in such a development. The chosen marketing alternatives lie on a multi-dimensional sales surface at points of tangency between equal-sales and equal-cost relationships with the selection process following the same decision rules as in the less complex examples sketched above.

PROFITABLE LEVEL OF OUTPUT

If no outside- and firm-imposed restrictions exist, or if, at least, those that do exist are ineffective in the sense that they do not prevent either the marketing or the production staff from reaching desired alternatives, then all points on the total-revenue-net-of-selling-costs curve

and on the total-production-cost curve will represent balanced marketing programs and balanced production programs. Given no effective non-profit-maximizing firm-imposed restrictions, top management would then select the output level where marginal revenue net of selling costs equaled the marginal cost of production.[14]

Since, under the above conditions, both the marketing and production programs would be balanced within themselves, the chosen level of output will be a position at which the marginal revenues net of selling costs are equal for all firm-controlled marketing factors, the marginal costs are equal for all firm-controlled production factors, and the marginal revenues net of selling costs are equal to the marginal costs of production.

At this point, all firm-controlled factors are fully exploited to where the last dollar spent on each just returns a dollar—i.e., for each factor the marginal contribution net of all costs (marketing and production, including the cost of the factor itself) is equal to zero.

When the total-revenue-net-of-selling-costs curve and the total-production-cost curve are both smooth instead of scalloped, the above equality position takes place where the slopes of the two curves are equal. If one or both of the two curves is scalloped instead of smooth, the equality of marginal revenue net of selling costs and marginal cost of production may occur more than once and, therefore, may not be a sufficient condition in itself. In such cases the profit maximizing solution is at the marginal equality point where the total-revenue-net-of-selling-costs curve lies furthest above the total-production-cost curve.

MARGINAL EQUALITY POINT

The point of marginal equalities must lie at or before the peak of the total-revenue-net-of-selling-costs curve. After this curve begins to turn down, the firm is confronted with declining total revenue net of selling costs and rising total production cost (average production cost may be falling because of economies of scale, but total production cost would be rising) so that profit declines.

Actually as a result of rising total production cost, the profit maximizing solution is likely to occur at an output level prior to the peak of the total-revenue-net-of-selling-costs curve rather than at the peak itself. Such a solution is presented in Chart IV for the case of a

CHART IV

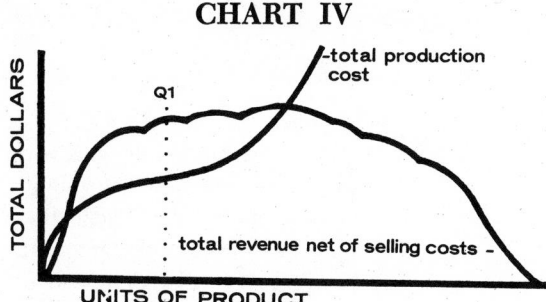

scalloped total-revenue-net-of-selling-costs curve and a smooth total-production-cost curve.

THE IMPACT OF RESTRICTIONS

In the examples which follow, it is always assumed that the stated restrictions are the only restrictions on the manipulation of the firm-controlled marketing and production factors. Furthermore, it is assumed that the marketing and production staffs always strive (within the limitations of any restrictions on their actions) to maximize total-revenue net of selling costs at each output level and to minimize total costs of production at each output level. Thus, when the discussion centers on the problem of balance within either the marketing or the production program, it is assumed that the discussion of balance refers to balance within the best obtainable marketing or production alternative at a specified level of output.

BALANCE ISN'T EVERYTHING

As indicated earlier, even poor alternatives can be balanced. Balance, therefore, is not of such high merit that the firm will select a balanced but poor marketing or production alternative over an unbalanced alternative that has a higher total revenue net of selling costs or a lower total cost of production. In effect, the proper derivation of the equal-sales contours in the sales function or of the equal-output contours in the production function should eliminate alternatives that were balanced but inefficient from consideration as these alternatives would lie beyond the specific contour for their sales or output level.

FIXED PLANT

Plant facilities may be fixed either because of a time restriction or a capital restriction. In either case, the marketing staff is not involved, and there is no effect on the total-revenue-net-of-selling-costs curve. At each output level, the marketing staff can reach the desired programs and can achieve a balancing within those programs in that the marginal revenues net of selling costs can be equated for all of the firm-controlled marketing factors.

The production staff, however, finds that certain desired alternatives are ruled out and that they have to move from a long run cost function to a short run relationship where fixed factors are involved. The production staff should balance the variable inputs in the production mix by equating the marginal costs of the variable factors to each other, but only at one output level can these marginal costs be equated to the marginal cost of increasing the plant size.

At low output levels the marginal cost of the plant is higher than that of the variable factors—in such a situation, the production staff would prefer to use less plant and more of the variable factors if it were possible. At high output levels the marginal cost of the plant is lower than that of the variable factors, and here the production staff would prefer to increase the amount of plant in their production mix and reduce the amounts of the variable factors.

In putting marketing and production data together, top management should equate the marginal revenues net of selling costs of the controlled marketing factors to the marginal costs of the controlled production factors which are not fixed. Only if, by chance, this equality occurs at that one point where the marginal cost of the plant equals the marginal costs of the firm-controlled variable production factors, would all of the marginal values be equal.

FIXED INDIVIDUAL BUDGETS

Situations in which the marketing staff is given a fixed budget for one of the firm-controlled marketing factors are quite parallel in their impact on total revenue net of selling costs to the effect of a fixed plant on the production-cost relationship. A major difference does arise in that, in the case of a fixed plant, it is assumed that the plant size can neither be reduced nor increased, while in the case of fixed

marketing budgets, it is generally acceptable to spend less than the fixed budget, if it should be advantageous to the firm to do so.[15]

Thus, at the lower output levels where the budget restriction is ineffective, the marketing staff can balance the marginal revenues net of selling costs for all marketing factors. At output levels where the budget restriction is effective, the marketing staff should equate the marginal values for the variable firm-controlled marketing factors to each other. At such levels, the factor restricted from increased use by the budget limitation has a marginal net revenue that is higher than the other controlled marketing factors. Thus, at these levels of output, the marketing staff would, if permitted, find it desirable to increase the amount of the fixed-budget item and reduce the amounts of the variable items.

For example, if a budget limitation restricted advertising outlays to level A in Chart I, a horizontal line drawn through A would establish the range of choice open to the marketing staff. Note that once the budget restriction becomes effective, the marketing staff must resort to economically inefficient methods simply because the advertising outlay cannot be increased—i.e., given budget restriction A in Chart I, 600 units of sales can be reached only by using an economically inefficient combination of advertising and personal selling. Also note that—given the fixed advertising budget and the assumed levels of the other firm-controlled marketing factors—the firm in Chart I cannot realize 700 or more units of sales regardless of how much personal selling effort it stands ready to use.

Budget restrictions on marketing factors do not affect the production-cost relationship. When the marketing and production data are brought together by top management, the marginal revenues net of selling costs for all the controlled marketing factors not restricted by budget limitations should be equated to the marginal costs of the controlled production inputs. If this takes place at levels of output where the budget limitations are ineffective, a complete balancing both within and between the firm-controlled marketing and production factors can be achieved.

An expanded example of the budget restriction case is the situation in which the marketing staff is given a fixed total marketing budget with no limitations on how it might be used. Here the budget should be allocated among the controlled marketing factors so that the marginal revenues net of selling costs from all the budget restricted factors are equal. Price would probably be the only controlled marketing factor not affected by the budget restriction.

Thus, after the budget restriction begins to force the firm away

from desired marketing alternatives, the marginal revenue net of selling costs for the price factor should be taken out of equality with the marginal values of the other controlled marketing factors. In the output range where the budget restriction is effective, the marginal revenues net of selling costs for the restricted factors should be equal to each other and larger than the marginal revenue net of selling costs for the price variable. Thus, at these output levels, the marketing staff would like to expand the use of the restricted factors and adjust price upward.

In reaching the decision on the level of output for the firm, top management should equate the marginal revenue net of selling costs for price to the marginal costs of the production inputs. If this equality occurs within the range of output where the budget restriction on the marketing staff is ineffective, the marginal revenues net of selling costs for the controlled marketing factors would all be equal to each other and to the marginal costs of the controlled production inputs.

Manipulation of the price factor may be restricted for the marketing staff through top management setting a minimum below which price cannot be lowered, a maximum above which price cannot be raised, or a specific price that can neither be lowered nor raised. The latter case is similar to the fixed plant situation in production.

Given an unchangeable price, the marketing staff should equate the marginal revenues net of selling costs at each output level for all firm-controlled marketing factors other than price. Probably at one output level, at least, the price dictated by top management will be ideal so that, at that output level—or levels—the marginal revenues net of selling costs can be equated for all the firm-controlled marketing factors.

At levels of output below the latter point, the marginal revenue net of selling costs for the price factor is lower than that of the other firm-controlled marketing factors. In selling these outputs, the marketing staff would like to be able to raise price and increase the amounts used of the other controlled marketing factors.

At the levels of output above the point where all the marginal revenues net of selling costs are equal, the situation is just reversed— i.e., the marginal revenue net of selling costs for price is relatively high. Here the marketing staff would like to lower price and reduce the amounts used of the other controlled marketing factors.

The setting of price has no impact on the production-cost relationship. In putting marketing and production data together, top management should select that level of output which equates the marginal

revenues net of selling costs for all the firm-controlled marketing factors except price to the marginal costs of all controlled production inputs. Only if this output level is also the point where the marketing program is in complete balance, would the firm be operated where all the marginal values of the firm-controlled factors were equal.

If the price set by top management is merely a minimum or maximum price, rather than an unchangeable price, the marketing staff can achieve balanced marketing programs for all output levels where the ideal price for the output level falls within the unrestricted ranges. If the solution to the level of output for the firm falls within this range of outputs, all firm-controlled factors would be balanced with their marginal revenues net of selling costs being equal to each other and to their marginal costs of production.

FIXED QUANTITY

Quantity, like price, can be fixed by top management through setting a minimum, a maximum, or a specific unchangeable level. If it is assumed that the fixed quantity level does not grow out of a restriction on any of the firm-controlled marketing or production factors, but rather reflects such desires of top management as (1) not growing beyond a certain point, (2) realizing some fixed percentage increase in sales, (3) achieving some stated share of the industry market, or (4) growing to some absolute size level, then the quantity restriction would have no impact on the total revenue net of selling costs relationship or on the production cost relationship. At all levels of output both the marketing and the production staffs would be able to achieve their desired balanced programs.

If output is to be at some unchangeable level, top management will find that the marginal revenues net of selling costs for the controlled marketing factors do not equal the marginal costs of the controlled production factors at the fixed level of output unless, by chance, the fixed level of output falls just at the output level where the total equality occurred. If output is set in the sense of stating a minimum or a maximum quantity, marginal revenues net of selling costs for the controlled marketing factors can be equated to the marginal costs of the controlled production factors only if this equality occurs within the range of accepted quantity levels. If such is not the case, the chosen level of output must fall on the stated minimum or maximum quantity. In these situations, all marginal revenues net of selling costs should be equated for the controlled marketing factors and the

marginal costs of production should be equated for the controlled
production factors; however, the two groups—marginal revenues net
of selling costs and marginal costs of production—would not be
equated to each other.

SUMMARY

Essentially, the marketing staff is viewed as having responsibility for
maximizing total revenue net of selling costs for each level of output.
Achieving the best possible combination of the controlled marketing
factors at a particular output level requires that the revenue net of
selling costs realized from the marginal effort expended on each of the
controlled factors be equal, and that no feasible change in any one or
any group of the controlled factors be able to improve the firm's total
revenue net of selling costs for that output level.

Ideally, when top management chooses the particular combination
of marketing and production programs for the firm, the marginal
values of the firm-controlled factors on both the marketing and production sides of the firm should be equal so that the net contribution
of the last dollar spent in any and all areas of the firm would be equal
to zero.

Generally, the marketing staff is not given an entirely free hand in
carrying out its responsibility, but rather finds itself confronted with
restrictions on its choice among alternative marketing plans as a
result of outside- and firm-imposed limitations on the actions it can
take. Thus, the marketing staff may well find that the above conditions cannot be realized; yet, they are conditions which are to be
pursued as far as possible.

If outside- or firm-imposed restrictions prevent either the marketing staff or the production staff from reaching otherwise desired
alternatives at particular output levels, top management should pick
the marketing and production combination which balances the marginal values for the unrestricted controlled marketing and production
factors and which thereby equates the marginal contribution net of all
costs for the unrestricted controlled factors to zero.[16]

In the process of evaluating specific manipulations of the firm-
controlled marketing factors, allowance must be made for anticipated
responses from those factors influenced but not controlled and for the
impact of any such responses, in turn, on the outcome of the original
manipulation of the controlled factors.

Furthermore, the marketing staff must incorporate into its evaluation of the alternative manipulations of the controlled factors, both the primary and secondary effects of the expected levels of those total revenue and/or selling cost influencing factors which are neither controlled nor influenced by the firm.

DATA FOR FRAMEWORK

It is well recognized that much of the data about the impacts and interrelationships of the various factors affecting total revenue net of selling costs are not known to the firm. Furthermore, it is recognized that some of these data cannot be objectively measured, while in the case of others, it is too costly in terms of time and money to measure them for the decision at hand either because the necessary time and money are not available to the firm or because, for the particular situation, the contribution of the objectively measured data is not deemed worth the cost of obtaining it.

What is maintained here is not that the marketing staff will have, or even will be able to secure, all the data demanded by the decision-making situation, but rather that (1) the decision must be made (if no action is taken, the implication is that it has been decided that inaction is the best course) and that (2) the final decision indirectly assigns a value, or at least a range of values, to all the unquantified variables involved.

Therefore, since the final decision can only be the correct solution under some set of assumed values for the unquantified variables; and since these unquantified variables will receive at least implied values, or ranges of value, through the final decision, it is best to attack the problem of estimating them head on.

The head-on approach has two merits. First, the estimating or "guesstimating" process used in the head-on approach at least rules out obviously impossible and highly improbable values for the unquantified variables, while such values might slip by undetected on an indirect assignment basis if a decision is reached by completely ignoring them.

Second, this approach will more clearly indicate the weaknesses in the quantitative estimates behind the decision so that significance of these weaknesses can be properly assessed in terms of their impact on the probability of a favorable outcome. In short, as its second contribution, the head-on approach makes the decision-maker more aware of when he is about to draw to an inside straight position.

ROLE OF FRAMEWORK

The role of the developed framework approach presented here is not to supply the answers to marketing problems, but rather to offer a consistent and reasonably inclusive frame of reference within which to search for the answers. The emphasis is on the nature of the problem, the wide range of variables, interrelationships among the variables which must be reckoned with, and the conditions that should be met.

Real-world decision-making situations may fall short of this framework for many reasons; yet, attempting to approximate the framework should result in improved marketing decisions through a more systematic and complete consideration of the variables involved, even though much of the evaluation is still done through executive judgment.

Thus, it is hoped that the presented framework has value as a tool for improving marketing decision-making. Furthermore, it is hoped that it conveys a better understanding of the marketing sector of the firm to individuals outside marketing, thereby fostering a more cooperative relationship between marketing and nonmarketing groups.

Throughout this article an effort has been made to integrate the presented framework with the standard approach to production relationships. It is hoped that this not only makes the framework more palatable to the theorist but also contributes to a better appreciation of the process of making marketing decisions and to a better understanding of the interrelationships among the factors affecting total revenue net of selling costs.

REFERENCES

1. P. J. Verdoorn, "Marketing from the Producer's Point of View," *The Journal of Marketing,* volume XX, 3, January, 1956, pp. 221–235.
2. Wroe Alderson, *Marketing Behavior and Executive Action* (Homewood, Illinois: Richard D. Irwin, Inc., 1957), particularly Chapter IV.
3. Albert W. Frey, *How Many Dollars for Advertising* (New York: The Ronald Press Company, 1955), particularly Chapter 4.
4. Alfred R. Oxenfeldt, "The Formulation of a Market Strategy" in Eugene J. Kelley and William Lazer, *Managerial Marketing: Perspectives and Viewpoints* (Homewood, Illinois: Richard D. Irwin, Inc., 1958), pp. 264–272.

5. D. M. Phelps, *Sales Management* (Homewood, Illinois: Richard D. Irwin, Inc., 1953). Also, John A. Howard, *Marketing Management: Analysis and Decision* (Homewood, Illinois: Richard D. Irwin, Inc., 1957), particularly Chapters I and II.

6. Total relationships are used throughout this paper rather than average relationships, because dealing with totals eliminates the danger of becoming engrossed with increasing profit per unit at the expense of total profits, and also because total relationships are one step closer to the underlying sales and production input data and to the concept of marginal increments than are average relationships. Selling costs are taken to include the costs associated with such activities as advertising, personal selling, physical distribution, and services. While variables such as product design and quality level are considered to be marketing variables in this paper, changes in such variables are treated as defining a new product with new revenue and cost functions. The costs associated with such changes would not be subtracted from total revenue in getting the total-revenue-net-of-selling-costs curve but rather would be handled on the production side through a shift in the total-production-cost curve.

7. Examples of the latter are goals to (1) maintain—or increase to some stated level—the firm's share of the market, (2) avoid inciting aggressive action from competitors, (3) keep financial control of the firm in the hands of the present ownership, (4) secure some stated rate of sales increase, (5) achieve some particular industrial and/or social power position for the firm's management, (6) maintain some minimum level of employment, (7) continue the firm's position of a leader in new product development or in product quality, or (8) carry out some stated social welfare goal.

8. The predicted outcome of any plan has a degree of uncertainty, but for some plans the degree of uncertainty is greater than for others; thus, the weighing of alternative plans has to include some element of discounting for uncertainty.

9. The range of commitments affecting marketing activities is quite large, e.g., (1) inventories may be excessive or short; (2) certain facilities and equipment may be owned, while others may be under long term leases which may include some penalty clause if the agreement is cancelled; (3) critical positions are already staffed and lines of authority and responsibility are established; (4) production licensing agreements may be in existence; and (5) channel agencies may claim certain territorial rights and may hold commitments from the firm involving some degree of specific marketing support.

10. A price reduction has a cost equal to the amount of the price reduction times the number of units that could have been sold at the higher price and a return equal to the increased number of units sold times the new price. A price increase has a cost equal to the reduction in units sold times the old price and a return equal to the amount of the

price increase times the quantity sold at the new price level. If in the case of a price reduction, the firm must absorb losses on dealer inventories, or if in either case there are costs of changing price lists and catalogues or other costs associated with the price change, such costs would have to be allocated over time and charged against the expected return from the proposed price change.

11. The equal-cost lines are straight lines since dollars spent on advertising are a perfect substitute for dollars spent on personal selling as far as total expenditures are concerned—i.e., there is a constant dollar cost rate of substitution between advertising and personal selling. Changes in prices of inputs related to the quantity used could be accounted for through departing from straight equal-cost lines or through inserting several sets of straight equal-cost lines with different slopes and relating the equal-sales contours to the set of equal-cost lines appropriate to the quantity of inputs involved.

   The equal-sales contours are illustrated as curved in a convex fashion toward the origin because advertising and personal selling are infrequently perfect substitutes for each other in their ability to create sales. For example, as marginal effort is transferred from advertising to personal selling, the marginal performance of the effort in advertising increases while that of personal selling decreases. Thus, if the total sales effectiveness is to be retained—i.e., if the firm is to stay on the same equal-sales contour—it will take larger and larger chunks of personal selling effort to balance reductions in advertising.

12. The result here is a function of both the situation and the variable(s) being considered—e.g., in certain situations advertising may have a range in which increasing returns occur.

13. Owing to the many variables having some effect on total revenue net of selling costs, it is difficult to generalize about just how the total-revenue-net-of-selling-costs curves would appear relative to each other. One would expect, however, to find that the highest segments at the low output levels were associated with relatively high prices while the highest segments at the high output levels were associated with relatively low prices.

14. Here, as throughout this discussion, it is assumed that at least one alternative yielding positive profits exists for the firm.

15. The marketing staff may, however, decide that it must expend its full budget—even though this means using an inefficient marketing program—in order to protect its long-run interest. For example, an excessive advertising budget may be fully expended simply because failure to do so may have an adverse impact on future requests for funds for advertising.

16. An alternative formulation would be to view the marketing staff as, in effect, the grand strategists of the firm operating within firm-

imposed restrictions determined by top management. In such a perspective, the production staff would be required to submit the production cost data to the marketing staff. The marketing staff would then proceed to move directly to the maximum long-run profit strategy consistent with the outside- and firm-imposed restrictions. Here the marketing staff could somewhat restrict the range of output over which it did extensive evaluations of marketing alternatives. It could also by-pass the marginal revenue net of selling costs concept, and move directly to dealing with marginal contribution net of all cost for the controlled marketing factors.

PART II | Tools and Techniques of the Decision Sciences in Marketing

Marketing applications of quantitative techniques basically take place at two levels: the descriptive level (Chapter 4 describes many of the new techniques at this stage) and the decision-making level (Chapter 3 provides articles on techniques at this level of executive decision making). Applications in the first (or lowest) level involve the classification and categorization of market segments, the processing of masses of data to yield useful information, and the determination of useful relationships. This "information search" technique is used in marketing to help the firm eliminate some of the uncertainty about the environment in which it operates and to provide information for management analysis.

chapter 3 | Decision Techniques of Marketing Management

Chapter 3 exposes the reader to many of the latest techniques employed by the decision maker. These approaches are the higher level methods of analysis used by marketing management to determine the expected outputs given certain decision inputs. After the evaluation of several promising courses of action, management compares the decision outputs of each alternative strategy to determine that one which seems to provide the highest expectation of achieving the marketing and firm objectives.

Traditionally, management has found it hard to determine which strategy maximizes its objectives, assuming that it has correctly defined the true goals of the company. This dilemma has caused marketers to take a new look at an old friend—the heuristic. In "Heuristic Models: Mapping the Mazes for Management," Charles Hinkle and Alfred A. Kuehn evaluate the new role and the potential of heuristic programming in market planning.

In "The Use of Mathematical Models in Marketing," Philip Kotler introduces the reader to the possible uses of models for decision making in marketing. Also Kotler reviews and evaluates the roles of calculus, matrix algebra, probability theory and simulation in solving business problems.

Two "glamour" techniques of management science that attract attention in marketing are simulation and Bayesian Statistics. Harold Weitz, in "The Promise of Simulation in Marketing," describes the advantages and disadvantages of this approach to making decisions.

The potential applications of Bayes Theorem described by Harry V. Roberts in "Bayesian Statistics in Marketing" would probably astound the Reverend Bayes. In this short article Roberts presents an example of the use of Bayesian statistics, then discusses the role of judgment (in the derivation of the *prior distribution*) and the potential contributions of the method. It is an excellent article for the lay marketer wishing to acquire an elementary understanding of Bayesian Statistics.

Heuristic Models: Mapping the Maze for Management

Charles L. Hinkle
Alfred A. Kuehn

One's business vocabulary sounds incomplete nowadays unless liberally sprinkled with such words as models, systems, decision theory, and digital computers. As management science evolves, the two interrelated concepts of models and systems are proving their usefulness in all functional areas of business—accounting, finance, production, and marketing.

Certain aspects of the application of mathematical models to business problems are presented here, with particular emphasis on the merits of heuristic approaches as aids to decision making. The discussion is directed toward those executives and researchers who have more than just a casual or academic interest in using models and computers in problem solving and embodies considerations of reality, efficiency, and costs.

HISTORICAL USES OF MODELS

GENESIS AND EVOLUTION. The term "mathematical model" may be defined in two parts: Mathematics is the science of relationships—a language, the quintessence of which is conveyed and explained by numerals and symbols. A model is the simplified representation of a concept, system, or process, and it becomes "mathematical" when expressed as a quantitative or logical relationship.

Among the earlier models developed in physics were Archimedes' law of levers, Galileo's law of the pendulum, and Newton's well-

known law of gravitation—all rather simple formulations by twentieth-century standards. Upon the heels of the development of the calculus, statistical theory, and the electronic computer there has been a surge of interest in things quantitative in the business community.

The use of mathematical models has recently had a phenomenal growth in business as a means of expressing relationships between variables, testing the validity of hypotheses, and developing decision rules. The practical applications of this technology increased manyfold with the emergence of the digital computer and its capacity to "remember" large amounts of information, its perseverance in making endless calculations, its ability to consistently follow a set of programmed instructions, and its speed in retrieving and processing data.

Business models may be classified as either descriptive or normative, or both. A descriptive model is useful for portraying the behavior of a system. Most marketing simulations are of this type. A normative model is intended to be a guide to business operations, prescribing rules of operation based upon the evaluation of relevant variables and the goals of the firm.

The two types of models are not necessarily strictly dichotomous, however. For example, a simulation model not only provides an approach to *describing* and analyzing systems, but, once constructed and tested, it may be applied to *predict* the effects of alternative policies, strategies, and decisions. In this sense, the descriptive model often provides the basis for developing the normative.

A MIXED BLESSING

DANGER AND OPPORTUNITY. That computer science has fomented a "second" industrial revolution of sorts, making possible the application of sophisticated aids for problem solving, is a mixed blessing for management. The Chinese have a word for "crisis" (*wei chi*) which is a combination of parts of the words for "danger" (*wei hsien*) and "opportunity" (*chi hui*).

The opportunities created by combining models and machines are legion and will constitute the focus of this article. Danger inheres in choosing the computer hardware, in developing appropriate models to help interpret the problem, and last, but certainly not least, in hiring the people who will develop the models and determine the quality of the output.

Closely related to the hazards posed by unqualified personnel and inadequate problem definition is the production of reams of output which covers in minute detail every aspect of the problem, print-outs

of so many numbers that meaningful analysis is either impossible or extremely difficult. Although it may be necessary to examine many different dimensions while learning the problems, the ultimate goal should be to refine these into a few signposts pointing toward succinct conclusions.

VALUE OF SIMPLICITY

COMPLICATIONS VS. SIMPLICATIONS. It may be easily surmised from reading the current management literature that model builders feel compelled to increase the complexity of all models on the assumption that intricacy is positively correlated with usefulness. While this premise is valid for some systems, we believe that it is a mistake to ignore simpler approaches which frequently will serve as well or almost as well. Furthermore, elaborate models are likely to be useful only when they are the result of a long-term program of research and development.

In the exploratory stages of a problem, the elementary plotting of points is very useful and, as a first step, generally to be preferred over more mathematical methods, unless, of course, the researcher has some a priori basis for choosing specific functions. Unsophisticated methods fail to furnish clear explanations of the phenomena under investigation, but they are desirable in approaching new problems for the first time. Even the most erudite probabilistic or econometric models will yield unreliable results if employed without careful planning and consideration of the problem, as well as a thorough understanding of the technique of analysis.

The computer, perhaps, unfortunately has made it easy for individuals to use analytic methods that they do not understand and models that do not fit the problem. Every model that is not a reasonably true representation of reality introduces distortions, and the best safeguard against such distortions is a sound knowledge of the technique being used and its assumptions as well as experience in applying it.

WHAT IS A HEURISTIC?

ALGORITHMS VS. HEURISTICS. To a mathematician, an "algorithm" is a specific computational procedure for numerical manipulation—a method of writing and performing any of the four basic mathematical operations. An example of a multiplication algorithm is $q \times r = s,$

which may have the values of $24 \times 3 = 72$, and which may be written in a number of other forms such as $(3X)\,(3) = 72$, depending upon the hypothesized relationships of the multiplicand and multiplier. In finance, the formula for the present discounted value of a stream of future earnings,

$$\sum_{n=0}^{\infty} \frac{1}{(1+i)^n}\, p(n)$$

is an algorithm. The stochastic equation,

$$M\hat{S}_{i,\,t} = \sum_{j=1}^{K} P_{ji} MS_{j,\,t-1}$$

used to predict market shares in some exponential models, is an algorithm. Algorithms that have played important roles in operations research include linear programming devices such as the simplex method and maximization procedures using the calculus. Whether relatively simple or extremely complex, *an algorithm guarantees optimal solutions to any complete set of data and any problem as posed by the model.*

A heuristic, in contrast to an algorithm, is a shortcut process of reasoning—in the models to be discussed here, a computerized rule-of-thumb—that searches for a *satisfactory, rather than an optimal, solution.* The heuristic, which reduces the time spent in the search for the solution of a problem, comprises a rule or a computational procedure which restricts the number of alternative solutions to a problem, based upon the analogous human trial-and-error process of reaching acceptable solutions to problems for which optimizing algorithms are not available.[1]

It may not be obvious why a less precise heuristic method should be used when an algorithmic technique assures a superior solution. A good reason is that algorithms demand quantitative inputs from a clearly structured problem cast in a reasonably restrictive framework, whereas heuristics are operable in problems that are much more complex and less well structured in terms of susceptibility to algorithmic methods. In addition, computation costs may be lower. Heuristic solutions need not be optimal to be of practical value; they need only represent some improvement in the solutions provided and the cost of application as compared with alternative methods available to management.

The activity of a digital computer when processing the flexible heuristic program closely parallels human mental activity in that it is

essentially inductive in nature and may even exhibit intuition and "learning" in improving its performance by adjusting the parameters itself, provided that it is appropriately instructed in the first place.[2] Because it is more human than deductive in solving problems by trial-and-error procedures, the heuristic program can inspire confidence only through repeated application and when the solutions compare favorably with those derived by alternative methods of analysis. Repeated proof may be thought necessary by some simply because the "certainty" associated with a deductive algorithm is necessarily lacking.

FLEXIBILITY

PROBLEM DEFINING. One of the major obstacles to developing a good model is getting a good definition of the problem. There is a risk in using an available algorithm because a researcher is likely to try to fit the problem to the familiar algorithm (for example, the linearity assumption in linear programming), especially if he knows little about the variable involved. The less the analyst knows about the situation under investigation, the more likely he is not to question the constraints imposed by the optimizing algorithms. To be sure, available heuristic routines may lead to somewhat similar problems. On the other hand, insofar as they are designed with greater flexibility, the researcher is required to choose among alternative formulations that are not available with the more restrictive algorithms.

The choice between a heuristic program and an optimizing algorithm for the solution of a specific problem must be made by comparing the error introduced into the operational decisions as a result of the algorithmic constraints in the modeling of the problem with the combined error of the suboptimality of the heuristic solution and its modeling errors. Final proof is possible only by comparing operational decisions reached via the two methods. In many problems, however, developing such final, conclusive evidence is not directly possible; thus, the vital element of managerial judgment is required to evaluate the reasonableness of the various outcomes against the reference point of empirical knowledge.

The surge of recent interest in heuristic approaches to problem solving has led to the development of computer programs designed to:

Schedule construction activity—smoothing materials handling and work flows.

Manage inventory,[3] also performed by optimizing quadratic programming.[4]

Balance assembly lines in automotive and electronic component plants.[5]

Schedule job shop assignments.[6]

Simulate the activities of the investment trust officer in a bank, performing evaluations that the officer could not do personally because of time limitations,[7] using the General Problem Solver.[8]

Locate warehouses.[9]

Consolidate orders for freight savings.

Schedule local truck delivery to many small customers.

Solve itinerary problems for traveling salesmen.[10]

Schedule airplane timetables for airlines.

Coordinate factors in new product introductions.

Select media schedules.

Discover proofs for theorems in logic and geometry.

Design electric motors and transformers.[11]

Lay out cutting patterns to reduce steel waste.

Play chess[12] and checkers.[13]

One may deduce that the practical applications of heuristic programming are limited because it is basically more elementary than certain sophisticated mathematical approaches. On the contrary, heuristic devices are being employed with considerable success (or are in stages of development nearing use) in a number of situations by a number of companies, a few brief examples of which follow.

LOCATING WAREHOUSES

WAREHOUSE LOCATION PROBLEM. The problem of warehouse locations has been considerably simplified by the use of heuristic programming, which helps to determine the locations that will be most profitable to the company by equating the marginal costs of operating the warehouses with cost savings and profit increments to be realized.

Warehouse networks are often considered from a number of viewpoints including:

Reducing transportation costs by permitting quantity shipments to the warehouse from the factory, rather than shipping small orders directly from factory to customers.

Grouping products from different plants for combined shipment to individual customers.

Speeding up deliveries to customers, which permits them to carry reduced inventories.

The heuristic program considers plant location with relation to raw materials, the kind of warehouse needed (automated, intermediate transfer point, etc.), and even preferred shipping and inventory arrangements (for example, air freight costs versus inventory costs).

It also must be noted that the inventory control problem embraces considerations other than cost minimization, as employed in economic lot size calculations. One should evaluate such problems from the profit maximization angle, considering, for example, that shipment delays may constitute costs in terms of customer good will and future orders. This frequently overlooked point illustrates the fact that canned approaches are fraught with potential errors, if the analyst fails to adjust the model to account for differences in costs, products, customers' alternatives, and so on. Warehouse cost structure is such a vital factor in pattern determination that a program used by a farm equipment manufacturer had to be recompiled and extensively modified before it could be used by a manufacturer of diversified electrical products.

ORDER CONSOLIDATION

ORDER CONSOLIDATION FOR FREIGHT SAVINGS. Traffic people work on this problem diligently, but time pressures—often allowing only thirty minutes to make a decision—make it difficult to achieve optimal solutions. The goal is minimum total cost, requiring a decision as to whether consolidation pays off. It is assumed that "to consolidate orders" implies the ability to ship over the same route, which leads to an evaluation of the cost of shipping alone versus shipping with another order. Choice is dependent on the number of available routes and the size of the order. In most sections of the country, a maximum of four orders may be grouped, with three stop-off charges, but at least one state's laws allow six orders to be grouped. Crossing certain state lines also involves different rate structures.

Obviously, then, order-consolidation poses many difficult obstacles to cost-minimization. Integer programming could solve the problem, if orders numbered eleven or less, but in actual runs the optimal has been achieved only after running seven hours on the IBM 7090 computer! This problem is now being solved heuristically in a few seconds on the 7070, and the savings for a large food company may amount

to as much as 8 percent of shipping costs. (A revised version of this order-consolidation program is being set up to run routinely for another company.) Cards are read into the company's computer, with daily changing inputs, and the print-out tells which orders to group, the preferred routes to be taken, and the total costs.

TRUCK SCHEDULING

LOCAL TRUCK DELIVERY SCHEDULING. Linear programming is used by a number of multiproduct, multiplant companies to assign orders to particular service points and to schedule deliveries. Elements entering the calculations include demand requirements, supply capacities, and cost structures. Such programs compute the optimal allocation of resources that will minimize the total costs of production, warehousing, and transportation. Computation costs and data availability are by no means trivial considerations for the large firms, but they pose especially serious limitations to the use of such approaches by small firms.

One relatively small company uses a heuristic model for scheduling deliveries to a number of small affiliated grocers. The data used by the company include number and types of trucks available, number of customers served, average time spent unloading at each customer location, distances between pairs of customers, and so on. Compared with former procedures, the heuristic scheduling device has been spectacularly successful.

The company could ill afford to pay the number of people who would be required to perform these calculations, even if it were not for consideration of prompt service to customers and opportunity costs attendant on delays. The over-all savings in this case would be more predictable, were it not for objections raised by the union to which the truck drivers belong, but even this constraint has not negated the overriding advantages gained through use of the heuristic search routine.

AIRLINE SCHEDULING

AIRLINE SCHEDULING. Scheduling, a giant headache for airline management, is very similar to the familiar "tramp steamer" problem, except that planes, unlike ships, are not the same craft going out and returning. With the inauguration of the supersonic transport, the time

required for loading and turn-around will become a crucial element in costs and profits. The airline heuristic of the future may well have to consider the containerization of passengers as well as baggage and freight.

The time element is already crucial for airlines, since, for maximum efficiency, the airplanes must fly when passengers want to fly, and service requirements that vary by cities as well as competitive schedules must be evaluated. Equipment must be available, and the right aircraft must be assigned to the right routes. Further, adding new airplanes causes major scheduling revisions. Restrictions imposed by the Civil Aeronautics Board are also decisive factors.

All of these parameters must be built into the program, making the optimizing algorithm impractical. Heuristic programming promises to be useful in developing satisfactory schedules, especially as the problems become more complicated with expanded geographical coverage, faster aircraft, changing public preferences, and the continuation of semiannual schedule changes in April and October.

MARKETING NOT AMENABLE?

HEURISTICS IN MARKETING. Many practitioners view with suspicion the use of quantitative tools in marketing; some think such devices are worthless. The nature of the model is frequently to blame for creating such attitudes, especially when the model represents only certain facets of actuality, producing results that are inconsistent with management's empirical knowledge of marketplace realities. "Canned" or "off-the-shelf" models or computer programs—algorithmic and heuristic—are seldom appropriate for more than the preliminary exploration of marketing problems.

Although marketing analysts have been among the most vociferous critics of classical economic theory and its *ceteris paribus* assumptions, it seems that the empirical work in marketing usually centers on one independent variable at a time. Many attempts have been made to relate the effects of advertising or price changes to sales volume while essentially ignoring other concomitant variables. Repeated failures of such research to produce clear-cut operational directives have contributed to the attitude on the part of both line managers and researchers that marketing is a complex maze of behavioral mechanisms not amenable to mathematical mapping. It is not paradoxical, then, that the building of mathematical models has received a less than hearty endorsement by many in marketing.

The task of building marketing models is arduous. For instance, just to identify an adequate, minimum set of variables in terms of which the problem can be defined and then to combine these factors into behaviorally meaningful and analytically tractable expressions is difficult. One must beware in adding variables that he is not merely adding confusion by reducing the signal-to-noise ratio in the system. Further, the mere fact that variables are included does not mean that "we are taking them into account," as is often stated when defining the independent variables in regression analysis. We are trying to take them into account, but this goal is an elusive one unless the actual interactions of the variables are in accordance with our hypothetical constructs. Just because the algebraic sign is "right" does not guarantee that our assumptions are correct.

Admittedly, it is more common in marketing to find classes of models with dubious correspondence to real life—based on vague assumptions and an internal logic lacking in consistency—than to find models which approximate the interactions of supply, demand, and related marketing effort. Even the flexible heuristic is less useful in the field of marketing than in the more structured situations, mainly because it is hard to get a good model of the problem in marketing.[14]

MARKETING APPLICATIONS

Nevertheless, there are two marketing applications in which the heuristic device has proved successful. One is the scheduling of new product introduction by coordinating clerical details, planning production runs to match market needs, summarizing results, and modifying strategy. Another is media selection, involving the development of schedules according to market characteristics and evaluation of such factors as the trade-off of placing advertisements on Saturday versus scheduling them on the major shopping days of Thursday and Friday. Given the constraints in these two classes of problems, the computer searches for better allocation as it juggles the inputs and evaluates thousands of alternatives in minutes, greatly reducing the time needed to arrive at the decisions.

Optimizing algorithms have proved popular in selecting media where reach and frequency constitute the major constraints in the decision process. However, although numerical data play a major role in media selection, the "creative function" of individual judgment and skill is a principal factor.[15]

Since the creative aspects are largely qualitative in essence, the

heuristic program will grow in popularity as an aid to media selection because its flexible nature permits the inclusion of symbolic terms neither amenable to expression as numerical variables or scalar and vector quantities nor specifiable in terms of profit maximization or cost minimization.[16]

Although new product introduction and media selection are two classes of problems that will be increasingly aided by heuristics, they can be accurately solved only to the extent that the computer is told how customers behave, which brings us full circle to the prerequisite that the problem must be learned in order to build suitable models. It is easy to develop simulation models if they are not expected to simulate very well. But if one intends to fit the variables in a meaningful way, then market simulations cannot be built in a day.

Constructing a realistic computer simulation of a market will continue to be extremely involved and painstaking. It is often helpful to break down the system being simulated into subsystems for which models can be built and tested independently. Thus, constructing a market simulation is a great deal like putting together a picture puzzle in which the individual subsystems, each involving a smaller number of variables, are joined into related parts and tested as subsystems. The proof of whether or not appropriate connections have been made comes in the testing of the completed design for logical alignment among its elements. Admittedly, this long-term view sometimes is thwarted by personnel turnover, making it necessary for newcomers to become familiar with work done previously. Similarly, consulting firms are frequently transient, making it difficult for a company to maintain continuity of effort.

MACHINE TIME AND COSTS

EFFICIENCY AND COSTS. When deciding between heuristic and algorithmic approaches, important considerations of time and costs are involved. Conceptually, integer programming could solve most of the complex business problems that have been solved by heuristic methods if there were a machine available to handle the massive calculations required by that algorithm. But costs become a major factor in cases like these. For example, the small-to-medium-size problem in warehouse location described above has been solved by heuristics in less than one minute on an IBM 704. The same problem solved by integer programming would probably require at least three months of IBM 704 time, provided the core were large enough to

store the problem. Since the time required to process integer programming problems increases exponentially as the size of the problem expands, it is clear that only very small and unimportant warehouse problems could be solved by the integer programming methods available today.

The heuristic program that took fifty seconds on the IBM 704 was run in less than ten seconds on the CDC 3600 (the program actually runs so fast on the 3600 computer that an accurate time estimate is difficult—more time is spent getting the program on and off the machine than it takes for the actual running). The original warehouse location program included inputs of fifty customers, twenty-five warehouses, and two products; the problem has since grown to over five hundred customers, more than three hundred warehouses, and twelve products. Arriving at optimal warehouse sites via integer programming could never be carried out today on a time schedule for practical application and would require machine time of such magnitude that the costs would, in all probability, not be justified.

The availability of machine time clearly becomes a crucial factor in the choice among models and methods of solution, and it is fairly evident that the magnitude of problems will grow at least as fast as the capacity of machines to solve them. Sizable savings in computational time and cost are possible with heuristic programming, savings that are further enhanced by larger machines.

To date, after application of the warehouse program with more than a dozen firms, no user has been able to devise an improved solution. One company has succeeded in effecting a cost improvement in machine time of three-fourths of one percent, realized by eliminating one of the constraints in the original set of parameters.

CONCLUSIONS

CONCRETENESS AND ABSTRACTION. It may seem disrespectful to apply Plato's teaching that business activities are suited only for misfits in a commercial context. Nevertheless, there is a moral for model builders in his narrative of mankind in the dark cave, a dialogue in which Socrates contrasts the material world of our everyday sense experience with the spiritual world of pure thought and truth.

By observing the shadows of images of outside action projected upon the wall of the cave, prisoners in the cave were to construct a model of the real world. A few individuals were allowed to emerge from their confinement to study the phenomena occurring outside,

using the new information to add to the basic structure of their original model. Ultimately, the chosen ones saw their own likenesses reflected in a pool, which enabled them to discover their relationship to what had already been observed. Until they left the somewhat abstract world of the cave to see the concreteness of the total arena, "truth (was to them) literally nothing but the shadows of the images."[17] Further, Plato believed that once these appointed thought leaders had attained a thorough understanding of real-life events, they had an obligation to share their knowledge of the world outside by going back among the captives in the dungeon to participate in their labors of learning.

The responsibility of the business model builder is the same. With so much at stake, it is imperative that he move from the easy generalities of basic mathematical statements to the hard particulars of the complex relationships prevalent in the system he proposes to describe. Perhaps the ideal situation would be for a company to have a qualified, highly experienced practitioner become an expert mathematician so that he could construct the models himself, but this is not likely to happen.

Managers can best facilitate model building by helping builders to learn the system, but they cannot realistically give researchers continuing free rein unless some results are forthcoming. Management is very interested in gambling on such projects, but it needs some confidence that there is a reasonable chance of success.

Occasionally, the researcher's experience is limited, and his judgment is sometimes naïve. Therefore, operating management must effect mutuality between practitioner and researcher and help model builders learn the system, achieving a fruitful synthesis of efforts. As practice not built on sound theory is likely to be useless, likewise theory not tested in practice is relatively meaningless to management. The utility of a model improves through testing—feeding empirical data into it to see how well it works, then making essential modifications, and testing it again.

Almost any model begins crudely and then is refined as it assimilates new information bearing on the problem at hand. But components added over a period of time do not linearly improve the model; rather, accuracy is likely to decrease and become asymptotic. Yet first-stage approximations to reality are inacceptable as long as modifications will enhance the productivity of the model without incurring marginal costs in excess of the marginal return.

Evaluation of the appropriateness of models is far from a simple task. Important questions in determining where the faults lie are:

Are parameters set incorrectly? Are minor program subroutines in error? Or is the entire structure of the model unsuitable to the problem? Not infrequently one finds to his dismay that the nature of the output provides few clues to the sources of error, particularly in large-scale simulation models.

The barriers hindering the consumer's purchase of a product—awareness, interest, desire, and action—have their analogue in management's acceptance of mathematical models. Awareness of progressive ways of doing things does not necessarily lead to interest, or if it does, the interest may be casual or even dilettantish. The desire to try such methods, once interest is aroused, may be thwarted by a lack of technical understanding and uneasiness in basing decisions on the findings. If the plateau of action is reached, management may grow discouraged with the rate of progress, become disillusioned, and revert to former habits which seem to be well-ordered and easier to comprehend. Once executives reject a technique, the staff specialist will find it tough sledding to sell them on another try.

Even when certain research approaches get the stamp of executive approval, it is quite another matter to persuade planners to utilize the results. There is often a wide gap between analysis and application, which points up a problem touched on but briefly in this article, the problem of a lack of communication and understanding between model builders and model users. There must be provided a suitable climate so that models and machines can make their maximum contributions to the enterprise.

Managerial decision making may proceed from postulates that are either explicit or implicit, either consistent or inconsistent. Probably no decision framework collectively exhausts all relevant factors that obtain in a situation. Yet adequate structure for use in decision making should permit the inclusion of all available information, because the more closely a logical mathematical system corresponds to the process it represents, the greater its usefulness to management.

Where initial data costs are concerned, it may not be so much a matter of dollar outlays for data as it is the ability to make full use of the information. For example, several companies that once considered panel data too expensive have come to look upon such data as well worth the investment. Of course, any data may be expensive at first, relative to the return in improved understanding, but cumulative gains from interrelated analyses can quickly reverse the imbalance as the models are improved and expanded with additional variables.

Just as one should not be satisfied with naive models, undue complexity is likewise wasteful in terms of the time necessary to erect the analytical framework, the costs of providing superfluous data to

satisfy the needs of the equations, the excessive consumption of machine time, and the ultimate danger that management may accept the output less critically than is called for by the basic nature of the problem. In connection with the last point Alfred North Whitehead said, "There is no more common error than to assume that, because prolonged and accurate mathematical calculations have been made, the application to some fact of nature is absolutely certain."

Caution is advised, especially for behavioral models, in the use of analytic methods such as regression analysis and linear programming. True, readily available analytic methods will speed the analysis, but may produce completely unreliable solutions if they are inconsistent with important aspects of the problem. The temptation of fitting problems to available techniques will usually inhibit the careful modeling of the behavioral systems and impede future progress because the foundations are unstable. Yet, as with simple graphical plotting, these convenient algorithms often help to identify functional relationships and can therefore be valuable as preliminary means of exploring various aspects of the system one is attempting to model.

There is a place for traditional optimizing algorithms as well as a place for heuristic problem-solving methods. Such techniques as linear programming, integer programming, quadratic programming, the calculus, and queueing theory are capable of solving a variety of scheduling and resource allocations problems, but there are limitations in the complexity and the size of the problems that can be adequately solved by such optimizing methods. Heuristic programming as a tool for problem solving comes into its own when the assumptions required by rigorous optimizing techniques are either inappropriate to the problem or when, as is frequently the case, the size of the problem prevents the practical application of such techniques.

REFERENCES

1. Herbert A. Simon and Allen Newell, "Heuristic Problem Solving: The Next Advance in Operations Research," *Operations Research,* VI:3 (May–June 1958), 1–10.

2. M. Gelernter and N. Rochester, "Intelligent Behavior in Problem-Solving Machines," *IBM Journal of Research and Development,* II (Oct. 1958), 336–345; and *ibid.,* 281–300.

3. Joseph Buchan and Ernest Koenigsberg, *Scientific Inventory Management* (Englewood Cliffs, N.J.: Prentice-Hall, Inc., 1963); and Herbert A. Simon and Allen Newell, "Information Processing in Computer and Man," *American Scientist,* LII:3 (Sept. 1964), 281–300.

4. C. C. Holt, F. Modigliana, J. F. Muth, and H. A. Simon, *Planning Production, Inventories, and Work Force* (Englewood Cliffs, N.J.: Prentice-Hall, Inc., 1960).

5. Maurice Kilbridge and Leon Wester, "A Heuristic Method of Assembly Line Balancing," *Journal of Industrial Engineering,* XII:4 (July–Aug. 1961), 292–298; and F. M. Tonge, *A Heuristic Program for an Assembly Line Balancing Problem* (Englewood Cliffs, N.J.: Prentice-Hall, Inc., 1961).

6. "Computer Planning Unsnarls the Job Shop," *Business Week,* April 2, 1966, pp. 60–61; and William S. Gere, Jr., "A Heuristic Approach to Job Shop Scheduling," unpublished doctoral thesis, Carnegie Institute of Technology, 1962.

7. P. E. Geoffrey Clarkson, *A Model of the Trust Investment Process,* Ford Foundation Award Dissertation (Englewood Cliffs, N.J.: Prentice-Hall, Inc., 1962).

8. A. Newell, J. C. Shaw, and H. A. Simon, "Report on a General Problem-Solving Program for a Computer," *Information Processing,* UNESCO, 1960, pp. 256–264.

9. Leon Cooper, "Location-Allocation Problems," *Operations Research,* XII:3 (May–June 1963), 331–343; and Alfred A. Kuehn and Michael J. Hamburger, "A Heuristic Program for Locating Warehouses," *Management Science,* IX (July 1963), 643–666.

10. Robert L. Karg, "A Heuristic Approach to Solving Traveling Salesman Problems," *Management Science,* X:2 (Jan. 1964), 225–248.

11. G. H. Goodwin, "Digital Computers Tap Out Designs for Large Motors Fast," *Power,* April 1958.

12. A. Bernstein, M. Roberts, T. Arbuckle, and M. H. Belsky, "A Chess-Playing Program for the IBM 704," *Proceedings of the 1958 Western Joint Computer Conference,* pp. 157–159; and A. Newell, J. C. Shaw, and H. A. Simon, "Chess Playing Programs and the Problems of Complexity," *IBM Journal of Research and Development,* II (Oct. 1958), 320–335.

13. A. L. Samuel, "Some Studies in Machine Learning Using the Game of Checkers," *IBM Journal of Research and Development,* III (July 1959), 210–229.

14. A. A. Kuehn, "Heuristic Programming: A Useful Technique for Marketing," *Proceedings of the American Marketing Association,* 1962, pp. 162–170; Herbert A. Simon and Peter A. Simon, "Trial and Error Search in Solving Difficult Problems: Evidence from the Game of Chess," *Behavioral Science,* VII:4 (Oct. 1962), 425–429.

15. "Selecting Media Creatively," *Printers' Ink* (Sept. 23, 1966), pp. 15 ff.

16. Samuel, *op. cit.*

17. Plato, *Republic,* VII.

The Use of Mathematical Models in Marketing

Philip Kotler

The modern marketing man has to be multilingual, for he obtains his material from many disciplines.

He must be able to converse with *economists* about marginal analysis, elasticity, and diminishing returns; with *psychologists* about projective techniques, latent needs, and nonrational behavior; with *sociologists* about acculturation, social norms, and subcultures; and with *statisticians* about standard error, least squares, and correlation.

Now another language—that of higher mathematics—is needed in marketing. Many marketing men are uncomfortable about this. They do not look askance at mathematical concepts, but they are a bit anxious because of a "language barrier." Fortunately, however, the language barrier is not insurmountable. Linear programing, waiting-line theory, and the like are simply unfamiliar names for some significant ideas.

The purpose of this article is to reduce some of the "mysticism" of the new mathematics by defining its vocabulary and illustrating its central ideas in the context of marketing.

DECISION MAKING

Quantitative analysis is not alien to the field of marketing. For many decades marketing research departments have conducted consumer surveys, prepared sales forecasts, and analyzed sales reports. A few practitioners have even used higher mathematics for complex problem-solving in marketing. But until recently the mathematical "sophistication" underlying the typical research project could be found between

Reprinted with permission from the *Journal of Marketing,* vol. 28, no. 4 (October, 1963), pp. 31–41, published by the American Marketing Association.

the covers of a textbook in elementary statistics. And much of the research has amounted to routine information gathering.

Today the emphasis is changing. The focus of research is on *decision making,* and not fact gathering for its own sake. The belief is spreading that models can be built which identify and relate the key factors in a problem situation, and which offer explicit directions for decision making.

Today's marketing executive is asked to distinguish carefully between alternative strategies in making a major decision. Each strategy will lead to one of several outcomes, depending in part upon events beyond the firm's control; and the possible outcomes for each strategy must somehow be weighed, to achieve an estimated value for that strategy. The values of the various strategies must be compared, and the executive must then attempt to select the strategy promising the highest value or payoff.[1]

THE TOOLS OF MATHEMATICS

The mathematician carries in his attaché case four basic tools, plus a *potpourri* of special models. His basic tools are *matrix algebra, calculus, probability theory,* and *simulation.*

Matrix Algebra

One tool is *matrix algebra,* by which large arrays of numbers in the form of *vectors* and *matrices* can be manipulated by rules similar to those found in ordinary algebra.

As a miniature example, suppose (6,000, 3,200, 5,000) is a *vector* (for our purposes, a single array of numbers) whose component numbers represent sales targets in three geographical markets —(say) East, West, and South, respectively. Past records show that on the average it takes ½ hour of sales effort and $1 of advertising expenditure to produce a sale in the first market; ¼ hour of sales effort and $2 of advertising expenditure to produce a sale in the second market; and ⅕ hour of sales effort and $3 of advertising expenditure to produce a sale in the third market. This information

[1] Two excellent articles illustrating this approach are Robert D. Buzzell and Charles C. Slater, "Decision Theory and Marketing Management," *Journal of Marketing,* vol. 27 (July, 1962), pp. 7–16; and Paul E. Green, "Bayesian Decision Theory in Pricing Strategy," *Journal of Marketing,* vol. 28 (January, 1963), pp. 5–14.

can be summarized in a *matrix* (for our purposes a rectangular array of numbers):

	SALES EFFORT (IN HOURS)	ADVERTISING EXPENDITURE (IN DOLLARS)
East	1/2	$1
West	1/4	$2
South	1/5	$3

To find the total hours of sales effort and dollars of advertising expenditure required to achieve the geographical sales targets, we multiply the vector by the matrix:

$$(6{,}000,\ 3{,}200,\ 5{,}000) \begin{pmatrix} 1/2 & 1 \\ 1/4 & 2 \\ 1/5 & 3 \end{pmatrix}$$

For example, we can call the vector A and the matrix B, and we then proceed to find their product, that is, A·B.

There are definite rules for the multiplication of a vector by a matrix (and for that matter, for the multiplication of two vectors or two matrices, etc.). In the example above, the product A·B is $(6{,}000 \times \frac{1}{2} + 3{,}200 \times \frac{1}{4} + 5{,}000 \times \frac{1}{5}, 6{,}000 \times 1 + 3{,}200 \times 2 + 5{,}000 \times 3)$ or, collecting terms, (4,800, $27,400). This new vector is the solution; and it means that the company must have enough salesmen to make 4,800 hours of calls, and also an advertising budget of at least $27,400.

Matrix algebra is essentially a symbolic shorthand for the manipulation of large arrays of data. It affords the advantage of economy in quantitative expression.

Calculus

The second tool which the mathematician brings to marketing is *calculus.* Using *differential calculus,* the mathematician can, among other things, determine what combination of inputs will maximize some output.

A marketing mix is a combination of inputs, such as price and advertising. Suppose that it were possible experimentally to vary the price input and the advertising input while controlling other factors. The effect of these variations on sales could then be recorded, and the profit implied by each level of sales estimated.

The task is to find an equation which best describes how profit

varies with variations in price and advertising. A form for such an equation as well as a method of estimating the coefficients (usually "least squares" regression) must be decided upon. Suppose the following equation is found to give a good fit to the data:

$$I = 320 - 2P^2 - 3P + 4\,PA - 7A^2 + 60A$$

On the left side of the equation is profit (represented by I). Profit is treated here as the *dependent variable,* because its value is conceived to depend upon the values taken on by variables listed on the right side of the equation. These *independent variables* are price (P) and advertising (A). The particular numbers in the equation are constants and coefficients, which are estimated by an appropriate statistical method.

If such an equation can be found, what unique mix of price and advertising would maximize profit? The nonmathematician can use trial and error to arrive at the profit-maximizing mix, but this will be frustrating and time consuming. The mathematician can determine this mix in a very short time by using calculus. Although this is not the place to explain the procedure, his calculations will show that the optimum price is $4.95, and the optimum advertising budget is $5.7 (in some appropriate unit).

The chief contribution of differential calculus to marketing is to enable a direct determination of optimal action where differentiable functions are involved. In fact, *marginal analysis* which is applied by economists to all kinds of decision situations—such as determination of the best price, or the number of salesmen—actually is a gross application of differential calculus.

Integral calculus, representing the other branch of calculus, is not used to find the maximum and minimum values of a function, but rather the *area* under a function, among other things. An area can have a meaningful marketing interpretation.

Suppose on a particular billing date that a department store ranks all of its charge accounts by dollar size. These charge accounts range from $0 to $198. The frequency distribution of all the accounts by dollar size is shown in Figure 1. The shaded area under the curve between $50 and $150 represents the percentage of all accounts falling in this range. How can this area be measured? It does not have the simplicity of a rectangle, triangle, or circle. This area, or other areas under the curve, can be readily measured through integral calculus, provided that the frequency distribution can be represented by a mathematical equation with certain properties.

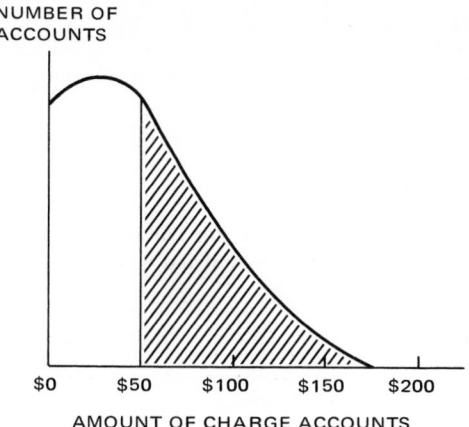

NUMBER OF
ACCOUNTS

$0　　$50　　$100　　$150　　$200

AMOUNT OF CHARGE ACCOUNTS

Figure 1　Frequency distribution of charge accounts

Probability Theory

The third important tool of the mathematician for use in marketing is *probability theory*.

How should the marketing man handle the uncertainty that surrounds legislation, consumer intentions, and competitors' acts? He can try to list all the possible consequences of a business move, along with their probabilities. The probabilities can be based on the frequency distribution of past outcomes for similar business moves, or on personal judgment. The assigned probability numbers must satisfy only two requirements:

1. The probability that a particular consequence will occur is given numerically by some number between 0 and 1 inclusive.
2. The sum of the probabilities of all possible consequences is 1.

Probability numbers can serve as "weights" for appraising various money (or utility) outcomes. Suppose the manufacturer has developed a new product and must hire and train a special sales force to sell it. The number of salesmen to hire will depend upon his estimate of market potential, among other things.

Suppose that he is uncertain whether there is a potential of 2,000, 3,000, or 4,000 units, and he is trying to decide whether to hire 60 or 70 salesmen. Too few salesmen will mean that some potential sales are never realized, and too many salesmen will mean that excess

selling costs are incurred. It would help to estimate the profits under different assumptions as to market potential and sales-force size. The estimates will depend upon an appropriate set of assumptions concerning product price, production costs, the effect of the number of salesmen on sales, and selling costs. A hypothetical set of profit estimates is shown in Table 1.

TABLE 1   **Estimated Profits for Different Combinations of Market Potential and Sales-Force Size**

		MARKET POTENTIAL		
		2,000 UNITS	3,000 UNITS	4,000 UNITS
Decision?	60	−$20,000	$50,000	$60,000
	70	−$40,000	$40,000	$70,000

If market potential is 2,000 units, the manufacturer will lose $20,000 with 60 salesmen and $40,000 with 70 salesmen. If market potential is 3,000 units, the manufacturer will earn $50,000 with 60 salesmen, and $40,000 with 70 salesmen. Finally, if market potential is 4,000 units, he will earn still larger profits. In this last case, the profit is higher with 70 salesmen because 60 salesmen are inadequate to tap the full potential.

Should the manufacturer hire 60 or 70 salesmen? By hiring 70, he has the opportunity to gain more but also to lose more. His decision will depend upon the personal probabilities he assigns to the three estimates of market potential. Suppose he quantifies his beliefs as follows: there is a .2 probability that the market potential is 2,000 units, a .3 probability that it is 3,000 units, and a .5 probability that it is 4,000 units. If this were a game of chance which the manufacturer could play repeatedly facing the same payoffs and the same probabilities, and if he had adequate funds, it would be easy to define a good decision rule: choose the act which has the highest *expected monetary value* (EMV). EMV is a weighted average of the alternative profit consequences of an act, the weights being the probabilities assigned to the alternatives. For the example we have:

EMV (60) = −$20,000 × .2 + $50,000 × .3 + $60,000 × .5 = $41,000.
EMV (70) = −$40,000 × .2 + $40,000 × .3 + $70,000 × .5 = $39,000.

The results present an interesting paradox. The manufacturer is optimistic about the market potential, and yet EMV is higher with 60 salesmen. His optimism is not quite strong enough.

The use of EMV as a decision criterion in a once-only decision is generally acceptable, if the best consequence is not too great nor the worst consequence too bad. Were the money stakes unusually high for the decision maker, it would be necessary to employ a utility index instead of a money index. This utility index can be constructed from preferences expressed by the decision maker between given sums of money and certain gambles. Instead of the maximization of EMV, the decision criterion would be the maximization of expected utility.[2]

Simulation

The great majority of marketing problems probably will remain intractable to ordinary mathematical solution. For example, the correct price to charge depends upon such elements as the future sales outlook, the possible reactions of competitors, the time lags of these reactions, the intended level of advertising support, ad infinitum. A complex phenomenon is characterized by feedbacks, distributed lags, uncommon probability distributions, and other features which render exact mathematical solutions difficult or impossible. But mathematicians are undaunted: "When all else fails, *simulate!*"

A simulation is essentially a hypothetical testing, as opposed to a field testing, of the consequences of alternative business decisions. The first step is the construction of a model which spells out how the key variables interact in the situation. The second step is the testing of alternative decisions on the model. Simulations can range from simple paper-and-pencil exercises to full scale computer analyses. The purpose is to speculate on the consequences of changing a price, or dropping small distributors, or introducing a new pattern of trade deals, before risking the irrevocable judgment of the marketplace.

The model used in the simulation may be *exact* or *probabilistic*. In an exact model, the effect of one variable upon another is known with certainty. In a probabilistic model, one of several effects might take place, and we presume to know only their respective probabilities.

Retail inventory control can be used to illustrate a probabilistic model. The problem is to adopt purchasing rules which will balance inventory losses against sales losses. Suppose a supermarket wishes to

reconsider its present purchasing policy with respect to one product—for example, eggnog. The daily demand for eggnog fluctuates, and each day of the week has its own demand distribution. Suppose that on a sample of past Tuesdays the number of quarts demanded has varied between 0 and 4, according to the probabilities shown in Table 2.

**TABLE 2   Probability Distribution of Demand
for Eggnog on Tuesdays**

NUMBER OF QUARTS DEMANDED	PROBABILITY	MONTE CARLO NUMBERS
0	.07	00–06
1	.20	07–26
2	.22	27–48
3	.33	49–81
4	.18	82–99
	1.00	

The third column of Table 2 consists of an allocation of 100 2-digit numbers (between 00 and 99) to all possible events in proportion to their probabilities. Thus, on 7% of the Tuesdays no eggnog will be demanded; so we assign 7 different 2-digit numbers (00 to 06 inclusive) to this event. Likewise, we assign 20 different 2-digit numbers (07-26 inclusive) to the event of 1 quart being demanded, etc.

We now go to a table of *random* digits. The digits are listed in this table in no apparent pattern. The fact is that each of the digits had the same chance of appearing on each trial. While there is no pattern, we know that all the digits will be approximately *equally* represented in a large sample of such digits.

We draw 2 digits at a time. If the first 2-digit number is 43, this can be looked up in the Monte Carlo column in Table 2 and would be interpreted as 2 quarts. In other words, on this Tuesday the demand at the supermarket is 2 quarts. By repeatedly drawing 2-digit random numbers, we can generate a characteristic picture of demand for a succession of Tuesdays.

We can use a different demand distribution, based on store records, for each day of the week. Then we can make assumptions about supply, such as a delivery period every other day and a decision rule to purchase (say) 3 quarts each time. With this information, we can manually or mechanically generate daily demand-and-supply quanti-

ties to learn the likely magnitude and frequency of excess inventories and shortages. We compare the average losses incurred under different purchasing rules and choose the loss-minimizing rule.

The probabilistic feature provides realism and has given rise to the name of *Monte Carlo* simulation. In the more complex simulations, a computer is used to produce the random numbers, interpret the events, make the necessary computations, and summarize the results. Computer simulation has been conducted on such marketing problems as media selection; department-store ordering and pricing; site location for retail outlets; and customer facility planning in retail outlets.

THE MAJOR MODELS

The tools of matrix algebra, calculus, probability theory, and simulation are fundamental in setting up and solving many of the models which have been developed to aid marketing executives in decision making. Some of these models are designed for *normative decision making,* and others for the *analysis of a process.* Most of them originated out of operations research activities.

The following models appear particularly "ripe" for marketing application:

1. Allocation models
2. Competitive strategy models
3. Brand-switching models
4. Waiting-line models
5. Critical-path scheduling models

Some of the examples below may seem too simple, if not contrived. However, the examples are illustrative only. Model building is not just a "fun" exercise for those who like to solve puzzles, but can be a serious attack on decision making in business.

Actually the final model for a real decision problem can be quite elaborate and represent a "hooking together" of several elementary models and techniques.

1. Allocation Models

The economic aspect of business decision making is the "allocation of scarce resources to competing ends." In marketing, the scarce resources may be salesmen who are too few to make all the desirable

contacts, or advertising dollars which are too limited to produce adequate exposure, or many other possibilities. Nevertheless, a decision must be made on how to allocate or *program* these limited resources to territories, classes of customers, and product lines.

Take, for example, the development of a media plan. The number of available media vehicles is very great. But when any particular product is considered, there are a number of constraints which severely delimit the range of media choice.

First, the advertising budget is finite. Second, the message must be directed at specific market segments (such as mothers in the case of a baby lotion); and certain media vehicles are more effective than others in reaching these segments. Third, the geographical distribution of the market segments imposes restrictions on the choice of media. Finally, the media vehicles or the advertiser, or both, may impose restrictions.

Nevertheless a large number of different media plans would satisfy all the constraints. Of these, which plan will be the most effective? An *effectiveness criterion* needs to be developed against which every feasible plan can be rated. In media selection, the criterion is the number of expected effective exposures, or some variant of this. *Programing* is one of the mathematical models that can be used for the discovery of an exposure-maximizing media plan.

As an example, a media plan is to be prepared consisting of the purchase of X_1 advertising units of medium 1 and X_2 advertising units of medium 2. Table 3 indicates the relevant characteristics of the two media.

TABLE 3   Selected Characteristics of Two Media

	MEDIUM 1	MEDIUM 2
Cost of an advertising unit	$ 2,700	$ 900
Maximum number of units	12	40
Minimum number of units	0	9
Total number of effective exposures per unit	720,000	360,000
Number of effective exposures in region 1 per unit	60,000	100,000
Number of effective exposures in region 2 per unit	660,000	260,000
Number of exposures to single women per unit	100,000	80,000
Number of exposures to college educated women per unit	400,000	40,000

The following constraints are made explicit in a discussion between the media planner and the advertiser:

1. The total advertising budget is $39,600.
2. At least 1,800,000 exposures are to be achieved in region 1, and 7,280,000 in region 2.
3. No more than 2,400,000 exposures are to take place among single women.
4. At least 2,000,000 exposures are to take place among college educated women.

The problem is to find the number of issues of the two media which would maximize the total number of effective exposures subject to the various constraints. A mathematical statement of the problem is given in Table 4.

TABLE 4   Mathematical Statement of Media Problem

Maximize	$720,000X_1 + 360,000X_2$			
subject to (1)	$2,700X_1 + 900X_2 \leq$	$39,600$	budget constraint
(2)	$X_1 \leq$	12	
(3)	$X_2 \leq$	40	individual medium
(4)	$X_1 \geq$	0	usage constraints
(5)	$X_2 \geq$	9	
(6)	$60,000X_1 + 100,000X_2 \geq 1,800,000$		regional constraints
(7)	$660,000X_1 + 260,000X_2 \geq 7,280,000$		customer charac-
(8)	$100,000X_1 + 80,000X_2 \leq 2,400,000$		teristics
(9)	$400,000X_1 + 40,000X_2 \geq 2,000,000$		constraints

Each constraint has been expressed as a mathematical inequality. For example, the budget constraint reads: The number of advertisements purchased in medium 1 (X_1) times their unit cost ($2,700), plus the number purchased in medium 2 (X_2) times their unit cost ($900), must be less than or equal to the budget of $39,600.

The second constraint reads: The number of advertisements placed in medium 1 must not exceed 12. The other inequalities are similarly interpreted.

The constraints have the effect of eliminating most combinations of X_1 and X_2 but there are still a large number of remaining combinations which would satisfy all the inequalities. But only one of these (usually) will also maximize the total number of effective exposures. Mathematical programing is the technique for finding the best solution.

In this simple case, the inequalities could be drawn on graph paper; and this would help to delimit the set of media plans (points) which would satisfy all of the constraints. Then there is a procedure for locating the best plan, the details of which are beyond the scope of this article.

The best plan calls for 8 advertisements in medium 1, and 20 advertisements in medium 2. This plan will cost exactly $39,600 and yield 12,960,000 exposures.

There are several types of mathematical programing. *Linear programing* implies that the criterion and the constraints in the problem can be represented by single-line segments. The essence of a straight line is that the slope is constant, which means that the ratio of a change in one variable to a change in the other is constant. For example, a linear cost function means that the cost of an additional unit is constant; and a linear exposure function means that the effect of an additional advertising exposure is constant. In other words, diminishing or increasing returns are ruled out in strictly linear models.

Since the assumption of constant marginal returns and costs is patently false in many situations, what explains the popularity of *linear programing models?* The answer is largely that the linear assumption is the easiest to work with and solve. As an additional consideration, many important functions are linear or nearly linear over much of their range.

A number of techniques are available for solving a linear programing problem, once it has been expressed mathematically. *Graphical solutions* are possible when the number of variables is not more than three. Alternatively, the *simplex algorithm* is an all-purpose method. The word "simplex" has nothing to do with "simple"; the *simplex* is a well-defined mathematical concept which has a geometric interpretation. An *algorithm* is a systematic method for testing various solutions; it guarantees that each successive solution will represent an improvement until the best solution is reached.

The term *non-linear programing* is reserved for a problem formulation where either some constraint(s) or the effectiveness criterion, or both, are not linear. One example is *quadratic programing,* which uses a second-degree curve for some of the constraints or effectiveness criterion, or both.

Integer programing is a variant so named because the optimal solution is constrained to consist of whole numbers. For example, suppose X_1 represents how many salesmen should be hired. If the answer is *not* constrained to be an integer, it could be a mixed decimal such as

9.4. What does it mean to hire 9.4 salesmen? Should the answer be "rounded" to 9 salesmen or 10 salesmen? The solution is not obvious, and the decision may involve a difference of many thousands of dollars. Integer programing is a way of avoiding the ambiguities of fractional answers.

Dynamic programing, the most complicated of the programing variants, is applied to problems where a series of consecutive *inter-dependent* decisions have to be made. Purchasing decisions, for example, must be made throughout the year; and today's decision must be made in terms of what it implies for the decision choices in the next period, which in turn will affect the decision choices in the following period, and so on.

In summary, a programing model is applied to problems where there seem to be many different ways to allocate resources. Constraints (usually in the form of mathematical inequalities) are introduced to reduce the number of admissible solutions. Then a search is made for that solution among the feasible set which is optimal in term of some effectiveness criterion. The programing model holds great promise for aiding in the solution of such important marketing problems as media selection; allocation of sales force; determination of the best product line in terms of a firm's resource base; site location, and selection of channels of distribution.

There are some specialized versions of the programing model which are useful in a marketing context. One of these is the *transportation model,* which defines the existence of several *origins* (such as warehouses) and *destinations* (such as retail stores), and the unit cost of shipping from every origin to every destination. Furthermore, the amount of goods available for shipment from each warehouse and the amount of goods ordered by each retail store are specified. Under the given constraints, the problem is to find which warehouses should ship their supplies to which stores, in order to minimize total transportation costs.

A sample problem is shown in Table 5—try to find the least-cost shipping allocation by trial and error. Mathematical analysis would show that there is a shipment allocation which would cost only $5,800. It is possible to convert this problem into a standard linear programing problem and then solve it by the simplex method. Alternatively, special techniques have been developed to solve the problem directly, using the format in Table 5.

The transportation model has been used for a number of years in some large companies to develop shipping schedules. It has a useful variant, called the *assignment model,* with promising applications to

TABLE 5   Unit Shipping Costs from Various Warehouses to Various Stores

WAREHOUSE	STORE 1	STORE 2	STORE 3	WAREHOUSE AVAILABILITIES ↓
A	$5	$3	$6	300
B	$2	$9	$4	200
C	$3	$7	$8	600
D	$6	$1	$4	500
Store requirements →	200	1,000	400	1,600

other problems than transportation. In the assignment model, the number of origins *equal* the number of destinations; and each origin is to be associated with *only one* destination.

As an example, suppose 4 salesmen are to be *assigned* to 4 territories. The salesmen have differing skills, and the territories are in different stages of development. The sales manager makes an estimate of the expected annual sales that would result from each man being assigned to each territory. This information is summarized in Table 6.

TABLE 6   Estimated Annual Sales from the Assignment of Different Salesmen to Different Territories

| | TERRITORY | | | |
SALESMAN	1	2	3	4
A	$90,000	$57,000	$82,000	$45,000
B	$73,000	$75,000	$40,000	$51,000
C	$60,000	$30,000	$51,000	$75,000
D	$92,000	$95,000	$75,000	$70,000

There are 24 (4x3x2x1) different possible assignments. Because this is a small-scale example it is not difficult to arrive at the total sales maximizing assignment by trial and error—A3; B1; C4; D2; total sales, $325.

In more complex examples, the number of possible solutions increases factorially, and a mathematical analysis is necessary. Incidentally, the model could be used for assignment of salesmen to other than territories, to different company products, or to different types of customers, for example.

Another problem is known as the *"traveling-salesman" problem.* Although not involving allocation, it has certain similarities to an assignment problem. A salesman must make calls in *n* cities. This means that there are *n* factorial possible routes. One of these routes would minimize the total travel *cost;* and another route (possibly the same) would minimize the total travel *time.* The problem is to find the "best" route in terms of whichever is the stated objective. To date, general solutions are lacking, but certain important theorems have been discovered, such as the fact that the best route never involves any crossing of paths; and mathematical solutions are available where special simplifying assumptions are made. A simulation approach also can be used to search for a reasonable solution.

2. Competitive Strategy Models

Profit outcomes are not only a function of the decision of a firm, but of this decision in conjunction with the decisions made by competitors. A marketing decision must be based on an estimate of what competitors are likely to do, even though their intentions may not be known in advance.

Game theory is the name given to the systematic investigation of rational decision making in the context of uncertainty concerning the moves of competitors. As an example, suppose Row and Column are the managers of two competing supermarkets. Every week, each of the managers chooses some item to promote as the "Special of the Week." Neither manager knows in advance what the other is going to feature. However, each can estimate the approximate profit that would result from every pair of possible choices. Suppose Row estimates the payoffs shown in Table 7.

TABLE 7   Payoffs Resulting from Various Strategy Combinations

		COLUMN	
		FLOUR	COFFEE
ROW	Sugar	4	1
	Tea	6	−2

The table is interpreted as follows. If Row featured sugar and his competitor featured flour, Row would gain 4 (say in hundreds of dollars); that is, more of the marginal customers will "flow" to his

store, and the profit derived from this extra trade is estimated as 4. And Column will lose 4.

If Row featured sugar and his competitor featured coffee, Row would gain only 1 on Column. If Row featured tea and his competitor featured flour, then Row would gain 6. However, if Row featured tea and Column featured coffee, Row would lose 2.

The problem is whether Row should adopt one item and feature it week after week (a *pure strategy*), or choose an item randomly each week according to a constant though not necessarily equal set of probabilities (a *mixed strategy*).

If Row is to use a pure strategy, should it be sugar or tea? According to one doctrine, he should make the move which would minimize his maximum possible loss (the *minimax rule*). Tea would lead both to the largest possible gain and the largest possible loss, whereas sugar at least guarantees to Row a small but steady gain of 1.

Furthermore, Column can minimize his maximum loss by featuring coffee, and he undoubtedly will. This is a stalemated game where, so long as the same payoffs persist, Row will feature sugar and Column will feature coffee; and it would not be to either's advantage to make a surprise change. On the other hand, there are other payoff matrices which possess no such equilibrium solution, and where a mixed random strategy could be employed to advantage.

The Row-and-Column example illustrates one of the simplest types of games: *a 2-person, zero-sum game*. Only two players are involved, and they transfer a fixed sum of money between each other. The term "zero-sum" is used because in each play the sum of one player's gain (positive) and the other player's loss (negative) is zero.

More interesting, but at the same time more mathematically difficult, are the *3-or-more person, non-zero-sum games*. The 3-or-more-person feature allows the formation of coalitions where certain players can gain more by not acting independently. The non-zero-sum feature refers to the fact that competitive actions may expand the size of the market (that is, the total stakes) in addition to shifting market shares.

Game models have been designed for a variety of military and political situations, but some have interesting marketing possibilities. One is a game of timing involving two duelists (competitors) who at a signal are to begin approaching each other at some constant uniform rate. Each has only one available bullet (a new product) and is free to fire it whenever he wishes, with the knowledge that his chance of hitting the opponent improves as the distance narrows. When should the duelist fire?

Another game involves distributing an army over several battle-

fields, with the knowledge that each battlefield is "won" by the side which has disposed more troops in that battlefield. How should an army distribute its troops (or a company distribute its salesmen) in this situation?

Another game, "gambler's ruin," involves two competitors with different initial endowments of capital. A coin is tossed repeatedly with a probability p that competitor A will win and a probability $1-p$ that competitor B will win. The game ends when the capital of one competitor is exhausted. Given specific data, it is possible to estimate such things as the probability of "ruin" for each gambler, and the likely duration of the game.

Although to date game models do not seem to have much predictive power, they do suggest a useful analytical approach to such competitive problems as pricing, sales-force allocation, and advertising outlays. They may help to clarify the strategic implications of such moves as surprise, threat, and coalition.[3]

Finally, game theory should be distinguished from *operational gaming.* The latter term describes the modeling of a game around a realistic situation, where the participants actually make decisions (often in teams), and where the results of their interacting decisions are reported and become the data inputs for the next round of decisions. A large number of management and marketing games have been developed and used both in formal management-training programs and in research settings.[4]

3. Brand-switching Models

Marketing executives must watch their *market share* just as much as their profits. Present customers can never be taken for granted.

The attitude of marketing executives toward brand switching is quite simple: the switching-out rate must be slowed down, and the switching-in rate must be increased. The factors affecting brand choice must be analyzed, and this knowledge applied where possible in order to alter existing brand-switching rates.

Switching rates can be estimated from data showing the individual brand choices made over time by a representative panel of consumers. Suppose three brands are involved, A, B, and C. We can ask what

[3] R. Duncan Luce and Howard Raiffa, *Games and Decisions* (New York: John Wiley & Sons, Inc., 1957); Martin Shubik, *Strategy and Market Structure* (New York: John Wiley & Sons, 1959).

[4] J. F. McRaith and Charles R. Goeldner, "A Survey of Marketing Games," *Journal of Marketing,* vol. 26 (July, 1962), pp. 69–72.

proportion of those who bought A in the last period purchased A again, and what proportions switched to B and C. These proportions for each product can be conveniently exhibited in matrix form. Table 8 is a hypothetical example.

TABLE 8   Hypothetical Brand-Switching Matrix

		To		
		A	B	C
	A	.70	.20	.10
FROM	B	.17	.33	.50
	C	.00	.50	.50

Note that each row adds up to 1.00. The first row reads: Of those who purchased brand A in the last period, 70% bought A again, 20% bought B, and 10% bought C. Thus, A retained 70% of its previous customers and lost 30%, with twice as many of its previous customers going to B as C. This means that B poses a more competitive threat to A than does C. The other two rows are interpreted similarly.

We have seen where A's ex-customers go. Where do new customers come from? This is revealed by column A, rather than row A. Note that A picks up 17% of the customers lost by B, and none lost by C. This is further evidence that A and B are in close competition.

The brand-switching matrix provides information about:

1. The *repeat-purchase rate* for each brand, indicated by the principal diagonal numbers. Under certain assumptions, the repeat purchase rate can be interpreted as a measure of brand loyalty.
2. The *switching-in and switching-out rate* for each brand, represented by the off-diagonal numbers.

But this is not all. If the switching rates are likely to remain constant, at least for the short run, the matrix becomes a useful tool in forecasting both the magnitude and speed of change in future market shares on the basis of the present market shares. Even where the switching rates change, if they change in a predictable way, a forecast of market shares is possible.

In this connection, important research has taken place to determine how switching rates are affected by price and promotion changes. Some of the products which have been studied in terms of brand

switching rates are margarine, frozen orange juice concentrate, and instant and regular coffee.[5]

4. Waiting-line Models

Waiting appears in many marketing situations—customers wait for service, and companies wait for both customers and deliveries. Waiting is of interest because it imposes a cost. The customer who waits in a supermarket line bears a cost in terms of more desirable alternative uses of her time. If she regards the waiting time as excessive, she may leave and buy elsewhere, and the cost of her waiting would be shifted to the supermarket.

While waiting time imposes a cost, so does the effort to reduce waiting time. The supermarket might reduce waiting time by adding more counters or personnel, or both. The decision problem is one of balancing the cost of lost sales against the cost of additional facilities. In marginal terms, the supermarket should increase its servicing facilities up to the point where the cost of an additional facility would just overtake the profits lost due to customer impatience.

The decision problem is illustrated graphically in Figure 2. The higher the average waiting time in the system, the greater the cost of lost sales (2), but the lower the cost of facilities and personnel (1). The two cost curves are added vertically to derive a combined cost curve (3). The lowest point on this combined cost curve indicates the average waiting time, W_1, which will minimize combined costs. The implied investment in service facilities is F_1. The lowest point on (3) can be found graphically, or through differential calculus if appropriate cost equations can be found.

The cost of additional facilities is not difficult to measure; but it is very difficult to measure the value of lost sales which take place due to customer impatience. People vary considerably in their attitudes toward waiting; and customer impatience is also a function of the difference between anticipated and actual waiting time, and anticipated waiting varies by situations. Also, customers who feel impatient may decide not to "abandon" the store if they think that alternative stores are no better.

Waiting line theory, also called *queuing theory,* is not designed to

[5] Lester G. Telser, "The Demand for Branded Goods as Estimated from Consumer Panel Data," *Review of Economics and Statistics,* vol. 44 (August, 1962), pp. 300–324; Alfred A. Kuehn, "A Model for Budgeting Advertising," in reference 2.

answer how much waiting time should be built into a system. This is primarily an economic question as shown in Figure 2.

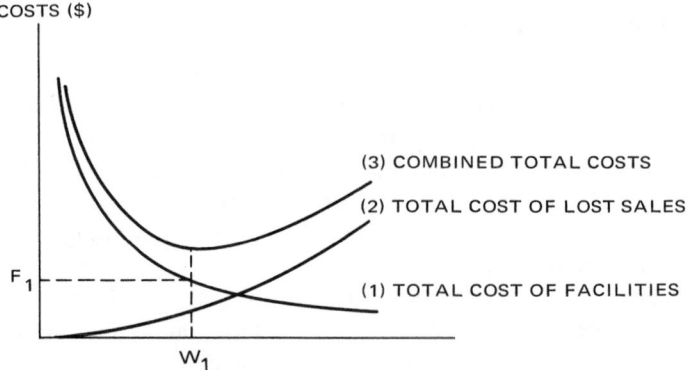

Figure 2   Costs as related to average waiting time

The theory is designed instead to handle two preliminary questions: What amount of waiting time may be expected in a particular system? How can this waiting time be altered?

The waiting time depends on four dimensions of the system:

1. *The inter-arrival time.* The time between arrivals into the system has a probability distribution which can be estimated from frequency data. The mean, standard deviation, and other characteristics of inter-arrival time can then be derived from the probability distribution.

2. *The service time.* The time between the initiating of a service and its completion can also be viewed as having a probability distribution.

3. *The number of service facilities.* The number affects the amount of waiting time.

4. *The service method.* Usually customers are serviced in the order in which they arrive (called first-in, first-out). But other methods are to give service to the most "important" customers first; to service the shortest orders first; and to service at random.

When these four dimensions are specified for a particular system, it is possible to estimate queuing characteristics, such as expected waiting time, expected queue length, and the variability of waiting time and queue length. For certain simple queuing situations, it is possible to derive these answers mathematically; but for more complicated systems, estimates can be derived through *simulation.*

If the system breeds long queues, the decision maker can simulate the effects of different hypothetical changes. In the case of a supermarket with a serious queuing problem on Saturday, four possible attacks are indicated by the dimensions. The supermarket can try to influence its customers to do their shopping on other days—this would have the effect of increasing the time between arrivals on Saturdays. Or the supermarket can decrease the service times, as by employing baggers to aid the cashiers. Or more service channels can be added. Or some of the channels can be specialized to handle smaller orders.

Most of the literature about queuing deals with facility planning for telephone exchanges, highways and toll roads, docks, and airline terminals. Yet retailing institutions such as supermarkets, filling stations, and airline ticket offices also face critical queuing problems; and marketing executives of such organizations can be expected to show increased interest in waiting line models.

5. Critical-path Scheduling Models

A technique called PERT (*Program Evaluation and Review Technique*) deals with the tactical questions of managing a complex project. As an example, consider new-product development.

Suppose that management has just finished reviewing and approving ideas for a new product. Some important tactical questions are: (1) What is the one best way to sequence the various activities which must be performed? (2) With normal departmental resources, how long will it be before the product is ready for sale? (3) What extra resources would be necessary to complete the project x weeks earlier?

Each new product will require the starting and completion of hundreds of different activities. The completion of an *activity* is called an *event*. As a simplified illustration, suppose the following six events must take place:

A. Corporate approval granted
B. Engineering and styling completed
C. Marketing analysis completed
D. Advertising campaign plans completed
E. Manufacturing preparation completed
F. Market testing completed

After these events are identified, a PERT analysis consists of three steps:

1. *Preparing a Program Network.* In what order should the above events take place? Certain events will be in a *priority* relationship, and others in a *concurrent* relationship.

The best way to see this distinction is to work backward from the terminal event. Before a market test can be started, let alone completed, two prior events must take place. The advertising campaign plans must be completed and the product must be manufactured.

But these two prior events are themselves in a concurrent relationship—the activities leading to the completion of each can be carried on concurrently. The next step would be to examine each of these events separately, to determine what events must precede each. When there are hundreds of events, the task of preparing a "network" for these events is neither easy nor free from ambiguity. But for the six events listed above, the most efficient network is fairly straightforward. By representing the events as circles and the activities as arrows connecting the circles, we would prepare the network shown in Figure 3.

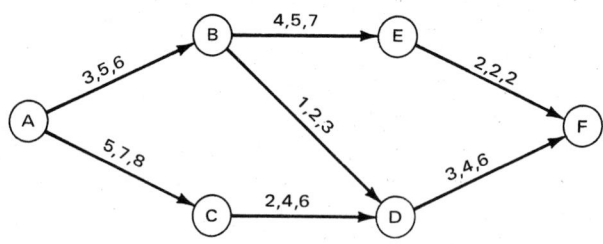

Figure 3   A PERT network

2. *Estimating Activity Times.* The department responsible for each activity is asked to estimate the *most likely time* to complete that activity, given the department's normal resources. This estimate is supplemented by both an optimistic and pessimistic estimate, again assuming normal departmental resources. For convenience, the three estimates are connected by commas and placed along side the activity arrows. (See Figure 3.) As an example, the department responsible for event B estimates that it will take between 3 and 6 weeks, with the most likely time being 5 weeks.

3. *Finding the Critical Path.* What is the earliest time the market test could be completed? It is necessary to trace back through all the paths which must be traveled, and the total time each will take.

There are three paths leading to the market test: ABEF, ABDF, and ACDF. On a *most likely time basis* (a different measure is used

in practice), path ABEF will take $5 + 5 + 2 = 12$ weeks; path ABDF will take $5 + 2 + 4 = 11$ weeks; and path ACDF will take $7 + 4 + 4 = 15$ weeks. This last path is, therefore, considered the *criticaι path;* since it must be traversed and it consumes the greatest sum of time, it sets the earliest most likely time for completion.

What is equally interesting is that events along a noncritical path, such as ABEF, can take place later than estimated without necessarily delaying the 15-week estimate for the project as a whole. In other words, activities along noncritical paths have some "slack" in their required completion time.

In actual applications, the network will be extremely complicated, and its characteristics would be very time-consuming to discern through manual calculations. However, a computer can be used to estimate the likely completion date and the slack times associated with the noncritical activities. Every few weeks a new computation is made, to reflect new information affecting the completion date. Alternative decisions about shifting resources can be simulated to see what effect they would have on completion time.[6]

PERT offers a number of benefits. It forces the various participants in the planning process to make careful estimates of activity completion time; it affixes responsibility; it highlights subtle interdependencies in the planning process; it suggests where resources may be shifted to shorten completion times; and it quantifies an estimate of meeting scheduled dates.

PERT will undoubtedly play an increasing role as a scheduling-and-control technique in the development of new products. It will also aid in the planning of other complex marketing projects such as advertising campaigns, special promotions, new-store development, and salesmen-training programs.

IMPLICATIONS

Operations researchers have developed a number of other models to analyze special situations—such as replacement models and sequencing models—but the ones described here have the most relevance for marketers. The major purpose served by these models is to "organize our ignorance."

[6] Robert W. Miller, "How to Plan and Control with PERT," *Harvard Business Review,* vol. 40 (March–April, 1962), pp. 93–104. For an alternative model to PERT, see Borge M. Christensen and J. R. Greene, "Planning, Scheduling, and Controlling the Launching of a New Product Via CPM," in reference 1.

Yet model-building is only half the task. The other half is to find the necessary data. Sophistication in model building must be matched by further refinement in marketing research procedures.

A more quantitative approach is needed for adequate decision making in marketing. Nonetheless, there are clear limitations. Many of the known variables cannot be handled mathematically, and all the variables are never known. Intuition and experience and judgment can not be transplanted into a machine.

There is the danger also that mathematics might be used by some to lend authority to some essentially ill-conceived decisions.

Marketing men will be subject to further mathematical name-dropping in written reports and at their conventions—cybernetics, information theory, econometrics, distributed lags, Bayesian decision theory, and so forth. Although these terms stand for perfectly good ideas, they should be viewed as part of a larger plan to advance knowledge, and not just represent verbal glibness.

Following is a list of some significant collections of readings and references on model building in marketing:

1. Wroe Alderson and Stanley Shapiro, editors, *Marketing and the Computer* (New York: Prentice-Hall, Inc., 1962).
2. Frank M. Bass and others, editors, *Mathematical Methods and Models in Marketing* (Homewood, Illinois: Richard D. Irwin, Inc., 1961).
3. Robert D. Buzzell, editor, *A Basic Bibliography on Mathematical Methods in Marketing* (Chicago: American Marketing Association, 1962).
4. Ronald Frank and others, editors, *Quantitative Techniques in Marketing* (Homewood, Illinois: Richard D. Irwin, Inc., 1962).
5. David W. Miller and Martin K. Starr, *Executive Decisions and Operations Research* (New York: Prentice-Hall, Inc., 1960), especially Chapter 9.

The Promise of Simulation in Marketing

Harold Weitz

Simulation, as a technique, is one of the most talked-about methods in the field of management science today in spite of a rather negating definition from Webster's dictionary which states: "Simulation is the act or process of simulating; to assume an appearance which is feigned or not true; to counterfeit; to imitate; the act of willful deception, and misrepresentation." The results of a recent survey[1] show how simulation is being applied to marketing problems; its strengths and weaknesses; the different forms, structure, and purposes of simulation models; and its promise as a technique for future marketing analysts.

RANGE OF APPLICATIONS

During the past decade, simulation has been increasingly applied to a wide spectrum of marketing problems, both theoretical and practical. The range of applications includes: management information systems design and evaluation, industrial demand analysis, investment analysis, pricing, pre-testing field interviewing plans, staffing of a service organization, physical distribution (including warehouse location), predicting media exposure, evaluating advertising-message effectiveness, marketing-games for training, and models for evaluating alternative market strategies.[2]

Reprinted with permission from the *Journal of Marketing*, vol. 81, no. 3 (July, 1967), pp. 28–33, published by the American Marketing Association.

[1] Harold Weitz, *"Simulation Models in Marketing,"* IBM Technical Report 17-192, IBM Advanced Systems Development Division, Yorktown Heights, N.Y. (1966).

[2] A description of the structure of each of these models, their characteristics, strengths, and weaknesses is included in footnote 1.

In spite of the clear and growing use of simulation in marketing, the full potential of this technique remains largely unexploited, at least insofar as can be ascertained from the applications described in the literature. (Clearly, many applications of simulation are not reported in the literature. Some successful applications may be of a proprietary nature; other unsuccessful applications may remain unpublicized.) The reasons for this are numerous. Market phenomena are complex processes and not clearly understood. Sufficient knowledge of the effects of market-mix variables has not been generally available and such relationships are necessary to the construction of viable and meaningful models.

Another reason lies perhaps in the kinds of skills traditionally brought to bear on marketing problems. Not only is knowledge of management science techniques (including simulation) necessary, but increasingly it is becoming clear that the skills of the behavioral scientist (psychologist, sociologist) and the economist are also needed to attack what is basically a socio-economic problem. Much of the emphasis in early management science was placed upon analytical techniques which yielded optimum solutions. Unfortunately, the solutions offered required a simplification of reality that often made the results grossly inadequate. Because of decreases in the cost of computation and in the cost of obtaining information, the utilization of management and behavioral-science personnel and, because of increasing pressures by management to make more effective utilization of marketing resources, the use of simulation should grow manyfold.

CLASSIFYING SIMULATION MODELS

The lack of a precise and universally accepted definition of simulation makes difficult any classification of the different kinds of simulation models. No widely accepted terminology is available, but many terms frequently used to describe certain characteristics of simulation models are included in a three-level classification which may be useful as a starting framework for looking at simulation. This classification is by:

1. *Purpose*
   a. Prognostic models
   b. Process or behavioral models
2. *Degree of System Definition*
   a. Tactical models
   b. Strategic models

3. *Structural Characteristics*
   a. Static/dynamic models
   b. Deterministic/stochastic models
   c. Aggregate/disaggregate models

Purpose of Simulation Model

Almost all simulation models constructed have as their ultimate aim a predictive capability. *Prognostic* models are primarily intended to simulate the results of a system, whereas *process* models seek to simulate the dynamics of the system itself as well as future results. The two types might be distinguished by considering the classic "black box." In one case (prognostic) the interest is simply in the outputs of the black box; in the second (process), primary interest lies in exploring the phenomena occurring within the "black box" and in constructing theories to describe that behavior.

Degree of System Definition

In a *tactical* model, one is generally interested in exploring the impact of alternate decision rules or parameter values within well-defined and well-understood structures. Questions raised by such a model may be:

a. What is the impact upon either the waiting time or the size of the queue if the service time is decreased?
b. What is the effort on a production system of alternative priority rules for assigning shop orders?

In both these cases, the mechanisms or elements within the system are well-defined, such as the distribution of time required to service individual customers, or the time required to machine parts. The *strategic* model applies when there is an interest in exploring the behavioral properties of ill-defined problems involving elements and relationships which are largely unknown or which are poorly understood, for example, consumer behavior. A model in which certain behavioral relationships are assumed is constructed and then tested against reality. The emphasis, as with process models, is on understanding the dynamics of a system so that a theory can be constructed. Once the theory has been sufficiently validated, the model can be used to simulate the outcomes of the system under a wide variety of conditions.

Structural Characteristics of Models

A *static* model would seek to describe or predict the total response of a system as if it occurred at a single instant of time; a *dynamic* model would seek to explore the changes occurring within the system over some period of time. A *deterministic* model would contain no probabilistic elements; a *stochastic* model would contain one or more elements, or mechanisms, involving random or probabilistic characteristics. An *aggregate* model is so structured that it can only answer questions of an aggregate nature, for example, the total response to an advertisement; a *disaggregate* model (there are various levels of aggregation or disaggregation) is so constructed as to yield information of a more detailed nature such as the number of men between the ages X and Y, having incomes beyond R and S who respond to an advertisement. Unlike the aggregate model, the disaggregate model can respond not only to a variety of detailed questions, but is by nature a more microscopic representation or model of the phenomena under study. An example of a disaggregate model would be one in which the behavior of each member of a hypothetical data bank of persons is individually simulated. Other terms could be added to further distinguish the structure of simulation models such as discrete or continuous, fixed or variable time intervals. The above characterization will suffice for our purpose.

This classification is intended more to clarify the nature and uses of simulation than it is to serve as a universal classification scheme. It is somewhat arbitrary and the categories are not completely unique; a single model may be classified as: process, strategic, dynamic, stochastic, and disaggregate.

THE ADVANTAGES AND DISADVANTAGES
OF SIMULATION

Marketing generally involves a complex environment about which relatively little is known with respect to predicting the *impact* of a marketing decision. Analytical optimization techniques, such as linear programing, frequently employ unrealistic simplifications as with a linear objective function (which is often not linear) that maximizes media exposure (which often is not the central problem). Another tool frequently employed is regression analysis which treats covari-

ance; it does not treat cause and effect nor get at the dynamic characteristics underlying market behavior. Although valuable, Markov and other kinds of probabilistic models which have been proposed for predicting consumer buying behavior (for example, brand loyalty) similarly employ simplifications which detract from their utility.

Frequently in developing an analytical approach, simplifications are made in order to arrive at a feasible and reasonable solution. These simplifications may augment the utility of a model but not if they permit too significant deviation from reality so that the results become of questionable value.

Some important advantages of simulation are:

1. Solutions to complex problems can often be obtained more readily through simulation than by analytical solutions. Simulation overcomes the deficiencies of other methods for dealing with complex, interacting, dynamic processes which marketing generally entails. This technique utilizes a set of mathematical and logical relationships which represent the essential features of the process being studied, however complex these relationships may be. Simplifications and assumptions are not required for simulation to the extent that they are demanded by analytical solutions.

2. Simulation offers an opportunity for relatively inexpensive experimentation, even where precise data is lacking. A simulation permits one to conduct a series of experiments on a computer or by hand computation, using the model developed to describe some process without recourse to actual field studies. It permits the use of data which may be known only imprecisely which after simulation studies is revealed to be relatively insensitive over a wide range of values.

3. Analytical models which can yield optimum solutions can frequently be developed as a result of simulation studies. Without reservation, a model which immediately and directly leads to an optimum solution is preferable to simulation. It is the difficulty which complex processes present that makes analytical solutions arduous and often questionable. Frequently, however, in developing and using a simulation model, insights are gained which, in turn, permit meaningful analytical solutions.

4. Simulation languages are available which offer further stimulation to the use of simulation because of lowered programming costs, and the relative ease of learning and applying simulation models to a wide diversity of problems. Just as FORTRAN is both easy to learn and less costly to program than machine languages, specially designed simulation languages are available which offer similar advantages. (The simulation languages most frequently used in the U.S.A. are:

the General Purpose System Simulator (GPSS), and SIMSCRIPT.) Additionally, these languages offer a conceptual view of a system, or process which facilitates the construction and programming of simulation models.

5. The non-technical manager can comprehend simulation easier than a complex mathematical analytical model, and, in fact, less sophistication may be required to develop it. In general, a simulation model is simpler to understand and explain, for it is in essence only a description of the behavior of some processes or phenomena.

Simulation does, however, have basic problems which should be recognized by the marketing analyst. It does not easily produce optimum solutions. Each simulation run is, in effect, a single experiment conducted under a given set of conditions as defined by a set of values for the input variables. To determine an optimum, or close to optimum condition, a number of simulation runs will be required sufficient for a response curve to be established.

Simulation may be time consuming. This follows from the necessity to conduct a number of different types or successive simulation runs as previously described. As the number of input variables increase, the difficulty in finding the optimum values for a set of strategic variables increases manyfold and requires careful design of experimental runs and optimum search methods; otherwise, there may be excessive and needless cost. When the question relates to finding an optimum value for a single input variable, for example, the advertising expenditure for media X, several runs will be required using various values of this variable. As additional input variables (that is, strategies) are examined, the number of possible combinations requiring exploration increase in factorial fashion.

Simulation may become a convenient or easy alternative to applying appropriate effort toward the development of an efficient analytical solution, ideally, required. As the ability to employ simulation increases, there may be a tendency to rely on this technique because of its relative ease of application. Simulation should be used where appropriate; it should not be substituted for the use of analytical techniques which may be more efficient.

THE POTENTIAL OF SIMULATION

Previously cited were areas of marketing in which simulation has already been applied. More sophisticated, viable, and valid models will continue to be developed in these and other areas. Promising

work is currently in progress. Furthermore, other aspects of marketing appear to be appropriate for the application of simulation.

Predicting Consumer Reaction to New Products

One area in which simulation should have significant impact in the future is that relating to the prediction of consumer reaction to new products. The capability of predicting a latent demand for a product not now on the market, without costly surveys, is certainly a desirable one. Such a capability would be based on the planned characteristics of consumers. It would answer questions relating to market potential: who would buy? What is the reaction of potential customers to the color, design, etc.? Knowledge, now unavailable, is required; research, now going on, offers some promise toward satisfying this "latent demand" objective. Volney Stefflre reported on techniques of product development which are based on the notion that "an individual behaves towards a new thing in a manner similar to the way he behaves towards other things he sees the new thing as similar to."[3]

Recently Abelson and Bernstein published a description of a model for the simulation of a referendum on the question of fluoride in the water supply.[4] The referendum simulation suggests techniques for simulating the test marketing of new products, as it would be for simulating an advertising campaign to answer the questions: what message? what media? and what frequency? The referendum model exposes some 500 hypothetical individuals having certain characteristics to a set of communication channels, each of which carries a particular message. The model specifies two processes by which each individual may change his attitudes:

a. by exposure to public assertions appearing in the communication channels, and

b. via conversations with others who have some stand on the issue and who may also make assertions.

Each simulated week an individual is subjected, with varying probabilities of exposure, to several communication channels and to particular assertions made in these channels. Rules determine if an

[3] Volney Stefflre, "Simulation of People's Behavior Towards New Objectives and Events," *The American Behavioral Scientist,* vol. 8 (May, 1965).

[4] Robert P. Abelson and Alex Bernstein, "A Computer Simulation Model of Community Referendum Controversies." *Public Opinion Quarterly,* vol. 27 (Spring, 1963).

assertion is accepted, depending on the individual's attitudes towards the communication source, previous acquaintance with the assertion, the congeniality of the assertion, and his previous position on the referendum issue. As a result of the model's exposure process, assertions may be accepted, resulting in changes in attitudes towards the communication sources, the probability of exposure to the various channels, and interest in the issue as well as one's position on the issue.

The model's conversational phase considers the level of interest of the individuals in the issue, their compatibility, their respective positions on the issue, their acquaintance with the assertion, and the social network of each. The model is indeed complex, incorporating reasonable hypotheses regarding human behavior. At a recent presentation, Bernstein outlined how this model could be adapted to test marketing.[5] He asserted that for the exposure process, this would require knowledge on what assertions people make about a particular class of products. Instead of assertions reflecting peoples' attitudes toward fluorides, for example, concern with the impact of fluorides on health, age, etc., the model would reflect attitudes toward the characteristics of a particular product class, for instance its taste, mildness, or color. Changes would also be required to indicate the locus of stores visited by a particular person, presumably to reflect upon product availability as well as in-store promotion. The effects of competitive efforts would also have to be considered. Although the approach presented was not sufficiently detailed to permit evaluation, it was, nevertheless, intriguing in its possibilities.

Predicting Market Share

Numerous consumer flow models have been designed to predict the expected product market share. These are commonly referred to as brand-shifting, or brand-loyalty models. They basically take the form of Markov, learning, or other kinds of probabilistic models. These models suffer numerous deficiencies, largely because their use requires assumptions which are unrealistic. They further exclude such relevant factors as sales promotion, advertising, and competition. The promise of simulation lies in its capability to consider complex but realistic conditions which minimize the need to make unwarranted simplifying assumptions.

[5] Alex Bernstein, "An Application of Simulation to Test Marketing." Paper presented at *First Annual Conference on Simulation in Business and Public Health.* American Statistical Association, New York Hilton Hotel, New York (March 2, 1966).

TABLE 1   Inter-Industry Input-Output for the National Economy

	INDUSTRY SECTORS	A	B	C	D	•	j
I	A	X_{AA}	X_{AB}	•	•	•	•
N	B	X_{AB}	X_{BB}	X_{BC}	•	•	•
P	C	X_{CA}	•	•	•	•	•
U	D	•	•	•	•	•	•
T	•	•	•	•	•	•	•
	i	•	•	•	•	•	•
	Total Output	A_T	B_T	C_T	D_T	•	•

Where $X_{BC} = \dfrac{\text{input from industry B to industry C}}{\text{total output of industry C, }(C_T)}$

Samuel G. Barton pointed to a conceptual model for short term sales prediction which deserves attention.[6] It encompasses many of the salient variables affecting a sale, such as advertising, pricing, and promotion. Although conceptual, it may offer a basis for a useful operational model for predicting short term sales, appraising the effectiveness of alternative test-market programs, and guiding the allocation of promotional efforts.

The short term prediction model views a consumer as being influenced at two different times: prior to the point of sale, and at the point of sale. The factors governing these influences are termed consumer momentum, customer intention to change, share of space, and consumer-deal offerings. The weight of these factors, a function of a complex of other factors, varies among the different classes of buyers, that is, new, new repeat, and old customers. To illustrate, the principal factors affecting intention to change include:

1. Share of new product announcements
2. Share of general advertising
3. Share of consumer deal advertising
4. Share of shelf and display stocks

Sufficient data with adequate understanding of market processes to implement such a model probably do not exist, but they may serve as a framework for development.

[6] Samuel G. Barton, "A Marketing Model for Short Term Prediction of Consumer Sales." *Journal of Marketing* (July, 1965), pp. 19–29.

Competitive Gaming Models

The value of market games, one of the forms which simulation may take, lies in their ability to introduce competitive forces explicitly into consideration. Here lies the potential of games as a vehicle for determining market strategy. Philip Kotler objects to most games because they treat consumers in a superficial way, as an aggregate which responds in some lagged and linear way to market decisions.[7] He outlined a competitive-market simulation which not only has a decision-rich marketing function but also has an environmentally rich market of individuals. His prime interest is in observing whether such a tool could be useful for company predictions.

Typically, the model would have a representative sample of 200 households, differentiated by socio-economic characteristics, through which the computer will cycle each week to determine a buyer's choice as a function of:

1. Socio-economic factors
2. Previous brand choices
3. Interim experience
4. In-store experience

The last two factors are a function of management's decisions; the former are attributes of the consumer. Such a model could be used as a game either with player-managers or without players when an input-decision rule defines a strategy. The latter condition removes the need for player roles.

Input-Output Analysis

Input-Output analysis has until recently been largely regarded as an economic tool. Its power rests on a table of coefficients (see Table 1) which relates the inputs and outputs of 81 industry sectors of the National economy to each other and to final demand. Using this table, one can determine, for example, the direct dollar value of iron and steel required by the automobile and other industries as well as the iron and steel purchased directly by the consumer. The table also shows the intermediate inputs required to make the iron and steel.

[7] Philip Kotler, "The Competitive Marketing Simulator—A New Management Tool." *California Management Review* (Spring, 1965).

From this basic table, a table of inverse coefficients can be derived representing the amounts of input from industry i necessary to produce one unit of final demand (the ultimate demand by consumers) for products of industry *j*.

Input-Output analysis has been used in a variety of ways to determine the effect on an industry of an increase in the gross national product, the effect upon an industry if sales of some major sector of the economy experiences a significant change, the impact of the Federal highways program upon the U.S. economy, the contribution of the tobacco industry, and the effects of proposed changes to the industrial structure of the Appalachia region. Variations of the input-output model have also been used to forecast total demand for the iron and steel industry.

Some large companies are reported to have individual input-output models (describing the relationships between the various components of the organization) which are coupled to a national input-output model.[8] Such company models are intended to provide greater control and predictive capabilities. Still other applications have been reported; these extend to such areas as evaluating poverty programs for the Office of Economic Opportunity and to evaluating proposed transportation systems.

Efforts by the U.S. Department of Commerce to develop input-output data are currently under way which would be frequently updated for a larger number of industry sectors. With such data the market analyst would have a potentially powerful tool at his fingertips. In addition to those uses mentioned, the following would be permitted.

1. Evaluating more precisely the effects of technological change, for example, as changes occur in the materials used in the manufacture of some product, they would be reflected in the entries to the input-output matrix.

2. measuring the full impact of a major new government program, such as a major increase in education, a new poverty program, or an economic development project for an economically poor community, and

3. estimating more precisely the future demand for products and services for each industry.[9]

[8] Wassily W. Lenotief, "The Structure of the U. S. Economy." *Scientific American* (April, 1965).

[9] Typical Brochure: *IBM Industry Information Service,* (Form No. 520-1373) IBM, Data Processing Division, White Plains, New York.

Several companies offering computer service, including IBM, have announced the use of input-output models to simulate the potential market for a wide range of industries. These services process proprietary data as required, and at the same time, permit referencing it automatically, if desired to data banks of information gathered and maintained for management use.

THE FUTURE

Simulation has already been used in many diverse areas of marketing. It would be difficult to discuss all the areas in which this technique can fruitfully be applied. New applications are being developed continually. Other areas having potential are: strategic long-range planning,[10] the selection of distribution channels, and the location of merchandise and displays in the supermarkets.[11]

The major advantage and stimulant to the use of simulation in marketing lies in its ability to deal with complex, dynamic, and interacting phenomena which are characteristics of marketing. If the processes or phenomena permit adequate description, they can be modeled and experiments can be simulated. Unlike analytical optimization solutions, simulation models, by avoiding over-simplification, tend to be better descriptions of reality.

Simulation will play an increasing role in the future marketing function. Before long, many companies will have a number of market simulators available. These will take diverse forms including that of the strategic, or competitive, gaming simulator. Such models will invariably be complex, representing the channels of distribution, the competition, the environment, the customer, and the firm.

There are those who say that such simulation will form the nucleus of a "war gaming center," typical of that of the Armed Services. Such a capability would readily permit one to investigate new strategies, to rapidly measure the impact of new marketing intelligence, and generally, to improve the operations of the firm. Such a center could be embedded within a larger framework—an Information System for Marketing Managers.

[10] Robert Weinberg, "Simulation Models for Planning Management Strategy." Paper presented at the *First Annual Conference on Simulation in Business and Public Health,* American Statistical Association, New York Hilton Hotel, New York, March 2, 1966.

[11] Alfred A. Kuehn, "Simulation of Consumer Behavior." Same reference as footnote 10.

The availability of more powerful and less costly computing systems, larger and more accessible storage devices, and more convenient input-output devices, which can be used with relative ease by the non-programmer, will hasten the development of the "war gaming center" concept. The "conversational" terminal and time-shared systems are further indications of trends narrowing the gap between the computer and the user.

Bayesian Statistics in Marketing

Harry V. Roberts

The application of statistics to marketing has grown substantially in recent decades. Yet statistics has remained more of a "sideshow" than an integral part of the process of decision-making. Too often, consumer surveys and sales analyses have been carried out with little thought about their contribution to management problems.

This is hardly surprising, because it is only recently that statistical theorists themselves have seen the potential contribution of statistics to decision-making and have begun to evolve a formal structure of *decision theory* that can actually be applied. Although the structure is still incomplete, its promise is bright. This structure is called *Bayesian statistics.*

The adjective "Bayesian" comes from Bayes's theorem, an elementary result of probability theory traceable to the Rev. Thomas Bayes, an English clergyman of the 18th century. His theorem typically, although not necessarily, plays an essential part in a Bayesian statistical analysis. Strangely enough, the really distinctive feature of Bayesian statistics is not Bayes's theorem but rather the personalistic interpretation of probability. That is, it is legitimate to quantify our feelings about uncertainty in terms of subjectively assessed numerical probabilities, even when confronted by a single unique decision and when there is no extensive past history on which to base the assessment of probabilities.

Assessments are made of probabilities of events that determine the profitability of alternative actions open to a decision-maker. Assessments are also made of profit (more generally, utility) for each possible combination of action and event. For each possible action, expected profit can be computed, that is, a weighted mean of the possible profits, the weights being the probabilities mentioned above.

Reprinted with permission from the *Journal of Marketing,* vol. 27, no. 1 (January, 1963), pp. 1–4, published by the American Marketing Association.

The action is chosen for which expected profit is highest. The dominating principle of decision, then, is maximization of expected profit (or utility).

AN EXAMPLE

Consider the following hypothetical, simplified, yet reasonably realistic marketing application.

A manufacturer of automobiles is testing a new direct mail approach B versus a standard approach A. An experiment is conducted in which each of the two approaches is tried out on random samples of size n (sample size $2n$ in total) from a large national mailing list. Suppose that $n = 100,000$, so that 200,000 is the total sample size of the experiment. During a three-month period, approach B has 761 sales and A has 753.

The problem is: should A or B be used on a national scale, or should a decision be deferred until more research has been done?

Suppose that additional evidence cannot be obtained and that a choice must be made between A and B. Many statisticians would suggest a test of significance. It turns out that the difference is not significant at any of the usual levels. What to conclude? One answer is that nothing can be decided from the experiment because A and B do not differ significantly. Another answer is that the standard method A should be continued because it is not significantly worse. Still another answer is that it does not matter whether A or B is used because they are not significantly different. The correct answer is that if all *other* considerations are evenly balanced, then the slight edge of B over A should be decisive.

While this common-sense answer can be given a justification of sorts by conventional statistical theory, it can be supported easily by a Bayesian analysis. Three assumptions about "all *other* considerations are evenly balanced" can be made explicit. First, it can be assumed that other evidence on the effectiveness of the two approaches is negligible by comparison with this statistical evidence. Second, it can be assumed that if the true effectiveness of each method were known, we would be willing to adopt the one with the higher effectiveness; that is, there are no differences in costs or side benefits: the "break-even" difference in true effectiveness is zero. Third, it can be assumed that the difference in effectiveness measured in sales rates per mailing is proportional to the difference in effectiveness measured in profit rates per mailing.

Under these assumptions a Bayesian analysis proceeds as follows. Compute a *posterior distribution* (posterior to the sample, that is) of the true difference of effectiveness between B and A. Under our present assumptions, Bayes's theorem shows that the posterior distribution of the true difference in sales rates per mailing can be approximated by a normal distribution with a mean of

$$\frac{761}{100,000} - \frac{753}{100,000} = \frac{8}{100,000} = .00008$$

and a standard deviation of

$$\sqrt{\frac{(.00761)\,(1 - .00761)}{100,000} + \frac{(.00753)\,(1 - .00753)}{100,000}}$$

$$= \sqrt{\frac{.00756}{100,000} + \frac{.00748}{100,000}}$$

$$= \sqrt{.0000001504}$$

$$= .00039,$$

where familiar classical formulas, $p_1 - p_2$ and

$$\sqrt{\frac{p_1 q_1}{n_1} + \frac{p_2 q_2}{n_2}}$$ are used in the calculation.

What does this mean? It means that we are attaching probabilities to the thing we are uncertain about, namely, the true difference in effectiveness between B and $A,$ and that these probabilities are summarized approximately by a normal distribution with the stated mean and standard deviation. Once we attach probabilities to the things we are uncertain about, we can implement the rule of decision: Choose that action for which expected profit is highest.

In our present example, it can be shown that this rule tells us to compare the mean of the posterior distribution, .00008, with the break-even point of true differential effectiveness, or 0. Since .00008 exceeds 0, we should choose appeal B.

Reasonably realistic numerical assumptions show that the expected superiority of B over A is $2,000,000. The assumptions are that the balance of the national mailing list has 50,000,000 names, and that the incremental profit per car sold is $500. Under these assumptions, 8 added cars per 100,000 names implies an expected differential profit of $(.00008)\,(50,000,000)\,(\$500) = \$2,000,000$. It is hardly a matter of indifference which approach is chosen.

The decision to choose B could, of course, be reached by unaided common sense. Even if the economic break-even point were different than zero, unaided common sense would still work. Suppose that it was judged that because of certain change-over costs, B would have to be at least .00020 units more effective than A to warrant its adoption. Then we would compare .00008 with .00020 and conclude that A should be retained, since .00008 is less than .00020.

THE ROLE OF JUDGMENT

Suppose, however, that other evidence is not negligible compared to the statistical evidence. For example, suppose that prior to the experiment management had felt that on balance A was better than B, but that the chances that they were wrong were enough to warrant the experiment.

More quantitatively, suppose that it had been judged that the odds were even that the true effectiveness of B over A did not exceed $-.00010$, but also that the odds were only even that the true effectiveness was within .00026 of $-.00010$. Note that .00010 is about 1.3% of the sales rate for A, and that .00026 is about 3.5% of it.

Moreover, management assumed that the normal distribution fitting these requirements, which will have a mean of $-.00010$ and a standard deviation of .00039, can be taken to be the *prior distribution* of the true difference in effectiveness. "Prior" simply means prior by comparison with the statistical evidence contemplated, which in this example was the experiment already described. Bayes's theorem again tells how this prior distribution should be revised in the face of sample evidence to arrive at a posterior distribution. It turns out to be approximately a normal distribution with mean

$$\frac{-.00010 + .00008}{2} = -.00001,$$

so that the decision would now go *against* approach B.

In order to make this calculation, the standard error of the sample difference, .00039, had to be used. It is an accident of this particular illustration that the reconciliation of judgment and sample evidence is achieved by a simple average; in general, the two would not be weighted equally. While the details of operation of Bayes's theorem will not be developed here, the important thing is that the theorem gives a formal reconciliation between managerial judgment, expressed

quantitatively in the prior distribution, and the statistical evidence of the experiment. This reconciliation might be much harder to arrive at by common sense alone.

Incidentally, managerial judgment is not, as assumed at the outset, likely to be given negligible weight by comparison with the experiment evidence. There is likely to be good reason to believe that the differential sales effectiveness of *A* and *B* is rather small, as in this last illustration, because the direct mailing itself has a relatively small influence on total sales.

THE PROBLEM OF SAMPLE SIZE

Turn now to a more difficult question, that of deciding whether additional evidence should be sought, and if so, how much. This question is really the problem of sample size.

To give a concrete illustration of how it is solved, let us revert to the situation in which prior evidence was negligible compared to that of a sample, so that the posterior distribution is normal with mean .00008 and standard error .00039. This posterior distribution now can be regarded as a *prior* distribution with respect to additional experimental information that might be obtained.

In addition to this prior distribution, an assessment must be made of four key economic quantities: (1) the incremental profit to the company (assumed constant) of an added car sold; (2) the size of the national mailing list; (3) the fixed cost of an experiment; (4) the incremental cost per name (assumed constant) on an experimental mailing list.

For illustration, take $500, 50,000,000, $10,000, and $0.25 for these quantities. The result of a numerical calculation is that a further experiment involving about 500,000 names for each approach— 1,000,000 in total—should be run, and then a final decision between *A* and *B* should be made based on the mean of the posterior distribution after that experiment. (The added or lost sales attributable to *B* during the experiment are not accounted for in this approximate calculation. The details of this calculation would be meaningless without a great deal more background than can be developed in a short exposition.[1])

[1] Robert Schlaifer, *Probability and Statistics in Business Decisions,* corrected impression (New York: McGraw-Hill Book Co., Inc., 1959), especially pp. 544–546.

POTENTIAL CONTRIBUTIONS

There are three potential contributions of Bayesian statistics illustrated by the example above:

1. How to choose between marketing alternatives on the basis of sample evidence when virtually no weight is to be given to managerial judgment.

2. How to choose between marketing alternatives on the basis of sample evidence when substantial weight is to be given to managerial judgment.

3. How to decide on how much research, if any, should be done before a final choice is made.

For completeness, there is a fourth potential contribution not indicated in the example above:

4. How to choose between marketing alternatives when no sample evidence is available: judgments would be expressed as a prior distribution, and the mean of this distribution would be compared with the break-even point.

IMPLICATIONS

Consider the importance of each of these contributions. The fourth, how to make a choice in the absence of sample evidence, is simply a way of formalizing what would otherwise be done informally and intuitively. It is like having a checklist to assure that nothing will be forgotten or given distorted importance.

The first, how to make a choice when the evidence is almost wholly statistical, can be made by common sense without Bayesian statistics. On the other hand, the Bayesian approach helps greatly to avoid errors that are common in practice, and especially those due to serious yet natural misunderstandings of traditional statistical methods.

The second, how to reconcile strong judgments with statistical evidence, is very difficult to do by common sense alone. The formal Bayesian apparatus is a great help.

The third, how to choose the best sample size, is not obvious at all to common sense. On no other problem are the recommendations of different statisticians likely to differ so much. The Bayesian calculation illustrated is the only defensible way to give an answer. Traditional statistical theory tells how to choose a sample size that will meet a specification for precision. It does not tell how much precision

should be specified, except to give informal advice that the benefits of added precision must be balanced against the cost of attaining it. Such informal advice is not an adequate guide.

Not all marketing problems can be answered as easily as the one given in this example. However, a substantial fraction of marketing problems are of this type, although perhaps more complicated, as where a choice must be made between three approaches, *A, B,* and *C,* where *C* might be no direct mailing at all. The Bayesian apparatus has been worked out for these problems. Moreover, the apparatus has been extended to certain other kinds of problems.

There was not sufficient realism in this example to make it completely convincing. One defect is that an experiment of this kind would have to be carried out in selected markets rather than in a random sample of a national mailing list. There is uncertainty as to how the differential effectiveness of *A* and *B* in Denver, for example, might compare with differential effectiveness in the rest of the country. A formal Bayesian apparatus exists for dealing with such problems.

Of course, much needs to be done to work out Bayesian solutions for common marketing problems. But much has already been done, and important problems can be solved now.[2]

The real difficulty in applying statistics to marketing is that until recently no theoretical bridge existed between "statistics" and "business judgment." For the first time we now know how to fit both these elements into the process of decision-making. In particular, no statistical analysis is complete unless "business judgment" is incorporated into it. It *does* matter, for example, what management thinks about the comparative effectiveness of *A* and *B* before statistical evidence on the question can be intelligently sought or analyzed.

Marketing statisticians cannot pursue the illusory goal of trying to provide "definitive answers" in the sense that scientific research is sometimes supposed to do. "Definitive answers" might require exorbitant sample sizes, and even then the answers might not turn out to be really definitive.

Likewise, marketing executives cannot leave statistics solely to the statisticians. They must communicate the essence of their judgment about marketing problems before statisticians can make a fully satisfactory technical contribution; and they must understand the underlying rationale of decision theory.

[2] *Ibid.* Also, Robert Schlaifer and Howard Raiffa, *Applied Statistical Decision Theory* (Boston, Division of Research, Harvard Graduate School of Business Administration, 1961).

| Statistical Tools for
Marketing Research

Much of the information used at the next level of quantitative applications flows from the techniques employed at this first level. Some
examples below serve to illustrate the relationship between information search techniques and decision-making methods:

1. A large metropolitan department store wishes a better method to
   discriminate between satisfactory and unsatisfactory credit applicants. It has a great number of completed application forms and has
   been able to label the applicants who fill out these forms as either
   satisfactory or unsatisfactory. On the basis of this information,
   management is able to construct a linear discriminant function,
   which can be used to classify new applicants as either "satisfactory"
   or "unsatisfactory" (in a manner that minimizes the probability of
   misclassification). However, this information only supplements the
   judgment of management; the profit potential of the *expected sales*
   of a subclassification of the unsatisfactory group may far outweigh
   the expected losses. In Chapter 4, William F. Massey renders an
   excellent discourse on the nature of discriminant analysis.

2. Sales Management gives a battery of tests to sales applicants to
   determine their suitability for sales careers. The application of
   factor analytic methods reveals that many of the tests are intercorrelated and thus have common factors. The number of tests is
   reduced to two and management has almost the same amount of
   information it gathers with five tests. Now management must give
   meaning to the extracted factors and determine if they are correlated with success in sales careers. Gwyn Collins provides even non-
   quantitative readers with an intuitive feel for factor analysis.

3. The sales management of a large concern wishes to determine which
   of three proposed point-of-purchase displays is most effective. It is
   felt that the display effectiveness varies among its three sales
   regions. To solve their problem, management uses a two-factor
   analysis of variance technique in conjunction with a latin-square
   sampling plan to eliminate sequence and store-size bias. It finds an
   "interactive" effect between region and type of display. Consequently, management uses different displays in different regions.
   The nature of ANOVA is explained by Gwyn Collins in "Analysis
   of Variance."

In summary, Part II provides the reader with an excellent review of the philosophy and techniques of the decision sciences in marketing. Parts IV and V probe into applications and more sophisticated theory of the above approaches to information search and decision making.

Analysis of Variance

Gwyn Collins

Analysis of variance is a technique for learning how important each of several factors may be in producing a result. Its fundamental idea is altogether simple, its development quite recent and its theoretical foundation a single mathematical theorem. It has wide application; regression and correlation, for instance, can be regarded as aspects of it. It is the basis of all modern experimental design.

The variance of a set of numbers is a measure of the way those numbers are scattered, a set of numbers which are widely scattered having a higher variance than one which is closely grouped together. The term has been given a precise meaning which enables the variance to be calculated: it is the sum of the squared differences between each number and the average of the set, divided by the number of independent members in the set.

Thus the variance of the five numbers 1, 2, 3, 4, 5 is one fifth of the sum $(3-1)^2 + (3-2)^2 + (3-3)^2 + (3-4)^2 + (3-5)^2$ which is ten fifths or two.

Similarly the variance of 7, 9, 11, 13, 15 is one fifth of $(11-7)^2 + (11-9)^2 + (11-11)^2 + (11-13)^2 + (11-15)^2$ which is 40 fifths, or eight. This larger variance reflects the greater scatter of the numbers 7, 9, 11, 13, 15.

The variance, of course, is not the only measure of scatter. But it has many convenient properties which have given it a special place in the theory of statistics.

One particularly useful quality, and the one used in analysis of variance, is associated with the sums of the squared deviation from the mean before they are averaged to give the variance. In fact the analysis of variance could be more accurately, though less elegantly,

Reprinted with permission from the *Journal of Advertising Research*, vol. 1, no. 6 (December, 1961), pp. 40–46. © Advertising Research Foundation, Inc. (1961).

described as the analysis of sums of squares. For these sums of squares are "additive"—a description which will be illustrated extensively. This term, "the sum of squares," will crop up with great regularity in this article. There is no statistical term for it, though "deviance" and "squariance" have been advocated; here we shall simply refer to it as the sum of squares and it will usually be quite clear which squares are being summed.

In the examples above, the sum of the squared differences between each number and the average of the group was, in the case of 1, 2, 3, 4, 5, equal to 10. For 7, 9, 11, 13, 15, it was 40. Now if we were to throw both sets of numbers together to form a new set of 10 numbers we would have 1, 2, 3, 4, 5, 7, 9, 11, 13, 15.

The average of these 10 numbers is 7 so their variance is one tenth of the sum $(7-1)^2 + (7-2)^2 + (7-3)^2 + (7-4)^2 + (7-5)^2 + (7-7)^2 + (7-9)^2 + (7-11)^2 + (7-13)^2 + (7-15)^2$, or 21. The sum of squares in this case is 210—much more than the sum of squares for the two sets of five added together, which is ten plus 40, or only 50. The interesting thing is that we can find the missing 160. If we substitute for the first five numbers their average repeated five times (there were five numbers in the set), and similarly replace the last five by *their* average repeated five times, we have: 3, 3, 3, 3, 3, 11, 11, 11, 11, 11. The sum of squares of this set is the missing 160.

This illustrates how the sums of squares of a set of numbers can be divided up. If a set of numbers is separated into two parts, the sum of squares of both together is equal to the sum of squares of the first, plus the sum of squares of the second, plus the sum of squares of the averages of each set weighted by its number of members.

Something else comes out of this example. Three different sums of squares and three different variances are involved.

Now if the first and second sets of numbers were both chosen at random from the same much larger population of numbers, we would expect their variances to be not very different from one another. Both would tend to be like the variance of the population from which they come.

We might also expect the variance of the composite of the two sets to provide an even better estimate of the population variance. Better, because it would be based on twice as many observations. Again, our small sets have averages and these averages will be scattered around the population average. *Their* variance, too, we would expect to be based on the population variance in some way. If it is, then it offers still another way of estimating the population variance. These two ways of estimating the population variance—from a composite

of samples and from the averages of those samples—are quite different. Clearly both estimates should be roughly the same, for the population variance is some fixed number. If they are not at all the same, then we must conclude that the hypothesis that the two different samples came from the same population is probably wrong.

Intuition tells us that here, somewhere, is a test which will tell whether different sets of numbers come from the same or different sources. What follows in this article is a more particular and elaborate phrasing of this testing procedure and of some of the ways of using it most efficiently. The procedure is known as the analysis of variance; the arrangement of situations where it can be used is generally called the design of experiments.

SAMPLES AND POPULATIONS

When we take samples from a large population and take measurements on each member of the sample, we expect these measurements to reflect those we would find in the total population. If we want to investigate the smoking habits of the nation, for instance, we interview only a sample of the population and then consider our sample as somehow reflecting the behavior of the whole population. In such a case we expect, if the sample has been well chosen, that averages calculated from the sample will be good estimates of averages in the population. We do not expect them to be exactly equal to the population average but they are usually close. The larger the sample, the closer we expect them to be. Moreover the amount of variation we find in the sample we would take as a good estimate of the variation in the population.

More precisely we can say that we expect sample averages to estimate population averages and sample variances to estimate population variances. Since the sample averages are scattered around the population average, we can and do speak of the variance of these sample averages as "the sampling variance of the mean." This sampling variance of the mean we expect to be smaller as the number in the sample gets larger. It can easily be shown that we may expect it to be one nth of the variance in the population, where n is the number of members in the sample. An obvious exception to this rule occurs when we expand our sample so that it eventually becomes the population itself. At that stage the sample average *is* the population average—there is no sampling variance of the mean. When the sample is large enough to be a significant proportion of the population, say

as much as a tenth, we make a simple correction (by multiplying it by the proportion of the population *not* included in the sample), but for present purposes we can suppose that the population is very large compared with the sample.

In computing an estimate of the variance of a population from a sample, we need a formula which will give us numbers that will in the long run (on enough samples) average out to the right value; that is, we need an unbiased estimator. Also we want one that gets closer and closer to the right value as we take larger and larger samples; this we call the property of consistency. Then we also need some way of telling how accurate our estimate is likely to be say nine times in ten, or 99 times in 100; that is, we want to know how the estimate will be distributed about the true value.

It can be shown that the sample variance is an unbiased, consistent estimate of the population variance. There is no more satisfactory way of estimating it.

So far we have been discussing a statistic—the variance. A statistic is just an index calculated from data, any data. We can calculate the variance, for example, from any set of figures no matter what the source of them. But if we want to make inferences about data we have to have some expectation of how the statistic is going to behave. These expectations we get from probability theory, a completely abstract mathematical discipline, which studies the distribution of *random variables,* and which has nothing to say about statistics. The trick is to find a random variable that we think, for various reasons, should describe the way in which our statistic behaves and whose probability distribution is known. Then we find the chance of getting a value of the random variable which departs as much from its expected value as the statistic we have.

Take, for instance, the ratio of the population variance estimated from the sample to the true population variance. The estimate from the sample should be fairly close to the true population variance so the ratio should be fairly close to one. Sometimes it will be rather more than one, sometimes rather less, but generally it is less likely that the ratio will be far from one than close to it.

Tables of the chi-square distribution, one of the best known in probability theory, list the probabilities of getting, by chance alone, values of this ratio beyond levels as great as or greater than one, and as little or less than one. Suppose we take a sample of ten members from a large population and find the sample variance half again as large as the population variance, we could find in a chi-square table that this happens only as often as one time in four by chance alone.

The ratio we find from calculating the population variance estimate divided by the true population variance is the statistic chi-square. The table we look in gives the chance of obtaining various values of the random variable chi-square. The statistic chi-square is calculated by the computational formula:

$$\frac{\text{population variance estimator from sample}}{\text{true population variance}}$$

Obviously variances of large samples are better estimates of the population variance than variances of smaller samples. The ratio of the sample to the population variance will more likely be near one with large than with small samples. In other words, the chi-square distribution differs for different sample sizes.

DEGREES OF FREEDOM

But this statement needs a slight modification. It is not the actual sample size that is important, but the number of *independent* members in it. If we took a sample of 100 store inventories from a retail audit and before tabulating them made up ten more, all identical with one another, each being the average of the 100 stores already reported, we would have 110 returns to analyze. But there would, in fact, be only 100 independent returns.

Similarly when we make an estimate of the population variance from a sample, if we knew the mean of the population we could calculate the estimate of the variance treating every member of the sample as independent. If, however, we use the sample to estimate the population mean first, we assume that there is an equation connecting the members of the sample with this fixed value, the mean, in the population. This is equivalent to losing one independent member of the sample. Imagine, for instance, that we have four members in a sample. Let them have measurements a, b, c, d. Now the sample average is one fourth of a + b + c + d. If we assume that this is equal to the population average (say μ), then a + b + c + d = 4μ.

Now the population mean μ is assumed known when we calculate the variance. Thus we could do without one member of the sample, say d, because d = 4μ − a + b + c. That is, d could be computed from μ and the independent values a, b and c. When the sample values are bound together by any equation like this, we say they are subject to a *constraint*. The number of independent values left in the

sample is called the number of degrees of freedom and the variance estimator is always the sum of squares divided by this number of degrees of freedom.

THREE ESTIMATES

When several samples are drawn from the same population we can estimate the variance of the parent population three ways. First we could put all the separate samples together and calculate their variance. Next we could consider just the means of each sample. If there were k samples, we know the sampling variance of the means is their sum of squares divided by (k-1), the number of degrees of freedom of this sum of squares. Since this is only one nth of the population variance, where there are n members in each sample, we can get another estimate of the population variance by multiplying this sampling variance of the mean by n. Finally we could get a third estimate of the population variance from the variances of each of the separate samples. These we would pool together by adding the sums of squares from each sample and dividing by the appropriate number of degrees of freedom.

We have mentioned that the sums of squares are additive; so are the degrees of freedom. For example, if we calculate the variance of the numbers 1, 2, 3, we have $\dfrac{(1\text{-}2)^2 + (2\text{-}2)^2 + (3\text{-}2)^2}{2} = 1$. The two in the denominator is the number of degrees of freedom of the sum of squares in the numerator. Similarly, the variance of 5, 6, 7, is 1. If we put both sets together we have a new set 1, 2, 3, 5, 6, 7 and its variance is

$$\frac{(4\text{-}1)^2 + (4\text{-}2)^2 + (4\text{-}3)^2 + (4\text{-}5)^2 + (4\text{-}6)^2 + (4\text{-}7)^2}{5} = \frac{28}{5},$$

where the five in the denominator is the number of degrees of freedom of the sum of squares in the numerator.

If, however, we had calculated an estimate of the population variance from a knowledge of the variance of the two separate groups we should have $\dfrac{(2 + 2)}{4} = 1$, where the four in the denominator is the number of degrees of freedom of the sum of squares in the numerator. Here two degrees of freedom have been lost; one was used in calculating the average of 1, 2, 3 and a second was lost in calculating the average of 3, 4, 5. To get this pooled variance of the

two samples we add the sums of squares from each and divide by the sum of their degrees of freedom.

Then we can make a third estimate of the population variance from the variance of the mean of the two separate groups around the mean of both together: $3 \left[\dfrac{(2\text{-}4)^2 + (6\text{-}4)^2}{1} \right] = 24$. Here again, the one in the denominator is the number of degrees of freedom of the sums of squares in the numerator. This overall variance was calculated to be $\dfrac{28}{5}$ and we see that both numerator and denominator can both be partitioned like this:

28 (the overall sum of squares) =
 2 (the sum of squares in the first sample) +
 2 (the sum of squares in the second sample) +
24 (the sum of squares of the means of the samples)
 5 (the overall number of degrees of freedom) =
 2 (the degrees of freedom from the first sample) +
 2 (the degrees of freedom from the second sample) +
 1 (the degrees of freedom from the sample of two means)

We noted that the chi-square shows how often various ratios of sample variance to population variance occur, and that the probabilities differed for different numbers of independent members of the sample. More succinctly, we can say that there is a chi-square distribution for each different number of degrees of freedom. Tables of this distribution appear in most statistical textbooks. They show how, when the number of degrees of freedom becomes very large as it does in large samples, the ratio of sample variance to population variance becomes very close to one and there is very little chance of getting a ratio as far away from one as say, .75 or 1.5.

Different samples from the same population usually give slightly different estimates of the population variances. Since the two sample variances are estimating the same thing, we would expect them to be of about equal size and their ratio, therefore, close to 1. One way of looking at it is this: Let V_1 and V_2 be two different sample variances used to estimate the population variance. The ration of V_1 to V_2 is V_1/V_2. Now suppose that the population variance is V, then we know the probability of getting various values of V_1/V for this ratio follows the chi-square distribution. We also know the probability of getting the various values of V_2/V, for this ratio, too, follows a chi-square distribution. Each ratio is associated with a certain number of degrees

of freedom depending on the number of independent members in the samples used to calculate V_1 and V_2. Now the ratio V_1/V_2 is equal to V_1/V divided by V_2/V so we see that the ratio of two sample variances drawn from the same population is the ratio of two quantities both of which have a chi-square distribution. Such a ratio is said to have an F distribution, another one of the half dozen best known probability distributions in the theory of probability. There will be a different F distribution for different numbers of degrees of freedom for both V_1 and V_2. In order to check how likely it is that a particular ratio of V_1 to V_2 should occur by chance alone, we have to know the degrees of freedom of V_1 and V_2. We can then look up tables of the F distribution. It provides us with a means of comparing sample variances and is the testing instrument of analysis of variance.

WHICH SOUP TASTES BEST?

A few simple examples will show how the technique is used and will indicate how, with a little ingenuity, it can be extended. Suppose six members of a small taste-testing panel are asked to rate four samples of soup for flavor. They give their ratings on a scale running from zero to ten, like this:

			Soups	
JUDGES	W	X	Y	Z
A	4	6	5	7
B	5	7	7	4
C	4	5	6	7
D	6	4	2	4
E	6	5	6	5
F	5	4	6	6
Average	$\frac{30}{6}$	$\frac{31}{6}$	$\frac{32}{6}$	$\frac{33}{6}$
Sum of squares	$\frac{24}{6}$	$\frac{41}{6}$	$\frac{92}{6}$	$\frac{57}{6}$

The question is: are all these soups alike to the raters, or do they differ?

One approach to this problem, especially if we were comparing just two soups, would be to calculate the average rating given to

each soup and use a standard statistical test to find whether the average ratings differed significantly. The kind of answer such a test gives is that two soups differ in their average ratings by an amount that would only be found as often as one time in twenty by chance alone. The trouble is that if we try this out for all pairs of soups there are six comparisons to make, and things that happen only one time in twenty by chance alone, start happening rather more often.

The analysis of variance approach is different. It consists of seeing the six ratings as a sample of ratings. There are then four such samples, one for each soup, and six members, one for each rating given, to each sample.

The sum of squares for the average ratings of each soup is $\dfrac{8047}{144}$ and weighted by the number of ratings composing each average is $\dfrac{8047 \times 6}{144}$. The comparison of the estimates of the population variance provided by the variance for each soup and the variance of the average ratings is then laid out in this form:

Source of Variation	Sum of Squares	Degrees of Freedom	Variance Estimate
Between soups	$\dfrac{5}{6}$	3	$\dfrac{5}{18} = .2778$
Within soups	$\dfrac{214}{6}$	20	$\dfrac{214}{120} = 1.7833$
Total	$\dfrac{219}{6}$	23	$\dfrac{219}{138} = 1.5870$

This illustrates the basic method of analysis of variance and, incidentally, the standard method of presenting it. Before considering how this could be complicated to deal with harder questions, it is appropriate to explain some assumptions that have been made implicitly.

In the first place, the test just described supposes that the soups each had some kind of true rating. But preventing us from having this true rating given to each soup each time are the perversity of the judges and the vicissitudes of the experimental situation which together add a random element to each true rating. This random element is assumed to afflict all the ratings of every judge and every

soup. It will vary in the amount it affects each figure but the degree to which this random element varies, and the frequency which it assumes various levels, is assumed to be described by the normal distribution. The F test assumes this is the case, but it is what statisticians call a "robust" test—one not very misleading even when the data being examined depart somewhat from the assumptions made about them.

Finally, we guess that the four "true" ratings of the soups are all the same and then we see how likely it is that we should get variance estimates which differ as much as they actually do.

Imagine, as the underlying mathematical model assumes, that the rating given to each soup is really a fixed number and that, unfortunately, these fixed numbers are veiled from sight by random additions and subtractions which affect all our data. The actual ratings we have are, according to this model, the "true ratings" seen, as it were, through a glass darkly.

A slightly more complicated mathematical model would take into account the fact that each judge might have his own tendency to be mean or generous with his ratings. The actual observed ratings would then be a composite of three parts: the particular soup being rated, the particular rating and the random variable obscuring these basic influences. This can be illustrated by the kind of data that the mathematical model assumes and the kind that we actually find in practice.

WHICH COPY IS BEST?

Suppose we used four different copy platforms to advertise a product and that each was tried in each of five cities, only one approach being tried in one city at a time. Suppose, too, that we have assumed that there is no pronounced order effect to copy platforms—that the effect of each on its success is negligible. The mathematical model, or at least, one mathematical model, of analysis of variance assumes that the "real" sales results, if only we could see them, would be like this:

| Copy Approach | CITY | | | | |
	A (+10)	B (−8)	C (+12)	D (+2)	E (−16)
I (+3)	+13	− 5	+15	+5	−13
II (−2)	+ 8	−10	+10	+0	−18
III (−2)	+ 8	−10	+10	+0	−18
IV (+1)	+11	− 7	+13	+3	−15

In this table the numbers in the main body of the table represent units sold, perhaps in thousands, above or below the average for all five cities and four copy platforms. The numbers in parentheses under each city and copy platform indicate the effect of that city or platform. Whatever copy approach is used in city A, for example, will sell ten units more than in the average city, and 20 units more than in city B. Similarly, Platform I will, city for city, always sell five more units than the average platform in that city and five units more than Platform II.

THE VEIL OF REALITY

Unfortunately, this is the kind of data that rarely turns up, least of all in marketing and advertising experiments where all sorts of complicating influences obscure these straightforward effects. In practice we might observe the following kind of information, which is no more than the previous table with each observation infected with a normally distributed random variable, and an overall average sale of 50 units in all cities with all campaigns.

Copy Approach	CITY				
	A	B	C	D	E
I	62	46	56	55	37
II	59	41	59	48	33
III	58	40	61	51	32
IV	63	43	58	54	34

The data in this table are much less informative. It is impossible to see, simply from inspection, whether the copy approaches differ significantly from one another.

The method of analysis, however, is simple and much as before. This time, instead of just computing the variances within columns and the variances between columns of the table, we add a new dimension. We compute the variance between the cities, that is, between the row means; then we compute the variance of all the figures in the table. Next by subtraction of the sums of squares and degrees of freedom of the rows and of the columns from the total sum of squares and degrees of freedom, we have a "residual" sum of squares and degrees of freedom. From these we can compute an estimate of the population variance which does not take into account the row (platform) or

column (city) effects. To determine whether the platforms differ significantly in effect, we compare the estimate of the variance from between rows with the residual variance; to determine whether different cities have a significantly different effect we compare the variance estimate from between cities with the residual variance. The actual analysis would look like this:

Source of Variation	Sums of Squares	Degrees of Freedom	Variance Estimate	F Ratio
Between cities	1990	4	497.50	$\dfrac{497.5}{4.93} = 100.9*$
Between copy approaches	35.8	3	11.93	$\dfrac{11.93}{4.93} = 2.42\dagger$
Residual	59.2	12	4.93	
Total	2085	19		

* The variance between cities is so large that it could have occurred by chance alone less than one time in 1,000. Different cities affect sales significantly.
† The variance between copy approaches could have occurred about one time in ten by chance alone. We would conclude from this evidence that the copy approach did not significantly influence sales.

In this table the "Residual" variance has been obtained by subtracting the sum of the between-city and between-platform variance from the total variance.

The same assumptions have been made in this analysis as in the earlier one. First, that the effects, in this case of city and copy platform, have a simple additive effect. The fact that a particular platform might be just right for one of the towns is the kind of effect that would violate this assumption altogether and cause this particular analysis to be quite misleading. Then it is assumed that the city and platform effects have all been obscured by a normally distributed random variable. If these assumptions are satisfied, the method offers a speedy means of judging whether an effect is important and assessing the degree to which it is.

This second example has shown an extension of the technique to deal with two influences acting simultaneously. The procedure can be extended much further and with ingenuity many experiments can be combined in one large-scale plan.

A simple but well known elaboration of the basic technique is to

test the effect of three different influences at once. The type of design most often employed is the Latin square. The basic principle is that the rows and columns of the table, such as we have employed in the example of copy approaches and cities, shall each represent a hypothesized influence. But another effect is also considered by applying it selectively to the observations represented by the cells of the square table.

We might, for example, wish to test the effect of four different advertising themes, four different price levels and four cities all at once. As before, we could lay out a square table which would describe not only our observations but our way of getting them. Each column of our table will represent a different city; each row a different advertising theme. The problem, then, is to experiment with price. This we do by applying each of the experimental prices in each city and with each advertising theme such that any one price appears once only in any city or with any theme. Then in analyzing the results we find the effect of price by adding together the sales from all cities with the same price level. The following table illustrates the procedure.

	CITY			
THEME	*1*	*2*	*3*	*4*
I	A	B	C	D
II	B	A	D	C
III	C	D	A	B
IV	D	C	B	A

In this table the price levels are denoted by A, B, C and D. Each appears once only in each row and column. Extra observations provided, for example, by an extra city, can be used, of course, but the table presents the minimum design required to test the third effect. The square in the illustration is not the only way of arranging prices within cities and themes. There are over 500 other arrangements possible.

Nor does the Latin square exhaust ingenuity in this direction. We could add another effect, say that of different packaging, and test that at the same time. If we denote few different packages by the Greek letters α, β, γ, δ, we can test their effect with the experimental design

Here the method of distributing the different packages and prices is self-evident. The important point is that every possible combination of price and package occurs. We have superimposed two Latin

	CITY			
THEME	*1*	*2*	*3*	*4*
I	αA	βB	γC	δD
II	γB	δA	αD	βC
III	δC	γD	βA	αA
IV	βD	αC	δB	γA

squares, one denoted by Latin letters, the other by Greek letters so that every pair appears once only. What is more, yet another treatment, say product variation, could be added, so that every pair of variations in product, packaging and price will occur once and only once.

The superimposition of Latin squares in this way is not always possible. We know it can be done if the number of treatments is a prime number or 4, 6, 8 or 9.

This is merely one of several ways of extending the simple basic techniques to serve elaborate ends. Whatever the complexity of the design employed, two things remain the same. First, the method of analysis will be the subdivision of sums of squares among different influences in order to make estimates of the population variance. Second, the analysis assumes that each influence acts independently and additively, and that the chance variations which appear in the experiment are normally distributed.

Multiple Regression Analysis—The Easy Way

Jack B. Landis

This paper is designed for researchers in the marketing and media fields. It systematically outlines a simplified procedure of multiple regression analysis, including a step-by-step description of the analytical process together with some of the concepts behind these procedures.

Multiple regression analysis can be extremely useful to the researcher who wishes to determine the relationships among a large number of factors. It offers a means of establishing such relationships without cumbersome cross-tabulations. These often involve division after division, which reduce subsample size to the point where conclusions are unreliable.

As in most technical expositions, the explanation of the method is more difficult than the actual process itself. But if the text is followed carefully and the examples worked out, the type of analysis outlined here can easily become a standard tool for any researcher with even a limited statistical background.

The only unique portion of this description of multiple regression analysis deals with the iteration process. However, in order that the entire process may be easily followed, a detailed description is given of the handling of a typical problem from start to finish.

In passing we should note that while large-scale multiple regression analyses are most efficiently handled by computers, there will always be smaller analyses for which short-cut calculator techniques are more appropriate. These smaller analyses are the subject of this paper.

Quite often in marketing or media research work it is desirable to know the relationship between two variables. For example, we may wish to learn whether a brand is bought more by large families or small, or whether a TV program is better liked by younger or older

Reprinted with permission from the *Journal of Advertising Research,* vol. 2, no. 2 (March, 1962), pp. 35–42. © Advertising Research Foundation, Inc. (1962).

people. As long as the goal of the analysis is one of pure description, a simple cross-tabulation or correlational analysis will suffice.

If, on the other hand, the researcher wishes to determine the "net" relationship between two factors, after the effects of other variables have been eliminated, more complicated statistical procedures are in order. For example, the sale of a product may be higher among larger families and *also* among the lower income groups. Since larger families tend to have lower income, is family size or income more closely related to the product's sales level?

Of course, with a simple problem of two or three factors, it is easy enough to cross-tabulate the data to find the answer to this question. But when nine or a dozen factors have to be considered, the sample would be so frequently subdivided that a reliable answer probably could not be obtained. In situations such as these, the process of multiple regression analysis can reveal the true relationship between each factor and some criterion variable while maintaining an adequate sample size.

Multiple and partial regression analysis is a method of examining the relationship between two variables while eliminating the influence of several other factors. In a usual multiple regression problem, one factor is called the criterion, while several other items are considered the independent variables. Inferentially, the independent factors are thought of as the "causes" while the criterion factor is the "effect."

Multiple and partial regression analyses have five primary values for the researcher:

1. To determine the relationship between one variable and a criterion factor while simultaneously removing the influence of other factors. Example: What is the relationship between family size and sale of Scotties when the influences of income, size of city, availability and price are eliminated?

2. To determine which of a set of factors is most related to the criterion factor. Example: Which of the following factors is most closely related to the sale of Ford cars: number of Ford dealers in the market, size of city, effective buying income, or percent of families owning a car?

3. To "match" two groups so that they are equivalent in important respects. Example: Differences between viewers and non-viewers in terms of age, family size, previous buying habits, etc. can be eliminated when studying the relationship between viewing and buying of the advertised product.

4. To formulate a predictive equation which allows for the calculation of expected levels of the criterion factor, given any combination

of values of the independent factors. Example: Estimates can be made of probable sales levels of Kodak cameras in various markets, knowing the average income level, sales in previous years, economic conditions, etc.

5. To gain inferences about additional factors which may be related to the criterion variable. Example: By examining the cases in which actual sales for Kodak do not agree with the estimates, inferences can be made about other factors which affect camera sales.

Five Steps

To most of us multiple regression analysis is unfamiliar and not often used in day-to-day work, even though a richer analysis would result from its application. Fortunately, a technique is available whereby problems involving a dozen or more factors can be solved relatively easily, with a minimum expenditure of time and money. The method, based on an iterative technique developed by the writer, can be carried out with a desk calculator by any clerk.

The procedure involves five steps, each a logical extension of the preceding step:

1. Assembly of the raw data
2. Computation of deviations
3. Computation of cross-products
4. Calculation of the cross-product matrix
5. Iteration to determine the solution

The first three steps are exactly the same as those of simple correlation procedures. The fourth step is common to any multiple regression analysis. The fifth step is new: it offers a simplified method for the solution of the simultaneous equations.

A Hypothetical Problem

Suppose ten families have been surveyed to learn their rates of TV viewing, i.e., the number of hours per week each watches TV. A multiple regression analysis is set up to find the relationship between the criterion variable of hours of TV viewed per week and the independent variables of family size, years the TV set was owned, and number of TV sets owned.

Now in order to help demonstrate the validity of the multiple regression analysis, let us construct a set of data in which the contribution of each of the factors is known beforehand. This will pro-

duce a viewing rate for each family in our sample. We can then determine if the technique will reproduce these original values when only the viewing rates and family descriptions are known. (It should be clearly understood that in a real regression problem, we would not know the true values for each of the factors in advance; to find them is the whole purpose of the analysis. But in this hypothetical case, we are starting with full knowledge of the values so that the accuracy of the answers can be demonstrated.)

For example, suppose the formula linking the factors of family size (F), years owned a TV set (Y), and number of TV sets (N) to TV hours viewed per week (T) is as follows:

$$T = 4.0F - 2.0Y + 6.0N + 4.$$

In other words, each family member adds four hours, each additional year of ownership decreases the viewing rate by two hours, and an additional set adds six hours of viewing. Then a family with three persons, who have owned a set for six years, and presently own two TV sets, would view for 16 hours ($4 \times 3 - 2 \times 6 + 6 \times 2 + 4 = 16$). The hypothetical set of data used in this problem was constructed in this way.

Step One—The Raw Data

Step one in the multiple regression analysis consists of assembling the raw data for each family in a table:

FAMILY	FAMILY SIZE (F)	YEARS OWNED TV (Y)	NUMBER OF TV SETS (N)	HOURS/ WEEK VIEW TV (T)
Anderson	1	2	1	10
Boyle	3	9	1	4
Cooper	5	10	2	16
Dennis	2	1	1	16
Endicott	4	2	2	28
Foster	3	7	1	8
Gerber	4	3	2	26
Healy	3	5	1	12
Ingram	2	5	2	14
Jones	3	6	2	16
Average	3	5	1.5	15

These are the data the researcher would have from our hypothetical survey. The question is whether he can—through multiple regression analysis—reproduce the values of F = 4, Y = −2 and N = 4 from which these data were generated.

His first analysis of these data might cross-tabulate each factor against the criterion of hours-per-week of TV viewing:

	AVERAGE HOURS PER WEEK TV IS VIEWED
Family Size	
1 or 2	13.3 hours
3	10.0
4 or more	23.3
Years Owned TV	
1 to 3	20.0
4 to 6	14.0
7 or more	9.3
Number of TV Sets	
1	10.0
2 or more	20.0

His interpretation of these figures would be obvious: viewing decreases with years owned TV, increases if a second set comes into the home, and is least in three person families. After a little thought, however, he might conclude that family size of three is related to long years of ownership, and that this fact may be influencing the levels obtained for this family size group. Perhaps multiple regression analysis can untangle this web of inter-relationships.

Step Two—Deviations

To set up a regression analysis, the next step is to compute for each family its deviation from the sample average on each factor. This shows whether it is above or below average on a given item. Thus the Andersons (Family A in the table below) are two persons less than average in family size (−2), have owned TV for three years less than average (−3), have one-half a TV set less than average (−0.5) and view five hours of TV less than the average family (−5). Notice that the sum and therefore the average of each column of deviations should be zero.

	DEVIATIONS			
FAMILY	F	Y	N	T
Anderson	−2	−3	−.5	− 5
Boyle	0	4	−.5	−11
Cooper	2	5	.5	1
Dennis	−1	−4	−.5	1
Endicott	1	−3	.5	13
Foster	0	2	−.5	− 7
Gerber	1	−2	.5	11
Healy	0	0	−.5	− 3
Ingram	−1	0	.5	− 1
Jones	0	1	.5	1
Average	0	0	0	0

Step Three—Cross-Products

The third step is to compute the sums of the cross-products of all combinations of two factors. These cross-products reflect the degree to which the various factors are interrelated. The cross-products are obtained by multiplying for each family the deviations for every combination of two factors and for each factor by itself; the results are then summed over the ten families in our sample. For example, for Family A the cross-product of F and Y is $-2 \times -3 = +6$; for Family B it is $0 \times 4 = 0$; for Family C, $2 \times 5 = 10$, etc. The total of the FY cross-products for all families in the sample is 15.

Where four factors are concerned, there are ten unique cross-products as shown above.

While the operation may look somewhat complicated in this example, all the computations can be made simply on a calculator. The individual cross-product need not be computed for each family, but only the cross-product sums. These can be obtained by accumulating individual cross-products in the "cumulative multiply" section of a desk calculator.

Care must be taken in this step to observe the laws of signs. Note that the sums of the cross-products for a factor with *itself* (such as FF) will always be positive; the cross-product sum for a combination of two *different* factors, however, may be either positive or negative such as YN and YT.

FAMILY	DEVIATIONS				CROSS-PRODUCTS									
	F	Y	N	T	FF	FY	FN	FT	YY	YN	YT	NN	NT	TT
A	−2	−3	−.5	−5	4	6	1.0	10	9	1.5	15	.25	2.5	25
B	0	4	−.5	−11	0	0	0	0	16	−2.0	−44	.25	5.5	121
C	2	5	.5	1	4	10	1.0	2	25	2.5	5	.25	0.5	1
D	−1	−4	−.5	1	1	4	0.5	−1	16	2.0	−4	.25	−0.5	1
E	1	−3	.5	13	1	−3	0.5	13	9	−1.5	−39	.25	6.5	169
F	0	2	−.5	−7	0	0	0	0	4	−1.0	−14	.25	3.5	49
G	1	−2	.5	11	1	−2	0.5	11	4	−1.0	−22	.25	5.5	121
H	0	0	−.5	−3	0	0	0	0	0	0	0	.25	1.5	9
I	−1	0	.5	−1	1	0	−0.5	1	0	0	0	.25	−0.5	1
J	0	1	.5	1	0	0	0	0	1	0.5	1	.25	0.5	1
Total	0	0	0	0	12	15	3.0	36	84	1.0	−102	2.5	25	498

Step Four—The Matrix

The preceding is the usual method of obtaining simple correlation coefficients. Here in Step Four we begin a special procedure, developed to simplify the job of extracting the values of each factor.

Let us assemble the ten cross-product sums obtained in the previous step in a table or matrix. The ten values are shown in the upper right part of the table and are repeated in the lower left half in a systematic fashion (inasmuch as FT = TF, FY = YF, etc.). This matrix summarizes all the relationships found so far:

	F	Y	N	T
F	12	15	3.0	36
Y	15	84	1.0	−102
N	3.0	1.0	2.5	25
T	36	−102	25	498

Note that all the relationships are positive except the one between Y and T. The minus sign shows that years-owned-TV and hours-of-viewing are negatively related: the longer a set is owned, the fewer the hours it is viewed. The four rows in the matrix actually describe the four simultaneous equations which are needed to determine the values for the three unknowns, F, Y and N. We will now describe a method which can find these values quickly and easily.

Step Five—The Iteration Process

In the fifth or "iteration" step in multiple regression analysis, our goal is to solve the four equations in the Step Four matrix for the unknown values of F, Y and N.

If we look along the first row, for item F, we see the degree of relationship between F (family size) and each of the other variables. In formula terms, this equation is: $12F + 15Y + 3.0N = 36$.

Now if we assume (temporarily) that Y and N are zero, we get $12F = 36$ and $F = 3$.

This is our first estimate of the value of F. It means that as family size increases by one member, they view, on the average, three more hours of TV per week.

Similarly the first estimates for Y and N can be computed:

$$84Y = -102 \text{ or } Y = -1.2$$
$$2.5N = 25 \text{ or } N = 10.0$$

Earlier, to obtain a value for F, we assumed that Y and N equaled zero. Now we know that they are not zero but -1.2 and 10.0 respectively.

Let us now put these new values for Y and N in the original equation in order to correct for our assumption that they were zero.

1. Original equation
   $12F + 15Y + 3.0N = 36$
2. Substituting for Y and N
   $12F + (15 [-1.2] + 3.0 [10.0]) = 36$
3. Obtaining value of Y and N
   $12F + (-18 + 30) = 36$
4. Correcting for Y and N
   $12F = 36 - 12$
5. Y and N eliminated
   $12F = 24$
6. New estimate of F
   $F = 2.0$

Now our estimate of F has gone from three to two. The difference is a correction warranted by the fact that Y and N were related to F and also to the criterion variable T. In similar fashion, we can compute a second estimate for Y and N to obtain the following figures:

FACTOR	1ST ESTIMATE	2ND ESTIMATE
F	3.0	2.0
Y	-1.2	-1.7
N	10.0	8.3

It can be seen that a third estimate for each variable could be determined in the same way, always using the most recent values when making corrections. This process, when followed for several iterations, will eventually produce a value for each factor in which no change is recorded from the previous estimate. At this point the process is complete and the solution has been obtained. This was done as shown below:

FACTOR	ESTIMATES							
	1ST	2ND	3RD	4TH	5TH	6TH	7TH	8TH
F	3.0	2.0	3.0	3.4	3.7	3.8	4.0	4.0
Y	-1.2	-1.7	-1.7	-1.9	-1.9	-2.0	-2.0	-2.0
N	10.0	8.3	7.1	6.7	6.3	6.2	6.0	6.0

So we see that with each additional family member, the viewing rate increases by four hours; with each additional year of ownership there is a decrease of two hours in viewing; a second TV set is associated with an additional six hours of viewing. These values are known as "b coefficients" and indicate the slope of the line describing the relationship between the independent variable and the criterion. For instance, each additional family member was related to four additional hours of TV viewing. A graph of this relationship would look as follows:

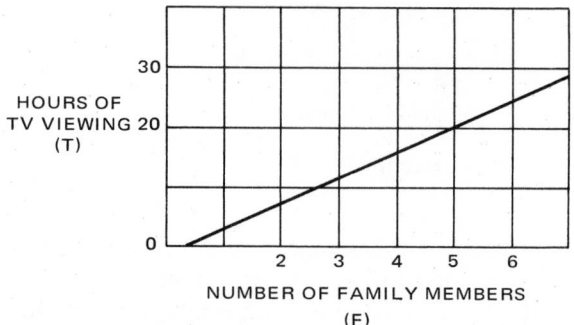

Note that the values obtained are the same values which we originally used to construct this set of hypothetical data. Q.E.D.— the multiple regression analysis has correctly indicated the values for each factor, using only the raw data which would be collected in a survey.

SIMPLIFIED CALCULATION PROCESS

Steps four and five were detailed so that the concept of iteration could be easily understood. Note that the method is a process of "pulling oneself up by one's own bootstraps." Given a first estimate which is a fair approximation, corrections are gradually made to home in on the true answer.

The actual computational procedure to be used in practice can be made much simpler than that above. The worksheet need be no bigger than one 8½ × 11 page!

Let us return to step four, in which the cross-product matrix had been developed. The set-up was:

	F	Y	N	T
F	12	15	3.0	36
Y	15	84	1.0	−102
N	3.0	1.0	2.5	25
T	36	−102	25	498

Divide each factor in a column by the bold-face diagonal terms. The "T" column is eliminated at this point, since it is not needed in the following computations.

	F	Y	N
F	1.0	.18	1.2
Y	1.25	1.0	.4
N	.25	.01	1.0
T	3.0	−1.2	10.0

Note that the numbers in the T row are the first estimates for F, Y and N.

Next, the first estimates are rotated 90 degrees so that they are adjacent to F, Y and N, respectively. At the same time, an X is substituted for the 1.0 at each diagonal:

	F	Y	N	1st Est.
F	X	.18	1.2	3.0
Y	1.25	X	.4	−1.2
N	.25	.01	X	10.0

To get the second estimate for F, the correction term is found by multiplying each item in the F column (except the diagonal X) by its corresponding first estimate and summing the products. In the example, the computation is $(1.25 \times -1.2) + (.25 \times 10.0) = 1.0$. This correction factor is then subtracted from the *first estimate* for F to arrive at the second estimate for F. (Second estimate for F = $3.0 - 1.0 = 2.0$.)

The iteration table would then look like this (cells in this first step are italicized):

	F	Y	N	1ST EST.	2ND EST.
F	X	.18	1.2	3.0	2.0
Y	1.25	X	.4	−1.2	
N	.25	.01	X	10.0	

Note that this second value is the same estimate arrived at previously by the longer process. Similarly, the second estimate for Y would be found by multiplying each item in the Y column (except the diagonal X) by its corresponding first estimate and summing the products. Here, however, we will use the *new* estimate for F (2.0) since this is the latest and best value for F we have. Thus, the formula for Y's second estimate is:

$$Y = -1.2 - [(.18 \times 2.0) + (.01 \times 10.0)] = -1.7$$

The iteration table would then look like this:

	F	Y	N	1ST EST.	2ND EST.
F	X	.18	1.2	3.0	2.0
Y	1.25	X	.4	−1.2	−1.7
N	.25	.01	X	10.0	

The second estimate for N follows the same procedure, multiplying the N column values by the appropriate estimate (using the second and latest estimates for F and Y) and subtracting the aggregate from the *first* N estimate.

The second estimate of N is found as follows:

$$N = 10.0 - [(1.2 \times 2.0) + (.4 \times -1.7)] = 8.3$$

Here's how the iteration table would look at each step as the third estimates for F, Y and N are derived. Note that the procedure for finding each succeeding estimate is similar to that used to obtain the second. Note also that the correction factor is always subtracted from the *first* estimate, not from the succeeding estimates:

	F	Y	N	1ST EST.	2ND EST.	3RD EST.
F	X	.18	1.2	*3.0*	2.0	*3.0*
Y	*1.25*	X	.4	−1.2	*−1.7*	
N	.25	.01	X	10.0	*8.3*	

Compute: $3.0 - (1.25 \times -1.7) + (.25 \times 8.3) = 3.0$

	F	Y	N	1ST EST.	2ND EST.	3RD EST.
F	X	*.18*	1.2	3.0	2.0	*3.0*
Y	1.25	X	.4	*−1.2*	−1.7	*−1.7*
N	.25	*.01*	X	10.0	*8.3*	

Compute: $-1.2 - (.18 \times 3.0) + (.01 \times 8.3) = -1.7$

	F	Y	N	1ST EST.	2ND EST.	3RD EST.
F	X	.18	*1.2*	3.0	2.0	*3.0*
Y	1.25	X	*.4*	−1.2	−1.7	*−1.7*
N	.25	.01	X	*10.0*	8.3	*7.1*

Compute: $10.0 - (1.2 \times 3.0) + (.4 \times -1.7) = 7.1$

Thus the entire method consists of systematic application of these computations, deriving at each step successively better estimates of the value of each factor. When followed through to the point of no change, the values of 4.0, −2.0 and 6.0 are obtained for F, Y and N respectively, as in the longer process.

Points to Check

Parts of the procedure should be double checked. Experience shows that errors are most likely to occur at these places:

1. In step two, see that each column of deviations adds to zero.
2. In step three, keep the minus and plus signs straight when multiplying two deviations to determine their cross-product.

3. In step four, see that the matrix is balanced, i.e., that the cross-products above the diagonal are the mirror-image of the cross-products below in terms of both the actual numbers and signs.

4. In step five, be sure that a correction is always subtracted from the *first* estimate when drawing succeeding estimates; a common mistake is to subtract the correction from the preceding estimate for that factor.

How much time does the iteration process (steps 4 and 5) take? Given competent clerical help, perhaps 30 to 60 minutes for a five-variable problem; perhaps three or four hours for a ten- or 12-variable problem. Certain shortcuts can reduce this time appreciably. These times compare with about a day for a five-variable problem, and four or five days for a ten-variable problem via the traditional Doolittle method.

Possible Shortcuts

1. Curiously enough, it is impossible to make a calculation mistake in the iteration process which would affect the final solution! An error will lengthen the process, but eventually the true answer will be obtained for the values of each factor.

2. Usually it is best to take only two-thirds of the indicated correction when obtaining the second estimate for the first factor (the second estimate for F in our hypothetical problem would thus be 2.5, instead of 2.0). The correction for the second item (Y) could be set at 80% of this indicated correction. These reductions apply *only* to the start of the process when obtaining the second estimate.

3. After a few iterations it can be seen that the value for each factor is "homing in." At that point it will speed up the process to guess (carefully!) the final answer and use this for the next estimate. With experience, accurate guesses are possible. For example, in our hypothetical problem it would have been possible to forecast the answers after the fourth estimate. Graphing the changes, of course, makes for a better guess.

4. If only two or three of the factors show big changes, work with these and ignore the rest until problem factors come into line.

If the answers must be accurate to several decimal places, work out approximate solutions accurate to only one or two places. Then when a stable solution is found, work out the final value to any degree of accuracy desired. As before, the final b coefficients are obtained

when the same value is found for each factor in two successive iterations.

Final Steps

Most of the work is now finished. For completion of the analysis, there remain only the usual steps of determining the following:

1. The predictive equation
2. Comparison of the actual and estimated levels for each family
3. The amount of variance accounted for
4. The multiple correlation coefficient (multiple R).

1. When values have been found for each of the factors, it is easy to construct a predictive equation to estimate the criterion values. We need only the constant in the equation. First the b value for each independent factor is multiplied by the average for the factor:

FACTOR	AVERAGE LEVEL (a)	b VALUE (b)	a × b
F	3	4.0	12.0
Y	5	−2.0	−10.0
N	1.5	6.0	9.0
Total			11.0

Together, at their average level F, Y and N account for a total of 11 hours of TV viewing. Since the average hours of viewing was 15, the constant for the equation is equal to 4.0, derived as follows: Constant $= 15 - (12.0 - 10.0 + 9.0) = 4$.

In effect, this means that if F, Y and N were each 0, a family would view 4 hours of TV.

Thus, the predictive equation is: $T = 4F - 2Y + 6N + 4$. Now if we learn that a family has three members, owned their set for three years, and has one TV set, we would estimate their hours of viewing in the following way: $T = 4F - 2Y + 6N + 4 = (4 \times 3) - (2 \times 3) + (6 \times 1) + 4 = 16$ hours.

Our best estimate is that this family would view TV 16 hours each week.

2. It is usually helpful to compute estimated values for each unit in the multiple regression analysis. Here we would use the regression

values (b coefficients) in conjunction with the levels of F, Y and N for each family in our sample.

FAMILY	FAMILY SIZE	YEARS OWNED TV SETS	NUMBER OF SETS	HOURS OF TV VIEWING	
				ACTUAL	ESTIMATED
Anderson	1	2	1	10	10
Boyle	3	9	1	4	4
Cooper	5	10	2	16	16
Dennis	2	1	1	16	16
Endicott	4	2	2	28	28
Foster	3	7	1	8	8
Gerber	4	3	2	26	26
Healy	3	5	1	12	12
Ingram	2	5	2	14	14
Jones	3	6	2	16	16
Average	3	5	1.5	15	15

In this hypothetical case we accounted for all the variation in the criterion factor, hence actual and estimated levels agree perfectly. In most real work this obviously is not the case.

By studying the actual and expected columns, it is easier to understand the meaning of the multiple R result. It is merely the simple correlation between the actual and estimated values. If our estimates are close to the observed levels then we have a high multiple R; if the estimates are poor we have a low multiple R. Thus, the multiple R is an expression of our ability to forecast levels of the criterion variable when we know the levels of the independent factors.

An additional step can often make the analysis more fruitful. We can examine the deviant cases—those in which the estimated values differ sharply from the actual. This may suggest an additional factor or two which should have been analyzed independently. Often an item can be unearthed in this way which will markedly increase the correlation.

In practice, list the large deviations, *either plus or minus,* between actual and estimate. Then examine them carefully in the light of any background knowledge about the subject matter, in a search for additional variables. If you find factors which might explain the deviations, enter them into a new multiple regression analysis.

3. We can determine the power of our procedures by calculating the amount of the total variation of the criterion factor which has been

accounted for by the independent factors. This is obtained by multiplying the b value for each factor by the cross-product of that factor with the criterion variable and summing the results:

Factor	Cross-Product with T	$\times$	b Value	=	Variance Accounted for
F	36 (FT)		4.0		144
Y	−102 (YT)		−2.0		204
N	25 (NT)		6.0		150
Total					498

$$R^2 = \frac{\text{Variance Accounted For}}{\text{Variance in Criterion}} = \frac{498}{498} = 1.0$$

In this hypothetical case we have accounted for 100% of the variation in the criterion. This would never happen in practice because of errors of measurement and/or unidentified factors. Here we *constructed* the hours of TV viewing for each family, based on the assumption that family size, years owned TV and number of sets are the only factors responsible for the number of hours the family views TV.

4. The last step is to compute the coefficient of multiple correlation. The meaning of this term is exactly the same as in simple correlational work: 1.0 means a perfect positive relationship; −1.0 is a perfect negative relationship; 0.0 denotes the absence of any relationship.

$$\text{Multiple } R = \sqrt{R^2}$$

in this case, 1.0. We have accounted for all the variance in hours of TV viewing, ergo we have a perfect correlation.

While the regression analysis has determined the b values for each independent factor in our hypothetical example, we still do not know which of the items, family size, years owned TV, or number of TV sets, is most important in accounting for variation in viewing time. At first glance it would seem that the b values fulfill this function, inasmuch as they indicate how much change in viewing time can be expected with each *unit* change in an independent factor; however, since the factors are measured in different units, their *relative* contribution in accounting for the criterion factor variation is not evident.

To determine the relative importance of each independent factor,

beta weights are calculated. Here we transform the data into standard
deviation units. This puts each item on a common footing.

We begin by calculating the standard deviation for each variable
directly from the original variance cross-products obtained (FF, YY,
NN and TT):

$$\text{Standard Deviation} = \sqrt{\frac{\text{variance cross-product}}{N}}$$

where N is the size of the sample (in this case, 10). The standard
deviation of each independent variable is then divided by the standard
deviation of the criterion variable. We set:

Factor	Variance Cross-Product	Variance / N	S.D.	Factor S.D. / Criterion S.D.
F	12	1.2	1.1	.16
Y	84	8.4	2.9	.41
N	2.5	.25	0.5	.07
T	498	49.8	7.1	—

Now the beta weights are computed by multiplying each of the
standard deviation ratios by the b value for the appropriate factor.
(Signs are ignored at this point.)

Factor	S.D. Ratio	×	b Value	=	Beta Weights
F	.16		4.0		.64
Y	.41		2.0		.82
N	.07		6.0		.42

Conclusion: years owned TV is the most important factor in explaining variation in time spent viewing TV, followed by family size and
number of sets owned.

One could have done this analysis himself in the time it took him
to read its explanation. This may be a good definition of a shortcut
method.

Discriminant Analysis of Audience Charactertistics[1]

William F. Massy

How similar are the audiences of two or more advertising vehicles? While most would agree, for example, that *Life* and *Look* readers are more nearly alike than those of *Life* and *New Yorker,* methods for quantifying these differences are rather unwieldly. The usual procedure is to collect data for each audience group on several interesting variables, compute the means of the variables, and then compare them among the audience groups. Thus, it might be found that *"Life* readers show more preference for Brand X than do those of *New Yorker,"* or *"Life* readers tend to be drawn from the Y socio-economic class, whereas *New Yorker* readers tend to be in the Z class."

While statements like these are very useful for sorting out gross differences in audience characteristics, they do not readily combine into a compact index of overall audience similarity. It is difficult to look at two columns of means and decide how different, on balance, they really are. The problem becomes much more complicated when comparing three or more audiences.

Reprinted with permission from the *Journal of Advertising Research,* vol. 5, no. 2 (March, 1965), pp. 39–48. © Advertising Research Foundation, Inc. (1965).

[1] This study was supported, in part, by funds made available by the Ford Foundation to the Graduate School of Business, Stanford University. Conclusions, opinions, and other statements are those of the author and do not necessarily represent those of the Ford Foundation. Computations were subsidized by and performed at the Western Data Processing Center, University of California at Los Angeles.

The author also expresses his appreciation to Herbert Taylor, who collected the data upon which this study is based in the Spring of 1962, as part of the requirements for the degree of Master of Science in Industrial Management at the Massachusetts Institute of Technology, and to Professor Thomas Lodahl of the Graduate School of Business and Public Administration, Cornell University, for making the information available. The data also are discussed in a previous paper by the author (Massy, 1963).

The method of N-way multiple discriminant analysis discussed in this paper can provide a set of aggregate similarity indices for a given number of audiences. Basically, the procedure attempts to "predict" which audience group an individual belongs to, based on the sets of group means discussed above, together with the set of sample variances and co-variances of the variables. That is, the individual is assigned to the audience group whose characteristics are most like his own. Since it is known beforehand which group the person actually belongs to, we can prepare a table of correct and incorrect classifications. This "score sheet" of correct and incorrect classifications, or *confusion matrix,* then provides the basis for the desired similarity indices. That is, the fewer the misclassifications of individuals to audience groups, the more distinct or dissimilar the audience groups.

This paper describes an application of the confusion matrix method in measuring the similarity of audiences for five Boston FM radio stations. But first let us examine the statistical underpinnings of N-way multiple discriminant analysis, starting with two-way analysis.

Two-way Discriminant Analysis

Two-way discriminant analysis, which deals with an arbitrary number of variables but only two populations, is becoming more common in marketing (see, for example, Banks, 1958; Evans, 1959; and Frank and Massy, 1963). The first step in this form of analysis is to estimate the coefficients in a linear discriminant function. Here is an example of this type of function, in terms of two hypothetical variables, X and Y.

$$f_i = c_X X_i + c_Y Y_i$$

The subscript i runs over the individuals included in the analysis.

A critical value of f is determined such that if an individual's f value is above the break-point he is classified in one group and if it is below he is assigned to the other. Hence the name "discriminant analysis": the function f is defined so that it discriminates between members of the two groups in the most efficient fashion.

Let us assume we have measurements on two variables for a sample of 18 drawn equally from two populations, A and B. Figure 1 presents the hypothetical scatter diagram for this sample. Now imagine that we draw a nineteenth observation, but do not know whether it belongs to A or B. The problem is to assign the new observation to either A or B in a way that minimizes the probability of misclassification.

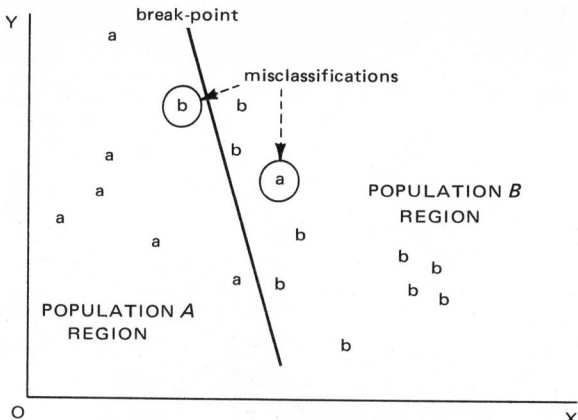

Figure 1 Discrimination of two hypothetical populations on two variables

In this case we would base our estimate of the coefficients (the c's) of the discriminate function on the information provided by the original 18 observations. Having values for the c's allows us to assign a value of f to any possible combination of X and Y, whether from our original sample or a new sample. Next, we use mathematical methods to estimate the probability that, given a particular value of f, the observation would fall in A. This probability distribution for A might look like the one given by the solid curve in Figure 2, which also presents a similar distribution for B, shown by a dotted curve.

Further, Figure 2 contains a vertical line which represents the discriminant or break-point value of f. The break-point is set half way between the means of f for A and B, so at this point an observation has about an equal probability of falling in A or B. The shaded areas on either side of the break-point give the total probability of misclassifying a particular observation.

The logic of two-way discriminant analysis is presented in greater detail in Frank, Kuehn, and Massy (1962), along with computing formulas. More detailed treatments can be found in the references cited in connection with N-way analysis.

N-way Analysis

Consider three populations of individuals (A, B, and C) describable in terms of two variables (X and Y). The populations might refer to audiences of three advertising media and the variables to audience attributes, such as family size and income. Figure 3 shows a hypo-

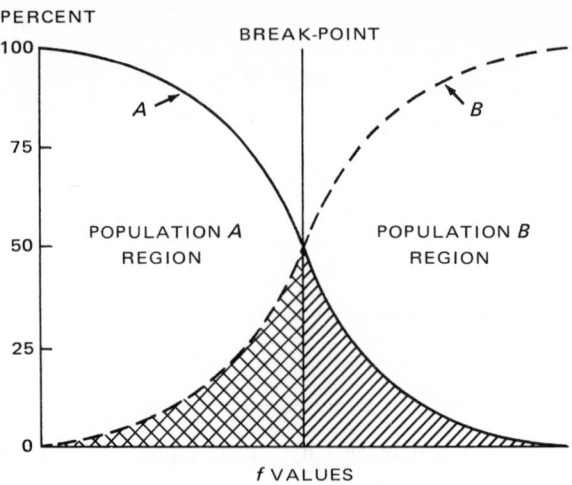

Figure 2 Probability that an observation will fall in population A or B

thetical scatter diagram for the attribute values of individuals in each of the three populations.

The discriminant problem here is to define three mutually exclusive regions (a, b, and c) which exhaust the X-Y space. The region boundaries should be set up such that when the X and Y values put an individual into a given region, it is more probable that he actually is a member of that population than of any other population. The problem is soluble provided that the variables are approximately normally distributed in each population, their respective variance-covariance matrices are about equal, and that the a priori probability for membership in each (i.e., the relative incidence of the groups in the overall population) is known. (These conditions also are required for the two-way case.)

In Figure 3, the lines separating the three regions represent loci of equal probability for their respective pairs of regions. To report that a given observation lies to one side of the threshold line is to say that the probability that the observation belongs in this region is greater than for any other region. Obviously, this "maximum probability criterion" does not preclude mistakes in classification. Six population A individuals are erroneously put in group C and one in group B. On the other hand, if the classification process were repeated many times with similar samples of individuals, this procedure would result in the lowest possible proportion of errors.

How are the regions determined? As in the two-way case, the

sample data are used to estimate the parameters of linear discriminant functions for the populations. These are denoted by the three broken half lines (Z_A, Z_B, and Z_C) in Figure 3. (Note: for the sake of simplicity, the discriminant function was not drawn in Figure 1; if it had, it would be shown perpendicular to the break-point line.) Once the parameters of these functions have been estimated, the boundaries are set so that each discriminant line (Z) bisects the angle between its respective boundary lines: thus Z_A bisects the angle between *ab* and *ac*. (This is equivalent to taking half the distance between the

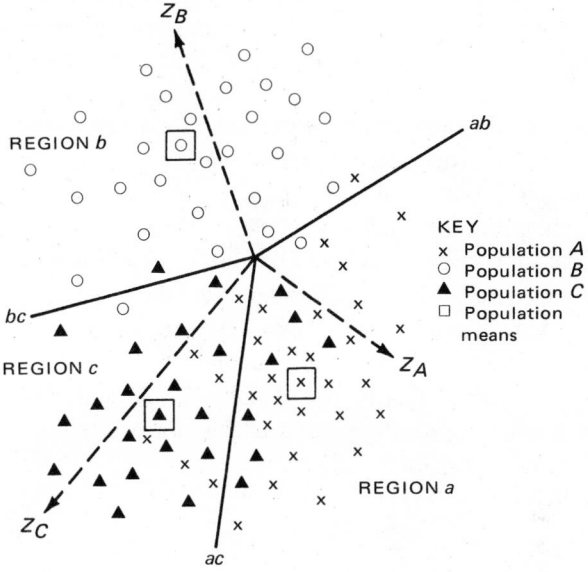

Figure 3   Acceptance regions for three hypothetical populations on two variables

discriminant means in the two-way case.) The analyst proceeds by first estimating the three sets of discriminant coefficients by mathematical methods shown in the special box on page 210, and then setting up boundaries for the acceptance regions on the basis of his initial results. While the means of the variables fall within the acceptance regions for their respective populations (this is a necessary condition), they do not have to lie on the discriminant lines.

Figure 3 also provides insight into using confusion matrices to evaluate the similarity of populations. Table 1 shows the correct and incorrect classifications for the example. The figures along the diagonal tell us that the number of correct predictions for *B* is greater

**TABLE 1   Predicted and Actual Population Membership
of Hypothetical Example**

ACTUAL:	PREDICTED:			TOTAL
	A	B	C	
A	20	1	6	27
B	1	25	1	27
C	7	1	19	27

than for either A or C. The off-diagonals indicate that a member of A is most likely to be misclassified as a C, and a member of C to be wrongly associated with A. Hence it makes sense to conclude that populations A and C are more nearly alike than are A and B, or B and C. Figure 3 corroborates this view, since the distance between the two swarms of points for the A-C pair is less than that between the points for either the B-C or B-A pair.

While the same conclusion could have been obtained by examining the six t ratios for the differences between the means of pairs of groups, this would greatly strain the analyst's ability to compare many numbers at once, even in this rather simple example. Another technique for measuring similarity, the Mahalanobis D^2 statistic (see Rao, 1952), is not as easy to understand and is not as closely related to the predictive efficacy of the discriminant analysis as the method of confusion matrices.

AN APPLICATION

Similarity of FM Station Audiences

Confusion matrices were used to evaluate the similarities among the audiences of five FM radio stations located in the Boston Metropolitan Area. The data for the study were collected by Herbert Taylor (1962) from a sample of families who owned at least one FM radio receiver. A mail questionnaire was used to obtain information on current station selections and some 47 socio-economic and consumption variables. Respondents were given a series of scales simulating the markings on a typical FM dial, and asked to note the position of the dial(s) on each FM receiver in the home, as of the time the questionnaire was filled out.

The sample consisted of returned questionnaires from about 380 families; 280 had sent in for Station *A*'s program guide and the rest were selected at random. The results given here are based on the 239 families for whom the station tuned to at response time could be unambiguously determined. Since the sample probably contains substantial biases, which may lead to false impressions about audience characteristics, station call letters have been withheld.

The first step in the analysis was to reduce the number of potential explanatory variables from 47 to some more manageable number. Factor analysis was used to obtain 12 new variates that could serve as summaries of the original set. (The definitions of the factor score variables are presented below in Table 4.) The factor loadings matrix upon which they are based is the same as that reported by Massy (1963).

The 12 summary variates were subjected to a five-way multiple discriminant analysis to predict which types of respondents listen to what radio station.

Table 2 gives the confusion matrix for the 12-variate five-way discriminant run for the sample of 239 families, under the assumption that a priori probabilities are equal for membership in any of the five audiences. (Compare Tables 5 and 6 to see the effects of using the sample population frequencies as a priori probabilities.) Entries on the main diagonal of the matrix denote correct classifications or hits, while the off-diagonal elements represent misses. The percentage of hits is 36.8 percent. A χ^2 test based on the Mahalanobis D^2 statistic found the differences between the means among the five groups to be significant at the .025 critical level. Thus we may conclude that at least one pair of station audiences are different on at least one of our 12 variables.

TABLE 2 Confusion Matrix for 12 Variates, Assuming Equal Probabilities

ACTUAL AUDIENCE:	PREDICTED AUDIENCE MEMBERSHIP:					TOTAL
	A	B	C	D	E	
A	*43*	13	8	21	14	99
B	16	*15*	15	13	13	72
C	3	5	*14*	5	4	31
D	2	3	5	*9*	4	23
E	2	1	0	4	*7*	14

Total Hits = 88; Percent Hits = 36.8%; χ^2 (48) = 72.4

We are better able to draw conclusions from the confusion matrix if we normalize the raw misclassification counts by dividing each by its row total. The new entries, presented in Table 3, represent the probabilities that an individual who is actually in a given station's audience will be so classified. Table 3 indicates that some combinations of stations are much more alike than others, as far as we can tell.

TABLE 3   Normalized Confusion Matrix for 12 Variates, Assuming Equal Probabilities

ACTUAL AUDIENCE:	PREDICTED AUDIENCE MEMBERSHIP:					TOTAL
	A	B	C	D	E	
A	*.43*	.13	.08	.21	.14	1.00
B	.22	*.21*	.21	.18	.18	1.00
C	.10	.16	*.45*	.16	.13	1.00
D	.08	.13	.22	*.39*	.17	1.00
E	.14	.07	.00	.29	*.50*	1.00

Station A has a fairly distinct audience profile, as indicated by the .43 on its diagonal; it is most strongly associated with Station D, and to a lesser extent with E and B. Station B's profile is little different from those of the other stations; it is somewhat more closely associated with A and C.

Station C has a strongly differentiated profile; its diagonal of .45 is almost three times as large as any of the misclassifications. C is weakly associated with B and D.

Station D has a fairly distinct profile, and is most nearly like Station C, followed by E. The Station E profile appears to be quite distinct, but the small sample size for E makes conclusions difficult.

It would be interesting to know whether the relationships given above are reciprocal. That is, if members of one group tend to be misclassified in a second group, are members of the second group in turn likely to be misassigned to the first group? In Figure 4 the arrows indicate the direction of misclassification for the two largest off-diagonal entries in each row of Table 3. The figure shows that, except for Station A, all relationships are reciprocal. Station A listeners tend to be disproportionately associated with Station D rather than B, even though B's listeners are more likely than D's to be associated (i.e., misclassified) with A.

Table 4 presents the coefficients of the 12 variables for the five

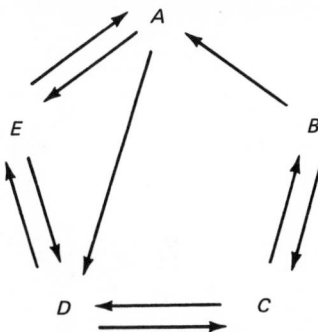

Figure 4   Association diagram for 12 variables (arrow indicates direction of misses)

discriminant functions. Each coefficient represents the effect of the variable on the probability of classification in the group corresponding to the particular discriminant function. As such, the coefficients are more sensitive measures of audience characteristics than a similar table of the means of the variables. Moreover, the discriminant coefficients take into account correlations among variables. For example, since older people obviously have fewer children living at home, the means for these two variables would tend to be highly correlated from group to group. The discriminant coefficient, on the other hand, gives us the effect of number of children at home, holding age constant, and vice versa.

Certain audience characteristics can be observed by looking at the extreme values of the discriminant coefficients for each variable in Table 4. A variable contributes most to the probability of classification in that station audience for which it is most positive. Conversely, negative coefficients indicate the extent to which high scorers on a variable are *not* likely to be associated with the particular audience. Variables whose coefficients are near zero for any group do not much affect the probability for that group.

Key Audience Characteristics

An analysis of the extreme positive and negative coefficients in Table 4 produced the following audience profiles:

TABLE 4 Multiple Discriminant Coefficients for Five Stations and 12 Variates

VARIABLES		STATIONS			
	A	B	C	D	E
1. Durables ownership (high scorers more likely to own dishwashers, freezers, washers, dryers, second cars)	−.18	−.53	+.27	−.74	−1.01
2. Age—older (+)	−.89	−.79	+1.18	+.38	−1.72
3. Social class I—higher occupational status	+.41	+.90	+.21	+1.22	+1.11
4. Music preference I—classical and opera (+) vs. popular (−)	+.03	+.06	−.26	+.11	−.01
5. Social class II—"lower middle class" (high scorers use credit, have low income and assets, tend to have older cars)	+.20	+.29	−.34	+.57	+.94
6. Automobile ownership (high scorers own newer cars, tend toward foreign, lower priced, and larger models)	+.96	−.01	−1.27	−1.04	+1.10
7. Music preference II—folk (+) vs. popular (−)	−.04	+.19	+.06	+.18	−.27
8. Source of entertainment (high scorers seldom "go out")	+.58	+.21	+.48	+.24	+1.04
9. Wife's status—working wife (+)	+.36	−.09	−.06	−.69	−.49
10. Music preference III—opera (+) vs. jazz (−)	+.28	+.35	+.55	−.13	+.77
11. "Individualism" (high scorers tend to like folk music, dislike trading stamps, and not own TV set or shop in discount houses)	−.27	+.20	+.71	+1.98	+.20
12. Program guide—sent in for Station A's guide (−)	+.31	+.43	+.18	+.25	+.22
Constant	−.26	−.19	−.38	−.38	−.33

Station A. Ownership of a bigger or newer car, or more than one car, contributes most strongly to classification in A's audience. Families that seldom "go out" to movies, sports, or cultural events also are disproportionately likely to be "A's." The younger the family the higher its probability of being in the A audience.

Station B. The probability of classification in B increases as the family rises in occupational status. It is highest if the family did not send in for A's program guide. Younger families, and families that indicate a preference for opera over jazz are more likely to be assigned to B.

Station C. Respondents assigned to C tend to be much older than average, and own fewer and/or older and smaller automobiles, and prefer jazz and popular music to opera. "Going out" contributes more to C's classification probability than to any other station. The same is true for sending in for A's program guide—Station C even is ahead of Station A.

Station D. "Individualism" contributes most strongly to the probability of classification in this audience. Next in importance is occupational status. Affluence in automobile ownership strongly inhibits the chances of being so classified.

Station E. High classification probabilities for E are strongly related to occupational status and automobile affluence, and inversely related to "going out" and durables ownership. Younger people are much more likely to be classified in this audience. The group is most likely to exhibit "lower middle class" values (Social class II). The extreme positive coefficient for opera versus jazz might best be regarded as a dislike for jazz.

Differences between pairs of coefficients indicate the extent to which the variable aids in discriminating the two audiences. The five stations permit ten different pair-wise comparisons of coefficients. Since this is an unwieldy number, we shall concentrate on the pairs that are not connected by any arrows in Figure 4. Our data indicate that the most widely separated stations in the discriminant space are *A-C, B-C, B-D,* and *C-E.*

A compared with *C.* *A* listeners are younger and much more likely to own newer, larger autos, and/or more autos than *C* listeners. On the other hand, families that "go out" often are much more likely to be classified in *C.*

B compared with *C.* The probability of classification in *B* rather than *C* increases as automobile affluence increases, and decreases with age.

B compared with *D*. "Individualism" increases the probability of membership in *D* relative to *B*. On the other hand, the *B*'s tend to be younger and more affluent on automobile ownership.

C compared with *E*. Age, automobile affluence, and durables ownership increase the probability of being classified in *C* relative to *E*. The same is true for a stated preference for jazz over opera. The *E*'s tend to "go out" more than the *D*'s, and are more likely to exhibit "lower middle class" behavior.

While a more extensive analysis of audience differences would be necessary in an actual study, the foregoing shows how the confusion matrix can be used to narrow down the comparison of pairs of discriminant coefficients. The same approach could be used to determine what pairs of means are most likely to exhibit significant differences. It represents an important reduction of the dimensions of the problem of defining essential differences between audiences, especially when a large number of audiences are to be compared.

Adding More Explanatory Variables

Adding new variables increases the predictive power of a multiple discriminant analysis, but does this also affect the structure of the confusion matrix and our ability to interpret associations between audience profiles? The following paragraphs present some evidence on this point.

Tables 5 and 6 present normalized confusion matrices based on discriminant runs with two and 25 explanatory variables, respectively. The sample sizes for the audience groups are the same as previously reported. The set of two variables in Table 5 was obtained through a factor analysis of answers to music preference questions. One variable

TABLE 5   Normalized Confusion Matrix for Two Music Preference Variates, Assuming Equal Probabilities

ACTUAL AUDIENCE:	PREDICTED AUDIENCE MEMBERSHIP:					
	A	B	C	D	E	TOTAL
A	*.31*	.14	.10	.11	.33	1.00
B	.26	*.15*	.21	.13	.33	1.00
C	.10	.19	*.45*	.16	.10	1.00
D	.17	.00	.30	*.26*	.26	1.00
E	.21	.21	.07	.14	*.36*	1.00

Total Hits = 67; Percent Hits = 28.0%; χ^2 (8) = 35.3

is positively associated with preference for classical and opera versus popular music. The second is positive on folk and negative on semi-classical and show tunes. The two-variable confusion matrix, then, is based only on stated preference for musical radio programs, and not on any socio-economic or demographic variables.

The 25-variable analysis in Table 6 used 17 original variables from the questionnaire, plus eight factor analysis scores covering the remaining 30 original variates. The 17 variables were chosen on the basis of communalities in the factor analysis that formed the basis for the results presented above. Variables with low communalities were not well summarized by the factor scores from that analysis and so did not contribute effectively to the 12-variable discriminant predictions. This defect was remedied by treating them separately in the 25-variate run.

TABLE 6   Normalized Confusion Matrix for 25 Variates, Assuming Equal Probabilities

ACTUAL AUDIENCE:	PREDICTED AUDIENCE MEMBERSHIP:					
	A	B	C	D	E	TOTAL
A	*.40*	.17	.10	.21	.11	1.00
B	.19	*.35*	.18	.12	.15	1.00
C	.13	.23	*.55*	.10	.00	1.00
D	.09	.09	.17	*.61*	.04	1.00
E	.21	.14	.00	.07	*.57*	1.00

Total Hits = 104; Percent Hits = 43.5%; χ^2 (100) = 148.4

Compared with a score of .368 for the original 12-variable analysis, the proportion of successful predictions drops to .280 for the two-variable case and climbs to .435 for the 25-variable run. Both χ^2's are significant at beyond the .005 critical level, which indicates that the discriminant functions are not illusory.

The association diagrams for these two runs show some interesting differences. In Figure 5 the two music preference variables show the same reciprocal, circular pattern noted in Figure 4 for the 12-variate analysis, except that the unexpected association of *A* and *D* has been replaced with a reciprocal link between *B* and *E*. Apparently the audiences of *B* and *E* share a measure of music preference similarity that is not reflected in the socio-economic and demographic profiles. The reverse seems to be true for Stations *A* and *D*.

The association diagram in Figure 6a for the 25-variable analysis

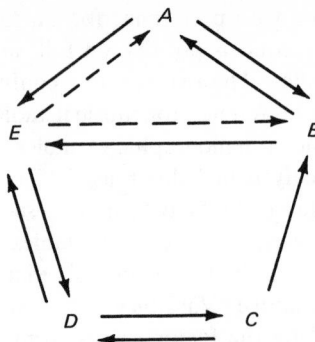

Figure 5   Association diagram for two music preference variables (arrows indicate direction of misses). The pair of dotted lines emanating from E represent the two off-diagonal elements tied for second place.

is not nearly as neat as for the other runs. As before, Stations A and B, B and C, and, to a lesser extent, A and D are reciprocally associated. But after this the relationships break down into an indistinct pattern. This result can be explained partly by the fact that there are few misclassifications for stations C, D, and E. This means that a shift in the classification of just a few individuals would make a substantial difference in the association diagram. The difficulty may be relieved by considering only the largest off-diagonal entries in Table 6; this is

Two Largest Misclassifications

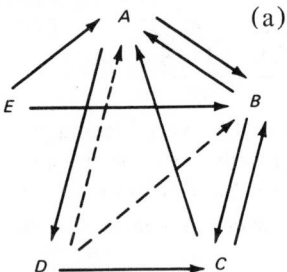

Largest Misclassification

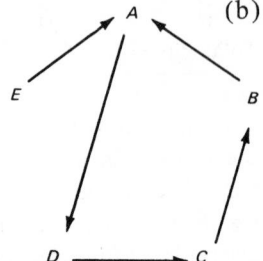

Figure 6   Association diagram for 25 variables. The pair of dotted lines (*a*) represent a tie.

shown in Figure 6b, which gives the same general pattern of associations already noted for the 12-variable case.

Adjusting the A Priori Probability

Heretofore we have assumed equal a priori probabilities of audience membership (i.e., the actual audience sizes are assumed to be equal). Substantially different results are obtained if the a priori probabilities,

the Π's in equation (5), are set equal to the sample frequencies rather than being assumed equal. This tends to make the predicted membership frequencies equal the actual ones, whereas no such condition was involved in the equal-Π case. It also increases the overall percentage of hits for the discriminant analysis, since the populations with larger sample frequencies tend to pick up more assignments than they would otherwise. We shall see, however, that it is not an unmixed blessing.

Table 7 presents the normalized confusion matrix for sample

TABLE 7 Normalized Confusion Matrix for 25 Variates, Sample A Priori Probabilities

ACTUAL AUDIENCE:	PREDICTED AUDIENCE MEMBERSHIP:					
	A	B	C	D	E	TOTAL
A	.77	.15	.04	.02	.01	1.00
B	.42	.44	.11	.00	.03	1.00
C	.39	.23	.39	.00	.00	1.00
D	.48	.17	.13	.22	.00	1.00
E	.57	.14	.00	.00	.28	1.00

Total Hits $= 130$; Percent Hits $= 54.5\%$; $x^2 (100) = 184.4$

a priori probability predictions based on the 25-variable discriminant run reported above. The resulting association diagram, based on the largest misclassification per station, is given in Figure 7. The percentage of hits is increased by 11 percentage points over the equal a priori probability results for the same variates reported in Table 6. Accuracy in classifying Station A and B listeners was increased more than enough to offset the decrease in accuracy for C, D, and E. Station D and E listeners, who have a low incidence in the sample, are now more likely to be assigned to Station A (which has the highest incidence) than in their own group.

This shift takes on more meaning after an examination of the association diagram for the run. When using sample a priori probabilities, stations A and B form a closed set of reciprocal associations, while C, D; and E are most likely to be misassigned to A. It appears that for sample sizes that are as unbalanced as the ones in the present study, using sample frequencies as a priori probabilities leads to results that reflect variations in sample size rather than true differences among the groups. If the equal a priori probability assumption is unpalatable it may be possible to utilize population rather than sample frequencies, provided that these are not so unbalanced as to obscure the relationships among groups.

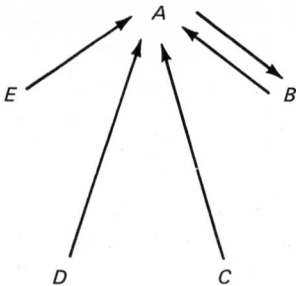

Figure 7   Association diagram for 25 variates, assuming sample probabilities

CONCLUSION

"How similar are the audiences of two or more advertising vehicles?" This article attempts to show how confusion matrices based on multiple discriminant analysis can provide the answer. Any survey which obtains audience data can be used as input for the analysis. The audience profile data may involve any questions that can be scaled and coded quantitatively; the socio-economic and consumption information used in the example is intended to be only suggestive.

Confusion matrix analysis has two advantages. First, it is a multivariate statistical technique: the interrelationships between the explanatory variables are taken into account statistically, the same as in multiple regression. Second, the results of the analysis are presented in a compact format that is easy to interpret and communicate. They represent information about the degree of overlap of station characteristics. This information also can be portrayed graphically in an association diagram. The relative advantage of this method over univariate analysis becomes greater as more audiences are to be compared. In addition, a multivariate test of the hypothesis that the means of all the variables are the same for all audiences is readily available.

The main problem with the confusion matrix approach is that while it indicates the relative degree to which audience groups differ from one another, it does not provide direct information as to the dimensions on which the differentiation occurs. The coefficients of the various discriminant functions provide information on the importance of each variable for each discrimination, but the large number of such

coefficients and the difficulties in comparing them from function to function make interpretation difficult. On the other hand, separate confusion matrix runs with different combinations of independent variables may provide insight into the combinations of each set of variables to the discriminant analyses. An example of this approach can be seen by comparing Figures 2 and 3, in which the association diagrams are based on two and 12 variables, respectively. In any case, confusion matrix analysis can suggest hypotheses to guide further work using other techniques.

Finally, the normalized confusion matrix bears a strong resemblance to the transition probability matrix defined in Markov chain models for brand switching behavior. Both consist of sets of conditional probabilities that subjects will participate in a particular class of behavior, given that they exhibit certain attributes. Of course, the similarity between the two approaches stops there, since multiple discriminant analysis is a purely statistical technique that assumes perfectly static behavior on the part of its subjects, while the Markov approach is based on a dynamic behavioral model. On the other hand, the use of confusion matrices to evaluate similarities among audiences is much the same as the approach advocated by Lipstein (1959) for examining similarities among brands. Clustering among sub-sets of the conditional probabilities provides the basis for the analysis in both cases.

THE MATHEMATICS OF DISCRIMINANT ANALYSIS

Here are formulas for discriminant calculations on three populations and an arbitrary number (p) of variables. The reader is referred to Kendall (1957, Chap. 9) for their proofs. Generalization to the case of N populations is obvious. Tests of significance in discriminant analysis are not considered here, but have been extensively treated by Rao (1952).

Assume that the variates for individuals in each population ($k = 1, N$) are normally distributed according to $N(X_q, q = 1, p)_k$, with identical variance-covariance matrices. Then the probability that an individual chosen at random will fall in population k is given by the product of the kth distribution at the point associated with that individual's X values times the a priori probability of membership in the kth group: $N_k \Pi_k$. (This formulation is the result of Bayesian logic.) The ratio of these posterior membership probabilities for populations 1 and 2 (say) is given by:

$$(1) \quad \log \frac{\Pi_1 N_1}{\Pi_2 N_2} = \sum_q \sum_j \sigma^{qj} (\mu_{1j} - \mu_{2j}) X_{qi} -$$

$$\tfrac{1}{2} \sum_q \sum_j \sigma^{qj} (\mu_{1q}\mu_{1j} - \mu_{2q}\mu_{2j}) + \log \frac{\Pi_1}{\Pi_2}$$

where: X_{qi} is the ith individual's value for the qth variate, and
μ_{kj} is the mean of the jth variate in the kth population.
σ^{qj} is the qjth element of the inverse of the variance-covariance matrix, which is the same for all the populations.

The first and last terms of this equation are the same as in the more familiar 2-way discriminant analysis; the most familiar case is for $\Pi_1 = \Pi_2$, where the last term drops out.

When the two posterior probabilities are equal, the left side of (1) is equal to zero, so we may rearrange terms and write:

$$(2) \quad \sum_q \sum_j \sigma^{qj} \mu_{1j} X_{qi} - \tfrac{1}{2} \sum_q \sum_j \sigma^{qj} \mu_{1q} \mu_{1j} + \log \Pi_1 =$$

$$\sum_q \sum_j \sigma^{qj} \mu_{2q} X_{qi} - \tfrac{1}{2} \sum_q \sum_j \sigma^{qj} \mu_{2q} \mu_{2j} + \log \Pi_2$$

Let us denote the first two terms on each side of (2) by Q_1 and Q_2, respectively, so that

$$(3) \qquad\qquad Q_{1j} + \log \Pi_1 = Q_{2j} + \log \Pi_2,$$

for $\Pi_1 N_1 = \Pi_2 N_2$. Setting $Q_{ki} + \log \Pi_k$ equal to Z_{ki} provides another simplification in notation, so that the final criterion for discrimination is

$$Z_{1i} \underset{<}{\overset{>}{=}} Z_{2i}.$$

We have already shown that if the equality holds, the ith individual's posterior probabilities for population membership are equal (then the discriminant procedure results in a tie—although this case is not important in practice since a tie may always be broken by carrying the results to a sufficient number of decimal places). If Z_{1i} is greater than Z_{2i}, it follows that the probability ratio of population 1 to 2 is greater than one and the individual should be classified in population 1. The reverse is true for Z_{1i} less than Z_{2i}. The functions Z_k correspond to the broken half-lines Z_k in Figure 3, while the boundary lines *ab, ac,* and *bc* are the loci of equalities among the various pairs of functions.

Operationally, the N-way discriminant procedure consists of finding the parameters of the N linear discriminant functions Z_{ki}, so that their values can be evaluated for each of the individuals in the sample:

$$(4) \qquad Z_{ki} = b_{0k} + b_{1k}X_{1i} + b_{2k}X_{2i} + \ldots + b_{pk}X_{pi}.$$

Expressions for the parameters are obtained from equations (2) and (3), and the definition of Z.

$$(5) \qquad b_{qk} = \sum_{j} \sigma^{qj} \mu_{kj}$$

$$b_{0k} = \sum_{q} \sum_{j} \sigma^{qj} \mu_{kq} \mu_{kj} + \log \Pi_k$$

There are a total of $N\,(p+1)$ parameters to be estimated from the data. Estimation is accomplished by substituting the sample means and variance-covariance inverse elements into (5): standard computer programs much like multiple regression programs exist and may be used to handle these calculations.

Once numerical estimates of the b's are available, all N of the discriminant values (the Z_{ki}) are calculated for each individual in the sample and each is assigned to the population for which his value is the largest. The terms involving $\log \Pi_k$ can be dropped from the equations if the a priori probabilities for all the populations are equal; this affects only the constant terms (the b_{0k}) in the discriminant functions. The confusion matrix for the analysis is formed by cross-classifying the counts of correct and incorrect assignments by the actual and predicted populations for the individuals in the sample.

REFERENCES

Anderson, T. W. *Introduction to Multivariate Statistical Analysis.* New York: Wiley, 1958.

Banks, S. Why People Buy Particular Brands. In Robert Ferber and Hugh Wales (Eds.). *Motivation and Market Behavior.* Homewood, Illinois: Richard D. Irwin, 1958.

Cooley, W. W., and P. R. Lohnes. *Multivariate Procedures for the Behavioral Sciences.* New York: Wiley, 1962.

Evans, F. B. Psychological and Objective Factors in the Prediction of Brand Choice: Ford versus Chevrolet. *Journal of Business,* vol. 32, no. 4, October 1959, pp. 340–369. Reprinted in Frank, R. E., A. A. Kuehn, and W. F. Massy (Eds.). *Quantitative Techniques in Marketing Analysis.* Homewood, Ill.: Richard D. Irwin, 1962.

Fisher, R. A. The Use of Multiple Measurements in Taxonomic Problems. *Annuals of Eugenics,* vol. 7, 1936, p. 179.

Frank, R. E., A. A. Kuehn, and W. F. Massy. *Quantitative Techniques in Marketing Analysis.* Homewood, Ill.: Richard D. Irwin, 1962.

Frank, R. E., and W. F. Massy. Innovation and Brand Choice: The Folgers' Invasion. *Proceedings* of the Winter Meeting of the American Marketing Association, Boston, December, 1963.

Kendall, M. G. *A Course in Multivariate Analysis.* London: Griffin, 1957.

Lipstein, B. The Dynamics of Brand Loyalty and Brand Switching. In *Proceedings: Fifth Annual Conference.* New York: Advertising Research Foundation, 1959, pp. 101–108. Reprinted in Britt, S. H., and H. W. Boyd, Jr. (Eds.). *Marketing Management and Administrative Action.* New York: McGraw-Hill, 1963.

Massy, W. F. Applying Factor Analysis to a Specific Marketing Problem. *Proceedings* of the Winter Meeting of the American Marketing Association, Boston, December, 1963.

Rao, C. R. *Advanced Statistical Methods in Biometric Research.* New York: Wiley, 1952.

Factor Analysis

Gwyn Collins

Factor analysis has become increasingly popular among advertising and market researchers. Its techniques and its terminology are, however, better known than the intentions which underly its purely mechanical procedures. Until quite recently, to become acquainted with factor analysis called for extensive reading of original papers, most of them scattered through the psychological journals. The publication of *Modern Factor Analysis* (Harmon, 1960), has changed this state of affairs considerably. This book brings together a large number of recent developments and ideas which are to be found in no other single source; at this time it is the most authoritative work on the subject. It is appropriate, therefore, to consider not just how to factor analyze, which this book explains with clarity and in detail, but the general intention of the factor analyst and, in broad conceptual terms, how his results are obtained and presented.

This article, however, will not discuss where and where not to use factor analysis. The general purposes of factor analysis have been stated as:

. . . to reduce the number of experiments the scientist must do to impose order on complex subject matter. It helps him (or his manager) decide which experiments should be done next. So many responses are caused by large numbers of stimuli that his factor analysis may be the only way the researcher can reach a conclusion—within his lifetime—about which stimulus variables are most important in producing the response he wishes to predict or control. (Ramond, 1961.)

This topic will not be elaborated further here.

Briefly factor analysis is a technique for representing a large num-

Reprinted with permission from the *Journal of Advertising Research,* vol. 1, no. 4 (June, 1961), pp. 28–32. © Advertising Research Foundation, Inc. (1961).

ber of measurements each made on many objects or persons in terms of some smaller number of artificial measurements. For instance, the results of twenty different tests for mechanical ability may be factor analyzed and from the analysis we might find that from just four indexes, or factors, for each person tested, we could reproduce all twenty scores with a high degree of accuracy. This kind of thing is the basis of factor analysis. Unfortunately for simplicity, there are many ways of doing it and something needs to be said about them and their points of difference.

Factor analysis is the collective name given to all these procedures for deriving factors from original measurements. Its central idea was suggested 75 years ago as a means of isolating the fundamental characteristics of convicted criminals; its techniques were first introduced almost 60 years ago by a British engineer, Charles Spearman, in an article on intelligence in a psychological journal. Since then its practice has been almost entirely confined to psychology, especially to the field of personality measurement. Spearman's paper was itself entitled "General Intelligence, Objectively Determined and Measured." It presented the technique as a means of resolving disputes about the meaning of intelligence, but the method he presented, and later elaborations of it, have served to feed controversy in this very area right up to the present time.

Professional mathematicians and statisticians have had little to say about factor analysis; mathematicians because the basic procedures have long been known and are relatively trivial, statisticians because the statistical problems of factor analysis such as that of estimating sampling errors, have appeared more or less beyond solution. To statisticians generally, factor analysis has exerted very little appeal; to some it is a dirty word.

The raw material of factor analysis is a table of original measurements. Suppose that we have many individuals a, b, c–to n and that we have measured each of them in various ways A, B, C–to M, all different. We can record the results in a matrix or rectangular table of numbers, like this:

INDIVIDUALS

TESTS	a	b	c	d	...	n
A	X_{Aa}	X_{Ab}	X_{Ac}	X_{Ad}		
B	X_{Ba}	X_{Bb}	X_{Bc}			
C						
D						
.						
.						
.						
M	X_{Ma}	X_{Mb}	X_{Mc}	...	...	X_{Mn}

where X_{Bc}, for instance, denotes the measurement B taken on individual c. This, of course, is just a straightforward tabulation of the result of each of the measurements. Since they may be taken on a very large number of people, this is normally a huge matrix.

FACTORS ARE FEWER

Now the object of factor analysis is to find certain new composite dimensions, or factors, say α, β, γ, δ etc., fewer in number than the original measurements, uncorrelated with one another and which contain all the information provided by them. Each individual would have a score on each of these factors though it would not be open to direct observation; instead it would have to be inferred from the original measurements. The result of measurement A taken on individual a has been written in the matrix of original measurements as X_{Aa}. Analogously we can write his hypothetical score on the artificial dimension α as $X_{\alpha a}$, on the dimension β as $X_{\beta a}$ and so on. The problem is to find new dimensions such that any individual's score can be reconstituted by adding together some proportion of each of his hypothetical scores. Moreover, these proportions must be the same for every individual.

These proportions obviously have great importance and are appropriately called *factor loadings*. Thus if X_{Aa} is written in terms of factor scores as:

$$X_{Aa} = pX_{\alpha a} + qX_{\beta a} + rX_{\gamma a} + \text{etc.,}$$

then we would write X_{Ab} as:

$$X_{Ab} = pX_{ab} + qX_{\beta b} + rX_{\gamma b} + \text{etc.},$$

where p, q and r, the proportions of the factors α, β and γ that are used to reconstitute the measurement A, are known as the factor loadings of measurement A on the factors α, β and γ.

An important point is that factor analysis only attempts to find factors which can be added in this simple way to get back to the original measurements. It is conceivable that the original measurements could be obtained by some more complicated way of putting factor scores together, but this possibility is not encountered in present day factor analysis. What we have described is an ideal which no procedure achieves.

TWO APPROACHES

The attempt to reconstruct original measurements from a smaller number of factors is in practice rarely, if ever, completely successful. Usually it can only be done approximately and this offers the factor analyst a choice. He can either go on extracting factors until he has enough to reconstitute the original measurements almost perfectly, or he can decide at the outset that he will look for those two, three, or however many factors he prefers, which do the best job of recreating the original measurements. These two approaches are really fundamentally different, though the difference is usually ignored. The first approach, that of taking out as many factors as necessary, starts with the observed data and seeks to represent it in another way in terms of factors uncorrelated with one another. The second approach, that of finding the "best" p factors (where p is some number decided upon beforehand) is an attempt to fit a mathematical model to the observed data. The first approach is more accurately described as *component analysis,* and the term *factor analysis* should perhaps be reserved for the second approach. The confusion between these two basic methods has arisen because the arithmetical routines of both are closely similar. No attempt is made in the remainder of this article to unscramble this well established confusion; both will usually be referred to indiscriminately as factor analysis.

Factor analysts start their work by summarizing the information from the matrix of original measurements by calculating the correlation coefficients between each pair of measurements. This is a starting point in picking out that which is common to the various measure-

ments. The correlation coefficients are then written in the form of a matrix like this:

	A	B	C	D	—	—	M
D	r_{AA}	r_{AB}	r_{AC}	r_{AD}			
B	r_{BA}	r_{BB}	r_{BC}	r_{BD}			
C	r_{CA}	r_{CB}	r_{CC}	r_{CD}			
A	r_{DA}	r_{DB}	r_{DC}	r_{DD}			
—	—	—	—	—	—	—	—
—	—	—	—	—	—	—	—
M	—	—	—	—	—	—	—

This matrix is obviously square for there are as many rows as there are columns and usually, since there are many less measurements than people, it is a much smaller matrix than that of the original measurements. Another point is that the part of the matrix above the diagonal running from top left to bottom right (called the *principal diagonal*) is reflected on the other side of it because, for instance, the correlation between C and A, r_{CA} is equal to the correlation between A and C, r_{AC}. Another point is that the principal diagonal consists of terms like r_{AA}, r_{BB}, r_{CC} and so on. Now it might be thought that these entries must necessarily all equal 1, for the correlation of any measurement with itself should be perfect. In this case, however, we are dealing with the *hypothetical* correlation which would be found between two actual measurements. Since there are always at least errors in measurement, we might expect such correlations to be high but not necessarily perfect. Just how the spaces in the main diagonal should be filled is an important issue in factor analysis.

Earlier, in discussing the matrix of original measurements, factor analysis was described as an attempt to express each of the measurements in terms of some linear combination of a lesser number of them where the new artificial measurements, or factors, are uncorrelated. If this were possible then we should describe the measurements as *linearly dependent:* if it is impossible we describe the measurements as *linearly independent.* Now if all the M measurements of the matrix of original measurements are linearly independent, we describe that matrix as having *rank* M. If, however, any one of the measurements could always be obtained by a combination of the others, the matrix would be said to have rank $(M-1)$ at most. In short, the rank of a matrix is the greatest number of linearly independent rows (or columns) to be found in it. Using these terms, we can say that factor

analysis aims to express the matrix of original measurements as a matrix of some reduced rank. Since it is easy to show mathematically that the rank of the correlation matrix is always the same as that of the original matrix (if all elements of the principal diagonal are made equal to one) from which it is derived, the same thing can be said of the correlation matrix.

FACTOR VS. COMPONENT ANALYSIS

At this point, however, it is worthwhile to make some distinction between factor analysis and component analysis. The factor analyst is interested in actually reducing the rank of the correlation matrix to the number of factors he thinks is appropriate in his mathematical model. The component analyst, on the other hand, is not interested in reducing the rank of the correlation matrix. He is interested instead in obtaining factors which are not correlated with one another such that the first will explain as much as possible of the original measurements, the second will explain as much as possible of that left unexplained and so on.

Now the factor analyst wishing to reduce the rank of the correlation matrix has one useful tool. It has been pointed out that the elements of the principal diagonal of that matrix are more or less undefined. If appropriate numbers are put in, the rank of the matrix can, under very general conditions, be considerably reduced. A correlation matrix of rank 10, for example, can be reduced to rank 6. That is, we can reduce the results of 10 measurements to scores on 6 factors, whatever the original scores are. In fact the correlations actually found between the different measurements may help to reduce the rank of the matrix still further.

There are, however, two points of view about these diagonal entries, which factor analysts call *communalities*. One point of view expressed by a statistician is:

Where the [communalities] are completely unknown one method of approach has been to regard them as being at choice; and in particular to assume that they are such as to minimize the number of factors. In general, this seems to assume, on Nature's part, a much more indulgent behavior than we have any right to expect, but it is interesting to see what happens in such cases. (Kendall, 1957, p. 43.)

The other point of view, often expressed by psychologists, is that the communalities are unique numbers which represent that portion

of each measurement which correlates with other measurements under consideration; they are not observed, but can be computed. This, however, seems to be a way of describing an aspect of the mathematical model of factor analysis rather than a statement of observable fact.

There is another useful way of looking at the meaning of the rank of a matrix. Suppose, for instance, that we have only two measurements for each of a number of individuals. We could, if we chose, represent the pair of measurements for each person as points on a graph. The distance of the point from one axis could be used to represent one measurement; the distance from the other axis could stand for the other measurement. Points then, represent persons and because their positions depend upon two measurements they are spread over a two dimensional space—a plane. If we had three measurements for each person we would, of course, need three different dimensions in which to represent them, and so on.

To this rule of n dimensions to represent n different measurements there is an interesting exception. If, for example, we have two measurements for each person and the second is, say, always three times the first, then the points representing persons will always fall on one straight line. Because both measurements can be expressed in terms of only one of them, only one dimension is necessary to represent both. Similarly, if three measurements are such that they can be expressed in terms of any two of them, all the points will lie in two dimensions and, in general, n different measurements not linearly independent can be represented in less than n dimensions.

If the original measurements were expressed in terms of factors uncorrelated with one another, we should be able to represent them diagrammatically in a space with as many dimensions as there are factors. In the graph each measurement would be denoted by a point whose distances from the axes (each of which represents a factor) would represent factor loadings. If lines are drawn to join each of these points to the origin the angle between any pair of them can be shown to be a simple function of the correlation coefficient between the measurements they represent (the correlation coefficient is the cosine of the angle). Observed correlations can be represented completely by angles between pairs of lines. In the case of three dimensions we may imagine a series of spokes sticking out in all directions from some fixed point as representing the original measurements—this, of course, is an illustration of the original measurements represented in a three dimensional space, that is by three factors. Now the factors are inferred from the correlation coefficients while the

correlation coefficients are derived from observed data. We cannot choose our correlation coefficients; we must put up with those we find. The factors, however, can be chosen in any way that we please, as long as they do the job of representing the original measurements.

Returning to our three dimensional example, the three factors can be represented as three axes perpendicular to one another with their origin at the common point of the lines standing for the original measurements. Now the only observable data expressed in the diagram are the correlation coefficients and these are denoted by the angles between the lines. These angles are, then, the only invariant part of the diagram. But it is clear that if the whole configuration of lines representing the original measurements were rotated with its origin held fixed, the lines would then occupy different positions with respect to the axes and would have to be described differently. In other words, when we represent a correlation matrix in terms of a number of factors, there are an infinite number of ways of doing it. Each of these corresponds to a different rotation of the factor axes relative to the lines representing the original measurements.

SIMPLE STRUCTURE

This is a problem which has exercised psychologists greatly. A number of criteria have been suggested for the "best" selection of axes. The most venerated of these is one proposed by Thurstone and called "simple structure." The use of "simple structure" is no more than the factor analytic expression of the principle of parsimony. Essentially, it is that each variable should be represented by as few factors as possible. The rules given by Thurstone for obtaining "simple structure" demand a certain amount of judgment from the analyst. In general "simple structure" means that the axes will be so chosen that a large number of the points representing the original measurements will be near the origin and many of them will be close to one axis or another.

More recently there have been a number of attempts to specify what is meant by "simple structure" in analytical terms. Two well known ones are referred to as the Varimax and Quartimax methods. Roughly speaking the Quartimax method is a method of rotating the axes so that each measurement is described in terms of as few factors as possible. The Varimax method, on the other hand, obtains a rotation of the factor axes so as to minimize the number of measurements in which any one factor occurs.

The various procedures that have been used in factor analysis very often provide different approximations to the same factor solution. Usually they can be translated into one another mathematically or, where their mathematical models differ, their differences are of course, the result of different initial assumptions made by the analyst. In the early days of factor analysis, this was not so clear and disputes between rival analysts were heated and sometimes abusive. One review of rival methods put it this way:

Factor theory may be defined as a mathematical rationalization. A factor-analyst is an individual with a peculiar obsession regarding the nature of mental ability or personality. By the application of higher mathematics to wishful thinking, he always proves his original fixed idea or compulsion was right or necessary. In the process he usually proves that all other factor-analysts are dangerously insane, and that the only salvation for them is to undergo his own brand of analysis in order that the true essence of their several maladies may be discovered. Since they never submit to this indignity, he classes them all as hopeless cases, and searches about for some branch of mathematics which none of them is likely to have studied in order to prove that their incurability is not only necessary but also sufficient. (Cureton, 1939, p. 287.)

Nowadays three procedures seem to share public favor. One of them, cluster analysis, is not a factor analytic method at all. It offers an insight into the way measurements group together in terms of their correlation coefficients. A far simpler procedure than factor analysis it is regarded by many as providing an approximation to it.

PRINCIPAL AXES METHOD

The method of factor analysis which has always seemed mathematically preferable is that known as the method of principal axes—this is in fact a component analysis. It achieves a unique resolution of the original measurements into factors. No subjective judgment is called for at any stage of the method. In this method the first axis is selected so that the sum of the squares of the distances of points from the axis is minimized. Successive axes, each perpendicular to the preceding axes, are chosen so as to minimize the squares of the distance of the points from the new axis. Factor loadings on each successive axis become smaller and smaller until the number of factors reaches the rank of the correlation matrix. Usually, the factor loadings on the first few factors can reproduce the correlation matrix very well and the

analysis is concluded when such a stage has been reached. Thus the method, a true component analysis, is sometimes used to select a limited number of factors in the same way as a true factor analytic method might.

CENTROID METHOD

The computations required by the method of principal axes are extremely laborious. The most popular method of factor analysis, and one which demands much less labor is the *centroid method,* proposed by Burt (1917) and developed by Thurstone (1931), which was originally intended as an approximation to the principal axes factor solution. Its solution, however, is not unique and some subjective judgment is called for when each set of factor loadings is computed. The *centroid method* selects the first factor axis to pass through the center of gravity of points representing the original measurements. The factor loadings of each measurement on this factor will go a long way toward reproducing the correlation matrix. The difference between the elements of the correlation matrix and those of the attempted reproduction of it, using the first centroid factor, is now regarded as a new correlation matrix and is attacked in the same way. To carry out the next stage, however, it is necessary to alter from positive to negative, or vice versa, all the correlation coefficients involving certain measurements. This selection of measurements for "reflection" of sign, however, is largely subjective.

Currently the principal axes method is gaining favor. Its relative mathematical purity makes it generally desirable and high speed computers have at last made it quite practicable. With the ascendancy of this method the most important questions nowadays in factor analysis are not how it should be done but what it means—and whether it should be done at all.

REFERENCES

Burt, Cyril. *The Distribution and Relations of Educational Abilities.* London: P. S. King & Son, 1917.

Cureton, E. E. The Principal Compulsions of Factor Analysis, *Harvard Educational Review,* vol. 9, 1939, pp. 287–295.

Harmon, Harry F. *Modern Factor Analysis.* Chicago: University of Chicago Press, 1960.

Kendall, M. G. *A Course in Multivariate Analysis.* London: Charles Griffin, 1957.

Ramond, Charles K. *Factor Analysis in Advertising Research.* Unpublished speech to the Statistical Methods and Operations Research Discussion Group, American Marketing Association, March 30, 1961.

Thurstone, L. L. Multiple Factor Analysis. *Psychological Review,* vol. 38, 1931, pp. 406–427.

Numerical Taxonomy in Marketing Analysis:
A Review Article

Ronald E. Frank
Paul E. Green

Marketing managers and researchers often comment on their difficulty in developing useful ways of classifying customers for formulating marketing policy. The source of the difficulty frequently stems from the abundance of alternative classification methods rather than from a lack of possibilities. Changes in our concepts of customer behavior have more often been associated with the generation of new measures of behavior than with the integration of existing measures. In 50 years, researchers have stopped focusing almost exclusively on customer socioeconomic characteristics as a basis for policy formulation and have begun considering a wide range of measures of sociological and psychological phenomena (such as personality, preferences, buying intentions, perceived risk, interpersonal influence) and an increasing number of measures of actual buying behavior (such as total consumption and brand loyalty).

Much of customer behavior has many factors—it is multidimensional. Researchers often sidestep its complexity by picking some unidimensional attribute assumed to be an indicator of the more complex phenomena to be understood. For example, in studies of household brand loyalty (with respect to frequently purchased, branded food products), the researcher often finds variables used to measure brand loyalty such as the proportion of purchases spent on the most frequently purchased brand or the proportion spent on the brand that is of central interest to the researcher. For many purposes, however, these might be too limited a measure of loyalty since they fail to approximate a full description of a rather complex phenomenon. Customers do not typically buy a single brand or even two brands.

Reprinted with permission from the *Journal of Marketing Research,* vol. 5, no. 1 (February, 1968), pp. 83–98, published by the American Marketing Association.

Many households purchase three, four, or five brands of a product. In addition, the subset of brands chosen for consumption will vary from household to household.

What procedure could be used to study the clusters of brands that different households consume? All possible combinations of brands could be computed and households sorted into respective classes, but this approach presents a few problems. How many combinations are there in a market with only twelve brands? There are over four million if the number of partitions resulting from grouping twelve brands into two or more clusters is added.[1] Even worse, one may want to measure the similarity of brand purchasing behavior not only for the combination of brands but also for the relative proportion of money spent on each brand.

This kind of classification problem is not unique to brand loyalty. How are television programs classified for similarity of audience profiles? Here, too, practitioners often use a single category as the basis for classification, such as the modal audience group, (for example, teenagers loyal to "Rat Patrol"). How should market areas for choosing test markets be grouped? How can a potential purchaser compare the performance specifications of a wide range of computers? How should the readership characteristics of a number of alternative magazines be compared?

Almost every major analytical problem requires the classification of objects by several characteristics—whether customers, products, cities, television programs, or magazines. Seldom are explicit classification systems with some combination of attributes, such as those used for measuring a customer's social class or stage in life cycle, found. Such classification systems typically represent self-imposed taxonomies; that is, taxonomies the researcher believes to be relevant because of a theory or prior experience.[2] Although this approach can

---

[1] The general formula [29] for finding all possible partitions of a given set of entities is

$$P(n,m) = \left[m^n - \sum_{i=1}^{m-1} m_{(m-i)} P(i) \right] / m!$$

where
    m is number of partitions; $m \geqslant 2$
    n is number of entities in set to be clustered; $n \geqslant m$
    $P(m)$ is number of distinct partitions containing exactly m clusters
    $m_{(m-i)}$ is $m(m-1)(m-2) \cdots (m-i+1)$.

[2] Taxonomies can be distinguished from classifications since they denote interconnections (usually a hierarchy) among characteristics of the objects—a less generic term than classifications. In practice, however, the terms are often used interchangeably.

be useful, it has limitations. Regardless of the complexity of reality, it is difficult to classify objects by more than two or three characteristics at a time. If reality requires greater complexity, researchers are severely constrained by their conceptual limitations.

The difficulty of seeing through this often bewildering maze is not unique to marketing, (not to mention business problems) as indicated by Sokal, an entymologist:

Classification is one of the fundamental concerns of science. Facts and objects must be arranged in an orderly fashion before their unifying principles can be discovered and used as a basis for prediction. Many phenomena occur in such variety and profusion that unless some system is created among them, they would be unlikely to provide any useful information [82].

A new technology, numerical taxonomy, has been developed, primarily in biology. It consists of a set of numerical procedures for classifying objects [83]. These taxonomic procedures may be called preclassification techniques since their purpose is to describe the natural groupings that occur in large masses of data. From these natural groupings (or clusters) the researcher can sometimes develop the requisite conceptual framework for classification.

Numerical taxonomy is still new, and to the authors' knowledge, only three articles in marketing have appeared [34, 50, 66]. This article introduces potential marketing applications of this set of techniques, giving some attention to their mathematical bases, current limitations, and assumptions. The following topics are discussed:

1. the nature of taxonomic procedures,
2. illustrative applications of taxonomic methods to marketing problems,
3. the assumptions and limitations of the procedures.

The authors feel that taxonomic methods will be used increasingly to describe complex marketing data. Hopefully, this article will alert more researchers to the potential of these methods and to some of the cautions associated with use.

THE NATURE OF TAXONOMIC PROCEDURES

Assume that there is a set of objects, such as people, products, advertisements, and marketing channels, each of which can be characterized by a measurement (or more generally, by an attribute score) on each

of a set of characteristics. The researcher has no external criterion for grouping the objects into subsets of similar objects; instead, he wants to identify natural groupings in the data, after which more formal models might be developed.

More formally stated, the problem is: How should objects be assigned to groups so there will be as much likeness within groups and as much difference among groups as possible? From this question four others arise: (1) what proximity measure is to be used to summarize the likeness of profiles, (2) after these likeness measures have been computed, how should the objects be grouped, (3) after the objects have been grouped, what descriptive measures are appropriate for summarizing the characteristics of each group, (4) are the groups formed really different from each other (the inferential problem)?

There are numerous taxonomic procedures for achieving the major objective. The following discussion illustrates the logic of one of them, followed by a brief overview of other kinds of procedures that have been developed. The purpose is to show the relevance of these techniques for establishing multidimensional classification systems, not to provide a definitive methodological statement.

An Example

Suppose that the objects of interest are television programs and the characteristics are (assumed independent) measures of the socio-economic profile of each program. Let us start with measures of two characteristics, number of teenagers (X_1) and number of adult men (X_2), for each of ten programs. Our problem is to find a way of grouping the programs by the similarity of their audience profiles. Figure 1 plots the programs in two dimensions.

Assume that two clusters of five programs each are desired. A start is to compute Euclidean distances of every point from every other point with the usual formula:

$$\Delta_{jk} = [(X_{1j} - X_{1k})^2 + (X_{2j} - X_{2k})^2]^{1/2}.$$

Points 1 and 2 in Figure 1 appear to be closest together. The first cluster would then be formed by finding the midpoint between Points 1 and 2, the centroid of the point coordinates. Then the distance of each point from this average would be computed and the point closest to this average would be added (here, Point 3). Similarly, Point 4 and then Point 5 would be added, giving a cluster of five programs as desired.

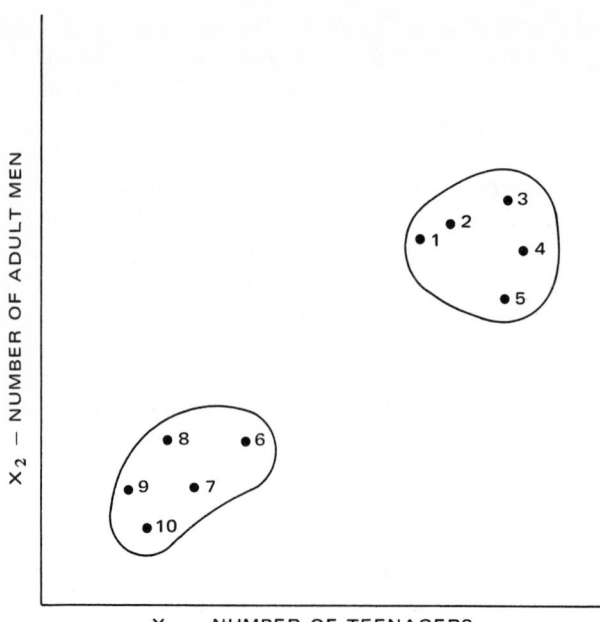

Figure 1   Illustration of taxonomic techniques (hypothetical)

Generalizing to More than Two Dimensions

In the previous illustration, only two measurements were considered for each point (television program). It is relatively easy to follow the procedure visually.[3] In practice there may be many measurements for each program; hence, the graphical procedure must be supplemented by a computational technique that can deal with several characteristics.

Several computer routines are available for this type of taxonomic analysis often called cluster analysis. For example, one computer routine used involves these steps:

1. Each characteristic is first converted to a standardized variate with zero mean and unit standard deviation.

---

[3] The typical Euclidean distance measure can be easily generalized to more than two dimensions as:

$$\Delta_{jk} = \left[\sum_{i=1}^{n} (X_{ij} - X_{ik})^2 \right]^{1/2}.$$

2. Euclidean distances are then computed for each of all possible pairs of points.

3. The pair with the smallest distance is chosen as the node of the first cluster, and the average of this pair is computed.

4. Additional points are added to this cluster (based on closeness to the last-computed average) until:
   a. Some prespecified number of points has been clustered.
   b. The point to be added to the cluster exceeds some prespecified distance-cutoff or threshold number.

5. The program then proceeds to the next pair of points which are closest together of all unclustered points, and the above process is repeated.

6. If desired, the program can be modified to allow points to be in more than one cluster.

7. The program can be further modified to shift points from cluster to cluster to obtain final clusters which are best in the sense of having the lowest average within-cluster distance summed over all clusters at a given stage in the clustering.

OTHER CLUSTERING TECHNIQUES

PROXIMITY MEASURES. This program is only one way to cluster points in multidimensional space. Other proximity measures and clustering techniques have been proposed by researchers in the biological and social sciences. With some simplification, the proximity measures can be categorized as:

1. distance measures,
2. correlation measures, and
3. similarity measures for attribute data.

The input data—nominal, ordinal, interval, ratio or mixed scales—often determines the proximity measure used to express pairwise relationships among the elements.

DISTANCE MEASURES. One kind of clustering technique based on Euclidean distance has already been described. Two problems exist with regard to this kind of measure: (1) correlated characteristics and (2) noncomparability of the original units in which the characteristics are measured [69]. The second problem is usually "solved" by standardizing all characteristics to mean zero and unit standard

deviation. Thus it is assumed that mean and variance among characteristics is not important in the grouping process.

The first problem can be handled two ways. A principal component analysis may be run on the characteristics and factor scores computed for the objects. Each component score may then be weighted by the square root of the eigenvalue associated with that component before computing the distance measure. A second approach uses the Mahalanobis [60] generalized distance in which the squared distances between objects is measured as a linear combination of the correlated measurements expressed in units of the estimated population dispersion of the composite measure. If the characteristics are uncorrelated and measurements are first standardized (mean zero and unit standard deviation), the square root of the Mahalanobis measure is equivalent to the Euclidean measure discussed.

In practice, distance measures of the kind just described are usually used when data are at least intervally scaled. Kendall [54], however, proposed a distance measure requiring only ordinally scaled measurements. Also, Restle [75] and others have shown that even nominally scaled data may be characterized in distance terms, in the sense of obeying the distance axioms. The resulting metric, however, may not be Euclidean.

CORRELATION MEASURES. Probably the most widely used proximity measure in clustering procedures involves the correlation coefficient.[4] Inverse factor analysis, the Q-technique, is a fairly widely used procedure in which objects replace tests in the computation of factor loadings. Clusters may then be formed by grouping subjects with similar factor loadings. Three problems are associated with this class of techniques. First, correlation removes the elevation and scatter of each object, thereby losing information. Second, in grouping objects by factor loadings, the analyst risks obtaining some objects that are split among clusters. Finally, the analyst must usually resort to an R-technique to interpret the clusters' characteristics according to their correlations with underlying factors.

SIMILARITY MEASURES. Similarity measures are often used in clustering when the characteristics of each object are only nominally scaled, for example, dichotomous or multichotomous. The usual notion of distance seems less applicable here (although it is still possible to use multidimensional scaling techniques to "metricize"

---

[4] If the characteristics are expressed in standard scores, the Euclidean distance between two objects is a monotone transformation of their correlation [18].

such data before clustering). Typically, however, the analyst tries to develop similarity coefficients based on attribute matching.

For example, if two objects are compared on each of eight attributes, the following might result:

ENTITY	ATTRIBUTE							
	1	*2*	*3*	*4*	*5*	*6*	*7*	*8*
1	1	0	0	1	1	0	1	0
2	0	1	0	1	0	1	1	1

The fractional match coefficient would be:

$$S_{12} = \frac{M}{N} = \frac{3}{8},$$

where M denotes the number of attributes held in common (matching 1's or 0's) and N denotes the total number of attributes. If weak matches (non-possession of the attribute) are to be deemphasized, the Tanimoto [76] coefficient is appropriate:

$$\text{Tanimoto } S_{ij} = \frac{\text{No. of attributes which are 1 for both objects } i \text{ and } j}{\text{No. of attributes which are 1 for either } i \text{ or } j, \text{ or both}}.$$

In this problem the coefficient would be $\frac{2}{7}$. Many other similarity measures have been developed that represent variations of the fractional match coefficient. (See [83].)

One interesting distance-type measure which can also be used for attribute matching is the pattern similarity coefficient, r_p, proposed by Cattell, Coulter, and Tsujioka [16]. In interval-scaled data, the coefficient compares the computed distance with that expected by chance alone:

$$r_{p(jk)} = \frac{E_i - \sum_{i=1}^{n} d^2_{(jk)}}{E_i + \sum_{i=1}^{n} d^2_{(jk)}},$$

where i is the number of dimensions, $d^2_{(jk)}$ is the squared Euclidean distance in standard units between entities j and k, and E_i is twice

the median chi-square value for i degrees of freedom. Cattell's coefficient has the convenient property of varying from $+1$ for complete agreement, 0 for no agreement, to -1 for inverse agreement.

The coefficient may also be adapted for dichotomous items as:

$$r'_p = \frac{E_i - d}{E_i + d} ,$$

where d represents the number of disagreements on d items.

Finally, some mention should be made of the mixed scale problem in which the characteristics are measured in different modes. One possibility is to degrade interval-scaled data into categories and use similarity coefficients. Another possibility is to upgrade nominally or ordinally scaled data. There seems to be no satisfactory solution to this problem although it is conceivable that some highly general measure of proximity, perhaps one derived from information theory, may be appropriate.

Clustering Routines

After the analyst has decided on some measure of pairwise proximity, he must still contend with the grouping process itself. A variety of approaches are possible. One major class of approaches to the clustering problem consists of hierarchical routines. For example, Edwards and Cavalli-Sforza [24] describe a clustering procedure (based on a least-squares technique) which first clusters the data into two groups. The procedure is repeated sequentially so that progressively smaller clusters are formed sequentially by splitting the original clusters. A hierarchical array is obtained. A variant of this procedure starts with clusters of one object each and builds new clusters hierarchically until one overall cluster results. This approach was described by Ward [93].

Other grouping routines use threshold or cutoff measures similar to the algorithm described earlier. Some procedures, for example, suggest selecting an object closest to the centroid of all the data to serve as a prime node around which other points are clustered until some threshold distance level is reached. An unclustered object farthest from the centroid of the first cluster may then be chosen as a new prime node. The process is continued, the third and subsequent prime nodes being selected on the basis of largest average distance from the centroids of clusters already formed.

Some grouping routines [24, 93] are highly metric since effective-

ness measures involve the computation of within-cluster variance around the centroid of the cluster members. Others [83] use only the proximity between an unclustered object and some single member of the clustered set as a criterion for set inclusion.

In Q-technique, objects are often clustered by highest factor loadings, a simple approach; but it does not use all available information.

Finally, there is the possibility of clustering by systematic space-density search routines in which the *n*-dimensional space is cut into hypercubes and the computer program counts the number of cases falling into each region. Relatively little work, however, has been done on this taxonomic routine.

Descriptive Characteristics of the Groups

Even after objects are grouped, each cluster must be characterized by its representative profile. In some instances the cluster's centroid is used as a description of its members. In others the actual profile of the object closest to the group's centroid may be used. As in choice of proximity measure and choice of grouping routine, however, the criteria for describing each group are usually ad hoc, a main problem being that *cluster* is still not a precisely defined term. Some of these problems and the inferential problem will be reconsidered later in this article.

ILLUSTRATIVE MARKETING APPLICATIONS

Some appreciation for the versatility and unresolved problems of taxonomic methods can be gained from the following short review of studies conducted by the authors in the past two years.

Clustering Analysis in Test Marketing

One of the earliest pilot applications involved the use of cluster analysis in the grouping of cities (standard metropolitan areas) for test marketing purposes [34]. Data for each of 88 cities were available on 14 measured characteristics, such as population, number of retail stores, percent non-white. A clustering program using the Euclidean distance measure grouped the cities into homogeneous five-point clusters. Centroids of each cluster in 14-space and average distances of each point from the grand centroid and from the centroid of its own cluster were obtained. As an alternative for comparison pur-

poses, the original data matrix was factored, and cluster analysis was performed on the resultant (standardized) factor scores.

The cluster analysis yielded some interesting findings. First, the cluster of five cities closest to the grand mean of all 88—Dayton, Columbus, Indianapolis, Syracuse, and New Haven—agreed well with various lists of typical cities prepared by such magazines as *Sales Management* and *Printers' Ink* indicating results consistent with industry judgment. This method also provides homogeneous groups of cities with centroids quite distant from the grand origin. Second, the combined procedure of factor analysis (and subsequent clustering of factor scores) indicated that two major dimensions, a city size construct and a demographic construct, explained most of the variance in the data.

This study was only a pilot effort. In practice, the marketing manager would use those city characteristics most relevant to his product line. The clusters could then serve as homogeneous blocks from which individual cities could be chosen to serve as treatment and control units, that is matched units for various experimental purposes.

Television Program Audience Profile Analysis

Grouping of television programs into clusters having similar audience profile, which was used to illustrate the nature of taxonomic procedures, comprises still another exploratory investigation currently in progress. American Research Bureau data for both day and evening programs in October, 1965, are the bases for this analysis. For each, program measures of the number of adult men and women in different age categories and the number of children and teenagers viewing the program are available. The primary objective is to group programs by viewer characteristics so that their grouping is a function of viewer reaction to content and casting—not to the effects of time of day, day of week, and lead-in programs.

The analysis is divided into two stages. The first is the adjustment of raw data for the effects of time of day, day of week, and lead-in programs. The adjustment is roughly analogous to making a cyclical adjustment in a time series analysis to ensure a cleaner set of data for studying trend movements. When variations in audience profile from program to program are caused primarily by the effect of program content and casting, the adjusted data are subjected to a taxonomic analysis. The first stage of the study is complete, and the taxonomic work is about to begin. (It will soon appear as a working paper [30].)

Patterns of Customer Brand Loyalty

At the beginning of this article the study of brand loyalty was used to illustrate the tendency for letting unidimensional measures represent customer behavior that may be multidimensional. In this study cluster analysis and Kruskal's algorithm [56] is used to characterize customer brand purchasing behavior. The objective is to develop more comprehensive classification systems for analyzing brand choice.

Chicago Tribune panel data for three product categories (carbonated beverages, regular coffee, and ready-to-eat cereals) for 1961 were used in the analysis. For each product category for each of 480 households, the percentage of units (based on weight) purchased by brand was computed.

Two different approaches were then taken. A Euclidean distance measure was used to group households that had relatively similar percentage distributions of brand purchasing behavior within a product. This is equivalent to studying brand loyalty for the bundle of brands households purchase. The results showed that with only one exception in the regular coffee market each cluster of households bought only one brand at a rate greater than the brand's overall market share. Although other brands were purchased, none was given this degree of favor. The only exceptions are the clusters containing several private brands. Households that purchase one private brand at a greater rate than its overall share are likely to purchase another with a similar degree of concentration. Customers who buy them may be less sensitive to differences in product characteristics, or the products themselves may be more similar.

A second approach organized the data by brand instead of by customer. This part of the analysis started with the transpose of the data matrix used, that is the data were organized by brand and within brand, by household. For each brand the percentage of purchases devoted to that brand by each of about 100 households was available. Euclidean distance measures characterized brand similarity by pattern of purchase requirements over households.

Results so far have provided few surprises and have raised more questions than can be answered here. For example in the cereal market, evidence appears that old standard brands (Kellogg's Corn Flakes, Cheerios, Wheaties) tend to serve segments which overlap, yet many health-oriented cereals (Special K, All Bran, Grape Nuts) tend to serve a somewhat different group of customers.

An Experimental Gaming Application

Another application of clustering was prompted by experimental data obtained in studying the relationship between risk taking (in a no-information-improvement context) and the propensity to acquire uncertainty-reducing information in an information-buying context [35]. Data were available for 42 men and women subjects on a variety of behavioral and personality variables.

Preliminary analysis using a variety of multivariate techniques showed little support for the study's primary hypotheses. Part of the problem was thought to be that different subjects were using different behavioral models; these differences became obscured in the process of data aggregation. Accordingly, each subject's behavior in the experiment was viewed as a point in task performance space, the axes of which were represented by the situational and personality variables comprising the experimental situation. Subjects were then clustered by their similarities to each other over the whole experiment.

This procedure produced various clusters of subjects—some supported the hypothesis and others suggested other kinds of behavioral models. The potentialities of this approach appear provocative in the examination of experimental gaming data generally. Perhaps even more interesting, however, is the application of this kind of approach to the design of behavioral experiments. Alternative explanatory models are the rule rather than the exception in experimental games. Before collecting any data the researcher could characterize the play of ideal subjects (those whose behavior corresponded to each alternative model) by points in experimental performance space. Levels of the experimental variables might then be chosen to maximize the discrimination among alternative models before the experiment is conducted.

Operational Characterization of Inter-Brand Competition

In another pilot study, cluster analysis helped to characterize inter-brand competition in the computer field [38]. Performance data were obtained for over 100 different computer models with installation date used to categorize them as first- or second-generation models. For each computer model, data were available on 12 measured characteristics, such as word length, execution time, digital storage,

transfer rate, and 10 categorical characteristics, such as whether the computer possessed Boolean operations, table look-up, and indirect addressing.

The data's mixed character (continuous variables and dichotomous features data) required a different approach from that typically used in cluster analysis. First, the attribute data were metricized by a multidimensional scaling technique [56]. A two-dimensional representation revealed that each computer model could be characterized by the dimensions of capacity (number of different features) and orientation (scientific versus business), as based on the particular pattern of zeroes and ones.

The resultant clusters, developed by a hierarchical grouping technique, displayed interesting characteristics from the standpoint of intermodel competition. For example, a machine's cluster of features appears to be idiosyncratic to the particular manufacturer, that is, each manufacturer tends to build all his machines with a particular set of features. Each manufacturer's complex, however, may vary from that of his competitors. It is interesting that only IBM had a model in each of the major clusters. However, the time period comparison—first- versus second-generation computers—indicated a trend toward all models having a greater number of features.

The measured variables were then analyzed separately, yielding two main dimensions—speed and size of computers. Finally, the measured data were dichotomized about the median of each characteristic (taken separately) and submitted to a combination multidimensional scaling and cluster analysis.

Figure 2 shows a two-space configuration derived from applying a nonmetric program to proximity measures developed from the above steps. After adjusting for intercorrelation of the characteristics [39], similarity measures were developed by tabulating the number of (weighted) matches for all computer pairs. The higher this number, the more similar each pair was assumed to be with respect to all 22 performance characteristics. For $n = 55$, there are 1,485 interpoint proximities as input to the program; only their rank order is required.

The two-space configuration of Figure 2 shows the boundaries of clusters formed (by another means) on a more precise configuration obtained in four-space. Such compression of results (into two-space) seriously distorts the makeup of Cluster 8; otherwise the clusters are fairly compact. It is interesting to note that Cluster 5 is composed of small, fairly slow, business-oriented machines, but Cluster 7 is characterized by large, relatively fast, scientific machines.

The complete study on which Figure 2 is based revealed that four

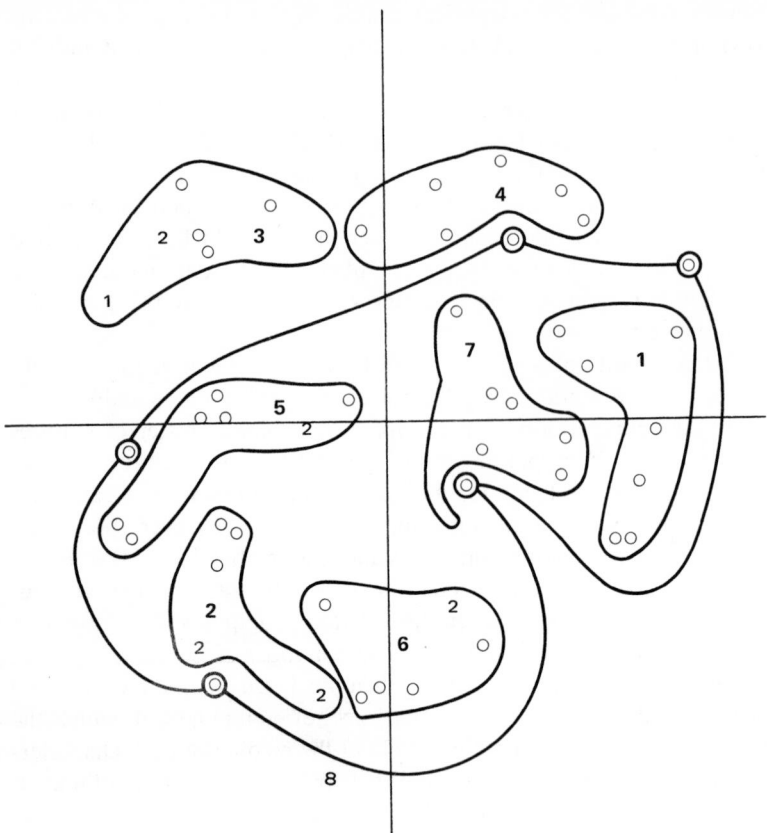

Figure 2   Two-space configuration of computer models in "performance space"

dimensions—speed, size, number of different features (qualitative characteristics), and orientation (scientific versus business)—appeared to adequately describe the computer market.

The possibilities of such performance-space analyses over time have potential for the study of product innovation and modification—particularly industrial products like electric motors and machine tools. In this approach a whole series of performance spaces could be viewed through time—their dimensions, number of points (models), and interrelationships among points could all be changing, reflecting changes in technology and inter-model competition. Such an approach would seem to indicate the data's fine structure better than the more traditional reliance on S-curves to describe product life cycles.

Physician's Media Reading Habits

In another study [41], numerical taxonomy was used to cluster reading profiles of both physicians and medical journals. The basic data consisted of zero-one matrixes in which each physician was classified as a light (zero) or heavy (one) reader of each of 19 medical journals. Each physician was also classified as one who lightly or heavily prescribed each of 29 therapeutic drug classes. Data were also available on the physician's speciality, age, and total weekly patient and prescription loads. The zero-one matrixes were again metricized by a multidimensional scaling program. Clusters of journals with similar, physician reading habits and clusters of physicians with similar journal profiles were developed.

Findings indicated that, within a given specialty, media reading profiles are not associated with such variables as physician age, total prescribing frequency, and product mix selection. However, the journal clusters provided an interesting output of the analysis by summarizing a diverse set of zero-one data. The marketing manager could use these clusters as a guide to media scheduling. For example, if he wishes to choose journals with high overlap of coverage, he can choose all journals within a given cluster. If, however, he wishes to emphasize diversity, he can choose one journal from each cluster.

From a methodological viewpoint, the interesting concept is the dual use of multidimensional scaling and cluster analysis. The first technique allows the researcher to make a concise description of the data—frequently interpretable in its own right—and the last allows him to organize the data into similar journal profiles that can then be subjected to further analysis.

Taxonomy in Psychometric Studies

Some mention should also be made of the usefulness of clustering procedures in psychometric studies involving perceptual and preference mapping. A recently completed study [36] involved the analysis of proximities data developed during a study of student perception of six graduate schools of business. Three modes of data collection—similarity triads, direct ratings, and the semantic differential—were used to collect proximity judgments.

In this study a hierarchical grouping method was used to develop clusters of respondents with similar perceptions of the six business

schools. That is, although the main objective of this study was the development of perceptual maps, cluster analysis was useful in partitioning the respondents into homogeneous groups with similar perceptions.

The results indicated that a two-space solution adequately portrayed the respondents' perceptions. From other data collected in the study, the dimensions of the space could be characterized as prestige of school and quantitativeness of its curriculum. Not inconsequentially all three data collection methods yielded fairly similar perceptual maps, on an aggregate basis. Moreover, differences in perceptual mappings were not generally explainable by respondent personal data, such as undergraduate major, previous work experience, graduate major. Only one variable, home state of respondent, appeared to influence his perception of the business schools in any significant way.

A similar study [37] involved a multidimensional scaling of professional journals typically read by marketing academics and researchers. Perception and preference data were obtained for eight journals, and respondents were clustered on the basis of similarity of perception and preference.

Figure 3 shows the results of applying a nonmetric clustering routine to the perception data [37]. Note that this program is hierarchical. Respondents 4 and 7 are first clustered because they had the highest proximity measure of the group. Respondents 2 and 11 are next clustered at level two, and so on, until all points are eventually in one large cluster. On the left-hand side of Figure 3 one can see how the proximity measure declines as more disparate points are clustered.

The results of this study indicated that preferences and perception were independent over stimuli, that is respondents clustered by commonality of perception were unrelated to clusters formed by commonality of preference.

ASSUMPTIONS AND LIMITATIONS OF CLUSTERING METHODS

Cluster analysis is not a single, cohesive set of techniques but rather a variety of procedures, each having a kind of ad hoc flavor and certain advantages and disadvantages. Some of the limitations are shared by all these techniques to some degree, but specific procedures have both advantages and disadvantages.

PROXIMITY MEASURE	12		05		07		04	03		11	02		06		08	01		10	09
1.8253	·	·	·	·	×	×	×	·	·	·	·	·	·	·	·	·	·	·	·
1.7745	·	·	·	·	×	×	×	·	·	·	×	×	·	·	·	·	·	·	·
1.7111	·	·	·	·	×	×	×	×	×	·	×	×	·	·	·	·	·	·	·
1.6871	×	×	×	·	×	×	×	×	×	·	×	×	·	·	·	·	·	·	·
1.5961	×	×	×	·	×	×	×	×	×	·	×	×	·	·	·	·	·	·	·
1.4724	×	×	×	·	×	×	×	×	×	·	×	×	×	×	·	·	·	·	·
1.3715	×	×	×	·	×	×	×	×	×	·	×	×	×	×	×	×	×	·	·
1.2901	×	×	×	×	×	×	×	×	×	×	×	×	×	×	×	×	×	·	·
1.1388	×	×	×	×	×	×	×	×	×	×	×	×	×	×	×	×	×	·	·
1.0558	×	×	×	×	×	×	×	×	×	×	×	×	×	×	×	×	×	·	×
0.8077	×	×	×	×	×	×	×	×	×	×	×	×	×	×	×	×	×	×	×

SUBJECT NUMBER

Figure 3   Illustration of hierarchical clustering routine

General Problems in Cluster Analysis

All clustering techniques have certain general analytical inadequacies because the data are used to generate the groupings. Illustrative questions are:

1. How many clusters should be formed?
2. If, as is usually the case, the characteristics of the objects are measured in different units, how can equivalence among metrics be achieved?
3. If the objects' scores along several dimensions are intercorrelated, how should these interdependencies be handled?
4. Even if the number of clusters can be determined in some satisfactory way, how does the analyst decide on the appropriate boundaries for clusters, summary measures of the characteristics of each cluster, and their statistical significance?

In some of the illustrative applications described here, the number of clusters was decided in advance. Increasing the number of clusters will tend to reduce the average within-cluster distance but, obviously, one must stop short of ending with each point being a cluster.

In addition, all data including variables originally interval-scaled were standardized to zero mean and unit standard deviation. Although this step enables the analyst to work with common metrics, it is assumed that central tendency and variability among dimensions are not important.

The problem of dealing with intercorrelated characteristics was pointed out in the test marketing illustration. In this study an alternative procedure was used in which the set of characteristics was first reduced to independent constructs by a principal component analysis before the cluster analysis. This procedure can lead to different clusters from those obtained by the first procedure that ignored the intercorrelations among characteristics. Finally, the researcher might wish to use the Mahalanobis generalized distance measure discussed by Morrison [66].

Appropriate boundaries and descriptive statistics of clusters are usually determined by the specific technique used—in many instances by a generalized distance function, the computation of centroids, and the use of a preset number of points or cutoff distances. Even so, it is fair to say that good measures of cluster compactness are not available. In the test marketing illustration each dimension included

in the analysis was given (manifest) equal weight in determining similarity. In a given situation one might choose to give a single dimension or some subset of dimensions more weight than others in defining proximity measures. Cluster analysis can be easily modified to take into account unequal weights, but this approach still largely varies with circumstances.

Still less is known about the inferential characteristics of clustering techniques. Unlike other multivariate techniques, such as discriminant analysis and principal component analysis, clustering techniques are much less structured, and little investigation has been made to date of their statistical properties.

Limitations of Specific Proximity Measures

In earlier sections of this article, the characteristics of specific proximity measures—distance measures, correlation techniques, similarity coefficients—were briefly described. Each measure suffers from certain specific limitations.

Distance measures are usually restricted to instances in which the objects' characteristics to be measured can be expressed as interval-scaled variables. This represents a limitation on the kind of variable meaningfully handled although Kendall's nonparametric measure (mentioned earlier) could be used to handle data that are scaled only ordinally and the researcher could develop non-Euclidean metrics.

In addition, the Euclidean measure suffers from the disadvantage that two objects may be viewed as different solely because their values on one variable differ markedly. Finally, it should be reiterated that the researcher would, in general, obtain different results by using original versus standardized data for the characteristics of the objects being clustered by this method.

Correlative techniques, such as Q-factor analysis, have an even more serious limitation because one must standardize over objects, thus losing mean and scatter information. That is, in this technique, each object is given the same mean and variance.

A second disadvantage is that rotation of factor axes (to get purer loadings) lends a certain arbitrariness to the procedure. Finally, also mentioned earlier, in this procedure objects may be split on factors, leading to uncertainty of the placement of an object into a specific group.

Similarity measures are flexible since they can be adapted to handle nominal, ordinal, and interval-scaled data. Furthermore, it can be shown that similarity measures can be metricized by multidimensional-

scaling procedures. Moreover, similarity measures are generally less sensitive to the impact of a single characteristic on the resultant dissimilarity of two objects than are the Euclidean distance measures.

However, similarity measures have their set of limitations. First, if a group is to be formed on the basis of overall matches, two objects may not be grouped even if they match well on some subset of characteristics. Conversely, an object may be in a group because it is similar to different members of the group on different subsets of characteristics.

Second, if a large number of characteristics are involved, objects which match may do so for accidental reasons, reflecting the noise in the data; and third, if some variables are dichotomous and others are multichotomous, the two-state attributes will tend to be more heavily weighted in the similarity measures. For example, if one attribute were broken down into 100 states, we would rarely find matches. Hence this attribute would receive little importance in the overall similarity measure.

Finally, if continuous data are discretized in order to use similarity measures, valuable information can be lost. The analyst is thus plagued with the problem of deciding both the kinds of attributes to include in the analysis and the number of states to be associated with each.

Choosing Appropriate Techniques

Numerical taxonomy invites some ambivalence by the analyst wanting to use the techniques. On one hand, the procedures are designed to cope with a relevant aspect of marketing description—the orderly classification of multivariate phenomena. On the other hand, the varying character of various proximity measures and clustering techniques—and the basic lack of structure at either the descriptive statistic or inferential statistic level—suggests that the analyst be cautious in applying them.

Until more structure is introduced, it seems prudent to conduct analyses in parallel where alternative proximity measures and grouping procedures are used [40]. Moreover, sensitivity analyses on synthetic data might be helpful in exploring the various idiosyncracies of alternative techniques. If the data are well clustered to begin with, similar results over alternative techniques will usually be obtained—but how often will these pleasant states of affairs exist? Though the authors believe numerical taxonomy can be useful in marketing analysis, they would urge prudence in its application and the sys-

tematic study of similarities and differences among alternative procedures. (The references may help to facilitate this study.)

REFERENCES

1. G. H. Ball, "Data Analysis in the Social Sciences: What About the Details?" *Proceedings Fall Joint Computer Conference,* 1965, 533–59.

2. B. M. Bass, "Iterative Inverse Factor Analysis: A Rapid Method for Clustering Persons," *Psychometrika,* 22 (March 1957), 105.

3. J. F. Bennett and W. L. Hays, "Multidimensional Unfolding: Determining the Dimensionality of Ranked Preference Data," *Psychometrika,* 25 (March 1960), 27–43.

4. A. Birnbaum and A. E. Maxwell, "Classification Procedures Based on Bayes' Formula," *Applied Statistics,* 9 (November 1961), 152–68.

5. Jack Block, "The Difference Between Q and R," *Psychological Review,* 62 (1955), 356–8.

6. ———, Louis Levine and Quinn McNemar, "Testing for the Existence of Psychometric Patterns," *Journal of Abnormal Social Psychology,* 46 (July 1951), 356–9.

7. R. E. Bonner, "Some Clustering Techniques," *IBM Journal of Research and Development,* 8 (January 1964), 22–33.

8. A. D. Booth, "An Application of the Method of Steepest Descent to the Solution of Simultaneous Non-linear Equations," *Quarterly Journal of Mech. Applied Mathematics,* 2 (December 1949), 460–8.

9. G. E. P. Box, "The Exploration and Exploitation of Response Surfaces: Some General Considerations and Examples," *Biometrics,* 10 (March 1954), 16–60.

10. S. H. Brooks, "A Discussion of Random Methods of Seeking Maxima," *Journal of Operations Research Society,* 6 (1958), 244–51.

11. ———, "A Comparison of Maximum Seeking Methods," *Journal of Operations Research Society,* 7 (1959), 430–57.

12. Cyril L. Burt, "Correlations Between Persons," *British Journal of Psychology,* 28 (July 1937), 59–96.

13. H. Cartwright, *Structural Models: An Introduction to the Theory of Directed Graphs,* New York: John Wiley & Sons, Inc., 1963.

14. Raymond B. Cattell, "r_p and Other Coefficients of Pattern Similarity," *Psychometrika,* 14 (December 1949), 279–98.

15. ———, "On the Disuse and Misuse of R, P, Q and O Techniques in Clinical Psychology," *Journal of Clinical Psychology,* 7 (1951), 203–14.

16. ———, M. A. Coulter and B. Tsujioka, "The Taxonometric Recognition of Types and Functional Emergents," in R. B. Cattell, ed., *Handbook of Multivariate Experimental Psychology,* Chicago: Rand McNally and Co., 1966, 288–329.

17. W. W. Cooley and Paul R. Lohnes, *Multivariate Procedures for the Behavioral Sciences,* New York: John Wiley & Sons, Inc., 1963.

18. C. H. Coombs, *A Theory of Data,* New York: John Wiley & Sons, Inc., 1964.

19. ———, "A Method for the Study of Interstimulus Similarity," *Psychometrika,* 19 (September 1954), 183–94.

20. Douglas R. Cox, "Note on Grouping," *Journal of American Statistical Association,* 52 (December 1957), 543–47.

21. Lee J. Cronbach and Goldine C. Gleser, "Assessing Similarity Between Profiles," *Psychological Bulletin,* 50 (November 1953), 456–73.

22. Frank M. duMas, "A Quick Method of Analyzing the Similarity of Profiles," *Journal of Clinical Psychology,* 2 (January 1946), 80–3.

23. ———, "On the Interpretation of Personality Profiles," *Journal of Clinical Psychology,* 3 (1947), 57–65.

24. A. W. F. Edwards and L. L. Cavalli-Sforza, "A Method for Cluster Analysis," *Biometrics,* 52 (June 1965), 362–75.

25. G. A. Ferguson, "The Factorial Interpretation of Test Difficulty," *Psychometrika,* 6 (October 1941), 323–29.

26. R. A. Fisher, "The Use of Multiple Measurements in Taxonomic Problems," *American Eugenics,* 7 (1963), 179–88.

27. W. D. Fisher, "On Grouping for Maximum Homogeneity," *Journal of American Statistical Association,* 53 (December 1958), 789–98.

28. Claude Flament, *Applications of Graph Theory to Group Structure,* New Jersey: Prentice-Hall, Inc., 1963.

29. J. J. Fortier and H. Solomon, "Clustering Procedures," Unpublished paper, International Symposium on Multivariate Analysis, University of Dayton, June 1965.

30. Ronald E. Frank, "Television Program Audience Similarities: A Taxonomic Analysis," University of Pennsylvania, December 1967, mimeographed.

31. Eugene L. Gaier and Marilyn C. Lee, "Pattern Analysis: The Configural Approach to Predictive Measurement," *Psychological Bulletin,* 50 (March 1953), 140–8.

32. J. A. Gengerelli, "A Method for Detecting Subgroups in a Population and Specifying Their Membership," *Journal of Psychology,* 55 (1953), 140–48.

33. L. A. Goodman and W. H. Kruskal, "Measures of Association for Cross Classifications," *Journal of American Statistical Association,* 59 (September 1964), 732–64.

34. Paul E. Green, Ronald E. Frank and Patrick J. Robinson, "Cluster Analysis in Test Market Selection," *Management Science,* 13 (April 1967), 387–400.

35. ———, "A Behavioral Experiment in Risk Taking and Information Seeking," Working paper, University of Pennsylvania, January 1967.

36. Paul E. Green and P. J. Robinson, "Perceptual Structure of Graduate Business Schools—An Application of Multidimensional Scaling," Working paper, June 1967.

37. ———, "Perceptual and Preference Mapping of Professional Journals," Working paper, May 1967.

38. ——— and F. J. Carmone, "Structural Characteristics of the Computer Market—An Application of Cluster and Reduced Space Analysis," Working paper, May 1967.

39. ———, "WAGS: An IBM 7040 Computer Program for Obtaining Weighted Agreement Scores for Multidimensional Scaling," Working paper, May 1967.

40. ———, "Cross Techniques Study—Computer Model Clustering," Working paper, August 1967.

41. ———, "A Reduced Space and Cluster Analysis of Physicians' Media Reading Habits," Working paper, September 1967.

42. H. H. Harman, *Modern Factor Analysis,* Chicago: University of Chicago Press, 1960.

43. C. W. Harris, "Characteristics of Two Measures of Profile Similarity," *Psychometrika,* 20 (1955), 289–97.

44. G. C. Helmstadter, "An Empirical Comparison of Methods for Estimating Profile Similarity," *Educational and Psychological Measurement,* 17 (1957), 71–82.

45. J. L. Hodges, Jr., "Discriminatory Analysis I: Survey of Discriminatory Analysis," USAF School of Aviation Medicine, Randolph, Texas, 1950.

46. Karl J. Holzinger, "Factoring Test Scores and Implications for the Method of Averages," *Psychometrika,* 9 (December 1944), 257–62.

47. Paul Horst, *Matrix Algebra for Social Scientists,* New York: Holt, Rinehart and Winston, 1963.

48. ———, "Pattern Analysis and Configural Scoring," *Journal of Clinical Psychology,* 10 (January 1954), 1–11.

49. K. J. Jones, *The Multivariate Statistical Analyzer,* Cambridge, Mass.: Harvard Cooperative Society, 1964.

50. J. Joyce and C. Charron, "Classifying Market Survey Respondents," *Applied Statistics*, 15 (November 1966), 191–215.

51. H. F. Kaiser, "Formulas for Component Scores," *Psychometrika*, 27 (March 1962), 83–7.

52. M. G. Kendall, *The Advanced Theory of Statistics*, Vol. 1, New York: Hafner Publishing Company, 1958.

53. ———, *Rank Correlation Methods*, London: Griffin Publishing Company, 1948.

54. ———, "Discrimination and Classification," London: CEIR Ltd., 1965.

55. J. B. Kruskal, "Nonmetric Multidimensional Scaling: A Numerical Scaling Method," *Psychometrika*, 29 (June 1964), 115–30.

56. ———, "Multidimensional Scaling by Optimizing Goodness of Fit to a Nonmetric Hypothesis," *Psychometrika*, 29 (March 1964), 1–28.

57. E. O. Laumann and L. Guttman, "The Relative Association Contiguity of Occupations in an Urban Setting," *American Sociological Review*, 31 (April 1966), 169–78.

58. J. C. Lingoes, "A Taxonometric Optimization Procedure: An IBM 7090 Classification Program," *Behavioral Science*, 8 (October 1963), 370.

59. ———, "An IBM 7090 Program for Guttman-Lingoes Smallest Space Analysis," Computer Center, University of Michigan, 1965.

60. P. C. Mahalanobis, "On the Generalized Distance in Statistics," *Proceedings National Institute of Science*, 12, India, 1936, 49–58.

61. F. Massarik and P. Ratoosh, *Mathematical Explorations in Behavioral Science*, Homewood, Ill.: Richard D. Irwin, Inc., 1965.

62. P. McNaughton-Smith, *et al.*, "Dissimilarity Analysis: A New Technique of Hierarchical Subdivision," *Nature*, 202 (June 1964), 1033–4.

63. Louis L. McQuitty, "Hierarchical Syndrome Analysis," *Educational and Psychological Measurement*, 20 (1960), 293–304.

64. ———, "Typal Analysis," *Educational and Psychological Measurement*, 20 (1960), 293–304.

65. ———, "Best Classifying Every Individual at Every Level," *Educational and Psychological Measurement*, 23 (July 1963), 337–46.

66. Donald G. Morrison, "Measurement Problems in Cluster Analysis," *Management Science*, 13 (August 1967), B-755–80.

67. Jum Nunnally, "The Analysis of Profile Data," *Psychological Bulletin*, 59 (July 1962), 311–19.

68. Charles E. Osgood and George J. Suci, "A Measure of Relation Determined by Both Mean Difference and Profile Information," *Psychological Bulletin*, 49 (May 1952), 251–62.

69. J. E. Overall, "Note on Multivariate Methods of Profile Analysis," *Psychological Bulletin,* 61 (March 1964), 195–8.

70. K. Pearson, "On the Dissection of Asymmetrical Frequency Curves," *Contributions to the Mathematical Theory of Evolution, Phil. Trans. of Royal Society,* 1894.

71. ———, "On the Coefficient of Racial Likeness," *Biometrika,* 18 (July 1926), 105–17.

72. R. G. Pettit, "Clustering Program: Continuous Variables," Advanced Systems Development Division, IBM, Yorktown Heights, New York, 1964.

73. C. R. Rao, "Tests of Significance in Multivariate Analysis," *Biometrika,* 35 (May 1948), 58–79.

74. ———, "The Utilization of Multiple Measurements in Problems of Biological Classification," *Journal of Royal Statistical Society,* Section B, 10 (1948), 159–203.

75. F. Restle, *Psychology of Judgment and Choice,* New York: John Wiley & Sons, Inc., 1961.

76. D. J. Rogers and T. T. Tanimoto, "A Computer Program for Classifying Plants," *Science,* 132 (October 1960), 1115–22.

77. P. J. Rulon, "Distinctions Between Discriminant and Regression Analysis and a Geometric Interpretation of the Discriminant Function," *Harvard Educational Review,* 21 (June 1951), 80–90.

78. R. N. Shepard, "The Analysis of Proximities: Multidimensional Scaling With an Unknown Distance Functions: I and II," *Psychometrika,* 27 (June 1962, September 1962), 125–40, 219–46.

79. ———, "Analysis of Proximities as a Technique for the Study of Information Processing in Man," *Human Factors,* 5 (February 1963), 33–48.

80. G. G. Simpson, "Numerical Taxonomy and Biological Classification," *Science,* 144 (May 1964), 712–13.

81. P. H. A. Sneath, "The Application of Computers to Taxonomy," *Journal of General Micro-Biology,* 17 (August 1957), 201–27.

82. R. R. Sokal, "Numerical Taxonomy," *Scientific American,* 215 (December 1966), 106–16.

83. ——— and P. H. A. Sneath, *Principles of Numerical Taxonomy,* San Francisco: Freeman & Company, 1963.

84. William Stephenson, "Some Observations on Q Technique," *Psychological Bulletin,* 49 (September 1952), 483–98.

85. S. A. Stouffer, *et al., Measurement and Prediction,* Princeton, N.J.: Princeton University Press, 1950.

86. Robert L. Thorndike, "Who Belongs in the Family?", *Psychometrika,* 18 (December 1953), 267–76.

87. Warren S. Torgerson, "Multidimensional Scaling: Theory and Method," *Psychometrika,* 17 (December 1952), 401–19.

88. ————, "Multidimensional Scaling of Similarity," *Psychometrika,* 30 (December 1965), 379–93.

89. Fred T. Tyler, "Some Examples of Multivariate Analysis in Educational and Psychological Research," *Psychometrika,* 17 (September 1952), 289–96.

90. Robert C. Tyron, *Cluster Analysis,* Edwards Bros., 1939.

91. ————, "Cumulative Communality Cluster Analysis," *Educational and Psychological Measurement,* 18 (March 1958), 3–35.

92. J. W. Tukey, "The Future of Data Analysis," *Annals of Mathematical Statistics,* 33 (March 1962), 1–67.

93. J. H. Ward, "Hierarchical Grouping to Optimize an Objective Function," *Journal of American Statistical Association,* 58 (March 1963), 236–44.

94. Joe E. Ward, Jr., and Marion E. Hook, "Application of an Hierarchical Grouping Procedure to a Problem of Grouping Profiles," *Educational and Psychological Measurement,* 23 (1963), 69–82.

95. Harold Webster, "A Note on Profile Similarity," *Psychological Bulletin,* 49 (September 1952), 538–9.

96. Joseph Zubin, "A Technique for Measuring Like-Mindedness," *Journal of Abnormal Social Psychology,* 33 (October 1938), 508–16.

Canonical Analysis: An Exposition and Illustrative Application

·   *Paul E. Green*
Michael H. Halbert
Patrick J. Robinson

The purpose of this article is to describe a specific multivariate procedure—canonical analysis—and to illustrate its use in a correlation study which grew out of an attempt to relate information buying behavior to various personality characteristics of subjects who participated in an experimental game. Unlike some other multivariate statistical techniques, such as factor analysis and discriminatory analysis, canonical correlation has received little attention in past reports of marketing research studies. Its potential advantages and limitations, and its relationship to other multivariate techniques, constitute the emphasis of this article.

The reader is no doubt familiar with multiple linear regression analysis, which can be appropriate when one wishes to predict the value of a single criterion variable from a linear function of a set of predictor variables.[1] In some instances, however, interest may not center on a single criterion variable; that is, the analyst may be interested in relationships between *sets* of variables or relationships within a single set. Canonical correlation is a subclass of multivariate analysis which, as defined by Kendall is that "branch of statistical analysis which is concerned with relationships of sets of dependent variates [12]."

One way to view the nature of multivariate techniques (*e.g.,* factor

Reprinted with permission from the *Journal of Marketing Research,* vol. 3, no. 1 (February, 1966), pp. 32–39, published by the American Marketing Association.

[1] Strictly speaking, multiple linear regression is to be distinguished from multivariate correlation in terms of assumptions underlying the model-fixed values for the predictor variables in the former, versus multinormal distributions in the latter.

analysis, discriminant functions, multivariate regression, canonical analysis) is in terms of the questions these techniques, considered generally, are designed to answer. In a marketing context we may encounter questions like the following:

1. We have assembled data on types of programs watched by a group of TV viewers. Can we identify various program types? If so, do any particular programs serve as "bellwhethers" of the listenership habits of various program types? Furthermore, can we arrange individuals in some type of meaningful order within a program class?

2. A sample of purchasers of a given product class can be measured in terms of a set of socioeconomic characteristics such as, income, occupation, living quarters, and so on. Can we assign purchasers to brands in the product class based on their socioeconomic profile?

3. A field experiment for a recently introduced product is designed, in which we are interested in several responses (awareness level, product preference, first purchase, repeat purchase) as related to several stimuli (advertising theme, media used to convey the message, frequency of ad placement). How can we test hypotheses regarding various "treatment" effects?

4. A researcher interested in the study of comparative marketing systems has multiple measurements (GNP, electricity, consumption, birthrates, literacy level, etc.) for 50 different countries. How can countries be grouped in terms of some overall measure of "similarity"?

5. A set of package designs is being tested on a large group of consumers. Two measurements—"esthetic appeal" and "functionality" —are developed from consumer responses to the various designs. In addition, the consumers take a set of personality tests. Can an index of design "satisfaction" (as associated with personality types) be constructed?

With the foregoing questions as background, a brief discussion of each major subclass of multivariate methods in terms of the objectives underlying each technique can now be made:

1. *In factor analysis* [8, 13, 16, 17] no particular variable is singled out as a criterion, or "dependent" variable. Rather, the analyst is concerned with any or all of the following purposes:

    a. Reducing a set of observed relationships (usually a correlation matrix) to a smaller, more parsimonious set of variables which can be used to reproduce the original set of intercorrelations with little loss of information.

b. Attempting to identify the reduced set of variables, either independent or related, in terms of dimensions or constructs of which the observed variables are linear combinations.

c. Determining index values for the individuals comprising the sample in terms of linear combinations of the underlying constructs.

2. In *linear discriminatory analysis* [14], the criterion variable is categorical, while the predicator variables are continuous measurements. The discriminant(s) is determined from known assignment of sample members to categories. The objectives of this class of techniques are to:

a. Predict an individual's group assignment to one of two or more categories on the basis of his scores on the set of measured characteristics.

b. Test whether the sample groups have arisen from a single population versus two or more populations.

c. Determine the relative importance of each predictor variable in making "optimal" assignments of individuals to categories.

3. In *multivariate analysis of variance* [1], the response criterion is multidimensional rather than unidimensional, as is the case with conventional analysis of variance procedures. For example, the analyst may be interested in testing various hypotheses regarding advertising copy design in terms of reader recall and preference. The objectives of this class of techniques are to:

a. Test the significance of differences among groups where the criterion variable is multidimensional.

b. Remove effects of uncontrolled variables (multivariate covariance analysis) so as to reduce the size of experimental error.

c. Provide "point" and interval estimates of pertinent criterion variables.

4. The distinguishing feature of *cluster analysis* [10] is that no assignment of individuals to categories is made in advance. For example, if the analyst has a set of socioeconomic measures for each of a sample of consumers, he may be interested in:

a. Setting up clusters of individuals who are "similar" with respect to a general socioeconomic configuration.

b. Determining some "best" number of clusters.

c. Determining whether overall cluster measures are significantly different.

5. In *canonical analysis* [5], the analyst is not concerned with a single criterion, multiple predictor relationship (as in ordinary multiple linear correlation) but, rather, with relationships among sets of criterion variables and predictor variables. His objectives are to:

a. Determine the maximum correlation between a set (of more than one element) of criterion variables and predictor variables.
b. Derive "weights" for each set of criterion and predictor variables, such that the weighted sums are maximally correlated.
c. Derive additional linear functions which maximize the remaining correlation, subject to being independent of the preceding set(s) of linear compounds.
d. Test statistical significance of the correlation measures.[2]

As can be noted from the above description, canonical analysis is a technique for dealing mainly with *composite* association between sets of criterion and predictor variables. Geometrically, it may be viewed as a measure of the extent to which a group of individuals occupies the same relative position in the space spanned by the criterion variables as it does in the space spanned by the predictor variables. The technique, then, does not force the investigator, on an *a priori* basis, to develop a single index to represent the set of criterion variables (in order, say, to run a single, "global" multiple linear correlation), or to compute a set of correlations for each criterion variable taken separately. Canonical analysis can also be used in prediction and, hence, can fill a function that traditional multiple regression serves.

An Illustrative Application of Canonical Analysis

In order to describe canonical analysis more adequately, a numerical illustration seems most appropriate. The data for this application were obtained from an experimental game [7]. Essentially, the subjects (36 business graduate students) were given prior information about the likelihood that a set of ten card decks belonged to one of two possible classes. They had the option, on the basis of prior information alone, to guess which class the deck they chose for betting purposes belonged to, or could, for a fixed cost per card, see some or all of the cards before placing their bet. The main purpose of the

---

[2] The above listing is not meant to be exhaustive but does cover the principal classes of multivariate techniques.

experiment was to see to what extent subject's intuitive behavior was consistent with current statistical decision models.

In this article interest centers not on average play, but on *individual* subject behavior and the possible relationship of this behavior to various personality variables; that is, attempting to explain *intersubject* differences in mode of play. Surprisingly, relatively little work has been reported on the relationship of risk taking and uncertainty reduction to personality characteristics. Scodel, Ratoosh and Minas [15] have reported the results of a set of betting exercises in which subject behavior was related to a set of personality test scores. They concluded that conservative (low payoff-high probability) players were more "other directed, socially assimilated" than less conservative (high payoff-low probability) players. Atkinson, et al., [2] and Becker and Siegel [4] have conducted various experiments related to risk taking and personality variables, but as Edwards [6] points out, little experimentation has been undertaken on the relationship of risk taking and personality.

In this study individual subject scores on several personality tests for each game participant were obtained. The relationship between a subject's "personality profile" and two behavioral charactristics which summarized each subject's game performance were of interest.

Characteristic 1: the subject's "sensitivity" attribute, is a categorical indicant of whether or not a subject varied the amount of information purchased in the experiment as a function of his prior uncertainty. For example, some subjects, having once decided upon some number of cards to purchase, continued to purchase this fixed number (or close to it) *independently* of the prior information which they received regarding the likelihood that the deck belonged to one of two possible classes. Other subjects *varied* the amount of additional information which they requested as a function of their prior information, buying less when prior uncertainty was low than when it was high.

Characteristic 2: the subject's "bias," is a measured indicant of how much information, in total, a subject bought over the whole trial sequence. Some subjects, for example, elected to purchase large amounts of information, whether or not purchasing variability about their specific average was related to prior information. Other subjects, of course, purchased relatively little information before placing their bets.

Thus, two criterion variables, sensitivity and bias, appeared to be describing different things about subject behavior. Moreover, the sample correlation between these two response variables was virtually

zero. No strong *a priori* grounds existed for combining these variables into a single criterion measure. That is, no logical basis was available for assigning so much weight to the sensitivity attribute and so much weight to the bias measure. Thus, if the association between these variables (*as a set*) with the set of predictor variables (personality test scores) is studied, a technique would have to be used which would permit description of an *overall* relationship between a set of two criterion variables and a set of several predictor variables. Canonical analysis is just such a technique. Moreover, its use would permit objective discovery of the weights to be assigned to each criterion variable, such that the resulting linear compound would be maximally correlated with the set of predictor variables.

The predictor variables (personality test scores) were represented by the following:

1. The Atwell and Wells Wide Range Vocabulary Test. Reputed to be a good indicator of general intelligence.

2. The Shipley Institute of Living Test. Purports to (conceptual portion) measure a subject's ability to "see patterns" or deal with abstraction and constitutes another type of intelligence measure.

3. The Gough Sanford Rigidity Test. Attempts to measure the extent of a subject's open-mindedness versus close-mindedness; that is, degree of attitude rigidity.

4. The Rotter Social Reaction Inventory Test. Purports to measure the degree of one's "felt control over his environment"; that is, the extent to which he feels that he can influence events versus viewing uncertainty in a more fatalistic manner.

5. The Hierarchy of Needs Test. Attempts to rate subjects with regard to need level, ranging from "lower-level" physiological needs to "higher-level" needs, such as esteem from others and self-actualization.

6. The Allport, Vernon and Lindzey Study of Values Test. Purports to classify subjects according to scores in the following classifications: theoretical, economic, aesthetic, social, political and religious.

7. The Gordon Personal Profile Test. Attempts to classify subjects according to test scores in personality classifications: ascendancy, responsibility, emotional stability and sociability.

All of the above tests are of the self-administered type. Subjects required, on the average, about two hours to complete the test battery. Some of the tests, *e.g.,* the Allport-Vernon-Lindzey, have separate scores for various subparts. In total, 20 predictor scores were available for each subject. In combination with the two criterion

variables, sensitivity and bias, a 22 x 22 matrix was required to summarize the intercorrelations. As might be surmised, however, many
correlation coefficients were not significant. Those test scores which
did not correlate well (alpha risk equal to 0.15 for the null hypothesis
$\rho = 0$) with at least one predictor were eliminated.

This step resulted in five predictor variables: (a) the Atwell-Wells
intelligence measure; (b) the Gordon measure for responsibility; (c)
the Gough Sanford measure of open-mindedness; (d) the Rotter
measure of "felt control over one's environment"; and (e) the Gordon
measure for sociability, which were used in the canonical analysis.
(Subsequent work using all 20 predictor variables, indicated, as expected, little improvement over the canonical correlation coefficients
based on only these five variables.)

The starting point for the canonical analysis is the correlation
matrix in Table 1.

Looking at the sample intercorrelations in Table 1, the following
can be seen:

1. The criterion variables, sensitivity and bias, are practically uncorrelated, the sample correlation coefficient being only 0.09.
2. Sensitivity (coded 0) versus nonsensitivity (coded 1) seems to be
associated with the predictor variables in the following way: The
higher the subject's I.Q., responsibility and sociability, the greater
his tendency to be sensitive to prior information; The higher his
attitude rigidity and degree of fatalism with respect to uncontrollable
events, the greater his tendency to be nonsensitive to prior information.
3. Bias (total amount of information purchased) seems to be associated with the predictor variables in the following way: The
higher the subject's I.Q., responsibility and sociability, the less the
tendency to exhibit high positive biases in information purchasing.
(The correlation coefficients relating the bias measure to the Gough-
Sanford and Rotter scores are so small as to be insignificant at the
0.15 alpha risk level.)

On an *a priori* basis the observed relationships appear to make
sense, but the problem is to determine the overall correlation between
the *set* of criterion variables (sensitivity and bias) and the set of
predictor variables. This is analogous to finding a coefficient of
multiple correlation if each criterion variable was considered separately.[3]

[3] A short mathematical description of canonical analysis may be found in the
Appendix.

TABLE 1 Correlation Matrix of Experimental Game Results

	1	2	3	4	5	6	7
Sensitivity measure	1.00	0.09	-0.27	-0.36	0.19	0.44	-0.23
Bias measure		1.00	-0.29	-0.23	-0.09	0.05	-0.29
Atwell-Wells I. Q.			1.00	0.22	-0.23	-0.23	0.07
Gordon responsibility				1.00	0.18	-0.17	0.07
Gough-Sanford rigidity					1.00	0.24	0.01
Rotter social reaction						1.00	-0.25
Gordon sociability							1.00

Essentially, two sets of weighting coefficients (a set for the criterion variables and a set for the predictor variables) were sought, such that if linear combinations of each set were formed (thus arriving at a *composite* variable representing each set) and correlated in a *two-variable* linear correlation, a higher correlation *for this particular set* of composite variables would be obtained than any other set of combinations which could be formed. As would be surmised, specific numbers satisfying the above criterion are called canonical coefficients. The technique develops these coefficients and also computes the canonical correlation index which would be obtained if the two composite variables were formed and carried through a two-variable linear correlation.

Two other considerations should also be mentioned before presenting the results. First, we were not necessarily limited to finding only one set of canonical coefficients for the criterion and predictor variables. In this problem another set of coefficients could be "extracted" for which the linear compounds would also be maximally correlated, subject to being independent of all previously obtained compounds within the criterion or predictor set, as the case may be. In general, if there are *r* criterion variables and *s* predictor variables, as many sets of canonical coefficients can be obtained as are represented by the smaller of the two numbers, *r* or *s*. Each new canonical correlation index, however, will be smaller than the preceding value. That is, the highest canonical correlation index will be related to the *first* set of canonical coefficients which are obtained by the technique.

Second, formulas are available (see Appendix) for testing the significance of the canonical correlation indexes under the usual assumptions involving multivariate statistical inference. (In this problem both canonical indexes turned out to be significant at the 0.05 alpha level; although, in view of the coded categorical variable, sensitivity, some question arises as to the appropriateness of the test.)

Proceeding now to the results, a canonical analysis was performed on the correlation matrix of Table 1. For illustrative purposes, a description of only the results for the first (maximally correlated) set of canonical coefficients and the associated canonical correlation index is given.[4] The canonical correlation index for this problem turned out to be 0.61. This index is interpreted as a measure of the *overall* correlation between the two sets of criterion and predictor

---

[4] The analyst may wish to extract additional canonical indexes if his interpretation of the resultant relationships is improved in so doing. In this respect the motivation is similar to extracting more than one factor in principal components analysis.

variables. (As in the usual case of multiple linear correlation, it has an upper limit of unity.) Notice that this value is higher than the correlation indexes for the original variables taken singly (see Table 1).

The set of canonical coefficients, also found by the technique, is shown in Table 2.

TABLE 2   Set of Canonical Correlation Coefficients for Criterion and Predictor Variables

VARIABLE	CANONICAL COEFFICIENT
Sensitivity measure	0.842
Bias measure	0.465
Atwell-Wells I. Q.	−0.341
Gordon responsibility	−0.516
Gough-Sanford rigidity	0.117
Rotter social reaction	0.358
Gordon sociability	−0.381

To show how the canonical coefficients in Table 2 are used, the standardized scores (mean equal to zero and standard deviation equal to one) of the first subject in the experiment are shown in Table 3. The linear compounds for the criterion and predictor sets, using the coefficients of Table 2, are also computed, leading to the two composite scores for Subject One:

$$-0.89 \text{ (criterion set)}$$
$$-0.80 \text{ (predictor set)}$$

Similarly, for the remaining 35 subjects, two composite values, $\overset{*}{x}_i$ and $\overset{*}{y}_i$ ($i = 2, 3, \cdots , 36$) can be computed. Then, if desired, these pairs can be plotted in conventional scatter diagram form. This two-variable plot is in the Figure.

If the two composite variables were now correlated, the same canonical correlation index (0.61) would be obtained as derived from the original analysis. The figure shows the regression lines for the linear regression of the criterion set Y on the predictor set X, and vice versa.

The slope coefficients for the two regression lines plotted in the figure are again:

$$\overset{*}{y}_c = 0.61 \, \overset{*}{x}$$
$$\overset{*}{x}_c = 0.61 \, \overset{*}{y}$$

TABLE 3   Illustration of Linear Compound Computation for Subject One

	Standard Scores	Linear Compounds
Sensitivity measure	−0.722	$\overset{*}{y_1}$: $0.842\,(-0.722) = -0.608$
Bias measure	−0.605	$0.465\,(-0.605) = -0.281$
		$\overset{*}{y_1} = -0.889$
Atwell-Wells I. Q.	0.741	$\overset{*}{x_1}$: $-0.341\,(\ 0.741) = -0.253$
Gordon responsibility	−0.183	$-0.516\,(-0.183) = 0.094$
Gough-Sanford rigidity	−1.124	$0.117\,(-1.124) = -0.132$
Rotter social reaction	−0.776	$0.358\,(-0.776) = -0.278$
Gordon sociability	0.606	$-0.381\,(\ 0.606) = -0.231$
		$\overset{*}{x_1} = -0.800$

Since we are dealing with standardized variates, both regression lines will pass through the origin of the coordinate system and the slope coefficients will equal the canonical correlation index, 0.61, by the relationships:

$$r_{y \cdot x} = b_{y \cdot x} \frac{\sigma_x}{\sigma_y}$$

$$r_{x \cdot y} = b_{x \cdot y} \frac{\sigma_y}{\sigma_x}.$$

These equations could be used for traditional prediction purposes. That is, if there was a set of personality test scores, say for some *new* individual, the linear compound $\overset{*}{y}_c$ could be estimated in two steps. First, compute the linear compound $\overset{*}{x}$ by substituting the subject's (standardized) test scores in the equation in Table 3. Then substitute this numerical value in the first of the above regression equations and find the appropriate $\overset{*}{y}_c$ value. This predicted value could then be compared with the linear compound obtained by substituting the subject's sensitivity and bias measures (in standardized form) in the linear compound $\overset{*}{y}$.

A few comments should also be made on the canonical coefficients of the predictor and criterion variables in the linear compounds, illustrated in Table 3. With respect to the predictor set note that the highest coefficient (-0.516) is associated with the Gordon responsibility test score, and the next highest coefficient (-0.381) is associated with the Gordon sociability score. With regard to the criterion set of variables, it appears that the sensitivity measure carries the higher coefficient (0.842), which is probably not surprising judging from the correlation coefficients summarized in Table 1. Thus, the appropriate weights to assign to the sensitivity attribute and bias measure are found, which result in maximal correlation with the set of predictor variables.

More important, the canonical coefficients enable one to ascertain the overall relationship between sensitivity-bias and the set of personality variables. It appears as though sensitivity and "unbiasedness" tend to increase with higher scores on I.Q., responsibility and sociability and decrease with higher scores on attitude rigidity and degree of fatalism with respect to uncontrollable events. This behavior is consistent with the interpretation given to the original correlation matrix in Table 1, but is now applicable to the overall relationship between the two sets of variables.

Additional Considerations in Canonical Correlation

The foregoing illustration hardly exhausts the various aspects of canonical analysis. For example, the technique can be extended to deal with correlations among *more* than two sets of data. That is, if in addition to the present variables, information is known about various socioeconomic variables for each subject, the technique could be extended to handle association among all three sets of data [11].

Furthermore, canonical analysis can be combined with other multivariate techniques for more efficient analysis, should the problem justify it. As an illustration, if one were dealing with a very large set of criterion and predictor variables, one could first conduct a factor analysis on each set and then run a canonical analysis on the principal components. One could also combine all variables into one factor analysis, separating the extracted factors into criterion-predictor versus independent factors for criterion and predictor variables, respectively. The analyst could then run a canonical analysis on the resultant sets.[5] Finally, one might wish to avoid canonical analysis altogether by finding the *first* principal component of the criterion set (by factor analysis) and then correlating scores on this component with the predictor variables, not unlike an ordinary multiple correlation problem.

Canonical analysis, like other multivariate techniques, is not without limitations. The two major assumptions underlying the model (when canonical correlation indexes are to be tested for statistical significance) are:

1. Both criterion and predictor sets are made up of interval-scaled variables.
2. The observed data represent a random sample of observation vectors drawn from the same multinormal universe.

In the illustrative application covered earlier the sensitivity attribute was a coded variable. As such, tests of significance of the canonical indexes are not strictly appropriate.

---

[5] It should be mentioned that, in general, one would not obtain the same results by using this method. As a matter of fact, dissatisfaction with some aspects of factor analysis gave rise to the development of canonical analysis in the first place. These alternative techniques are merely listed to show some of the possible ways in which a given multivariate problem might be analyzed.

The assumption of multinormality (and, hence, linearity) can also be restrictive if statistical significance is to be ascertained. As in traditional multiple correlation, the analyst may be able to make suitable transformations in order to achieve linearity, but in dealing with small samples, the linearity assumption must usually be made by necessity; experimental error is typically large enough to mask the possibility that nonlinearity is present. As the number of variates increases, however, the multivariate extension of the central limit theorem indicates that moderate departures from multinormality probably do not lead to serious errors in the application of significance tests which are based on multinormal distributions.

The computational labor involved in conducting canonical analysis

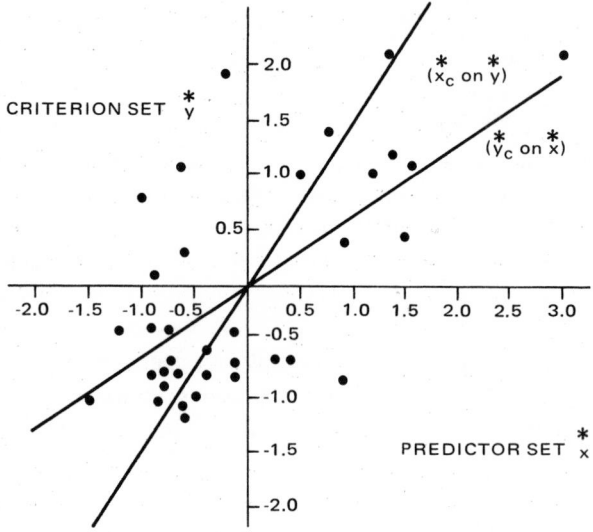

Figure 1   Scatter plot of linear compounds

is usually such as to require a computer for handling problems of any realistic size. Fortunately, many "canned" programs are available. The particular program used in the above illustrative problem was part of the "Biomedical Package" of U.C.L.A. Cooley and Lohnes [5] also provide flow charts and FORTAN programs for canonical analysis.

The use of canonical analysis in marketing research has been virtually nonexistent to date, although other multivariate techniques (discriminatory analysis, factor analysis) are beginning to find in-

creasing application. It would seem that the limitations of canonical analysis are no more or no less than those of other multivariate procedures, and that lack of application in marketing research studies to date is principally due to lack of familiarity with the technique. If the analyst is primarily interested in the *overall* relationship between *sets* of dependent variables, canonical analysis is an appropriate method to describe this relationship. Its use can free the investigator from (a) having to pick a single criterion variable from two or more possible criterion variables or (b) arbitrarily weighting the set of criterion variables, in order to fit the problem into the standard format of multiple correlation analysis.

SUMMARY

This article has shown how a relatively little-used technique, canonical analysis, may be helpful in the analysis of marketing problems in which the analyst must deal with sets of criterion and predictor variables. In the example shown, it turned out that the sensitivity measure was the criterion variable with the higher "loading," and that the Gordon Personal Profile measures, responsibility and sociability, appeared to contribute most to the overall correlation. The first canonical correlation index was 0.61, which was significant at the 0.05 alpha risk level.

Also included were a short description of possible extensions of canonical analysis, the relationship of this technique to other multivariate procedures (e.g., factor analysis), and the major limitations of the method in analyzing multivariate data. Finally, it is of interest to note that personality variables (at least those measured by these tests) were not able to explain much of the intersubject variation in game-playing behavior. This is, of course, not to say that personality characteristics generally do not influence risk attitudes, but only that the problem of identifying relevant personality constructs is far from solved.

TECHNICAL APPENDIX

In canonical analysis the objective is to find two sets of coefficients, represented by the vectors a and b, which maximize the correlation between the canonical variables y_i and x_i as defined below:

$$\overset{*}{y_1} = a_1 y_{11} + a_2 y_{12} + \cdots + a_r y_{1r} \, ; \qquad \overset{*}{x_1} = b_1 x_{11} + b_2 x_{12} + \cdots + b_s x_{1s}$$

$$\overset{*}{y_2} = a_1 y_{21} + a_2 y_{22} + \cdots + a_r y_{2r} \, ; \qquad \overset{*}{x_2} = b_1 x_{21} + b_2 x_{22} + \cdots + b_s x_{2s}$$

$$\overset{*}{y_n} = a_1 y_{n2} + b_2 y_{n2} + \cdots + a_r y_{nr} \, ; \qquad \overset{*}{x_n} = b_1 x_{n1} + b_2 x_{n2} + \cdots + b_s x_{ns}$$

In the problem of this article $n = 36$ and the vector a is a two-component vector representing experimental gaming results, while the vector b is a five-component vector representing personality test scores. The y_{ij} and x_{ij} are expressed in standard scores (zero mean and unit variances).

The analysis proceeds by partitioning the matrix of intercorrelations R as follows:

$$R = \begin{bmatrix} R_{11} & \vdots & R_{12} \\ \cdots\cdots & \vdots & \cdots\cdots \\ R_{21} & \vdots & R_{22} \end{bmatrix},$$

where

R_{11} = intercorrelations among the r criterion variables,
R_{22} = intercorrelations among the s predictor variables,
R_{12} = intercorrelations of criteria with predictors,
R_{21} = the transpose of R_{12}.

The appropriate canonical equation can be written in two ways:

$$(R_{11}^{-1} R_{12} R_{22}^{-1} R_{21} - \lambda I) a = 0,$$

and

$$(R_{22}^{-1} R_{21} R_{11}^{-1} R_{12} - \lambda I) b = 0.$$

If the last equation is used, the appropriate characteristic roots, λ_k, must be found which result in the determinant of the characteristic equation being equal to zero. That is, find

$$| R_{22}^{-1} R_{21} R_{11}^{-1} R_{12} - \lambda I | = 0.$$

Then obtain the vector b associated with λ. The vector a is found by solving:

$$a = \frac{R_{11}^{-1} R_{12} b}{(\lambda)^{1/2}}.$$

In our problem, the appropriate eigenvalues λ_1 and λ_2 were 0.372 and 0.123, respectively, leading to canonical correlation indexes of:

$$r_{c1} = (\lambda_1)^{1/2} = 0.61,$$
$$r_{c2} = (\lambda_2)^{1/2} = 0.35.$$

The associated vectors for each canonical correlation index were:

$a\,(\lambda_1) = (\;\;0.84\;\;\;\;0.47);\;\; b\,(\lambda_1) = (-0.34 - 0.52\;\;0.12\;\;0.36 - 0.38)$
$a\,(\lambda_2) = (-0.55\;\;\;\;0.89);\;\; b\,(\lambda_2) = (-0.58\;\;0.12 - 0.50 - 0.67 - 0.50).$

To find the appropriate canonical variates $\overset{*}{y}$ and $\overset{*}{x}$ we have (illustrating for the first eigenvalue λ_1):

$$(a_1\,a_2) \begin{bmatrix} y_{11} & y_{12} & \cdots & y_{1,\,36} \\ y_{21} & y_{22} & \cdots & y_{2,\,36} \end{bmatrix};$$

$$(b_1\,b_2\,b_3\,b_4\,b_5) \begin{bmatrix} x_{11} & x_{12} & \cdots & x_{1,\,36} \\ x_{21} & x_{22} & \cdots & x_{2,\,36} \\ \cdot & & & \cdot \\ \cdot & & & \cdot \\ \cdot & & & \cdot \\ x_{51} & x_{52} & \cdots & x_{5,\,36} \end{bmatrix},$$

where the y_{ij} and x_{ij} values are the standardized observations.

The significance of each canonical variate may be tested by the so-called lambda test of Bartlett [3]. Also, see [9]. For the first root λ_1

$$\Lambda = \prod_{k=1}^{r} (1 - \lambda_k); \qquad r < s.$$

Λ is approximately distributed under the null hypothesis as:

$$\chi^2 = -[N - 0.5(r + s + 1)] \ln \Lambda,$$

with degrees of freedom:

$$r \cdot s$$

In general, after t roots are removed:

$$\Lambda' = \prod_{k=t+1}^{r} (1 - \lambda_k),$$

and the appropriate degrees of freedom are:

$$(r - t)\ (s - t).$$

In the problem of this article, both characteristic roots, λ_1 and λ_2, were significant at the 0.05 alpha risk level.

REFERENCES

1. T. W. Anderson, *Introduction to Multivariate Statistical Analysis,* New York: John Wiley & Sons Inc., 1958.

2. J. W. Atkinson, *et al.,* "The Achievement Motive, Goal Setting, and Probability Preferences," *Journal of Abnormal Social Psychology,* 60 (1960), 27–36.

3. M. S. Bartlett, "The Statistical Significance of Canonical Correlation," *Biometrica,* 32 (1941), 29–38.

4. S. W. Becker and Sidney Siegel, "Utility of Grades: Level of Aspiration in a Decision Theory Context," *Journal of Experimental Psychology,* 55 (1958), 81–5.

5. W. W. Cooley and P. R. Lohnes, *Multivariate Procedures for the Behavioral Sciences,* New York: John Wiley & Sons Inc., 1962.

6. Ward Edwards, "Behavioral Decision Theory," *Annual Review of Psychology,* 12 (1961), 473–98.

7. P. E. Green, M. H. Halbert and J. S. Minas, "An Experiment in Information Buying," *Journal of Advertising Research,* 4 (September 1964), 17–23.

8. H. H. Harmon, *Modern Factor Analysis,* Chicago, Ill.: University of Chicago Press, 1960.

9. D. L. Heck, "Charts of Some Upper Percentage Points of the Distribution of the Largest Characteristic Root," *Annals of Mathematical Statistics,* 31 (1960), 625–42.

10. R. N. Howard, "Classifying A Population into Homogeneous Groups," *Proceedings of the Cambridge Conference on Operations Research,* Cambridge, England, September 14–8, 1964.

11. Paul Horst, "Relations Among *m* Sets of Measures," *Psychometrika,* 26 (1961), 129–49.

12. M. G. Kendall, *A Course in Multivariate Analysis,* New York: Hafner, 1957.

13. D. N. Lawley and A. E. Maxwell, *Factor Analysis as a Statistical Method,* London: Butterworths, 1963.

14. W. F. Massy, "On Methods: Discriminant Analysis of Audience Characteristics," *Journal of Advertising Research,* 5, (March 1965), 39–48.

15. A. P. Scodel, Philburn Ratoosh and J. S. Minas, "Some Personality Correlates of Decision Making Under Conditions of Risk," in D. Willner, ed., *Decision, Values and Groups,* New York: Pergamon Press, 1960, 37–69.

16. Hilary Seal, *Multivariate Statistical Analysis for Biologists,* New York: John Wiley & Sons Inc., 1964.

17. L. L. Thurstone, *Multiple Factor Analysis,* Chicago, Ill.: University of Chicago Press, 1947.

PART II REFERENCES

Bass, Frank M. et al., Editors, *Quantitative Techniques in Marketing* (Homewood, Illinois: Richard D. Irwin, 1961).

Buzzell, Robert D., and Slater, Charles C., "Decision Theory and Marketing Management," *Journal of Marketing,* July, 1962.

Crawford, C. Merle, "Shotgun Marriage of Mathematics and Marketing," *Business Horizons,* Summer, 1966.

Frank, Ronald, Massy, William F., and Morrison, Donald G., "Bias in Multiple Discriminant Analysis," *Journal of Marketing Research,* August, 1965.

Frank, Ronald, et al., Editors, *Quantitative Techniques in Marketing* (Homewood, Illinois: Richard D. Irwin, 1962).

Levin, Richard I., and Lamone, Rudolph P., *Linear Programming for Management Decisions* (Homewood, Illinois: Richard D. Irwin, 1969).

Massy, William F., "Bayesian Multiple Discriminant Analysis," Graduate School of Business, Stanford University, Working Paper Number 58, (July, 1965).

Massy, William F., and Savvas, J. D., "Logical Flow Models for Marketing Analysis," *Journal of Marketing,* January, 1964.

Sheldrick, S. B., "Computers in Marketing," *Marketing,* October, 1967.

Weiss, Doyle L., "Simulation for Decision Making in Marketing," *Journal of Marketing,* July, 1964.

PART
III

Research into
Consumer Behavior

The rate of advancement in marketing is jointly determined by progress on two broad fronts: first, marketing relationships must be structured through the advancement of theory and the empirical verification of theory; and second, theory must be restructured in operational terms for use by marketing management. Both fronts are directed by one common objective: the satisfaction of consumer needs and desires at a profit. Thus, the theory of consumer behavior provides a foundation for the research activities of marketing and much needs to be done to solidify its theoretical base. Also, marketing strategists find that optimal policy making is dependent upon knowledge of consumer preferences, innovative behavior, and brand choices.

5 | Quantitative Analysis of Consumers

Drive a hard bargain, then make a liberal settlement. This always leaves the other man willing to do business again.

—R. A. LONG

The main thrust of "Methods of Estimating Consumer Preference Distributions" is the demonstration of the correct philosophy of marketing science. Ralph L. Day argues that "Marketing should be more concerned with applying useful tools and theories from the behavioral and quantitative sciences than in trying to develop a pure science." Day feels that more should be determined about the usefulness of tools from "psychology, mathematics, and statistics" in the analysis of marketing problems.

Markov chain models have provided an intriguing approach to the study of brand loyal consumers. Searching for a method to predict aggregate consumer movements among brands, theorists noted the similarity of gas particle movements among different gases in a closed container and consumer movements among product brands. It was felt that the model which described the process toward *gas equilibrium* could also predict *consumer equilibrium*.

In Markov chain models, the probability that a consumer will purchase a given brand is dependent upon prior purchases; in the case of first order Markov chains the probability of brand purchase is dependent only upon the last brand purchased. Thus, the *first order* model assumes that the consumer learns from his *last* purchase, but his learning extends no further than this last purchase.

Ronald A. Howard provides the reader with a basic view of Markov chains in "Stochastic Process Models of Consumer Behavior." Howard succinctly differentiates between the *probabilistic* view of Markov chains and the more commonly held notion of *percentage* changes under certainty. Under the latter viewpoint brand shares are predicted with certainty, while stochastic models predict *expected values* with their concomitant *variances*. Howard explains why empirical data fail to fit the Markovian Process Model of Consumer Behavior explicitly; the researchers lose sight of the dispersion that is to be expected from any probability process.

While a great deal has been written on the potential of Markov chains in the explanation and the prediction of consumer behavior, not many empirical studies are available for examination. Very few real world situations are feasible for study, since the assumptions of the Markov model are very stringent, and parameters are constantly shifting (for example, demographic characteristics change; competitors are not very cooperative and change their advertising, price, and other policies; and the legal environment may shift).

The consumer innovator is considered to be the key element in the diffusion of new products and innovation. As such, the ability to distinguish innovators from non-innovators becomes a key problem for marketing management and depends to some extent upon socio-economic characteristics of consumers. Robertson and Kennedy attempt to use such characteristics as *venturesomeness, social mobility, privilegedness, social integration, interest range, status concern,* and *cosmopolitanism* to *discriminate* in the prediction of consumer innovators. Multiple discriminant analysis (described in Section 3) is the instrument used in classifying consumers as either innovators or non-innovators, and the results of this study suggest that venturesomeness and social mobility explain most of the innovative behavior of most consumers.

What are the underlying characteristics which seem to account for the consumer preferences of a given product? Jean Stoetzel utilizes classical factor analysis to discover the answer to this question for a given class of wines. Forcing French consumers to rank a set of wine brands according to preference, Stoetzel runs intercorrelations between brand rank scores, and then utilizes the resultant matrix of correlation coefficients to extract factors and factor loadings through use of the *Centroid Factor Rotation Method.* This article serves a two-fold purpose: first, it shows that common factors explain consumer preferences ascribed to brands; and second, it demonstrates the usefulness of quantitative methods in marketing research and marketing management. Consumer behavior must be understood before any phase of marketing within the firm can be adequately organized and planned.

Methods of Estimating Consumer Preference Distributions

Ralph L. Day

The rapidly increasing use in marketing of the techniques of quantitative analysis and the concepts of the behavioral sciences has led many to conclude that marketing is becoming a science. I prefer to think, however, that the practice of marketing is becoming more professional and, as a result of this, various "contributing sciences" and other professional fields are becoming sources for more sophisticated methodologies.

It appears that marketing is now more like the professional areas of engineering and medicine were in their early stages of development than like the social and behavioral sciences. Therefore, marketing should be more concerned with applying useful tools and theories from the behavioral and quantitative sciences than in trying to develop a "pure science." This philosophical orientation to marketing is reflected in the research discussed in this article. It presents the application of theories and tools from psychology, mathematics, and statistics to the analysis of problems which are of interest to marketing practitioners.

THURSTONE'S WORK

Since the preference distribution concept is concerned with measurement of aspects of the human choice process, it is not surprising that its roots can be found in the work of measurement-oriented psychologists. The idea of estimating frequency distributions of consumer preference can be traced to the work of L. L. Thurstone, a psycholo-

gist widely known for his work in psychometrics and psychophysics. In an article published in 1945, Thurstone suggested the prediction of the outcome of political elections or "the relative consumption of competing commodities" by developing estimates of the *average affective values* of candidates or products and the *discriminal dispersion* around these mean subjective values on a psychological continuum.[1] Thurstone suggested the estimation of frequency distributions on each stimulus by psychophysical methods, such as the method of successive intervals, and pointed out that such distributions might be normal, skewed, or even bimodal in form. He then presented a method for predicting the proportions of first choices for each of several stimuli (political candidates, competing products, etc.) when the distributions (affective dispersions) are known.[2]

While the specific procedures advocated by Thurstone do not appear to have been widely used in the analysis of consumer preferences for competing products, considerable interest has been evidenced in the past three years in methods utilizing his concept of a frequency distribution of consumer preferences.[3] The first two articles reporting the measurement of distributions of preferences for physical attributes of products appeared at almost the same time in the fall of 1962. These were "A Short Method of Estimating a Distribution of Consumer Preferences," by Purnell Benson[4] and "Strategy of Product Quality," by Alfred A. Kuehn and Ralph L. Day.[5] I will briefly discuss the approaches presented in these articles and in subsequent published papers and will conclude with a discussion of some as yet unreported aspects of my own research on preference distribution analysis.

BENSON'S CURVE

BENSON'S METHODS. A major portion of the extant literature on the estimation of preference distributions has been contributed by Purnell H. Benson, a former professor of sociology who now has his own consulting firm.[6] Dr. Benson's earlier work on the measurement of consumer preferences was directed toward the determination of the optimal level of a product attribute. He developed functions which related the degree of like or dislike to the level of product characteristic. The optimum value was then determined by differential calculus.[7] Recognizing that this model required the highly unrealistic assumption of homogeneous tastes across the population, Benson shifted his attention to fitting a distribution curve which would depict

the proportions of the population preferring various alternative levels of the product.

In his initial paper on preference distributions, Benson approached the fitting of preference distribution curves as a "practical research problem." He rejected the systematic testing of many product forms as impractical and costly.[8] His methods were designed to estimate the preference distribution directly from data obtained in field product tests, utilizing a minimum number of product versions. The study which he reported in his 1962 paper (disguised data) involved two widths of a food-wrapping material. He presented the test items to a sample of consumers and asked them to indicate with reference to each sample if they would like more of the characteristic (width), about the same, or less. He summarized his results as follows:[9]

	ITEM A (10-INCH WIDTH)	ITEM B (14-INCH WIDTH)
Prefer less width	15%	63%
Prefer about the same	5%	9%
Prefer more width	80%	28%

Using a table of areas under the normal curve, Benson located the boundary points of the above classifications in terms of standard derivations away from the mean according to the included and excluded areas. The resulting "distribution of consumer preferences" is as shown in Figure 1.[10] With the normal curve thus positioned on a linear scale of the product characteristic (width of the food wrap in

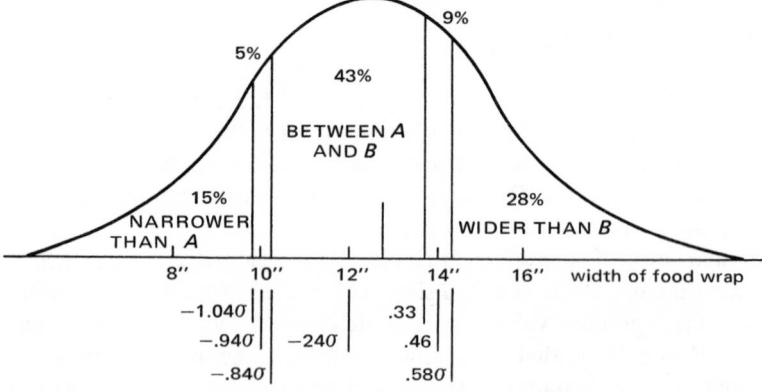

Figure 1   A preference distribution curve fitted by Benson's method

inches), Benson accepts the areas under the curve as indications of the proportions of the population preferring various values of the characteristic.

Benson recognized (in his 1962 article) the possibility that preferences might not be normally distributed. He pointed out that the distribution for some characteristics might be skewed and that in the case of multiple end-uses for a product there might be a multimodal distribution. He did not suggest a procedure for recognizing the existence of multimodality but did suggest an approach to checking for skewness. He proposed that the midpoint between his two test items on the scale of values on the characteristic under study be used as a third point. A cumulative frequency curve fitted to these points would then be compared with a family of ogive curves for skewed distributions. In a more recent article,[11] Benson did not mention this procedure but suggested that data similar to that obtained for the first two items should be obtained for a third item as a means of checking for skewness. If the discrepancy between the deviate associated with the new item and that predicted for it by the initially fitted normal curve is substantial, Benson suggests that a skewed curve be fitted and provides a method for transforming normal deviates.

Benson's recent publications suggest fitting distribution curves to data related to intangible "product attributes such as flavor, appearance, style, and convenience"[12] which cannot be measured directly in the laboratory. He proposes the use of scales whose values have no actual physical counterpart. For example, he suggests a "more-less" scale for the flavor of a dessert.[13] Using an approach similar to that used in physical attributes, Benson estimates a distribution of choices over a "measurement-free" scale of values. By assuming a two-way normal distribution, Benson extends his analysis to two dimensions for "measurement-free" data.[14] He displays his multivariate results as a "scatter dot diagram" which graphically depicts the relative densities of the joint choices on the more-less scales for the two intangible product characteristics. Benson now offers as a routine service to his clients the estimation of preference distributions in one dimension for physical or tangible characteristics and in two dimensions for intangible factors.

KUEHN MODEL DIFFERENT

THE KUEHN PREFERENCE MODEL. The approach to the estimation of preference distributions originated by Professor Alfred A. Kuehn of Carnegie Institute of Technology differs from the Benson approach

in both its underlying assumptions and its methodology. Where Benson fits preference distribution curves directly to product test data, the Kuehn model involves the analysis and interpretation of product test data in terms of a probabilistic model of consumer choice in the product test situation. While Benson estimates distributions of preferences for physical characteristics from a limited number of test items and projects his scale of values from the test items, the Kuehn method requires systematic testing over the range of feasible values on the characteristic under study. While more complex and more difficult to apply, the Kuehn method requires fewer advance assumptions about the shape of the preference distribution and provides additional information on the ability of consumers to recognize differences.

The Kuehn model requires the identification in advance of the feasible range of values of a characteristic which can be incorporated in a product. A scale spanning this range in equal steps is established as the base line of the distribution to be estimated. The assumption is made that each consumer will prefer some level of the characteristic to all other levels. The steps on the scale then represent the possible "most preferred" levels with which consumers can be associated. The "preference distribution" is determined by estimating the proportions of the population who prefer each of the various levels to all other levels.

It is assumed that the consumer has less than perfect ability to recognize which of two samples has a level of product characteristic closest to his "most preferred" level. The heart of the Kuehn method is a probabilistic model of choice in the pair comparison situation. The probability that a consumer will choose the test item with a level of the characteristic closer to his most preferred level on the scale is a function of the particular level he prefers, his basic ability to recognize differences in the value of the characteristic incorporated in products, and the actual values of the characteristic incorporated in the two test items. This is expressed mathematically as follows:

$$p^i_{jk} = \frac{d^{|j-i|}}{d^{|j-i|} + d^{|k-i|}} \tag{1}$$

where i represents the level on the scale which the consumer prefers to all other levels.

j and k represent the two levels which are incorporated in the two test items.

d is the "discrimination parameter" which reflects the basic ability of consumers to recognize differences in the level of the characteristic.

For a particular product test, the value of i runs from 1 up to n where n is the particular number of steps used in the scale of values of the characteristic. The values of j and k are specified by the levels of the characteristic contained in the items of a particular pair but vary as different pairs of test items are used in the pair comparison tests.

The expected results of a paired comparison product test in terms of the proportion preferring level j to level k can be expressed as a summation of the p's for each segment times the proportion of the population preferring that segment. Where the w_i are these unknown proportions and P_{jk} is the proportion of the sample testing j against k saying they prefer j to k, we have:

$$P_{jk} = \sum_{i=1}^{n} p_{jk}^i \cdot w_i \qquad (2)$$

Each pair of test items containing a unique combination of levels of the characteristic (steps on the scale) provides an equation. The resulting system of simultaneous equations is solved for the values of the w_i which are estimates of the proportions of the population preferring each level of the product characteristic.

The values obtained by this method are free of any prior assumptions about the shape of the preference distribution and can take on virtually any form. The resulting distribution might be multimodal, rectangular, highly skewed, or normal. The shape of the distribution is specified by the data and not by the researcher.[15] In addition to the estimate of the proportions of the population preferring the various levels, the solution also provides a value of the parameter d. This parameter is a measure of the consumer's ability to recognize differences and is likely to be as valuable to the manufacturer as knowledge of the shape of the preference distribution. The value of d is useful in estimating how much difference in the level of the characteristic is needed for recognition by consumers, in estimating the number of different versions needed to provide products at all points on the scale, and in evaluating the "preference share of the market" which a present or proposed product would have.

COMPUTER SIMULATION

A Simulation Method for Preference Analysis. The Kuehn approach clearly offers major advantages over the "rough and ready" methods used by Benson but the costs of using it are relatively high.

The equation system of the Kuehn method is quite complex and is frequently difficult to solve. I have developed a method for fitting preference distributions which seeks to retain most of the advantages of the Kuehn method while gaining some of the advantages of the relatively simple direct fit approach of Benson. The basic idea is to conduct the systematic pattern of tests[16] required in the Kuehn approach and then fit a preference distribution curve to the results by computer simulation.[17]

A researcher studying preference for a product characteristic will usually have an idea of the shape of the underlying preference distributions before he designs his experiment, although it is necessary only to identify the relevant range of values on the scale in order to design the pair comparison experiment. When a complete pattern of paired tests is done (every level tested against every other level), the summary of total choices will suggest the shape of the underlying distribution. In many cases the researcher can be reasonably confident of the shape of the distribution curve after examining the product test results in light of previous beliefs about the shape of the distribution of preferences. When a specific distribution can be hypothesized with some degree of confidence, computer simulation can provide a relatively simple method of fitting the curve and obtaining an estimate of the discrimination parameter. The Kuehn model is utilized but is used in reverse gear, so to speak. The proportions of the assumed distribution are assigned as the values of the w_i in the equations. Then product tests are simulated with this "known" population to obtain the number choosing each item in each paired comparison test. The resulting equations are:

$$C_j = \sum_{i=1}^{n} p_{jk}^i \cdot A_i \cdot N_{jk}$$

$$C_k = \sum_{i=1}^{n} (1 - p_{jk}^i) A_i \cdot N_{jk}$$

(3)

where the A_i are the areas under the hypothesized curve on each segment of the product characteristic scale.

N_{jk} is the number of consumers in the test.

C_j and C_k are the numbers choosing levels j and k.

A simulation run is made by estimating a value for d (see equation 1) and then solving for all the C_j and C_k and summing the results. These

simulated results are then compared to the actual field results with a χ^2 test of goodness of fit. Iterating on the value of d, the best fit value of d is found. If the simulated test results have a high degree of statistical fit to the results obtained in the actual field tests, the hypothesized distribution and the "best fit" value of d are accepted as useful estimates of the population values. If the best obtainable fit is "rejected by the data," then either another hypothesized distribution can be tried or an analytical solution to the Kuehn model should be computed.

The simulation method was developed and tested in connection with a study of preferences for the amount of chocolate flavoring materials in chocolate ice cream which I conducted on the Pennsylvania State University campus. Five test batches of chocolate ice cream were formulated by ice cream specialists in the Dairy Science Department to span the range from the mildest chocolate level which they thought any appreciable number of consumers would prefer up to the strongest level they thought any appreciable number would prefer. The test batches were carefully controlled to hold all aspects of the ice cream constant except for the amount of chocolate. Each of the five test batches was tested against every other batch in a systematic paired comparison field experiment involving 928 student subjects. The total choices (adjusted for variations in sample size) are shown in column 1 of Table 1.

TABLE 1   Five-Segment Study

Test Batch	(1) Field Test Results*	(2) Field Test Results†	(3) First Simulation	(4) Second Simulation
1	184.6	199	175	195
2	220.6	238	211	230
3	202.8	218	228	230
4	183.5	198	211	196
5	136.5	147	175	149
Total	928.0	1,000	1,000	1,000

* Adjusted for variation in sample size.
† Adjusted to a sample size of 100 per test for ease of comparison with simulated output.

When the study was being designed, it had seemed reasonable to assume that the distribution of preferences for the "chocolatiness" of ice cream among the student population would be approximately normal. Although the actual results appeared to be skewed, it was not

obvious that they were incompatible with a normal underlying preference distribution. Therefore, a simulation model was developed by assigning a standard normal distribution over a preference scale corresponding to the five test batches with each of the interior segments one standard deviation wide. In other words, the A_i of equations (3) were assigned the values .0669, .2417, .3830, .2417, and .0669. Starting with a guess of d safely on the low side, the field test was simulated and the results were compared to the actual results using a χ^2 test of goodness of fit. An increment was added to the value of d and the process was repeated until the value of d giving the best possible fit to the observed results was found. These results, shown in column 3 of Table 1, did not provide a good statistical fit, and the hypothesis that preferences were normally distributed over the five levels was rejected.

Although casual analysis of the results suggested that the underlying distribution was skewed to the right, the prior belief that preferences were normally distributed seemed to justify the investigation of the possibility that the apparent skewness was the result of "piling up" on the end of a scale which did not adequately span the range of levels of "chocolatiness." In other words, a possible explanation was that there should have been another step on the low end of the product characteristic scale. To test this assumption, a normal curve was allotted in the same manner as before to a six-segment scale so that the values of the A_i were .0027, .1360, .3413, .3413, .1360, and .0227. The product tests were simulated as before for five test batches of the product but with the new six-segment underlying distribution. The results obtained with the value of d giving the best possible fit are shown in column 4 of Table 1.

The fit of these simulated results to the actual field results was quite good. A value of χ^2 as large as that obtained could occur by chance more than 50 percent of the time. Therefore, the six-segment normal distribution and the "best fit" value of d were accepted as useful approximations of the population values. The value of the parameter d which was obtained ($d = .65$) suggests a moderate degree of ability to recognize differences in "chocolatiness" in ice cream.

SECOND PREFERENCE MODEL

The simulation results seemed to be sufficient evidence of error in the initial estimate of the relevant range of the product attribute to justify a new field preference experiment with chocolate ice cream. I had a

new batch of ice cream formulated with one step less chocolate than the batch which had previously had the least chocolate. This batch was designated as level 0 to avoid renumbering the previous test batches. This new test batch was then tested in pair comparison tests against each of the original five levels. The results were combined with the results from the previous study and are shown in column 1 of Table 2. The results now appear to be reasonably symmetrical

TABLE 2   Six-Segment Study

TEST BATCH	FIELD TEST RESULTS*	FIELD TEST RESULTS†	SIMULATION RESULTS
0	170.8	179	200
1	250.4	262	255
2	285.0	298	295
3	264.1	277	295
4	257.1	269	255
5	205.6	215	200
Total	1,433.0	1,500	1,500

* Adjusted for variations in sample size.
† Adjusted to a sample size of 100 per test.

across the six test batches. A χ^2 test reveals no significant difference between the number preferring lower levels and the higher levels.

A similar test applied to the results obtained with the original five test batches showed that the number preferring the lower levels was significantly higher than the number preferring the higher levels. Thus, the combined product test results clearly support the hypothesis that the distribution of preferences for the quantity of chocolate flavoring materials is symmetrical and had a lower mean value than was supported in advance of the first field preference experiment.

As a further test of the second simulation model, the results of systematic paired comparison tests of the six test batches were simulated and compared to the observed results (Table 2). The best fit of the simulated results to the observed results was obtained with approximately the same value of d that provided the best fit to the original data (five test batches). The fit was good (significant at the 5 percent level), further supporting the conclusion that a normal curve fitted to the six segments in the way described earlier provides a useful approximation of the distribution of preferences for "chocolatiness" in chocolate ice cream in the sampled population (Penn State students). While additional testing of the simulation method of fitting prefer-

ences curves and obtaining estimates of discrimination ability is needed before its usefulness can be appraised fully, I have found these early results highly encouraging.

CONCLUSIONS

Three approaches to the estimation of distributions of consumer preferences have been briefly discussed. The Benson method treats the fitting of distributions as a "practical research problem" and fits curves directly to data with simple procedures. The more complex Kuehn method fits a distribution without prior assumptions about its shape and also provides an estimate of the basic ability of consumers to recognize differences in the product attribute being studied. A method of fitting distributions and estimating discrimination ability by computer simulation was described and illustrated with the results of two large field preference experiments. It is simpler to apply than the Kuehn method and is proposed for those cases where the researcher's prior assumptions are supported by preliminary analysis of product test data.

REFERENCES

This article is based on material presented at the Thirty-Fifth Annual Conference of the Southern Economic Association to the session on "Quantitative Techniques Applied to Marketing," sponsored by the Southern Marketing Association, Nov. 12, 1965, at Miami Beach, Florida. The research was supported by grants from the Graduate School of Industrial Administration, Carnegie Institute of Technology, the Central Fund for Research of the Pennsylvania State University, and by the Ford Foundation through a Faculty Fellowship for Research on Business for the 1964–1965 academic year.

1. L. L. Thurstone, "The Prediction of Choice," *Psychometrika,* X (Dec. 1945), 237–253.

2. *Ibid.,* 241–247.

3. For example, see Harper W. Boyd, Jr., and Ralph Westfall, *Marketing Research: Text and Cases* (rev. ed.; Homewood, Illinois: Richard D. Irwin, Inc., 1964), pp. 697–699. This book contains a section entitled "Preference Distribution Analysis."

4. Purnell Benson, *Journal of Applied Psychology,* XLVI (Oct. 1962), 307–313.

5. Alfred A. Kuehn and Ralph L. Day, *Harvard Business Review*, XL:6 (Nov.–Dec. 1962), 100–110.

6. Consumer and Personnel Studies, Inc., Madison, New Jersey.

7. Purnell Benson, "A Model for the Analysis of Consumer Preferences and an Exploratory Test," *Journal of Applied Psychology*, XXXIX (Oct. 1955), 375–381.

8. Purnell Benson, "A Short Method for Estimating a Distribution of Consumer Preferences," *Journal of Applied Psychology*, XLVI (Oct. 1962), 307–313.

9. *Ibid.*, 308.

10. *Ibid.*, 309.

11. Purnell Benson, "Fitting and Analyzing Distribution Curves of Consumer Choices," *Journal of Advertising Research*, V (March 1965), 28–34.

12. *Ibid.*, 33.

13. Purnell Benson, "Distribution of Consumer Choices for Qualitative Food Characteristics," *Food Technology*, XVIX (May 1965), 116–119.

14. *Ibid.*, 118.

15. For a discussion of various shapes of consumer preference curves, see Kuehn and Day, *op. cit.*, 104–107.

16. For a detailed discussion, see Day, "Systematic Paired Comparisons in Preference Analysis," *Journal of Marketing Research*, XXIX (Nov. 1965).

17. Ralph L. Day, "Simulation of Consumer Preference," *Journal of Advertising Research*, V (Sept. 1965), 6–10.

Stochastic Process Models of Consumer Behavior[1]

Ronald A. Howard

A colleague and I recently reviewed the literature in quantitative marketing. We read papers, talked to people, and found that although Markov chain analysis is an impressive phrase in marketing at the moment, many of the really practical problems that we face when we try to apply this analysis to actual consumer populations have never been solved. These discrepancies between theory and practice are discussed here.

I am reminded of a recent brochure intended to explain this new Markovian technique to the businessman. The brochure described customers who purchase periodically in time—every week or every month. Of course, when we look at actual consumer purchase patterns we find that consumers are not nearly so obliging—they may go for a number of weeks without purchasing anything. To make this behavior consistent with the assumptions of the brochure model it was necessary to postulate a "No Purchase" brand and to say that customers bought this fictitious brand when their history showed they made no purchase at all. I have always found this treatment of the irregular purchase problem very dissatisfying.

This is only one objectionable feature of the conventional Markovian analysis. Another is the implicit assumption that customers are cooperative in the way they change brands. Suppose we have a market where customers divide their purchases among three brands, A, B, and C. The transition probability matrix for this market specifies the

Reprinted with permission from the *Journal of Advertising Research,* vol. 3, no. 5 (September, 1963), pp. 35–42. © Advertising Research Foundation, Inc. (1963).

[1] Extension of remarks presented at the Eighth Meeting of the Operations Research Discussion Group of the Advertising Research Foundation, Inc. in New York City on November 21, 1962. Jerry Herniter of Arthur D. Little, Inc. and I have worked closely on both the technical and practical aspects of quantitative marketing for some time; I owe to him my interest in the subject.

probability that a customer who bought each brand as his last purchase will purchase each brand next time. Suppose that a customer of brand A has probability ½ of repurchasing A, ¼ of purchasing B, and ¼ of purchasing C. We would expect that if brand A had 100 customers at the end of one period, these customers would be distributed among brands A, B, and C during the next period by sampling according to the transition probabilities.

The brochure mentioned and most of the other work I have read is not consistent with this interpretation. The concept used is not that each customer of brand A has a probability ½ of buying brand A next time, but rather that exactly half the customers of brand A will return to brand A for their next purchase. In other words, if 100 customers start out in brand A, they determine by lot which 50 customers are going to return to brand A next time, and the remaining 50 customers count off "one-two, one-two" to decide who is going to each of the brands B and C.

We see that the Markov chain analysis is not being used as it was originally intended, but rather as some kind of flow model. There is no statistical element in what is going to happen to the population of customers of the given brand. They are assumed to divide themselves among brands on a subsequent purchase occasion in strict proportion to the pertinent transition probabilities.

The problem we have just discussed is the problem of aggregation: If you have a stochastic model of individual customers, how do you combine this individual behavior to obtain a model of the whole market? It is a question that has received too little attention.

We have now mentioned two important problems with present approaches. A third is the following: Suppose you have made some market tests in the past and determined a Markov transition matrix for customers. Now you are ready to run another test. How do you combine the information you have from past studies with the information that you obtain on the present test in order to get the most appropriate estimate of the transition matrix at the present time? In other words, how do you combine prior information with experimental results?

These, then, are the three problems on which I would like to comment: first, the problem of describing interpurchase times; second, the problem of aggregation; and third, the problem of estimation of transition matrices using prior knowledge. Let us begin with the problem of aggregation.

THE AGGREGATION PROBLEM AND THE VECTOR MARKOV PROCESS

What we would like to say with respect to aggregation is not that if we have 100 customers buying brand A now, 50 customers will turn up as brand A customers at the next purchase, but rather that each of the 100 customers of brand A has a probability ½ of becoming a brand A customer next time. This means that, instead of thinking about ordinary Markov processes that consider how a unit will behave when it is subjected to random forces, we must consider how a whole population of units behaves when it is subjected to the same forces. Let us call this kind of process the vector Markov process.

It is easy to describe the vector Markov process in formal terms. Let $c_i(n)$ be the number of customers of brand i at time n. For the moment we shall consider the time variable n to be discrete; we shall relax this assumption later. We assume that each customer in an N-brand market makes transitions from one brand to another at successive instants in time according to some transition probability matrix P. The problem is to determine the statistics of the number of customers of each brand i at time n if we have some initial number of customers of each brand i at time 0, $c_i(0)$.

The first thing we can say is that the number of customers of brand i at time n is going to be a random variable; we cannot say with certainty how many customers will be purchasing brand i at time n. Let us assume temporarily that all customers at time 0 purchase brand k: brand k has c_k customers; all other brands have no customers. Consider one such customer of brand k at time 0. He will either be a customer of some particular brand j at time n or he will not be a customer of that brand at that time. What is the probability that a customer who started in brand k will be a customer of brand j at time n? It is $\phi_{kj}(n)$, the multi-step transition probability that a process starting in state k at time 0 will be in state j at time n. This multi-step transition probability is easily derivable from the transition matrix for the Markov process, P.

Because we assume that customers act independently of each other, each of the c_k customers in brand k has the same probability $\phi_{kj}(n)$ of purchasing brand j after the expiration of n time periods. Thus we expect that the number of customers of brand j at time n will be given by the binomial probability distribution with probability of success $\phi_{kj}(n)$ and number of trials c_k.

We now have the probability distribution of the number of customers of brand j at time n under the assumption that all customers were originally brand k customers. Of course, in an actual situation we will not be starting out with all customers purchasing the same brand but rather each brand i will have some initial number of customers c_i. Each customer of each brand will be acted upon independently by the process. Those customers who go from brand 1 at time 0 to brand j at time n will have one binomial distribution; those who go from brand 2 to brand j over the n periods will have a second binomial distribution, and so forth. The total number of customers of brand j at time n will have a distribution that is the convolution of all these binomial distributions. The formal expression is

$$p\{c_j(n) = m\} = \overset{N}{\underset{i=1}{*}} p_B[m|c_i, \phi_{ij}(n)]$$

Here $*$ is a symbol for manifold convolution and $p_B[m|c_i, \phi_{ij}(n)]$ is the binomial probability of m successes in c_i trials with probability of success $\phi_{ij}(n)$.

This rather complicated expression is worth examining. It says that if you want to know the probability distribution of the number of customers of brand j at time n, you have to convolve N different binomial distributions, each of which has a number of trials equal to the number of customers originally in each state and a probability of success given by an n-step transition probability for the underlying Markov process.

From a more general point of view, what we really desire is not simply the probability that there are m customers in brand j at time n but rather the joint probability distribution of the number of customers in all states. We would like to know

$$p\{\dot{c}_1(n) = n_1, c_2(n) = n_2, \ldots, c_N(n) = n_N\}$$

This quantity is, in fact, given by a multinomial distribution which would be even more complicated. Let us concentrate, therefore, on the one marginal distribution of the number of customers purchasing brand j at time n.

In practice we are especially interested in certain of the moments of the distribution of the number of customers in brand j at time n. For example, what is $\bar{c}_j(n)$, the expected number of customers in brand j at time n? Since the distribution of $c_j(n)$ is the convolution of N dif-

ferent binomial distributions, the mean of $c_j(n)$ must be just the sum of the means of the various binomial distributions. Recalling that the mean of a binomial distribution is just its probability of success times its number of trials, we can write

$$\bar{c}_j(n) = \sum_{i=1}^{N} c_i \phi_{ij}(n)$$

In row vector-matrix notation this equation is:

$$\bar{\underline{c}}(n) = \underline{c}(0)\ \Phi(n) = \underline{c}(0)\ P^n$$

Here we have written the n-step transition probability matrix $\Phi(n)$ in its most usual form as the nth power of the transition probability matrix P.

The variance of the $c_j(n)$ distribution, $\overset{V}{c_j}(n)$ is also easily derived. The variance of the number of customers of brand j at time n is just the sum of the variances of the N binomial distributions that are convolved to produce the $c_j(n)$ distribution. Since the variance of a binomial distribution is equal to the number of trials times the probability of success times one minus the probability of success we obtain directly

$$\overset{V}{c_j}(n) = \sum_{i=1}^{N} c_i \phi_{ij}(n)[1 - \phi_{ij}(n)]$$

If we define a quantity $v_{ij}(n)$ by

$$v_{ij}(n) = \phi_{ij}(n)[1 - \phi_{ij}(n)]$$

then we can write $\overset{V}{c_j}(n)$ in the form

$$\overset{V}{c_j}(n) = \sum_{i=1}^{N} c_i v_{ij}(n)$$

Finally, by using a variance matrix $V(n)$ with elements $v_{ij}(n)$ we can write this equation in matrix form as

$$\overset{V}{\underline{c}}(n) = \underline{c}(0)\ V(n)$$

We could calculate other moments of the $c_j(n)$ distribution by similar methods if they should be needed.

AN AGGREGATION EXAMPLE

An example will serve to illustrate the necessary computations. Suppose that two brands, 1 and 2, share a market. It has been decided to model a customer in this market by a two-state Markov process. State 1 corresponds to his having purchased brand 1 last; state 2, brand 2. It is found that a customer has a probability 0.8 of repeating a purchase of brand 1 and a probability 0.7 of repeating a purchase of brand 2. The transition probability matrix for the process is, therefore,

$$ P = \begin{bmatrix} 0.8 & 0.2 \\ 0.3 & 0.7 \end{bmatrix} $$

The probability that a customer who buys brand i as his zero-th purchase will pruchase brand j on his nth purchase is the multi-step transition probability $\phi_{ij}(n)$. The matrix of these multi-step transition probabilities, $\Phi(n)$, is given by the nth power of the transition probability matrix P. The first few of these matrices are easily evaluated.

$$ \Phi(1) = P = \begin{bmatrix} 0.8 & 0.2 \\ 0.3 & 0.7 \end{bmatrix} $$

$$ \Phi(2) = P^2 = \begin{bmatrix} 0.7 & 0.3 \\ 0.45 & 0.55 \end{bmatrix} $$

$$ \Phi(3) = P^3 = \begin{bmatrix} 0.65 & 0.35 \\ 0.525 & 0.475 \end{bmatrix} $$

$$ \Phi(4) = P^4 = \begin{bmatrix} 0.625 & 0.375 \\ 0.5625 & 0.4375 \end{bmatrix} $$

We see, for example, that the 12 element of $\Phi(3) = P^3$ is 0.35. This means that there is a probability 0.35 that a customer who bought brand 1 at his zero-th purchase will buy brand 2 as his third purchase.

It is possible to write a simple expression that specifies $\Phi(n)$ for any value of n:

$$ \Phi(n) = \begin{bmatrix} 0.6 & 0.4 \\ 0.6 & 0.4 \end{bmatrix} + (0.5)^n \begin{bmatrix} 0.4 & -0.4 \\ -0.6 & 0.6 \end{bmatrix} $$

This expression brings into view what is perhaps the most important and common property of the Markov process—its tendency to achieve a limiting probability distribution over its states that is independent of where it is started. In this case, as n increases, $\Phi(n)$ tends more and more closely to the matrix

$$\Phi = \begin{bmatrix} 0.6 & 0.4 \\ 0.6 & 0.4 \end{bmatrix}$$

This matrix shows that after a large number of purchases, the customer will buy brand 1 with probability 0.6, brand 2 with probability 0.4, independent of which brand the customer purchased originally.

We are especially interested in the vector Markov process. We have already found $\Phi(n)$; the variance matrix $V(n)$ is computed from the elements of $\Phi(n)$ by multiplying each element by the difference between that element and one. We obtain

$$V(n) = \begin{bmatrix} 0.24 & 0.24 \\ 0.24 & 0.24 \end{bmatrix} + (0.5)^n \begin{bmatrix} -0.08 & -0.08 \\ 0.12 & 0.12 \end{bmatrix}$$
$$+ (0.25)^n \begin{bmatrix} -0.16 & -0.16 \\ -0.36 & -0.36 \end{bmatrix}$$

We have now completed all necessary preliminary calculations and can begin analyzing a vector Markov process. Suppose that the manufacturer of brand 1 conducted a panel study to see what happens to the buyers of his product. He selects 100 customers whose last purchase was brand 1 and observes their future purchases. What does our model predict about his observations? The initial vector of customers is $c(0) = \begin{bmatrix} 100 & 0 \end{bmatrix}$. The vectors giving the means and variances of the number of customers who buy each brand as their nth purchase is easily derived from our basic equations

$$\bar{c}(n) = c(0)\,\Phi(n) = \begin{bmatrix} 60 & 40 \end{bmatrix} + (0.5)^n \begin{bmatrix} 40 & -40 \end{bmatrix}$$

$$\overset{V}{c}(n) = c(0)\,V(n) = \begin{bmatrix} 24 & 24 \end{bmatrix} + (0.5)^n \begin{bmatrix} -8 & -8 \end{bmatrix} + (0.25)^n \begin{bmatrix} -16 & -16 \end{bmatrix}$$

We shall write these vectors for a few values of n:

$$\bar{c}(1) = \begin{bmatrix} 80 & 20 \end{bmatrix} \qquad \overset{V}{c}(1) = \begin{bmatrix} 16 & 16 \end{bmatrix}$$

$$\bar{\text{c}}(2) = [70 \quad 30] \qquad \overset{\text{v}}{\text{c}}(2) = [21 \quad 21]$$

$$\bar{\text{c}}(3) = [65 \quad 35] \qquad \overset{\text{v}}{\text{c}}(3) = [22.75 \quad 22.75]$$

$$\bar{\text{c}}(4) = [62.5 \quad 37.5] \qquad \overset{\text{v}}{\text{c}}(4) = [23.4375 \quad 23.4375]$$

$$\vdots \qquad\qquad\qquad \vdots$$

$$\bar{\text{c}}(\infty) = [60 \quad 40] \qquad \overset{\text{v}}{\text{c}}(\infty) = [24 \quad 24]$$

We see from the first component of $\bar{\text{c}}(2)$ that 70 customers are expected to purchase brand 1 as their second purchase. The first component of $\overset{\text{v}}{\text{c}}(2)$ shows, however, that a variance of 21 is to be associated with this number. Therefore, if the manufacturer observed that, say, 74 customers had in fact bought brand 1 as their second purchase, he would have no reason to doubt the Markov model. If, however, 80 customers were found in this category, the fundamental applicability of the model would be brought into question. Because of the requirement that the total number of customers always be 100, such a test need be applied only to the population of one state in a two-state system. This special property of the two-state system is also revealed by the equality of the components of $\overset{\text{v}}{\text{c}}(n)$.

Figure 1 illustrates the type of fluctuations to be expected in the occupancy of state 1. We would expect the actual population to lie within the one standard deviation band with a probability of about

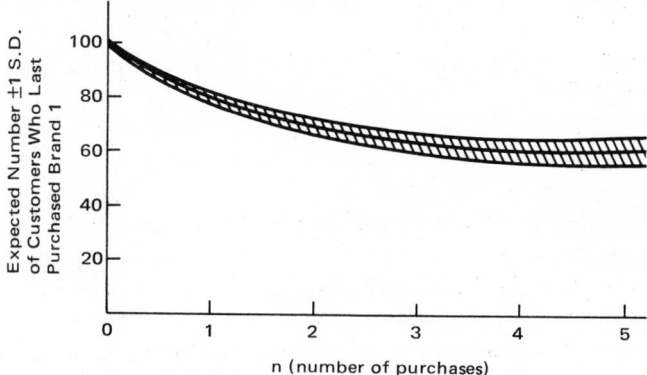

Figure 1   One standard deviation band for occupancy of state 1 on successive transitions $\bar{\text{c}}_1(n) \pm \sqrt{\overset{\text{v}}{\text{c}}_1(n)}$

2/3. The actual population will fall outside a band of twice this width with a probability of about 1/20.

The vector Markov process thus has an important use in establishing the validity of a Markov model. Notice that the fluctuation of the number of customers buying each brand is predicted to continue into the indefinite future. Although after many purchases have been made the manufacturer expects 60 customers of his original 100 to be buying brand 1, a variance of 24 persists. Therefore fluctuations from 55 to 65 will not be unusual variations in the number of customers in state 1. Perhaps this is the most important observation that arises in using the vector Markov models—that even when a population has achieved steady-state behavior, the number of customers in each state is expected to vary.

Now that we have developed the analysis of the vector Markov process it is easy to see the assumption that is being made when the customers of a brand have their purchases divided among the various brands in the following month strictly according to the transition probabilities. The assumption is that the actual flow will be the expected flow. Even if the simple Markov process were a perfect model for individual customer behavior, the predictions made for the population of customers would be uncertain because of the inherent randomness of the cumulative behavior.

The main point to make about the aggregation problem is that if you assume a Markov model for customer behavior, you must state whether you think this model applies to the individual customer or to the market as a whole. If you model the whole population by the Markov transition matrix, then you are dealing with the Markov process as a flow model, not as a stochastic process. If the Markov model is applied to the individual customer then there will be a fluctuation in the number of customers purchasing each brand in the steady state; this fluctuation can be predicted by the methods we have discussed.

The use of Markov models is most typically a two-step procedure. First, the model is formulated and verified on a small sample of customers using special tests or panel data. Then it is applied to make predictions about the entire population. The vector Markov process model or a variant is essential to the first step. It is unnecessary in the second because the large numbers of customers involved make percentage fluctuations negligible.

We have left an important issue still in the air. A manufacturer is not nearly so much interested in what brand a customer will buy on his nth purchase as he is in the combination of this information with

a knowledge of when the nth purchase will be made. So we must revert to the first problem we mentioned, that of representing random inter-purchase times.

RANDOM INTERPURCHASE TIMES—
THE SEMI-MARKOV PROCESS

If you actually examine consumer panel data for one family unit you find quite a random pattern of purchases. You see that on January 1 the customer bought brand A, on February 13 he bought brand B, and maybe on February 20 he bought brand B again, and so forth. The purchase pattern is far from regular even if we allow for possible interruptions. Fortunately, there is no need to assume that the time between purchases is a constant, and thereby create the necessity for fictitious "No Purchase" brands; all we must do is expand our concept of a Markov process.

The regular Markov process is defined by transition probabilities p_{ij} that specify the probability of making a transition from state i to state j. This transition is assumed to require exactly one time period, such as a week or a month. Let us consider a generalization of this model where the probabilities of transitions are again governed by quantities like p_{ij} but where the time to go from one state to another is a random variable. We shall let τ_{ij} be the time required for a transition from i to j. It is selected from a density function $h_{ij}(.)$ that depends on the transition to be made.

The generalized Markov process we have described is called a semi-Markov process. The regular Markov process is just a special case of the semi-Markov process where all the density functions for transition times $h_{ij}(.)$ are impulses at one time unit. The so-called continuous-time Markov process is the special case where the density functions, also called holding-time distributions, are exponential density functions. A semi-Markov process is described by a transition probability matrix P and by a holding time matrix H with elements $h_{ij}(.)$.

A fundamental quantity of interest for a semi-Markov process is its interval transition probability matrix $\Phi(t)$. The element $\phi_{ij}(t)$ of this matrix is the probability that a system that entered state i at time zero will be in state j at time t. The interval transition probabilities satisfy the equation

$$\phi_{ij}(t) = \delta_{ij}\left[1 - \sum_{k=1}^{N} p_{ik}\int_0^t d\tau\, h_{ik}(\tau)\right]$$

$$+ \sum_{k=1}^{N} p_{ik} \int_{0}^{t} d\tau \, h_{ik}(\tau) \, \phi_{kj}(t - \tau) \quad t \geqslant 0, \, 1 \leqslant i, j \leqslant N$$

$$\delta_{ij} = \begin{cases} 1 & i = j \\ 0 & i \neq j \end{cases}$$

Calculation of the interval transition probabilities sometimes poses problems. In many cases it is possible to use transform methods to solve the equations; in others digital computation is advisable.

A RANDOM INTERPURCHASE TIME EXAMPLE

Let us consider a simple example of the semi-Markov process in marketing. Every customer in a two-product market is assumed to alternate his purchases of the two products. A possible interpretation is the purchase of television picture tubes and the brighteners that can be used when they get old. A customer is considered to be in state 1 if he last purchased a brightener and in state 2 if he last purchased a tube. The density function for the time a brightener will last is shown in Figure 2; the density function for the lifetime of a tube is shown in Figure 3. This semi-Markov process can be represented by the transition probability matrix

$$P = \begin{bmatrix} 0 & 1 \\ 1 & 0 \end{bmatrix}$$

and the holding time matrix

$$H(t) = \begin{bmatrix} \underline{\quad\quad} & 4e^{-4t} \\ te^{-t} & \underline{\quad\quad} \end{bmatrix}$$

Thus the customer in state 1 must go to state 2; his time for this transition (time to purchase a tube) is drawn from the density function $4e^{-4t}$. Similarly, a customer in state 2 must go to state 1; the time for this transition (time to purchase a brightener) is drawn from the density function te^{-t}.

We might ask two interesting questions of the model. Given that a customer purchased a brightener at time zero, what is the probability that he will have a brightener as his last purchase at time t? And the same question, except with tube instead of brightener. The answers to these two questions are $\phi_{11}(t)$ and $\phi_{22}(t)$. They have been cal-

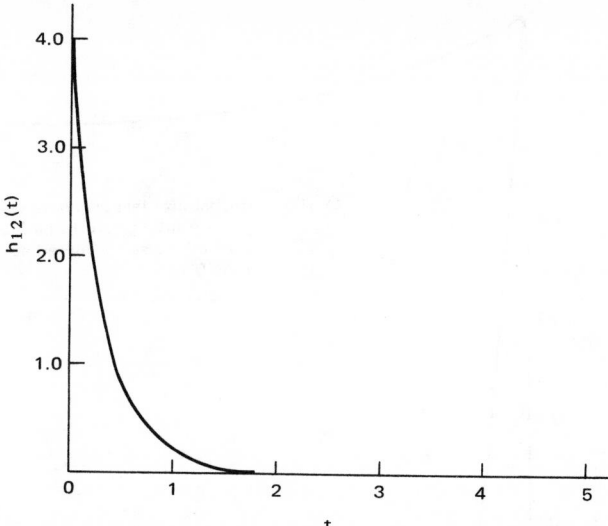

Figure 2   Density function for lifetime of brighteners $h_{12}(t) = 4e^{-4t}$

culated using transform methods and plotted in Figure 4. Notice how quickly the information that a customer purchased a brightener at time zero loses its value as time passes. The probability that the customer's last purchase was a brightener approaches 1/9; that it was a tube, 8/9. This means that we would expect the ratio of brighteners to new tubes in the population to be about one to eight.

A number of interesting questions could be based on this model. We could, for example, find the effect on the market of making tubes last longer. We could also modify the model to allow the purchase of a new tube instead of a brightener when the original tube wore out; but these are details. So is the fact that the present example could be considered as a continuous-time Markov process.

The important point is that we have models available that do not

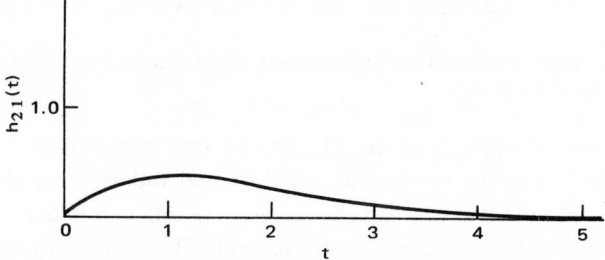

Figure 3   Density function for lifetime of picture tubes $h_{21}(t) = te^{-t}$

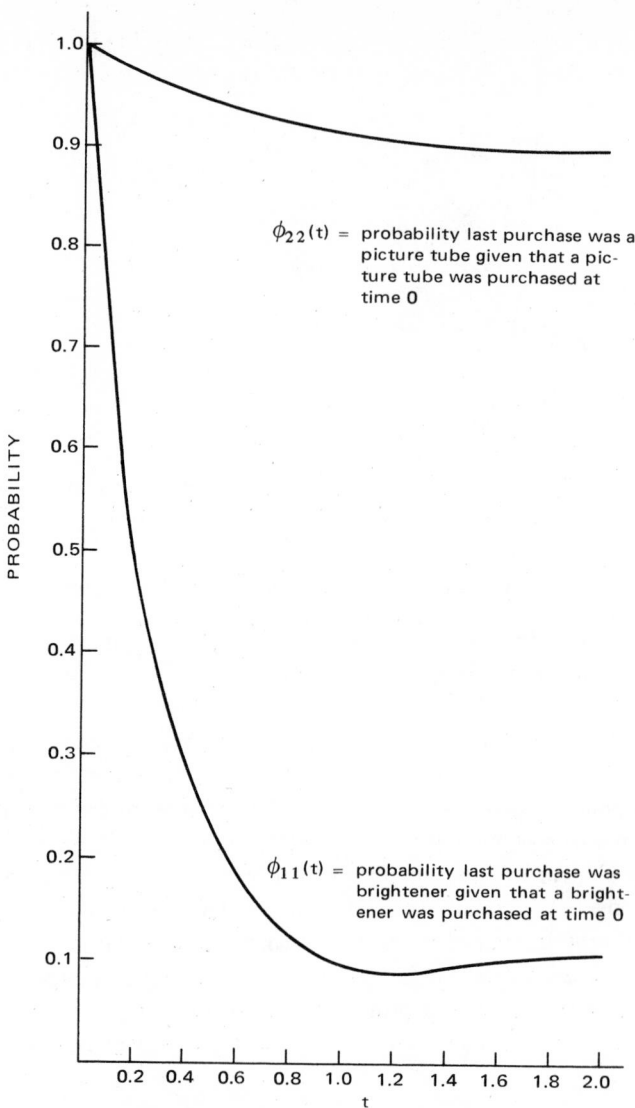

Figure 4   Interval transition probabilities for the semi-Markov model of the television problem

require the assumption of equally spaced purchases—time between purchases can be as random as you like and different for different products. For the first time we can see ways of taking into account differences in package size or product use rate. The generality afforded by the semi-Markov process is impressive.

How is the semi-Markov process used in analyzing panel data? The transition probability matrix P is estimated from the data by noting the fraction of times that a purchase of brand j follows purchase of brand i, regardless of the time interval separating the purchases. There is no need to divide time arbitrarily into two-week or two-month intervals. Then, as an entirely separate matter, a histogram of the time between purchases of brands i and j is plotted. This histogram is an estimate of the holding time distribution for this transition, $h_{ij}(.)$. This calculation is performed for all pairs of brands to construct the holding time matrix H.

When the transition probability matrix P and the holding time matrix H are known, the semi-Markov process structure can be used for all the predictions currently made by ordinary Markov models—future market shares, transition rates, etc. The semi-Markov process provides a powerful model for individual consumer behavior because it frees us from the discrete-time restriction. Of course, the remarks made on the aggregation problem with respect to ordinary Markov processes apply with equal force to semi-Markov processes.

THE ESTIMATION PROBLEM

We shall just briefly discuss the third problem, that of combining experimental results with prior information. Suppose that you have the good feeling for the form of the transition probability matrix for a certain product and then you obtain additional data on actual transitions, either from a test situation or from a consumer panel. How are you going to incorporate the new test data with your prior knowledge? The solution to this problem lies in current research. We have been able to place it in a Bayesian framework. Prior knowledge about the transition probability matrix can be expressed in terms of continuous distributions over the probabilities in this matrix. If these distributions are chosen judiciously, it is possible to combine the prior knowledge with the experimental results by simple arithmetic computations. The result of these computations is a new set of continuous distributions over the transition probability matrix that will generally have smaller variances than the previous distributions. It is fair to say that these techniques, although very promising, are not at the state of development of the other areas we have discussed.

SUMMARY

Previous research in Markovian market models has not squarely faced the issues of random inter-purchase time, aggregation, and estimation of transition matrices. We have discussed some approaches that can make contributions on each of these problems. Perhaps the most important point to make is this: We all realize that Markovian analysis is no panacea for marketing problems. We have found some cases where it was an excellent approach and others where it was of little value. In any case, we can only benefit by using those Markov models appropriate to the phenomena we are studying.

Prediction of Consumer Innovators: Application of Multiple Discriminant Analysis

Thomas S. Robertson
James N. Kennedy

INTRODUCTION

The successful diffusion of new products depends on an understanding of the consumer innovator. This article reports on using multiple discriminant analysis to predict innovators and to assess the importance of several innovator characteristics.

Two multiple discriminant equations are generated. The first, a short-cut method permitting manual calculation, is based on the assumption that the variables studied are independent. The second requires a computer but considers whatever interdependence is present.

The findings here are based on an empirical inquiry into the adoption of a new small home appliance product. The characteristics studied came from literature on new product diffusion from various academic disciplines.

INNOVATOR CHARACTERISTICS

The characteristics of consumer innovators are ill-defined. Although some 800 studies on the diffusion of new ideas and practices have been reported in sociology, direct application of these findings to the marketing of consumer products is questionable.

As defined in sociology, innovators are the first 2.5 percent of the community's potential adopters to purchase. In marketing, a 10 per-

Reprinted with permission from the *Journal of Marketing Research*, vol. 5, no. 1 (February, 1968), pp. 64–69, published by the American Marketing Association.

cent figure has gained some recognition. An innovation is loosely defined as any product that consumers perceive to be new. Adoption or innovative behavior is the process of accepting and purchasing the innovation. Diffusion means the spread of the item from the manufacturer to ultimate users.

A model of innovator characteristics follows. This model is based on agricultural findings summarized by Everett M. Rogers [18], on a major research effort tracing a new drug's diffusion in the medical community [6], and on four innovative behavior studies in the marketing discipline [1, 4, 10, 16]. The characteristics selected are not exhaustive but are of most general importance in previous research.

Venturesomeness

Rogers uses venturesomeness as a summary concept to characterize agricultural innovators.

The major value of the innovator is venturesomeness. He must desire the hazardous, the rash, the daring, and the risking [18, p. 169].

Venturesomeness is operationally defined in this study as willingness to take risks in the purchase of new products. Risk-taking by consumers has been investigated in several recent marketing studies [3, 8].

Social Mobility

The Tastemaker studies by Opinion Research Corporation conclude that innovators are the mobiles in society [1]. Social mobility means movement on the societal status hierarchy. Here, upward social mobility is measured and defined by prior and anticipated movement on the social class ladder.

Privilegedness

Income level frequently has correlated with innovative behavior [4, 19]. Privilegedness is financial standing *relative* to other community members. Richard P. Coleman applied the privilegedness concept to the compact car and color television markets and found, for example, that color television innovators were overprivileged members of each social class [7].

Social Integration

Social integration is defined as the person's degree of participation with other community members. This variable has been important in the agricultural studies and the medical diffusion study [18, 6], but it has not been directly tested in the consumer goods' area.

Interest Range

Katz and Lazarfeld found degree of interest in a consumption area to be "strongly related" to opinion leadership [14]. A common assumption has been that innovators are more interested in the consumption area in which they innovate [22]. The Tastemaker studies further suggest that innovators may be committed to a wider range of interests or values than non-innovators [1] . The hypothesis of interest range will be studied here.

Status Concern

Status concern is the person's need to be noticed and admired. The variable is not explicitly derived from diffusion research but from Veblin's treatise on conspicious consumption [20]. The conspicuousness of innovations and the resulting attention may prompt innovative behavior. Air-conditioners, for example, were a highly conspicuous item and this affected their pattern of diffusion in the Philadelphia neighborhood studied by Whyte [21]. Bourne, on reference group influence, cites the product's conspicuousness as perhaps the main attribute in whether purchase will be susceptible to reference group effect [5].

Cosmopolitanism

How oriented the person is beyond his community is referred to as cosmopolitanism. Findings from the agricultural and medical studies emphasize that innovators have cosmopolitan outlooks. The physician innovator, for example, subscribed to more medical journals, attended more out-of-town professional meetings, and visited more out-of-town medical institutions and teaching hospitals [13].

Hypotheses

Innovators will have distinguishing characteristics from non-innovators. The formulation and direction of each hypothesis is based on previous research findings. Innovators will be:

1. more venturesome in their consumption behavior than non-innovators,
2. more socially mobile,
3. relatively more financially privileged,
4. more socially integrated,
5. interested in a wider range of consumption areas,
6. more status concerned,
7. more cosmopolitan in outlook.

RESEARCH DESIGN

Research was done in one reasonably well defined social system, the middle class suburban community of Deerfield, Illinois. Innovators were operationally defined as the first ten percent of the community's members to adopt the small home appliance innovation under investigation. Penetration of this product in the community was 11 percent at the time of the study, one year after the product's introduction. Non-innovators were those who did not purchase the product.

The sample had 60 innovators and 40 non-innovators. This breakdown was preferred to allow more opportunity to trace the flow of information that innovators used. Innovators were chosen systematically from the community's geographic areas where the product's penetration was greatest. The sampling procedure selected every other household owning the innovation for inclusion in the sample. By a random number procedure, non-innovators were selected from each block on which an innovator was chosen. Thus it was hoped that certain demographic variables would be controlled for the innovator and non-innovator subsamples.

A telephone street-address directory was used in sample selection and interviews were arranged by telephone. Under these controlled procedures, response rate was about 80 percent. The only known biases are the exclusion of unlisted telephone number households, no telephone households, and some working wife households.

In-home personal interviews, lasting about 90 minutes each, were done by professional interviewers. The female head of household was the spokesman for each family consumption unit because she represented the family's opinions best and she was more open to depth interviewing.

Table 1 gives the questionnaire items measuring venturesomeness and social mobility characteristics. For example, the venturesomeness characteristic is assessed by four measurement components. The answers to these components can all be arranged on seven-point scales from highly venturesome to highly non-venturesome. The mean of the several components gives an overall venturesomeness score for the person. The same procedure was followed for the remaining variables.

Four coders handled the coding of the open-ended material. Over 90 percent consistency was obtained using guidelines set by the head researcher.

LINEAR DISCRIMINANT FUNCTION

The objective of the multiple discriminant analysis is to produce a linear function that will distinguish innovators from non-innovators. Weights are assigned to the variables such that the ratio of the difference between the means of the two groups to the standard deviation within groups is maximized. The discrete nature of the dependent variable suggests discriminant analysis rather than regression analysis, which has as an assumption that the dependent variable is a random variate.

The linear discriminant function can be expressed as [9]:

(1) $$Z = w_1 x_1 + w_2 x_2 \ldots + w_n x_n.$$

Here, $x_1 \ldots x_n$ represent the independent variable while $w_1 \ldots w_n$ represent the discriminant coefficients, or *weights,* to be applied to the independent variables. Z will be called the person's point score. Based on the point score, it should be possible to predict innovators and non-innovators.

Discriminant analysis also allows the researcher to determine the relative importance of the independent variables. The importance value, proposed by Mosteller and Wallace [17], measures the contribution of each variable to the difference in the average point scores between the two groups ($\bar{Z}_I - \bar{Z}_N$).

TABLE 1 Examples of Questionnaire Items

CHARACTERISTIC	MEASUREMENT COMPONENTS	QUESTIONNAIRE ITEMS
Venturesomeness	Attitude toward innovative behavior	How do you feel about buying new things that come out for the home?
	Actual adoptions of home appliances	Which of the following items do you have for your home?
	Willingness to buy hypothetical innovations	How willing would you be to buy the following items immediately after they come on the market?
	Self-perception on represented innovator characteristics	In regard to new products on the market, I am: (last-first . . . leader-follower, etc.)
Social mobility	Continuity or change in friendship patterns	What about *your* friends and the friends that *you and your husband* have together. Where do you know them from? How long have you known them?
	Neighborhood mobility patterns	What do you dislike about your neighborhood? If you move, what kind of neighborhood would you like to move to? Why?
	Occupational mobility	What is your husband's occupation? What position did your husband hold before this one?
	Locational mobility	How long have you lived at this address? How often have you moved within the last five years?
	Organizational mobility	How often do you give up one organization and join another?

Given that one mean value is exactly at the average of the innovator group and another at the average of the non-innovator group, then the difference in score is a measure of the importance $[Y_i]$ of the variables, indicating the contribution it makes to the total difference in innovator versus non-innovator point scores.

(2) $$Y_i = w_i \bar{x}_{iI} - w_i \bar{x}_{iN} = w_i(\bar{x}_{iI} - \bar{x}_{iN}).$$

Here, w_i is the discriminant weight for the variable under consideration while $\bar{x}_{iI}$ is the mean score of the innovator sample for this variable and $\bar{x}_{iN}$ is the mean score of the non-innovator sample. The discriminant weight may be determined manually if the covariance of the variables involved is assumed to be zero. Otherwise, the computations should be made using a regression analysis or discriminant analysis program.

Thus, if independence of the variables is assumed, the weights may be computed directly from the relationship:

(3) $$w_i = (\bar{x}_{iI} - \bar{x}_{iN}) / (\sigma_{iI}^2 + \sigma_{iN}^2)$$

where $\bar{x}_{iI}$ is the average for the *ith* characteristic in the innovator sample and $\bar{x}_{iN}$ is the average in the non-innovator sample. The respective variances of the *ith* characteristic are represented by

$$\sigma_{iI}^2 \text{ and } \sigma_{iN}^2 [17].$$

Significance of the point-score distributions is tested using the difference between the average point scores for innovators and non-innovators.

(4) $$D = \bar{Z}_I - \bar{Z}_N$$

Using this value and the appropriate degrees of freedom, the various significance tests can be approximated [12, p. 379].

APPLICATION

Manual Technique

The first step in the analysis was to compute discriminant weights using (3), assuming zero covariance among the variables. The objective was to quickly identify the important variables and to provide guidelines for the final computer analysis.

Mean scores and manually computed weights for innovators and non-innovators are summarized in Table 2. Means are based on a

TABLE 2 Mean Values of Characteristics, Discriminant Weights, and Importance Values[a]

Characteristic	Inno-vator Mean (N = 60)	Non-inno-vator Mean (N = 40)	Manual Computations	
			Weight	Impor-tance
Venturesomeness[b]	4.88	4.12	3.59	2.73
Social mobility[b]	3.93	3.20	2.02	1.47
Privilegedness[c]	3.68	3.25	1.77	0.76
Social integration[c]	4.13	3.78	1.97	0.69
Status concern	2.00	1.73	1.72	0.46
Interest range	5.27	5.00	1.25	0.34
Cosmopolitanism	2.77	3.03	−1.41	0.37
Unweighted total	26.66	24.11	Difference	6.82

[a] Mean values based on a seven-point scale except status concern where a three-point scale was used.
[b] Difference between means significant at $p < .01$ (t test).
[c] Difference between means significant at $p < .05$ (t test).

maximum possible score of 7, except for the status concern variable, where the maximum possible score is 3. Differences in mean scores from variable to variable may be comparable; yet, as will be seen, the importance values resulting can vary significantly as a function of the variances.

The discriminant function is designed to give high point scores (Z values) to the innovator group and to give low point scores to the non-innovator group. These Z values represent the combination of weighted characteristics for each person. It is possible to set a cutoff point so that the cost effects of misclassifying innovators and non-innovators are minimized. This cutoff point can then be used to predict innovators and non-innovators from other samples. The model's functioning, therefore, gives maximum significant difference between the means of the two groups by assigning optimum weights to the independent variables.

Based on the manually derived discriminant function and optimum cutoff points, 82 percent of the innovator group and 63 percent of the non-innovator group could be correctly classified. This discriminant function also gave importance values for the several variables, which indicated that venturesomeness and social mobility together accounted for about 62 percent of the point score difference between innovators and non-innovators.

The manually derived discriminant function, therefore, proved useful for gaining insight concerning the data. Its value is that of an approximating device. It is also helpful in evaluating the effects of various methods of coding and parameterizing the variables.

Computer Technique

The input data for the computer analysis was respondent scores on the seven characteristics (independent variables) and a dummy dependent variable. The dependent variable was assigned values of (100) $(n_2)/(n_1 + n_2)$ for innovators and (100) $(-n_1)/(n_1 + n_2)$ for non-innovators. A regression analysis program was then used to generate discriminant function weights (actually regression coefficients), the coefficient of multiple correlation, and a test of significance (F test). The covariance among the variables was, of course, considered. Discriminant function weights and importance values are in Table 3. Each importance value is also transformed into its relative importance compared with the other variables.

TABLE 3   Discriminant Weights and Importance Values by Computer

CHARACTERISTIC	WEIGHT	IMPORTANCE	RELATIVE IMPORTANCE
Venturesomeness	3.59	2.73	35%
Social mobility	3.08	2.25	29
Privilegedness	2.04	0.88	11
Social integration	2.44	0.85	11
Status concern	0.95	0.26	3
Interest range	0.59	0.16	2
Cosmopolitanism	−2.86	0.74	9
Total		7.87	100%

Venturesomeness makes the greatest contribution in discriminating between the two groups. Its importance value, 2.73, may be interpreted as the contribution this variable makes toward overall innovative behavior, or, more strictly, the contribution toward the overall difference between the average point scores of innovators and noninnovators. Its relative value is 35 percent.

The social mobility characteristic with an importance score of 2.25 accounts for 29 percent of the point score difference between innovators and non-innovators, while privilegedness and social integration each have relative contribution values of 11 percent. Status concern and interest range account for only 3 percent and 2 percent, re-

spectively, of the difference between innovator and non-innovator point scores, and are of minor importance here.

Cosmopolitanism, finally, has a negative weight with an importance value of .74. This value can be interpreted as a positive localism score and accounts for 9 percent of the difference between group point scores. A high cosmopolitanism score reduces the likelihood of innovative behavior.

The Z score distributions are in Table 4. The cutoff point that minimizes cost effects of misclassification is dependent on: (a) the proportion of innovators and non-innovators in the population and (b) the cost of misclassifying a member of either group. The two misclassification costs may be considered as: (1) the loss of profit from not selling an appliance to an innovator and (2) the cost in-

TABLE 4   Point Score Distributions

| POINT SCORE RANGE | INNOVATORS | | NON-INNOVATORS | | DENSITY RATIO P_I/P_N |
	PERCENT P_I	CUMU- LATIVE	PERCENT P_N	CUMU- LATIVE	
57.6–60.0	1.7				∞
55.1–57.5	5.0	6.7			∞
52.6–55.0	8.4	15.1			∞
50.1–52.5	11.7	26.8	7.5		1.56
47.6–50.0	18.3	45.1	5.0	12.5	3.66
45.1–47.5	23.3	68.4	20.0	32.5	1.17
42.6–45.0	18.3	86.7	17.5	50.0	1.05
40.1–42.5	10.0	96.7	7.5	57.5	1.33
	a				
37.6–40.0	0.0	96.7	20.0	77.5	0.00
35.1–37.5	3.3	100.0	7.5	85.0	0.44
32.6–35.0			7.5	92.5	0.00
30.1–32.5			5.0	97.5	0.00
27.6–30.0			0.0	97.5	0.00
25.1–27.5			2.5	100.0	0.00

a Cutoff score that minimizes misclassification cost if the population contains 10 percent innovators and the ratio of costs, C_c/C_{LP}, is .10.

volved in canvassing a nonbuyer. Members of a population are classified as innovators if the following relationship is satisfied [2]:

$$(6) \qquad p_{I(Z)}/p_{N(Z)} \geqslant (C_c/C_{LP})\,(q_N/q_I).$$

The values $p_{I(Z)}$ and $p_{N(Z)}$ are the percentages of innovators and non-innovators in the sample with point score Z. The frequency or

density ratios, $p_{I(z)}/p_{N(z)}$, are in the last column, Table 4, for each of the groupings. The proportion of innovators and non-innovators are represented by q_I *and* q_N, respectively; the canvassing and loss-of-profit costs are C_c and C_{LP}.

For example, if the ratio of canvassing cost to loss-of-profit is .10, and ten percent of the population are innovators, the value for the right-hand side of (6) is .90. The ratios, computed in Table 4, exceed this value in the class intervals for point scores above 40. The estimated cutoff that minimizes the cost of misclassification is, therefore, 40. That is, if the point score of a particular respondent is above 40, he would be called an innovator and canvassed; if his score is 40 or below, he would be called a non-innovator and not canvassed. This strategy minimizes the cost effects of misclassification for the sample estimates.

The cutoff point that minimizes the number of respondents misclassified in the sample can also be determined by (6). Here, the cost effects are considered to be equal, and the ratio C_c/C_{LP} is, therefore, 1: Since the sample has 60 innovators and 40 non-innovators, the ratio of q_N/q_I is assumed to be .67. The optimum cutoff point, minimizing misclassification in the sample is also 40 since the ratios for point scores above 40 in Table 4 exceed .67.

It can also be seen that the density ratios do not decrease steadily, as might be expected, because of the relatively small sample number of innovators and non-innovators.

The significance of the discriminant function was evaluated by an F test [15]. The F value obtained, 2.767, suggests that the discriminant function could discriminate between innovators and non-innovators ($P < .05$). The multiple correlation coefficient was .417.

The task of validation is not yet finished, however. As shown by Frank, Massy, and Morrison [11] and by Mosteller and Wallace [17], bias can occur in multiple discriminant analysis if the discriminant function is applied to the same sample data used to estimate the function.

The primary cause of this bias is due to errors of sampling when estimating the means of the population, upon which the discriminant coefficients are based [11, p. 252].

A further possible source of bias is search bias which enters when a researcher seeks the best predictive variables. This bias is of no significance in this study because all hypothesized variables were used in the discriminant function.

The method for validation consists of splitting the sample data and using one-half the data to derive the discriminant function and then applying this function to the remaining data [11]. This procedure can help isolate the effect of sampling errors by the decrease in discriminant power from the analysis subsample to the applied subsample.

Here, two validation runs were made. Data were divided into two series—odd and even. A linear discriminant function was computed for each series and applied against the analysis series and the applied series. Thus four combinations emerge: odd-odd, odd-even, even-even, and even-odd.

Results (Table 5) show a drop in the percentage of correct classifications when the discriminant function is applied to new data. This is caused by sampling variation in the original computation of the weights. The F tests were not significant because of reduced sample sizes. Overall results based on the discriminant function should be regarded as tentative rather than conclusive. There is evidence that predictive ability was improved. Each percentage improvement can potentially translate into an increase in sales volume.

DISCUSSION

Review of the innovative behavior literature from several disciplines suggested probable characteristics of consumer innovators. These characteristics were measured for consumer innovators and non-innovators, and discriminant analysis was applied to test the value of the composite of characteristics for predictive purposes and the discriminating value of each characteristic.

Results of manual and computer techniques did not differ greatly, despite the assumption of zero-covariance in the manual method. The manual method is a good approximating device and at an early stage in a research project can be used to test the value of the hypotheses in discriminating ability.

For the present set of findings, it appears that two variables, venturesomeness (willingness to take new product risks) and social mobility (movement up the social class hierarchy) account for most of the innovative behavior difference between innovators and non-innovators of new home appliances. The astute marketer of such product innovations would seem to have his best chance for initial sales success with an appeal to venturesome, socially mobile people.

Characteristics also important are social integration (degree of

TABLE 5 Results of Validation Tests

	TOTAL	EVEN DATA		ODD DATA	
		EVEN-EVEN	EVEN-ODD	ODD-ODD	ODD-EVEN
Percentage correctly classified					
Innovators ($N = 60$)	96.7%	83.3%	76.7%	100.0%	93.4%
Non-innovators ($N = 40$)	42.5	65.0	60.0	45.0	30.0
Total ($N = 100$)	75.0	76.0	70.0	78.0	68.0
F value	2.767	1.004		0.928	
Multiple correlation coefficient	.417	.379		.366	

participation with others), privilegedness (financial standing relative to other community members), and cosmopolitanism (orientation beyond the local community), the only negatively related variable. The status concern and interest range variables are of minor importance here. The marketing program for an appliance innovation should perhaps further emphasize the socially integrated, privileged, and non-cosmopolitan characteristics of innovators.

The present set of findings about adoption of new home appliances suggests, therefore, promotional and market segmentation strategies. Achieving initial market penetration would seem to depend on appeals to the characteristics of importance. A revised marketing strategy would be needed after the innovator penetration level was secured in order to appeal directly to the characteristics of non-innovators. In fact, varying promotional appeals might be appropriate throughout the buildup of market share.

REFERENCES

1. *America's Tastemakers,* Research Reports Nos. 1 and 2, Princeton, N.J.: Opinion Research Corporation, 1959.
2. T. W. Anderson, *An Introduction to Multivariate Statistical Analysis,* New York: John Wiley & Sons, Inc., 1958, 130–1.
3. Raymond A. Bauer, "Consumer Behavior as Risk Taking," in Robert S. Hancock, ed., *Proceedings of the American Marketing Association,* Chicago, June 1960, 389–98.
4. William E. Bell, "Consumer Innovators: A Unique Market for Newness," in Stephen A. Greyser, ed., *Proceedings of the Winter Conference of the American Marketing Association,* Chicago, 1963, 85–95.
5. Francis S. Bourne, "Group Influence in Marketing and Public Relations," in Rensis Likert and Samuel P. Hayes, Jr., eds., *Some Applications of Behavioral Science Research,* Paris: UNESCO, 1957, 217–24.
6. James S. Coleman, Elihu Katz, and Herbert Menzel, *Medical Innovation: A Diffusion Study,* Indianapolis: The Bobbs-Merrill Company, 1966.
7. Richard P. Coleman, "The Significance of Social Stratification in Selling," in Martin L. Bell, ed., *Proceedings of the 43rd National Conference of the American Marketing Association,* Chicago, December 1960, 171–84.
8. Scott M. Cunningham, "Perceived Risk as a Factor in the Diffusion of New Product Information," in Raymond M. Haas, ed., *1966 Fall Proceedings of the American Marketing Association,* Chicago, 1966, 698–721.

9. Ronald A. Fisher, *Statistical Methods for Research Workers*, London: Oliver and Boyd, 1958, 285–9.

10. Ronald E. Frank and William F. Massy, "Innovation and Brand Choice: The Folger's Invasion," in Stephen A. Greyser, ed., *Proceedings of the Winter Conference of the American Marketing Association*, Chicago, 1963, 96–107.

11. ———— and Donald G. Morrison, "Bias in Multiple Discriminant Analysis," *Journal of Marketing Research*, 2 (August 1965), 250–8.

12. Cyril H. Goulden, *Methods of Statistical Analysis*, New York: John Wiley & Sons, Inc., 1952, 378–93.

13. Elihu Katz, "The Social Itinerary of Technical Change: Two Studies on the Diffusion of Innovation," *Human Organization*, 20 (Summer 1961), 70–82.

14. ———— and Paul F. Lazarsfeld, *Personal Influence*, Glencoe, Ill.: The Free Press, 1955.

15. Maurice G. Kendall, *A Course in Multivariate Analysis*, London: Charles Griffin and Co., Limited, 1957.

16. Charles W. King, "Fashion Adoption: A Rebuttal to the 'Trickle Down' Theory," in Stephen A. Greyser, ed., *Proceedings of the Winter Conference of the American Marketing Association*, Chicago, 1963, 108–25.

17. Frederick Mosteller and David L. Wallace, "Inference in an Authorship Problem," *Journal of the American Statistical Association*, 58 (June 1963), 275–309.

18. Everett M. Rogers, *Diffusion of Innovations*, New York: The Free Press, 1962.

19. ————, "Characteristics of Agricultural Innovators and Other Adoptor Categories," *Studies of Innovation and of Communication to the Public*, in Wilbur Schramm, ed., Stanford: Stanford University Press, 1962, 63–97.

20. Thorstein Veblen, *The Theory of the Leisure Class*, New York: The Macmillan Company, 1912.

21. William H. Whyte, Jr., "The Web of Word of Mouth," *Fortune*, 50 (November 1954), 140–3, 204–12.

22. Gerald Zaltman, *Marketing: Contributions from the Behavioral Sciences*, New York: Harcourt, Brace & World, 1965, ch. 3.

A Factor Analysis of the Liquor Preferences of French Consumers

Jean Stoetzel

Practical reasons account for the introduction of motivation research in the field of market study. When it becomes desirable to influence consumer behavior and attitudes, a simple assessment is no longer adequate and there is an obvious need for a deeper knowledge of their roots. The word "motivation" expresses this concept of psychological causality.

But the very concept of causality is by no means a simple one, as many Western thinkers have repeatedly observed. Aristotle felt that it was necessary to distinguish among four kinds of causes. In modern times, Malebranche and Hume have demonstrated that in the realm of psychology as well as in physics, we are utterly unable to comprehend the effectiveness of a given cause, and that—however vivid—our spontaneous intuitions of causality are hollow and meaningless.

It would be a mistake to dismiss these remarks by scornfully characterizing them as philosophical. It is most important to be fully aware of what we are searching for. In the perspective of behavioral psychology, when we face the matrix of simultaneous preferences expressed by a group of consumers or voters, what corresponds to the popular concept of causality is simply the unique configuration or pattern made up by the diverse phases of stimulus situation, the characteristics of the subjects and their behavior. And it is quite significant, I believe, that in French or German, the word *motif* or *motiv* is used to convey that very idea of a pattern in the field of architecture or music. It appears that in psychology, too, the notion of motivation can be resolved conceptually into that of a pattern. Needless to say, however, such structures are never given in actual experience, but are only intellectual constructions.

Reprinted with permission from the *Journal of Advertising Research* vol. 1, no. 2 (December, 1960), pp. 7-11. © Advertising Research Foundation, Inc. (1960).

This inevitably leads us to the concept of the model. A model is a system of relationships, mathematically expressed, apt to reach a high degree of complexity, and such that when experience has set the values of the parameters, the values of all the variates can be deduced in agreement with the nearly inexhaustible data of observation.

METHOD

Such models of preference for several items by a population are made available through factor analysis. At first it appears that the individual choices between the several items are correlated, so that given a choice by an individual, all his other choices can be forecast within determined probability limits. Later the whole matrix of correlation coefficients can be rationally computed from an appropriate set of variates characteristic of the items preferred.

The intended goal has thus been reached; a complex system of relationships has been established through which individual preference judgments, not one at a time but simultaneously, can be deductively reproduced. The principles of this reproduction are the factors—abstract mathematical parameters computed without any personal interference by the analyst. The analysis may thus be called entirely objective in the sense that anyone making use of the same procedure will find the same results. This feature gives way, as will be made clear later, to the possibility of turning over the burden of computation to machines.

Human judgment, however, is needed at the next stage when assumptions are formulated concerning the significance of the factors. Still, those assumptions themselves can be operationally expressed and consequently can be experimentally tested. The conclusions of the study are quantitatively phrased. Not only are the preferred items ranked by their loadings in the factors, but also the contribution of each factor to the variance of the empirical data is quantitatively assessed.

The preceding statements obviously need concrete illustrations. For this purpose, we will make use of a body of data gathered in the course of a market survey made in February 1956 by the French Institute for Market Research (ETMAR).

Personal interviews were conducted February 9–21, 1956 with 2,014 adult men and women who constituted a representative cross-section of the French population selected by quota sampling methods. All information was obtained in the home, in 161 different localities,

by interviewers habitually employed by ETMAR. A total of 1,442 completed interviews were obtained, for a completion rate of 70 percent.

In the course of this survey, the following question was asked:

Which of the following liquors do you personally like best? You are requested to classify them by ranking on top the one you like best, ending up with the one you like least.

(A card with the following items was shown the subjects.)

ARMAGNAC	KIRSCH	RUM
CALVADOS	MARC	WHISKEY
COGNAC	MIRABELLE	LIQUEURS

RESULTS

Product-moment correlation coefficients were computed between the nine simultaneous choices requested from each respondent (see Table 1). The ranks given to Armagnac and Cognac on the one hand, and to Kirsch and Mirabelle on the other, showed positive, rather high correlations (.37 and .25). Armagnac, Calvados, Cognac and Marc were negatively and rather strongly correlated ($-.38$ and $-.39$) with Liqueurs. Rankings of Kirsch, Mirabelle, Rum and Liqueurs were negatively correlated with the other rankings. Most correlation coefficients with Whiskey ranks were small, the most noticeable exception being the Whiskey-Liqueurs correlation, which was rather highly negative, $-.24$. To sum up, the whole matrix of the 36 correlation coefficients revealed a rather clear-cut pattern of preferences by French consumers.

We can now turn to the factor analysis of this matrix. The procedure used was Thurstone's centroid method. Three factors have been extracted.

The analysis was discontinued after the extraction of the third factor because the third residual matrix was such that two-thirds (22/36) of the figures were less than or equal to three standard errors of the corresponding correlation coefficients. The values for the correlations deduced from the three factors differed 21 times out of 36 from the actually observed correlation coefficients by a quantity less than or equal to three standard errors.

This table, and still more clearly a tri-dimensional geometrical representation, show again what was clear from the correlational

TABLE 1 Correlations Between Rankings of the Nine Liquors

	ARMAGNAC	CALVADOS	COGNAC	KIRSCH	MARC	MIRABELLE	RUM	WHISKEY
Calvados	.21							
Cognac	.37	.09						
Kirsch	-.32	-.29	-.31					
Marc	.00	.12	-.04	-.16				
Mirabelle	-.31	-.30	-.30	.25	-.20			
Rum	-.26	-.14	-.11	-.13	-.03	-.24		
Whiskey	.09	.01	.12	-.14	-.08	-.16	-.20	
Liqueurs	-.38	-.39	-.39	.90	-.38	.18	.04	-.24

Table 2 gives the factor loadings for the different liquors.

TABLE 2   Loadings in the Three Factors

ITEMS	FACTOR I	FACTOR II	FACTOR III
Liqueurs	0.64	0.02	0.16
Kirsch	0.50	−0.06	−0.10
Mirabelle	0.46	−0.24	−0.19
Rum	0.17	0.74	0.97[1]
Marc	−0.29	0.66	−0.39
Whiskey	−0.29	−0.08	0.09
Calvados	−0.49	0.20	−0.04
Cognac	−0.52	−0.03	0.42
Armagnac	−0.60	−0.17	0.14

[1] This figure is certainly too high and should not exceed the maximum of .64. A reiteration of the factor analysis, bringing about progressively better approximations of the communalities, would very likely lessen it.

matrix; the similarity in the rankings of Armagnac and Cognac, Kirsch and Mirabelle and also the main differences already observed. In addition, factor analysis puts those similarities and those differences in a complex order and reveals, in the abstract but strict sense of the word, *factors,* that is to say, the causes of these similarities and differences. Passing from the abstract to the concrete, from the mathematical to the psychological, is indeed delicate. We shall now proceed with this kind of interpretation by way of illustration.

DISCUSSION

The largest loadings in the first factor are, in order, those of Liqueurs, Kirsch, Mirabelle and the smallest those of Calvados, Cognac and Armagnac. We are inclined to surmise that the first factor discriminates between sweet and strong liquors. We conclude that this distinction between sweet and strong liquors is the first principle upon which consumer preferences are based. Let us emphasize this point: this principle is the first, not only in the sense that it has been analyzed first, but also in the sense that it is the most important. It is in effect this first factor which (except for Rum and Marc) contributes most to the variance in preferences.

The second factor ranks the preference judgments in an entirely

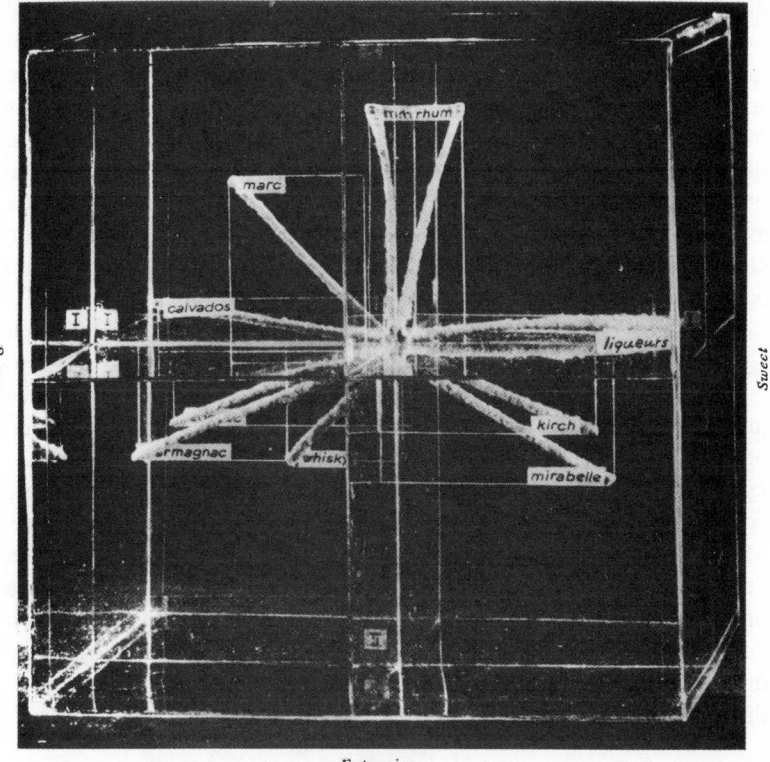

Figure 1   A GRAPH OF THE FACTOR MATRIX. This is a photograph of a plastic model which graphs the factor matrix. Since there are three factors accounting for liquor preferences, the graph is three-dimensional. The first axis runs across the page and represents, left to right, the dimension strong to sweet. Calvados, for example, is strong; liqueurs are sweet. The second dimension is inexpensiveness, and this runs up and down the page. Rum, for example, is inexpensive and exhibits plenty of this factor. The third dimension is less easily seen because it runs into the page. It represents local or national preference. The direction toward the reader shows local preference; national preference is indicated by positions away from the reader.

One interesting feature of this diagram is that it indicates the correlation between various preferences. Kirsch, for instance, enjoys about the same factor loadings as Mirabelle; and, the two liquors are, as we see from their neighboring positions in the model, positively correlated in preference.

different dimension. This is quite natural since it is an essential property of the factors to be mathematically independent. The largest loadings characterize the preference judgment on Rum and Marc; the smallest on Armagnac and Mirabelle. A likely interpretation of this factor, which is given here only as a possibility, is that it is related to the price, low or high, of the different items. These differences in the prices of the several items, it may be observed in passing, need not be established objectively on the retail market. It is sufficient that they be so perceived psychologically by the respondents. This interpretation could be tested in a separate survey.

The third factor reaches its maximum in the case of Rum and Cognac, its minimum with Mirabelle and Marc. We have reasons to interpret it as related to the sociological variability of preference judgments within the public. A study of the mean rating given to each of the items throughout the different geographic regions of France (see Table 3) shows that the loadings in Factor III are negatively correlated with the variance of the mean ratings in the case of Marc, Mirabelle, Calvados, Kirsch and Armagnac, all of which enjoy a definite traditional preference in some region or another. In the case of the other liquors, for which regional differences are felt to a much lesser degree, it is likely that a more detailed study would show some other variable such as sex or socio-economic level to correlate with their loadings in Factor III.

CONCLUSION

This example may substantiate faith in the possible contribution of factor analysis to the problem of motivation. In the case studied, our interpretation of consumer behavior would be the following.

The major principle of liquor preference in France is the distinction between sweet and strong liquors. The second motivating element is price, which can be understood by remembering that liquor is both an expensive commodity and an item of conspicuous consumption. Except in the case of the two most popular and least expensive items (Rum and Marc), this second factor plays a much smaller role in producing preference judgments. The third factor is concerned with the sociological, and primarily the regional, variability of the judgments.

Consequently the recommendation of a systematic use of factor analysis in market studies seems justified. This procedure, as may have been noticed, leads to no change in the usual techniques of sam-

TABLE 3   Mean Preference Ranks by Region

REGIONS	ARMAGNAC	CALVADOS	COGNAC	KIRSCH	MARC	MIRABELLE	RUM	WHISKEY	LIQUEURS
The North	4.90	4.30	3.75	4.85	5.78	4.46	4.51	7.65	4.79
Normandy, Brittany	4.77	3.68	3.80	4.16	6.62	4.97	4.48	7.92	4.42
The Loire	4.42	4.62	4.16	4.23	6.75	4.15	4.82	7.94	4.41
Burgundy, Champagne	4.23	4.75	4.26	3.80	4.57	3.66	4.99	7.95	5.01
The East	5.21	5.87	3.92	3.51	5.92	3.65	4.29	7.81	4.65
West and Central	4.57	5.56	3.15	4.78	6.04	4.20	4.01	7.81	4.23
Aquitaine and Languedoc	3.62	5.53	3.32	4.86	6.36	5.17	4.06	7.65	4.35
Mediterranean and Alpine	4.36	5.49	3.99	4.85	5.45	4.95	4.63	7.90	4.24
Paris	3.92	4.89	3.64	4.16	6.25	4.14	5.25	7.01	4.74
Grand Mean	4.43	5.04	3.77	4.33	5.98	4.35	4.64	7.77	4.54
Variance	.2393	.2446	.1186	.2314	.3926	.2224	.1584	.0195	.0737

pling and interviewing. The main reason why factor analysis has been used only on rare occasions in market research is probably that it requires rather laborious calculations. This difficulty is entirely overcome today thanks to electronic calculating machines. The preceding analysis was entrusted to l'Institut Européen de Calcul Scientifique of IBM-France. Once a program has been established, an IBM 704 electronic machine is fed with the ordinary punch cards of the market study at the rate of 150 per minute, during which time all significant data are read and enregistered and all arithmetic computations performed. Results are then printed at the speed of 100 lines a minute. Preliminary and final manipulations included, the working time was less than three-quarters of an hour.

We believe that factor analyses carried out under such conditions open up far-reaching and novel possibilities to market and opinion research.

REFERENCES

Britt, Stewart Henderson, *Consumer Behavior and the Behavioral Sciences* (New York: Wiley and Sons, 1966).

Ehrenberg, A.S.C., "An Appraisal of Markov Brand-Switching Models," *Journal of Marketing Research,* November, 1965.

Evans, Franklin B., "Psychological and Objective Factors in the Prediction of Brand Choice; Ford Versus Chevrolet," *Journal of Business,* October, 1959.

Green, Paul E., "Bayesian Classification Procedures in Analyzing Customer Characteristics," *Journal of Advertising Research,* May, 1964.

Hamberg, Morris and Atkins, Robert J., "Computer Model for New Product Demand," *Harvard Business Review,* March–April, 1967.

Herniter, J. D., and Magee, J. F., "Customer Behavior as a Markov Process," *Operations Research,* January, 1961.

Kuehn, Alfred A., "Consumer Brand Choice—A Learning Process?" *Journal of Advertising Research,* December, 1962.

Kuehn, Alfred A., and Day, Ralph L., "Probabilistic Models of Consumer Buying Behavior," *Journal of Marketing,* October, 1964.

Lipstein, Benjamin, "A Mathematical Model of Consumer Behavior," *Journal of Marketing Research,* August, 1965.

Lipstein, Benjamin, "The Dynamics of Brand Loyalty and Brand Switching," *Annual Conference of the Advertising Research Foundation,* September, 1959.

PART IV | Marketing Management

The complexity of the marketing process and the heavy losses which frequently result from poor decision making have placed extreme pressures on marketing scholars and practitioners to find ways in which to improve the existing decision-making process. Part IV focuses on the application of operations research to the major decision areas with which marketing management is concerned—namely, pricing decisions, product decisions, communication decisions, channel and physical distribution decisions. In each of these decision areas, the tolerable range for error has diminished to disturbingly narrow limits. The applications discussed in the following sections will demonstrate some of the ways in which management science has helped the marketing manager reduce this uncertainty.

chapter 6 | Pricing Decisions in Marketing Management

While it is true that managerial decision making has always involved more art than science, management science is bringing about a change in the art form from an *ad hoc* seat-of-the-pants approach based on intuition to one based on systematic analysis and synthesis *supported* by intuition, judgment, and experience. In the first article of this section, William R. Darden develops an approach to product pricing which provides a formal structure within which the decision maker can fully utilize his judgment and experience. In this way, judgment and experience become the plus ingredients in the pricing decision rather than its entire foundation. Furthermore, Darden's discussion of the obstacles to optimal product pricing points up the need for an operational approach to product pricing.

The next article in this section is one of three in Part IV written by a leading marketing scholar, Professor Paul Green of the University of Pennsylvania. In each of these articles, Professor Green demonstrates the application of one of the most powerful analytical tools used in recent years—Bayesian decision theory.

The great power of Bayesian statistics is that it allows a subjective interpretation of probability. Given the decision maker's experience and "feel" of the environment within which he operates, the decision maker in most cases has a great deal of information concerning the states of nature relevant to his decision problem. In Bayesian decision theory, this information is made explicit and used as a basis for determining the probabilities assigned to each state of nature.

In summary, Bayesian decision theory provides the executive with a formal decision framework, a rational procedure for including all relevant data in a given decision problem. By formalizing what otherwise might be done intuitively, Bayesian decision theory adds a new dimension—greater scope and impact to the manager's decision-making function. Professor Green discusses the application of this "tool" to the pricing problem and in general discusses how Bayesian statistics forces a more rigorous approach to the marketing planning problem. In subsequent sections of Part IV, Green discusses the application of Bayesian statistics to product and advertising problems.

One of the more interesting pricing problems in marketing is that faced by marketers of industrial goods and construction companies. In this situation, channels of distribution are direct and the inquiry/bid system is used for buying and selling products. In "How to Price Industrial Products," Arleigh W. Walker develops the identical argument as later generalized by Darden. Pricing is not performed on a rational basis and to a great extent relies on the intuition and experience of seasoned sales managers. However, Walker's approach to pricing begins with known probability distributions of percentage bid values above and below market level. Since a great deal of published information exists on the inquiry/bid environment, the Walker approach shows great promise.

Finally, Darden and Robin explore the potential of "price programming" in the evaluation of multiproduct price strategies. Price programming provides a systems approach to viewing and evaluating market strategies within the context of total firm constraints.

An Operational Approach to Product Pricing

William R. Darden

The best brains in the business and academic worlds labor to provide the product pricer with a repertoire of sophisticated techniques and approaches, and he continues pricing products in his usual manner. While the economist expounds use of concepts of demand and marginal analysis, the pricer uses experience, intuition, and cost-plus. While the statistician calls for probability and payoff tables, the pricer uses experience, intuition, and cost-plus. While the professional expounds the use of price elasticity and cross-elasticity concepts, the pricer again uses experience, intuition, and cost-plus.

OBSTACLES TO OPTIMAL PRODUCT PRICING

Why does the pricer persist in this "irrational" behavior? This question seems to evoke answers from academicians and professionals that are as "irrational" as the pricer's behavior. Actually, the answers are simpler than presupposed and are all in the form of obstacles to "optimal" pricing. Some of these obstacles are:

1. The pricer does not have the time, nor the interest, to read and digest the latest literature on pricing, even if it were directly applicable in practice, which it is not.

2. In many cases the objectives of the pricer may be quite different from the objectives assumed in the literature for arriving at optimal guides to action.

3. The typical pricer usually has many product lines, and in each product line he may have many products. Thus, the time that he may allot to pricing each product may be very small.

4. Also, while the pricer recognizes that many products are substitutes or complementary to each other, he has no way to quantify or measure these effects properly.

Reprinted with permission from the *Journal of Marketing,* vol. 32, no. 2 (April, 1968) pp. 29–33, published by the American Marketing Association.

5. The product pricer also has problems in determining competitor reactions to price strategies. The direction and degree of *price* reactions is a prime trouble area.

6. Again, the pricer does not have the methods, time, or money to measure demand curves or other consumer response curves properly. From experience, intuition, and judgment he must make hypotheses about future decision relationships. Future positive feedback increases the belief in these hypotheses, while negative feedback decreases the belief in these hypotheses. With negative feedback, the pricer begins to investigate his "key" hypotheses, sequentially, and these may be revised.

The above "obstacles" do not begin to show the difficulties of the "complete" pricer. The "complete" pricer must deal with all the myriad combinations of price, advertising, sales promotion, personal selling, place, and product. Heuristically, he must hypothesize about the degree to which competitors will react to his price change and in what form this reaction will occur. The product pricer must "guess" —on the basis of his present hypotheses—what blend of marketing decisions will go best with a given price, and he must in turn determine what effect the given price will have on the sales of other products in the product line (both in the short run and in the long run). To continue with the latter thought, the product pricer must coordinate pricing policy with channel decisions, product decisions, and promotion decisions. *This coordination must take place through time,* not only at a point in time (as economic analysis often assumes).

It is not surprising, then, that the product pricer cannot predict the quantity demanded for a given price during a given period. However, it is probable that the product pricer does use an implicit, informal method of determining a sales volume range for a given price. Thus, it is believed that most product pricers *do* consider more than cost and turnover in pricing. It is hypothesized in this paper that many pricers use experience and intuition to arrive operationally at hypotheses which serve as a basis for price making. The purpose of this paper, then, is to formalize, heuristically, an operational approach to pricing, given the beliefs of the pricer.

PROFIT VARIANCE AND PRICE LIMITS

The central concept of the proposed pricing approach is exemplified in Figure 1. Assuming some given price, P_1, the breakeven chart in Figure 1 can be easily produced. The typical marketing executive will determine the most likely quantity demanded at P_1—in this case, Q_M.

Now the marketing student determines the most likely profit at Q_M, as well as the breakeven quantity, Q_B. This approach is likely to be repeated for several prices, yielding respective profit and breakeven quantities for each price. Actually, the marketer is using repetitive breakeven analysis to feel out demand.

In addition, the marketer may determine optimal advertising and sales promotion for each price, which in turn also affects the profit and breakeven quantities received for each price. It is also recognized that the final most likely price is that which reflects judgments about competitive reactions.

Now the price investigator can estimate for a given price a pessimistic quantity demanded and an optimistic quantity demanded. These estimates are Q_P and Q_0, respectively, for price P_1 in Figure 1. Thus the pricing specialist has three sales volume estimates at a given price, P_1: a most likely estimate (Q_M), a pessimistic estimate (Q_P), and an optimistic estimate (Q_0).

Rationale and Uses of Quantity Estimates

In the Program Evaluation and Review Technique, commonly called PERT, the planner is faced with the problem of estimating times required for accomplishing particular activities. In order to draw upon the judgment and experience of the superintendent or foreman in charge of completing the activity, and at the same time eliminate bias, the planner asks for three time estimates. These time estimates include an optimistic estimate, a pessimistic estimate, and a most likely estimate. In the cases of optimistic and pessimistic estimations, the planner counsels the estimator to choose times that have a chance of 1 in 100 of occurring. The rationale behind this counsel is that such estimates can be used to approximately fit a beta probability density function to the time occurrence of the given activity.

The same rationale lies behind the estimations of Q_P, Q_M, and Q_0 at P_1 in Figure 1. The marketer is unsure what future volume will be generated by the projected marketing mix (including, of course, the price, P_1). For example, the degrees to which competitors may react, the change in marketing environment, and changes in company implementation effectiveness are all subject to varying degrees of change. However, using the three quantity estimates and assuming a beta probability distribution, the price-maker can determine a sales volume which stands a 50-50 chance of occurring. This volume will be called "largest expected volume" and is denoted by Q_E. Borrowing from PERT network analysis, the following formula yields an approximation of Q_E, using the three quantity estimates:

$$1 \qquad Q_E = \frac{Q_P + 4\,Q_M + Q_0}{6}$$

An important characteristic of this approach is the flexibility of the beta distribution. It allows the volume estimator to make the extreme volume estimates asymmetrical around the most likely volume, if he so chooses. Thus, the probability distribution fitted to the volume estimates may be positively skewed, negatively skewed, or symmetrically distributed.

Variance of the Sales Volume

In addition to yielding the "largest expected volume" for a given price, this "operational approach" produces a good estimate of the volume variance. Using again the volume estimates at P_1, the marketer can compute this approximate variance with Equation 2 shown below:

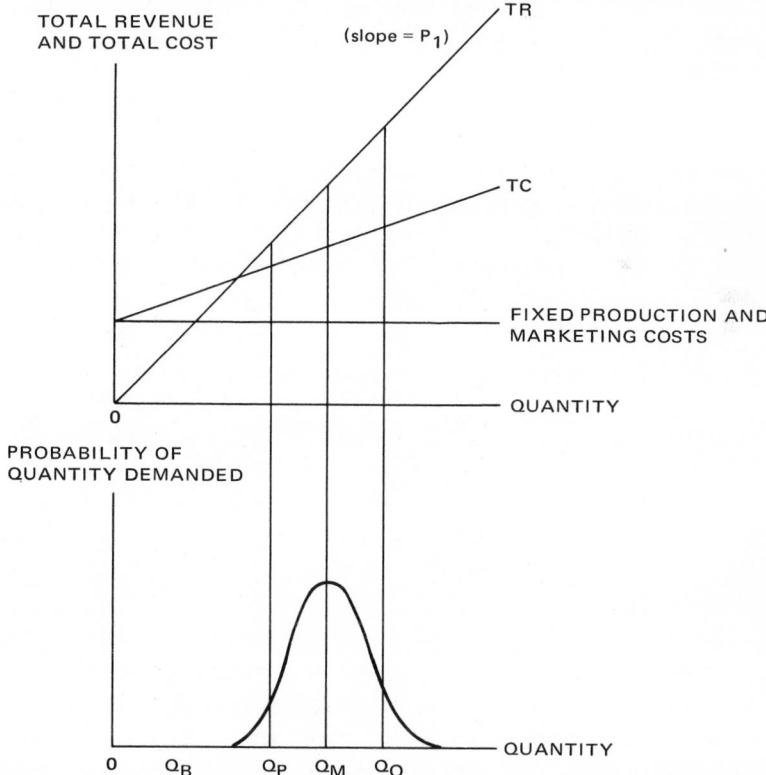

Figure 1 At a given price (P_1), the use of three volume estimates to fit a beta probability distribution

Price Range and the "Operational Approach"

The major strength of the "operational approach" lies in its ability to draw on the experience and judgment of marketing specialists in the firm. The knowledge in regard to competitor reactions, market changes, consumer behavior, and company implementation effectiveness should to a great degree be reflected in the estimates of volume at a given price. Using a repetitive approach, the same analysis can be made for several prices.

Specifically, the pricer wishes to determine some upper and lower limits for prices that must be investigated. Figure 2 shows a special type of demand curve (or curves). This demand curve actually represents three demand curves: the first (D_0) indicates optimistic quantity estimates at various prices; the second (D_M) shows most likely sales volume at all prices; and the third (D_P) shows pessimistic estimates. These three curves generate three total revenue curves in Figure 2: the optimistic revenue curve, the most likely revenue curve, and the pessimistic revenue curve.

The marketer begins at a high price level, decreasing the price until at a given price (in this case P_1) the pessimistic quantity estimate generates only enough revenue to just break even (BEP_1). At a higher price P_{1+}, the volume Q_{P1-} will not cover costs and at a lower price P_{1-}, the volume Q_{P1+} will generate profits. The price (P_1) which accompanies Q_{P1} becomes the upper price limit, ensuring the firm that it will do better than break even over 99% of the time at this price.

In order to establish a lower price limit, in Figure 2, the marketer lowers the price past P_1 until a price is reached which allows the pessimistic revenue curve to break even again (BEP_2). At P_2, such a situation occurs and this price, again, will generate profits 99% of the time.

The marketer has now "bracketed" the feasible prices available to him. This price range may be so small that the respective quantity estimates of the two extreme prices may overlap; however, this seems unlikely in most cases.

The price range determined above provides a very conservative price zone for analysis. Actually, there are other criteria which provide a wider range of prices for investigation. For example, the product pricer could determine the upper and lower price limits on the basis of the largest expected quantity estimates. The probability of breaking even using this criterion (at either price limit) drops from

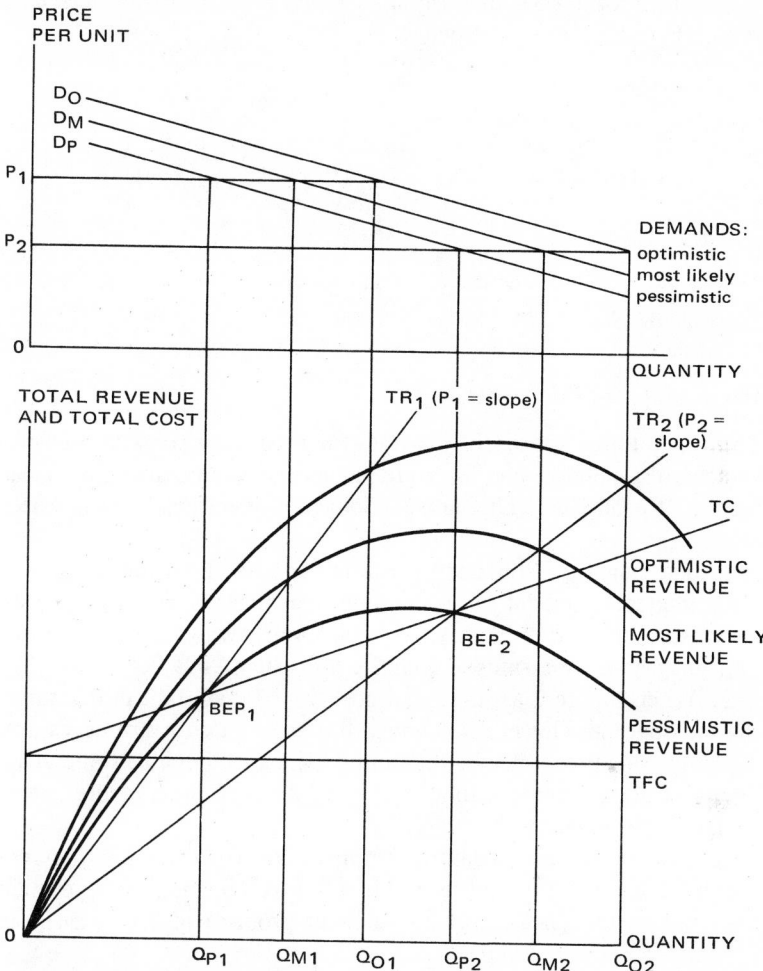

Figure 2   Determination of feasible price range through the interaction of pessimistic, most likely, and optimistic demands with cost curves

.99 to .50. Another criterion, the most likely quantity estimate, provides a compromise, most likely guide, and, depending upon the individual industry and market, may prove the most feasible criterion for most firms.

After the upper price limit ($P_1 = P_U$) and the lower price limit ($P_2 = P_L$) have been determined, the firm may wish to find the largest expected quantities and the quantity variances at each price limit.

From this information, the largest expected profit can be determined at both P_U and P_L as shown below.

$$Q_{E1} = \frac{Q_{P1} + 4\,Q_{M1} + Q_{O1}}{6}$$

Expected Profit $= PR_E = Q_{E1}\,(P_U) - TFC - (V)Q_{E1}$
Where V = Average Variable Cost
TFC = Total Fixed Cost

Now the same information can be determined at the lower end of the price bracket.

Implications for Pricing Strategy

The "operational approach" provides the product pricer with a formal vehicle to summarize and integrate his various hypotheses into a clear picture of economical alternatives. Some considerations for the pricer are:

1. The quantity estimates for the upper price limit and the lower price limit may overlap. For example, the upper limit may have an optimistic quantity estimate of 500,000 units, while the lower price limit may have a pessimistic quantity estimate of 499,000.

2. While Figure 2 assumes that costs remain constant in determining the upper and lower price limits, this assumption is not necessary. Thus, the pricer can change marketing blends to optimize some given objective at each price without changing the usefulness of the operational approach.

3. The use of three quantity estimates for a given price *does not* require that pricing specialists within a firm reach complete agreement as to forecasted sales. Thus, the difficult problem of "consensus" in pricing is largely overcome.

4. Once the product pricer has "bracketed in" the upper and lower price limits, he can use a sequential approach to test the expected profitability of intermediate prices.

5. The product pricer can not only compute and compare expected largest profits, but he can also compute and compare quantity and profit variances at various prices. There is no guarantee that quantity variances will be similar at different prices; therefore, a product pricer may be willing to accept a lower expected largest profit at some price in exchange for a much smaller variance (in other words, the pricer may be willing to trade off expected profit for a greater degree of certainty).

CONCLUSION

In general, the product pricer must use experience, intuition, and cost to price products. The pricer cannot wholly rely on sophisticated techniques and theory for optimal pricing of products. If it can be accepted that product pricers must rely on "operational" techniques for pricing then it would appear that one of the principal tasks of the marketing academician is the exploration of these approaches. Thus, major contributions can be made to marketing by providing marketing management with operational approaches which allow the executive to efficiently use his hypotheses about the decision situation. Bayesian decision theory is one move in this direction; however, the complexity of its methodology, as well as the problem of determining subjective probabilities for the various alternative outcomes of a given price strategy, prohibit its use by most product pricers.

This paper presents an operational approach to pricing that takes into consideration the above complexities and provides a formal vehicle to quantify the pricing hypotheses of businessmen. The approach involves no change in thinking. However, the methodology does allow use of a sequential approach and probability theory.

Bayesian Decision Theory in Pricing Strategy

Paul E. Green

Since the publication of Robert Schlaifer's pioneering work, *Probability and Statistics for Business Decisions,*[1] the Bayesian approach to decision making under uncertainty has received much comment, pro and con, by theoretical and applied statisticians alike.

However, in contrast to the large number of theoretical contributions being made to decision theory in general and Bayesian statistics in particular, reported applications of these procedures to real-world problem situations have been rather meager. Applications appear especially lacking in the marketing field.

In highly oversimplified terms, the Bayesian approach to decision making under uncertainty provides a framework for explicitly working with the economic costs of alternative courses of action, the prior knowledge or judgments of the decision maker, and formal modification of these judgments as additional data are introduced into the problem.

In the Du Pont Company, the decision theory approach, often augmented by computer simulation, has been used experimentally over the past few years in a variety of market planning applications, ranging from capacity expansion problems to questions concerning the introduction of new products and long-range price and promotional strategy. The application to follow concerns the use of Bayesian decision theory in the selection of a "best" pricing policy for a firm in an oligopolistic industry where such factors as demand elasticity,

Reprinted with permission from the *Journal of Marketing,* vol. 27, no. 1 (January, 1963), pp. 5–14, published by the American Marketing Association.

[1] Robert Schlaifer, *Probability and Statistics for Business Decisions* (New York: McGraw-Hill Book Co., Inc., 1959). In addition, two excellent general articles dealing with the Bayesian approach are: Harry V. Roberts, "The New Business Statistics," *Journal of Business,* vol. 33 (January, 1960), pp. 21–30, and Jack Hirshleifer, "The Bayesian Approach to Statistical Decision—An Exposition," *Journal of Business,* vol. 34 (October, 1961), pp. 471–489.

competitive retaliation, threat of future price weakness, and potential entry of new competitors influence the effectiveness of the firm's courses of action. Although the content of this case is apocryphal, its structure has been compounded from actual situations.

No attempt will be made to describe even superficially all of the many facets of the Bayesian approach to decision making under uncertainty. The content of this article is focused on only two main considerations.

First, in dealing with actual marketing situations, for example, pricing problems, the opportunity to obtain field information may be nonexistent. Second, in dealing with actual marketing problems, the complexity of the situation may force the analyst to develop a problem structure in much greater detail than has been described in the literature.

AN ILLUSTRATIVE APPLICATION

Since early 1955, the Everclear Plastics Company had been producing a resin called Kromel, basically designed for certain industrial markets. In addition to Everclear, three other firms were producing Kromel resin. Prices among all four suppliers (called here the Kromel industry) were identical; and product quality and service among producers were comparable. Everclear's current share of Kromel industry sales amounted to 40%.

Four industrial end uses comprised the principal marketing area for the Kromel industry. These market segments will be labeled A, B, C, and D. Three of the four segments (B, C, and D) were functionally dependent on segment A in the sense that Kromel's *ultimate* market position and rate of approach to this level in each of these three segments was predicated on the resin's making substantial inroads in segment A.

The Kromel industry's only competition in these four segments consisted of another resin called Verlon, which was produced by six other firms. Shares of the total Verlon-Kromel market (weighted sums over all four segments) currently stood at 70% Verlon industry, and 30% Kromel industry. Since its introduction in 1955, the superior functional characteristics per dollar cost of Kromel had enabled this newer product to displace fairly large poundages of Verlon in market segments B, C, and D.

On the other hand, the functional superiority per dollar cost of

Kromel had not been sufficiently high to interest segment A consumers. While past price decreases in Kromel had been made, the cumulative effect of these reductions had still been insufficient to accomplish Kromel sales penetration in segment A. (Sales penetration is defined as a market share exceeding zero.)

In the early fall of 1960, it appeared to Everclear's management that future weakness in Kromel price might be in the offing. The anticipated capacity increases on the part of the firm's Kromel competitors suggested that in the next year or two potential industry supply of this resin might significantly exceed demand, if no substantial market participation for the Kromel industry were established in segment A. In addition, it appeared likely that potential Kromel competitors might enter the business, thus adding to the threat of oversupply in later years.

Segment A, of course, constituted the key factor. If substantial inroads could be made in this segment, it appeared likely that Kromel industry sales growth in the other segments not only could be speeded up, but that ultimate market share levels for this resin could be markedly increased from those anticipated in the absence of segment A penetration. To Everclear's sales management, a price reduction in Kromel still appeared to represent a feasible means to achieve this objective, and (even assuming similar price reductions on the part of Kromel competitors) perhaps could still be profitable to Everclear.

However, a large degree of uncertainty surrounded both the overall attractiveness of this alternative, and under this alternative the amount of the price reduction which would enable Kromel to penetrate market segment A.

PROBLEM STRUCTURING AND DEVELOPMENT OF THE MODEL

Formulation of the problem required a certain amount of artistry and compromise toward achieving a reasonably adequate description of the problem. But it was also necessary to keep the structure simple enough so that the nature of each input would be comprehensible to the personnel responsible for supplying data for the study.

Problem components had to be formulated, such as: (a) length of planning period; (b) number and nature of courses of action; (c) payoff functions; and (d) states of nature covering future growth of the total Verlon-Kromel market, inter-industry (Kromel vs. Verlon)

and intra-Kromel industry effects of a Kromel price change, implications on Everclear's share of the total Kromel industry, and Everclear's production costs.

Initial discussions with sales management indicated that a planning period of five years should be considered in the study. While the selection of five years was somewhat arbitrary, sales personnel believed that some repercussions of a current price reduction might well extend over several years into the future.

A search for possible courses of action indicated that four pricing alternatives covered the range of actions under consideration:

1. Maintenance of status quo on Kromel price, which was $1.00/lb.
2. A price reduction to $.93/lb. within the next three months.
3. A price reduction to $.85/lb. within the next three months.
4. A price reduction to $.80/lb. within the next three months.

Inasmuch as each price action would be expected to produce a different time pattern in the flow of revenues and costs, and since no added investment in production facilities was contemplated, it was agreed that cumulative, compounded net profits over the 5-year planning period would constitute a relevant payoff function. In the absence of any unanimity as to the "correct" opportunity cost of capital, it was decided to use two interest rates of 6 and 10% annually in order to test the sensitivity of outcomes to the cost of capital variable.

Another consideration came to light during initial problem discussions. Total market growth (for the Kromel or Verlon industry) over the next five years in each market segment constituted a "state of nature" which could impinge on the Everclear's profit position. Accordingly, it was agreed to consider three separate forecasts of total market growth, a "most probable, optimistic, and pessimistic" forecast.

From these assumptions a base case was then formulated. This main case would first consider the pricing problem under the most probable forecast of total Verlon-Kromel year-by-year sales potential in each segment, using an opportunity cost of capital of 6% annually. The two other total market forecasts and the other cost of capital were then to be treated as sub-cases, in order to test the sensitivity of the base case outcomes to variations in these particular states of nature.

However, inter- and intra-industry alternative states of nature

literally abounded in the Kromel resin problem. Sales management at Everclear had to consider such factors as:

1. The possibility that Kromel resin could effect penetration of market segment A if no price decrease were made.
2. If a price decrease were made, the extent of Verlon retaliation to be anticipated.
3. Given a particular type of Verlon price retaliation, its possible impact on Kromel's penetration of segment A.
4. If segment A were penetrated, the possible market share which the Kromel industry could gain in segment A.
5. If segment A were penetrated, the possible side effects of this event on speeding up Kromel's participation in market segments B, C, and D.
6. If segment A were not penetrated, the impact which the price reduction could still have on speeding up Kromel's participation in segments B, C, and D.
7. If segment A were not penetrated, the possibility that existing Kromel competitors would initiate price reductions a year hence.
8. The possible impact of a current Kromel price reduction on the decisions of existing or potential Kromel producers to increase capacity or enter the industry.

While courses of action, length of planning period, and the payoff measure (cumulative, compounded net profits) for the base case had been fairly quickly agreed upon, the large number of inter- and intra-Kromel industry states of nature deemed relevant to the problem would require rather lengthy discussion with Everclear's sales personnel.

Accordingly, introductory sessions were held with Everclear's sales management, in order to develop a set of states of nature large enough to represent an adequate description of the real problem, yet small enough to be comprehended by the participating sales personnel. Next, separate interview sessions were held with two groups of Everclear's sales personnel; subjective probabilities regarding the occurrence of alternative states of nature under each course of action were developed in these sessions. A final session was held with all contributing personnel in attendance; each projection and/or subjective probability was gone over in detail, and final set of ground rules for the study was agreed upon. A description of these ground rules appears in Table 1.

TABLE 1 Subjective Probabilities and Data Estimates Associated with Everclear's Pricing Problem

1. If Kromel price remained at $1.00/pound and market segment A were not penetrated, what market share pattern for Kromel industry sales pounds would obtain in segments B, C, and D?

BASE ASSUMPTION—KROMEL INDUSTRY SHARE

	SEGMENT B	SEGMENT C	SEGMENT D
1961	57.0%	40.0%	42.0%
1962	65.0	50.0	44.0
1963	75.0	80.0	46.0
1964	76.0	84.0	48.0
1965	76.0	84.0	50.0

2. If Kromel price remained at $1.00/pound, what is the probability that Kromel would still penetrate market segment A?

PROBABILITY OF PENETRATION—SEGMENT A

1961	.05
1962	.10
1963	.20
1964	.25
1965	.40

3. Under price strategies $.93/pound, $.85/pound, and $.80/pound, what is the probability of Verlon industry price retaliation; and given the particular retaliation (shown below), what is the probability that Kromel would still penetrate market segment A?

PRICING CASE (ENTRIES ARE PROBABILITIES)

VERLON INDUSTRY RETALIATION	$.93 CASE	$.85 CASE	$.80 CASE
Full match of Kromel price reduction	.05	.15	.38
Half match of Kromel price reduction	.60	.75	.60
Stand pat on price	.35	.10	.02

GIVEN A PARTICULAR VERLON RETALIATORY ACTION, THE PROBABILITY THAT KROMEL WOULD STILL PENETRATE SEGMENT A

	$.93 CASE			$.85 CASE			$.80 CASE		
	FULL MATCH	HALF MATCH	STAND PAT	FULL MATCH	HALF MATCH	STAND PAT	FULL MATCH	HALF MATCH	STAND PAT
1961	.15	.20	.35	.20	.40	.80	.75	.80	.90
1962	.25	.30	.60	.30	.60	.90	.80	.85	.95
1963	.35	.40	.65	.40	.75	.95	.85	.90	1.00
1964	.60	.65	.75	.70	.65	.98	.90	.95	1.00
1965	.65	.70	.80	.75	.80	.98	.95	.98	1.00

4. If penetration in market segment A were effected, what is the probability that Kromel would obtain the specific share of this segment (a) during the first year of penetration, and (b) during the second year of participation?

SHARE	FIRST YEAR	SECOND YEAR
25%	.15	.00
50	.35	.00
75	.40	.00
100	.10	1.00

5. If Kromel penetration of market segment A were effected, what impact would this event have on speeding up Kromel industry participation in segments B, C, and D?

Segment B—Would speed up market participation one year from base assumption shown under point 1 of this Table.

Segment C—Would speed up market participation one year from base assumption shown under point 1 of this Table.

Segment D—Kromel would move up to 85% of the market in the following year, and would obtain 100% of the market in the second year following penetration of segment A.

6. Under the price reduction strategies, if Kromel penetration of market segment A were *not* accomplished, what is the probability that Kromel industry participation in segments B, C, and D (considered as a group) would still be speeded up one year from the base assumption shown under point 1 of this Table?

PROBABILITY OF SPEEDUP

$.93 Case	.45
$.85 Case	.60
$.80 Case	.80

7. If Kromel price at the end of any given year were $1.00/pound, $.93/pound, $.85/pound, or $.80/pound respectively, *and* if market segment A were not penetrated, what is the probability that present competitive Kromel producers would take the specific price action shown below?

IF KROMEL PRICE	ACTION	PROBABILITY
@ $1.00/pound	$1.00/pound	.15
	.93	.80
	.85	.05
	.80	.00
@ $.93/pound	.93	.80
	.85	.20
	.80	.00
@ $.85/pound	.85	1.00
	.80	.00
@ $.80/pound	.80	1.00

8. Under each of the four price strategies, what is the probability that competitive (present or potential) Kromel producers would add to or

initiate capacity (as related to the price prevailing in mid-1961) in the years 1963 and 1964? (No capacity changes were assumed in 1965.)

COMPETITOR	$1.00/POUND	$.93/POUND	$.85/POUND	$.80/POUND
R	.50	.20	.05	.00
S	.90	.75	.50	.20
T	.40	.10	.05	.00
U	.70	.50	.25	.00
V	.70	.50	.25	.00

TIMING AND AMOUNT AVAILABLE BEGINNING OF YEAR

COMPETITOR	1963	1964
R	10 million pounds	20 million pounds
S	12	20
T	12	20
U	6	12
V	6	6

USE OF TREE DIAGRAMS

The large number of alternative states of nature which were associated with inter- and intra-industry factors necessitated the construction of "tree diagrams" for each pricing alternative. These diagrams enabled sales management to trace the implications of their assumptions. Figure 1 shows a portion of one such tree diagram.

A word of explanation concerning interpretation of the probability tree is in order. The two principal branches underneath the *$1.00 case* refer to the event of whether or not Kromel penetrates segment A in the first year of the planning period. Sales personnel felt that a 5% chance existed for penetration, hence the figure .05000 under A.

However, if A were penetrated, four market participations were deemed possible: 25, 50, 75 and 100% carrying the conditional probabilities of .15, .35, .40 and .10 respectively.

Multiplication of each conditional probability, in turn, by the .05 marginal probability leads to the four joint probabilities noted in the upper left portion of the chart.

Next, if Kromel did not penetrate segment A during the first year, a probability of .80 was attached to the event that competitive Kromel producers would reduce price to $.93/lb. Multiplying the conditional probability of .80 by .95 results in the .76000 probability assigned to

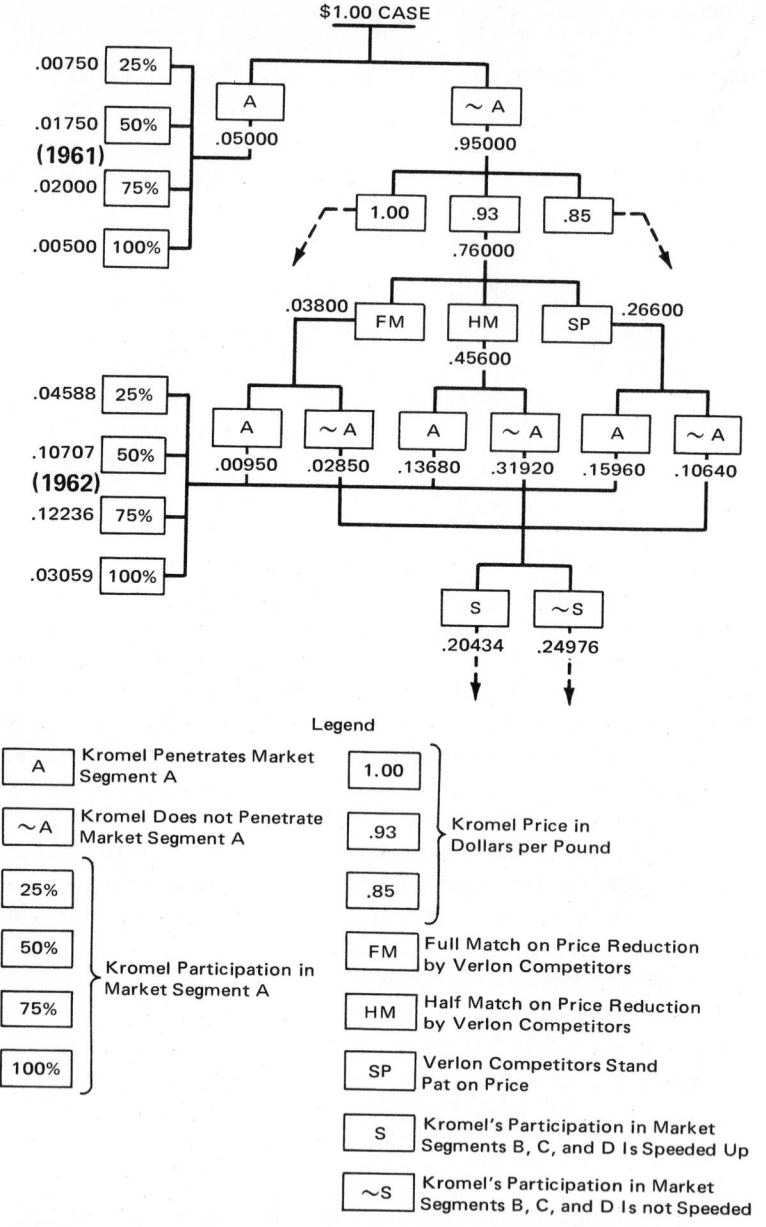

Figure 1   Portion of a "tree diagram"; Kromel price simulation

the joint event, "did not penetrate segment A and Kromel price was reduced to $.93/lb."

However, if Kromel price were reduced to $.93/lb., Verlon retaliation had to be considered, leading to the joint probabilities assigned to the next set of tree branches. In this way probabilities were built up for each of the over-400 possible outcomes of the study by appropriate application of the ground rules noted in Table 1.

A mathematical model was next constructed for determining the expected value of Everclear's cumulative, compounded net profits under each price strategy. See Table 2.

TABLE 2   Kromel Model–Expected Value of Cumulative, Compounded Net Profits

The mathematical model used to determine the expected values of Everclear's cumulative, compounded net profits was as follows:

$$CCN(X_k) = \sum_{j=1}^{n} p_j \cdot \sum_{i=1}^{m} [(1+r)^{m-i} T \{ (D_{ij} - Z_{ij})(K_{ij}M_{ij}) \}]$$

$$Z_{ij} = \emptyset(K_{ij}M_{ij})$$

$CCN(X_k) =$ Expected value of Everclear's cumulative, compounded net profits under each X_k price strategy ($k = 1, \ldots, 4$).

$p_j =$ Probability assigned to the j th outcome ($j = 1, 2, \ldots, n$).

$r =$ Interest rate per annum, expressed decimally.

$T =$ Ratio of net to gross profits of Everclear's Kromel operation (assumed constant in the study).

$D_{ij} =$ Kromel price in $/pound in the i th year ($i = 1, 2, \ldots, m$) for the j th outcome.

$Z_{ij} =$ Cost in $/pound of Everclear's Kromel resin in the i th year for the j th outcome. (This cost is a function of the amount of Kromel pounds sold by Everclear.)

$\emptyset =$ Function of.

$K_{ij} =$ Everclear's over-all market share of Kromel Industry sales (in pounds) in the i th year for the j th outcome (expressed decimally).

$M_{ij} =$ Kromel Industry poundage (summed over all four market segments) in the i th year for the j th outcome.

This model was then programed for an electronic computer. The simulation was first carried out for the base case assumptions regarding total Verlon-Kromel market growth and cost of capital. Additional runs were made in which these assumptions were varied.

RESULTS OF THE COMPUTER SIMULATIONS

The computer run for the base case showed some interesting results for the relevant variables affecting Everclear's cumulative, compounded net profits position at the end of the planning period. These results are portrayed in Figures 2 through 4.

Figure 2 summarizes the cumulative probability of Kromel's penetration of market segment A (the critical factor in the study) as a function of time, under each pricing strategy. As would be expected,

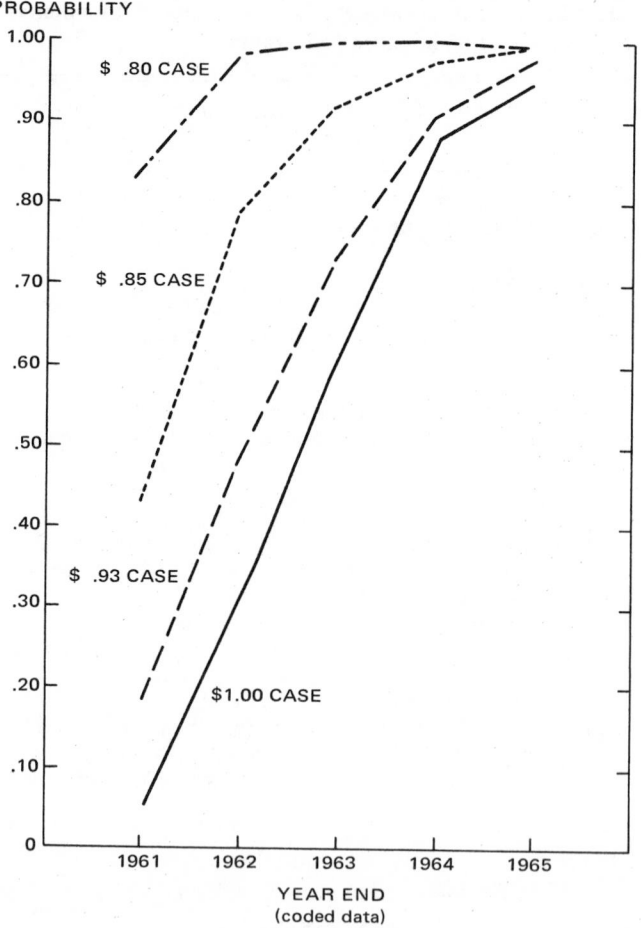

Figure 2   Cumulative probability of Kromel's penetration of market segment A (as a function of time and initial price)

Paul E. Green **355**

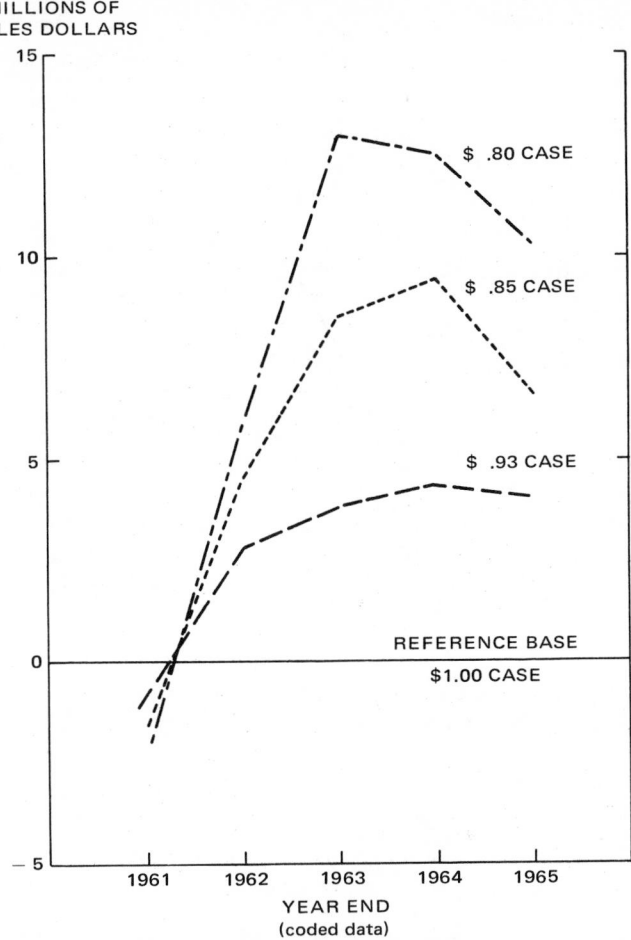

Figure 3 Kromel sales volume—Everclear Plastics Co. (incremental sales dollars generated over $1.00 case)

the lowest price strategy, the *$.80 case,* carried the highest probability of market penetration. However, the cumulative probability approached 1, that *all* price strategies would eventually effect penetration of market segment A by the end of the simulation period. This behavior stems from the impact of price decreases assumed to be initiated by Kromel *competitors* (if penetration were not initially effected under the original price strategies) which in turn changed the probability of Kromel's penetration of segment A in later years, since this probability was related to price.

Figure 3 shows the expected incremental sales dollars (obtained by

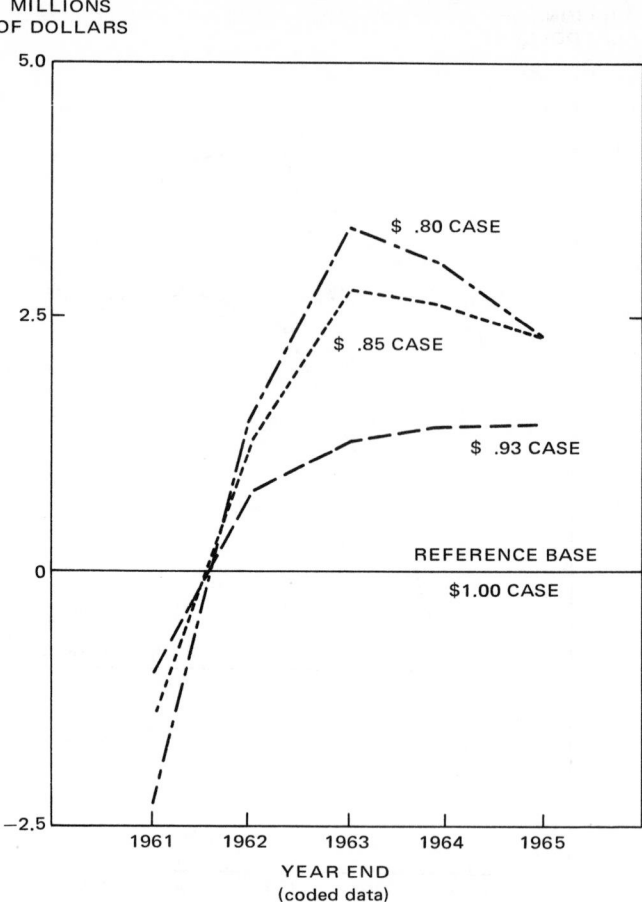

MILLIONS
OF DOLLARS

Figure 4   Compounded year-by-year net profits of Everclear Plastics Co. (compound rate equals 6% annually)

subtracting the expected outcomes of the *$1.00 case,* used as a reference base, from the expected outcomes of each of the other three cases respectively) generated for Everclear under each price strategy. While some tapering off in average sales dollars generated from the price reduction cases compared to the *$1.00 case* can be noted near the end of the simulation period, this tapering off is less pronounced than that which would be experienced by the total Kromel industry.

The reason for this different pattern is that the price reduction strategies (by reducing the probability of future capacity expansion on the part of existing and potential Kromel competitors) led to gains in

Everclear's market share, relative to market share under the *$1.00 case.* These increases in Everclear's market share, under the price reduction strategies, partially offset the decline in incremental sales dollar gains (experienced by the Kromel industry near the end of the period) and thus explain the difference in sales patterns that would be observed between Everclear and the Kromel industry.

Figure 4 summarizes the behavior of Everclear's average, year-by-year (compounded) net profits performance again on an incremental basis compared to the *$1.00 case.* As would be expected, time lags in the penetration of segment A, under the price reduction strategies, result in an early profit penalty compared to the *$1.00 case.* This penalty is later overbalanced by the additional sales dollars accruing from earlier (on the average) penetration of segment A under the price reduction strategies versus the status quo price case.

The overall performance of each pricing strategy on Everclear's cumulative, compounded net profits position (expected value basis) at the *end* of the 5-year planning period is shown in Table 3. These values were obtained by application of the formula shown in Table 2.

Table 3 shows that all of the price reduction strategies yield ex-

TABLE 3   Cumulative, Compounded Net Profits—Everclear Plastics Co. (1961–65)

Price Strategy	End of Period Profit Position
$1.00 case	$26.5 million
.93 case	30.3 million
.85 case	33.9 million
.80 case	34.9 million

pected payoffs which exceed the *$1.00 case.* These additional profits stem from two principal sources: (a) the higher profits generated in the middle portion of the planning period, as a function of the increased probability of effecting penetration of market segment A, and its associated effect on Kromel industry sales in market segments B, C, and D; and (b) the higher market share for Everclear, resulting from the influence of the price reduction strategies on lowering the probability of capacity expansion and/or entry by Kromel competitors (existing or potential). These combined factors overbalance the lower profit margins per pound associated with the price reduction strategies compared to the *$1.00 case.*

However, a relevant question arose concerning the influence of the more favorable market share factor (under the price reduction cases) on the outcomes of these strategies vs. the *$1.00 case.* Suppose that no favorable difference in market share were obtained under the price reduction strategies compared to the no-price reduction case. That is, suppose the probability that lower Kromel price would discourage future competitive expansion of Kromel industry capacity in the 1963–64 period were zero. How would this affect Everclear's profit position?

In order to test the impact of this variable on Everclear's cumulative, compounded net profits, the market share factor was held constant at the trend level estimated under the no-price reduction, or *$1.00 case,* over the simulation period. This analysis resulted in the information given in Table 4.

It is clear from Table 4 that the market share factor is important

TABLE 4   Profit Position–Market Share Held Constant

(Everclear's Cumulative, Compounded Net Profits; 1961–65)

PRICE STRATEGY	END OF PERIOD PROFIT POSITION
$1.00 case	$26.5 million
.93 case	26.9 million
.85 case	27.4 million
.80 case	25.2 million

in producing Everclear's higher profit position as associated with the price reduction alternatives noted in Table 3. If increased share for Everclear were *not* obtained in the 1963–65 period (relative to the share expected under the *$1.00 case*), all strategies would yield close to equal payoffs. That is, over the planning period, the increased sales volume resulting from earlier (on the average) penetration of segment A under the price reduction strategies just about balances the less favorable profit margins associated with these strategies.

However, beyond the planning period, all strategies have for all practical purposes accomplished penetration of segment A. The impact of *higher market share* for Everclear thus assumes an important role toward maintaining higher payoffs for the price reduction cases versus the *$1.00 case.*

When computer run results were analyzed for the sub-cases (vary-

ing the total market forecast and cost of capital variables), it was found that the study outcomes were not sensitive to these factors. Although the absolute levels of all payoffs changed, no appreciable change was noted in their relative standing.

In Summary

This illustration has shown two principal findings regarding the expected payoffs associated with the alternative courses of action formulated by Everclear: (a) all price reduction strategies result in higher expected payoffs than that associated wtih the status quo pricing case and of these, the *$.80 case* leads to the largest expected value; (b) the higher payoffs associated with the price reduction strategies are quite sensitive to the assumption that Everclear's future market share would be favorably influenced by reductions in Kromel price.

Everclear's management is now at least in a position to appraise the *financial implications* of its marketing assumptions in order to arrive at a reasoned selection among alternative choices.

IMPLICATIONS

The preceding illustration indicates the extent of problem detail which can be (and frequently must be) introduced to reflect adequately the characteristics of real market situations. Nevertheless, this illustration omits some important features of Bayesian decision theory.

First, payoffs were expressed in monetary terms (cumulative, compounded net profits) rather than utility, in the von Neumann-Morgenstern sense, as discussed by Schlaifer.[2] One assumes implicitly, then, that utility is linear with money. As tempting as this assumption may be, some small-scale studies at Du Pont in which attempts were made to construct empirical utility functions raise some questions regarding the assumption of linearity. However, this feature of the Bayesian approach may well take many years of further education and development before it may find regular application on the industrial scene.

Second, while a plethora of Bayesian prior probabilities were used in this problem, no mention was made of analyzing sample data and calculating *posterior* probabilities. How does one investigate states of nature in problems of this type? Certainly the problems of conducting meaningful experiments are hardly trivial in pricing problems, or the general area of market planning.

[2] Ibid, Chapter 2.

Third, just how detailed a structure can be warranted, particularly when the imputs to the problem are largely subjective in character? One may obviously over-structure as well as under-structure a problem. This *caveat*, however, applies to all model building. While sensitivity analysis may be used to shed light on which variables "make a difference," the fact remains that the model-building process is still based largely on the builder's intuitive grasp of problem essentials and the interplay between analyst and decision maker. The structure of the problem discussed in this article turned out to be complex precisely because the variables included *were* deemed important by the decision maker(s). And part of the analyst's job is thus to examine the impact of supposedly important variables on the relevant payoff junction and then feed back his findings to the decision maker.

Finally, in conducting this study, realistic problems have a way of generating quite a lot of arithmetic detail, for example, a multi-stage set of alternative states of nature and payoffs. Implementation of the Bayesian approach must, therefore, frequently be aided by recourse to a high-speed computing device. Moreover, a computer model also facilitates the task of running sensitivity analyses concerning either changes in probabilities originally assigned to states of nature or changes in the payoff values related to any particular combination of state of nature and course of action.

Our experience has indicated that the Bayesian approach, even coupled with the ancillary techniques of computer simulation and sensitivity analysis, does not offer any foolproof procedure for "solving" market planning problems. Still, it would seem that this method *does* offer definite advantage over the more traditional techniques usually associated with market planning. Traditional techniques rarely consider *alternative* states of nature, let alone assigning prior probabilities to their occurrence. Moreover, traditional market planning techniques seldom provide for testing the sensitivity of the study's outcomes to departures in the basic assumptions.

At the very least, the Bayesian model forces a more rigorous approach to market planning problems and offers a useful device for quickly finding the financial implications of assumptions about the occurrence of alternative states of nature. In time, this procedure coupled with a more sophisticated approach to the design, collection, and interpretation of field data appears capable of providing an up-to-date and flexible means to meet the more stringent demands of dynamic decision situations, so typical in the problems faced by the marketing manager.

How to Price Industrial Products

Arleigh W. Walker

For marketers of industrial goods and construction companies, pricing is the single judgment that translates potential business into reality. Yet pricing is the least rational of all decisions made in this specialized field.

Careful study and analysis govern every aspect of business judgment, from manufacturing techniques through market surveys that can reliably describe potential sales. But pricing is left to the experience and intuition of the sales manager, and while no one deprecates his hard-earned experience and acutely developed sixth sense, the pricing function should be as precise and scientific as human knowledge can make it. Because the natural imprecision of human judgment makes it impossible to account accurately for all the factors which affect competitive bidding, this article offers a pricing formula to complement executive judgment in industrial marketing.

I shall try to show that the application of mathematical probabilities in determining the impact of even small price changes can yield better results than a sales manager's intuition. The human factor remains, however, whatever formulas are applied; and later I shall discuss it as an element in bidding.

THE BIDDING PROCESS

Great segments of industry buy and sell through the process known as the inquiry/bid system. This bidding process is used not only for custom-engineered products but for standard manufactured items as well. A buyer generally sends inquiries only to respected companies

able to produce in conformity with his requirements, and equal consideration of all bidders is usual.

Bidding is a continuous process for most industrial companies. Batteries of engineers, estimators, and salesmen are constantly occupied with the search for new business and handling the flow of inquiries received from companies and governmental units wishing to purchase manufactured items. In varying degrees this flow represents new business available to a supplying company, and it is possible to approximate closely the dollar worth of the inquiries even before estimating.

Because bids are the sums of variable quantities arrived at through estimation, bids from different companies for identical items will vary, even when internal costs are essentially the same for all competitors. The market level is therefore not a specific value for a given item, but rather a band, or spectrum, of prices with fairly well-defined empirical limits for each industry.

PROBABILITY IN BIDDING

I have defined market level as the mean of a group of bids, not the low bid. The purchase is generally made at the low bid, but market level is the price at which all companies are aiming.

If actual bid results were not available, it would be possible to assume that the intent of the bidders would result in a normal distribution of bids clustered about the market level. Published bid results are available by the thousands, however, and by reducing each set of bids to an average price, and percentages above or below the average, a cumulative total of bids at each percentage can be determined. I have performed this statistical exercise for many actual sets of bids for water supply and water treatment projects over a two-year period and have plotted the resulting totals. They are shown in Exhibit 1.

To obtain useful deductions from such data it is necessary to treat the material mathematically. It is reasonable to assume that if I continued to plot bid results indefinitely, the deviations in the totals of some bid values would be eliminated. The resulting curve would approach the appearance of the familiar normal probability curve, and now one can with justification postulate that in a series of bids reaching for an unknown market level, a normal probability distribution will result. By defining the market level as the mean of the price band, we can predict the chances of success in bidding at percentages above or below the market level.

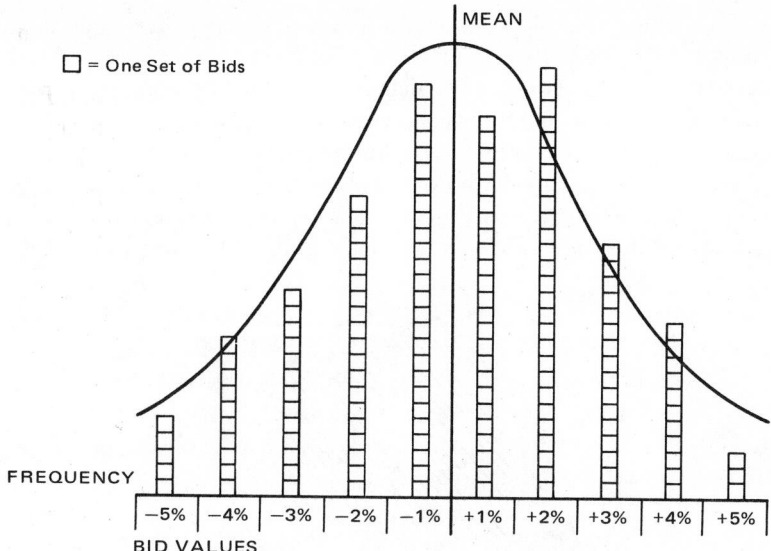

MEAN

☐ = One Set of Bids

FREQUENCY

| −5% | −4% | −3% | −2% | −1% | +1% | +2% | +3% | +4% | +5% |

BID VALUES

Exhibit 1 Range of bids for water supply and treatment equipment according to variation from the mean (market level)

PRICE LEVEL/MARKET SHARE

For a given distance along the horizontal axis of the probability curve, the area under the curve to the left or right of that point represents, respectively, the probability of success or failure.

The success probability equals the market share. This is so because, by mathematical definition, the success probability describes the percentage of low bids, in a series of bids, at a definite price level above or below the mean of all bid sets. If in 10% of all bid sets the low bid is 2% above the average of all bids for that product, then 10% of the market for the product can be captured by pricing it 2% above the average bid price.

The bid range depends on the predictability of costs, and where unknown factors are likely to affect costs, the bid range naturally will be larger than in situations where costs can be accurately forecast. Most industries obtain sufficient control over unknown factors to be able to estimate costs closely, and observation of many bid sets indicates that a 10% bid range adequately covers most bidding situations without excluding a significant number of erratic bids. The bid range, however, must be determined by observation for each industry.

Calculating success probabilities at various price levels enables us to plot the market share against the price level. After a series of success probabilities (or market shares) is arbitrarily chosen, we can determine the horizontal ordinate corresponding to each figure in the series from standard normal distribution tables.

Since any point on the horizontal axis that defines a success area also defines a failure area, to define, say, a 30% success probability (as shown in Exhibit 2), it is necessary to read the tables for a 20%

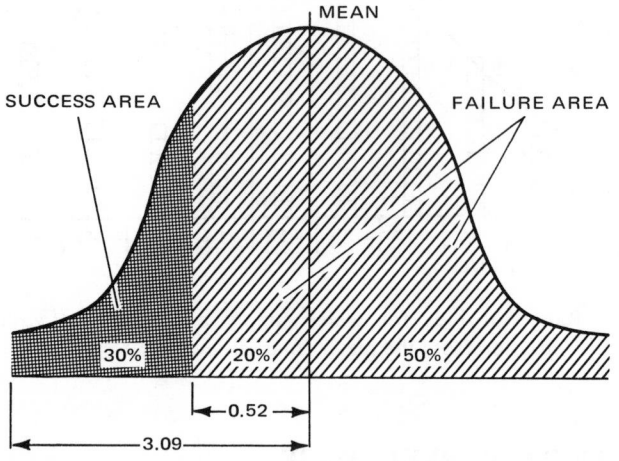

Exhibit 2   Determining bid percentage resulting in a 30% market share, using a 10% bid range

complementary area. Here one finds that 3.09 defines half the area of the curve, and, for a 30% success probability, the ordinate is 0.52. After prorating the ordinate in the equivalent bid range of 5%, one finds that to obtain a 30% market share it would be necessary to bid 0.84% above the market level, according to this calculation:

$$\frac{0.52}{3.09} \times 5\% = 0.84\%$$

This simple calculation is repeated until enough coordinates are obtained to define the curve shown in Exhibit 3. This curve is constructed for a 10% bid range; for a 20% bid range each unit on the horizontal axis would be doubled, and for a 5% bid range each unit would be halved.

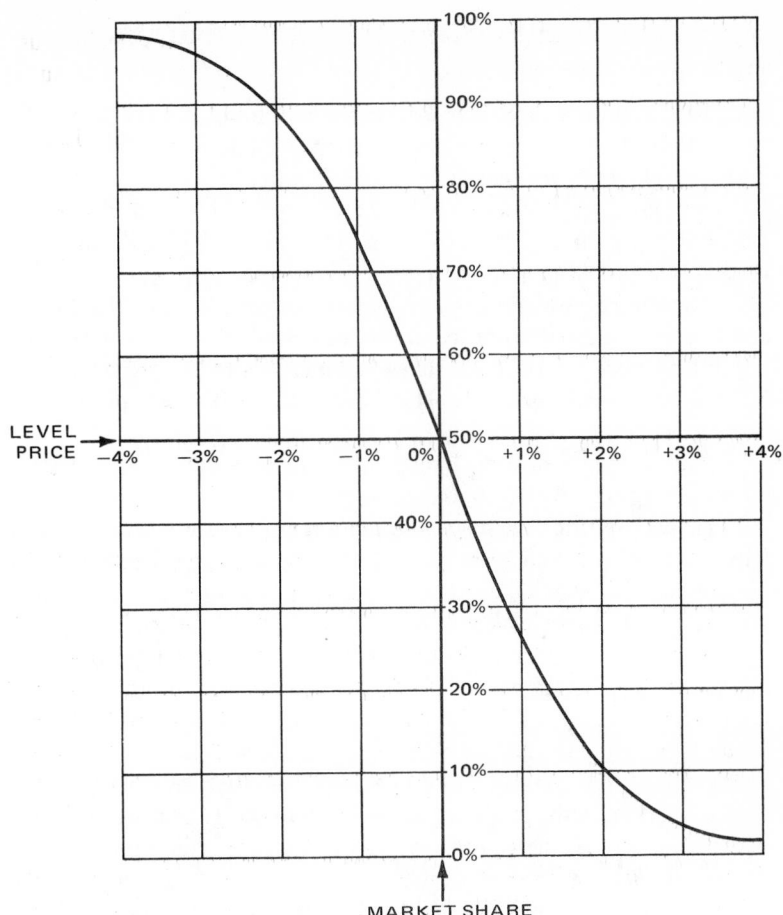

Exhibit 3 Price level/market share curve

EMPLOYING THE CURVE

The price level/market share curve has great utility as a management tool. A company can, for instance:

Determine the market level, in light of the market share for the preceding period and of the profit applied to the company's bids.

Optimize profits by weighing a price increase against the decreased volume that would result.

Apply the curve to different products and different territories hand-

ling the same product, since the curve is set down in terms of percentages above or below the mean.

Following are two examples of how to use the curve:

Example A. A prospective bidder wants to determine his optimum profit margin, knowing the market share required.

1. Summarize the value of all business that will be bid during the next bidding period. (The total of all inquiries to be bid in the next week is $4,000,000.)

2. Determine how much business is required to absorb fixed costs and pay the expected profit, based on historical price levels. (According to historical data, half the sales volume goes to pay the $500,000 in fixed expenses incurred weekly. Therefore, $1,000,000 in business is required.)

3. Divide Step 2 by Step 1 to get short-term market share. (Dividing $1,000,000 by $4,000,000 equals 25%.)

4. Enter the price curve on the market share axis, move horizontally to the curve, and then vertically to the price level axis. (Read horizontally from 25% on the market share axis to the curve, then vertically to the price level axis.)

5. For each territory and product, find the profit margin from the market level tabulation constructed from past bid information and adjust the margin based on Step 4. (Add 1% to the market level price for all bids during the next week.)

Example B. A company that currently has 20% of a $1,000,000 weekly market, with a 10% profit level ($20,000), wants to find out whether higher volume at a lower profit percentage is desirable.

The company has the capacity to handle 25% of the market without increased fixed costs. Management is certain that the rise in volume will not upset the market because of the large number of competitors bidding.

From the curve it can be seen that at a 20% market share the company's price level is 1.35% above the market level, and that to obtain a 25% market share the price level must be reduced to 1.05% above the market. Since it is known that the present volume is yielding a 10% profit margin, the new profit would be:

$$10\% - (1.35 - 1.05) = 9.7\%$$

In a $1,000,000 weekly market the company's $250,000 in sales then would produce a profit margin of $24,250. Since the company would enjoy a gross profit increase of $4,250 a week, it would be wise to increase the volume by decreasing the margin.

Determining Pricing Policy

To arrive at a pricing policy with confidence, the sales manager must have available a range of facts. He must know the percentage of available business that his company obtained in the last period and the profit margin at which that business was conducted. He must also know the volume of business available to him in the next period and the percentage of that business needed to pay his fixed costs and return the expected profit.

Where the sales of a product are too small to draw conclusions with confidence, the sales force must obtain information on lost jobs. Admittedly it is sometimes not easy to discover the successful bidder's name and price, but it must be done to avoid pricing blindly. Persistence is the prime requisite in getting bid information for the home office.

In most cases, the salesmen most successful in this regard are those who realize that their company's efforts and money have been spent at the purchasers' request, and that some compensatory information is in order. In most industrial operations, the feedback of bid information is routine and the data necessary to use the price level/market share curve are always available. Where complete sets of bid results are available, calculation of the market level is easily performed by averaging the applied profit margin for all projects. The profit margin on a competitor's bid is found by translating that bid into a profit percentage applied to the investigator's costs for the same product.

A sample bid tabulation for one product in one sales territory is given in Exhibit 4. If Bidder C makes the evaluation, he knows that his estimated cost was $43,218. Using this cost figure Bidder C calculates the profit margin on all bids, arriving at an average of 15.1%.

BIDDER	PRICE		INVESTIGATOR'S COSTS		GROSS PROFIT	GROSS PROFIT PERCENTAGE
A	$50,249	—	$43,218	=	$7,031	14.0%
B	50,415	—	43,218	=	7,197	14.3
C	50,757	—	43,218	=	7,539	14.8
D	52,300	—	43,218	=	9,082	17.4
					Average	15.1%

Exhibit 4   Determination of market level for one product in one sales territory

Where only the low bid figures are available, the same procedure is followed, but the average of all profit margins on low bids will not define the market level. To arrive at the market level profit percentage, the average scatter of bids must be taken into account by adding 1.10% to the low bid profit margin average.

The 1.10% is the difference between the market level and the average of all low bids, as stated on the price level/market share curve at a 25% market share. According to the laws of probability, half the bids below the market level will occur at less than 1.10%, and half will occur at more than 1.10%. If the industry bid range is 20%, then 2.20% should be added to the average of all low bids to obtain the market level.

Having obtained information on product sales from each sales territory, the sales manager can tabulate market level profit margins as shown in Exhibit 5. For the next bidding period, which naturally equals the average time necessary to prepare bids, the value of all current inquiries can be assessed. This is the total market.

	PRODUCT			
TERRITORY	W	X	Y	Z
Northeast	10%	9%	12%	6%
Mid-Atlantic	11	10	13	6
South	11	11	15	6
Midwest	10	10	14	6
Southwest	11	11	16	6
West	11	12	15	6

Exhibit 5   Typical market level table for all sales territories

Accounting for Fixed Costs

All companies calculate fixed cost absorption rates based on anticipated sales. These rates are derived by dividing the sum of all indirect costs, such as engineering, accounting, administration, sales, and depreciation, by the expected direct costs associated with the projected sales volume.

The overhead absorption rate so derived is true for one sales volume only, and is therefore an approximation. But it is useful in determining the market share needed at existing price levels. By totaling the dollar value of all inquiries quoted and knowing the amount of fixed costs that can be absorbed in each unit, the required market share of

existing business can be determined. By entering the price level/market share curve on the market share axis and moving horizontally to the curve, then moving vertically to the price level axis, the recommended adjustment for profit margin can be found.

When the quoted work is awarded, the actual market share can be calculated and the prices adjusted to focus on the required market share.

Steadying the Sales Rate

The rate of taking business is fully as important as market share. The most profitable rate of sales is equal to the required market share; that is, the rate of sales throughout the year should be as even as possible, without wide fluctuations. Some industrial and contracting companies go on sales sprees to load up on work, then "coast" while the present work is performed, after which another sales rush is held. Repeating the cycle is costly, as shown in Exhibit 6.

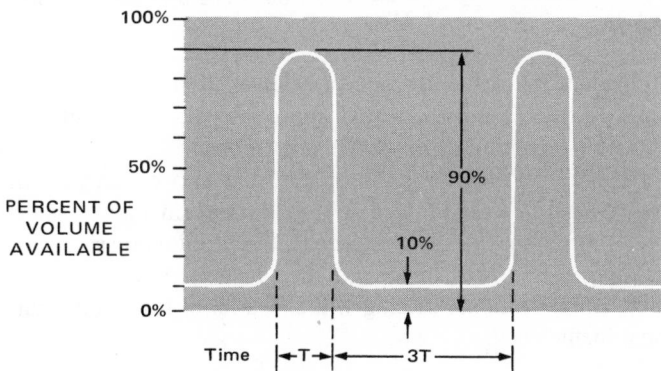

Exhibit 6   Results of a fluctuating rate of sales

This exhibit portrays graphically what happens when a company regulates its production load by its pricing. If we designate T as the time during which the price level is lowered to take 90% of the available business, and 3T as the time necessary to manufacture that volume of business, we can calculate the profit margin on the average rate of sales. (To dramatize the comparison between a fluctuating rate of sales and a level one, I have arbitrarily selected sales volumes of 90% and 10%.)

The average rate of sales is determined by dividing the area under the curve for one cycle, by the time elapsed for that cycle. As a formula, the calculation is as follows:

$$\frac{\text{Area under curve}}{\text{Time elapsed}} = \frac{.9T + 3T\,(.1)}{4T} = 30\%$$

From the price level/market share curve, we note that:

Margin @ 30% rate of sales $= +0.80\%$ (above market level)

This is the relative profit margin if a level 30% rate of sales is used. Again consulting the curve, we find that:

Margin @ 90% $= -2.1\%$ (below market level)
Margin @ 10% $= +2.1\%$ (above market level)

And to obtain the weighted average margin, we use the following calculation:

$$\frac{.9T\,(-2.1) + .3T\,(+2.1)}{1.2T} = \frac{-1.27T}{1.2T} = -1.06\% \text{ (below market level)}$$

It is readily evident that a steady rate of sales of 30%, as compared to the fluctuating rate described, would improve profit by the sum of 1.06% and 0.80%, or 1.86%, above the market level.

Based on a 10% profit margin on sales, the above comparison would show a profit increase of 18.6% from a uniform rate of sales. If a 5% profit margin on sales was expected, the profit increase would be an astounding 37%. It is important then to employ a consistent pricing policy, since irrational pricing will cause more lost profit than organizational inefficiency.

HUMAN FACTOR = X

The pricing formula does not and will not supplant the sales manager's judgment; it merely complements his experience and intuition. Shrewd bidding and sales techniques are valuable, but the human factor can still reduce precise mathematical calculations to worthless theory. I shall discuss some of these considerations briefly.

Bias in Bidding

Individual prejudice sometimes influences bidding so much that it fits no normal pattern. Bias can be traced to a close personal relationship between a salesman and a buyer, to the fact that one bidder has sup-

plied the buyer most of the time, or to real or fancied differences in service.

Regardless of the reason, any sales manager can soon detect bias by observing whether he gets a reasonable share of the purchaser's business. When bias against his company is known to exist, the sales manager must adjust the success probability upward to perhaps 80% or 90% for a particular bid.

Pricing can be used as a competitive weapon to create favorable bias in a preferred customer. Realizing that certain customers have more potential than others, an astute sales manager will depart from a broad pricing policy to obtain the lion's share of that customer's business. Becoming the major supplier for a key customer can result in future favorable bias, permitting the supplier to obtain not only most of the customer's business but the full market price as well.

The purpose of salesmanship in a business dependent on winning bids is to obtain inquiries and create favorable bias in the buyer. But often salesmanship has little effect other than to counterbalance the salesmanship of competitors. Only on rare occasions will a buyer who is favorably disposed toward a supplier permit him to reduce his bid below that of the original low bidder. Countless bidding situations have shown that salesmanship without the right price is usually value-less, while the right price without salesmanship may still result in success.

No Vacuum in This Business

"Don't leave any money on the table" is the old adage that supposedly guides sales managers in bidding. Behind this statement is the realization that a bid must be low, but not by much, to be successful.

It is possible for a company taking a small percentage of the business available to have little or no effect on the market level. And it is theoretically possible for such a company to obtain its business far below the market level, while the stronger companies maintain the market level.

The converse is not true, however, since the low end of the price band determines who receives the business. There is therefore an upper limit to the profit margin available to the small company; but there is no lower limit for a company that does not dominate its industry.

As in the physical world, inertia exists in the market. Prices and market shares, like objects, remain at rest until set in motion by external forces. Healthy markets with established market shares will hold steady until a sudden decrease in available volume causes one competitor to try to hold his dollar volume constant, thereby increas-

ing his share of the market. If the market responds quickly, and an immediate flood of business comes to the offender, other bidders will launch a fierce competitive counterattack.

The result is price warfare, with prices spiraling downward to the no-profit level, at which all bidders are desperately trying to stave off disaster by merely absorbing fixed costs. History has shown that sudden attempts to change market shares end with approximately the same market shares but at deflated prices. Quick gains made by defying a market in equilibrium cause the market to exact retribution on all competitors, not just the offender. The law of equilibrium in the market is immutable.

In view of human weakness, it is probably of little value to point out that industry is better off maintaining market shares at the equilibrated price level than trying to achieve the impossibility of quick market growth. Only individual discipline will hold prices at a profitable level.

Faced with a shrinking available volume, prudent managers find that retrenchment by cutting fixed expenses is the only solution. Overcapacity is synonymous with poor management, and production capacity must be governed by the market share available.

CONCLUSION

The pricing formula I have described is a means of optimizing present conditions. Although it should not be used for greedy assaults on the market, it is useful in taking advantage of normal fluctuations occurring in the available business volume. Over a period of time the pricing formula will steadily strengthen the user's market share.

Consider that a 1% profit increase where the normal profit on sales is 10%, is equivalent to a 10% gain on return on investment. And also consider that a 1% profit increase over a normal profit on sales of 5% represents a 20% improvement in return on investment. It becomes apparent that the casual process of marking up costs, repeated thousands of times daily by sales managers using their intuition, has more effect on a company's profit position than the most stringent austerity program.

The price level/market share curve enables management to complement intuition with logic in pricing products. By so doing, management can remove human inconsistency from the profit judgment and thereby optimize its market position.

Consideration of the factors that affect the curve will help management, faced with either shrinking or expanding markets, to make decisions which will strengthen the market for all participants.

A Systems Model for Price Programming

William R. Darden
Donald P. Robin

As companies have become larger, output, which is usually the domain of the production department, and pricing, which is properly the domain of marketing, are separated from each other by far too wide a gulf. Friction easily develops between the two departments when marketing suggests how production should allocate its time and resources. The reasons for this friction can be traced to both departments. For example, the suggestions which come from marketing too often do not represent the overall price-demand situation. Also, too frequently marketers fail to recognize the constraints faced by production. But production personnel are also to blame; market demand situations produce very real constraints, and producing a product without considering these can easily lead to non-optimizing behavior. The goal of this paper is to combine the above mentioned problems of marketing and production into a framework for integrated executive analysis. Since this model crosses somewhat sacred boundaries, it is properly classified as a systems approach.

The method employed to effect the desired solution consists of a simple programming model. Within the model the authors have included constraints from production and market demand. More specifically, this approach demonstrates an operational approach to multi-product price analysis within the context of interdepartmental constraints. Therefore, the final solution of the model yields information valuable to both production and marketing personnel.

Scope

In price analysis, the economics of various price strategies traditionally compare generated volumes to the costs of producing and marketing these levels. This paper proposes that such an approach is misleading

Not previously published.

and, in the case of multi-product strategies, leads to the shrouding of many important pricing relationships. In general, the traditional approach of using cost-volume-revenue figures can result in the following difficulties:

1. Certain hidden costs are not considered; for example, the opportunity costs of allocating productive capacity to other products is hard to ascertain.
2. Traditional breakeven analysis tends to concentrate on one product or one group of products at a time, without considering product combinations.
3. Without viewing a price strategy as a *set* of prices for product combinations, it is difficult to understand the various consequences that are possible—given the uncertainty faced by all product pricers.
4. And traditional price approaches are vulnerable to suboptimimal decisions, since attention is directed toward the market. A *systems* framework for pricing is desirable.

Operational marketing managers have recognized such problems over a long period of time and have felt frustrated in their efforts to structure their real-world problems to fit the price-cost-volume models advocated by theorists. Their attempts are admirable; however, it is felt that a pricing structure is needed which removes the dollar-cost shroud and presents pricing from a systems viewpoint.

Approach to the Paper

This paper concentrates on the operational aspects of integrating market demand analysis into the production programming problem. The approach to this task is composed of the steps listed below:

1. A linear programming product allocation problem is introduced with the simplistic assumption of unlimited demand. Inventories are not considered.
2. The more usual case of the downward sloping demand curve is considered. That is, price strategies are now a possibility for the executive. Pricing and production decisions are treated in a constrained environment—and simultaneously.
3. The model considers the case of risk in demand forecasting and how to price and produce optimally under these conditions.

UNLIMITED DEMAND EXAMPLE

The Market

Let us assume that the MAPRO Company sells two products—*A* and *B*. The marketing department of the firm is in an enviable position, for at current market prices it can sell as many units of *A* and *B* as its production department can hope to produce; that is, its demands are for all practical purposes unlimited. From the demand side, an economist would probably explain that this is a firm in a pure competition market (See Figures 1-A and 1-C). At higher prices, not one

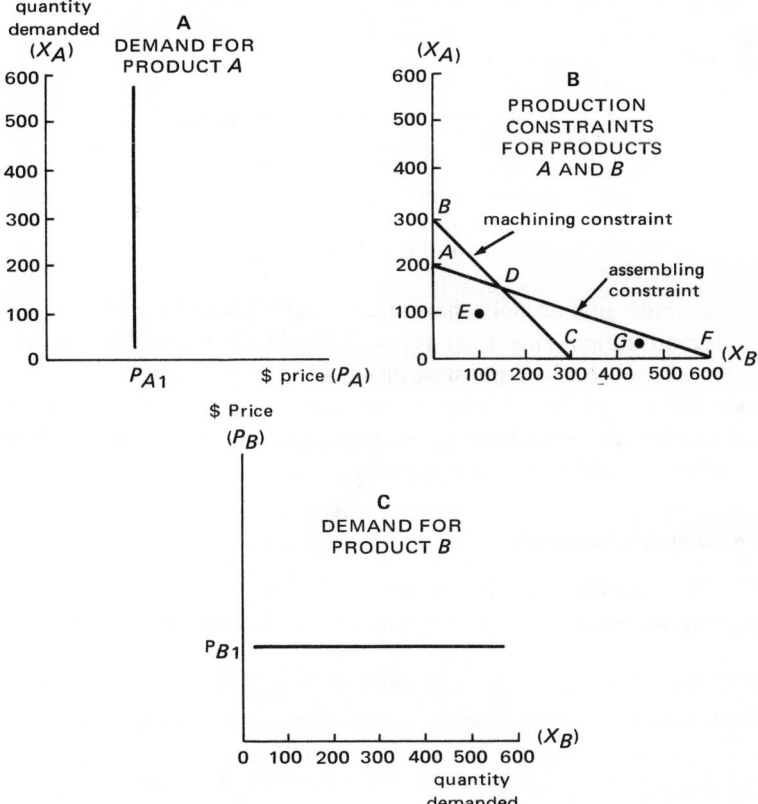

Figure 1 Typical linear programming problem with perfectly elastic product demands and no price option available to the market strategist

unit could be sold; however, at the market prices of each (respectively P_{a1} and P_{b1} per unit of A and B), the firm can sell an infinite number of units. Thus only firm short run supply constraints are important in the event profits are being maximized or losses minimized.

Production Consideration

Linear programming (from now on referred to as LP) assumes that there is a *linear* objective function which is to be optimized (maximized or minimized) subject to a set of N *linear constraints* with M *variables*. The objective function of the MAPRO Company is mathematically stated below.

$$C_t = C_1 X_A + C_2 X_B \text{ (objective function)}$$

where:

$C_t =$ total contribution from the manufacture
       and sale of A and B
$C_1 =$ per unit contribution of Product A
$C_2 =$ per unit contribution of Product B
$X_A =$ quantity of A manufactured and sold
$X_B =$ quantity of B manufactured and sold

We notice immediately the objective function to be maximized is total contribution—not total profit. The objective function *must* be linear; therefore, since per unit profit varies with volume, the difference between price and average variable cost can be substituted for per unit profits—assuming that average variable cost (V) and price are *invariant with production* volume.

Production Constraints

The MAPRO Company has only two production constraints: machining and assembly. Table 1 shows that Product A and Product B *com-*

TABLE 1

	1 UNIT PRODUCT A	1 UNIT PRODUCT B	TOTAL CAPACITY HOURS
Machine Center	3 hours	3 hours	900 hours
Assembly Center	6 hours	4 hours	1200 hours
Unit Contribution	$100	$50	

pete for the total machine time (900 hours) and the total assembly time (1200 hours). These constraints can be mathematically stated below as inequations.

$$1.\quad 3X_A + 3X_B \leqslant 900$$
$$2.\quad 6X_A + 4X_B \leqslant 1200$$

The analysis can now proceed in one of two directions to find a solution for X_A and X_B which maximizes the objective function: (1) the simplex method, or (2) the graphical approach. The simplex approach involves the conversion of the inequations into equations through the use of slack or artificial variables and the inversion of the matrix of coefficients of this set of equations toward an optimizing solution for X_A and X_B.[1]

The graphical method is somewhat less universally applicable and is rarely used for more than two products. However, this approach is particularly useful for the purposes of the demand analysis which follows.

Solution

In Figure 1-B lines *BC* and *AF* are full production center utilization curves. For example, straight line *BC* includes all the possible combinations of *A* and *B* which can be produced when *all machinery capacity* is utilized and when considering machinery as the only needed production center. Line *AF* is the full-utilization curve for assembly and both lines show the upward limits to production caused by that capacity. Thus area *OADC* is the solution space, since we have *less than or equal to* constraints. For example, although maximum utilization of machinery and assembling is not reached, it is possible to produce 100 units of *A* and 100 of *B* (point *E*), while it is not possible to produce 50 *A's* and 400 *B's* (point *G*), since there is not enough machining capacity available.

The traditional approach to solving the product allocation problem of the MAPRO Company involves testing the solutions at the extreme points by substituting these values (coordinates of points *D, A, B,* and *C*) into the objective function and then choosing that solution which is maximum. We would suspect that point *A* (200-*A*, 0-*B*) would be the contribution maximizing solution; however, the analysis below

---

[1] See for example R. W. Metzger, *Elementary Mathematical Programming* (New York: John Wiley & Sons, Inc., 1963).

indicates that point D optimizes the objective function (yielding $22,500 contribution).

I. Extreme Point A (200-A, O-B)
C_{ta} = Total contribution at point A
= $C_1 X_A + C_2 X_B$
= $100 (200 units) + $50 (0 units) = $20,000

II. Extreme Point D (150-A, 150-B)
C_{td} = $100 (150 units) + 450 (150 units) = $22,500

III. Extreme Point C (O-Z, 300-B)
C_{tc} = $100 (0 units) + $50 (300 units) = $15,000

While the discussion to this point has centered on the production constraints, the reader is reminded that demand has also been considered. The assumption of pure competition and the ability of the market to absorb an unlimited quantity from this producer at the market price eliminates the problem of market constraints.

PRICE ADMINISTERED DEMAND

Demand poses no problem for the MAPRO Company when (as in the above analysis) it is considered to be in a perfect or pure competition industry. In this environment, the marketing department of MAPRO does not encounter difficulties in determining product prices, since the intersection of industry demand and industry supply automatically sets the product prices that each firm must face. However, let us hypothetically change the market environment of the industry in which MAPRO competes. In this new environment, MAPRO can now administer its pricing policies.

Assumptions

Marketers recognize that the demands of the products within the product line may be independent, complementary, or competitive; product line cross-elasticities are well recognized. The analysis below assumes complete independence between the demands of Product A and Product B. The framework also assumes that market forecasting is perfect; that is, the quantities demanded at various prices for both Product A and Product B are known with certainty (later this assumption is to be removed).

In Figure 2, the demand curve of Product A (shown in Figure 2-A

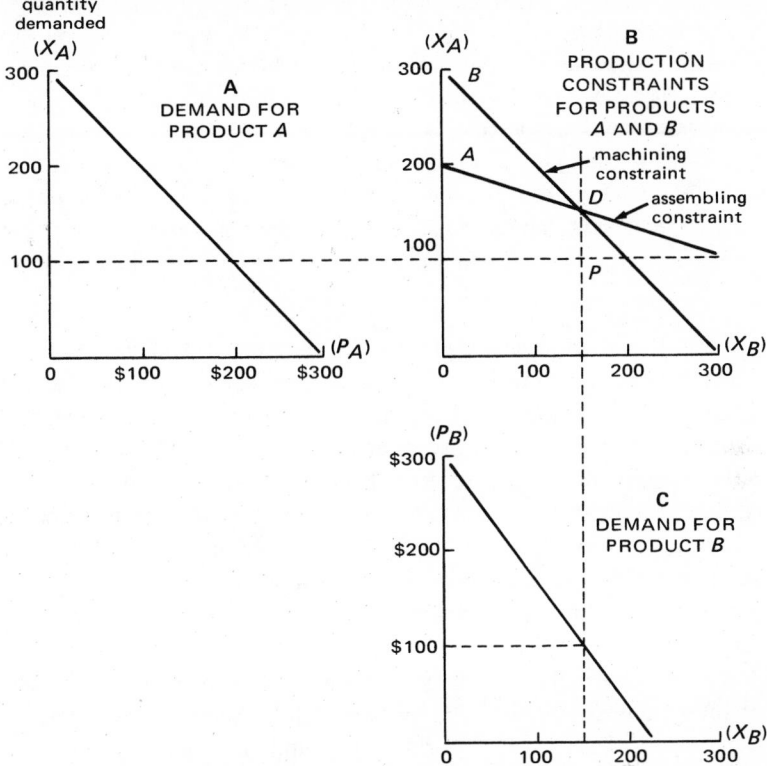

Figure 2   The integration of pricing analysis into production program-ming analysis

to the left of the product possibilities curve) and the demand curve of Product *B* (shown below the graphical presentation of the linear production constraints) are included to provide a graphical picture of the strategies available to top management. It is now easy to as-certain that prices of $200 per unit of *A* and $100 per unit of *B* gen-erate demand volumes which lie within present production capabilities.

Price Strategy Analysis

At a price of $200 per unit of *A*, the quantity demanded is 100 units. If the possibility of stockout or inventory on hand is precluded, Product *A* demand becomes a horizontal line which may be extended to the LP graph. The final solution for the LP problem *must lie* on this line because of its positioning (see Figure 2). Conversely, the same analysis can be made for Product *B* at a price of $100 per unit. A

vertical equality is generated on the LP graph and if management does not wish *stockouts* or *inventory* the final solution must also lie on this vertical line. Point P is the only solution which satisfies all pertinent conditions, that is, it lies on both the horizontal and vertical demand equalities, as well as meeting the production constraints.

But the market analyst knows that at times it is wise to carry inventories and sometimes it is even smart to take *stockouts;* that is, not to satisfy the present demand fully. It is also apparent from Figure 3 that *excess capacity* exists and that price decreases can cause the respective quantities demanded of each product to increase.

PROFIT OPTIMIZATION WITHIN PRODUCTION CONSTRAINTS. The above discussion shows that the executive choice of price is not arbitrary. In fact, marketers are prone to set price in a manner that maximizes contribution or profit, or at least minimizes losses. In this process, marketing executives are likely to forget that production constraints may exist and the resulting volumes demanded of products A and B may be greater than the possible production volume of Product $A,$ or greater than the needed production volume of Product $B,$ or greater than quantities of *each* which can be manufactured in the given time span.

Let us follow the reasoning of the marketing manager as he sets about maximizing profits. The problem will be made somewhat easier than is possible in the real world by providing him with the following *structural* assumptions. First, independence between the demands of Products A and B is assumed; that is, price changes of one product in no way affect the demand of the second. Second, marginal cost is constant for all feasible ranges of production. Third, classical *ceterus paribus* demand conditions are assumed; that is, advertising of the company and competitors, competitors' prices, etc., all remain constant. While the synergistic effects of marketing mix interaction are recognized, short run decisions are assumed to be made with advertising, research and development expenditures and other operating expenses already budgeted. Within certain planning horizons, such assumptions do not deviate far from reality. The rational marketer would now proceed to define his objective function as below:

$$X_i = f_i\,(P_i)$$

$$\text{Profit} = \sum_{i=1}^{N} [(P_i - V_i)\,X_i] - T$$

$$= \sum_{i=1}^{N} [(P_i - V_i) \, f_i(P_i)] - T$$

where:

P_i = price of the product
X_i = quantity demanded of the product
V_i = unit variable
T = fixed production and operating expenses
N = the number of product ($N = 2$)
i = the given product

In the case of a straight line demand curve, equation (2) becomes a quadratic objective function defined in terms of P_i. Solution is then possible through the use of well-known quadratic programming techniques, which consider the maximal solutions within linear production constraints.[2]

UNCERTAINTY AND PRICE PROGRAMMING

While the foregoing model clearly shows the relationship between markets and manufacturing, it leaves certain fundamental questions unanswered. For example, how is uncertainty integrated into the model? And how are inventories treated? In this section, an operational approach is suggested to handle both uncertainty and inventories.

Operational Product Pricing

In a previous article it has been urged that operational pricing models be developed which harness the experience and intuition of managers.[3] In brief, one approach involves estimating optimistic, pessimistic and most likely quantities demanded at selected prices. For a given price strategy, management has a range of possible outcomes and a probability distribution can be assumed which describes the possibilities of the various outcomes within this range.

More importantly, three demand curves can be estimated by connecting groups of similar type quantity estimates through the range

[2] P. Wolfe, "The Simplex Method for Quadratic Programming," *Econometrica,* vol. 37 (1959), pp. 382–398.

[3] Bill R. Darden, "An Operational Approach to Product Pricing," *Journal of Marketing,* vol. 32 (April, 1968).

of selected prices. Panel A in Figure 3 describes the results for Product *A;* optimistic, pessimistic, and most likely demand curves are created. Similarly, the same conditions are created by Product *B* in panel C of Figure 3.

Price Strategy and the Region of Expectancy

Let us consider a product mix price strategy of $200 for *A* and $100 for *B*. From Figure 3 it can be seen that three demand estimates for

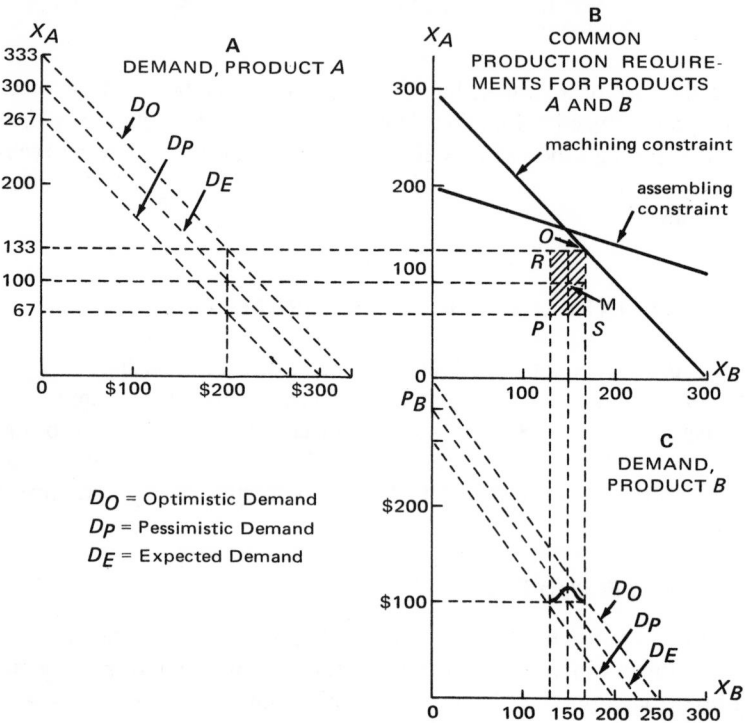

Figure 3   The operational determination of the "region of expectancy" for a given combination product price strategy

each product can now be projected over to the production possibilities graph (panel B). The intersections of the optimistic and pessimistic demand quantities now form a rectangle which can be termed the "Region of Expectancy." Management is almost 100 percent sure that all possible combinations of quantities demanded of the two products (within the given price strategy) will fall within this area. A methodology exists to convert the three demand curves for each product into an "expected" product demand curve. For *purposes of*

exposition let us assume that the *most likely* demand curves for Products *A* and *B* are actually *expected* product demand curves.

Point *M* in panel B, Figure 3, depicts the *expected* combination of products that are to be demanded; point *P* represents the most pessimistic combination; and point *O* is the most optimistic quantities of *A* and *B* that can be sold at $200 and $100, respectively. The closer a given point is to *M,* the greater the probability that this combination of sales will accrue with one given price strategy.

MAXIMUM PROFIT PRICE STRATEGY. From the above illustration, it is seen that the optimum combination of prices to charge is dependent upon the subjectivity of management. Three extreme alternatives exist for the prices: first, management can be conservative and choose a price strategy which maximizes optimistic quantity profits (Figure 4, panel A); or management may wish to price and produce

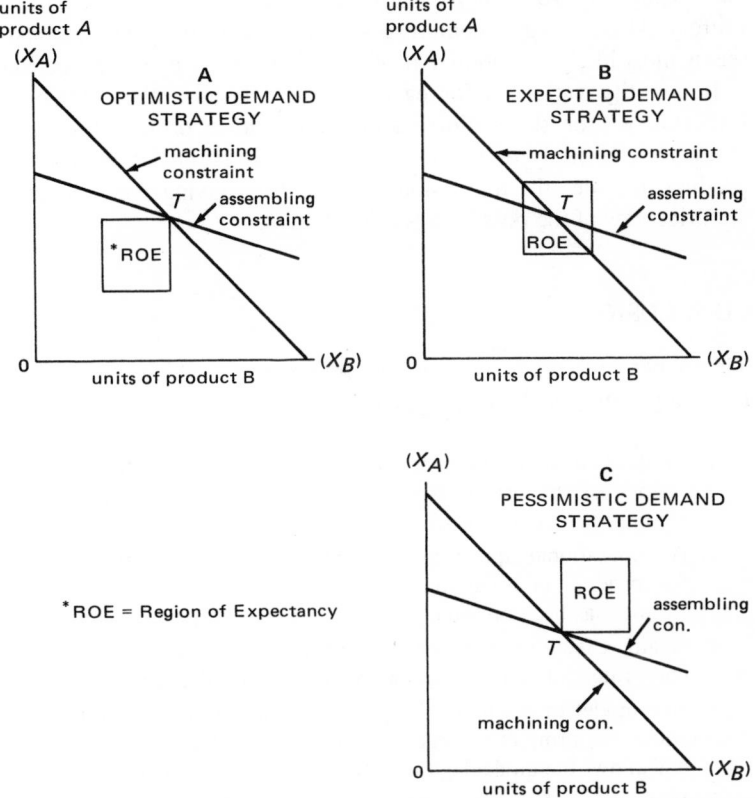

Figure 4   Example of optimistic, expect, and pessimistic price strategies and their respective effects on the "region of expectancy"

at *expected* levels of demand (panel B); or management may feel that pricing strategy and production should be selected to optimize pessimistic demand profits—yielding an expectancy region as in panel C. Optimization procedures under any one of the three strategies is the standard non-linear programming procedure, for which numerous *canned* programs are available.

The only difference in solution between strategies is the estimated demand curves used in the computations. Where management wishes to minimize the chances of *stockout,* optimistic demand curves should be used in the computations. Here, large inventories are likely to be carried, since optimistic production levels are to be maintained.

At the other extreme, the use of pessimistic demand curves in profit maximization results in stockouts. Production levels over the long run are too low to satisfy the upward demand variance.

Use of the "expected" demand optimization criterion results in minimizing the probability of either a stockout or being left with inventory. This strategy—combined with a predetermined *safety stock*—seems most likely to optimize profits through many operating periods.

If quantity variances for each price are known, the "Region of Expectancy" for the optimal solution of either of the three price strategies can easily be determined. Six standard deviations for each product provides the dimensions for the *Box,* giving the strategist a pictorial view of the possibilities that he faces.

CONCLUSION

This paper presents a price programming model which possesses the following operational advantages for the marketer.

1. Production opportunity costs are exposed and tied directly to the actions of the pricer. No longer must the pricer make decisions behind the shroud of cost.

2. An operational approach to optimizing the three price strategies for product combination within the context of production constraints has been presented.

3. Again, executive experience, intuition, and understanding are incorporated into an operational model for price decision making.

4. The model draws upon the pertinent constraints from other areas within the firm. This reduces the probability of suboptimal strategies and allows the model legitimately to be termed a *systems* model.

5. In view of the above, marketing and production can now work together toward the overall objectives of the firm.

Other Factors to Consider

Some additional factors which can be incorporated into this approach include the following:

1. More than two products can be introduced into the model. While the results are not as pictorially satisfying, the same management information can be entered into multiproduct linear and non-linear computer programs for solution of optimal prices within production constraints.

2. It is possible to treat the demands of products, whose sales are highly correlated, and who share common production requirements, into one group for analysis as one dimension. This greatly reduces the problem of analysis for firms with hundreds of different products. In this case the problem of *complementary* and/or *competitive* demands can be "grouped" out.

3. But where the demands of the product are interdependent (as opposed to independent product demand relationships assumed in the model), relationships can be built into the model to reflect the rate and direction of shift of the expected demands of other *complementary* and/or *competitive* products caused by the projected change in the price of Product *A*. Variances in most cases can be assumed constant for many products when compared before and after the shifts of their expected demands.

4. Obviously, as many linear constraints as are applicable to the programming problem can be included in this systems analysis. Many constraints which are curvilinear can easily be approximated by two or more *linear* constraints. Other marketing mix response curves can be integrated into the analysis as desired.

Product Decisions in Marketing Management

The importance of new product development to business firms is well recognized. Indeed the survival and growth of firms depends largely on their ability to maintain a steady stream of new-product ideas. Furthermore, there is ample evidence demonstrating that most new products are failures. This fact has placed an increasingly heavy burden on marketers to search for more effective means of evaluating new product decisions.

At each stage of the new development process—search, screening, profit analysis, product development, product testing, and commercialization—operations research has played an important part in developing more effective decision aids. Philip Kotler, in the first article of this section, describes a methodology for improving decisions necessary at the third stage—profit analysis. At this stage the new product, having survived the search and screening stages, must be analyzed for its profit potential. Kotler shows that it can be misleading to confine the analysis to one specific conception of the product's characteristics and marketing mix. If variations in the marketing mix influence profit potential of new products, how can the best marketing mix be found? Kotler suggests an answer and shows how the estimated profit potential of this best mix provides the basis for determining whether the new product should be developed.

In "Product Characteristics and Marketing Strategy," Gordon Miracle develops a model which permits the marketing manager to study in a systematic fashion the significant relationships between product characteristics and *each* of the elements in the marketing mix. The model may provide the basis for predicting, or justifying, a marketing mix for a product with given characteristics.

In the third article of this section, Professor Green demonstrates how Bayesian decision theory "provides a rich set of techniques for dealing with the complex problems that attend new product development."

Marketing Mix Decisions for New Products

Philip Kotler

Companies are increasingly recognizing that new products are basic to their survival and growth. According to one study "it is now commonplace for major companies to have 50% or more of current sales in products new in the past ten years." [1]

At the same time, the development of new products is a costly and risky business undertaking. Some new product ideas turn out to be technically unfeasible after good money has been spent and others turn out to be commercially unsuccessful after still more good money is gone. As many as three out of four new products introduced on the market may fail to attain commercial success.

Thus management finds itself in a dilemma: it must develop new products and yet the odds weigh heavily against their success. The answer lies in making the innovation function a more rational process through administrative reforms and improved decision-making procedures. Management is coming to recognize the desirability of centralizing responsibility for overseeing the process in new product committees and departments. Furthermore, it is recognizing the need for better theory and decision procedures at each stage of the new product development process (*search, screening, profit analysis, product development, test marketing,* and *commercialization*). At each stage, a basic decision is called for on whether to abandon the project or continue it. The purpose of this paper is to describe a methodology for improved decision-making at the third stage, that of profit analysis.

THE PROFIT ANALYSIS STAGE

Suppose a new product idea has been screened and found to be compatible with the company's objectives and resources. The next task is to evaluate the profit potential of the product. In practice, this evalua-

Reprinted with permission from the *Journal of Marketing Research,* vol. 28, no. 1 (February, 1964), pp. 43–49, published by the American Marketing Association.

tion tends to be conducted in the following manner. On the basis of inspiration or previous research, management develops a particular conception of product attributes and a marketing program for the new product. Based on this specific conception of the marketing mix, management develops two different estimates. One is an estimate of the required sales volume to break even. The other is an estimate of the sales volume which is likely to be stimulated by the marketing mix. If the sales potential estimate comfortably exceeds the break-even volume estimate, the product idea is judged to be profitable. If profits promise to be large in relation to the required investment, the product idea is likely to pass to the fourth stage, that of product development.

Yet a more refined model for the analysis of new product profit potential is both desirable and practical. Instead of considering only one marketing mix and whether break-even volume is likely to be achieved under it, the more refined model provides for a simultaneous evaluation of the profit potential of several marketing mixes. The refined model can be illustrated by the following example:

The ABC Electronics Company is a small manufacturer of transistors and clock radios and is presently engaged in reviewing other electronic products for possible addition to the product line. One of these is a small portable tape recorder. Small novelty tape recorders have appeared recently on the market, and they retail at prices between $20–$50. The company's marketing research department has surveyed the market and found that interest in this type of unit is substantial and growing.

An executive committee is appointed to examine the potential profitability of this product. The production department estimates that $60,000 would have to be invested in specific new equipment and facilities and that this investment would have an estimated life of five years. The accounting department submits that the product would have to absorb $26,000 a year of general overhead to cover the value of supporting facilities, rent, taxes, executive salaries, cost of capital, etc. The marketing department advises that the product be supported initially with an advertising budget of approximately $20,000 and a personal selling budget of approximately $30,000 and furthermore that it should be priced at approximately $18 F.O.B. factory with no quantity discounts. Finally, the various operating departments estimate that the new product would involve a direct material and labor cost of $10 a unit.

In the light of these estimates, should the ABC Electronics Company develop this new product? Is the marketing mix proposed by the marketing department sound?

What Is the Break-Even Volume?

The first step in the business analysis of a new product idea is to estimate how many units would have to be sold in order to cover costs. This break-even volume is found by analyzing how total revenue and total cost vary at different sales volumes.

Total revenue at any particular sales volume is that volume times the unit price adjusted by allowances for early payment, quantity purchases, and freight. The adjustments are fairly straightforward and total revenue as a function of sales volume is generally simple to estimate.

The total cost function is more difficult to estimate. Total costs often bear a non-linear relationship to output. It is difficult enough to establish the shape of the total cost function for existing products because the statistical data are impure; the total cost function for a new product is even more difficult to estimate because the statistical data are nonexistent. But as a practical matter, the break-even analyst usually assumes a linear total cost function. This assumption may be faulty for very low and very high levels of output but may be sufficiently accurate for intermediate levels, according to some recent statistical cost studies [3].

The total cost function is composed of variable and fixed cost elements. In the example, variable costs are assumed to be constant at $10 a unit. The following fixed costs are found in the example. The tape recorder requires additional fixed investment of $60,000 with an estimated life of five years. On a straight line basis, this amounts to an annual depreciation cost of $12,000. The new product is also charged $26,000 a year for its share of general overhead. This figure presumably represents a long-run estimate of the opportunity value of the corporate resources required to support this new product. In addition, the company is considering an annual exepnditure of $20,000 on advertising and $30,000 on personal selling. Fixed costs therefore add up to $88,000 ($12,000 + $26,000 + $20,000 + $30,000).

The break-even volume can now be estimated. At the break-even volume (Q_B), total revenue (TR) equals total cost (TC). But total revenue is price (P) times the break-even volume and total cost is fixed cost (F) plus the product of unit variable cost (V) and break-even volume. In symbols:

$$TR = TC$$
$$P \cdot Q_B = F + V \cdot Q_B$$

Combining similar terms, and solving for Q_B, we find that

$$Q_B = \frac{F}{P - V}$$

$P - V$ is the difference between price and unit variable cost and is called the unit contribution to fixed cost. It is $8 in the example. The company would have to sell 11,000 units ($88,000 ÷ $8) to cover fixed costs.

At this point it would be useful to express the break-even volume (Q_B) not as a constant but rather as a function of the elements in the marketing mix. The break-even volume will vary with the product price and the amount of marketing effort devoted to the new product:

$$Q_B = \frac{\$12{,}000 + \$26{,}000 + A + S}{P - \$10} = \frac{\$38{,}000 + A + S}{P - \$10}$$

where A = advertising budget
S = sales budget
P = unit selling price to wholesaler

In Table 1, eight alternative marketing programs are listed for this product along with the implied break-even volumes. In the case of mix #5, the company could sell as few as 4,143 tape recorders to break even; while in the case of mix #4, the company would have to sell as many as 23,000. This high sensitivity of the break-even volume to the marketing mix decision is often overlooked in profit analysis.

TABLE 1   Minimum Volume Requirements as a Function of Marketing Mix

	SOME POSSIBLE MARKETING MIXES			BREAK-EVEN VOLUME Q_B
	PRICE	ADVERTISING	SALES BUDGET	
1.	$16	$10,000	$10,000	9,667
2.	16	10,000	50,000	16,333
3.	16	50,000	10,000	16,333
4.	16	50,000	50,000	23,000
5.	24	10,000	10,000	4,143
6.	24	10,000	50,000	7,000
7.	24	50,000	10,000	7,000
8.	24	50,000	50,000	9,857

The eight marketing mixes in Table 1 are a small sample from the very large number of mixes which could be used to market the new tape recorder. They were formed by assuming a high and low level for each of the marketing variables and elaborating all the combinations. Suppose executive opinion held that $16 is a price on the low side while $24 is a price on the high side; and that $10,000 is a low budget for advertising and personal selling respectively, and $50,000 is a high budget. This yields eight strategy combinations (2 · 2 · 2 = 2^3) and makes the marketing mix problem manageable.

Each mix is a polar case. For example, mix #1 represents the common strategy of setting a low price and spending very little for promotion. This works well when the market is highly price conscious, possesses good information about available brands, and is not easily swayed by psychological appeals. Mix #4 represents a strategy of low price and heavy promotion. The interesting thing about this mix is that it produces a high sales volume but also requires a high sales volume to break even. Mix #5 consists of a high price and low promotion and is used typically in a seller's market where the firm wants to maximize short-run profits. Mix #8 consists of a high price supported by high promotion; this strategy is often used in a market where buyers are sensitive to psychological appeals and to quality. The other mixes (#2, 3, 6, 7) are variations on the same themes, with the additional feature that different assessments are made of the comparative effectiveness of advertising and personal selling. But it should be noted that while the division of a given budget between advertising and personal selling affects the actual sales volume, it does not affect the break-even volume.

Different marketing mixes not only imply different break-even volumes, but also differences in the sensitivity of profits to *deviations* from the break-even volume. For example, the break-even volume is approximately the same for mixes #1 and #8. Yet the high price, high promotion character of #8 promises greater losses or greater profits for deviations from the break-even volume. This is because there are higher fixed costs under mix #8 but once they are covered, additional volume is very profitable because of the high price.

Break-even analysis is necessary, but not sufficient by itself to identify the optimal marketing mix. It indicates what volumes have to be achieved but does not indicate what volumes are likely to be achieved. Missing is an account of how various elements in the marketing mix will affect the actual volume of sales.

Ideally the company requires a demand equation showing sales volume as a function of price, advertising, personal selling, and other

important marketing mix elements. Such equations are difficult enough to derive for established products where there are historical data, let alone for new product ideas where there are none. Yet though the product is only an idea at this stage, there are some research procedures which can yield useful information for estimating sales. A survey could be made of the attitudes and interests of various consumers toward alternative product features and prices. It might help to develop some prototypes of the tape recorder in order to get firsthand reactions. The survey may indicate what socio-economic groups constitute major prospects for this product. The approximate number of persons in each prospect group can be estimated from census data. In addition, an analysis can be made of the relative strength of competitors in different segments of the market. Since information is expensive to collect, a Bayesian analysis of the value of specified types of additional information should be performed at each juncture [2].

Through this type of research and analysis, the executives will have a better idea of what sales volumes are likely to be achieved with different marketing mixes. For each particular mix, the executives can develop a subjective probability distribution of possible sales volumes. The mean of this probability distribution shows the expected sales volume for this marketing mix. Let the expected sales volume be denoted by Q. The fourth column in Table 2 shows an (hypothetical) expected sales volume for each of the eight marketing mixes. It should be noted that sales are expected to move inversely with price and directly with the amounts spent on advertising and personal selling. However, increased promotion is expected to increase sales at a diminishing rate.

What Is the Best Marketing Mix and the Implied Profit Level?

At this point, the expected volume (Q) and the break-even volume (Q_B) can be compared for each mix. The results are shown in column 6 of Table 2. The greatest extra volume $(Q - Q_B)$ is achieved with mix #1. But extra volume is not a sufficient indicator of the best mix. The extra volume must be multiplied by the unit value $(P - V)$. A high price mix delivering a small extra volume may be superior to a low price mix delivering a large extra volume. Therefore $Z = (P - V) \cdot (Q - Q_B)$ has to be calculated for each marketing mix. These results are shown in column 7 of Table 2.

Z is a measure of the absolute profits expected from different marketing mixes. Of the mixes shown in Table 2, mix #5 appears to promise the largest amount of profit. This mix calls for the product

TABLE 2 A Comparison of Expected Volume (Q) and Break-Even Volume (Q_B) for Various Marketing Mixes

	(1)	(2) MARKETING MIX		(3)	(4)	(5)	(6) VOLUME ABOVE BREAK-EVEN	(7) ABSOLUTE PROFITS
	P	A	S		Q	Q_B	$Q - Q_B$	$Z = (P - V)(Q - Q_B)$
1.	$16	$10,000	$10,000		12,400	9,667	2,733	$16,398
2.	16	10,000	50,000		18,500	16,333	2,167	13,002
3.	16	50,000	10,000		15,100	16,333	−1,233	−7,398
4.	16	50,000	50,000		22,600	23,000	−400	−2,400
5.	24	10,000	10,000		5,500	4,143	1,357	18,998
6.	24	10,000	50,000		8,200	7,000	1,200	16,800
7.	24	50,000	10,000		6,700	7,000	−300	−4,200
8.	24	50,000	50,000		10,000	9,857	143	2,002

to be sold at a high price with little promotional support. This strategy is often used when a company believes its product has been smartly designed and essentially sells itself. But before ABC Electronics can be sure that it has found the best marketing mix, or that the product should be produced at all, it must examine some additional issues.

1. *The profit estimates for the eight marketing mixes may not be equally reliable.* The profit estimates were derived from prior cost and sales estimates. Management may have a varying amount of confidence in these different estimates. Suppose management has much more confidence in its sales estimate for marketing mix #6 than #5. This greater confidence may arise because the executives have more experience in using strategy #6. The choice they face is between a highly uncertain profit expectation of $18,998 and a more certain profit expectation of $16,800. Most managements have a risk aversion and are willing to accept a strategy with a lower expected profit if the accompanying risk is *sufficiently* less. However the specific amount of trade-off of expected profits for risk reduction will vary among managements.

How can management's taste for risk be measured and introduced into the formal analysis? There are at least two different ways to accomplish this. One is through the preparation of an indifference map in which management expresses its preferences between different combinations of expected profit and risk. Let us recall that in considering each marketing mix, management developed a subjective probability distribution of possible sales outcomes. Only the mean, Q, of the distribution was used. Now assume that the standard deviation of this distribution is used as a measure of risk. A low standard deviation means that management is fairly sure of the sales outcomes and a high standard deviation means that management is very unsure. The standard deviation of the profit estimate can be calculated from the standard deviation of the sales estimate.[1] Let us use σ_z to denote the standard deviation of estimated profit. Let (Z, σ_z)* represent the ex-

---

[1] Expected profit is given by $Z = (P - V) (Q - Q_B)$. Suppose both Q and Q_B are estimated with some uncertainty. The uncertainty of Q reflects the difficulty of estimating sales; and the uncertainty of Q_B, the break-even volume, reflects the difficulty of estimating costs. Suppose further that the degree of uncertainty in estimating sales is independent of the degree of uncertainty in estimating costs. Let σ_Q and σ_{QB}, the standard deviations, represent the respective degrees of uncertainty. Then σ_z, the standard deviation of profit, can be derived by applying elementary theorems on variances. Specifically, $\sigma^2_{ax} = a^2\sigma^2_x$ and $\sigma^2_{x+y} = \sigma^2_x + \sigma^2_y$. Applying these theorems to $Z = (P - V) (Q - Q_B)$, $\sigma_z = (P - V) \sqrt{\sigma^2_Q + \sigma^2_{Q_B}}$.

pected profit and standard deviation of profit, respectively, of the marketing mix with the highest Z; in our example, this is mix #5 and assume it is ($18,998, $12,000). Then management can be asked to list other (Z, σ_z) such that it is indifferent between them and (Z, σ_z)*. For example, management may be indifferent to ($18,998, $12,000), ($16,000, $6,800), ($13,000, $4,200), ($10,000, $2,000), and ($7,000, $0). An indifference curve has been fitted through these sample points in Figure 1. The region to the left of this curve consists

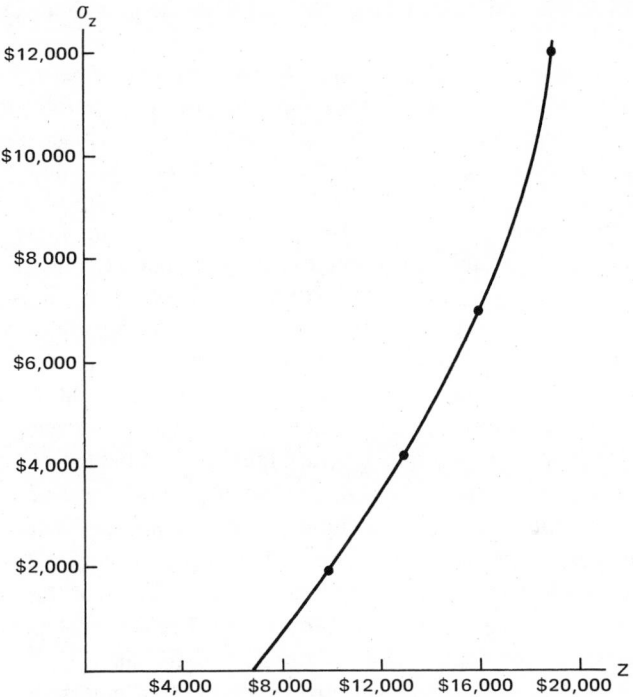

Figure 1   Company indifference curve for expected profit (Z) and risk (σ_z)

of inferior profit situations while the region to the right of this curve consists of superior profit situations. Then the (Z, σ_z) for the other marketing mixes can be plotted. If these points all plot in the inferior region, then mix #5 remains the best mix, subject to further qualifications. If any points plot in the superior region, the foregoing procedure can be repeated to establish a new indifference curve to the right of the old one and the remaining contending points can be tested again.

If management has difficulty in thinking of risk in terms of standard

deviations, an alternative procedure can be used instead. Management can be asked to express its preferences between various gambles where the risks are stated. The preferences become the basis for preparing a corporate utility scale for various money sums. For a management with risk aversion, the chance to earn twice the profit tends to carry *less* than twice the utility. For each marketing mix, the possible profit outcomes are re-stated as utility outcomes. Then the probabilities are used to find the expected utility for that marketing mix. The best marketing mix can be defined as the one with the maximum expected utility [5].

2. *The absolute profit estimates for the eight marketing mixes must be converted into rates of return on investment in order to choose the best marketing mix and to decide whether to develop the new product at all.* For example, management estimates that 5,500 units will be sold in the first year with marketing mix #5 and 8,200 units will be sold with marketing mix #6. But mix #6 will tie up more dollars than mix #5 because production, inventory, and marketing are carried out on a larger scale. For each mix, Z should be expressed as a ratio to the required investment. Mix #5 is still likely to stand out as the best choice in the example. But now a second question also can be answered: is the expected rate of return greater than the company's target rate of return? The company is not likely to develop a new product whose expected rate of return falls short of the target rate.

3. *The use of expected profits ignores the variability and duration of profits implied by different initial marketing mixes.* At the outset, it should be emphasized that management is *not* trying to determine a permanent marketing mix to be used over the lifetime of this product. Both costs and sales will change over time because of competition, market saturation, business fluctuations, and the like. The company may start with mix #5 and if strong competition enters the market with a reduced price, the ABC Electronics Company may find it expedient to change its mix. It may reduce its price and/or change its promotion. Either reaction is tantamount to adopting a new marketing mix.

By examining different marketing mixes in the profit analysis stage of new product development, the company is trying to ascertain an initial strategy and its implied initial profit level. Thus $18,998 represents the amount of profits expected in the first year with mix #5. The company is interested in discovering the strategy which will enable it to recover as much cost as possible as soon as possible because of the difficulty of foretelling the fate of the product beyond a

few years. Yet it is also a fact that the initial marketing mix can have an important effect on the company's long-run success with this product. A low price, medium promotion mix like #2, in creating a high initial sales volume, tends to bring about an earlier saturation of the market and hence a shorter period of profits. Mix #5, because it employs a high price and brings high profits, is likely to induce an early influx of competition which also tends to shorten the period of good profits. The long-run implications of the initial mixes must be considered. The solution ultimately may lie in simulating on a computer different time sequences of mix decisions under alternative assumptions and events to derive some indication of alternative profit possibilities.

4. *The previous analysis assumes that no marketing mix has been overlooked which might yield a higher expected profit than the eight listed mixes.* The sales estimates (Q) in Table 2 can be viewed as a sample from a larger universe of executive opinion concerning the functional relationship Q = f (P, A, S). It may be possible to find an equation which closely describes these estimates. The equation could then be solved to estimate expected sales, and ultimately profits, for marketing mixes which were not explicitly considered by the executives. For example, a plausible mathematical form for demand functions is the multiple exponential:

$$Q = kP^aA^bS^c$$

where k = a scale factor
a = the price elasticity
b = the advertising elasticity
c = the personal selling elasticity

The multiple exponential equation has provided a useful fit in several demand situations [4]. This form fits quite well the sample values of (Q) in Table 2. This is more by design than by accident. The least squares equation is

$$Q = 100,000 \, P^{-2}A^{1/8}S^{1/4}$$

Price has an elasticity of −2, that is, a one percent reduction in price, other things equal, tends to increase unit sales by 2 percent. Advertising has an elasticity of $\frac{1}{8}$ and the sales budget has an elasticity of $\frac{1}{4}$. The coefficient 100,000 is a scale factor which translates the dollar magnitudes into the appropriate physical volume effects.

Several of the preceding equations can now be drawn together:

$$Z = (P - 10)(Q - Q_B) \qquad \text{(1) profit equation}$$

$$Q = 100{,}000\,P^{-2}A^{1/8}S^{1/4} \qquad \text{(2) demand equation}$$

$$Q_B = \frac{38{,}000 + A + S}{P - 10} \qquad \text{(3) break-even volume equation}$$

The best marketing mix was defined initially as the one which maximized Z, that is, profits. Solving equation (1) in terms of (2) and (3), Z can be rewritten as:

$$Z = (P - 10)\left(100{,}000\,P^{-2}A^{1/8}S^{1/4} - \frac{38{,}000 + A + S}{P - 10}\right)$$

$$Z = (P - 10)(100{,}000\,P^{-2}A^{1/8}S^{1/4}) - 38{,}000 - A - S$$

$$Z = 100{,}000\,P^{-1}A^{1/8}S^{1/4} - 1{,}000{,}000$$
$$P^{-2}A^{1/8}S^{1/4} - 38{,}000 - A - S \qquad (4)$$

Thus Z is a function of three marketing variables.

The next step is to find that unique set of values of P, A, and S which maximizes Z in (4). This is a problem in differential calculus. The work is carried out in the appendix where the following values emerge:

$$P = \$20$$

$$A = \$12{,}947$$

$$S = \$25{,}894$$

$$Z = \$26{,}735$$

It is interesting to compare this mix with mix #5 which yielded the highest Z of the eight mixes considered in Table 2. Mix #5 called for a price of $24 and an advertising and sales budget of $10,000 each. The new calculation calls attention to the possibility that a somewhat lower price, a slight increase in advertising expenditure, and a substantial increase in personal selling expenditure might boost profits by several thousand dollars. Thus it may be possible to employ mathematical analysis to overcome the limitations of considering only a small set of marketing mixes. Though we have illustrated this in terms of Z, a more complicated mathematical analysis can be prepared for finding the best marketing mix under conditions of uncertainty, differ-

ent investment requirements, and more than three marketing variables.[2]

SUMMARY AND CONCLUSIONS

The overall challenge of new product development is to weed out the impracticable ideas as early as possible and to process the remaining ideas as efficiently as possible. The profit analysis stage is where a product idea which has been found to be compatible with the company's objectives and resources must be analyzed for its profit potential. It is not sufficient to confine the analysis to one specific conception of how the product will look and be marketed, though this is the typical practice. For the marketing mix will influence both the costs and the sales of the new product, and it is not obvious in advance which mix will maximize expected profits.

The method outlined in this article requires management to develop estimates of likely costs and sales under different marketing mixes on the basis of the best available information. These estimates become the raw data in an analysis which seeks to determine the best marketing mix and whether this mix promises a sufficient level of profits, in the face of uncertainty and the required investment, to justify developing the product. Admittedly there is no way to prove that the suggested analysis does in fact lead to better decisions at the profit analysis stage. Its claim is that it calls attention to the relevant factors and outlines a systematic way to consider them.

APPENDIX

The objective is to find the unique set of values of price (P), advertising (A), and personal selling (S), which maximize profits (Z) in the equation:

[2] It possesses a number of plausible properties. First, it provides that the effect of a specific marketing variable depends not only upon its own level but also on the levels of the other marketing variables. Thus a price of $16 will have one demand effect if advertising and selling are each set at $10,000 and another if advertising and selling are each set at $50,000. This interdependency does not exist with linear equations. Second, the exponential equation shows diminishing marginal returns to increases in the advertising and sales budgets and this accords with intuitive expectations. Finally, the exponents represent the respective elasticities of the marketing variables, provided there is no intercorrelation between the independent variables.

$$Z = 100{,}000\ P^{-1}A^{1/8}S^{1/4} - 1{,}000{,}000\ P^{-2}A^{1/8}S^{1/4}$$
$$- 38{,}000 - A - S \tag{1}$$

First find the first three partial derivatives of Z and set them equal to zero:

$$\frac{\delta Z}{\delta P} = -100{,}000\ P^{-2}A^{1/8}S^{1/4} + 2{,}000{,}000\ P^{-3}A^{1/8}S^{1/4} = 0 \tag{2}$$

$$\frac{\delta Z}{\delta A} = 12{,}500\ P^{-1}A^{-7/8}S^{1/4} - 125{,}000\ P^{-2}A^{-7/8}S^{1/4} - 1 = 0 \tag{3}$$

$$\frac{\delta Z}{\delta S} = 25{,}000\ P^{-1}A^{1/8}S^{-3/4} - 250{,}000\ P^{-2}A^{1/8}S^{-3/4} - 1 = 0 \tag{4}$$

Rearrange the terms in (2):

$$\frac{\delta Z}{\delta P} = 100{,}000\ P^{-2}A^{1/8}S^{1/4}(20\ P^{-1} - 1) = 0 \tag{2a}$$

Assuming that $P \neq \infty$, $A \neq 0$, and $S \neq 0$, it follows that
$(20\ P^{-1} - 1) = 0$ or
$$P = \$20 \tag{5}$$

Next, rewrite (3) and (4):

$$12{,}500\ P^{-1}A^{-7/8}S^{1/4}(1 - 10\ P^{-1}) = 1 \tag{3a}$$

$$25{,}000\ P^{-1}A^{1/8}S^{-3/4}(1 - 10\ P^{-1}) = 1 \tag{4a}$$

Divide (3a) by (4a), term for term:
$½\ A^{-1}S = 1$
$$S = 2A \tag{6}$$

Next substitute (5) and (6) in (3a):

$$12{,}500(20^{-1})(A^{-7/8})(2A)^{1/4}[(1 - 10(20^{-1}))] = 1$$
$$A = \$12{,}947 \tag{7}$$

Substitute (7) in (6):
$$S = 2(12{,}947) = \$25{,}894 \tag{8}$$

The optimal marketing mix (P, A, S) is ($20, $12,947, $25,894). The executives would forecast that this mix would produce a sales volume of:

$$Q = 100{,}000^{-2}A^{1/8}S^{1/4}$$
$$= 100{,}000(20^{-2})(12{,}947^{1/8})(25{,}894^{1/4})$$
$$= 10{,}358$$

The break-even volume implied by this mix would be:

$$Q_B = \frac{38{,}000 + A + S}{P - 10}$$

$$= \frac{38{,}000 + 12{,}947 + 25{,}897}{20 - 10}$$

$$= 7{,}684$$

Finally, profits (Z) under the optimal mix would be:
$$Z = (P - V)(Q - Q_B)$$
$$= (20 - 10)(10,358 - 7,684)$$
$$= \$26,735$$

REFERENCES

1. Booz, Allen, and Hamilton, *Management of New Products,* third ed., 1960.

2. P. E. Green, "Bayesian Statistics and Product Decisions," *Business Horizons,* 5 (1962), 101–109.

3. J. Johnston, *Statistical Cost Analysis,* New York: McGraw-Hill, 1960.

4. E. Nemmers, *Managerial Economics,* New York: John Wiley and Sons, 1962, 96ff.

5. R. Schlaifer, *Probability and Statistics for Business Decisions,* New York: McGraw-Hill, 1959, Chapter 2.

Product Characteristics and Marketing Strategy

Gordon E. Miracle

According to Webster, a science is "any branch or department of systematized knowledge considered as a distinct field of investigation or object of study." By this definition, marketing certainly may be designated as a science, albeit a science in the early stages of development. Scholars and students of marketing are concerned with the collection, analysis, and interpretation of marketing knowledge; and some progress has been made in systematizing and classifying marketing phenomena.

In recent years social scientists have begun to employ a method known in the physical sciences as *systems analysis*. As one social theorist has observed:

As judged by history of the physical, biological, and social sciences, study in any field is apt to begin with a none-too-ordered description of phenomena in the field, followed by a cataloguing of them on bases that seem to make sense. As understanding grows, the systems of classification become more closely related to the functioning of interacting elements. Gradually, generalizations about functioning are reached which are useful in predicting future events. As the generalizations gain in rigor, they take the form of analytical models of the behavior of the elements being studied. They take the form, that is, of systems.[1]

The development of marketing knowledge seems to be going through similar stages.

A system is a set of interdependent or interacting elements. The investigation of the factors that determine the state of the system is

Reprinted with permission from the *Journal of Marketing*, vol. 29, no. 1 (January, 1965), pp. 18–24, published by the American Marketing Association.

[1] Everett E. Hagen, *On the Theory of Social Change* (Homewood, Illinois: The Dorsey Press, Inc., 1962), p. 4.

called systems analysis. This type of analysis may be applied to a business firm as well as to a society or other organization. Exogenous and endogenous factors may be examined to determine their influences on the firm in its movement toward an equilibrium.

Exogenous factors influencing the business firm include a profusion of economic, sociological, political, and cultural circumstances and trends. Endogenous factors influencing the movement of a firm toward equilibrium include the several elements in a firm's marketing program, usually described as the firm's marketing mix. The marketing mix, in its general form, includes decisions and activities of business firms in the areas of product policy, channel policy, promotional policy, and pricing policy.[2]

The term "marketing mix" suggests a relationship between interacting elements. The development of the term constituted a step forward in the classification of interrelated marketing efforts. Although more is becoming known about the relationships among elements of the marketing mix, it is still common practice to think of it as a blend of marketing efforts, essentially nonquantifiable, the development of which often depends on experience, judgment, and perhaps a measure of good fortune.

The concept of a system provides a means of improving further the framework within which we think about the interrelationships between and among marketing activities. After all, a business firm engages in marketing activities (endogenous factors in the system) in order to adapt to its environment (exogenous factors). This adaptation is intended to move the firm toward an equilibrium in which the level of operation is such that the goals of the firm are being achieved.

THE CHARACTERISTICS OF GOODS THEORY

An observable relationship exists between the characteristics of a product and the approximate marketing mix for that product. This is by no means a startling assertion. However, up to the present, there appears to be no systematic statement of the relationships between product characteristics and *each* of the elements in the marketing mix.

Historically, one of the most widely accepted classification of goods has been that of convenience, shopping, and specialty goods. The defi-

---

[2] Neil H. Borden, "A Note on the Concept of the Marketing Mix," in Eugene J. Kelley and William Lazer, Editors, *Managerial Marketing: Perspectives and Viewpoints* (Homewood, Illinois: Richard D. Irwin, Inc., 1958), pp. 272–275.

nitions of these goods are based on consumer buying habits.[3] They focus on consumer behavior and assist in answering questions as to why the consumer "shops" for some goods but not for others. Although the classification is helpful in guiding marketing policies, it is not altogether satisfactory.[4] If a businessman classifies his product in the traditional manner, the relationships between product classification and marketing policies still may be quite uncertain.

The theory presented here is a revision and an extension of "The Characteristics of Goods Theory" proposed by Leo V. Aspinwall.[5] But whereas Aspinwall discusses the characteristics of goods theory only in respect to channels of distribution and promotional policy, the theory presented here is broadened to include the areas of product and pricing policy.

Definition of Product Characteristics

If product characteristics are to be utilized to explain marketing policies and methods, each distinguishing characteristic must be reasonably stable during the period of time the explanation is to be valid. Also, each characteristic must be universal in the sense that it is to some degree a feature of all products.

A product is defined by most modern marketers as the sum of the physical and psychological satisfactions the buyer receives when he makes a purchase.[6] For example, when he makes a purchase the consumer receives an article with certain physical characteristics, or a service with certain features; he receives the item at a convenient location; he is able to purchase at a convenient time; he receives an item about which he has some knowledge (from the salesperson or from consumer advertising).

While the product may not be absolutely perfect from the point of view of each consumer, producers and sellers usually attempt to offer a "total product" that suits a large number of consumers reasonably

---

[3] Melvin T. Copeland, "Relation of Consumers' Buying Habits to Marketing Methods," *Harvard Business Review,* vol. 1 (April, 1923), pp. 282–289.

[4] Richard M. Holton, "The Distinction Between Convenience Goods, Shopping Goods, and Specialty Goods," *Journal of Marketing,* vol. 23 (July, 1958), pp. 53–56.

[5] Leo V. Aspinwall, "The Characteristics of Goods Theory," in William Lazer and Eugene J. Kelley, Editors, *Managerial Marketing; Perspectives and Viewpoints* (Homewood, Illinois: Richard D. Irwin, Inc., 1962), pp. 633–643.

[6] Harry L. Hansen, *Marketing: Text, Cases, and Readings* (Homewood, Illinois: Richard D. Irwin, 1961), p. 312.

well. The "bundle of utilities" purchased by the consumer is "collected" by incurring product development costs, channel costs, promotional costs, and other marketing costs. The "total product," in a broad sense, includes all of the features and conveniences for which the consumer pays in the retail selling price of the item.

Considerable ambiguity often exists in the definitions of product characteristics, consumer characteristics, and market characteristics. The amount of time and effort spent in purchasing a product may *seem* to be a consumer characteristic. But if convenience of location is part of the "bundle of utilities" and hence part of the "total product" for which the consumer pays, it seems reasonable that the "short" length of time the consumer spends searching for a place to buy a pack of cigarettes is a characteristic of the product. The "convenience" is provided as one feature in the "bundle of utilities." Another way of stating this point is that the nature of the product determines how much time (or what kinds of effort) consumers will wish to spend in buying the product. Thus, "consumer" and "market" characteristics may be described in terms of product characteristics.

Redefining consumer and market characteristics in terms of product characteristics permits development of a single list of characteristics instead of several.

Classification of Products

Observation of a large number of "products" indicates certain "product characteristics":

1. Unit value
2. Significance of *each* individual purchase to the consumer
3. Time and effort spent purchasing by consumers
4. Rate of technological change (including fashion changes)
5. Technical complexity
6. Consumer need for service (before, during, or after the sale)
7. Frequency of purchase
8. Rapidity of consumption
9. Extent of usage (number and variety of consumers and variety of ways in which the product provides utility)

By reviewing a list of products (for example, candy bars, hardware, radios, automobiles, and electronic computers) the variations in product characteristics can be observed in detail. Unit value ranges from

low to high; the significance of each individual purchase to the consumer ranges from low to high; and so on down the list.

Products such as candy bars would be rated low for the first six characteristics, and high for the last three. For electronic data processing equipment, the opposite would tend to be true for each product characteristic. Hardware items or radios would be rated somewhere between. Thus, if products are arrayed on a continuum, they might range from such items as cigarettes and razor blades at one extreme, to steam turbines or large specialized machine tools at the other.

For convenience in exposition, it was decided to "break up" the array of products into five arbitrarily chosen groups, ranging from one extreme to the other, and including in each group some examples of items with similar product characteristics. The following groups were chosen:

Group I: Examples are cigarettes, candy bars, razor blades, soft drinks.

Group II: Examples are dry groceries, proprietary pharmaceuticals, small hardware items, industrial operating supplies.

Group III: Examples are radio and television sets, major household appliances, women's suits, tires and inner tubes, major sporting and athletic equipment.

Group IV: Examples are high quality cameras, heavy farm machinery, passenger automobiles, high quality household furniture.

Group V: Examples are electronic office equipment, electric generators, steam turbines, specialized machine tools.

Table 1 shows the variation in product characteristics for each group.

It is, of course, an artificiality to classify products by groups; and it would be more accurate to place products on a continuum, or within a spectrum ranging from one extreme to another. Leo Aspinwall utilizes the "color classification" to express the idea of gradation of products on the basis of their characteristics. He utilizes red and yellow as the extremes of the spectrum, indicating that the blend of these colors produces orange—in fact, various shades of orange. Products in Group I would be classified as "red" goods. Products in Groups II, III, IV, and V range from orange to yellow.

A product might not always remain in the same classification. It might fall initially into Group III or IV; then, as larger numbers of consumers gradually accept it, as time and effort spent in purchasing is reduced, as consumer needs for service decline, and as other characteristics change, the product may move into Group II, or even

TABLE 1   Product Characteristics of Five Groups

PRODUCT CHARACTERISTIC (SEE LIST)	I	II	III	IV	V
			GROUP		
1	Very low	Low	Medium to high	High	Very high
2	Very low	Low	Medium	High	Very high
3	Very low	Low	Medium	High	Very high
4	Very low	Low	Medium	High	Very high
5	Very low	Low	Medium to high	High	Very high
6	Very low	Low	Medium	High	Very high
7	Very high	Medium to high	Low	Low	Very low
8	Very high	Medium to high	Low	Low	Very low
9	Very high	High	Medium to high	Low to medium	Very low

Group I. At a later time marketers may succeed in improving or differentiating a product so that it is again in Group III or IV.

PRODUCT POLICY

An important aspect of marketing is the determination of the number of variations in products that are to be offered: the degree of product homogeneity or heterogeneity.

The problem for the businessman is to determine the effective demand for various product features—for example, style, color, model, quality level, and durability. The marketer must communicate this knowledge effectively to designers and production personnel, so that a product line can be developed that is consistent with the desires of consumers, the state of technology, the firm's capabilities, and other uncontrollable factors.

If the *unit value* or size of purchase is low, frequently the product will be highly standardized; perhaps only on variety within a brand category will be offered for sale—for example, Baby Ruth candy bars or Lucky Strike cigarettes. Likewise, if the *significance of each individual purchase* is low, and if the *time and effort spent in the pur-*

chasing process is low, product variety offered by each manufacturer tends to be low. Also, when the *rate of technical change* is low, few varieties tend to be offered; manufacturers are able to develop a product that remains suitable to consumers for an extended period of time.

Also, *technically simple* products often tend to be standardized to few varieties or a single variety. Likewise, a lack of *consumer need for service* often is associated with a standardized product. These characteristics with a rating of low or very low are typical of products in Group I.

On the other hand, *very high frequency of purchase, rapidity of consumption,* and *broad usage of the product* by a large number of consumers of diverse types, typically are associated with products in this group. Therefore, as indicated in Table 2, *a suitable product policy for products in Group I is to keep very low the varieties of products offered for sale.*

TABLE 2   Product Policy

PRODUCT GROUP	DEGREE TO WHICH A MANUFACTURER OFFERS PRODUCT VARIETIES (FOR EXAMPLE: STYLE, COLOR, MODEL, FLAVOR, PRICE) TO CONSUMERS				
	ONLY ONE, OR VERY FEW VARIETIES	FEW VARIETIES	SEVERAL VARIETIES	MANY VARIETIES	DIFFERENT VARIETY FOR EVERY SALE
I	X				
II		X			
III			X		
IV				X	
V					X

For products in Groups II, III, and IV, with successively higher values of characteristics 1 through 6 and successively lower values of characteristics 7, 8, and 9, the number of varieties offered tends to increase. At the other extreme, for products with a very high value for characteristics 1 through 6, and a very low value for characteristics 7, 8, and 9, the other extreme is reached in respect to the number of varieties offered.

Usually each product is "custom built" or "custom installed" according to the needs of each customer; every product sold is different from that sold to another customer.

MARKETING CHANNEL POLICY

Channel policies include selection of the types of distributors and number of each type. Intensity of distribution usually refers to the number of distributors utilized, from among those which might be suitable. A policy of intensive distribution means utilization of all available outlets regardless of their characteristics.

The selection of distributors according to their capability and suitability is called selective distribution. A policy of highly selective distribution is understood to mean the utilization of only a few (selected) outlets. The extreme case would be for a manufacturer to utilize no middlemen at all, that is, to sell directly to consumers or users, and either assume the wholesale and retail functions or pass them on to the consumer or user.

Intermediate policies, between the extremes of intensive and selective distribution, are indicated in Table 3. Moderately intensive dis-

TABLE 3   Marketing Channel Policy

Product Group	Intensity of Distribution				
	Intensive	Moderately Intensive	Some Selectivity	Considerable Selectivity	Highly Selective, or Direct Sale to Customers
I	X				
II		X			
III			X		
IV				X	
V					X

tribution refers to the situation in which products are sold in a wide variety of outlets, but somewhat limited in certain classes. Some selectivity in distribution refers to the policy of selling products through a large number of outlets but limited somewhat to those with desired characteristics. Considerable selectivity means that the number and types of outlets are limited to those with specifically desirable characteristics.

When the unit value is very low; when the significance of each individual purchase is low; when little time and effort are spent in the

purchasing process; when the rate of technological change is low; when the product is not complex technically; when consumers need little service; and when the frequency of purchase, rapidity of consumption, and extent of usage are high, highly intensive distribution usually is preferred over selective distribution. At the other extreme, when the values of characteristics are just the opposite, highly selective distribution is the rule. Various intermediate values of characteristics for products in Groups II, III, and IV suggest a range of policies between the extremes.

Note also that products in Group I typically are sold through a relatively long channel of distribution, while products in Group V often are sold through the shortest of channels direct to user or consumer.[7] In fact, in Table 3 the phrase "length of channel" could be used with some validity instead of "intensity of distribution."

PROMOTIONAL POLICY

A major aspect of promotional strategy is to decide how much effort is to be placed on mass media consumer advertising vis-a-vis the amount of effort on personal selling.

For products in Group I, observation suggests that the emphasis usually is on consumer advertising. In the extreme case a firm may have no salesforce at all. On the other hand, products in Group V depend almost entirely upon personal selling effort, although advertising in trade magazines may play a supplementary role. Products in Groups II, III, and IV require a combination of consumer advertising and personal selling, as illustrated in Table 4.

PRICING POLICY

The pricing policy of a firm depends upon the degree to which a firm has control over price. If the firm has no control, if prices are set "in the market place" by custom or by any other means beyond the control of the firm, there is no need for the firm to have any pricing policy at all (except to sell or not to sell at the going price).

Thus, a starting point in establishing a firm's pricing policy is to specify the degree of control which the firm has over price. It is only

[7] Aspinwall, op. cit., p. 635.

TABLE 4 Promotional Policy

	RELATIVE EMPHASIS ON MASS MEDIA CONSUMER ADVERTISING AND PERSONAL SELLING				
PRODUCT GROUP	SOLD ALMOST ENTIRELY BY CONSUMER ADVERTISING	SOLD PRIMARILY BY CONSUMER ADVERTISING	CONSUMER ADVERTISING AND PERSONAL SELLING BOTH NEEDED; NEITHER OF PRE-DOMINANT IMPOR-TANCE	SOLD PRIMARILY BY PERSONAL SELLING	SOLD ALMOST ENTIRELY BY PERSONAL SELLING
I	X				
II		X			
III			X		
IV				X	
V					X

after this has been ascertained that the businessman can turn to the specific tasks of price determination and price administration.

The degree of control that a firm has over price of its products seems to vary according to the enumerated product characteristics. As shown in Table 5, firms have little control over prices of items in Group I, relatively more control in the middle groups, and the highest degree of control in Group V.

Pricing policies are established with regard to (1) the degree of variation from customer to customer, and (2) the degree of adherence

TABLE 5 Pricing Policy

	DEGREE TO WHICH SELLER CONTROLS PRICE				
PRODUCT GROUP	VERY LITTLE	SLIGHTLY	MODER-ATELY	SIGNIFI-CANTLY	SUB-STANTIALLY
I	X				
II		X			
III			X		
IV				X	
V					X

to list prices versus dependence on negotiating the price for each sale. As can be observed in Table 6, products in Group I usually show little variation in price, whereas prices of products in Group V change relatively more frequently and often are substantially different for different customers purchasing similar products. Concomitantly, the prices of products in Group V are likely to be established independently for each sale. The prices of products in Group I are not often negotiated in this manner.

TABLE 6   Pricing Policy

PRODUCT GROUP	VARIATIONS IN PRICES OVER TIME, SHORT TERM, SEASONALLY, CYCLICALLY, OR BY CUSTOMER CATEGORIES				
	STABLE	SLIGHT VARIATION	MODERATE VARIATION	SIG- NIFICANT VARIATION	SUB- STANTIAL VARIATION
I	X				
II		X			
III			X		
IV				X	
V					X

THE MARKETING MIX

By way of summary, the marketing mix for products in Group I should be substantially as follows:

1. Relatively little effort and money spent on product development. Since a standard variety of the product is suitable for a broad group of customers, there is relatively less need for frequent change than for products in other groups.
2. Considerable effort spent in achieving intensive distribution. Products must be available quickly and conveniently.
3. Heavy consumer advertising—little or no personal selling. Consumers typically are pre-sold by advertising.
4. Relatively little effort and time spent on pricing. Firms have little control over price; variations in price are relatively infrequent; prices are not negotiated between seller and consumer.

At the other extreme, we would expect to find that products in Group V usually are:

1. Custom built.
2. Sold directly from manufacturer to user.
⌐ Sold primarily by salesmen, rather than advertising.
4. Sold on the basis of an individually negotiated price.

The marketing mix of products in Group V would involve relatively heavy efforts in the area of product policy; the marketing channel would be short, perhaps direct; personal selling is relatively more important than mass media; and considerable time and effort are spent on the determination and negotiation of price.

The marketing mix of products in Groups II, III, and IV can be characterized as modifications of the two extremes.

CONCLUSIONS

Knowledge of the product characteristics can be utilized to predict the nature of the marketing mix which is suitable for a given product. The prediction is, of course, an approximate *ideal* for a product with given characteristics. As a practical matter, the ability of a firm to engage in the indicated marketing methods may be limited in a number of ways, such as financial capabilities, or availability of personnel with the requisite skills, or management talent.

The primary contribution of the present theory is a modest increase in the analytical character of the marketing mix. Hopefully the next steps will be to develop more precise measures of the functional relationships among the elements in the marketing mix.

Businessmen may find the present theory handy as a shorthand method of ascertaining an appropriate marketing mix for a new product. Or if policies not in accordance with the theory are being followed, a businessman may be well advised to review carefully the reasons for his policies. It may even happen that the characteristics-of-goods theory will point the way to profitable policy changes.

As another example, a firm faced with the need to justify in a court of law its past marketing methods might use the theory as a broad framework to illustrate the reasons for its past decisions. Or the model might serve to direct the attention of researchers into relevant channels, or provide assistance to executives in the tasks of organizing marketing facts as a basis for making marketing decisions.

Bayesian Statistics and Product Decisions

Paul E. Green

In today's fast-moving technology the need for good decision making in the development of new and improved products is only too apparent. Typically, development of a new product from invention to commercialization is expensive and fraught with uncertainty regarding both technical and marketing success. On the one hand, it is not uncommon to find that development costs exceed discovery costs by fifteen or twenty times. On the other hand, the ratio of products successfully commercialized to total products placed on the market (let alone those that reached at least some stage of development) has been variously quoted as ranging from one in five to one in twenty.

As apparent as the need for improved decision making in this area is, there has been a dearth of good analytical techniques for dealing with the uncertainties that plague the development manager. While the product developer can (and usually does) enlist the aid of such data gathering services as market, process, and cost research, a formal apparatus for integrating these various sources of information has been conspicuous by its absence.

In recent years, however, a growing body of quantitative procedures for dealing with decision making under uncertainty has emerged from the disciplines of applied mathematics, statistics, and the behavioral sciences. Under the generic title of "statistical decision theory," these techniques show promise for assisting the decision maker in making rational choices under uncertainty. One of the most relevant and complete sets of tools is known as Bayesian decision theory. The pioneering development of this approach, as applied to business problem solving, is credited to Robert Schlaifer.[1]

Reprinted with permission from *Business Horizons,* vol. 5, no. 3 (Fall, 1962), pp. 101–109, published by Indiana University.

[1] Robert Schlaifer, *Probability and Statistics for Business Decisions* (New York: McGraw-Hill Book Co., Inc., 1959). In addition, two excellent expository articles dealing with a description of Schlaifer's work are: Harry V.

The purpose of this article is to show the relevance of the Bayesian approach to product development decision making. More specifically, we shall illustrate how these techniques can be used to help answer two persistent questions related to each stage in the development of a new product:

1. Should we make a decision *now* (with respect to passing a product along to the next development stage vs. terminating the project), or should we *delay* this decision until some future date, pending the receipt of additional information regarding the new product's chances for commercial success?

2. Given a decision on *when* to make the decision, *what* action ("go" vs. "stop") should we take?

The power of the Bayesian approach as applied to these basic questions is described in two parts. First, we shall review the nature of the costs associated with moving too slowly vs. too quickly through the product development process. Second, an illustrative case will show how these groups of costs can be introduced within a Bayesian framework to guide both the "when to" and "what to do" classes of decisions. However, the richness of Bayesian statistics goes well beyond the scope of this illustration. The concluding section of this article discusses some of the more general aspects of Bayesian decision theory.

TIME-RELATED COSTS

The ultracautious decision maker tends to incur sizable costs when he delays each development decision until he has assembled enough information to make the choice patently clear. These costs are partly associated with time and partly associated with the cost of the information gathering activity itself (which also takes time to accomplish).

An illustration should make clear the nature of these time-related costs. Assume that a new chemical product has reached the development stage where the company must either (1) decide now whether to construct a semiworks unit or to terminate the project, or (2) delay, pending the receipt of additional information regarding the anticipated outcomes associated with the alternative to proceed. Apart from sunk costs (that is historical costs, not relevant from an economic stand-

Roberts, "The New Business Statistics," *Journal of Business,* XXXIII (January, 1960), 21–30, and Jack Hirshleifer, "The Bayesian Approach to Statistical Decision—An Exposition," *Journal of Business,* XXXIV (October, 1961), 471–89.

point), termination at this point would result in a payoff of zero. The decision to proceed, however, is related to a series of future decisions up to and including commercialization before a positive payoff could be forthcoming. From the standpoint of delay, the decision maker should be concerned with how these conditional payoffs would be expected to change between now and some future time for viewing the same set of choices that he presently faces. Moreover, in multistage decisions, a present commitment does not demand that the project be continued in subsequent periods, should later information suggest project termination.

If the decision maker decided to delay his choice, pending the receipt of additional information, it should be clear that at least three groups of costs can be associated with delay.[2] First, as a function of delay time, the present value of all future revenues attendant with commercialization would be reduced as a consequence of delaying the start of the receipt of these revenues until a more distant time. This type of delay cost merely gives recognition to the time value of money.

Second, also as a function of delay time, the present value of all future revenues attendant with commercialization could be lowered as a consequence of the increased risk of competitive imitation or supersedure of the product (at the hands of competitors or conceivably of a future product of the decision maker's own research organization).

Finally, gathering the information obviously costs money and incurs time for its development. If one assumes some linear relationship of money spent for information with the period required to obtain the information, then this cost also can be associated with the time variable.

Certain implications obviously stem from the preceding listing of delay costs. If required target rates of return are low (that is, a low opportunity cost of the company's capital exists), and/or the threat of competitive retaliation is low, and/or the costs of data gathering are low, a relatively small penalty is attached to delay. Conversely, when these costs are high, a larger penalty is attached to the delay option.

On the other side of the coin, an impatient decision maker who eliminates or gives short shrift to vital steps of information gathering runs the risk of incurring sizable costs associated with acting under a high degree of uncertainty (and perhaps costs associated with "crashing" the program, that is, telescoping development steps, as well). The

---

[2] In the case of interdependent activities, a fourth category of cost could include the penalty associated with delaying some other necessary activity not in the project directly affected, that is, equipment design groups might not be able to switch efforts easily over to another job, thus incurring costs of transition.

behavior of these groups of costs can be viewed as a function of time, which, in turn, is a function of the amount of information collected.

Again, discussion of the preceding illustrative problem should make clear the nature of the costs associated with moving too quickly. Building a semiworks is related to a series of future actions leading to ultimate commercialization. In point of fact, however, these future actions may never be undertaken. The decision maker may delay any single decision while awaiting new data and, in multistage decisions, he will frequently have the opportunity to reevaluate the venture before making subsequent commitments.

Thus, the decision maker must view the change in payoff associated with the go vs. no-go decision now vs. the payoff associated with delay of this decision, pending receipt of additional data. Why collect additional data at all? Additional data would be collected for the purpose of reducing the variance associated with the estimated distribution of payoffs related to acting now. A simple example should clarify this concept.

If the option to build the semiworks now is a "sure thing," that is, no matter what information that could conceivably be developed on, say, potential sales, could change the decision, then it is obvious that additional information (cost-free or not) is irrelevant. On a more realistic basis, however, some potential sales levels (say, zero sales) would obviously favor the option of no-go. The essence of this concept can be expressed in Bayesian terms as the expected[3] cost associated with acting under uncertainty. That is, the difference in payoff between taking the best act now (in the light of current uncertainties) and taking the best act under perfect information about future events represents the expected value of perfect information; and, hence, the upper limit that the decision maker should spend for additional information if it could be collected immediately and would be without error.

Other things equal, it is clear that when the costs of uncertainty are large the decision maker could suffer by moving too rapidly to the next stage of the development process. On the other hand, if the costs of wrong decisions are low, he should move rapidly.

It is thus implied that gathering additional information would at least reduce, if not eliminate, the cost of uncertainty; otherwise the information would not be gathered. It is further implied that time and

---

[3] The adjective "expected" is applied here in the usual statistical sense. That is, expected costs are weighted averages found by multiplying each admissible cost by the probability of incurring it and then adding these products. The weights (probabilities) sum to unity.

money would be spent on the information gathering activity until the sum of the expected costs associated with information collection and delay and the expected costs of acting under uncertainty was minimal. Otherwise, a shorter or longer delay period would produce lower expected total costs. Figure 1 represents conceptually the behavior of the costs associated with moving too slowly vs. moving too quickly with respect to some stage in the development of a new product.

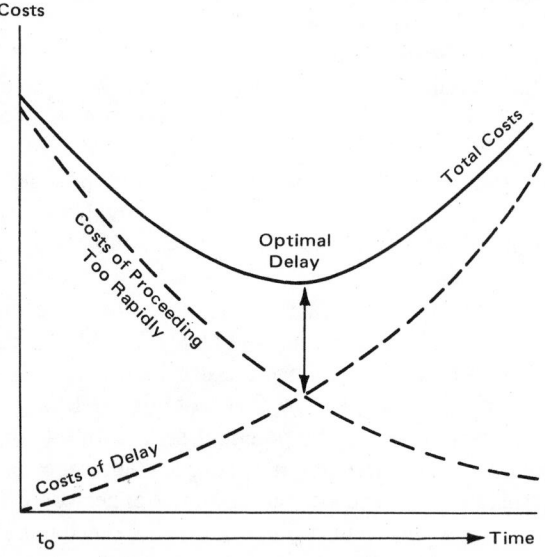

Figure 1   Behavior of total costs: proceeding too rapidly vs. too slowly

APPLYING BAYESIAN THEORY

While the preceding remarks have focused on the nature of the costs associated with moving too quickly vs. too slowly at any stage in the development process, we must still illustrate how Bayesian decision theory utilizes these costs to provide a rationale for answering both the "when to" and "what to do" questions. The following illustration is deliberately simplified to deal with the simplest of cases, a one-stage choice.[4]

___

[4] In more realistic (but more complex) illustrations, a multistage decision process—for example, pilot plant to semiworks to commercial plant with possible information steps in between—may have to be used. The techniques of dynamic programming are frequently appropriate here. See R. Bellman, *Dynamic Programming* (Princeton, N.J.: Princeton University Press, 1957).

Assume that a point has been reached in the development of a new product regarding whether or not a semiworks should be constructed now vs. delaying this decision (pending receipt of further market information). To be more explicit, three options will be considered:

1. Build a semiworks vs. terminate project now
2. Delay this decision until one period (year) into the future
3. Delay this decision until two periods (years) into the future.

Options 2 and 3 imply, of course, that better marketing information than now exists could be secured over the next year or two and that the more extensive this inquiry, the better the quality of the information. However, the development of the additional marketing data will cost something itself and will delay subsequent steps toward commercialization.

Some present marketing information, which is rather imprecise, indicates that four alternative forecasts of potential sales, given commercialization, bracket the possible levels of future sales. Subjective probabilities[5] have been stated for the occurrence of each forecast and, given each forecast, it has been possible to calculate the payoff, given commercialization. These data are noted in Table 1 where F_i stands for each sales forecast deemed admissible and $P(F_i)$ stands for the likelihood that the decision maker assigns to the occurrence of each forecast.

Under the go alternative, Table 1 indicates that if forecasts F_1 or F_2 actually occurred, negative payoffs (in present value terms) would result, while under the more optimistic forecasts, F_3 or F_4, payoffs

TABLE 1 Conditional Payoffs and Expected Values (in millions of dollars)

Acts	F_1	$P(F_1)$	F_2	$P(F_2)$	F_3	$P(F_3)$	F_4	$P(F_4)$	EP
Go	−$12	.15	−$1	.30	$5	.45	$10	.10	$1.15
No-go	$ 0	.15	$0	.30	$0	.45	$ 0	.10	$ 0

[5] The term subjective probability refers to the degree of belief the decision maker wishes to assign to the occurrence of each admissible event. This degree of belief is expressed numerically along a scale ranging from zero to one and reflects the experienced judgments of the decision maker. All weights are assigned so as to obey the postulates of probability theory. For a full discussion of the so-called school of personalistic or subjective probability, see the excellent book by L. J. Savage, *The Foundations of Statistics* (New York: John Wiley & Sons, Inc., 1954).

would be positive. According to the Bayesian approach the expected payoff (EP) of the go option is found by summing over the product of each payoff times its probability. The present value of future returns of the no-go alternative (termination) is, of course, zero.[6] In this oversimplified problem situation, the decision maker—in the absence of the opportunity to collect additional market information—would go with the project, that is, construct the semiworks. The expected payoff associated with this alternative is $1.15 million.

More realistically, however, the decision maker frequently has the option of delaying his decision pending the receipt of additional data regarding the occurrence of the alternative sales forecasts. These additional data will cost something to collect, delay construction time, and rarely, if ever, be perfectly reliable.

One-Year Delay Option

We shall first consider the one-year delay option.[7] For purposes of illustration we will assume that a delay of one year in construction would have the following results: (1) the cost of delayed revenues amounts to payoffs that are only 91 percent of the former payoff (interest rate equal to 10 percent annually); (2) the firm's market share would drop from 100 percent, under the no-delay case, to 75 percent because of the resulting greater lead time for competitive imitation; and (3) the cost of collecting additional information concerning

---

[6] A project payoff of zero, on a present value basis, would imply that the project's cash flow back (over its anticipated life) would just be sufficient to pay back all cash outlays and to earn some net rate of return, say 10 percent, on the present value of those outlays. Adoption of the no-go alternative thus assumes that other projects exist that could just earn this return; an opportunity cost concept is involved here.

[7] Although not explicitly shown above, it is relevant to note that the expected value of perfect information (EVPI) is $2.10 million. As mentioned earlier, this provides an upper limit on funds that could be spent on the collection of additional data, which could be collected immediately and would forecast perfectly which event would actually occur. To obtain EVPI, subtract the expected payoff of the best act in the light of current uncertainties from the expectation of the payoffs associated with the best acts (given the actual occurrence of each event):

EVPI = [.15 ($0 million) + .30 ($0 million) + .45 ($5 million) + .10 ($10 million)] −$1.15 million

The result is $3.25 million − $1.15 million, or $2.10 million.

This calculation may be interpreted as follows. If the decision maker could purchase a "perfect" forecasting device that would tell him which event would actually occur, it is clear that before the purchase he must still apply his prior probabilities as to which event the device would indicate; he would then be able to take the best act associated with the event specified.

future sales would be $150,000. However, information obtained at this early stage of development is assumed to be only 70 percent reliable. That is, if the market survey results indicate f_1 (namely, that forecast F_1 will occur), there is a 30 percent chance that this information could have been assembled if the true underlying sales potential were not F_1 but really F_2, F_3, or F_4.

All of the assumptions of our simple expository case can be summarized in Figure 2, which should be examined by working from

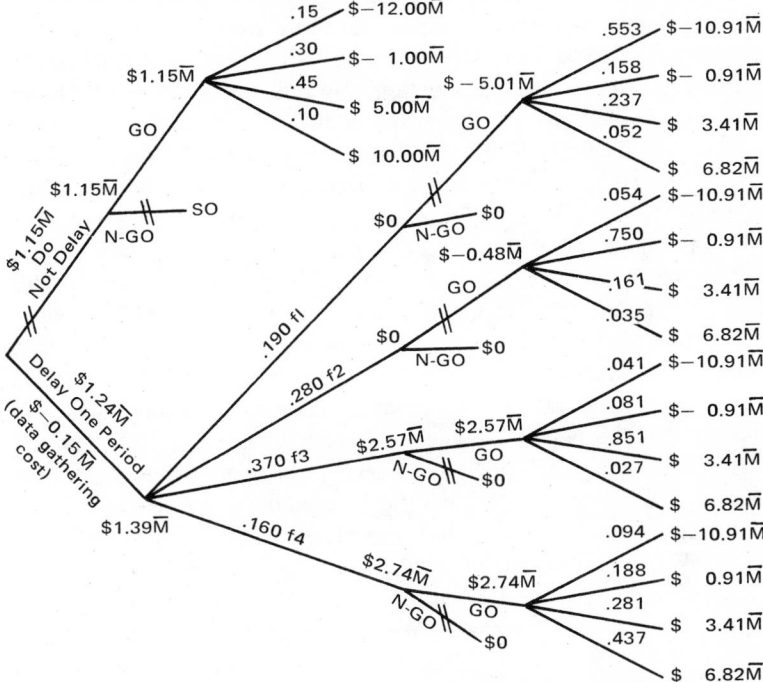

Figure 2   Build semiworks—terminate project now vs. one-period delay

right to left. To illustrate, the upper branch (do not delay) summarizes the results of Table 1. The conditional payoffs under each forecast, given go, are −$12 million, −$1 million, $5 million, and $10 million. Multiplying these payoffs by their respective probabilities and summing the results yields, of course, the expected payoff of $1.15 million. Since this is clearly higher than the $0 associated with no-go, this latter alternative is blocked off, and the best alternative, *given no delay*, is go.

However, the second main branch of the tree is still to be evaluated. The conditional payoffs, −$10.91 million, −$0.91 million, $3.41

million, and $6.82 million at the extreme right of the lower branch, reflect the penalties associated with (1) the discount penalty for delay and (2) the effect on the firm's market share, due to delay if the product were successful (see author's note).

If the market survey information indicates f_1 (that forecast F_1 is the best estimate), then, as noted earlier, some probability exists that this survey information could have been developed if the true underlying sales forecast were not F_1 but F_2, F_3, or F_4. If f_1 *is* observed, however, the best action to be taken after the survey is no-go—terminate the project. Hence, the go alternative branching from f_1 is blocked off. Similar results pertain to survey results f_2. Under survey results f_3 and f_4, however, the resulting best action is to build the semiworks. On an expected payoff basis, collecting the additional information produces a gross payoff of $1.39 million. From this gross figure must be subtracted the $0.15 million cost of collecting the information, yielding an expected payoff of $1.24 million associated with the one-year delay option.

The power of this technique is found in the recursive nature of solution. That is, the two payoffs, $1.24 million and $1.15 million, *summarize completely the whole series of moves along the decision tree.* Moves have been optimally planned from this point forward by, in effect, solving the problem backward. Thus, the decision maker is assured that the best decision now (which happens to be delay one period) has been derived by considering the relationship of this decision to the future decisions that the decision maker visualizes.

AUTHOR'S NOTE: Notice that several sets of new probabilities appear along the sub-branches of the lower main branch of Figure 2. These probabilities are derived by application of Bayes's theorem, a central tenet of this approach. We shall need to compute marginal, joint, and posterior probabilities. Their meaning will be made clear in the computations to follow.

First we consider the calculation of the *marginal* probabilities, .190, .280, .370, and .160 appearing beside the market survey results f_1, f_2, f_3, and f_4, respectively. These calculations are shown in Table 2. The cell entries represent joint probabilities (the probability assigned to the joint occurrence of each survey result f_i and each underlying event F_i). For example, the joint probability of survey result f_1 and event F_1 occurring is found, under the oversimplified assumptions of our problem, by multiplying the conditional probability, $P(f_1|F_1)$, by the prior probability, $P(F_1)$, which the decision maker assigned to F_1; $.70 \times .15 = .105$. The conditional probability of observing survey results f_1, given the fact that the true underlying forecast is F_2, is

**TABLE 2   Marginal and Joint Probabilities under
the One-Period Delay Option**

SURVEY RESULTS	JOINT PROBABILITIES F_1	F_2	F_3	F_4	MARGINAL PROBABILITIES
f_1	.105	.030	.045	.010	.190
f_2	.015	.210	.045	.010	.280
f_3	.015	.030	.315	.010	.370
f_4	.015	.030	.045	.070	.160
	.150	.300	.450	.100	1.000

assumed equal to .10. (Similarly, for the sake of simplicity, the probability of obtaining the survey result f_1 if the true forecast is F_3 or F_4 is also assumed to be .10.) Hence the joint probability of survey result f_1 and event F_2 occurring is, by way of illustration, $P\ (f_1|F_2)$ • $P\ (F_2) = .10 \times .30 = .030$ as shown in the second column of row f_1. The other cell entries are computed analogously.

The *marginal probabilities* f_1, f_2, f_3, and f_4 are then found by merely summing over the column entries for each row $-P\ (f_1) = P\ (f_1$ and $F_1) + P\ (f_1$ and $F_2) + P\ (f_1$ and $F_3) + P\ (f_1$ and $F_4)$ or .190 = .105 + .030 + .045 + .010. Also note that the marginal probabilities, found by summing over rows for each column F_i, are simply the prior probabilities that the decision maker had originally assigned to the occurrence of these four events.

We can next proceed to the calculation of the *posterior probabilities,* $P\ (F_i|f_i)$, and to a brief description of how Bayes's theorem can be used to derive them. These calculations are shown in Table 3.

Table 3 can be explained as follows: Under the assumptions of our problem it was noted that each survey result was deemed to be

**TABLE 3   Posterior Probabilities under
the One-Period Delay Option**

SURVEY RESULTS	POSTERIOR PROBABILITIES F_1	F_2	F_3	F_4	TOTAL
f_1	.553	.158	.237	.052	1.000
f_2	.054	.750	.161	.035	1.000
f_3	.041	.081	.851	.027	1.000
f_4	.094	.188	.281	.437	1.000

only 70 percent reliable in correctly "calling" the event assumed to be most strongly associated with it. Suppose, however, that we really did observe a particular survey result, say f_1. Under our assumptions it is more likely that event F_1 "caused" this specific result than events F_2, F_3, or F_4. Still, the other events could have caused this result. We would like to reason backward, so to speak, in order to determine how likely it is that F_1 was the underlying event, now knowing that f_1 has occurred.

Given that we have observed f_1, it is clear that only the joint probabilities along row one of Table 2 are now relevant. We should next wish to partition the total (marginal) probability associated with f_1 (.190) among the four events, F_1, F_2, F_3, or F_4, which could have produced this survey result. Hence the first row of Table 3 is derived by merely dividing each entry in Table 2 (.105, .030, .045, and .010) by the marginal probability (.190) associated with f_1. In summary, *before* observing f_1 we would have assigned the prior probabilities .15, .30, .45, and .10 to events F_1, F_2, F_3, and F_4, respectively. *After* having observed f_1 we would then revise these probabilities to .553, .158, .237, and .052, respectively, so as to reflect the fact that the observance of f_1 was deemed more likely under F_1 than under F_2, F_3, or F_4. Analogous considerations apply to the calculation of posterior probabilities shown in the remaining rows of Table 3.

Bayes's theorem formalizes this notion in terms of the following formula:

$$P(F_i|f) = \frac{P(f|F_i) \cdot P(F_i)}{\sum_{j=1}^{n} P(f|F_j) \cdot P(F_j)}$$

In terms of our problem, the posterior probability assigned to, say, event F_1, given that survey result f_1 was observed, is:

$$P(F_1|f_1) = \frac{.105}{.105 + .030 + .045 + .010}$$
$$= \frac{.105}{.190}$$
$$= .553$$

The appropriate marginal and posterior probabilities (as derived in Tables 2 and 3) appear along the subbranches of the lower main branch in the tree diagram of Figure 2. We can now proceed to

discuss which act we would choose, given the occurrence of each admissible survey result.

Two-Year Delay Option

We now consider the third option: delaying the decision pending a two-year inquiry into the sales potential of the product.[8] In this case we will assume that: (1) cost of deferred revenues amounts to payoffs that are only 83 percent of the payoffs under the no-delay case; (2) the anticipated market share would drop to only 50 percent of the market; (3) market survey costs increase to $300,000; but (4) the reliability of the resultant information increases to 90 percent.

Figure 3 summarizes this second analysis. The upper main branch of the decision tree, covering the no-delay case, is exactly the same as that in Figure 2. All payoffs and probabilities in the lower main branch, however, are adjusted in accordance with the changed assumptions just enumerated by developing tables analogous to Tables 2 and 3. Solution of the problem again proceeds from right to left, always choosing the best alternative for each subbranch of the tree.

The upshot of this analysis is that the two-year delay option produces a lower expected payoff than the no-delay option. In other words, the costs associated with delaying the venture more than outweigh the gains expected through increased reliability of the sales information. For this reason the lower branch of the tree is blocked off in Figure 3.

In summary, it has been shown, via the preceding simplified examples, how costs associated with delay can be balanced against the costs associated with the higher costs of uncertainty related to moving a development along too quickly.

The preceding illustrative case has touched upon some aspects of Bayesian decision theory but has by no means exhausted the many facets of this approach.[9] As could be inferred from our preceding illustration, the Bayesian approach to decision making under uncertainty provides a framework for explicitly working with the economic

---

[8] Numerous other combinations could be evaluated ranging from the case where construction of the semiworks and start of the marketing studies are begun simultaneously through various degrees of overlap in timing. No new principles would be involved. Payoffs would, of course, reflect the cost of project "takedown and salvage" if the marketing survey results were to indicate a change in action from go to no-go after construction had already been started.

[9] A full and lucid description of these features can be found in *Probability and Statistics for Business Decisions*.

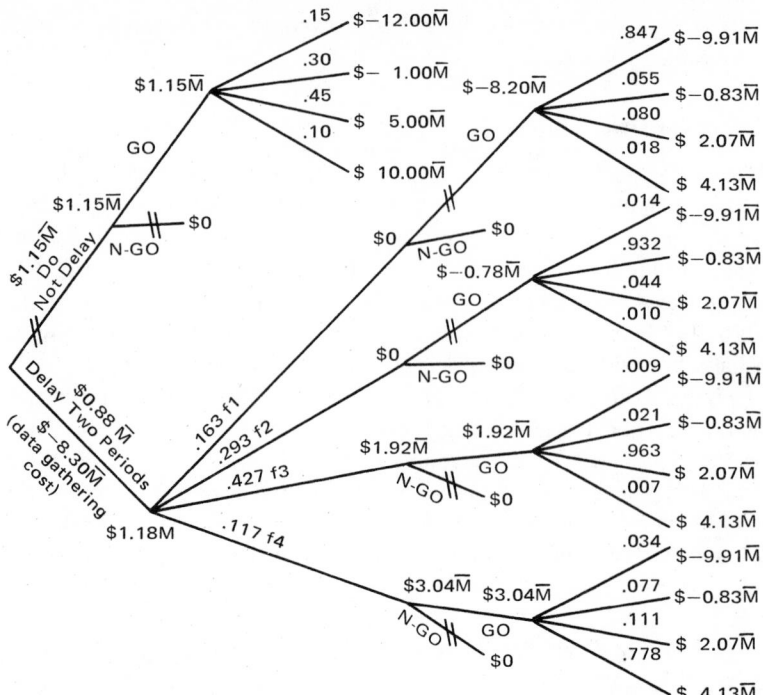

Figure 3   Build semiworks—terminate project now vs. two-period delay

costs of alternative courses of action, the prior knowledge or judgments of the decision maker regarding the occurrence of states of
nature affecting payoffs, and the conditional probabilities of observing
specific events, given each state of nature.

The Bayesian approach to decision making under uncertainty provides a rich set of techniques for dealing with the complex problems
that attend new product development. This is not to say that the
relevant probabilities used in this approach can be developed easily
or quickly. Rather, granting that decisions must be made in any event,
Bayesian analysis represents a rational procedure for including all
relevant data and for dealing explicitly with the gains vs. costs associated with the option to "purchase" new information bearing on
the problem. Coupled with ancillary techniques such as computer
simulation and sensitivity analyses, it seems fair to say that this set of
tools constitutes the most powerful analytical apparatus of its class
currently available to the product development manager.

chapter 8 | Communication Decisions In Marketing Management

Despite the fact that communication expenditures represent the major portion of most firms' marketing budgets, the decision sciences have played a limited role in providing guidance to advertising management. The nature and complexity of the decisions required of advertising specialists coupled with the scarcity of detailed and accurate data probably account for the limited success of applications in this area. Nevertheless, the work done thus far represents an important first step. The potential usefulness of the decision sciences in solving advertising problems has stimulated a great deal of research activity which will undoubtedly lead to solid advances within the next decade.

What do the decision sciences offer the advertiser? Green, Robinson, and FitzRoy explore current, past, and future mathematical approaches to the budgeting of advertising. Particularly important is their discussion of the major difficulties encountered in developing realistic models of advertising effectiveness.

Paul Green, in the second article, shows how Bayesian decision theory might be applied in advertising.

Another powerful and widely applied technique in the decision sciences is linear programming. In the past decade, there has been a large volume of research in the application of this technique to the problem of media selection.

In general, linear programming helps the decision maker determine how he can best use the resources of a business to achieve a specific objective when the resources have alternate uses. In the media selection problem, the advertising budget represents the scarce resource. The alternative uses of this budget are the many types of media and advertising units which must be considered before a specific media mix or schedule is adopted. The objective, then, is to allocate the budgeted advertising money among the different media to achieve the most effective advertising program.

The last article of this section focuses on the application of linear programming to the allocation of the advertising budget. Engel and Warshaw present simple examples to show precisely how linear programming is implemented, and discuss both the advantages and disadvantages of the technique.

Advertising Expenditure Models: State of the Art and Prospects

Paul E. Green
Patrick J. Robinson
Peter T. FitzRoy

Marketing managers acknowledge the importance of advertising and sales-promotion activities to the over-all competitive posture of the firm, and are generally eager to implement new techniques to improve the position of the firm. Despite this fact, quantitative techniques of a model-building nature have had relatively little impact on marketing managers.

This article explores current, past, and future mathematical approaches to the budgeting of advertising. First, a discussion is presented of some difficulties encountered in developing realistic models of advertising effectiveness. This is followed by a review of significant trends in model construction, and examination of recent research activity in a new class of models. These adaptive promotion models show promise for mitigating some of the problems associated with earlier efforts in this field.

MAJOR PROBLEMS

Several writers have commented on the paucity of actual applications of mathematical models for determining total promotion budgets and their allocation over products, territories, time periods, media, and so forth.[1] This dearth of applications does not appear to be a reflection

Reprinted with permission from *Business Horizons,* vol. 9, no. 2 (Summer, 1966), pp. 73–80, published by Indiana University.

[1] For example, Robert D. Buzzell, *Mathematical Models and Marketing Management* (Boston: Graduate School of Business Administration, Harvard University, 1964), p. 3; Peter Langhoff, ed., *Models, Measurement and Marketing* (Englewood Cliffs, N.J.: Prentice-Hall, Inc., 1965), p. 6; and Kristian S. Palda, "Sales Effects of Advertising: A Review of the Literature," *Journal of Advertising Research,* IV (September, 1964), pp. 12–16.

of the lack of model-building activity in this field; a recently compiled bibliography lists over 160 references on the subject.[2] Rather, the difficulty appears to stem from a general lack of realism of the models in characterizing advertising effectiveness and unavailability of appropriate data for making the models operational. Some of the major difficulties associated with the modeling of advertising processes are:

1. A great number of strategies may be adopted in marketing situations. In addition to advertising, some of the firm's controllable variables that influence sales are the product's characteristics, the price of the product, and the distribution system employed. Also, in a very real sense, outlays for marketing efforts compete with the monetary requirements of other activities pursued by the firm.
2. It is difficult to determine the outcome of any course of action. Even if a particular strategy is implemented, it is not generally known how external variables (consumer tastes, income, and the like) interact with the firm's course of action. Usually the information available to the firm is limited, at best, to probability distributions of sales response.
3. In any marketing situation, the effects of competitive action must be considered. Competitors do not remain indifferent to the firm's past performance and, hence, the firm must be able to adapt courses of action to changes in its environment.

In summary, sales response to advertising may be generally characterized as a probabilistic process involving many variables and whose parameter values are changing over time. This is one of the frontiers of modern mathematics. In contrast, the previous successes of model building, as applied to production and inventory processes, reflected mathematical techniques that were better understood—for example, the one-variable calculus.

Not the least of the difficulties to be faced in implementing mathematical formulations of advertising effectiveness is the problem of determining appropriate measures for the variables linking advertising and other marketing or nonmarketing inputs with sales. For example, it is generally assumed that the total dollars spent on advertising is a meaningful figure which represents, in some sense, an aggregate "communications level." Yet this assumption ignores the variability of effectiveness in individual advertisements. In addition, the functional form of the equation may, and the values of the variables certainly will, change with time and over situations, at any point in time.

---

[2] David H. Badger, *Mathematical Models and Advertising*, unpublished M.B.A. thesis, Wharton School of Finance and Commerce, University of Pennsylvania, 1965.

Finally, the interaction problem appears to be as significant as the measurement problem. If one is viewing promotional expenditures as just another form of investment outlay, the decision to spend some specific amount for advertising has to be compared to the returns anticipated from alternative uses of company funds, for example, their use in research and development, production, or finance. But the return anticipated with a given total promotional budget will depend on the way the budget is allocated. That is, the total return and allocation problems are intertwined.

For these and other reasons the solution of the *total* promotional problem is generally considered to be too complex for our current state of knowledge. Consequently, most model-building efforts have reflected attempts to break down the problem into components:

> Determination of the "optimum" total promotional budget, independent of its allocation
>
> Allocation of the budget among different promotional means, for example, advertising, personal selling, and merchandising
>
> Selection of media
>
> Scheduling advertisements within media
>
> Determination of the importance of advertising quality and the extensiveness of ad pretesting.

Such fragmentation of the promotional mix problem introduces the dangers of suboptimization. An example is temporal suboptimization where short-run profits may be achieved at the expense of long-run profits.

Another type of suboptimization is associated with limited objective approaches,[3] in which intermediate variables, such as exposure ratings, recall, and the like, are substituted for sales data. Such approaches are currently quite popular in the advertising research literature.[4] Two elements are usually missing, however: the rules of transformation, by which these intermediate variables are to be translated into sales, and the appropriate cost data. Such approaches cannot provide answers to the economic problem of how much to spend on advertising, even assuming that subdecisions are coupled loosely enough to justify solving the problem on a component-by-component basis.

[3] See "Sales Effects of Advertising," p. 13.

[4] Russell H. Colley, ed., *Defining Advertising Goals for Measured Advertising Results* (New York: Association of National Advertisers, 1961).

Some appreciation for later changes in model building, and their logical culmination in the formulation of adaptive models, can be gained by considering briefly the nature of earlier efforts that *were* concerned with the economics of budget determination rather than with limited objectives.

EARLY EFFORTS

Early Models

The early developers of promotional decision models owe a sizable debt of gratitude to the marginal analysis provided by microeconomics. As early as 1952, Rasmussen proposed a model for determining optimal advertising budget size that was based on a direct application of the marginal analysis.[5] Dorfman and Steiner followed essentially the same approach but added a second control variable—price.[6]

In the allocation of the total budget (among areas, media, products, and so on) the model proposed by Nordin also involved utilization of the calculus and Lagrange multipliers.[7] While solution techniques differed in the case of the Maffei and Friedman models,[8] the formulation of the model followed essentially the same structure. The models were static and deterministic. Little or no attention was paid to the problems of measuring the appropriate response functions; rather, one picked a response function that "looked realistic" and was "mathematically tractable."

Encouraged by the interest of large advertising agencies, allocation models were extended to problems of media mix determination. Although technical details on these models are sparse, it appears that

---

[5] Arne Rasmussen, "The Determination of Advertising Expenditures," *Journal of Marketing*, XVI (April, 1952), pp. 439–46.

[6] Robert Dorfman and Peter O. Steiner, "Optimal Advertising and Optimal Quality," in Frank M. Bass and others, eds., *Mathematical Models and Methods in Marketing* (Homewood, Ill.: Richard D. Irwin, Inc., 1961), pp. 203–19.

[7] J. A. Nordin, "Spatial Allocation of Selling Expense," in *Mathematical Models and Methods in Marketing,* pp. 178–94.

[8] Richard B. Maffei, "Planning Advertising Expenditures by Dynamic Programming Methods," *Management Technology*, I (December, 1960), pp. 94–100, and Lawrence Friedman, "Game-Theory Models in the Allocation of Advertising Effectiveness," in *Mathematical Models and Methods in Marketing,* pp. 230–44.

mathematical programming techniques (linear or convex) are representative of the class of solution procedures that are being used.[9] Efforts have also been expended on simulation models of media effectiveness.[10]

Field Studies

While many were building models with little benefit of empirical support, some firms were becoming aware of the need to conduct field experiments of sufficient scope to develop reliable estimates of promotional effectiveness. The mechanism of response to promotion was considered to be a "black box" in which the detailed mechanism for transforming advertising inputs into sales outputs was unknown. Interest centered on the measurement of sales response to planned variations in promotional outlays. Field tests of promotional effectiveness drew upon the principles of statistically designed experiments. For the most part, however, the experiments were one-shot affairs; it was implicitly assumed that the sales response function would remain stable over the subsequent time periods in which the experimental findings were to be used.

In the last three or four years interest has centered on the use of Markov processes in modeling the brand-switching processes of consumers. This work has led to considering sales response functions in a probabilistic rather than a deterministic sense. Grossack and Kelly have discussed the possible compatibility of this approach with promotional budget determination.[11] Here again, however, it is conjectural as to whether the type of model used, a stationary switching matrix, really characterizes the dynamics of the market.

Work is also proceeding on incorporating "quality" variables in advertising budget determinations. Gross has considered the implications of this variable on the extent of ad pretesting that should be

[9] See William T. Moran, "Practical Media Decisions and the Computer," *Journal of Marketing,* XXVII (July, 1963), pp. 26–30; *Mathematical Models and Marketing Management,* p. 60; and Ralph L. Day, "Linear Programming in Media Selection," *Journal of Marketing Research,* II (June, 1962), pp. 40–44.

[10] Alex Bernstein, "Computer Simulation of Media Exposures," sixth meeting of the Advertising Research Foundation Operations Research Discussion Group, New York, 1961.

[11] Irvin M. Grossack and Robert F. Kelly, "Measuring Advertising Effectiveness: Use of the Probability Transition Matrix," *Business Horizons,* VI (Fall, 1963), pp. 83–88.

undertaken before making selections among alternative ads.[12] But, unfortunately, little is known about the accuracy and reliability of ad pretesting techniques.

During the past year, however, some model builders have been devoting effort to *adaptive* models of sales promotion. The motivation for this most recent research has stemmed from dissatisfaction with earlier models which usually assumed static, deterministic response functions of known form and parameter values. For the first time, model builders appear to be considering the pressing need for recurrent measurement and the modification of decision parameters to reflect changes in uncontrolled variables over time.

In short, the problem is now being recognized as not lack of allocation algorithms (computational routines), but lack of techniques for systematically updating models as uncontrollable variables in the model change over time or space. To be sure, present adaptive models are overly simple. For example, they do not reflect adequately the influence of competitors on the firm's sales response. However, current modeling efforts are starting to cope with the nonstationary nature of marketing phenomena. Adaptive models represent a major step forward in the development of operational procedures for promotional budget determination that are coupled with ongoing field experiments for systematically monitoring the effectiveness of the model.

CURRENT EFFORTS: ADAPTIVE CONTROL PROCESSES

Adaptive control and adaptive models have been explained in a work by Bellman:

> When faced with uncertainties . . . the common sense approach is to learn from experience. As the process unfolds we should be able to learn more and more about the unknown structures and unknown parameters. . . . Processes of this type . . . will be called adaptive control processes.[13]

Adaptive models, then, are feedback models, in which the decision maker collects data, in a formal sense, on the performance of the

[12] Irwin Gross, "How Many Ads Does it Pay to Pretest?" tenth meeting of the ARF Operations Research Discussion Group, New York, March 10, 1964, pp. 1–18.

[13] Richard Bellman, *Adaptive Control Processes* (Princeton, N.J.: Princeton University Press, 1961), p. 201.

process under consideration. These data are then used to modify future decisions. That is, one not only implements some present course of action but, concurrently, "buys" information for making future decisions.

Adaptive Models

In adaptive models no attempt is made to predict the effects of all variables. Instead, the emphasis is on detecting changes in the process caused by changes in these variables, and on the parallel concept of cost and value of information.[14] The value of the data is measured by the *improvement* in the decision as a result of better knowledge of the sales response function; this improvement may continue indefinitely. The cost of data acquisition is simply the out-of-pocket cost of continuous data collection as well as lost opportunity costs incurred in willingly forgoing some assumed optimal level of advertising for the purpose of being able to gain experimental information about the changing sales response function.

To consider the process stationary is to imply that the world is not expected to change and that a static model would be adequate. Obviously, this is rarely the case in marketing environments. If the process were stationary, an optimal policy would be to spend as much as possible on data acquisition early in the process, since the benefits will accrue for all future periods. In marketing, however, measurements tend to be perishable; knowledge of customer demand a year ago is usually less valuable than knowledge of customer demand last month.

Adaptive models can be either macro or micro models. Their essential feature is that they include only a few of the important variables and make no attempt to postulate (in detail) the mechanism ruling the process. (A physical example of the reasonableness of this approach is Boyle's Law, which Boyle was able to formulate despite his lack of awareness of modern atomic theory.)

Evolutionary Operation

An example of adaptive modeling that has had some application in production processes is evolutionary operation (EVOP). The rationale of this technique has been summarized thus:

"It is nearly always inefficient to run an industrial process to pro-

---

[14] Paul E. Green, "Bayesian Decision Theory in Advertising," *Journal of Advertising Research,* II (December, 1962), pp. 33–41.

duce product alone. A process should be run so as to generate product plus information on how to improve the product."[15] The technique is quite simple and is illustrated in the accompanying figure.

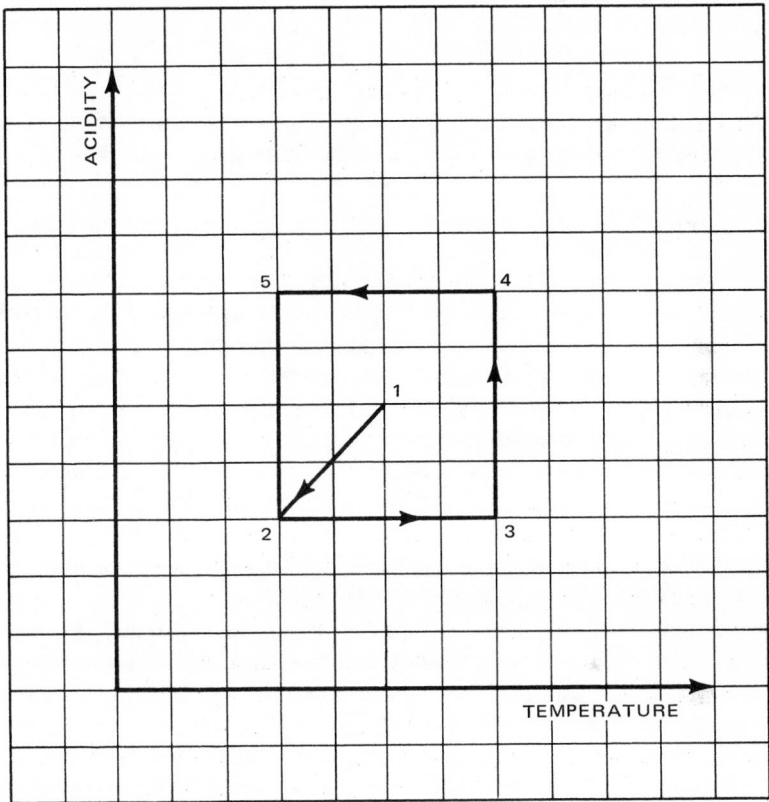

Figure 1   An illustration of evolutionary operation

Suppose that temperature and acidity are the two production variables whose current values are represented by point 1 in the chart. Then the values represented by the points 2 through 5 are tried, in sequence, and the effect on cost and quality of the product observed. A new starting point is then selected, and the cycling process continues. An important consideration in EVOP is that experimental levels are set that are within the tolerance limits of the process; this is done so as to reduce the risk of manufacturing off-specification products

[15] George E. P. Box, "Evolutionary Operation," *Applied Statistics,* VI (June, 1957), p. 81.

while process information about optimal control levels is being accumulated.

In theory, a similar procedure could be used in promotion where, for instance, advertising or personal selling efforts or both are varied in the above fashion. One major difficulty develops, however, in that EVOP requires a large number of process cycles to detect the effect of each parameter value on the yield of the process. Moreover, the relative experimental error of production processes would seem to be much smaller than its counterpart in marketing processes.

Adaptive Promotion Models

Efforts to construct adaptive models of advertising effectiveness are quite recent. Only a few models have been proposed; to the authors' knowledge, none is actually being applied in industry. Their value at this time appears to be in terms of future potential rather than current applicability.

Howard has used an adaptive model in the study of such non-stationary processes as consumer brand switching.[16] For example, a consumer's probability of purchasing a particular brand may change over time as a function of such variables as price, dealing activity, availability of brand, advertising, and so on. Moreover, the time between changes may not be predictable.

From consumer panel data one can obtain the consumer's purchase sequence. The *observed* pattern of choices will reflect in some way the changes in the statistical parameters describing the process. Given assumptions about the probabilistic characteristics of the change process and the observed purchase sequence, Howard shows how one can revise probability distributions about the statistical parameters of the process. The solution technique is based on statistical decision theory.

While Howard does not deal explicitly with the problem of advertising budget determination, his model provides a way of making general statistical inferences about nonstationary processes. The interesting innovation is that the statistical parameters of the model are viewed as random variables, which are, in turn, governed by probabilistic processes. One could, of course, continue this process of increasing the

---

[16] Ronald A. Howard, "Dynamic Inference," *Operations Research,* XIII (September, 1965), pp. 712–33. Also, see John U. Farley and Melvin J. Hinich, "Tracking Marketing Parameters in Random Noise," in *Proceedings of the Fall Conference* (Washington, D.C.: American Marketing Association, 1965), pp. 365–69.

level of abstraction at which stability of the system is assumed. The output of lower-level processes would then be viewed as nonstationary.

Little has proposed an adaptive model for dealing explicitly with the problem of promotional budgeting.[17] The model assumes a sales response function (quadratic) in which one of the parameters of the function is considered a random variable, subject to change over time. He proposes a procedure for determining simultaneously the level to spend for advertising and the departures (type of experiment) to make from this "best" level for purchasing information about the value of the random variable for each time period.

Little's model also has a mechanism for combining new data about the parameter—derived from continuous field experiments—with historical information for the purpose of updating the statistical description of the sales response function. Thus, the decision maker may change advertising expenditures from period to period, based on systematic updating of the model, while also monitoring the process through ongoing field experimentation.

FitzRoy is also concerned with the problem of setting the total advertising level, period by period.[18] Again, his model assumes that the functional relationship between sales revenue and promotion involves certain parameters, represented as random variables, whose statistical properties are only partially known. If perfect knowledge of these parameters were available, the optimum promotional level could be calculated using techniques of the calculus. Instead, a policy must be determined which is asymptotically optimal. That is, under fairly mild conditions, the policy converges to the optimal policy as more information on the process becomes available.

As a further consequence of this lack of perfect knowledge, the model has two decision variables:

1. The promotional level that must be set period by period
2. The information level, that is, how much should be spent each period to estimate the unknown process parameters. (It is realistically assumed that an error of measurement is associated with this estimate.)

[17] John D. C. Little, *A Model of Adaptive Control of Promotional Spending* (Cambridge, Mass.: Sloan School of Management, Massachusetts Institute of Technology, 1965).

[18] Peter T. FitzRoy, "An Adaptive Model of Promotional Expenditure Determination," in *Proceedings of the Fall Conference* (Washington, D.C.: American Marketing Association, 1965), pp. 370–76.

The promotional level is set using the best available information. FitzRoy then shows that, with this policy, the promotional level does converge to the optimal value.

Data acquisition expenditures in the model are set to minimize the sum of two costs: the direct cost of the information gathering and the cost resulting from decisions taken on the basis of imperfectly estimated parameter values. While the first is an out-of-pocket cost, the latter is an opportunity cost resulting from making nonoptimal decisions on the basis of less-than-perfect information about the parameter values. This opportunity cost, in turn, consists of two parts: one cost due to the uncertainty in the process and a second cost due to the error in estimation.

Other work is undoubtedly going on in adaptive promotional models; these brief, nontechnical descriptions only illustrate this trend. Moreover, it is clear that adaptive models can, in principle, be designed for other marketing decision classes, for example, new-product development, inventory levels for various links in the distribution chain, price markdowns in retailing, and so on. Our purpose here has been only to illustrate the conceptual nature of adaptive processes and show some examples of this type of model-building activity.

Clearly, any prediction assumes some stability over time in the phenomenon being predicted. In adaptive models, the stability in the model is assumed at a higher level of abstraction. In this way, lower-level processes may appear quite unstable, a condition all too familiar to the marketing manager. Current modeling efforts are aimed toward characterizing this nonstationary nature by the development of higher-level models which, in a sense, incorporate learning through systematic updating via repetitive field experimentation.

Implications for the Future

One might gather from the preceding discussion of adaptive processes that much work remains before mathematical models for promotional budget determination will be deemed sufficiently realistic to capture much of the complex character of marketing phenomena. Still, present research appears to be focusing on many of the major considerations—ad quality, sales response measurement, and model updating—which earlier models either ignored or assumed away.

What of future research efforts in this field? In our judgment, future modeling efforts will continue to emphasize the adaptive character of promotional budget determination and the concomitant need to incorporate response measurement via experimental design procedures

as a continuing program. Such probabilistic information processing systems may well justify the cost of setup and maintenance.

We also speculate that future research will delve more deeply into the decision processes which managers actually use. Heuristic programming techniques are already being used on an experimental basis in the attempt to explicate the decision rules that managers use to reduce alternatives to some manageable subset and to modify courses of action as new information becomes available.

Finally, we visualize that model builders will be expending more effort on studying the behavior of current optimal models in interactive settings. For example, if all competitors are using the same model, what happens to its optimality properties? Simulation provides a way to examine the sturdiness of so-called optimal models when employed in an interactive environment in which competitors are endowed with varying degrees of sophistication.

This is, of course, not to say that the use of mathematical models in promotional budget determination will quickly assume routine status. But, if anything, the promulgation of quantitative methods in promotional budget determination seems to be more limited by measurement inadequacies than by suitable computational routines for finding optimal outputs, once reliable input values are determined.

Bayesian Decision Theory in Advertising

Paul E. Green

The perplexing and vexing job of measuring the effectiveness of advertising has few parallels in industrial problem solving. The paucity of
relevant information on sales changes as a function of changes in the
quantity or quality of advertising is a reflection of several factors:

1. The mix situation—sales response is usually affected by other
actions (e.g., changes in price, product properties, distribution channels, personal selling, marketing services) which the firm may employ.

2. The environmental situation—a particular firm's sales response
may be affected by the interaction of its courses of action with corresponding activities of its competitors as well as by changes in consumer tastes, income levels, and other broad economic considerations.

3. The temporal situation—sales response to advertising can reflect the cumulative effect of past stimuli as well as current levels.

4. The correlative situation—in instances where the researcher can
measure the relation between advertising effort and intermediate response variables, like changes in consumer attitudes and message
recall, he must still consider the problem of how changes in intermediate variables are correlated with the primary dependent variable,
sales.

With all these complexities, advertising decisions are still made
every day, which might suggest that either the advertising manager
has a level of courage possessed by few other decision makers or else
takes comfort in the feeling that his associates and competitors can
do no better.

While the preceding statement is not to be dismissed lightly, this
article takes the point of view that (a) the experienced judgments of
advertising executives should be explicitly incorporated as part of the

Reprinted with permission from the *Journal of Advertising Research,* vol. 2,
no. 4 (December, 1962), pp. 33–41. © Advertising Research Foundation, Inc.
(1962).

decision process; but (b) these judgments should be modified by research findings in instances where this information-gathering activity is economically justifiable. Our stance is then somewhere between those "anti-researchers" who insist that advertising problems can best be solved on intuitive grounds alone and the "naive empiricists" who claim that the facts will always speak for themselves.

During recent years some interesting techniques have been developed for coping systematically with decision-making under uncertainty, and hence with decisions required in advertising. Many theories of making rational choices under uncertainty have been formulated. Scholars from a variety of disciplines, e.g., mathematics, statistics, economics, and psychology, have addressed themselves to the problem. And it is not surprising that the term "rationality" itself hardly enjoys universal acceptance among decision theorists.

Rather than try to cover all the proposals dealing with the subject, this article emphasizes only one. But this particular approach, known as Bayesian decision theory, is unusually complete and relevant to the real-world problems of the advertising executive. The origins of the approach go back to the work of an eighteenth century English clergyman, the Reverend Thomas Bayes, who developed a theorem for using observed evidence to modify prior judgments concerning different possible "causes" of the evidence. The modern form of Bayesian analysis has been developed during the last decade and reflects the combined efforts of many distinguished contributors.

This article is an attempt to explain the rudiments of the Bayesian approach and its potential applicability to advertising decisions. First, the major aspects of the theory will be discussed in terms of simple illustrations. Second, an illustrative decision problem associated with the advertising area will be outlined and the use of Bayesian theory in its resolution described. Finally, the advantages and limitations of the Bayesian approach in dealing with the complexities of real-world marketing problems will be discussed and some speculative comments offered regarding the future use of these techniques in business. A list of source readings is provided at the end of this article for the reader who wishes to explore the subject in more detail.

FUNDAMENTALS OF BAYESIAN THEORY

The Bayesian approach to decision-making under uncertainty, like other decision theories, is primarily normative. That is, if one grants its underlying assumptions, then a decision maker *should* choose ac-

cording to what the approach prescribes. This is not to say that all decision-making should incorporate this approach—many decision problems under uncertainty are not worth the effort to formalize—or that all decision makers *actually* employ this approach, either formally or intuitively. Moreover, Bayesian theory in itself offers no guide to developing the substance of the inputs (e.g., alternative courses of action or payoff functions) to the choice problem. Like any model it must start and end somewhere and must abstract from the tremendous complexity of real situations.

As background to a description of the approach, consider the following rather disparate problem situations as illustrative of decision-making under uncertainty. In our first situation an advertising manager is faced with the problem of whether or not to increase the level of product advertising in a particular marketing area. In our second situation a hungry but fastidious diner is faced with the less enervating options of ordering a ham sandwich vs. the specialty of the house in a restaurant he has never before frequented.

Both these problems possess a common structure. First, each decision maker possesses alternative courses of action, a necessary condition in order to have a problem. Second, we may assume that each decision maker wants to achieve certain objectives. The advertising manager may wish to earn a maximum return on his advertising investment; our hungry diner may settle for achieving a state of well-being which is not later marred by a need for bicarbonate of soda. It is clear that three components of a problem consist of a decision maker, alternative courses of action, and a payoff function which translates the possible consequences of each action into some measure of the success with which a certain objective or combination of desired objectives is attained.

As our mythical advertising manager reflects on his problem, he realizes that under some levels of response to increased advertising effort the additional advertising would pay for itself in terms of the profits from increased sales volume, while under other levels of response—certainly at zero level—pay-offs will be higher if he does not increase his advertising expenditures. Presumably his deliberations include the possible effects of competitors' options for changing their levels of advertising, and the resultant impact on total industry sales and his firm's market share. Our hungry restaurant patron realizes that under some quality levels of the cuisine, selecting the house specialty will lead to greater satisfaction, while under lower quality levels the more prosaic ham sandwich offers higher satisfaction. The trouble is that in each instance our decision maker does not know for certain

the underlying "facts of life" and must deal with payoffs which are conditional upon which of several possible events occurs.

Decision theory formalizes this notion of uncertainty; given a particular action, the underlying possible events are called *states of nature*. While decision theory assumes that the decision maker can characterize the possible states of nature relevant to his problem, it is assumed that he does not know for certain which state of nature will occur.

In most situations, however, the decision maker has had experience in facing at least broadly analogous situations and has been exposed to the events preceding his particular problem situation of the moment; e.g., he may well feel that some of the possible events are more likely to occur than others. Bayesian decision theory formalizes this notion by assuming that it is possible to assign numerical weights, in the nature of betting odds, such that they obey certain requirements for consistency. In Bayesian parlance, these numerical weights are called *prior probabilities*. Sometimes they may be based on long run, "objective" experience with very similar problems, while in other instances they may be more "subjective" in nature. A natural measure for the degree of uncertainty possessed by the decision maker thus becomes the breadth of possible states of nature which he feels should be included and the nature of his probability assignment over this set of possible events.

In many instances the decision maker can attempt to improve his view regarding the likelihood that each state of nature is the "true" underlying event *before* having to take final action. That is, he may elect to "experiment" before making a terminal choice among alternatives. Our perplexed advertising manager may conduct a test campaign before deciding whether to increase the total level of promotion. In the restaurant case our hungry but cautious patron may observe the reactions of other diners, sound out the waiter's opinion, or evaluate the quality of his soup course before deciding which entree to order.

But gathering additional data usually involves a cost, and rarely are data so reliable as to foretell perfectly the true state of nature. Decision makers usually must cope with both experimental and systematic error.

Bayesian decision theory deals with the experimental problem in three principal ways: (1) should additional data be collected at all before choosing a terminal action; (2) given the wisdom of assembling more data, how much data should be collected and in what way; and (3) how can the decision maker revise his prior judgments in the light of this new experimental evidence?

In essence, Bayesian statistics considers the utility or economic consequences attached to alternative acts under different events, the prior judgments of the decision maker regarding the likelihood of occurrence of alternative events, and the potential or actual modification of his prior judgments based on new data. We can now turn to a discussion of the *criterion* by which choices are made under the Bayesian approach, and an explanation of the role which Bayes's theorem plays in the revision of prior probabilities.

Both the preceding aspects can be illustrated by means of a simple numerical example, the classical Bertrand Box problem (Fry, 1928, pp. 121–122). We shall describe Bayes's theorem first.

Assume that we have three boxes which we shall call *A, B,* and *C.* Outwardly the boxes look alike. We are told that box *A* contains two gold coins, box *B* contains a gold and a silver coin, and box *C* contains two silver coins. The boxes are put in random order on a table top and we are allowed to make a simple "experiment," namely, to choose a box at random and, without observing the contents of the box, draw a single coin. Suppose that the coin drawn happens to be gold. Based on this "experimental" evidence we are asked to state the probability that the remaining coin is also gold, i.e., that box *A* was chosen.

We can reason as follows. Before we were given the datum that the first coin drawn was gold, our prior probability of drawing box *A* was one-third. This assumes that our state of knowledge with respect to the characteristics of each box led to a special case of the Bayesian approach, the assignment of an equiprobable measure over all states of nature: *A, B,* and *C.* A person who thought that he possessed extrasensory perception might not wish to make an equiprobable assignment at all; Bayes's theorem handles either case.

We can next ask ourselves the following question. Given the choice of each box, *A, B,* and *C,* respectively, how likely is it that we would have observed a gold coin? Had we chosen box *A* it is clear that we must observe a gold coin on a single draw from the box since *both* coins in *A* are gold; thus a probability of unity is correct. Given that box *B* was chosen, the probability is one-half that our first draw would have produced a gold coin, since box *B* contained one gold and one silver coin. Given that we chose box *C,* it is clear that the chances of drawing a gold coin are zero, since both coins in *C* are silver. The above probabilities are called conditional probabilities and can be identified as $P(g|A) = 1.0$; $P(g|B) = 0.5$; and $P(g|C) = 0.0$, respectively.

From here it is but a short step to Bayes's theorem. Figure 1 shows

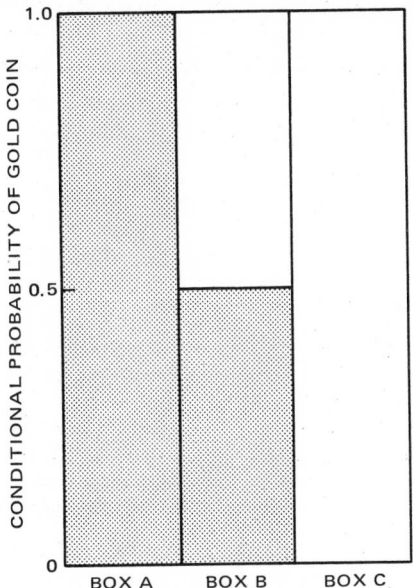

Figure 1   Bertrand Box problem: pictorial representation of probabilities

a diagrammatic representation of the problem. The area of the rectangle is first divided into three vertical strips of equal area, which
represent the prior probabilities of drawing box *A, B,* or *C*. Next, the
conditional probabilities are pictured by shading the area of each
strip in proportion to the probability of observing a gold coin. Thus,
all of strip *A* is shaded, half of strip *B* is shaded, and none of strip *C*
is shaded.

Since in performing our "experiment" we have *observed* a gold
coin, we must *revise* our prior probabilities to reflect this new information; that is, *only* the shaded area is now relevant. Moreover, the
shaded area under each vertical strip represents the combined occurrence of (1) choosing a particular box *and* (2) getting a gold coin;
these are joint events. Now if we partition the *shaded* area between
the relevant boxes *A* and *B* it is clear that two-thirds of *this* total area
is contained in the vertical strip *A;* hence the revised probability of
having drawn box *A* is now two-thirds, vs. a one-third probability of
having drawn box *B*. Obviously, given our information that the coin
is gold, we have *not* drawn box *C*.

Bayes's theorem merely formalizes this approach and can be shown
algebraically as follows: Let $P(S_i|E)$ equal the probability that some
state of nature, S_i, underlies the occurrence of some event E, given

that E was observed. In our problem S_i might stand for the box A and E might represent the appearance of the gold coin. Let $P(E|S_i)$ equal the conditional probability of observing E, given S_i; and $P(S_i)$ equal the prior probability assigned to the occurrence of each state of nature. Then Bayes's theorem can be stated as follows:

$$P(S_i|E) = \frac{P(E|S_i) \cdot P(S_i)}{\sum\limits_{j=1}^{n} P(E|S_j) \cdot P(S_j)}$$

If we were to substitute in the above general formulation to find, for example, the probability that box A was drawn, given the observance of a gold coin, we can use the following notation:

$$P(A|g) = \frac{P(g|A) \cdot P(A)}{P(g|A) \cdot P(A) + P(g|B) \cdot P(B) + P(g|C) \cdot P(C)}$$

$$= \frac{1 \cdot \frac{1}{3}}{(1 \cdot \frac{1}{3}) + (\frac{1}{2} \cdot \frac{1}{3}) + (0 \cdot \frac{1}{3})}$$

$$= \frac{2}{3}$$

From our previous discussion we already know this solution, $\frac{2}{3}$, agrees with our intuitive analysis of the problem. Notice that the revised or "posterior" probabilities, $P(S_i|E)$, are conditional upon a particular observed event; the appearance of a silver coin would have changed the posterior probability assigned to box A from two-thirds under the gold coin case to zero.

The criterion for choosing among courses of action under the Bayesian approach is actually quite simple: choose that act which leads to the highest *expected* or, in effect, weighted average payoff. We can modify our Bertrand Box example to illustrate this criterion.

Assume that we have the option to bet or not bet that we will choose box A from the three boxes on the table. Suppose we would win \$1.00 if A were drawn, but would lose \$.60 if box B were drawn and would lose \$.50 were we to draw box C. Suppose further that we are not allowed to run an "experiment" before betting, i.e., not allowed to observe one of the two coins in each box.

A pictorial representation of these initial ground rules appears in the upper branch of the "tree" diagram shown in Figure 2. Looking at the extreme right of the upper branch we note the conditional payoffs, namely, \$1.00, \$−.60, and \$−.50, associated with drawing

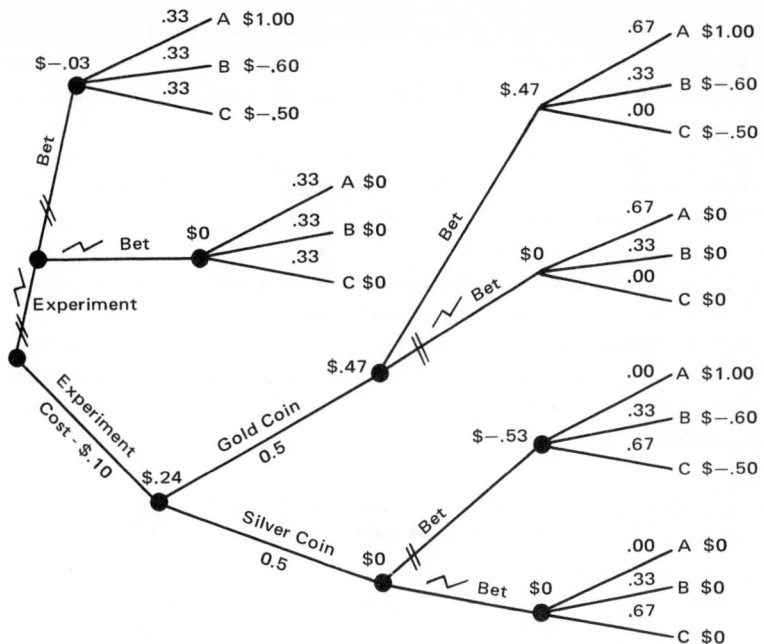

Figure 2   Decision tree: Bertrand Box betting problem

box *A, B,* and *C,* respectively. To find the *expected* payoff associated with "bet," we merely multiply these payoffs by our prior probabilities, ⅓, ⅓, and ⅓, and sum the products, leading to a negative expected payoff of $−.03; that is, we would *lose,* on an expected value basis, three cents per bet. Obviously, if maximizing expected monetary value is our criterion we would select the "no bet" action with an expected payoff of zero.

Consider one more modification of the problem. Assume that *before* we decide whether to bet or not we are allowed to observe one coin from the box chosen. To conduct this "experiment" we are charged a cost of $.10. Conditional payoffs are the same as before. The major difference is that we can delay our choice of whether to bet or not until *after* we have observed the results of our experiment, and it will cost us $.10 to run the experiment.

The lower branch of the "tree" diagram of Figure 2 summarizes the features of this strategy. If we look at the extreme right portion of the lower branch, following the sub-branch labeled "gold coin," we note the probabilities: .67, .33, and .00. These represent the posterior probabilities derived from applying Bayes's theorem on the assumption that a gold coin is observed. Notice that the expected payoff asso-

ciated with "bet" is $.47, clearly higher than that associated with "do not bet." Therefore the double slash through the "no bet" sub-branch indicates that if we observed a gold coin we would choose the "bet" rather than "no bet" act.

Before the fact, however, it is possible that we may observe a silver rather than a gold coin. Following this branch and looking at the posterior probabilities: .00, .33, and .67 for *A, B,* and *C,* respectively, the expected payoff associated with "betting" is very poor, namely, $−.53. It is clearly to our advantage *not* to bet if we observe a silver coin; hence the double slash through the "bet" sub-branch. But we must still compute the probabilities of getting a gold vs. silver coin, respectively. These are known as marginal probabilities and their calculation along with the calculation of joint probabilities is shown in Table 1.

TABLE 1 Calculation of Joint and Marginal Probabilities for the Bertrand Box Problem

	Box A		Box B		Box C		Marginal
Gold coin	⅓	+	⅙	+	0	=	½
Silver coin	0	+	⅙	+	⅓	=	½
Marginal	⅓	+	⅓	+	⅓	=	1

The chance of getting a gold coin is found by merely adding the joint probabilities of the combined events: gold and *A,* gold and *B,* and gold and *C.* This sum equals ½ or 0.5. A similar result pertains to the probability of observing a silver coin. Since under the ground rules of the problem, a gold or silver coin must be observed, these probabilities sum to unity.

Now we may obtain the expected payoff of $.24 by again averaging over the payoffs associated with the *best* act taken after the observance of each possible result of the experiment, i.e., $.24 = (0.5 × $.47) + (0.5 × $0). The expected payoff must then be reduced by $.10, the cost incurred in using this strategy, leading to a *net* expected payoff of $.14. This figure is still higher than the $0 associated with the best act under "do not experiment"; hence we double slash the upper main branch of the tree.

To summarize, our best strategy is (1) to conduct our experiment and (2) then take the best act after observing the experimental results. If we do this, our expected payoff after deducting the cost of the experiment is $.14.

AN ADVERTISING ILLUSTRATION

Our preceding description of the Bertrand Box problem, while pointing out some of the fundamentals of Bayesian theory, was nevertheless a bit removed from the class of problems with which the advertiser
deals. Our next example, although also oversimplified and hypothetical, is drawn from the advertising field. We shall illustrate the use of
Bayesian anslysis in evaluating the decision implications of a point-of-
purchase merchandising experiment.

The Hilbert Vending Co. was a small firm specializing in the sale
of soft drinks vended by machine. Its chief competitor, Alder San
Vending, had been increasing its share of the market, largely at Hilbert's expense. Mr. Hilbert, in noting the persistent decline in his firm's
market share, asked his sales manager, Mr. McNoon, for an explanation. Mr. McNoon believed that the principal reason for their competitor's gains stemmed from the fact that Alder San's vending
machines were much more appealing; what with lavish chrome trim
and colored lights which simulated a flow of bubbles, their shininess
contrasted with the rather drab and strictly functional appearance of
Hilbert's machines. Since both firms offered the same variety of drinks
and product quality was also comparable, Mr. McNoon could offer no
other reason for Alder San's comparative gains.

After a sleepless night, Mr. Hilbert hit upon what appeared at
first blush to be a solution to the decline in his firm's market share. He
speculated that by adding a more modern plastic front to his machines,
a music box which played a thirst-inducing jingle, and a special slot
which provided a fortune cookie with each drink, he could recapture
his lost share in short order. With obvious glee he summoned Mr.
McNoon to his office and explained his new strategy.

Mr. McNoon listened patiently to the new scheme and promised
to report back to Mr. Hilbert as soon as he had obtained some information bearing on the problem. After several consultations with vending machine engineers, he told Mr. Hilbert that costs incurred in
machine conversion, including lost profits on sales which could have
been made during the conversion period, would amount to $48,000, a
cost of $480 per machine for the 100 machines which Hilbert owned.
Moreover, the gross margin per dollar of sales would decline from 30
percent to 25 percent, due to higher materials cost (the fortune
cookies) and more expensive machine maintenance. But if smaller
cups and a weaker syrup solution were used, present margins could
be maintained.

Mr. Hilbert insisted on the maintenance of present quality and quantity. He then asked McNoon just how much monthly increase in sales per machine would be needed to justify the conversion expense and the lower gross margin. After careful calculation, McNoon replied that monthly gross sales would have to increase $200 (over next year's forecasted level of $200 per machine) just to break even.[1] This assumed that a one-year payoff of the added investment was required. His interest in a short payout period resulted from the fear that Alder San Vending would probably imitate the innovation relatively quickly if a marked reversal occurred in the trend of their share.

Mr. Hilbert, a bit sobered by the financial implications of his strategy, still felt that the idea had merit. He proposed an experiment as follows: (1) take 15 of Hilbert's present vending machines as prototypes and convert them to the new design; (2) choose 15 other Hilbert machines as a control; (3) select at random 30 different machine locations; place the 15 converted machines in half these locations and the control group in the second half, positions being selected at random; (4) after recording sales for each machine for one month, place the converted machines in locations in which the control machines had been installed, and vice versa, and record sales for each machine during the second month; (5) at the end of the two-month period, for each machine location, subtract the observed sales of the control machines from the observed sales of the converted machines; and (6) calculate the mean difference in sales over all locations.

Under Mr. Hilbert's direction the experiment was carried out. The average *increase* in sales of the converted machines amounted to $190 per machine per month.[2] The sample standard deviation of the sales differences, which was based on 30 observations, amounted to $82. At this point Mr. Hilbert was concerned with which course of action he should take. Noting that the sample result was $10 under the $200

---

[1] The breakdown value (μ_b) of $400 sales per machine per month, on the assumption of 100 machines in operation, is found by the equation:

$$.25\,\mu_b = .30\,(\$200) + \frac{\$48,000}{12 \times 100}$$
$$.25\,\mu_b = \$60 + \$40$$
$$\mu_b = \$400$$

In terms of differences, an *increase* of $200 over next year's $200 monthly sales level, anticipated without conversion, would be required.

[2] A more interesting but more complex question is whether or not the experiment should have been undertaken at all. That is, would the expected gain in information be worth the cost incurred to get the information? Questions of this type are called "preposterior analysis" in Bayesian statistics, and go beyond this introductory illustration.

increase required to break even, Mr. Hilbert was saddened and perplexed.

Mr. McNoon, who had been trained in Bayesian statistics, replied that he could render assistance. First, he asked Mr. Hilbert what betting odds he would have chosen before undertaking the experiment, concerning the possible real difference in sales if the new strategy were adopted across the board. Mr. Hilbert replied that in his judgment he could not conceive of any chance that the mean sales difference could be negative, i.e., that present Hilbert machines could outsell the newer design. Upon further reflection he felt that he could quantify his betting odds in even more explicit terms, as shown in Table 2.

TABLE 2 Mr. Hilbert's Prior Probabilities for Vending Machine Problem

PROBABILITY ASSIGNMENT	MEAN SALES DIFFERENCE; NEW VS. OLD (DOLLARS PER MACHINE PER MONTH)	EXPECTED VALUE
0.00	Under $100	$ 0.00
0.10	$100— 150	12.50
0.30	150— 200	52.50
0.50	200— 250	112.50
0.10	250— 300	27.50
0.00	Over $300	0.00
1.00		$205.00

Mr. McNoon replied that if Mr. Hilbert had acted on the basis of his prior judgments *alone,* he would have proceeded with the conversion of all machines to the new design, since the mean difference would have exceeded the $200 increase per machine per month deemed necessary to break even. But with the sample results available, Mr. McNoon wondered if the conversion of all machines was still desirable. McNoon first addressed himself to the question: how likely was it that we would get the experimental results we did get under each one of the states of nature Mr. Hilbert thought possible to occur?

To answer this question, Mr. McNoon first calculated the conditional probability of getting the sample difference, $190, under each possible state of nature, using the midpoints of the ranges shown in Table 2. The results are noted in Table 3. In order to arrive at Table 3, Mr. McNoon first calculated the standard error of the mean, $\sigma_{\bar{x}}$, by the conventional formula: $\sigma_{\bar{x}} = \sigma_x / \sqrt{n}$. Since his sample n equalled 30,

TABLE 3　Conditional Probabilities for Vending Machine Problem

POSSIBLE DIFFERENCES	MIDPOINT	$Z =$ $(\bar{x} - \mu)/\sigma_{\bar{x}}$	ORDINATE	$P(\bar{x}|\mu)$
$100—150	$125	(190-125)/15	.00004	.00004 $\triangle$ $\bar{x}$/15
150—200	175	(190-175)/15	.24200	.24200 $\triangle$ $\bar{x}$/15
200—250	225	(190-225)/15	.02833	.02833 $\triangle$ $\bar{x}$/15
250—300	275	(190-275)/15	.00000	.00000 $\triangle$ $\bar{x}$/15

he was willing to assume that the population standard deviation was equal to the sample measure ("large sample" theory). Hence, $\sigma_{\bar{x}} = 82/\sqrt{30} = 15$. The fourth column, labeled "Ordinate," represents the height of the standardized normal curve at each Z value shown in the third column. The last column, $P(\bar{x}|\mu)$, represents the conditional probability of getting the sample difference, $190, given the midpoint of each admissible interval of mean sales differences. This probability is a product of "height" (ordinate) times "width" ($\Delta\bar{x}/15$) of the density function.

Mr. McNoon was then ready to apply Bayes's theorem in a fashion similar to its use in the Bertrand Box problem. He proceeded to reconstruct Table 4.

Mr. McNoon derived Table 4 by combining Mr. Hilbert's prior probabilities (Table 2) with the conditional probabilities calculated in Table 3, and in a manner similar to the Bertrand Box example calcu-

TABLE 4　Posterior Probabilities for Vending Machine Problem

STATE OF NATURE	PRIOR PROBABILITIES	CONDITIONAL PROBABILITIES	JOINT PROBABILITIES	POSTERIOR PROBABILITIES
$125	.10	.00004 $\triangle$ $\bar{x}$/15	.000004 $\triangle$ $\bar{x}$/15	.00
175	.30	.24200 $\triangle$ $\bar{x}$/15	.072600 $\triangle$ $\bar{x}$/15	.84
225	.50	.02833 $\triangle$ $\bar{x}$/15	.014165 $\triangle$ $\bar{x}$/15	.16
275	.10	.00000 $\triangle$ $\bar{x}$/15	.000000 $\triangle$ $\bar{x}$/15	.00
			.086769 $\triangle$ $\bar{x}$/15	1.00

lated the posterior probabilities. Next McNoon applied the posterior probabilities to the admissible states of nature and derived a new expected value based on the combined judgmental and sample evidence: E.V.=.00 (125)+.84 (175)+.16 (225)+.00 (275)=$183.

To Mr. Hilbert's dismay, the expected value of the new strategy turned out to be less than the $200 mean sales difference required to justify the conversion strategy. So complete was his dismay that he decided to forego the collection of any additional sampling information. As a matter of fact, he decided—on the basis of then current judgment—to sell the merchandising idea *and* his business to Alder San Vending. His competitor bought the business but not the idea. When last heard from, Messrs. Hilbert and McNoon had formed a consulting firm specializing in advertising research.

SUMMARY

As the reader may readily surmise, this expository article has covered only a few of the many features of Bayesian analysis.

First, we have tried to show via the simple Bertrand Box example some of the computational aspects of the Bayesian approach and how, given each possible state of nature, the analysis is affected by such considerations as (a) the economic consequences attached to alternative courses of action, (b) the prior judgments of the decision maker, and (c) the conditional probabilities of observing specific events.

Second, we have attempted to cast a typical, if oversimplified, merchandising problem into the Bayesian framework. Emphasis was placed on the combining of experimental evidence with prior judgments about the occurrence of possible events (mean sales difference between the converted vending machines vs. the old machines), which influenced the decision of not adopting the new point-of-purchase merchandising strategy.

For a full and lucid discussion of other aspects of the Bayesian approach, e.g., optimal ways to sample, best size of sample, correction for anticipated bias in survey results, etc., the reader is referred to Robert Schlaifer's excellent book (1959). Our concluding comments pertain to some of the pragmatic problems encountered in implementing the Bayesian approach in real problem situations.

First, in realistic settings the breadth of the problem frequently necessitates use of a computer to derive expected payoffs (see Green, 1961). Second, sensitivity analyses offer a means to find out how critical is the choice of some best act to the prior probabilities used or to the values entered in the payoff matrices. That is, calculations can easily be made to detemine if some best act remains "best" under a variety of different conditions. Implementation of the Bayesian ap-

proach may thus involve fairly elaborate models of the problem situation in order to reflect adequately the characteristics of the system.

The question of whether or not a formal approach of this type is *necessarily* better than unaided intuition is still moot. Our own still limited experience in using this approach on an experimental basis in the Du Pont company suggests that Bayesian analysis provides a means for checking the internal consistency of the assumptions underlying the problem, and forces the decision maker to structure his thoughts and quantify, if crudely, his degree of uncertainty about the pertinent states of nature and the sequence of events or decisions which may be involved in the future. Not infrequently the primary impact of the approach occurs at the formulation stage; final crank-out of the results of the analysis may well be anticlimactic.

As an assist to the decision maker's judgment, decision theory should begin to be able to make a significant contribution as more firms familiarize themselves with the techniques and start applying them to actual problems. As may have been inferred from this simplified exposition, Bayesian decision theory is not "anti-data" at all. Rather, it looks at advertising experimentation or data gathering in general in the cold light of its net gain—if any—toward reducing the cost of uncertainty. Finally, the approach provides a formal way to incorporate the information right into the decision problem rather than the less direct, if more classical, adherence to the magic ".05 level" of significance.

SOURCE READINGS AND REFERENCES

Business Week. "Math Plus Intuition Equals Decision." *Business Week* (March 24, 1962), pp. 54–60.

Buzzell, Robert D. and Charles C. Slater. "Decision Theory and Marketing Management." *Journal of Marketing,* vol. 26, no. 3 (July 1962), pp. 7–16.

Chernoff, H. and L. E. Moses. *Elementary Decision Theory.* New York: John Wiley & Sons, Inc., 1959.

Fry, Thornton C. *Probability and Its Engineering Uses.* New York: D. Van Nostrand Company, Inc., 1928.

Green, P. E. "An Application of Bayesian Decision Theory to a Problem in Long Range Pricing Strategy." *Journal of the American Statistical Association,* vol. 57, no. 298 (June, 1962), p. 490. (Abstract)

————. "Decision Theory and Chemical Marketing." *Industrial and Engineering Chemistry,* vol. 54, no. 9 (September, 1962), pp. 30–34.

————. "Bayesian Statistics and Product Decisions." *Business Horizons,* vol. 5, no. 3 (Fall, 1962), pp. 101–109.

————. "The Computer's Place in Business Planning: A Bayesian Approach." In Alderson, W. and S. J. Shapiro (eds.), *Marketing and the Computer.* Englewood Cliffs, N. J.: Prentice-Hall, Inc., 1962.

Hirshleifer, J. "The Bayesian Approach to Statistical Decision: An Exposition." *Journal of Business,* vol. 34, no. 4 (October, 1961), pp. 471–489.

Luce, R. D. and H. Raiffa. *Games and Decisions.* New York: John Wiley & Sons, Inc., 1957.

Raiffa, H. and R. Schlaifer. *Applied Statistical Decision Theory.* Cambridge, Mass.: Harvard Business School Press, 1961.

Roberts, H. V. "The New Business Statistics." *Journal of Business,* vol. 33, no. 1 (January, 1960), pp. 21–30.

Schlaifer, R. *Probability and Statistics for Business Decisions.* New York: McGraw-Hill Book Company, Inc., 1959.

Schlaifer, R. *Introduction to Statistics for Business Decisions.* New York: McGraw-Hill Book Company, Inc., 1961.

Allocating Advertising Dollars by Linear Programing

James F. Engel
Martin R. Warshaw

Advertisers and advertising agencies alike have recently shown increased interest in the use of mathematical programing to allocate advertising expenditures to media, and the technique of linear programing has received special attention. Indeed, about a year ago full-page ads in the *Wall Street Journal* stated that linear programing had shown one client how to get "$1.67 worth of effective advertising for every dollar in his budget."

Ralph Day [3] led the way in explaining how L.P., as we shall call it, might be applied to the allocation of the advertising appropriation. We attempted to implement Day's suggestions, and it became quite clear that the difficult problems in the L.P. approach pertained to the identification and evaluation of important marketing variables. A great deal of this delineation and quantification was, of necessity, judgmental in nature. Once these definitions and subjective appraisals of marketing variables had been made, however, the mathematical problem was rather straightforward and presented no major difficulties.

It is our purpose to delve more deeply into the problem, beginning where Day and others leave off, by suggesting through simple examples how one might implement the L.P. approach. Also, the strengths and weaknesses of L.P. will be stressed to help the thoughtful advertiser judge how this promising tool might be used in his organization. Since the mathematical model of L.P. and the methods of solution have been well documented in technical terms by Spivey [9], Churchman, Ackoff, and Arnoff [2], Dorfman, Samuelson, and Solow [4], and others, we shall proceed directly to a simple statement of the mathematical model.

Reprinted with permission from the *Journal of Advertising Research,* vol. 4, no. 3 (September, 1964), pp. 42–48. © Advertising Research Foundation, Inc. (1964).

(1) Maximize (or minimize)
$$f = p_1 x_1 + p_2 x_2 + \ldots + p_n x_n$$
(objective function)

(2) subject to
$$a_{11} x_1 + a_{12} x_2 + \ldots + a_{1n} x_n \leqq b_1$$
(linear constraints)
$$a_{21} x_1 + a_{22} x_2 + \ldots + a_{2n} x_n \leqq b_2$$
$$\overline{\phantom{a_{m1} x_1 + a_{m2} x_2 + \ldots + a_{mn} x_n}}$$
$$a_{m1} x_1 + a_{m2} x_2 + \ldots + a_{mn} x_n \leqq b_m$$

(3) and $x_i \geqq 0 \quad (i = 1, \ldots, n)$.
(non-negativity constraint)

Hence L.P. is uniquely applicable to problems where the purpose is to maximize (or minimize) a given linear function under several constraining conditions represented by linear inequalities.

Equation (1) is called the objective function. The x's represent the variables in the problem, while the p's express the contribution or value of each x to the objective function. If, for example, the objective function to be maximized is the number of prospects reached by a given media assortment, the x's would be "dollars invested in individual media," and the p's "prospects reached by each medium per dollar invested."

The first constraints are designated by the inequalities (2). The symbol $\leqq$ means "less than or equal to," and $\geqq$ means "greater than or equal to." The b's refer to maximum quantities of resources or capacities available, and the a's indicate the extent to which each x uses up or consumes the resource or capacity b. For instance, b_1 may refer to the total advertising budget, which cannot be exceeded by the number of dollars invested in the various media. Factor b_2 may specify the number of insertions allowed in magazine x_2. The flexibility allowed in placing constraining conditions is one of the real strengths of the L.P. approach. Finally, inequality (3) specifies that all x's in the optimal solution either must assume a value of 0 or some positive number.

Day [3] indicates more specifically the manner in which the general L.P. model is applied to allocation of advertising dollars:

In the linear programing media mix model, the objective function shows how particular advertising units contribute to "total advertising effectiveness." The system of inequalities reflects the restrictions imposed on the solution values of the variables by the budget, the characteristics of available media, and other environmental conditions. The nonnegativity requirements prevent infeasible solutions involving negative values of the variables. Solution of a correctly formulated model will then indicate the

particular advertising units to be included in the media schedule and the number of uses of each which will result in the greatest "total advertising effectiveness" obtainable from a given budget (p. 42).

The rest of this article analyzes two examples to show how one moves from the general L.P. problem to a specific application. The simplest application of L.P. to media allocation is illustrated in the solution of the McGraw-Edison case [8]. The Pennsylvania Transformer Division of McGraw-Edison manufactures transformers used by industrial plants, schools, public institutions, commercial construction projects, and hospitals. The plant engineer usually makes the purchase decision, so the objective is to maximize the number of plant engineers reached, given budgetary and other constraints. The company has $25,000 to spend on industrial advertising, and data are available on markets reached by various media. Since ten media are available for analysis, the objective function assumes the following general form:

$$\text{Maximize } f = p_1 x_1 + p_2 x_2 + \ldots + p_{10} x_{10}$$

where the x's are the number of dollars invested in the various media and the p's represent the number of plant engineers reached in each magazine per advertising dollar invested.

We computed the values of the p's by dividing the total number of plant engineers reached by the six-time bulk page rate in each medium. The data shown in Table 1 were gathered:

TABLE 1

MAGAZINE	PLANT ENGINEERS REACHED/COST PER INSERTION		PLANT ENGINEERS REACHED PER DOLLAR
x_1 Consulting Engineer	0/475	p_1	0
x_2 Electrical Construction	12,000/792	p_2	15.15
x_3 Electrical World	24,000/730	p_3	32.87
x_4 Power	44,000/890	p_4	49.44
x_5 Plant Engineering	52,000/918	p_5	56.65
x_6 Electrical West	8,000/456	p_6	17.54
x_7 Electrified Industry	44,000/756	p_7	58.20
x_8 Public Power	0/700	p_8	0
x_9 Electric Light and Power	16,000/680	p_9	23.53
x_{10} Transmission and Distribution	23,000/575	p_{10}	40.00

Thus the objective function becomes:

$$\text{Maximize } f = 0x_1 + 15.15x_2 + 32.87x_3 + 49.44x_4 + 56.65x_5$$
$$+ 17.54x_6 + 58.20x_7 + 0x_8 + 23.53x_9 + 40.00x_{10}.$$

With only $25,000 to spend, a budgetary constraint must be established:

$$x_1 + x_2 + \ldots + x_{10} \leqq \$25,000.$$

In addition, constraints must be fixed to prevent more dollars being invested in any one monthly magazine than is necessary to buy 12 insertions. (*Electrical World* is published weekly but insertions have been limited to 12 for purposes of exposition.) Therefore, these constraints are added:

x_1	$\leqq$ 5,700	x_6	$\leqq$ 5,472
x_2	$\leqq$ 9,504	x_7	$\leqq$ 9,072
x_3	$\leqq$ 8,760	x_8	$\leqq$ 3,300
x_4	$\leqq$ 10,680	x_9	$\leqq$ 8,160
x_5	$\leqq$ 11,016	x_{10}	$\leqq$ 6,900

This problem is of the general L.P. form and can be solved by the Simplex method [9, 6], a procedure which moves the objective function from one feasible solution to the next until a solution is reached in which the objective function has the greatest value given the constraining conditions. An IBM 7090 computer was programed for the Simplex method, and an optimal solution indicated that an investment of $4,912 (roughly 5.5 pages) in *Power* (x_4), $11,016 (12 pages) in *Plant Engineering* (x_5), and $9,072 (12 pages) in *Electrified Industry* (x_7) would maximize the number of plant engineers reached for $25,000.

Obviously, we do not need a computer to solve such a simple problem (which suffers from lack of necessary refinements). It is apparent that some media are better than others for reaching desired objectives, and we need some form of "effectiveness rating." In other words, the media buyer must be certain that he has chosen the media which best match the audience as specified by his objectives. Audience dimensions such as age, income, location should be included in the objective function so that an "optimal" solution maximizes not only the number reached but readers who are likely to be prospects. Let us call this phase of effectiveness rating the "audience profile match."

In addition, media must be analyzed in terms of certain qualitative characteristics, such as the appropriateness of their editorial climate for the product advertised and their proven past ability to provide advertising readership. This second phase of effectiveness rating will be called the "qualitative rating."

Another problem was formulated to illustrate an approach to effectiveness rating. Here the problem is to spend $1,000,000 on advertising of women's electric razors in consumer magazines using full-page, four-color, non-bleed advertisements. Twelve media were singled out for analysis: *Cosmopolitan* (x_1), *Mademoiselle* (x_2), *Family Circle* (x_3), *Good Housekeeping* (x_4), *McCall's* (x_5), *Modern Romances* (x_6), *Modern Screen* (x_7), *Motion Picture* (x_8), *True Confessions* (x_9), *Woman's Day* (x_{10}), *Seventeen* (x_{11}), and *Ladies' Home Journal* (x_{12}).

The first step in effectiveness rating is to determine what parts of the market to reach. Suppose that we discovered through multiple correlation analysis that the desired market is composed of women who are: (1) white; (2) 18 to 44; (3) have incomes of $7,000 or more; and (4) live in metropolitan areas. Using the Starch Consumer Magazine Report, we next analyze various media possibilities in terms of these characteristics to arrive at the "audience profile match." In addition, we estimated each magazine's ability to deliver a good potential audience through data on the number of electric shavers bought by readers in the past year. A large percentage of purchases was considered a favorable indication, and these data were useful in the qualitative rating.

If the problem were approached in a manner similar to the McGraw-Edison case, the objective function would be framed in terms of the number of women reached by each magazine divided by the page rate. With the introduction of the effectiveness rating a great many different schemes could be employed. What we did, though, was to devise a rating scale, ranging from 0 to 1.00, to encompass both the profile match and qualitative rating. The total number of women reached by each medium is multiplied by this factor value to arrive at total "effective audience."

Assume that a multiple correlation analysis showed age to be the most important discriminator of prospects. Age would be assigned a weight in the total rating to reflect its relative importance, as would other facors. In the problem at hand we specified what each factor should contribute to the effectiveness rating as follows:

	Maximum Contribution
Age (18–44)	.40
Bought shaver	.30
Income ($7,000 or over)	.15
Metropolitan location	.10
White	.05
Total	1.00

The rating scheme could be modified to reflect any additional values which management assumes to be important. For instance, we could have employed another scale ranging from 0.5 to 1.0 to reflect ratings of the appropriateness of editorial climate. The actual form of the effectiveness rating, then, is entirely dictated by the tasks to be accomplished and the data available.

The profile match is obtained by analyzing each magazine's audience on the various dimensions and then assigning a factor weight. A conversion system, of course, is necessary for this purpose, and in a sophisticated approach one perhaps would derive the conversion scale by expressing the various magazines' characteristics in terms of standard deviations of their distributions. Thus, if the proportion of readership aged 18–44 for the magazines under consideration averaged 50 percent with a standard deviation of 5 percent, a specific magazine with 55 percent of its readership aged 18–44 might be assigned a $+1$ (one standard deviation above the mean). Another magazine having only 40 percent of its audience in the 18–44 bracket would be assigned a -2. To eliminate negative weights, -3 standard deviations might be termed a zero with the scale running up to a $+6$ for a magazine three standard deviations above the mean.

A much simpler conversion scale is used here for expository purposes. Here is the conversion scale for each factor:

Age (18–44) (0 to .4)		Income ($7,000 or More) (0 to .15)	
Under 50%	.0	Under 25%	0
50–55	.1	26–30	.03
56–60	.2	31–35	.06
61–65	.3	36–40	.10
66 or over	.4	41 or over	.15

WHITE (0 TO .05)		METROPOLITAN AREA (0 TO .1)	
Under 85%	0	Under 50%	0
85–90	.01	51–55	.03
91–95	.03	56–60	.06
96 or over	.05	61 or over	.10

PREVIOUSLY BOUGHT SHAVER (0 TO .3)	
Under 4%	0
5–6	.1
7–8	.2
9–10	.3

To illustrate the effectiveness rating procedure, let us take a hypothetical magazine, *Woman's World*. Assume that the audience data shown below are available on market coverage (from Starch Magazine report or the individual medium). Converting the data, these weights would be applied:

	AUDIENCE	WEIGHTS
Age 18–44	59%	.20
Income $7,000 or over	31	.06
White subscribers	96	.05
Metropolitan coverage	61	.10
Puchased shaver in last 12 months	7	.20
		.61

Suppose this magazine reaches 5,070,492 women. Multiplying this total by a factor of .61 gives an effective audience of 3,093,000 women. Dividing this by the four-color, full-page rate ($29,100) gives "effective readings per dollar spent" of 106. This final figure will appear in the objective function as the coefficient of the variable (x).

Using the above procedure for each magazine produced the following objective function:

$$\text{Max } f = 158x_1 + 263x_2 + 106x_3 + 108x_4 + 65x_5 + 176x_6 \\ + 285x_7 + 86x_8 + 120x_9 + 51x_{10} + 190x_{11} + \\ 101x_{12}.$$

With the budgetary constraint:

$$x_1 + x_2 + \ldots + x_{12} \leqq 1,000,000.$$

And the usual non-negativity constraint:

$$x_i \geqq 0 \quad (i = 1, \ldots, 12).$$

Also constraints again were established to prevent assigning more than 12 insertions to any of these monthly magazines. Suppose, however, that management had good reason to limit the maximum insertions to less than 12 for media x_2 and x_{12} (for example, 7 and 2 insertions respectively). Thus the constraints are:

$$
\begin{aligned}
x_1 &\leqq 58{,}080 & x_7 &\leqq 52{,}380 \\
x_2 &\leqq 30{,}075 \ (7) & x_8 &\leqq 53{,}580 \\
x_3 &\leqq 349{,}000 & x_9 &\leqq 57{,}960 \\
x_4 &\leqq 288{,}000 & x_{10} &\leqq 333{,}000 \\
x_5 &\leqq 407{,}400 & x_{11} &\leqq 72{,}360 \\
x_6 &\leqq 52{,}380 & x_{12} &\leqq 81{,}200 \ (2)
\end{aligned}
$$

Suppose further that the client company has specified certain minimum expenditures in magazines x_2, x_3, x_5, and x_{10}. Therefore:

$$
\begin{aligned}
x_2 &\geqq 13{,}275 \\
x_3 &\geqq 58{,}166 \\
x_5 &\geqq 33{,}950 \\
x_{10} &\geqq 27{,}750
\end{aligned}
$$

Finally, management declared a maximum expenditure of \$280,000 in magazines x_3, x_9, x_{10}, and x_{12} and specified the investment of exactly \$85,870 in magazines x_1 and x_8. Thus:

$$
\begin{aligned}
x_3 + x_9 + x_{10} + x_{12} &\leqq 280{,}000 \\
x_1 + x_8 &= 85{,}870
\end{aligned}
$$

The above problem is obviously more complex than the McGraw-Edison case, and it is no longer possible to visualize a solution readily. Imagine the difficulties if 50 media were employed with a more complex set of constraints! Also, a variety of subjective restrictions could have been used as alternatives to those shown above. The strength of L.P. is that for every configuration of subjective constraints, we can readily solve the corresponding problem. Indeed, management might be presented with two or more solutions showing the impact of changes in the subjective constraints upon the optimal solution.

The Simplex method of solution was used on the computer, and an optimal solution to the above problem directed that we make these purchases:

	MEDIUM	
x_1	Cosmopolitan	$ 58,080
x_2	Mademoiselle	30,075
x_3	Family Circle	194,290
x_4	Good Housekeeping	288,000
x_5	McCall's	180,484*
x_6	Modern Romances	52,380
x_7	Modern Screen	52,380
x_8	Motion Picture	27,790
x_9	True Confessions	57,960
x_{10}	Woman's Day	27,750
x_{11}	Seventeen	72,360
x_{12}	Ladies' Home Journal	0

* Includes reinvested discounts.

After the initial allocation it was necessary to reconsult Standard Rate and Data Service to find the extent of volume discounts which the firm had earned. We discovered that an additional $41,549 was available for expenditure. The Simplex solution indicates, within bounds, where to invest these additional funds. In the problem at hand, it was indicated that the additional dollars should be invested in *McCall's*.

An important point to keep in mind is that quantity discounts could not have been built into the original statement of the problem. The cost function would then have been nonlinear, and L.P. would no longer have been applicable. Nonlinear programing methods are available, but the solution would become decidedly more complex [5, 10].

As suggested earlier, management should not view the Simplex solution as the final phase in the L.P. approach. It might be quite useful, for example, to engage in a sensitivity analysis by changing the weights used in the effectiveness rating, especially those based on subjective evaluation. If rather large changes can be made in these weights without changing the optimal solution, it is evident that the solution is not dependent on precise evaluations of qualitative characteristics. If, however, the optimal solution changes with slight variations in these weights then it is obvious that the quality of the solution can be little better than the quality of the effectiveness rating procedure.

Let us now state more specifically the steps in a well-conceived L.P. media allocation procedure:

1. Establishment of specific advertising objectives.
2. Procurement of data on the relative importance of various characteristics of the market to be reached through multiple correlation analysis or other means.
3. Procurement of data on audiences of various candidate media. Often these data are stored in the computer, thus permitting quick access.
4. Application of an effectiveness rating procedure encompassing two phases: audience profile match and qualitative factor rating.
5. Quantification of all constraining conditions, including budgetary limits, limits on media availability, and other environmental factors.
6. Application of an L.P. computational procedure.
7. Analysis of the resulting media plan to determine its sensitivity to various factors in the effectiveness rating and to changes in constraint conditions.

The L.P. approach has important strengths and weaknesses which must be recognized by all potential users, and each point will be examined.

ADVANTAGES OF L.P. APPROACH

1. L.P. forces management to make precise definitions of markets to be reached. Instead of guesses or hunches, data must be developed which characterize markets along several dimensions. The net result of such analysis cannot help but increase the effectiveness of media allocation.

2. L.P. requires a quantification of factors which are highly qualitative in nature. Editorial climate is perhaps a highly subjective factor yet management must take this media characteristic and others of a similar nature into account when engaging in media selection.

3. L.P. creates a definite need for audience profiles of various media. The occasional media audience study no longer will suffice, and instead careful audience profile information must be provided with the regularity of ABC sworn circulation data. L.P. is certain, therefore, to stimulate the collection of a wealth of previously unavailable facts.

4. L.P. can be applied to problems involving a variety of media. Although we have discussed only magazines, there is no reason why all possible media cannot be included in the L.P. approach. If data are available, all media can be considered in the same terms, making it feasible to consider vastly more media at a time than would be possible without the aid of a computer.

5. L.P. can be used by advertisers and agencies of *any* size. No mumbo jumbo in the methodology limits this approach only to large firms. Furthermore, it is not necessary to confine L.P. to allocations approaching astronomical sums. Indeed, the allocation of a few thousand dollars can become sufficiently complex to warrant use of the computer, especially when one considers the potential costs of an ineffective allocation.

6. L.P. allows the blending together of many factors. As Maneloveg [7] points out:

> In the past we have worked at it with stubby pencils and people, many people. However, no matter how much time and how many people, we have had too many factors to contend with. The real advantage of an electronic computer to us then—its principal purpose—is to give us an opportunity to change these relationships, to juggle with them, to work with them while at the same time keeping all of them in the forefront of the operation and to end up with an effort that examines the whole not individual pieces of media . . . the way, incidentally, our customers view the campaign that we're putting together (p. 6).

LIMITATIONS

1. L.P. is applicable only if all relationships in the problem are linear or if it is appropriate for management purposes to regard them as so. This is a marketing decision, not a mathematical one. As noted above, the requirement of linearity in cost functions did not permit inclusion of quantity discounts in the initial allocation. Yet the resulting allocation may fail to achieve the maximum discount which might have become available if dollars were allocated differently. It is difficult to maximize discounts unless constraints require only large purchases of individual media, but, on the other hand, such constraints may unduly limit the solution space to large buys and thereby force an ineffective allocation.

The assumption of linearity becomes more crucial in another respect. Although the cost functions in both examples required purchases of full pages, fractional page purchases appeared in the allocation. The problem arises because the Simplex approach does not guarantee the purchase of only full pages. The cost of a half page, for example, is not half of the page rate, so it may be incorrect to assume that purchases of fractional pages are optimal. In other words, the cost function for various page sizes is actually nonlinear. Then what is the advertiser to do when his answer calls for 4.83 pages? Is he safe in

rounding this figure to 5.00? He probably would not err greatly if he does, but he still must recognize the danger of arriving at a nonoptimal allocation if he rounds off on a large scale. Furthermore, cost structures may not depart so far from linearity as to preclude meaningful answers. The only feasible way in which to guarantee nonfractional purchases, however, is to use "integer programing," and we are experimenting with this approach.

Finally, it is assumed that successive purchases in a media all contribute the same value to the objective function. It must be recognized that multiple exposure of a given prospect may become increasingly less effective, thus introducing nonlinearity into the response function. This problem may be crucial, but we cannot avoid it without resorting to more complex nonlinear programing methods.

2. Solutions were arrived at without consideration of audience duplication and accumulation. Because of audience overlap, purchase of two or more magazines should result in a total audience that is less than the sum of the individual audiences. Although the Agostini [1] constant may permit estimates of nonduplicated audiences, his approach requires data that are not available on a consistent scale, especially if one is comparing a magazine and a television show. Furthermore, whereas duplication and accumulation of *prospects* are the only truly relevant considerations, existing data are confined entirely to total audiences. Thus at present the L.P. approach cannot solve effectively the duplication and accumulation problems.

3. Comparable data are not always available for various media in terms of audience dimensions. More and better media data are required before L.P. can achieve its potential.

4. Finally, resulting solutions give a very misleading illusion of definiteness. Solutions are only as good as the data and assumptions upon which they are built. Weaknesses in data or in analysis of the problem will be compounded, so good judgment is vital.

CONCLUSION

The approach to L.P. and media allocation described here obviously needs considerable refinement. And it should be abundantly clear that the major problems arise in identifying and quantifying the important marketing variables—not in application of the L.P. computational procedure. L.P. is not a magical device that relegates responsibility for management decisions to computers and their programers. Indeed, the successful use of L.P. involves three essentials: (1) defining market

targets; (2) rating media in terms of their effectiveness in reaching these targets; (3) developing and quantifying monetary and non-monetary constraints which limit feasible solutions. Thus judgment responsibilities of the media executive are *sharpened,* not eliminated. The only thing eliminated is laborious clerical work.

Let us conclude by observing that L.P. is not a breakthrough and that it involves very little more than systematizing steps which have long been followed by successful advertisers. The real gain comes in the time saved and the ability to handle complex problems with greater ease and to deal quickly with alternative subjective evaluations of constraints and weighting factors. We hope the glamor which quantitative methods now hold does not cause advertisers to overlook the inescapable difficulty of identifying and evaluating the important marketing variables. If this problem is fully recognized, then L.P. is not likely to be blighted in its infancy, as was motivation research, by exaggerated and commercially-motivated claims of a few zealous spokesmen.

REFERENCES

1. Agostini, J.-M., "How to Estimate Unduplicated Audiences," *Journal of Advertising Research, 13* (March 1961), pp. 11–14.

2. Churchman, C. West, Ackoff, Russell, L., and Arnoff, Leonard E., *Introduction to Operations Research* (New York: Wiley, 1957).

3. Day, Ralph L., "Linear Programming in Media Selection," *Journal of Advertising Research, 2* (June 1962), pp. 40–44.

4. Dorfman, Robert, Samuelson, Paul A., and Solow, Robert M., *Linear Programming and Economic Analysis* (New York: McGraw-Hill, 1958).

5. Dorn, W. S., "Non-Linear Programming—A Survey," *Management Science, 9* (January 1963), pp. 171–208.

6. Garvin, W. W., *An Introduction to Linear Programming* (New York: McGraw-Hill, 1960).

7. Maneloveg, Herbert, *Linear Programming,* paper presented at the Eastern Annual Convention (New York: American Association of Advertising Agencies, November 1962).

8. McGraw-Edison Company, *ICH 6m67* (Boston: Intercollegiate Case Clearing House, 1961).

9. Spivey, W. Allen, *Linear Programming: An Introduction* (New York: Macmillan, 1963).

10. Wolfe, Philip, "The Simplex Method for Quadratic Programming," *Econometrica, 27* (July 1959), pp. 382–398.

chapter | Channels and Physical
9 | Distribution Management

Another major decision area for the marketing manager is the establishment of channels for his products and the solution of problems
associated with the distribution of these products. Given the complex
interrelationships that exist within the distribution structure, the
marketer's task is indeed a difficult one.

In the first article of this section, Bruce Mallen shows how an
integration of economic price theory and the marketing channel can
aid in the development of a marketing theory and its application to
the important area of marketing channels. More specifically, Mallen
shows how the marketer's concept of a channel can be injected into
the economist's concept of a market.

Heskett, in the second article, examines the temporal aspects of
the physical distribution system. According to Heskett, there has been
much emphasis placed on the spatial dimension. He points out
that "if an integrated, accurate method of analyzing and controlling
physical distribution systems is to be developed, time instead of space
will be the relevant unifying dimension to be used."

Introducing the Marketing Channel
to Price Theory

Bruce Mallen

Most of the various areas of marketing such as promotion, advertising, selling, pricing, product development, and distribution can be enriched by economic theory.

But one area in particular has had very little integration with economic theory—the marketing channel. "The final price of an article is not a simple thing arrived at as a result merely of the interaction of the forces in play at the point of sale and purchase. It is compounded of a whole system of interlocking price relationships reaching back through the retailer, the wholesaler, the manufacturer, and all the other marketing agents who may have had a hand in the movement of the product to the point of ultimate sale. It is the final fruit of an elaborate price structure complicated by such conditioning and obscuring factors as quantity allowances, credit terms, delivery arrangements, and services rendered at each of the several stages through which the product passes in its often devious and tortuous way to the point of final sale."[1]

DEFINITION OF CHANNEL

Trade channels and channels of distribution are synonymous with marketing channels. Resource channels are also synonymous, but they involve marketing channels from a buying rather than a selling standpoint.

In a wide sense, channels are all the "flows" extending from the

Reprinted with permission from the *Journal of Marketing,* vol. 28, no. 3 (July, 1964), pp. 29–33, published by the American Marketing Association.

[1] Ralph S. Alexander, "Marketing's Contribution to Economics," in Robert A. Solo, Editor, *Economics and the Public Interest* (New Brunswick: Rutgers University Press, 1955), pp. 71–72.

producer to the user. "A channel of distribution may be thought of as the combination and sequence of agencies through which one or more of the marketing flows move. . . . In its simplest form, a channel is limited to the movement of one unit of goods in one flow. . . . In its more complicated forms, the channel includes all combinations and sequences of all the agencies used in all the flows, possibly with an indication of the quantitative importance of each. It may apply to a whole class or type of goods and to a company, a trade, or an industry. In its most complex form, it describes typical or actual flows of broad classes of goods (say consumers' goods or industrial goods) or charts the marketing structure as a whole."[2]

This definition refers to the flows of physical possession, ownership, promotion, negotiation, financing, risking, ordering, and payment; and it is accepted by many authorities.[3] Under this concept, such diverse agencies as railroads, warehouses, factors, advertising agencies, and marketing research agencies would be included as channel members.

However, the concept of channels to be used here involves only two of the above-mentioned flows: ownership and negotiation. The first draws merchants into the channel definition, and the second draws agent middlemen. If any major processing is undergone, the channel ends. For example, the route from cotton farmer to textile mill to garment manufacturer to consumer is not one channel, but several.

ECONOMIC MARKETS CLASSIFICATION

How can the marketing man's concept of a channel be injected into the economist's concept of a market? This is a crucial question, as the concept of a market place is central to microeconomic price theory.

Economists look upon a market as the exchange mechanism between buyers and sellers. Thus, the exchange mechanism between a manufacturer as a seller and a wholesaler as a buyer is one market. A second market is the exchange mechanism between the wholesaler as a seller and the retailer as a buyer. Finally, the exchange mechanism between the retailer as a seller and the consumer as a buyer is a third market. Thus, a manufacturer-wholesaler-retailer-consumer channel can be looked upon as a series of three markets.

[2] Ronald S. Vaile, E. T. Grether, and Reavis Cox, *Marketing in the American Economy* (New York: Ronald Press, 1952), pp. 121 and 124.

[3] David A. Revzan, *Wholesaling in Marketing Organization* (New York: John Wiley & Sons, Inc., 1961), p. 109.

The type of market can be defined according to its degree of competitiveness, which depends to a great extent on the number of buyers and sellers in a market. Some possible combinations are shown in Table 1.

TABLE 1   Classification of Economic Markets

SUPPLIERS (SELLERS)	MIDDLEMEN (BUYERS)	MARKET SITUATION
Pure competitor	Pure competitor	Pure competition
Oligopolist	Pure competitor	Oligopoly
Monopolist	Pure competitor	Monopoly
Pure competitor	Oligopsonist	Oligoposony
Pure competitor	Monopsonist	Monopsony
Oligopoly	Oligopsonist	Bilateral oligopoly
Monopolist	Monopsonist	Bilateral monopoly
Monopolist	Monopolist	Successive monopoly

The classification of economic markets in Table 1 is based primarily on the degree of concentration and number of suppliers (manufacturers or middlemen) on the selling side, and the degree of concentration and number of middlemen on the buying side of the market.

1. The smaller the number and the greater the degree of concentration on the selling side, the less purely competitive and the more monopolistic that market becomes.
2. The smaller the number and the greater the degree of concentration on the buying side, the less purely competitive and the more monopsonistic that market becomes.
3. Where this diminishing number and increasing concentration are "working" on both sides of the market, the closer that market moves to bilateral monopoly.

In an oversimplified way, it can be said that:

1. Pure competition means many sellers and many buyers.
2. Oligopoly means few sellers; monopoly means one seller.
3. Oligopsony means few buyers; monopsony means one buyer.
4. Bilateral oligopoly means few buyers and few sellers; and bilateral monopoly means one buyer and one seller.
5. Successive monopoly means one seller selling to buyers, each of whom is in turn the only reseller in the next market of the channel series.

The more monopolistic the selling side, the higher the price will tend to be; and the more monopsonistic, the lower the price.

Aside from the number of micro-units involved, these definitions include specifications for degree of product differentiation (none in pure competition); degree of resource mobility and ease of entry (complete in pure competition); and degree of artificial restrictions (none in pure competition).

Because of these other specifications, definitions of other types of markets not mentioned above arise, such as monopolistic competition (pure competition changed by product differentiation); but these will not be dealt with here.

THEORIES IN THE CHANNEL-PRICE AREA

Several theories and concepts should be adapted to a channel situation. These include vertical conflict, simple monopoly, successive monopoly, vertical price relationship, monopsony and oligopsony, bilateral monopoly and bilateral oligopoly, countervailing power, inventory thoery, and price level theory.

Channel-price theory as derived from economic theory is useful in studying the conflicting interaction of channel member firms, but is not very useful in understanding their cooperative interactions.[4] Thus, while such theory concentrates on how the total channel profit is shared among members, it does not adequately show how cooperation is used in increasing the total.

Vertical Conflict

Palamountain isolated three forms of distributive conflict.[5]

1. Horizontal competition—this is competition between middlemen of the same type; for example, discount store versus discount store.
2. Intertype competition—this is competition between middlemen of different types in the same channel sector; for example, discount store versus department store.
3. Vertical conflict—this is conflict between channel members of different levels; for example, discount store versus manufacturer.

[4] For the cooperative aspect, see Bruce Mallen, "A Theory of Retailer-Supplier Conflict, Control and Cooperation," *Journal of Retailing,* vol. 39 (Summer, 1963), pp. 24–32 and 51.

[5] Joseph C. Palamountain, *The Politics of Distribution* (Cambridge: Harvard University Press, 1955).

The first two forms, especially the first, are well covered in ordinary economic analysis. Horizontal competition is what usually is referred to as "competition," while intertype competition can be referred to as "distributive innovation."

Vertical conflict, neglected in usual microeconomic discussion, is the type which is of special interest here. Microeconomics usually treats this area simply (too simply) as the ordinary relationship between buyer and seller; but this overlooks channel member conflict.

It is apparent that a principal factor differentiating vertical conflict from horizontal and intertype competition is that it is so directly a power conflict. Power relationships among horizontal competitors occasionally are significant, but this power usually is narrowly limited. . . . In the plane of vertical conflict, however, power relationships are direct, obvious, and important to the extent that the market is imperfect.[6]

In essence, any type of channel market—where both buyers and sellers are channel members—is vertical conflict.

Simple Monopoly[7]

If one channel member is a monopolist and the others pure competitors, the consumer pays a price equivalent to that of an integrated monopolist; and the monopolist member reaps all the channel's pure profits; that is, the sum of the pure profits of all channel members. Pure profits are, of course, the economist's concept of those profits over and above the minimum return on investment required to keep a firm in business.

Assume that the retailer is the monopolist and the others (wholesalers and manufacturers) are pure competitors, as for example, a single department store in an isolated town. Total costs to the retailer are composed of the total cost of the other levels, plus his own costs. No pure profits of the other levels are included in his costs, as they make none by definition (they are pure competitors).

The retailer would be in the same buying price position, so far as the lack of suppliers' profits are concerned, as would the vertically integrated firm. Thus, he charges the same price as the integrated monopolist and makes the same profits.

If the manufacturer were the monopolist and the other channel

---

[6] Ibid., pp. 52–53.

[7] Alfred R. Oxenfeldt, *Industrial Pricing and Market Practices* (New York: Prentice-Hall, Inc., 1951), Chapter 7, Part I, Section A.

members pure competitors, he would calculate the maximizing profits for the channel, and then charge the wholesaler his cost plus the total channel's pure profits, all of which would go to him since the others are pure competitors. The wholesaler would take this price, add it on to his own costs, and the result would be the price to retailers. Then the retailers would do likewise for the consumer price.

Thus, the prices to the wholesaler and to the retailer are higher than in the first case (retailer monopoly), since the channel's pure profits are added on before the retail level. The price to the consumer is the same as in the first case. It is of no concern to the consumer if the pure profit elements in his price are added on by the manufacturer, wholesaler, or retailer.

Thus, under integrated monopoly, manufacturer monopoly, wholesaler monopoly, or retailer monopoly, the consumer price is the same; but the prices within the channel are the lowest with the retailer monopoly, and highest with the manufacturer monopoly. Of course, the nonmonopolistic channel members' pure profits are not affected by this intrachannel price variation, as they have no such profits in any case.

Successive Monopoly[8]

Successive monopoly—that is, monopoly at two or more successive channel stages—can lead to a higher price than an integrated monopoly for the consumer and members, if no agreement is reached among the monopolists.

If there are two monopolies in a channel, such as a manufacturer monopolist and a wholesaler monopolist, the former may still try to gain all the pure profits of the channel, as described in the previous "monopoly" section.

Temporarily the price to the wholesaler would be the manufacturer's costs plus the total channel's pure profits. Under these circumstances, the wholesaler would have to charge the retailer the price the former paid the manufacturer plus his own costs. He could not add on pure profits as the manufacturer has kept them all for himself.

However, unlike the situation when the wholesaler was a pure competitor and was forced to receive no pure profits, this wholesaler can now cut back on the supply he will sell to the retailer, in order to maximize profits. This reduction in supply will increase the price to the retailer more than when the wholesaler was a pure competitor and only the manufacturer was a monopolist. The retailer must now

[8] Ibid., Chapter 7, Part II, Section B.

pay not only the costs of the wholesaler and manufacturer, but also the pure profits of both.

The cutback in supply of the wholesaler will also reduce his purchases from the manufacturer, and cause the latter's profits to fall. The manufacturer may then recalculate his pricing policy to take account of his profit decline. He may make agreements with the wholesaler such that both their profits are maximized instead of allowing either of them to try to obtain all of the channel's pure profits.

Vertical Price Relationship

The indeterminateness of the successive monopoly analysis (as the latter cannot predict price without knowing the nature of the members' agreement or disagreement), can be aided by an analysis by E. R. Hawkins.[9]

As well as assuming that the channel members know the shape of the final consumer demand curve, Hawkins assumes that they know the demand curves that they themselves face. (Of course, the consumer demand curve is the one faced by the retailer.) With this assumption he can arrive at the particular price at every level.

Monopsony and Oligopsony[10]

A monopsonistic or oligopsonistic channel member can obtain lower buying prices. His selling price depends on the market structure on his selling side. If it is competitive, he passes on his low buying price to the next level; and if it is not, he may simply increase his margin.

The mass retailer may be a monopsonist on some products and a competitor on others. He may also be a monopolist or competitor on his selling side, no matter what is his buying role.

Thus, he can be a monopsonist and a (seller) competitor with one product, and have a different combination with others. His role is often oligopsonist and competitor, and he would thus pass on his price savings to consumers.

[9] E. R. Hawkins, "Vertical Price Relationship," in Cox and Alderson, Editors, *Theory in Marketing* (Homewood, Illinois: Richard D. Irwin, Inc., 1950), Chapter 11.

[10] Joe S. Bain, *Pricing, Distribution and Employment* (New York: Henry Holt and Company, 1953, revised edition), pp. 382–394.

Bilateral Monopoly and Bilateral Oligopoly[11]

Bilateral monopoly, where the selling channel member is a monopolist and the buying channel member is a monopsonist, is rare. Depending on the bargaining power of each, the price to the buying member may be lower or higher.

One authority believes that price to the oligopsonist (or monopsonist) depends on who possesses the dominant bargaining power. If the monopolist (oligopolist) has it, then the price will be higher. "It will be noted that the tendency of bilateral monopoly (between a monopolistic seller and a monopsonistic buyer who is in turn a monopolistic reseller) is to arrive at a price-quantity solution for the final market—to which the monopsonist resells—the same as would be reached if the monopolist and the monopsonist were members of a single firm with a monopoly in the final market. There are no added output restrictions because of the passage of the good first through a bilateral monopoly market on its way to the final market. . . . However, any monopolistic output restriction in a final market (where the buyer resells) will remain."[12]

But Wroe Alderson says that experience shows bilateral monopoly actually makes for a lower price to the consumer relative to monopoly.[13] It is from this ability to offer the consumer a low price, rather than the ability to exploit him with a monopoly price, that these large channel members derive their power.

Countervailing Power[14]

Countervailing power—the ability of a buying channel member to offset the power of a selling member when competition dissolves as a regulator—is similar to bilateral monopoly. However, proponents of

---

[11] Richard B. Helflebower, "Mass Distribution: A Phase of Bilateral Oligopoly or of Competition?" in Robert D. Buzzell, Editor, *Adaptive Behaviour in Marketing* (Chicago: American Marketing Association, 1957); Fritz Machlup and Martha Taber, "Bilateral Monopoly, Successive Monopoly and Vertical Integration," *Economica,* vol. 27 (May, 1960), pp. 101–117; Bain, op. cit., pp. 394–396.

[12] Bain, op. cit., p. 485.

[13] Wroe Alderson, "Factors Governing the Development of Marketing Channels" in Richard M. Clewett, Editor, *Marketing Channels for Manufactured Products* (Homewood, Illinois: Richard D. Irwin, Inc., 1954), pp. 5–34.

[14] John K. Galbraith, *American Capitalism, The Concept of Countervailing Power* (Boston: Houghton Mifflin Co., 1956, revised edition), Chapter 9.

this theory claim that big sellers automatically cause the rise of big buyers.

Various authors have discussed the validity of countervailing power.[15] In summary, it can be said that although there are various reasons for the rise of mass retailing and although these retailers are not always so effective in countervailing big producers, nevertheless countervailance is an important pricing-channel dynamic.

Inventory Theory[16]

Inventory theory stresses the role of merchants' stocks in times of changing consumer demand:

1. The tendency of channel members to absorb increases in demand through inventory increases rather than price increases.
2. Their tendency to absorb demand decreases through price decreases rather than inventory decreases.

Price-Level Theory

It appears obvious that the level of prices (a macroeconomic rather than microeconomic concept) in one channel sector must influence the price level in another sector. However, this may not hold true for the short run.

One study concludes that short-run wholesale price index changes are not useful in predicting consumer prices, nor are they paralleled by retail price index changes.[17] Aside from purely structural differences in the make-up of these indexes, the difference is explained by the following: price variations of seasonal goods, differences in distribution costs at different channel levels, cumulating tendency of fixed percentage markup pricing, different competitive situations at different channel levels, varying level of inventories, desire of price stability, and different elasticities of buyers at various channel levels.

[15] For example, Alex Hunter, "Notes on Countervailing Power," *The Economic Journal,* vol. 68 (March, 1958), pp. 89–103.

[16] Wilford, J. Eiteman, *Price Determination* (Ann Arbor: Bureau of Business Research, Report No. 16, School of Business Administration, University of Michigan, 1949).

[17] Helen B. Jung and Theodore R. Gates, "Do Retail Prices Follow Wholesale Prices?" in Stanley C. Hollander, Editor, *Explorations in Retailing* (East Lansing: Michigan State University, 1959), pp. 48–51.

THE CHALLENGE TO THEORISTS

Quentin L. Coons' challenge to the economic theorist must be met.[18] And it must be met in a constructive fashion. There is a definite need to integrate marketing thought into economic theory—not only channel concepts, but concepts from all the marketing areas. Some of the attacks on marketing by economists are a direct result of this failure to integrate these concepts. Moreover, the meeting of this challenge will aid in the development of a marketing theory and increase the reality of economic theory.

[18] Quentin L. Coons, "Marketing's Challenge to Economics," *Journal of Marketing,* vol. 27 (July, 1963), pp. 11–15.

A Missing Link in Physical Distribution System Design

J. L. Heskett

Undue, misplaced emphasis on spatial matters in physical distribution has prevented effective measurement of physical distribution activity and the development of truly valid system planning methods. There is evidence of both a macro- and micro-economic nature to support this view.

MACRO-ECONOMIC SYMPTOMS

Economists and economic geographers have placed major emphasis on spatial (distance-oriented) measures of business.

The early studies by von Thünen[1] related to land use were landmarks in two senses of the word. Not only did they mark the beginning but also the direction of the work in economic geography for decades to follow. There was little reason for von Thünen to be concerned with other than spatial matters in his work. The areas near the city-state which he described by concentric rings emanating from the city center were relatively small and regularly described; and because of regular topography and limited traffic they were accessible to the city center in an inverse relation to their distance from it. He observed few irregularities in the pattern of agriculture resulting from the displacement of lower income crops by higher income crops on land of increasing value.

Assuming that perishability of agricultural products was of limited relevance, or only substantiated the spatial framework of von Thünen's

Reprinted with permission from the *Journal of Marketing,* vol. 30, no. 4 (October, 1966), pp. 37–41, published by the American Marketing Association.

[1] Johann Heinrich von Thünen, *Der Isolirte Staat in Beziehung auf Landwirthschaft und Nationalökonomie* (Berlin: Schumacher-Zarchlin, 1875).

theory by varying directly with crop value, temporal time-oriented considerations justifiably were given no emphasis in the theory.

Pursuing our landmarks further, we come to the work of Weber.[2] His relatively rich models of industrial location considered as variables: (1) the nature of raw material components and finished products, that is, whether they were localized or ubiquitous, weight-losing or pure; (2) the relative location of a two-dimensional plane of raw material sources and finished-product markets; and (3) the magnitude of labor (production) costs at all possible locations.

He assumed that both transportation costs and transit times were linear in relation to distance. If transportation "rates" of Weber's day and in his country were comparable to ours today, we know that the first part of his assumption is true, *if* we confine ourselves to a single method of transportation and disregard fixed costs.

Again, given the regular topography of his models and the limited transport alternatives of his day, it is understandable that he would assume time equated to distance to the extent that temporal aspects of the problem remained unmentioned. This assumption was to continue unduly to influence students of the subject for some time.

Among Weber's successors, various economists[3] with their linear market models, and also economic geographers of the location-theory school, neglected even to pay lip service to the model irregularities introduced by varying degrees of accessibility measured in units of time. The work of the latter group exhibits the lengths to which researchers have gone to eliminate inconstancies of time in formulating theory. For example, Lösch presumably did not choose the state of Iowa by accident as the area for much of his research in this country.[4] It provided him with a somewhat homogeneous economy, laced regularly with transport arteries, and sufficiently compact and landlocked to rule out most alternative modes of transportation. Only in

---

[2] Alfred Weber, *Über den Standort der Industrien* (Tübingen: Mohr, 1909), translated by Carl J. Friedrich as *Alfred Weber's Theory of the Location of Industries* (Chicago: University of Chicago Press, 1929).

[3] For example, Harold Hotelling, "Stability in Competition," *Economic Journal,* vol. 39 (March, 1929), pp. 41–57; F. Zeuthen, "Theoretical Remarks on Price Policy: Hotelling's Case with Variations," *Quarterly Journal of Economics,* vol. 47 (February, 1933), pp. 231–253; and Edward H. Chamberlin, *The Theory of Monopolistic Competition* (Cambridge: Harvard University Press, 3rd edition, 1938), Appendix C.

[4] August Lösch, *Die Raumliche Ordnung der Wirtschaft* (Jena: Gustav Fischer Verlag, 1940), translated from the 2nd revised edition of 1944 by William H. Woglom with the assistance of Wolfgang F. Stolper, *The Economics of Location* (New Haven: Yale University Press, 1954).

the work of Dean is there an effort to consider effects of irregular topography and the impact of transportation technology in locations.[5]

Of the regional scientists placing major emphasis on techniques of input-output analysis, a great deal of empirical work has been done by Isard.[6] But his most extensive published study did not have to deal with temporal aspects of the supply and distribution problem in determining what would be produced and where it would be stored. Those items in the petroleum-product family studied in which interregional (international) transportation was a factor were relatively homogeneous. One method of transportation, by water, was feasible. Inventory costs, while a variable, probably were not sufficiently important to influence the results of the analysis very much.

The concept of accessibility employed by graph theorists suggests the opportunity for the eventual use of *time rather than distance* in its computation. However, major studies of this type thus far have been concerned with the impact of alternative network investments on cumulative nodal accessibility for transportation networks containing only one mode of transport.[7] At such time as they are developed to the point where transportation systems describing modes with widely varying characteristics are superimposed upon one another, a consideration will be necessary of cumulative times rather than distances in measuring the degree of accessibility inherent in various systems and system combinations.

Only urban geographers appear to have placed some emphasis on temporal aspects of distribution on a somewhat macro-economic level.[8] This is natural, because the subject commodity of their location studies invariably has been people. And commuters or shoppers

[5] William H. Dean, Jr., *The Theory of the Geographic Location of Economic Activities, Selections from the Doctoral Dissertation* (Ann Arbor: Edwards Brothers, Inc., 1938).

[6] Walter Isard, Eugene W. Schooler, and Thomas Vietoriez, *Industrial Complex Analysis and Regional Development* (New York and Cambridge: John Wiley & Sons, Inc., and the Technology Press of the Massachusetts Institute of Technology, 1959), especially pp. 96–97.

[7] For representative works, see William L. Garrison, "Connectivity of the Interstate Highway System," in *Papers and Proceedings* (Philadelphia: Regional Science Association, 1960), pp. 122–137; and Karel Kansky, *Structure of Transportation Networks,* Department of Geography Research Paper no. 84 (Chicago: University of Chicago, 1963).

[8] For example, Lowdon Wingo, Jr., *Transportation and Urban Land* (Washington: Resources for the Future, Inc., 1961), especially pp. 43–62; and David L. Huff, "Defining and Estimating a Trading Area," *Journal of Marketing,* vol. 28 (July, 1964), pp. 34–38.

tend to measure distance in minutes, not miles. Their location decisions and consequently the "face" of the community, are altered by the factor of time.

By no means is this a complete list of examples; but each of the works mentioned has in some measure confused the issues related to system design at the micro-economic level.

MICRO-ECONOMICS OF SPACE AND TIME

The micro-economics of physical distribution systems concern two major cost categories: transportation and inventory.

The former are incurred in the connecting links on a distribution network. The latter are experienced primarily at system nodes, but also while goods are in transit. Costs of freight transportation approximated $60 billion and of inventory carrying $30 billion in the United States in 1964.

These major cost areas have spawned a number of models which can be grouped into related categories. Transportation costs, in combination with volumes of goods in movement, typically have provided the heart of location models regardless of whether the model has employed a linear-programing, center of gravity, or other approach. On the other hand, inventory models have been directly concerned with inventory costs. Accordingly, it can be said that:

1. Location models have been *spatially oriented* to date, while inventory models have and will always be *temporally oriented*.
2. A physical distribution system can be described completely for analytical purposes *only in terms of its inventories,* but not in terms only of its transportation elements.

If an integrated, accurate method of analyzing and controlling physical distribution systems is to be developed, time instead of space will be the relevant unifying dimension to be used.

Orientation of Location and Inventory Models

To date, the most popular approaches to location problems have been spatially oriented. The center-of-gravity method has been one of minimizing ton-miles accumulated between supply and demand points on a system. Where varying rates have applied to the ton-miles involved, a weighted ton-mile measure has been used. Nevertheless, with

the exception of Bowersox's use of transit time between a grocery warehouse and retail outlets in an urban setting,[9] the object of center-of-gravity models has been to minimize distance rather than time.

Linear programing models for location invariably have employed transportation costs between potential system nodes.[10] To the extent that transportation costs are assumed to be linear in relation to distance, this is a spatial measure. Finally, in the most extensively used models, based on heuristic programing, distance is the factor employed to describe nodal relationships.[11]

In contrast, inventory models have no spatial orientation in the context of the definition given earlier. The relationship of a demand point to its supply point is stated in terms of time for all models allowing uncertainty. Of course, the relevant time is not transit time between inventory locations, but rather the order-cycle time required to complete the course of communications and order shipment, extending from the point of order to the supply point and back again to the point of delivery.

A major preoccupation with the time dimension is characteristic of proponents of both optimization models and simulation models for inventory management.[12]

In total, a physical distribution system can be described in terms of its inventories and their determinants. But this requires a description of inventories in transit as well as at nodal points on a network. Thus, a system of three plants, two distribution warehouses, and ten markets arranged as in Figure 1 can be conceived of as having over 100 inventory "cells" of all or some goods in a product line.

The figure shows only 45 of the more important cells. Momentarily, any one cell or even most cells may be empty. Over time, however, all eventually may contain something. The elimination of a warehouse in Figure 1 would eliminate not 1 but 15 inventories and probably affect many of the remaining 30.

[9] Donald J. Bowersox, "An Analytical Approach to Warehouse Location," *Handling & Shipping,* Vol. 11 (February, 1962), pp. 17–20.

[10] For example, William J. Baumol and Philip Wolfe, "A Warehouse Location Problem," *Operations Research,* Vol. 6 (March–April, 1958), pp. 252–263.

[11] Alfred A. Kuehn and Michael J. Hamburger, "A Heuristic Program for Locating Warehouses," *Management Science,* vol. 9 (July, 1963), pp. 643–666.

[12] For examples of the former, see John F. Magee, *Production Planning and Inventory Control* (New York: McGraw-Hill Book Co., 1958), and Robert B. Fetter and Winston C. Dalleck, *Decision Models for Inventory Management* (Homewood, Illinois: Richard D. Irwin, Inc., 1961). An illustration of the latter is provided by Jay W. Forrester, *Industrial Dynamics* (Cambridge and New York: The M.I.T. Press and John Wiley & Sons, Inc., 1961), especially pp. 137–186.

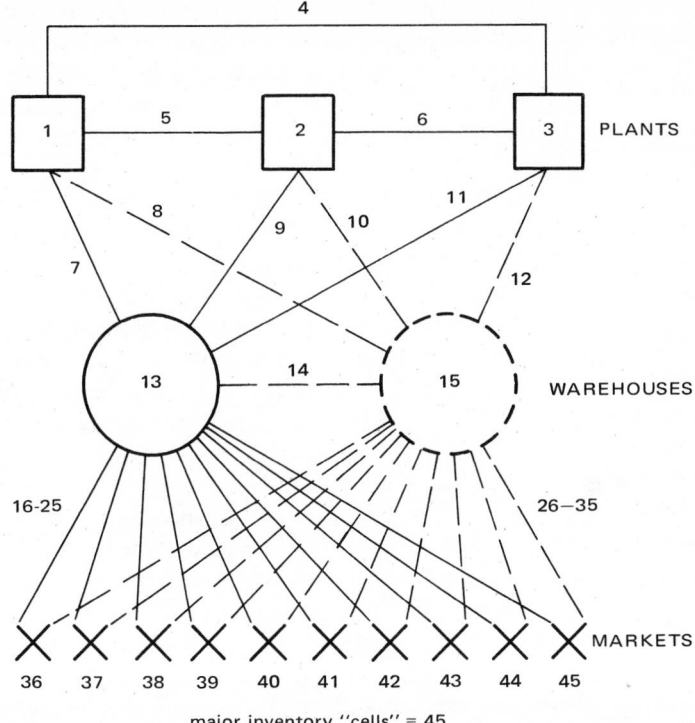

Figure 1 Designation of inventory cells in a system for physically distributing goods from three plants through two distribution warehouses to ten markets

Notice that the network in Figure 1 is dimensionless. Both distance and time are unsatisfactory dimensions for the graphic description of a physical distribution system. The shortcomings of distance as a measure have been discussed. Time as a determinant of inventory levels in various cells is a promising but confusing measure, for it takes on different meanings for inventories in transit, as opposed to those at nodal points.

The level of in-transit inventories is directly influenced, among other things, by transit times between a given set of nodes in a system. A different time period, that required for the completion of an order cycle, is relevant for a determination of the inventory levels at a nodal point.[13]

---

[13] Donald J. Bowersox implies this in his article, "Total Information Systems in Logistics," in J. L. Heskett, Editor, *Business Logistics—Appraisal and Prospect* (Stanford: Stanford University Graduate School of Business, 1965), pp. 109–122.

The first of these statements requires a re-evaluation of the assumption implicit in most location models—that in the location of one or more facilities on a network, a minimization of distance weighted by the freight volume to be moved between relevant existing nodes and the proposed nodes (least ton-mile points) will somehow lead to minimum transit times.

As has been pointed out above, where various transport methods can be employed to traverse a given distance, neither time nor cost necessarily bears a close relationship to distance.

On the other hand, the relevance of order-cycle times to nodal inventories requires an examination of the implicit assumption (stretched one step further) that distances between network nodes are somehow related to order-cycle times for goods ordered and shipped between them. The rationale for the assumption logically might be the direct relationships between distance and transit time on the one hand, and transit time and order-cycle time on the other.

However, time in transit represents roughly only 40% of total order-cycle time.[14] Furthermore, in a sample of means of order-cycle times for two categories of products, carefully measured several years ago, the relationship between order-cycle times and distances for shipments moving from various manufacturers to a distribution warehouse was so low as to be almost meaningless. More specifically, the coefficients of determination were .11 and .16 for drug and candy products, respectively.[15]

One additional argument can be given for the lack of relevance of spatially-oriented location models for the problem of physical distribution system design. Nearly all location models devised to date have had cost (weighted distance) minimization as their primary objective.[16] Unless demand is assumed constant regardless of a system design, cost minimization has little to do with profit maximization in a physical distribution system. In addition, the costs minimized in available

---

[14] Evidence of this is presented in Richard A. Johnson and Donald D. Parker, "Optimizing Customer Delivery Service with Improved Distribution," *Business Review,* vol. 21 (October, 1961), pp. 38–46, at p. 44; and in Paul R. Stephenson, *Manufacturers' Physical Distribution Service Knowledge and Penalties: An Experimental Analysis,* unpublished Master's thesis deposited in the library of The Ohio State University, 1963.

[15] Unpublished research by the author in collaboration with John Rider and Paul R. Stephenson.

[16] The one known exception is that reported in Frank H. Mossman and Newton Morton, *Logistics of Distribution Systems* (Boston: Allyn and Bacon, Inc., 1965), pp. 245–256, in which the effect of location on service and hence demand is explored in the context of a conventional location model.

spatial models often are not inclusive of all those incurred in physical-distribution activities.

In contrast, the time-oriented inventory model for conditions of uncertainty as a matter of course allows a consideration of order-cycle time and dependability as two of the determinants of demand. By facilitating the consideration of both demand (revenue) and costs, this type of model lends itself more readily than the spatially-oriented model to planning with a profit-maximization objective.

CONCLUSIONS

Location and inventory models can be used as the basis both for planning and operational control of logistics system elements. Even where both types of models have been employed in the same company, however, their dimensional inconsistencies have prevented their integration.

Concentration on spatial relationships in physical supply and distribution, although the product of nearly a hundred years of effort in the formulation of macro-economic theory, has not yielded a valid comprehensive approach to the description and analysis of physical distribution systems.

Rather, such a system can be viewed most productively as a set of actual or potential inventory cells linked and partially determined by time—transit time for those inventory cells in network links, order cycle time for those cells at network nodes.

Time rather than distance will be the unifying dimension of an integrated model for helping plan and control a logistics system. This model—adapted to each company's special needs—will combine elements of a temporally-oriented location model with an inventory model to produce information for planning purposes and a set of devices for the control of various elements of a company's logistics system.

REFERENCES

Charnes, A., Cooper, W. W., DeVoe, J. K., and Learner, D. B., "DEMON: Decision Mapping Via Optimum GO-NO Networks—A Model for Marketing New Products," *Management Science*, vol. 12, no. 11, July, 1966, pp. 865–887.

Duesenberry, Warren, "CPM for New Product Introduction," *Harvard Business Review,* July–August, 1967.

Forrester, Jay W., "Advertising: A Problem in Industrial Dynamics," *Harvard Business Review,* March–April, 1959.

Hawkins, Edward R., "Price Policies and Theory," *Journal of Marketing,* January, 1954.

Montgomery, David B., and Webster, Frederick W., Jr., "Application of Operations Research to Personal Selling Strategy," *Journal of Marketing,* January, 1968.

Pessimier, Edgar A., "Forecasting Brand Performance Through Simulation Experiments," *Journal of Marketing,* April, 1964.

Quandt, R. E., "Estimating the Effectiveness of Advertising: Some Pitfalls in Econometric Methods," *Journal of Marketing Research,* May, 1964.

Slater, Charles C., and Mossman, Frank H., "Positive Robinson-Patman Pricing," *Journal of Marketing,* April, 1967.

Urban, Glen L., "SPRINTER: A Tool for New Product Decision Makers," *Industrial Management Review,* Spring, 1967.

Vidale, M. L., and Wolfe, H. B., "An Operations Research Study of Sales Response to Advertising," *Operations Research,* June, 1961.

Weinberg, R. S., "Multiple Factor Breakeven Analysis: The Application of Operations Research Techniques to a Basic Problem of Management and Control," *Operations Research,* April, 1956.

Wong, Yang, "Critical Path Analysis for New Product Planning," *Journal of Marketing,* vol. 28, no. 4, October, 1964.

PART V | Market Information

The marketing information system is the basic structure which supports the work in the decision sciences. In a sense, then, the most important evolution taking place today is centered on the way in which information is processed and utilized.

The central theme in Chapters 10 and 11 of Part V is the concept of a marketing information system. What is a system? What is a system designed to do? In what way has concept of a marketing information system changed the traditional role of marketing research? How much is information worth? How would you measure the value of information? These are some of the questions that the reader should keep in mind as he reads the articles in Part V.

chapter 10 | Marketing Research and Marketing Information Systems

Since the marketing research department is the primary source of marketing information, we must examine the impact of the decision sciences on the traditional marketing research functions.

The application of the decision sciences to marketing problems places new demands on the kind and quality of information generated by the marketing research department. The implications are quite clear. Marketing research must concern itself more with integrating information flows with decision requirements. Furthermore, the information flows to the various decision points must be accurate and timely, whether the decision point be a machine, a man, or a department.

In the first article of this section, Brien and Stafford present the case for expanding traditional marketing research into marketing information systems. Today, the information needs of the marketer are substantially compounded, making the need for the implementation of marketing information systems all the greater.

In "Model Building in Marketing Research," Massy and Webster attempt to bring together the elements common to both quantitative and behavioral applications to marketing management. Both the quantitative and behavioral disciplines use scientific methodology in their approach to marketing problems.

The next article in this section, by Harder and Lindell, demonstrates the application of the PERT technique (described in Chapter 8) in marketing research.

In "How to Build a Marketing Information System," Cox and Good review some of the characteristics and advantages of a marketing information system and of the current state of the art. They then discuss some of the decisions necessary in developing the system. Despite the difficulties involved in implementing such an all-embracing system, the pressure to move in this direction is very great.

While areas other than marketing have used the techniques of information systems, Belden Menkus, in the final article, argues that the marketing function has been relatively untouched. According to Menkus, "the information needs of marketers demonstrate the almost classic failure of systems men to deal more than superficially with the functioning organization."

Marketing Information Systems: A New Dimension for Marketing Research

Richard H. Brien
James E. Stafford

Business enterprise in the United States is caught in an ironic dilemma: our economic system generates a massive volume of data daily, and the rate of information generation appears to be increasing exponentially; yet most managers continue to complain that they have insufficient, inappropriate, or untimely information on which to base operating decisions.

In 1958, Adrian McDonough observed: "Half the cost of running our economy is the cost of information. No other field offers such concentrated room for improvement as does information analysis."[1] Today, a decade later, the need for efficient information management is even greater, perhaps especially for marketing management since its job is to match the firm's products with dynamic markets. Marketing is inextricably caught up in the "Communications Revolution." The new era, "The Age of Information," will emphasize the information gathering and processing structure of the organization.

It is the contention of this article that the problem of securing adequate decision information for marketing must, and now can, be seen from a broader perspective than previously has been the case. In seeking to establish a new outlook on a matter it is often helpful to cast the problem in new terms. The new perspective from which this inquiry will be launched is that of "managerial systems." The process of developing timely, pertinent decision data for marketing management can now be characterized more meaningfully, even if somewhat prematurely, as the functioning of a "marketing information system" rather than simply as "marketing research."

Reprinted with permission from the *Journal of Marketing,* vol. 32, no. 3 (July, 1968), pp. 19–23, published by the American Marketing Association.

[1] "Today's Office—Room for Improvement," *Dun's Review and Modern Industry,* vol. 73 (September, 1958), p. 50.

THE ROLE OF MARKETING RESEARCH

Where does research fit into the marketing management process? If the marketing concept—with its emphasis on integrated decision-making—were widely accepted and implemented, the answer would be fairly clear. Research would be used to analyze specified relationships in the various functional areas of marketing, but the emphasis would be on its use in a coordinated, systematic fashion in order to make the total marketing strategy of the firm more efficient. (See Figure 1.)

Research findings would serve at the outset as a basis for establishing objectives and formulating an apparently optimal plan. At this stage the role of research essentially would be *to predict* the results of alternative business decisions (for example, a "penetration" price versus a "skimming" price, or information dissemination through salesmen rather than through advertising). (See the "A" feedbacks in Figure 1.)

If the research effort were extended full cycle, periodic post hoc studies would be conducted *to evaluate* the execution of specific aspects or phases of the marketing program. ("B" feedbacks in Figure 1.) In this role, research would provide the basis for control, modification, or redirection of the overall program.

Control and modification (or redirection), in sum, represent *reformulation,* and the "B" feedbacks (evaluative) in fact would become "A" feedbacks (formulative), for the succeeding stage of the marketing program. This condition simply underscores the fact that marketing management is an ongoing process, or—in the newer terminology—a dynamic system.

Formulative and evaluative information can also come *from inside the firm,* notably from the accounting department. This information flow typically is not considered part of "marketing research." It is definitely an integral part, however, of a marketing information system.

Under the marketing concept, research should also help to anticipate new profit opportunities for the firm in the form of new products or services. ("C" feedback in Figure 1.) In many U.S. industries—especially consumer goods industries—the rate of product innovation, the rate of new product failure, and the cost of new product failure are all extremely high and still rising. To survive in such dynamic markets the firm must try to develop a sensitivity to changes in consumer behavior and in the conditions that influence behavior, both of which create opportunities for successful new products.

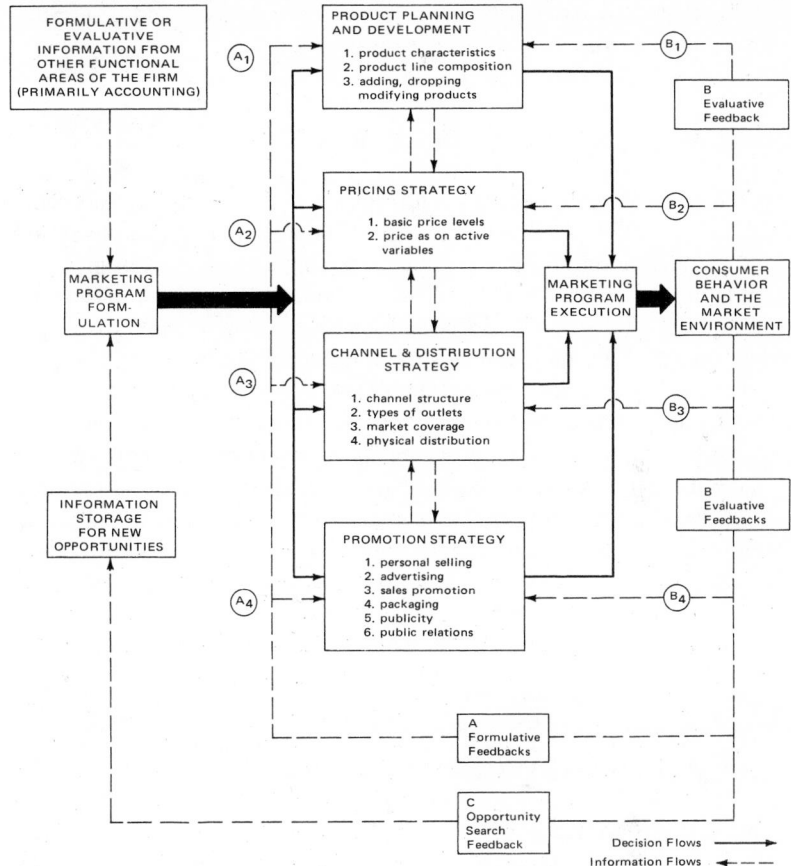

Figure 1 The marketing management process and information flow

It is meaningless to talk of a new product without considering at the same time the related marketing decisions (the rest of that product's marketing mix) that will have to be made. This consideration would bring the cycle back to the formulative role of research (the "A" feedbacks), suggesting again that marketing research really *should be a coordinating agent.* Each marketing decision should be thought of as an input in the dynamic system, and research should be used as an agent to assist in phasing the inputs. The common goal of the decision inputs is the profitable satisfaction of consumer needs or wants; this brings the matter back to the marketing concept, and the package seems reasonably complete. In fact, if marketing research and the marketing concept had this kind of relationship in widespread

practice, the case for marketing information systems would be considerably weakened.

RESEARCH BY FITS AND STARTS

A recent survey revealed that unfortunately there is still considerable confusion and wide divergence of opinion regarding the definition and managerial implications of the marketing concept.[2] Especially disappointing was the failure of many companies to cite customer-orientation and integrated decision-making as important aspects of the concept. One of the consequences of this narrow view has been the evolution of marketing research somewhat "by fits and starts."

A widely used definition of marketing research is "the systematic gathering, recording, and analyzing of data about problems relating to the marketing of goods and services."[3] Unfortunately, the research procedure has tended to be unsystematic, to emphasize data collection per se instead of the development of decision-pertinent information, and to concern itself with isolated problems almost on an ad hoc basis. "There is a widespread failure to visualize marketing research as a continuing process of inquiry in which executives are helped to think more effectively."[4]

TOWARD MARKETING INFORMATION SYSTEMS

The systems approach to marketing management is breathing new life into marketing research. The emphasis that systems theory places on interaction and integration in the decision-making process makes it clear that the particularistic, "brush-fire" approach that has characterized traditional marketing research is rapidly becoming obsolete. What is needed is "a *marketing intelligence* system tailored to the needs of each marketer. Such a system would serve as the ever-alert nerve center of the marketing operation."[5]

[2] Martin L. Bell, *Marketing: Concepts and Strategy* (Boston: Houghton Mifflin Company, 1966), p. 10.

[3] Committee on Definitions of the American Marketing Association, Ralph S. Alexander, Chairman, *Marketing Definitions: A Glossary of Marketing Terms* (Chicago: American Marketing Association, 1962), pp. 16–17.

[4] Joseph W. Newman, "Put Research Into Marketing Decisions," *Harvard Business Review,* vol. 40 (March–April, 1962), p. 106.

[5] Lee Adler, "Systems Approach to Marketing," *Harvard Business Review,* vol. 45 (May–June, 1967), p. 110.

The "nerve center" concept is the theme used by Philip Kotler who has drafted a blueprint for a new organizational unit within the firm, the Marketing Information and Analysis Center (MIAC).[6] MIAC represents a complete overhaul and expansion of the marketing research department into a comprehensive executive marketing information service.

Definition of MIS

Despite minor variations in terminology, it is clear that many of the critics of the narrow view of the role of marketing research are advocating a common concept—"the concept of careful search to generate flow of ideas and information which will help executives make better decisions."[7]

The notion of a sustained flow of decision-information leads to the term, "marketing information system," defined as follows:

A structured, interacting complex of persons, machines and procedures designed to generate an orderly flow of pertinent information collected from both intra- and extra-firm sources, for use as the bases for decision-making in specified responsibility areas of marketing management.

It will be helpful to take a closer look at the essential components of the definition: first, a *structured, interacting complex.* The important notion here is that the marketing information system is a carefully developed master plan for information flow, with explicit objectives and a home in the formal organization. Successful information systems will not evolve spontaneously within the organization, nor will they result if their creation is left exclusively to information technicians. Donald Cox and Robert Good point out that a characteristic common to each of the companies that so far has had success with its marketing information system is the *support of top management.*[8]

A marketing information system is a structured, interacting complex of *persons, machines, and procedures,* requiring the coordinated efforts of many departments and individuals, including:

Top management
Marketing management, brand management

---

[6] Philip Kotler, "A Design for the Firm's Marketing Nerve Center," *Business Horizons,* vol. 9 (Fall, 1966), p. 70.

[7] Newman, op. cit., p. 106.

[8] Donald F. Cox and Robert E. Good, "How to Build a Marketing Information System," *Harvard Business Review,* vol. 45, no. 3 (May–June, 1967), p. 149.

Sales management
New product groups
Market research personnel
Control and finance departments
Systems analysts and designers
Operations researchers, statisticians, and model builders
Programmers
Computer equipment experts and suppliers.[9]

It is clear that in traditional management terms both line and staff personnel inevitably will be involved in any marketing information system. Decision-makers will have to be a great deal more precise in specifying their information needs, and a complete crew of information specialists will be called upon to satisfy them.

What is not clear is the determination of the most effective organization pattern for implementing and administering the system. In fact, the organization problem is probably the greatest deterrent to the more rapid and widespread diffusion of the information systems concept. The question, like many others in the area of organization structure, is not generically answerable; each firm's system will have to be tailor-made.

One of the major factors that makes it meaningful to talk of information systems is the tremendous improvement since World War II in information handling *technology and machinery*. The building of the first primitive computer, only slightly more than two decades ago, has been designated the beginning of a revolution in the information sciences.

There has been some confusion, however, about the relationship between computers and information systems. They are not synonymous; nor is either the sine qua non of the other. The system is the structure and procedure of the entire organization's communicative process; the computer is a processing device that may or may not be included in the information system.

The consideration of the use of computers has, however, forced many organizations to pay explicit attention to their information systems. "The flexibility and power of the new tool, as well as its great cost, has caused many managers to think for the first time of formally planning their information flows and processing functions."[10]

[9] Ibid.

[10] Frederick G. Withington, *The Use of Computers in Business Organizations* (Reading, Mass.: Addison-Wesley, 1966), p. 3.

Business information systems include many machines other than the computer and some of them promise to have an impact on future systems that will rival the computer's influence. In particular, data copying, storage, and retrieval machines have greatly expanded management's information processing capability.

It is estimated that in 1966 some half a million duplicating machines spewed out 400 billion copies.[11] At the same time, a new document storage system was developed permitting the storage of up to 500,000 single-page documents on a single 7,200 foot reel of videotape. This means that roughly 20,000 articles or chapters from books could be stored on one reel with a retrieval time measured in seconds.

But the physical capacity to generate and process fantastic volumes of data at very high speed is an asset only if the types of data to be gathered and the sources from which they are to be elicited are carefully prescribed. The definition of a marketing information system alleged that it is *designed to generate an orderly flow of pertinent information, collected from both intra- and extra-firm sources.*

Computer-based Reporting Systems

Internal information includes fundamental records of costs, shipments, and sales and any analyses of these that can be made to measure the firm's performance (distribution cost analysis, market shares by product and region, and the like). The computer and more progressive accounting departments that see their role as the provision of management information rather than as simply "score-keeping" have been two of the most important contributors to the integration of such data, on a regular basis, into the marketing information flow.

Many companies are experimenting with "computerized marketing information" in an attempt to shorten the delay between the performance of their products in the market and the receipt of performance reports. In doing so, they stand to sharpen their strategy by gaining valuable lead-time over their competitors.

One producer and nation-wide marketer of consumer goods gets monthly reports on 3,000 key accounts 20 days earlier than before, thanks to computer-based reporting systems. Each account is compared with its performance at the same point in time during the previous year and with the company's current total volume in the

[11] E. B. Weiss, "The Communications Revolution and How It Will Affect All Business and All Marketing," a special issue reprinted from *Advertising Age* (Chicago: Advertising Publications, Inc., 1966), p. 22.

particular market zone. Also provided are gross daily tabulations for each package size of each brand by geographic district.

When the doors open each morning at another company, a major grocery products mnaufacturer, marketing management has a complete sales analysis and inventory position as of closing time the previous day. The data are fed by teletypewriter from the company's sales offices and warehouses to a central computer which analyzes the day's orders. In addition, each salesman is required to "mark sense" his daily call reports and send them in to headquarters each evening for computer analysis. Once accumulated, these reports on the in-store impact of frontings, shelf positions, and point-of-sale materials provide marketing management with an up-to-date retail product-movement picture.[12]

Integrating Research into the MIS

The most important notion in these examples is that a timely, basic data flow has been established to chart the firm's progress and raise warning signals when there is a marketing malfunction. Such a framework will make additional data needs much clearer, allowing special supplementary information to be collected, *as needed,* from external sources through surveys, panels or experiments. At this point, then, the proper order will have been established: *the need for conducting "marketing research" and the technique to be used will be determined in the context of specific managerial information requirements.*

Such an approach will help assure that any data gathered are *pertinent,* another important aspect of the definition of a marketing information system. It is perhaps a more grievous sin to collect unnecessary or redundant information than it is to fail to collect any data at all about a particular matter. Superfluous information costs money to develop and wastes decision-makers' time; it represents a serious misallocation of managerial resources. It must be remembered, the definition asserts, that the data generated are to be used as *the bases for decision-making in specified responsibility areas of marketing management.*

Thus, the questions of the types of data the information system is to generate and the sources from which it is to elicit the data really can be answered only in the framework of a careful designation of the organizational decision-structure and the specification of the informa-

---

[12] Ibid., pp. 13–14.

tion requirements for the decision process. In fact, according to many organizational theorists, information processing and decision-making are inseparable in practice. A decision occurs only on "the receipt of some kind of communication, it consists of a complicated process of combining communications from various sources and it results in the transmission of further communications."[13]

Mr. Paul Funk, executive vice-president of McCann/ITSM, contends that marketing information management *is* the basic business of business:

> Only by putting together an over-all construction of the total marketing process; only by identifying—and in most instances by visualizing—inter-relationships, information flows, concurrent and sequential work patterns and critical decision points can one truly grasp control of the bewildering and complex range of activities engaged in by the present-day major corporation.[14]

The pursuit of marketing information systems, then, really involves much more than expanding and automating the data gathering process. It is an inextricable part of the larger pursuit of more efficient forms and methods of organization for marketing management.

We Are Running Late

There is ample evidence that marketing decision-making is becoming more complex, making the need for a systematic approach to information management all the greater. First, there is a growing complexity of the areas that have to be managed, largely a function of the tendency toward larger scale enterprise. Second, as expanded marketing effort takes the firm across existing environmental frontiers, whether geographic, economic or social (or, more likely, all three), the information needs of the enterprise are substantially compounded. It is highly likely that the most crucial constraint currently imposed on the growth of international marketing, for example, is the dearth of pertinent decision-information.

But perhaps the most compelling argument for marketing information systems is the "Information Explosion" itself. The world's store

[13] John T. Dorsey, Jr., "A Communication Model for Administration," *Administrative Science Quarterly,* vol. 2 (December, 1957), p. 309.

[14] "Why Industrial Marketers Aren't Using Computers," *Industrial Marketing,* vol. 51 (November, 1966), pp. 88–89.

of knowledge has allegedly doubled during the past decade and is expected at least to double again in the next decade.

Information, including management information, is growing by the microsecond and even nanosecond. We cannot turn off the flow. We had therefore better learn to control it—and we are already running late.[15]

[15] Howell M. Estes, "Will Managers Be Overwhelmed by the Information Explosion?," *Armed Forces Management,* vol. 13 (December, 1966), p. 84.

Model-Building in Marketing Research

William F. Massy
Frederick E. Webster, Jr.

The constantly increasing influence of a scientific approach to the study and practice of marketing, and management in general, is one of the most salient developments of our decade. There have been very few attempts, however, to relate the various developments to one another. The current literature is rich in reports of the application of operations research techniques, such as mathematical programming, queuing theory and Bayesian decision theory, to marketing problems. Then there are the statistical model builders with their multiple correlation, maximum likelihood, and factor analyses. Concepts from the behavioral sciences, such as cognitive dissonance, selective perception, and opinion leadership—to indicate only three of the ideas contributed by psychology and sociology—are equally glamorous. No wonder many of us are confused by the volume and diversity of this new influx—the uncounted speeches, articles, and books that implore us to embrace some new and distinctively different concept or methodology.

The confusion generated by many voices often talking in seemingly contradictory terms has obscured the basic likeness of the various "scientific" approaches. Proponents of the application of quantitative and behavioral concepts to marketing are really striving for the same goal. The objective of each, very simply, is to inject *the scientific point of view* into the management decision process. Their common argument is that problems must be attacked systematically, facts obtained by means of measuring procedures with known properties, alternatives evaluated as objectively as possible and, finally, the results of problem-solving activity presented in a form that permits equally systematic analysis of outcomes, after the fact. Thus, each problem and its solu-

Reprinted with permission from the *Journal of Marketing Research,* vol. 1, no. 2 (May, 1964), pp. 9–13, published by the American Marketing Association.

tion could effectively add to the storehouse of knowledge being accumulated by the firm and, hopefully, by the marketing profession as a whole.

A set of unifying principles is needed—a broad conceptual framework for relating these apparently separate scientific approaches and showing the relevance and domain of each's importance. We hope to contribute to the desired structure by showing that the roles of the operations research specialist on the one hand, and the statistician, the behavioral scientist, and the marketing research analyst on the other, are mutually supporting so far as the solution of management problems is concerned. We shall also try to indicate the way existing marketing research departments can maximize their contribution to the use of scientific methods in marketing.

THE RELATIONSHIP BETWEEN BEHAVIORAL AND OPTIMIZATION MODELS

Applications of the scientific method to marketing problems can be grouped into two classes of study: (i) behavioral relationships and (ii) normative decision rules. Models of behavior reflect known or conjectured facts about the world. (We shall see that they may or may not stem specifically from the "behavioral sciences.") They are designed to describe how individuals or firms *do behave*. Optimization models, on the other hand, suggest how economic units ought to behave if they are to achieve some explicitly stated objective, such as the maximization of profits. Separation of models into these two classes is an important step toward rationalizing the scientific approach in marketing.

The distinction between behavioral and optimization models can be better understood if we compare it with the similar dichotomy involving a business firm's controllable and uncontrollable variables. In marketing, controllable or policy variables include the product, price, promotion, and channels of distribution. Consumer and trade behavior, and the factors that influence it, are generally considered uncontrollable by the individual marketing organization. A third class, criterion variables, can be defined in terms of the other two types:

Criterion = F (controllables and uncontrollables), where the notation $y = F(x)$ is read "y is a function of (depends upon) x." A more specific example of this kind of relationship might be:

$$\text{Sales} = F \text{ (price and consumers' income)}.$$

Here a firm's sales volume is assumed dependent upon its price and consumers' incomes. The former is a controllable variable while the latter is uncontrollable, so far as an individual company is concerned. These relationships are examples of behavioral models. Consumer purchasing behavior leads to sales, and this activity depends upon the product cost and the income available to support its consumption. By attempting to specify the form of this functional relationship, a firm may well come to understand more clearly the nature of its market. If the function can be determined with relative accuracy, it can forecast sales for particular price levels, given existing consumer income conditions. By itself, the behavioral model suggests no value judgment about whether the activity whose nature it reflects is "good" or "bad" —from either the viewpoint of a particular business firm or anyone else. Rather, it attempts to summarize and hopefully quantify the behavior patterns of certain groups participating in the marketing system, in order to improve understanding and provide better forecasts of future behavior.

Optimization models play the opposite role: they provide the value judgments that a manager needs in order to make decisions. The decision maker cannot change the form of the behavioral relationship between the controllable and uncontrollable variables on the one hand, and the criterion variables on the other. He can, however, react to it by adjusting his policies to yield the best possible criterion value, given the current status of the uncontrollable factors. Where decisions are amenable to formal treatment, optimization models provide systematic methods for deciding what policies will maximize the criterion variables.

An optimization model based on the example given above might well involve the maximization of profits through adjustment of the controllable variable (price), conditional on the uncontrollable variable (income). As every beginning economics student knows, the optimality conditions for this situation are that marginal revenue be equated to marginal cost. Total revenue, and hence marginal revenue, are linked to price by the behavioral model. So is marginal cost, since costs are assumed to depend partly upon the firm's output level, which in turn depends upon the price variable. The optimization model for this situation suggests that the decision maker set his price at the level at which marginal revenue equals marginal cost. If consumer income and the behavioral relationship between price and sales (given income) are known, and the necessary information about costs is available, the optimization model provides the information necessary for price setting.

Optimization models provide the linkage between behavioral relationships and such criterion variables as profits or sales. They are designed to help decision makers use their knowledge about the world wisely. But it is important to remember that the results obtainable from the best optimization model can be only as good as the behavioral information that is used as input to the model.

The use of optimization models tends to be associated with the operations research analyst, since the better known tools of his trade (e.g., mathematical programming and statistical decision theory) are designed to find policies that will maximize profits or minimize costs. But it is not unusual for the operations researcher to find himself building behavioral as well as optimization models because no appropriate behavioral relationships are available for the situation he wants to study. In fact, the effective application of optimization models to marketing problems has been hindered by the lack of reliable descriptive models of market behavior. Attempts to bridge this gap with intuitively developed models, based on tenuous assumptions, have not produced convincing results. Many applications of valid optimization models have been open to criticism because of the weakness of their support of behavioral models. Discussions of optimization models in the marketing literature have sometimes been unconvincing because the validation of behavioral assumptions has been left to the reader, who may be unable to bridge the gap sufficiently to see the relevance of the proposed normative techniques.

There has been no lack of published expository material on the use of optimization models in marketing. For example, linear programming and constrained marginal analysis have been discussed in an excellent article by Baumol and Sevin [1]. Statistical decision theory has been well covered in articles by Roberts [13], Green [6], and Buzzell and Slater [2]. Kotler [7] reviews these and several types of optimization models. The mathematical details of the techniques can be readily obtained from any good operations research textbook. So far, however, there has been little attempt to exhibit examples of behavioral models as important entities forming a distinct class within the "scientific approach," *per se*. The following examples are a modest start in this direction.

SOME BEHAVIORAL MODELS REVIEWED

Perhaps the best known behavioral model to appear in the marketing literature was developed by Vidale and Wolfe [14], who studied actual sales results for selected products in carefully controlled markets.

They were able to identify three parameters in the relationship between sales and advertising: (1) the "sales decay constant"; (2) the "sales response constant"; and (3) the "saturation level." The sales decay constant is a measure of the tendency for sales to decrease in the absence of advertising. The sales response constant expresses the change in sales dollars resulting from a change in advertising dollars. The saturation level is that level of advertising activity above which no additional sales can be obtained. Based on these empirically estimable parameters the model was mathematically extended to predict the sales gain resulting from an advertising "pulse" and the return on capital invested in advertising for particular products.

Palda [11] explored another model for assessing the response of sales to advertising. Working with yearly time series data for the Lydia H. Pinkham Company, he found that advertising expenditures affected sales not only in the current year, but in subsequent years as well. The effect of a given year's investment was greatest in the ensuing period, and then declined gradually to zero with the passage of time. Palda's attempts to estimate the numerical values of the paramenters of this "distributed lag model" were generally successful.

Cyert and March have reported a successful attempt to build a model of pricing behavior for the department store appliance buyer. Once again, this model was based upon an emipirical study. Cyert and March used the tool of logical flow analysis to model the buyer's decision-making process for price-setting. This model was then put on a computer and the resultant simulation was successful in predicting more than 90 percent of the prices set by this buyer, *to the penny* [5].

Kuehn's [8] model of the brand switching behavior for customers of a frequently purchased product draws heavily upon psychological learning theory. His approach was based on a Markov probability structure, which can be used to predict the probability that a consumer will buy a particular brand on his next outing given knowledge of the last brand he purchased. Rather than assume that the transition probabilities were constant for each family in the sample, however, he arranged his model so that the sequence of brands bought on several preceding occasions affected the odds on the next one. This is equivalent to saying that consumers learn to like (or dislike) particular brands through exposure and use. The mathematical relationships used to express this relationship were based on the work of certain experimental psychologists, and the empirical estimates of the parameters were obtained by using actual marketing data.

Cox [3] has developed a behavioral model for the relationship between available product information, customer self-confidence, and persuasibility in the personal selling context. "Subjects were asked to

evaluate 'two brands' of nylon stockings and to indicate how confident they were about their evaluation. The stockings were in fact identical, except for the identifying letters R and N. After making the evaluations (on 18 attributes) subjects heard a tape-recording of a salesgirl's opinion that Brand R stockings were better—on six attributes. Subjects then re-evaluated the nylons; evaluated the salesgirl; indicated how confident they were about their evaluations of the salesgirl; answered some questions on stocking buying habits and attitudes; completed three personality tests (one of which was a measure of self-confidence); and finally provided information on their age, education, marital status, and income" [4]. It was found that subjects who ranked either "high" or "very low" in self-confidence were less likely to change their evaluations of the stockings after being exposed to the "persuasion" than those who fell in the medium range. A theoretical explanation of the phenomenon was proposed, based on the empirical findings of the study.

All of these results have an important element in common: *they are based upon the formal analysis of some kind of empirical data.* All attempt to provide an explanation of an aspect of the real world, and in each case the findings are presented in a form that allows testing by other researchers using their own fresh samples of data. They are all models of human behavior, either at the level of the individual or averaged over identifiable groups of people. The behavior is modeled as it appears to exist in the world and not as the researcher or some decision maker might want it to exist.

The citations demonstrate that neither the *language* in which a behavioral model is couched nor the source of the assumptions on which it is based determines the quality of the result [9]. Vidale and Wolfe started from what appear to be "common sense" assumptions about the form of the response of sales to advertising, estimated the parameters of this relationship statistically from empirical data, and extended the scope of the model by means of mathematical manipulations. Palda also used the language of mathematics in presenting his model; he based his work on economic theory and some empirical findings of econometricians. Cyert and March based their results on direct observations of the behavior of their subject; they used the language of the logical flow diagram. Kuehn used a mathematical model developed by the quantitative learning theorist in psychology. Cox's work was also derived from psychological underpinnings, although his models were more verbal in character than any of the others. (Note that hypotheses derived from verbal models can be tested quantitatively.) In spite of their diversity of approach, all the models attempt to shed light on human behavior as it is affected by marketing variables. Each

used the assumptions and techniques that seemed to be most appropriate to the situation, and each contributed to the needs of management decision makers.

ROLE OF THE MARKETING RESEARCH FUNCTION

Marketing research departments have a vital role to play in bringing together behavioral models and optimization models. This role may take them considerably beyond the limits of marketing research as it has been defined in many industrial firms.

Marketing research has been defined by the American Marketing Association as "the gathering, recording, and analyzing of all facts about problems relating to the transfer and sale of goods and services from producer to consumer" [12]. To achieve validity and reliability, marketing research measurement procedures and methods of analysis must conform to generally accepted scientific standards. That is, they must be objective and, at least in principle, in a form that can be checked through replication. There is no doubt that the marketing researcher falls into the category of "scientist" as discussed in this paper. Yet the experience of many firms would indicate that market research has failed to live up to its promise. Some facts obtained through research are of questionable relevance for management, and others that are potentially important are not organized or presented in an effective fashion. Why is it that some highly professional research efforts fail to have the impact on marketing decisions that was originally expected by both the researcher and the management sponsor?

The AMA definition of marketing research stresses both measurement and analysis, but many studies concentrate on the former and leave the latter to the intuition of management. What is analysis in the marketing research context? In fundamental terms, it means building a predictive model of some aspect of individual, group, or organizational behavior and relating the model to the problem of management decision making. Both behavioral and optimization models are necessary for the effective utilization of marketing research data. The professional researcher can make a significant contribution to the modeling process. Indeed, the marketing researcher must concern himself with analysis and, subsequently, model-building, if he is to help management get full mileage out of market research data.

How far should a typical marketing research department try to carry the modeling process? While the answer to this question depends upon the attitudes of management, the existence of other staff departments within the company (e.g., an organized operations research

group), and the particular skills available within the department itself, it appears that marketing researchers should generally concentrate on behavioral rather than optimization models. There are two reasons for this view.

1. The resources required for building and testing behavioral models are more compatible with the skills traditionally associated with the marketing research function than are those necessary for work in the area of formal optimization methods. The competent behavioral modeler must first of all have a working knowledge of inferential and descriptive statistics. Techniques based on regression, discriminant, and factor analyses are extremely useful in this kind of work, for example. He must have the ability to express relationships between variables in mathematical terms, and be able to deduce the behavioral implications of particular models. Use of the computer for statistical analysis and the exploration of complex models through simulation is rapidly becoming important.

On the other hand, the behavioral model builder often does not need the level of mathematical ability required to find optimal solutions to particular decision problems. Leaving the underpinnings of statistical theory aside, the behavioral analyst uses mathematics as a language for the description and analysis of phenomena rather than as a method for the *solution* of complex mathematical problems. While sophistication is a must in either case, the inventory of mathematical techniques required for the former is much smaller than it is for the latter.

Finally, the behavioral model builder requires conceptual inputs from the behavioral sciences, and from the distilled experience of managers themselves. He must know how and where to find empirical data that are compatible with the postulates of his behavioral model. These requirements represent a fairly direct extension of the marketing researcher's present role.

2. Optimization analysis can be more effectively handled outside the marketing research department. The rationale for this view is clear if the company in question has an organized operations research group. Members of this organization will be trained in the application of formal optimization methods to management problems. If operations research has not been applied to marketing problems in the past, progress in behavioral model building within the marketing research department should provide increasing opportunities for applications in the future. The differences between the skills required for handling the two types of models suggest that a division of labor between the two scientific approaches is in order. Of course there will be a strong

need for continuing effective liaison between these two research groups.

The marketing research department's role in optimization analysis may be more controversial in companies without an organized operations research function, but the generalization given above can still be defended. It can be very difficult for the empirical specialist, who must often spend considerable time studying behavioral phenomena that may be fairly narrow in definition, to switch gears and reconsider his work within the global framework of management's problems. The marketing research professional may not fully understand the objectives of the company or the constraints within which its policies must be formulated; and there is always a danger that he will miss important questions not covered by his department's work. Behavioral analysis must be guided by management's decision needs, but in application it is directed toward phenomena that exist outside the company. In contrast, the actual decision process and the optimization models that contribute to better decision making are oriented inward, conditional upon external factors. It is hard to wear both hats at the same time.

Newman's [10] concept of the "research generalist" is designed to fill this gap between the professional researcher and the management decision maker. The role of the research generalist is defined as: (1) establishing mutually satisfactory relationships between the two parties through effective exchange of information about objectives and findings; (2) suggesting and planning an effective research program and seeing to it that appropriate kinds of resources are brought to bear on the problem; and (3) helping to implement the results of the research by working with the marketing manager. In the context of this article, the research generalist has the responsibility for (i) helping to determine what areas of market behavior need to be explored and what kinds of models will be appropriate, and (ii) helping management achieve better decisions based on the information contained in the completed behavioral model. If possible, the research generalist should call upon the services of operations research analysts for formalizing optimization procedures, just as he relies on the marketing research department for behavioral research.

SUMMARY

In summary, we have argued that the relationship between behavioral and optimization models has often been obscured. While these two manifestations of the scientific method in business are different by

virtue of their subject matter and skill requirements, they share a common orientation and neither can fully succeed without the other. The application of optimization techniques to marketing problems has sometimes been less than fruitful because of a failure to understand the importance of the underlying behavioral model that specifies the relationships among the variables of the problem. Formal optimization methods can succeed only if they are built upon sound behavioral foundations. Even where decision problems are too complex to be amenable to formal treatment, the marketing manager can increase the effectiveness of his judgment by using whatever rigorously determined behavioral information is available.

Progress in the application of scientific methods to marketing can be expedited if we continually keep in mind the relationship between the marketing researcher (who studies behavioral phenomena), the operations analyst (who prescribes problem solutions), and the research generalist who can help bridge the gaps between the scientific approaches and between them and marketing management.

REFERENCES

1. William J. Baumol and Charles H. Sevin, "Marketing Costs and Mathematical Programming," *Harvard Business Review,* 35 (September–October 1957), 52–60.

2. Robert D. Buzzell and Charles C. Slater, "Decision Theory and Marketing Management," *Journal of Marketing,* 26 (July 1962), 7–16.

3. Donald F. Cox, "Information and Uncertainty: Their Effects on Consumer Product Evaluations." Unpublished doctoral dissertation, Graduate School of Business Administration, Harvard University, 1962.

4. —— and Raymond Bauer, "Self-Confidence and Persuasibility in Women." Unpublished paper, Graduate School of Business Administration, Harvard University, September 1962, 6.

5. R. M. Cyert and J. G. March, *A Behavioral Theory of the Firm,* Englewood Cliffs, N.J.: Prentice-Hall, Inc., 1963.

6. Paul E. Green, "Bayesian Decision Theory in Pricing Strategy," *Journal of Marketing,* 27 (January 1963), 5–14.

7. Philip Kotler, "The Use of Mathematical Models in Marketing," *Journal of Marketing,* 27 (October 1963), 31–41.

8. Alfred A. Kuehn, "Consumer Brand Choice—A Learning Process?" in R. E. Frank, A. A. Kuehn and W. F. Massy, *Quantitative Techniques in Marketing Analysis,* Homewood, Ill.: Richard D. Irwin, Inc., 1962, 390–403.

9. William F. Massy and Jim D. Savvas, "Logical Flow Models for Marketing Analysis," *Journal of Marketing,* 28 (January 1964), 30–37.

10. Joseph W. Newman, "Put Research Into Marketing Decisions," *Harvard Business Review,* 40 (March–April 1962), 105–112.

11. Kristian S. Palda, "The Measurement of Cumulative Advertising Effects." Unpublished Ph.D. dissertation, Graduate School of Business, University of Chicago, 1962.

12. "Report of the Definitions Committee," *Journal of Marketing,* 12 (October 1948), 210.

13. Harry V. Roberts, "Bayesian Statistics in Marketing," *Journal of Marketing,* 27 (January 1963), 1–4.

14. M. L. Vidale and H. B. Wolfe, "An Operations-Research Study of Sales Response to Advertising," *Operations Research,* V (June 1957), 370–81. Reprinted in Bass *et al.* (eds.), *Mathematical Models and Methods in Marketing,* Homewood, Ill.: Richard D. Irwin, Inc., 1961, 363–374.

Using PERT in Marketing Research

Virgil E. Harder
Frank R. Lindell

The basic methodological aspects of marketing research are readily available. Any good marketing research text, for example, offers a "list" of items that must be investigated if one is to properly research a given basic marketing objective. When a researcher tries to use this list, however, certain practical problems face him.

To structure the problems in a meaningful way, the following question is posed: How can a marketing department (or investigator) provide systematic order to the research methodology when determining the feasibility of producing and marketing a new product? How well that question is answered depends upon how well the department or investigator determines

The areas (task objectives) to be researched

The sequence of interrelationships of the areas

The cost of researching each area

The time schedule for researching each area.

A workable body of methodology exists whereby one can determine the areas to be researched. The other aspects of the marketing research program, however, are not yet as well set forth in the literature. The element lacking is a means for integrating the various methodological aspects of the research program into some sort of system or network[1] that allows for control of:

Reprinted with permission from *Business Horizons,* vol. 9, no. 1 (Spring, 1966), pp. 91–102, published by Indiana University.

[1] For a general discussion of systems theory in business, see Richard A. Johnson, Fremont E. Kast, and James E. Rosenzweig, *The Theory and Management of Systems* (New York: McGraw-Hill Book Company, Inc., 1963).

When (in terms of time) *what* (the task objectives) shall be done by *whom* (in terms of resources)

When (in terms of quality) *what* (the task objectives) is complete.

Controls are necessary if one wants to make efficient allocation of resources, funds, and so on to the various task objectives. In addition, feedback is needed to permit measurement of performance against the task objectives, budget allocations, and time allocations. Thus, a desirable addition to existing marketing research methodology would be a technique that allows the integration of sequence, time, and feedback with the various task objectives. The result would be a system or network of established schedules for the marketing research program. Such a technique already exists—PERT (Program Evaluation and Review Technique). The purpose of this article, therefore, is to illustrate how PERT can be used in marketing research as a technique to integrate the various task objectives into a network or system. Selections can be made from many marketing objectives—for example, determination of the feasibility of moving into a new market or new area with an existing product, or attempting to increase share of market. The selection of a particular marketing objective for illustration and elaboration in this article is, therefore, purely a device of convenience in order to make the discussion more meaningful.

THE POTENTIAL OF PERT

PERT is based on the concept that in any program there are three variables: time, resources, and technical performance.[2] Since its inception by the armed services (during the development of the Polaris missile), the technique has won prominence as a useful tool in development of prototype items such as ships, airplanes, and missiles. Much credit has been given PERT for the successful completion, in compliance with an established schedule, of many production items. If PERT can be successfully used as a technique in the area of production, then such a technique should offer potential for similar use in marketing research—since the principal difference is mainly the form of the end product.

Successful use of this method depends upon integration of the various research task objectives into a sequential system. The investigator

[2] United States Air Force, *Pert-Time System Description Manual,* I (September, 1963), p. I-1.

must arrange the task objectives into a sequential order—into a network. To illustrate the mechanics of this network-building procedure, a PERT program for a hypothetical product is used in this article. The objective is to build a network of task objectives (in sequence) that are necessary in evaluating the feasibility of producing and marketing a new product. After the mechanics for using the technique have been explained, it will then be possible to visualize how portions of the network or system can be eliminated and other portions expanded to adapt the procedures to studies with varying degrees of complexity.

THE MECHANICS

Before detailed PERT networks can be developed, a general program plan must be devised that consists of the large and most important phases of the marketing study. These broad areas are set up schematically in Figure 1, which is a broad picture of the scope, sequence, and

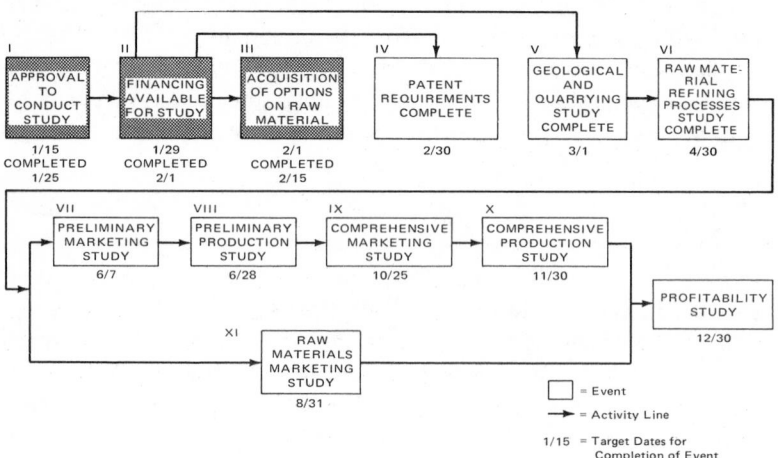

Figure 1   General PERT program for a new-product study

anticipated schedule for completion of the study. More detailed supplementary PERT programs are then designed for each of the broad phases. For the moment, however, the implications and mechanics of the PERT program are limited to the general program as illustrated in the figure.

The arrows on the joining lines (called activity lines) indicate the sequence required for satisfactory completion of the study. Boxes (or circles, or triangles, or the like) indicate events—the culmination of

activities. As the chart indicates, it is not necessary to complete all events in the order shown. For example, acquiring options on raw materials does not constrain the completion of the patent requirements event. Therefore, no activity arrow is shown between events III and IV. Instead, event II (the availability of financing) is shown—with an activity arrow—as governing the completion of event IV. The same is true of event V, since the acquisition of options on neither raw materials nor patent rights restrains the geological study.

Two phases of the market study could be conducted simultaneously. Activity arrows from events VII through X indicate the comprehensive path for conducting the product-market study. Results of the preliminary market study should reveal the feasibility of conducting a preliminary production study. Should the results of event VIII indicate that the item could be produced at a reasonable price, the signal would be given for a more comprehensive market review. The feasibility of investing the money required for a full-scale production study would be based upon the outcome of event IX.

While the product study is being conducted, it is possible to study the marketing of other materials obtained from the ore deposit. Such simultaneous study could include the feasibility of selling by-products from refining processes or raw materials in pit-run condition. This market study could be conducted with two possible end goals under consideration. Should the product study look promising, income could result not only from marketing the finished goods, but also from marketing various extracted raw materials or various refined by-products, or both. Since simultaneous market studies of this type, or others which involve one or more unrelated products, do not depend upon the outcome of each other, they are graphically shown by parallel activity lines—such as that shown for event XI in Figure 1.

Completion of both the product study and the raw materials study is shown as a constraint on completion of the profitability study. This is the case because the former would provide sufficient information to consider alternate courses of action before making final recommendations.

Other information of value to management is readily available from Figure 1. The dates immediately below each event box indicate the desired schedule date for completion. Events I, II, and III are shown as having already been completed (with cross-hatched lines). The date of completion is shown below the schedule dates. Thus, managers are able to evaluate quickly whether the program can be expected to remain on the proposed schedule. Event I was finished ten days later than originally planned. In an attempt to prevent the whole study

from lagging behind, however, financing (event II) was provided more rapidly than originally anticipated. Although event II was only two days late, event III slid fourteen days beyond the schedule date. Since event III does not constrain any downstream activity, a delay at this point will not affect other portions of the study.

Suppose management is reviewing this chart on March 15. Since events IV and V are scheduled for completion on Feb. 30 and March 1 respectively, visual inspection immediately reveals that events IV and V are both behind schedule. Concern over the delay should be concentrated on event V because it has direct impact on the proposed schedule dates for all other portions of the study.

Detailed Planning

Once the PERT chart for the broad plan is completed, the investigator then prepares detailed charts for each activity line shown on the master plan. As an example, the required activities between events VI and VII are portrayed in Figure 2. In this chart, the various activities that must be conducted to complete the preliminary market study are shown.

Figure 2 provides at a glance an immediate picture of the interdependency between events. For example, the activity line tying events VII-1 and VII-2 indicates the need for knowledge of where products will be moved before the appropriate channels of distribution can be properly evaluated. The sequencing of events VII-6 and VII-7 points out the importance of evaluating competitive reaction before the annual sales can be intelligently evaluated for purposes of completing the necessary accounting studies.

Location of all the events on the chart is such that the sequence of completion for a well-conducted study is shown. Figure 2 is only a suggested format; for most studies, a more complete and detailed description would be desirable.

More Information Possibilities

A PERT chart can be expanded to provide marketing management with useful tools in addition to the descriptive pictures of the sequencing of events. As an example, consider the activity line in Figure 2 between events VI and VII-9. Here a description of the activity being conducted is given below the line, which in this case covers the approximation of production costs. Above the line and within parentheses is the number 2, which in this example denotes the number of

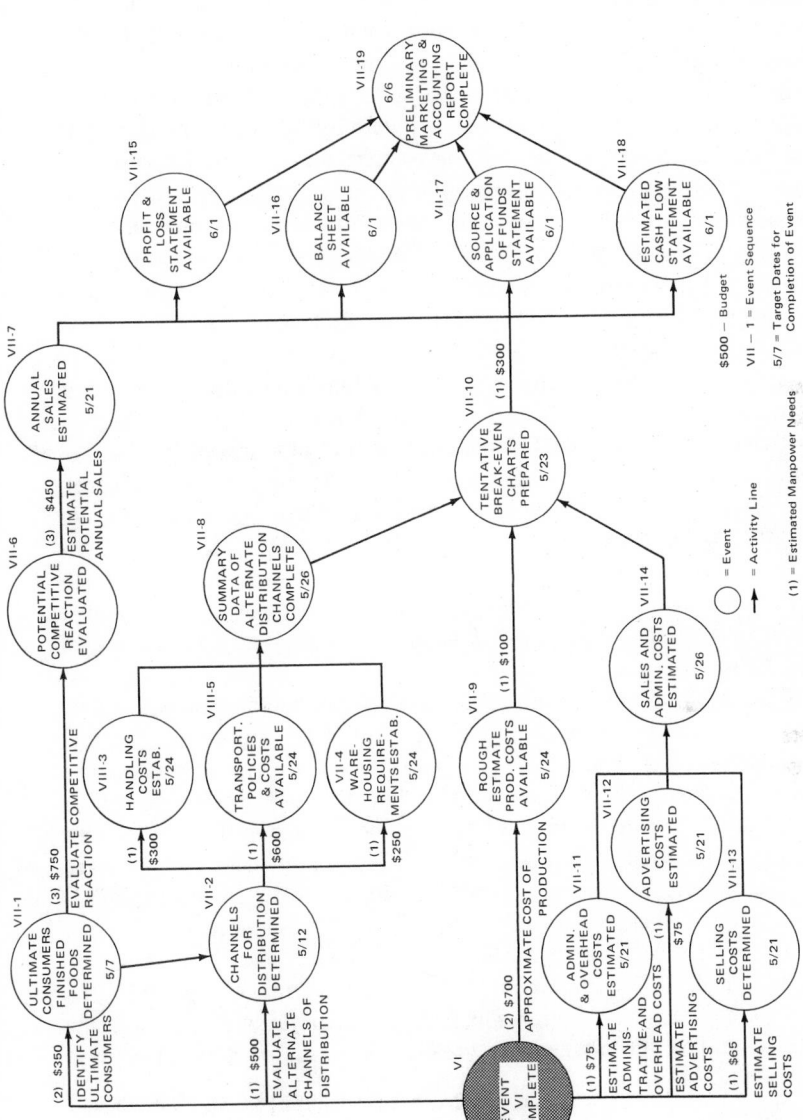

Figure 2   The achievement of Event VII (from Figure 1)

employees involved with this phase of the program. The number could be altered to show man-hours, days, weeks, or even the name of the responsible individual.

Financial information pertaining to each phase of a study can also be shown on the chart. The amounts shown in Figure 2 are in the form of budget estimates, established before the study started, to serve as a guide for the responsible individual. By adding a budget figure for each activity, it is possible to visualize the way the expenses are allocated; this in turn facilitates the development of a realistic total budget for the complete study. If, upon completion of each phase of the study, the actual cost is entered on the chart, the marketing department has a ready reference of expenditures in relation to allocated budget. This systematic feedback permits management to detect problem areas as they occur. This accessibility to allocation and costs also facilitates the control function, which management must exercise in bringing the study to a successful culmination.

PERT provides the marketing department of any firm or investigator with a useful tool for planning studies of varying degrees of complexity. In addition to providing a pictorial network of the method for conducting the study, this approach offers a versatile tool for evaluating the status of a program at any time. A well-organized and well-maintained PERT chart can provide rapid answers (feedback) pertaining to schedule status, financial position, and expenditure of manpower.

Only the most basic and elementary PERT principles have been set forth in this article—deliberately so, in order to not clutter the discussion with technical jargon. The PERT technique has been refined to the point where complex, specialized "language" of application can be used;[3] likewise, the technique has been the springboard to more complex systems, such as CPA (critical path analysis).[4] One need not learn all the technical language in order to apply the PERT technique, although some, such as that set forth in this article, is helpful.

The charts used in this article have likewise been kept relatively simple. The more complex and/or detailed the marketing study, the more complex and detailed must be the charts (system). And the more complex the system, the greater the need for a technical lan-

---

[3] See, for example, Federal Electric Corporation, *A Programmed Introduction to PERT* (New York: John Wiley & Sons, Inc., 1963).

[4] See, for example, Yung Wong, "Critical Path Analysis for New Product Planning," *Journal of Marketing*, XXVIII (October, 1964), pp. 53–59; or Ferdinand K. Levy, Gerald L. Thompson, and Jerome D. Wiest, "The ABC's of the Critical Path Method," *Harvard Business Review*, XLI (September–October, 1963), pp. 98–108.

guage. Thus, the basic PERT concept is flexible and easily adapted to expansion or reduction to meet specific marketing task requirements, but, as expansion takes place, the need for a larger technical vocabulary is more pressing.

Success in the use of the PERT technique depends not so much upon learning the mechanics as upon achieving a state of mind. In other words, PERT is based on a concept—the concept of *integrating.* One can integrate only sequence (first this, then that), or cost (budget, manpower, and so on), or time (this by such-and-such a time, that by so much later than this). Or, one can integrate the several variables simultaneously—probably the more desirable objective. The PERT technique has already been well crystallized with a language to facilitate its use. Thus, its adaptation to marketing research problems should be fairly simple—if one does not let himself become cowed by the technical sophistication and complex jargon which is available but not necessary to its successful application. It can be used in simple format; it is so used. Most important of all, it is and can be used effectively in marketing research.

How to Build a Marketing Information System

Donald F. Cox
Robert E. Good

Recently the marketing vice president of a company whose sales volume is $350 million asked, "How should we go about developing a marketing information system? I don't mean one that will keep track of orders and shipments, but a system giving our marketing managers information that will help them make better decisions about pricing, advertising, promotion, product policy, sales force effort, and so forth."

He asked the question of us because, since early 1966, we have been studying the attempts of 15 major U.S. corporations to develop a sophisticated marketing information system, or MIS. We have talked with executives at companies such as Chemstrand, Coca-Cola, General Electric, General Foods, IBM, Lever Brothers, Pillsbury, Schenley, and Westinghouse.

Although this field is relatively new, most of the technical aspects of developing a MIS are no longer an obstacle. Nevertheless, few companies are very far along in taking advantage of an approach which, its users agree, has great potential.

In this article we will attempt to provide some guidelines which might help answer the inquiring market vice president—and others with similar questions. First we will present a brief review of some of the characteristics and advantages of a sophisticated MIS, and of the current "state of the art." Then we will identify some of the key decisions which must be made by top management in the MIS development process. In each case we will present a distillation of the experience of the companies studied as an aid in making these critical management decisions.

Reprinted with permission from the *Harvard Business Review,* vol. 45, no. 3 (May–June, 1967), pp. 145–154. © 1967 by the President and Fellows of Harvard College; all rights reserved.

WHAT IT IS AND CAN DO

A MIS may be defined as a set of procedures and methods for the regular, planned collection, analysis, and presentation of information for use in making marketing decisions. This of course is a step beyond logistics systems, which handle inventory control, orders, and so forth.

It is desirable first to differentiate between the two major components of such systems—*support systems* and *operating systems*. Support systems include those activities required to generate and manipulate data—i.e., market research and other data gathering, programming, and data processing. Operating systems are those that use the data as an aid to planning and controlling marketing activities.

This article is concerned mainly with the development of three types of marketing operating systems—those designed for control, for planning, and for basic research. In Exhibit 1 we summarize some of the applications and probable benefits of each type of system (assuming increasing degrees of sophistication) and present examples of systems now operating. The following are examples of marketing systems we have observed, with some of the advantages the companies claim for them.

1. Control Systems

These provide continuous monitoring (sometimes through exception reporting) and rapid spotting of trends, problems, and marketing opportunities. They allow better anticipation of problems, more detailed and comprehensive review of performance against plans, and greater speed of response. For instance:

IBM's Data Processing Division has developed a MIS which district sales managers can interrogate through a time-sharing computer terminal located in an executive's office. A manager punches a typewriter-like keyboard and receives an immediate print-out of information such as:

Sales (or rentals) to date—broken down by product code, type of customer, and branch making the sale.

Sales in relation to goals.

Combinations of information which relate to sales, customer classifications, product codes, and so forth.

	Applications	Benefits	Examples
Control Systems	1. Control of marketing costs	1. More timely computerized reports	1. Undesirable cost trends are spotted more quickly so that corrective action may be taken sooner
	2. Diagnosis of poor sales performance	2. Flexible on-line retrieval of data	2. Executives can ask supplementary questions of the computer to help pinpoint reasons for a sales decline and reach an action decision more quickly
	3. Management of fashion goods	3. Automatic spotting of problems and opportunities	3. Fast-moving fashion items are reported daily for quick reorder, and slow-moving items are also reported for fast price reductions
	4. Flexible promotion strategy	4. Cheaper, more detailed, and more frequent reports	4. On-going evaluation of a promotional campaign permits reallocation of funds to areas behind target
Planning Systems	1. Forecasting	1. Automatic translation of terms and classifications between departments	1. Survey-based forecasts of demand for complex industrial goods can be automatically translated into parts requirements and production schedules
	2. Promotional planning and corporate long-range planning	2. Systematic testing of alternative promotional plans and compatibility testing of various divisional plans	2. Complex simulation models both developed and operated with the help of data bank information can be used for promotional planning by product managers and for strategic planning by top management
	3. Credit management	3. Programmed executive decision rules can operate on data bank information	3. Credit decisions are automatically made as each order is processed
	4. Purchasing	4. Detailed sales reporting permits automation of management decisions	4. Computer automatically repurchases standard items on the basis of correlation of sales data with programmed decision rules
Research Systems	1. Advertising strategy	1. Additional manipulation of data is possible when stored for computers in an unaggregated file	1. Sales analysis is possible by new market segment breakdowns
	2. Pricing strategy	2. Improved storage and retrieval capability allows new types of data to be collected and used	2. Systematic recording of information about past R & D contract bidding situations allows improved bidding strategies
	3. Evaluation of advertising expenditures	3. Well-designed data banks permit integration and comparison of different sets of data	3. Advertising expenditures are compared to shipments by county to provide information about advertising effectiveness
	4. Continuous experiments	4. Comprehensive monitoring of input and performance variables yields information when changes are made	4. Changes in promotional strategy by type of customer are matched against sales results on a continuous basis

Exhibit 1   Benefits possible with a sophisticated MIS

The data are current to within three or four days, allowing the manager to keep up to date on marketing problems and opportunities and on progress in relation to goals.

Schenley has installed the so-called SIMR (Schenley Instant Market Reports) system which allows key executives to retrieve (via video display desk consoles and printers) current and past sales and inventory figures for any brand and package size (or combination) for each of 400 distributors. SIMR furnishes information in less than one second after a query, compared with many minutes or even hours under its former computer and manual system. Furthermore, since the computer does the calculations, managers have great flexibility and near-instant speed of response in making many types of comparisons of sales and inventory positions, such as:

How a brand is doing in any size or in all sizes in any market or in all markets.

How a distributor is doing with a particular brand.

How a bottle size is doing by distributor, state, or region.

How a market is doing by month or has done since the end of the previous fiscal year.

"We can get answers literally while we are still formulating the questions," states Bernard Goldberg, president of Schenley's marketing subsidiary. "Needed information is available so quickly that it helps us think."[1]

2. Planning Systems

These furnish, in convenient form, information the marketing executive requires for planning marketing and sales programs. At least three major consumer goods producers, for example, are developing "data books" for product managers. The books bring together the basic information a product manager needs to formulate annual marketing plans and to "replan" during the course of the year. Putting the information into one book, rather than in a welter of reports, not only saves time, but it also enables all product managers in a group or division to base their plans on the same data. Consequently, their superiors

---

[1] *Industrial Data Processing Applications Report* (S_3), Business Publications International, Division of OA Business Publications, Inc., 1965.

are able to review comparable information quickly when considering the plans for approval.

At a more sophisticated level, planning systems allow simulation of the effects of alternate plans so that the manager can make a better decision. For instance:

Pillsbury's system enables marketing managers to obtain sales forecasts for each of 39 sales branches, supported by varying levels of trade promotion. The marketing manager asks the question, "What will sales be in each branch if we spend x dollars on trade promotions in comparison with .75x dollars and with 1.2x dollars?" Pillsbury does not claim that the system is perfect—it is obviously no better than the assumptions on which the simulation is based—but it has had a surprisingly good "batting average" in accuracy. It has great value to marketing managers because it allows them to look at alternate plans in each of the 39 sales branches; this was never feasible before.

A large pharmaceutical company has developed an even more complex model. The company has programmed an artificial panel representing the nation's population of doctors. Every week the company simulates each doctor's prescription decision for every patient he "sees." (Commercial research services are available which provide information on the incidence of symptoms of illness and the "patient mix" of the various medical specialists.) The doctor considers the symptoms "presented" by each patient and decides whether to prescribe a drug and, if so, which type and brand. His decision is based on factors such as his experience with the drug, current attitudes, exposure to the advertising of various brands, exposure to detail men, and word-of-mouth information from other doctors. The simulation even includes a "forgetting routine" which causes a doctor to forget from time to time some of the information he has acquired.

While the company does not disclose how the simulation model is being used, it certainly is capable of generating extremely sophisticated marketing planning. For example, marketing managers can test the effects on share of market and sales of variations in amount, type, and timing of advertising and simultaneously test the effects of variations in frequency of detail men's calls. On a broader basis, the system can be used to screen a number of alternative marketing programs to select the most promising ones to be actually test marketed.

Perhaps the ultimate in sophistication is a marketing planning system which reviews alternatives, then actually makes decisions and takes action. Thus, several large retailing organizations have developed systems that review sales trends and inventories and then place orders for merchandise.

The most advanced unit of this type we have seen is not a marketing system; rather, it buys and sells securities in a stock brokerage house. Still in the future are marketing systems that decide the amount and timing of advertising and price promotions in each of several dozen sales districts.

3. Basic Research Systems

These systems are used to develop and test sophisticated decision rules and cause-and-effect hypotheses which should improve ability to assess effects of actions and permit greater learning from experience. For instance:

A large consumer goods company is developing a MIS which, among other things, stores in computer memory the characteristics of each advertisement run (color versus black and white, nature of illustration, amount of copy, and so forth) and readership and attitude change scores for each ad. The purpose is to be able to relate ad characteristics to effectiveness measurements under different conditions and with different types of consumers by systematically studying "experience."

Most companies find it difficult to relate advertising to sales because there are so many important "uncontrollable" variables which are nearly impossible to take into account in an unsophisticated MIS. One large consumer goods producer has developed a MIS which for the first time allows the company to collect, store, and retrieve advertising, sales, and other marketing data at a level of detail which makes possible much better controlled studies of the relationship of advertising to sales.

CURRENT PROGRESS

The examples which we have presented probably represent the most sophisticated types of MIS now in existence. While we have not surveyed the 500 largest corporations in the country, we have screened more than 50 companies and have reviewed more than 100 current articles on information systems. As far as we have been able to determine, the current state of the art is something like this:

Very few companies have developed advanced systems, and not all of these are in operation. Some might even best be classified as subsystems, since they relate to only a portion of the marketing decisions made.

Some companies, perhaps 15, are actively upgrading their systems to a

high level. Of these, about half seem to be progressing well; the others have been much less successful.

Many other companies are contemplating plans to develop sophisticated systems.

The reasons why marketing systems have not developed to the same extent as, say, production, logistics, or financial systems are not "technical." Marketing research technology (data gathering), computer technology (data handling), and analytical procedures (e.g., mathematical model building) are all sufficiently advanced to permit companies to build effective marketing systems.

Although insufficient time has elapsed since the installation of most advanced marketing information systems to allow a precise assessment of benefits, the users of sophisticated systems with whom we have talked are virtually all very enthusiastic about their systems, even though many see room for improvement.

DEVELOPING THE SYSTEM

Because many of the technical problems of developing sophisticated support systems have been solved and many users are gratified over the results, why are there so few advanced marketing information systems in operation? And why have some companies succeeded more than others in realizing the potentials of the MIS?

One characteristic of the more successful companies is striking. In every case, at least some members of top management have seen the promise of the technique and have viewed its development as a top management responsibility. They have devoted a great deal of time, thought, and effort to guiding (and sometimes actually protecting) the development process. Unfortunately, it is widely believed that the job of building a MIS can be turned over to a technical staff group. This has not proved to be the case. Information systems are not merely technical appendages (developed by technical people) that are easily meshed with most existing marketing planning and control systems.

The best way to show why participation of top management is necessary is to pose five key questions which must be answered in the process of instituting a sophisticated MIS. In our opinion, each is a management question:

1. How should we organize to develop a better MIS?
2. How sophisticated should our marketing systems be?

3. What development strategy should we follow—do we attempt to build a "total" system in one move, or in stages?

4. What should be the major characteristics ("macro specifications") of our system?

5. How much should we spend on developing and operating a MIS?

While the field is too new to permit comprehensive and conclusive statements about all its aspects, we can present some guidelines and working hypotheses that are worthy of management's consideration.

Readying the Organization

The starting point in organizing for MIS development is not the establishment of a marketing systems group. The starting point is a review and appraisal of the entire marketing organization and of the policies that direct it. As James Peterson, vice president, grocery products marketing at The Pillsbury Company, pointed out to us:

"We realized we couldn't develop a marketing control system until we had clearly and sharply defined the responsibilities of our marketing managers. If the system was to measure their performance against plans, we had to specify precisely what each man was accountable for."

Some companies, for instance, have failed to decide whether a product manager is accountable for unit sales and market share, for sales revenue, for marketing profit, or for net profit. Until responsibilities and spheres of activity are clearly defined, it is virtually impossible to build a marketing control system. In fact, specification of who is accountable for what automatically determines many of the control system's characteristics.

Management must next decide how to organize MIS development activities. Our observations show that this is a much more complex problem than might be assumed. Sophisticated systems require the coordinated efforts of many departments and individuals, including:

Top management.

Marketing management, brand management.

Sales management.

New products groups.

Market research personnel.

Control and finance departments.

Systems analysts and designers.

Operations researchers, statisticians, and model builders.

Programmers.

Computer equipment experts and suppliers.

The contribution of each group of course depends on its specialized talents and interests in the system. Programmers cannot define managers' information needs, and managers usually cannot program. No one person knows enough to accomplish all phases of MIS development.

Furthermore, sophisticated systems do not fall into a company's traditional data handling domains, such as the market research department or the accounting and control department, because an essential feature of a good MIS is that it integrates and correlates marketing and financial data.

Many companies we have observed have not really come to grips with the difficult problem of providing the organizational arrangements and leadership necessary for successful MIS development. They have not answered the question of who is responsible for MIS design, planning, and development. Why is there a leadership vacuum? Partly because top management does not fully appreciate the requirements and implications of the MIS, and partly because it has an understandable reluctance to disturb entrenched and powerful departments.

The approaches which have been tried in an attempt to solve the problems of organization and leadership can be characterized as:

"Clean piece of paper" approach.

Committee approach.

Low-level approach.

Information "coordinator" approach.

"CLEAN PIECE OF PAPER" APPROACH. This involves drawing a new organization chart. The argument goes that the financial and accounting departments and market research departments have developed as much from growing data gathering and processing capability as in response to management information needs. In the pre-computer era, it was rarely possible to correlate marketing and accounting data in a sophisticated manner and on a regular basis for presentation to management. Now it is possible, but the marketing data are supplied by one set of departments and the accounting data by another. In the absence of coordination and compatibility, line management must often do its own correlating. Therefore the "ideal" procedure is to abolish the traditional information gathering and processing departments and establish a management information department.

While this may represent an "ideal" solution, it is not feasible in most companies. Traditions and positions are too well entrenched. Furthermore, it would not solve all the problems. For one thing, it would not ensure the development of a MIS geared to management needs. For another, no management information department could supply all of the data the system needed, such as reports from the field sales organization.

COMMITTEE APPROACH. Some companies have established MIS committees. They are excellent vehicles for communicating points of view and for joint learning and sharing in the experience of developing a MIS. They can create shared awareness of compatibility and coordination problems and of the need to resolve them.

The committee approach alone, however, is not the answer. Because meetings and committee assignments consume time, it is difficult to involve busy line managers. Furthermore, it is not easy to get anyone to carry out assignments in addition to his regular job. Finally, a committee of peers, chaired by a peer, is not always able to exert the leadership which may be required. Committees of this kind simply lack "clout." And at times clout may be the only thing that will accomplish necessary changes.

LOW-LEVEL APPROACH. Some companies have assigned the task of MIS development to a junior member of the market research department—often as a part-time assignment. This reflects a total lack of understanding of the difficulty of the task, and the outcome is predictable. The man, no matter how clever he is, lacks the time and the clout to overcome the organizational and psychological barriers he encounters. Such an assignment has led to the resignation of more than one bright young research man.

INFORMATION "COORDINATOR" APPROACH. Some companies, while retaining traditional departmental boundaries, have appointed a top-level executive to the post of information czar or "coordinator," sometimes called "director of marketing systems." We have observed that men who are capable of understanding both management information needs and systems problems can make substantial progress in MIS development in this position—*when* they enjoy top management support. But it is a delicate position; one coordinator we know preferred not to have any formal title until, after a year, he had established good working relationships with the various departments. Furthermore, even a sensible and sensitive information manager must establish organizational lines that encourage the coordinated efforts of the affected departments and divisions of the company in the design and the accomplishment of the MIS plan.

For many companies this approach has the best chance of success. We suggest that management designate the director of marketing systems as a "prime contractor" who develops MIS plans and specifications, and coordinates and reviews the work of the various "subcontractors" or suppliers contributing to the program. Such a prime contractor-subcontractor approach has proved in military and civilian applications to be effective in handling projects or tasks that require the utilization of many talents and capabilities, not all of which exist in the department or organization directly involved.

For the prime contractor to be effective he must have cost control. It is therefore advisable to use an interdepartmental billing system. The prime contractor is responsible for the overall budget, and negotiates with users (marketing managers) to determine their information needs and to obtain from them the funds required to develop and operate a MIS that would meet these needs. He also arranges to compensate the various supplying departments, such as the systems group for programming, for their services.

Management must also determine the prime contractor's organizational location. It is essential that he represent the department or division which will use (and pay for) the MIS. For a variety of reasons, not one of the companies studied having a central or corporate systems department (responsible for support systems) has designated that group as the "prime contractor" for operating its MIS. They view the corporate systems group as an important supplier of technical advice and of programming and data processing services for the marketing departments. But in the large companies, at least, final authority and responsibility for MIS development, where such authority has been designated, generally rests with the marketing department.

Of the several arguments for this practice, the most important is that the expertise of corporate systems groups is usually in support systems (programming and data processing). Effective development of marketing planning and control systems requires a management, rather than a technical support systems, orientation. Furthermore, effective MIS can be developed only by people who understand users' problems and who can be responsive to users' needs.

How Sophisticated?

Someone must decide on the level of sophistication of the MIS to be developed. This decision should, of course, be based on a review of the company's needs and the costs of meeting them.

Equally important, the abilities of managers must be considered. To

develop and use effectively some of the more sophisticated systems that have been described, managers must be able to:

Define specific information needs.

Develop analytical approaches and models.

Make explicit their planning, decision-making, and control processes and procedures.

Interpret and use sophisticated information.

One of the characteristics of the more advanced MIS is automation of certain aspects of the marketing management process. But it is first necessary to make the process explicit. For instance, to develop exception-reporting systems, managers' exception or "control" criteria must be articulated. Simulation models cannot be built into the system until managers have spelled out the characteristics of the different elements of the company's marketing system (consumers, distributors, competitors, and so forth) and have attempted to define how these elements interact.

If a company already has a well-articulated set of decision rules as to what constitutes an "execution," it would not be difficult to build an automated exception reporting system. Such a system could be developed, for the marketing manager who says,

I always like to know about all situations in which sales, profits, or market share are running 4% or more behind plan. Furthermore, in any exceptional cases I also require the following diagnostic information: prices, distribution levels, advertising, and consumer attitudes.

The problem is, as has been well documented in a Marketing Science Institute study,[2] that many marketing managers, particularly those at the operating level, do not use explicit planning and control systems. They do not make their decision rules and exception criteria explicit. In short, they are not equipped to contribute to the development of a sophisticated MIS, nor are they comfortable with it once it is operating. Though related to research information, their decisions often are highly intuitive. The problem seems less severe at higher management levels, partly because top management control systems are more explicitly articulated than those at the operating level.

[2] D. J. Luck and Patrick J. Robinson, *Promotional Decision Making* (New York, McGraw-Hill Book Company, Inc., 1964).

SYSTEM-MANAGER BALANCE. It is important that a balance be maintained between management sophistication and MIS sophistication. As a company upgrades the latter, so must it raise the former.

In a "steady state" (before anyone tinkers with the marketing system) there usually seems to be a correspondence between management sophistication and information quality. Managers usually get the quality of information they ask for. Though they may complain of a lack of good information and blame one or more of the information supplying departments, questioning often reveals that in most cases they have not been asking for better information in any specific way.

If, as we have suggested, the two "quality levels" are roughly in balance, what happens when only the level of information quality is raised significantly? Our prediction is that this would not lead to better decisions. In fact, the reverse may be true, as the result of the confusion and resentment generated by the manager's inability to deal with the more sophisticated information.

Information quality can be upgraded much more rapidly than management quality. It is easy to throw the management system out of balance by installing a sophisticated MIS, but there seems to be little point in doing so. A more positive approach is to develop a master plan for improving the system, but make the improvements gradually—say, over several years. Marketing control systems like Schenley's or IBM's, described earlier, are easier to develop and use than those like the pharmaceutical company's simulation-based planning system. So a company might first install a marketing control system and subsequently, as managers gained experience in using it, develop advanced planning systems.

"Complete" Systems

While an attempt to develop a highly sophisticated "total" marketing system at the outset has a high probability of failure, it *is* desirable to build a complete subsystem at one time—even if it is only a part of what will eventually be the company's total system. To illustrate:

A company develops a first-rate exception reporting system that will quickly present "exceptional" sales results to the marketing manager. Very likely he will be faced with more problems than ever before, because of the system's ability to monitor large amounts of detailed information. It will be difficult (and dangerous), however, for the manager to act on this information. Before he can take intelligent action, he must also know whether the deviations from plan are the result of deviations in sales effort, of unusual competitive

activities, or of other factors. To be complete, therefore, the system must also include a diagnostic procedure.

"MACRO" SPECIFICATIONS. Apart from decisions on the general characteristics of the system to be used, the company must determine the overall or "macro" MIS specifications. Besides the type of system to be developed, the most important considerations are the nature of the data bank, the form and the method of data display and presentation, and computer selection.

We should, however, underscore here the necessity of ensuring the participation in these decisions not only of top management but also of the line managers. In most cases we have studied, and in all of the least successful instances, the marketing systems developers have failed to involve line managers in the process of developing macro specifications. In many cases where systems developers have made the effort, they have found it difficult to elicit the views of busy line managers in the brief periods available in typical interviews or meetings. The systems developers subsequently present the managers with a fait accompli—which may or may not work.

A more effective approach is to involve the managers in an extended session, lasting days if necessary, in which a consensus on overall MIS specifications can be reached. In these sessions the group should develop flow charts of the "system"—or total environment in which the company operates—and designate critical decision points, identify the information they require for planning and controlling marketing (or other management) activities, and make cost/benefit analyses of alternative designs before agreeing on one design. This approach not only helps ensure a system that is keyed to management's needs, but also allows management to defer a decision on the size of the MIS development budget until it has assessed the alternative systems.

"MICRO" DATA BANK. Perhaps the most essential element in upgrading a system is a bank or file based on disaggregated or "micro" data. These are data recorded and stored in the lowest level of aggregation and detail—such as the size, price, time, and location of a single purchase of a product.

As Professor Arnold E. Amstutz of M.I.T. has commented:

At the heart of every successful information system is a disaggregated data file. . . . As new inputs are received they are maintained along with existing data rather than replacing or being combined with existing information. . . . The existence of a disaggregated data file facilitates system evaluation. . . . In the first stages of system development it is simply impossible

to anticipate the direction of later advancement. Aggregate data files may preclude highly profitable system modification. The disaggregated data file provides the flexibility which is the prerequisite of intelligent system evolution.[3]

In designing the data bank it is important to provide for common denominators in different sets of data, so that the correlation and analysis potential of the MIS can be realized. This means that such elements as the geographic, time, and responsibility boundaries of different types of data must be compatible to permit meaningful comparisons.

A disaggregated data bank gives the system the flexibility required for future upgrading. The alternative is to try to anticipate all possible future uses of the system and to agree on aggregated units (like aggregating all package sizes of a brand), aggregated time periods (a week, month, or quarter), and aggregated geographical areas (sales territories or regions).

Management must weigh the greater cost of a disaggregated data bank against the possibility that future conditions or new insights may call for analyses which are precluded because the data have been aggregated. Since most people who have participated in MIS development admit that they are unable to foresee all important management information needs, and since most current systems are likely to evolve to increasing stages of sophistication, the prudent decision would be to develop a disaggregated data bank—*if* the company can afford it.

PRESENTATION AND FORMAT. Developing a sophisticated MIS involves resolving the matters of what information should be presented, how it should be presented, and to whom.

One important aspect of this question is the degree of executive-system interaction desired. At the extreme of "distance," executives receive information in the form of regular reports. With somewhat closer but not complete interaction, the manager can make special requests for information from the data bank. At the extreme of "closeness," the manager can obtain almost instantaneous computer response with a time-sharing or on-line system. Consider Schenley's experience:

Schenley has installed a video display and retrieval system. Of interest is the fact that the new system carries little new information; indeed, the

---

[3] "The Marketing Executive and Management Information Systems," in *Science, Technology and Marketing,* 1966 Fall Conference Proceedings of the American Marketing Association, p. 76.

same data were generated previously in the form of computer print-out. The information in paper form, however, was too voluminous and unwieldy to use. What the new retrieval and presentation system has achieved is simply to make data much more usable for management.

On-line systems such as Schenley's have a tremendous advantage in speed of access to information. Critics of these systems argue that managers do not need to know what happened as of the close of business yesterday.[4] This may be true. But there are benefits in being able to receive split-second responses. A manager's willingness to formulate questions and get data on which to base decisions may depend on the ease and speed with which he can retrieve answers from the computer. Although it is too early to tell whether the cost of this capability can be justified, large companies should seriously consider experimenting with this type of system.

COMPUTER SELECTION. The computer requirement for a company's MIS will, of course, depend on the system's performance specifications and the decisions management has made on each of the preceding design problems. While technical help is necessary in the decisions on equipment, management has the responsibility for making certain that the hardware chosen will meet the MIS needs and specifications at the time of installation, which may be some years away. In this respect, managers should recognize that they probably will learn many new ways to use the computer, such as new marketing planning, control, decision, and research applications, given some experience with an improved MIS. So even with the most careful planning, demands for computer capacity are likely to expand faster than anticipated.

Cost and Value

It is difficult to generalize about how much a MIS will cost—or how much it will be worth. Usually there is not a large increase in data gathering costs, since many companies now have available to them much of the raw data required. Cost increases result from data storage and transforming the raw data into useful information. It is extremely difficult to determine MIS development costs, since many companies lack accounting arrangements, like interdepartmental billing, which allow them to keep track of the total cost of the manpower contributing to the program.

[4] See John Dearden, "Myth of Real-Time Management Information," *Harvard Business Review,* May–June, 1966, p. 123.

On a "best estimate" basis, we are aware of simple or partial systems which have cost only a few thousand dollars. At the other extreme, one complex marketing system we know of must have cost several million dollars. A large company with sales in the $500 million range should expect to invest several hundred thousand dollars (plus equipment charges) to develop a relatively sophisticated, computer-based MIS. And development costs will not end there, since after the first stage is operational, it is probable that management will want to upgrade the system continually.

If top executives authorize expenditures of this magnitude, they are likely to want a justification of the value of the system. Usually, computer-based information systems, such as those used for accounting, have been justified mainly on the ground that they reduce personnel and other administrative costs. Few advanced marketing information systems could be justified on the basis of cost reduction.

However, that test alone is not appropriate for a MIS. The main purpose of a MIS is to help the marketing manager make more profitable decisions, not to reduce data handling and paperwork costs. So a MIS should be evaluated in terms of its estimated effects on marketing efficiency.

Determining how much a MIS could increase marketing effectiveness is not an easy task. The involvement of management in developing overall specifications should help in making an estimate, however imprecise, of system benefits. In addition, the decision on a budget for MIS development need not be made in a single giant step. Rather, it is possible to attain system sophistication in discrete increments, involving a series of smaller budgeting decisions and cost/benefit evaluations.

CONCLUSION

Marketing men in many of the large corporations we studied are almost uniformly enthusiastic about the promise of the computer-based, advanced MIS. Relatively few such systems are now operating, however, and many companies have had indifferent success in deriving benefits from them.

In the more successful companies, the following patterns have been evident:

The development of the MIS has been viewed as a management responsibility, including both top management and operating line management.

Formal organizational lines have been drawn to provide leadership in use of the technique—usually including the appointment of a high-level information coordinator or "prime contractor" who develops plans and coordinates the efforts of the departments involved.

The prime contractor reports to the user group, such as the marketing department, rather than to the central systems group.

Line managers participate in developing overall specifications for the MIS.

The sophistication of the system is balanced with that of the managers who use it.

Systems development typically proceeds in manageable stages, rather than in attempts to develop "total" systems at once.

The system is based on a disaggregated data bank which allows managers to retrieve analyses in the form they want without having to specify all their information needs in advance.

Investments in systems development and operation are justified not on the basis of cost reduction, which is often irrelevant with the MIS, but on an estimate of the system's ability to help managers make more profitable marketing decisions.

It is evident that a good deal of faith is required to make substantial investments in the MIS—whose benefits by and large are still unproven. Yet more and more companies are demonstrating their faith. And some of the pioneers already claim their faith is justified.

Information Systems in Marketing

Belden Menkus

Essentially, marketing is a communicative phenomenon; its needs and problems are those of information manipulation. Yet the lack of adequate information handling techniques in the marketing function demonstrates the failure of systems men to deal more than superficially with the "total" corporate enterprise.

Within a relative handful of years the concepts and methods of integrated information handling have completely altered our essential approach to management. Yet the vital marketing function has been relatively untouched by the transformation. In no other area of business operations have the techniques of information systems been less used. In no other area of business do they have greater unrealized potential.

Information systemizing has immediate application to such fundamental areas of marketing as product line development, pricing structure, distribution operation, sales force management, advertising, and sales forecasting. Systematic information manipulation can help marketers find the answers to such basic questions as: What level of advertising expenditure is realistic in a specific product market situation? Is it preferable to work through a distributor or to sell direct in a given sales situation? What is a valid measure of the salesman's use of his time? What are reliable, yet universal, measures of advertising effectiveness?

WHAT ARE THE MARKETING FUNDAMENTALS?

Essentially marketing is a communicative phenomenon. Its needs and problems are those of information manipulation—gathering, evaluat-

Reprinted with permission from the *Systems and Procedures Journal*, vol. 14, no. 4 (July–August, 1963), pp. 10–14, published by the Systems and Procedures Association.

ing and using data. Marketing fundamentals embrace five interrelated functions in a broad operative process:

First—product design—translating the idea into a marketable item.

Second—manufacturing—translating production drawings into a deliverable product.

Third—advertising and sales—translating the customer's desire into a verified order.

Fourth—physical distribution—translating the customer order into promptly delivered goods.

Fifth—billing and collection—translating the customer order into cash in hand.

So long as a marketing organization (or any other organization, for that matter) functions properly there is a firmly established pattern of information flow within its component parts.

It is best to distinguish between information *pattern* and information *system*. Information *pattern* is the actual manner in which information moves through the organization. In theory, this flow may be compressed formally into rigid, slow-moving, organizational channels of communication. More likely in practice it breaks out of these channels and moves rapidly and somewhat erratically through informal, personal contacts.

Information *system* is an attempt to discipline and to refine the already existing information pattern. The basic objectives of this effort are to assure that all essential information is made available, and that effective and efficient use is made of all available information.

In the corporate marketing information situation we are dealing with more than a simple buyer and seller relationship. The marketer is at the center of a dynamic complex of communicative relationships. These intricate interrelationships defy simple meaningful reduction to a mere handful of multi-column statistical reports.

At one and the same time the marketer is involved in a continuing information pattern that touches his supplier, producer, sales organization, competitor, and the community at large, as well as his ultimate consumer.

Each marketer is, intrinsically, a part of the larger community, without regard to the nature or extent of either his competition or his customers; but those points of the basic marketing information pattern that touch the community and the competitor are beyond the scope of this presentation. The first relationship involves the interchange of information inherent in the community's role in our free economy as both regulator and promoter of the marketer's basic activities. The latter relationship involves the fascinating area of corporate informa-

tion security, a discipline of growing importance and increasing sophistication.

We concern ourselves, then, with those segments of the marketing information pattern that touch the supplier, the producer, the sales organization, and the ultimate consumer.

The manufacturing operation is subordinated to the overall marketing objective. Manufacturing is not an end in itself. It functions only to provide the raw material for the marketing operation. In other words: The organization does not exist merely to produce. It exists, instead, to market what it produces.

The supplier has a vital stake in the total marketing enterprise. His position is one of a partner. He should be vitally involved in product design, production continuity, and all of the other dynamic factors in the marketing process to which he is functionally related.

STANDARD SPECIFICATIONS NEEDED

Organizationally, the purchasing function is the point at which contact is made with the supplier. It demands articulate, highly competent professionals who know the supplier's specialty as well as he does. This is not the place to put men who have failed to produce satisfactorily elsewhere in the organization.

WHAT COMMUNICATION FAILURES CAN DO

Ideally, the purchasing function should maintain a continuing, realistic, and effective relationship with the supplier. Too often, however, purchases are made on price comparisons alone, without regard to optimum quality or to ultimate supplier resources. Or, delivery schedules are developed arbitrarily without regard to the best use of supplier capabilities. In some instances, due to a total lack of genuine communication, the supplier does not really know or understand what the marketer wants or needs.

The classic example of the basic marketing information problem is the predicament faced by the maker of a certain brand of packaged laundry bleach. The powdered chemical is packed in an envelope of soft, clear plastic. The product package is designed to dissolve completely when dropped into the hot water in the washing machine. This permits the bleach powder to mix quickly and directly with the wash water. A simple process, but the situation becomes complicated when the company finds a new source for the plastic envelope. Top manage-

ment is still congratulating itself for finding a cheaper envelope when the complaints start to come in from customers. Briefly, the new envelope is a crucial several millimeters thicker and is of a different chemical composition than the envelope used when the product package was developed. The results: Packages totally refuse to dissolve in wash water, sealing their contents inside. Or, the packages do not fully dissolve, leaving damaging blobs of plastic on clothing or in the machine itself.

There's an immediate moral to be drawn here—accountants, budgeteers, and other economic theorists notwithstanding—the cheapest product is not always the best buy. Cost considerations must be balanced by those of quality and suitability.

There's also another simple point to be taken: the availability of information and the correct use of it could have prevented this corporate error. And we'll return to this example later on.

The first step in improving information flow with suppliers lies in transforming the procurement function from passive to active. It is all too common for purchasing men to know nothing of their suppliers and their problems. It is not rare to find men in responsible procurement positions who have never been inside the plants of the suppliers with whom they deal. The answer probably lies in converting the basic function into one of liaison and expediting.

We must revise the recently developed interrelated ideas of value analysis and quality control. Rather than remaining static means of evaluating intrinsic product worth and supplier performance, these functions must become vehicles for coordinating product needs and delivered value. The twin restraints and disciplines of value analysis and quality control will not achieve full effectiveness until they become the basis for a genuine interchange of information between marketer and supplier.

In moving from ordinary hunch and intuition buying to intelligent purchasing we must come to regular reliance on standard specifications for routine procurement. A computerized system for product ordering and related inventory control will remain two-dimensional unless it is related to the specifications involved in the procurement process. A system for reducing product wants to written specifications is a commonly overlooked normal outgrowth of a program for written administrative directives—whether they are known as procedures or anything else.

The distinctions between supplier and producer dissolve when product manufacture is contracted out to a supplier facility. The basic information pattern problem for both marketer and producer is ending the isolation of production functions from the basic marketing

process. As already noted, the interrelated disciplines of value analysis and quality control will achieve maximum effectiveness in the manufacturing process when they become the media for a dynamic information interchange. Organizationally, the manufacturing function must be tied to sales operations. Conceptually, it must be made customer conscious. To begin with, the basic objectives of manufacturing must become product quality and craftsmanship. In our obsession with cost-conscious efficiency we have produced the desired statistics, but have lost all concern for the real value of what we have produced.

In addition, the manufacturing function must receive information "feed back" from both the sales operation and the customer. Product orientation of the sales force must be a continuing responsibility of the manufacturing function. As our technology becomes increasingly more complicated the order will more often go to the man who better understands application of his product—including the special features and the limitations. Essential information interchange will not take place when sales management acts to separate sales and manufacturing—as when field men or distributors are brought in for extended sales conference periods that carefully exclude all contact with production people.

Development of equipment descriptions and instructions must not be left to the fanciful devices of advertising people. A comprehensive and accurate presentation must not be set aside for one that is visually appealing and nothing else.

Periodic product revision must be built into the continuing manufacturing process. Applied creative effort and validation of ideas are inherent in the initial product design activity. They must be repeated. Product revision must be manufacturing's continuing corrective to customer reaction, both negative and positive.

To return to our example of the envelope for the bleach packets: Information flowing from customers directly or through the sales force should have alerted manufacturing to the inadequate performance of the plastic envelopes. It remains a paradox of modern marketing: Decision-makers will spend vast amounts to communicate with their customers. Yet, they will purposely make it difficult if not impossible for their customers to communicate with them.

INFORMATION NEEDS ARE THREE-FOLD

It should be noted here that in dealing with these areas of information flow we are dealing with both long range and short range immediate problems. In theory they can be separated. In the dynamic situation of

actual operations these considerations are intermingled. A constant corrective action is possible only where information flows freely and continuously through the marketing information complex. And we are dealing with quality as well as quantity. Thus, it will not always be possible in the commonplace, straight, statistical table to analyze the significance of:

> Buying pattern differences among customer classes in one market area and in all market areas.
> Order volume differences in product lines among customer classes in a given market area and in all market areas.
> Product item turnover differences in a single market area and all market areas in terms of damage and obsolescence.

In areas such as these mere numbers and statistical relationships are not necessarily indicative of anything significant.

Information needs of the sales organization are themselves three-fold in nature. These categories are not mutually exclusive but somewhat overlapping. The communicative relationship involves the advertising, distributor, and sales representative activities. Primarily, each must act as the intermediary in customer communication with the marketer. In addition, each needs a new appreciation of the quality of the information with which he is dealing. This demands accuracy, integrity (which is not necessarily the same thing as accuracy), and a respect for the native intelligence of the customer.

In general this means that you can not lie to all of the people all of the time—without being discovered. Failure to recognize this has meant for at least one manufacturer the gradual loss of business in all product areas and the abandonment of several in which he had traditionally operated. Specifically this means that you cannot continue to tell people that delivery can be made in two weeks from the factory when it has never been made in under six months, or that the equipment can be operated by anyone when it takes a graduate engineer to do the job.

All three information areas—advertising, distributor, and sales representative—must be kept aware of price changes, product revisions, and similar activities "back at the ranch." All are as much partners in the basic marketing operation as is the supplier.

Information interchange between the marketer and all three should determine the basic customer contact priority, and the relative importance of each item in each product line. Thus, you must deal with such questions (sometimes on a seasonal or market cycle repetitive basis)

as "Is there a secondary market?" Thus, in this instance, one might need to ask more specifically:

> Can an item being sold now to commercial decorators for painting work also be sold through hardware and garden supply outlets to the home handyman?
>
> Can this be done in all market areas or in just selected ones?
>
> Can this be done seasonably, or is it possible to market the item in this fashion throughout the year?

Customer preferences and similar factors are in constant change. Thus, both the answers and the questions must undergo continuing revision based upon the dynamic information interchange we have already mentioned. For one further example, grocery merchandisers have failed to make their distribution along the lines of regional preferences sufficiently flexible to react to the increased mobility of our population beyond regional boundaries.

NO PLACE FOR "BUG LETTERS"

Finally, we come to the marketer's direct communicative relationship with his customers. As we have noted before, marketers need to rediscover accuracy, integrity, and respect for the native intelligence of the customer. The marketer needs to realize that his communication with the customer is a two-way proposition. The customer needs to know that he is important to the marketer.

Thus, suppose the dealer fails to honor the marketer's product warranty, and the customer writes the marketer about it. The customer shouldn't get a "bug letter" telling him a sad story about the problems of competitive pressures in that particular industry.

The customer must always know that his problems and his complaints are important. The writer knows of one small firm that is gradually gaining control of its segment of the office equipment market from a number of massive corporations which have competing product lines. The secret: Management of that smaller firm gives personal attention to every letter of complaint—or suggestion—that comes in. And, each one of these letters is circulated among the production and sales segments of the organization, for each must react in detail to the basic idea in the letter, no matter how odd or off-beat it may be.

To return again to our powdered bleach marketer. In line with the firm's traditional manner of doing things, complaining customers re-

ceived vague form replies to their letters. These complaints were round-filed (in effect), and not shared with the sales and production people. Nothing was done until a major distributor went to the top man in the concern at the time falling sales in that product line became obvious.

But, to compound the basic error, the company refused to inform either its sales force or its customers of the problems. Thus, sales of this product line continued to drop. And the company failed to make realistic use of its production lot control system by calling in the defective products. Thus, quantities of this merchandise continued to reach customers long after the basic production error had been corrected.

THE CLASSIC FAILURE

The marketer's communicative relationship with his customer must be *comprehensive, meaningful* and *clear*.

Comprehensive means that he tells the essential story about the product. Too often the customer reads a lengthy, elaborate, and colorfully illustrated pamphlet designed to introduce a product to him, but he is unable to find out its cost, size, speed, and other vital facts.

Meaningful means that he uses significant terms to tell his story. For instance, a marketer won't impress a young mother by telling her that his product won't need servicing for three years. He will impress her by telling her that the same product won't need servicing until her two-year-old child is ready for kindergarten. The harried young mother doubts her youngster ever will make it to kindergarten.

Clear means that he uses short, colorful, and almost obvious words to tell his story. For just one instance, it is far better to say that a product will last and last instead of referring to its reliability.

In concluding this discussion we face the impact of all of these matters upon men working with systems in general and management information systems in particular. The information needs of marketers demonstrate the almost classic failure of systems men to deal more than superficially with the functioning organization. And these needs demonstrate that in the present state of development of the management information art it is deceptive to speak of a "total" system.

chapter 11 | Simulation and Computer Applications in Marketing Management

To a large extent, the success of many of the techniques of management science in both their theoretical development and their application is due to the development of the electronic computer. In fact, there is ample evidence to indicate that the progress in management science has paralleled the progress in the area of electronic computers. The computer has made it possible to attack large-scale problems, which otherwise would have been impossible or economically impractical to solve.

The first article of this section focuses on the changes in retailing functions brought about by the unity of the decision sciences and the computer. The experiences of a number of different companies are discussed throughout the article giving the reader an exposure to various areas of application.

The last article of this section centers around the application of simulation, in general, and a game, in particular. Simulation is an approach to problem solving widely used in the decision sciences. The primary ingredient in any simulation experiment is the model of the system being studied.

The simulation technique allows the researcher to build relatively complex mathematical models of various marketing systems. It has been increasingly applied to a wide range of marketing areas including pricing, pre-testing field interviewing plans, physical distribution, advertising, consumer behavior, and marketing training games. Given a mathematical model of the system being studied, simulation is then used as a technique to run experiments on the model. Experiments in this sense mean that parameter values are varied for each solution run of the model. By examining the results of many such experiments, the response characteristics of the model can be observed and analyzed.

In "A Simple Marketing Game," Broadbent shows how a game might be used to train marketing managers. The game described here does not require a computer, since the computations necessary are relatively easy to perform. Games such as the one described and, in particular, more complex ones, should help participants gain a better understanding of the total marketing process.

Computers Begin to Solve the Marketing Puzzle

Electronic data processing is furnishing the technique whereby "total systems" can be developed and implemented to provide fast, precise data for marketing decisions. Already, it is giving the buyer a new role; as it develops, it will transform the role of salesman and bring many other changes in retailing.

Routinely, every evening at J. C. Penney stores across the country, a chain of events begins that reflects the changing nature not only of retailing but of every other marketing practice.

The small, punched tickets that have been taken off merchandise sold during the day are dispatched to either New York City or Los Angeles. There the tickets, coded to describe the merchandise to which they were attached until it was sold, are fed into machines that transfer the information to punched cards. From cards, the data can be put on magnetic tape or fed directly into electronic digital computers.

The computers have been programmed to know what each store should stock of so-called "staples"—men's shirts, socks, ladies' hose, lingerie, and similar goods.

Every two weeks, a computer will match a store's planned stock level against merchandise sold in that store; and, when a store needs merchandise, the computer will send out an order to buy, along with shipping instructions.

THEORY INTO FACT. A retail store doesn't have to be as large as Penney—1,700 stores and $2-billion annual sales—to use computers in this way to control its stock level and ordering procedures. A score or so of stores around the country are using some variant of the system. In fact, some local chains, such as Woodward & Lothrop in Washington and Goldblatt Bros. in Chicago, use more complex and sophisticated systems to give them daily reports of stocks and sales.

In theory, it has always been true that a store's buyers could give management a daily report of stock conditions and what was sold the preceding day—just as in theory someone in almost any business gets the pertinent marketing figures every day. But as a matter of hard, cruel fact—as opposed to theory—this just hasn't been so.

The importance of what Penney and other companies are doing is simply this: They are turning the computer with its fantastic computational speed into a new marketing tool. It may be just a big adding

machine, as is often said, but it adds at a speed that hardly gives a man a chance to have a second thought.

LEGERDEMAIN. A customer of Owens-Illinois Glass Co. had that brought home to him recently. He had ordered some containers from O-I's Libbey Products Div., changed his mind, and called to cancel the order. He couldn't cancel; the shipment was already at his plant.

This disconcerting legerdemain was possible because Owens-Illinois is one of the hundreds of U.S. companies that are managing production, finished inventory, and distribution with a mathematical system controlled by computers.

O-I's data processing headquarters in Toledo (10 computers and 100 people) is connected by wire to 100 different sales and manufacturing locations. An order comes in, the computer determines whether the product ordered is in stock, indicates where it is, and sends a release and shipping order to the warehouse, or orders to a plant to make it.

What the customer who couldn't cancel was relying on is an order-shipping-billing procedure that is passing from the industrial scene. Normally, weeks elapsed between the time a salesman took your order and you got the shipment and the invoice. At Owens-Illinois, says Thomas H. Browning, manager of data processing, electronic data processing cuts the time to no more than 35 hours.

OVER THE WIRE. Helping to reduce the order-shipping-billing time is a system tying the computer that manages inventory to a data transmission network employing any one of a group of devices known as a Data-Phone. It is an adaptation of a normal telephone and is used with what the trade calls a "terminal" (the exact designation varies according to who makes it).

Together they transmit voice and numeric signals. Instead of a salesman dropping around to fill out an order pad, orders are filed by punched card or tape over wires direct to the supplier's receiving equipment, where they are put into form to go into the computer.

At Beals, McCarthy & Rogers, Inc., a large Buffalo industrial distributor, the combination of computer-managed inventory and Data-Phone ordering in the past four years has meant a reduction of inventory of $200,000 and a sales increase of more than $2-million, according to Frederick L. Davis, the company's marketing manager. When you can know faster, and fill quicker, what your customers are ordering, you can carry a smaller stock.

It works if you're the customer, too. When you can get faster

as its charge accounts so well organized they can be used for
tive merchandising.

blatt Bros., Inc., in Chicago, one of the most sophisticated EDP
the country, even has a Data-Phone system to transmit daily
orts of tapes from its 29 stores in the area to its State Street
arters store.

RS' NEW ROLE. Management's daily report of stock condition
ly changing one hallowed role in department stores: the pre-
e of the buyer. Since retailing began, buyers have been the
figures, responsible for keeping their stores stocked with salable
adise. But because of the enormous increase in the number of
store now carries, the buyer has become too busy with a
count of stock to try to know what the customer wants and

OP-equipped stores, management knows before the buyer does
noving and what isn't. Some buyers find this disconcerting
In the words of Jack Jacobson, Goldblatt's director of elec-
ata processing, they "don't trust computers and are not ana-
inclined."

thers use the freedom EDP has given them to get out on the
ce more to see what customers are like. Jack Hanson, senior
sident of Macy's New York, says buyers now have a chance
back into the market where they were 30 years ago, to get
ices and better merchandise."

y's merchandise planning and control manager, Emerson
ees another advantage to the end of physical stock-taking
's counts stock only every quarter): "Instead of being under
ter counting stock, the sales clerk can be standing up taking
ustomers."

SE WEAPON. Putting accounts receivable—customer's charge
records—on the computer might seem to be only another
ng procedure. But it can be a merchandising weapon of profit-
cision. Macy's has more than 1.3-million charge accounts on
tape. Depending on what it is told to do, the computer will
those accounts any way the store wants them—by alphabet,
number, by size of average charge.

ong ago Macy's had its computer print out a list of all charge
rs of the Herald Square store who lived in four counties, and
em to a special after-hours sale of furniture and furnishings.
esults can't be measured precisely because nothing like it had
ne before; but compared with other special sales using radio
ct mail, the computer-based effort cost less and sold more.

delivery you can carry a smaller inventory. Davis reports it is common
now for his customers to do without general stores and tool cribs
entirely. Normally, placing an order costs $15 and up; a BM&R cus-
tomer has reduced this by 17%.

TAKING OVER. The computer is flashing with dazzling speed across
the panorama of marketing—which takes in the entire relationship
between the designer of a product, the manufacturer, seller, buyer,
and user.

Electronic data processing not only is managing inventory in nation-
wide chains of retail stores; it is telling large department stores which
customers are the best prospects for certain merchandise, is "advising"
a food company when to offer special "deals," is giving rifle-accuracy
to the calls of an apparel manufacturer's salesmen, is forecasting crop
yields for a canner, giving greater precision to the selection of media
by advertising agencies.

There are still plenty of skeptics. A computer guided by programmers unfamiliar with the specific industry so thoroughly fouled
up one heavy equipment maker's replacements parts production that
it took two years to untangle. Most retailers, particularly supermarkets,
are loath to use computers as anything but bookkeepers.

TOO LATE? Strictly marketing uses of EDP, going beyond inventory
management, are still uncommon in U.S. business. But those who have
sampled its magic are convinced the hour is late for the laggards. In a
shockingly matter-of-fact way, a department store man in an Eastern
metropolis says: "Our competition is finished; they can't compete
with us any more. They started too late with their [EDP] systems and
now we are getting so much of the business they'll never be able to
afford the system to do the job."

His competition is about as old, as well-established, and as outwardly prosperous as his own store. But in the age of the computer,
the hands on marketing's clock are at half-past eleven—30 minutes
before the witching hour. The use of EDP is about to become routine
in many marketing operations which until now have defied systemiza-
tion.

Only a year ago, Richard F. Neuschel, a director of McKinsey &
Co., wrote in Marketing and the Computer:

In none of the major functions of American business has the impact of the
computer been so lightly felt as in marketing. Yet, in none of the major
functions is its potential so great.

I. THE DATA COLLECTORS GO TO WORK

The potential of EDP in marketing is great simply because of a pervading belief that there are not enough good, hard numbers in marketing to make a fair-sized computer work up a mild sweat.

In the book, *Decision Exercises in Marketing,* Dr. Arnold Corbin, professor of marketing at New York University, Dr. George Blagowidow, and Dr. Claire Corbin, write:

To many people, marketing . . . is regarded as a business function in which most decisions are highly qualitative in nature and strongly rooted in intangible factors. . . . Hence marketing decisions are often made on the basis of hunch, guess, or intuition, rather than on a rational analysis of the measurable relationships among the principal variables involved.

John F. Stolle, a Booz, Allen & Hamilton vice-president and specialist in operations research, comments that "marketing is the most difficult area to get quantification in."

You hear that strain throughout business: EDP, to do any good, needs hard data, tons of them, needs them fast—and there is a lack of data all through the marketing stream.

The automobile industry is about the only one that really knows who buys each of its products, where the customers live, and other useful bits of information about them. In contrast, another consumer goods manufacturer refused to advertise in Indianapolis because his records show no sales there; actually, his Chicago distributor serves Indianapolis retailers, but the manufacturer's own positive information about sales stops at the distributor level.

BRIDGING THE GAP. Yet, it simply isn't true that data do not exist in marketing; they exist in probably greater quantities than in any other business function. Until now there has never been a means to collect the information or to analyze it fast enough for it to be useful.

With the "peripheral" equipment associated with the computer— input-output devices such as the Data-Phone, tape, ticket and card readers, and high-speed printers, for feeding information to the computer and getting it out—the vast gap between collection of information and its analysis has been bridged.

Archibald J. McGill, an industry manager for the Data Processing Div. of International Business Machines Corp., figures that only 5% of the solution of what he calls the distribution problem is the com-

puter, and 95% is the system. "Input-o nificance in distribution than the comput

There are computers whirring and b ness—for the accounting department. N devices, the marketing department also tion for the computer to work on.

The Machine Knows What's in Stock

While the retailer is by no means in the being done in stores around the countr how much can be done.

You can see the future best, perhaps, in Washington, D.C. There, C. Rober nance, has installed what many authorit EDP system in the country. Soon, Wo every morning will get an 81-page rep pany's nine stores, will give the prev department, by dollar amounts, and a year-to-date and the trend of sales. A re will also be available.

The key to this astonishing flood of f for which McBrier designed the keyboa and nine from top to bottom, in add salesperson can punch in everything sto every detail of every transaction is recor

Each evening the information on t scanner and "exploded" into separate accounts payable, inventory manageme functions.

MORE AND MORE. When additional year and next, Woodward & Lothrop' connection from cash register to comp computer when a clerk checks the cred even a daily report on the sales perfo selling floor.

Other big department store operatio Woodward & Lothrop is doing; Josep one step away from a voice response on puter keeps up to date a list of accou other, should not be honored. Bullo

Coast
imagin
Gol
users i
sales r
headqu

BUY
is alrea
eminer
leading
merch
items
physic
when.
At
what's
indeed
tronic
lyticall
But
floor o
vice-pr
to "ge
better
Pen
Tolle,
(Penne
the co
care of

PRE
accoun
accoun
able p
magne
break
by hou
Not
custom
invite t
The
been d
and dir

Smaller Stock, but More Stores

In food retailing, the problems are different from those in a department store, and EDP has scarcely penetrated the retail end of food distribution.

For one thing, food retailing is about the most hidebound of all businesses dealing with the consumer. For another, a food store's after-tax profit is normally less than 2% on sales—so operators look at the cost of EDP and blanch. Yet, their low rate of return is in itself a reason to get involved with EDP; it offers opportunities for cutting costs and raising profits.

In food processing and warehousing, though, EDP has cut deep, mostly by use of an IBM-developed system known as Impact Inventory Management Program and Control Technique. All major food manufacturers, as well as other companies that sell through supermarkets—Scott Paper Co. and Procter & Gamble Co., for example—have data links between sales offices, plants, distribution and shipping points, and are managing production, warehousing, and shipping by computer-programmed economics.

LATEST LINK. The newest trend is a data link between a manufacturer and a distributor for the automatic ordering of staple items.

This has barely started. Kellogg Co. warehouses are linked with warehouses of Safeway Stores, Inc., on the West Coast and of Wakefern Food Corp., a distributor for a group of New Jersey supermarkets. Pillsbury Co. has a similar hookup with Spartan Stores, Inc., a small chain in the Grand Rapids (Mich.) area—after having proved the procedure in experiments with Kroger Co. and Super Valu Stores, Inc.

Savings with this sort of system can be sensational; James Rude, Pillsbury director of information services and systems, quotes a Spartan official as saying the chain can save enough in lead time and storage to build another store.

There is no longer any question about the marketing power of a data link between supplier and customer. The clincher is what has happened in industrial selling.

Save Customers and Prepare for Systems

The data link between supplier and customer originated on the West Coast with Ducommun, Inc., an industrial distributor, about three years ago [BW, Jul. 21, '62, p. 64]. It is now in use all over the coun-

try, but has reached perhaps its most influential and precedent-setting level in the Houston area.

"Ordermation"—a very well-suited term coined by Industrial Distribution, a McGraw-Hill magazine—was just beginning to be known in Houston when J. K. Bevel, purchasing agent at Hughes Tool Co., took a worry to Jack P. Cunningham, whose Cunningham Bearing Co. does an annual volume of about $1.5-million. Bevel wanted to cut down on the time his buyers were spending in placing repetitive orders, and thought an automatic ordering system would do it.

But he was aware of one danger: When you have a number of distributors in an area, each may use a different system; so a customer dealing with more than one distributor could wind up with a roomful of incompatible systems. Bevel warned Cunningham that, as a customer, he would use one data transmission system and expect his suppliers to conform. But that way, he pointed out, a single distributor could wind up with as many as 18 different systems.

TAKING OFF. From this came the Houston Industrial Distributors Assn. With an IBM salesman coordinating the efforts—the IBM 1001 in conjunction with the Data-Phone is the common transmission device—the association now has 30 distributors "on line" to 10 customers. It will take 40 to 50 customers for the system to remain economically feasible. Cunningham hopes the idea "will really take off once the results begin coming in from the customers already participating."

Although the Houston operation is being studied by groups of industrial distributors in other parts of the country—and is bound to be a pattern—ordermation has not aroused universal enthusiasm. Distributors' reservations come mainly from unfamiliarity with EDP; some fear the system will make them lose contact with customers.

That fear is not shared by Owens-Illinois Glass Co.'s Thomas Browning. He asks: "How much does it mean, for example, if we can cut delivery time for a good customer from six days to one day? It may not mean much in one case; in another, it may mean that we have retained business that might have gone elsewhere. How do you measure that?"

GOAL. The data link alone, of course, cannot make a radical cut in delivery time. It is an essential input, though, to a procedure that goes a long way toward the goal of building a "total information system." And that is the goal at Owens-Illinois, at General Mills, Scott Paper, Procter & Gamble, Hotpoint Div. of General Electric, and other long-

time EDP users. Westinghouse Electric Corp. is one of the very few companies that already has a total system.

To such companies, inventory management, sales analysis, a rapid order-shipping-billing cycle, though rewarding in themselves, eventually become as routine as the coffee break. But they are a necessary preliminary to more complicated and challenging EDP work—getting the information to use in making the decisions that bring higher profits.

THE ULTIMATE QUESTION. There's an example of where this is heading in the Carborundum Co., which has been using computers for about 10 years and, says Group Vice-President Robert W. Lear, is "still experimenting." Carborundum, with more than 1,000 programs on computers, is ready for the next plateau, which is defined best by a series of questions Lear asked in a recent speech:

Which of our districts, salesmen, distributors, customers, markets, and products are the real profit producers? How much does it cost to make a sales call? What does it cost to process an order item? If it's four bucks, can we afford to continue accepting five-buck or even twenty-five-buck orders without some kind of a surcharge or premium?

What was the return on investment from our last promotion? Did we even try to calculate it? Which is more profitable—a direct sale, or one through a distributor? Did our last price adjustment take into consideration the distribution cost for each item, or did we just study our factory gross margins and assume an arbitrary average for everything below the line?

Those questions get to the heart of the reason for using computers in marketing, for you can't answer them without getting data. Then, for the first time in marketing, management can ask the question: "What if . . . ?"

II. MARKETING BY MATHEMATICS

Dr. Wendell R. Smith, president of the Marketing Science Institute, tells of a former business associate who constantly used computers to ask the question: "What if . . . ?" He explained to Smith:

I can ask the computer without starting a rumor. If I went to the controller and asked him what would happen to our profits if we dropped a certain product line, it would be all over the plant before lunch that we were getting ready to go out of that particular business.

Storage in a computer of mathematical models that simulate a market or that duplicate a marketing situation is perhaps the ultimate contribution EDP can make to marketing.

C. A. Swanson, manager of P&G's Data Processing Systems Dept., lists four things his company expects from EDP: savings of money, accuracy, speed, and "doing things not otherwise possible."

There is wide agreement that model-building and simulation is perhaps the most significant of those things not otherwise possible without a computer. As of now, an electronic digital computer is the only device that can handle variable on top of variable and give management a choice of alternatives while there's still time to make a decision.

CHANGING MANAGEMENT. In a masterful little book, *Mathematical Models and Marketing Management,* published by the Harvard Business School last year, Prof. Robert D. Buzzell wrote:

The model-builder offers a general, systematic approach to the analysis of management problems. To the extent that this approach is accepted and implemented, fundamental changes may take place in the practice of marketing management.

The biggest change that model-building is bringing about in marketing management is almost defamatory to mention: It is forcing management to plan, and to define its goals. To John Stolle, of Booz, Allen & Hamilton, one of the things that has slowed down the use of EDP and model-building in marketing is simply the fact that "it exposes the non-planners."

As Buzzell brings out, few developments in marketing have churned up so much skepticism and downright suspicion among marketing executives as model-building and simulation. The man who rose through the ranks from salesman to vice-president for marketing usually has little sympathy for the "fellow who's never met a payroll"— and into that category fall most of the mathematicians who are skilled at model-building and simulation.

But already models are regulating some marketing programs.

It's Better Than a Crystal Ball

Just about a year ago, Chrysler Corp.'s top management asked its planners the sort of question with which all marketing efforts must begin, for it was about the future.

"Can you tell us what the market for heavy trucks will be in 1970?"

The market analysis broke out the significant components of the heavy truck market for every year back to World War II. They determined the relationship of truck sales, by weight class, to population, national income, industrial production, and so on.

In about a month, they had a mathematical model—a simulation—of the heavy truck market. They found that of 36 variables in the model only about a dozen had substantial significance. Applying these variables in different combinations, they plotted the range for heavy truck sales in 1970.

Shortly afterward, Chrysler made an effort to merge with Mack Trucks, Inc., but was restrained by the Justice Dept.

WHAT'S NEW? There was nothing new in the Chrysler people's approach to the problem. Examination of past relationships—multiple regression analysis—is a standard statistical technique, and mathematical models are ancient.

The new thing was the speed with which the analysts were able to process an enormous amount of data and in only a month or so give management the information needed for a decision. That speed was due to the electronic computer.

LIGHT ON LAMPS. General Electric Co. (one of its divisions was the very first to put the computer to work on business problems, in 1954) has at least two models routinely assisting marketing management. One is in the Photo Lamp Dept. This division has 2,000 distributors, who customarily order in September (Christmas is the peak selling time for photo lamps) and pay in January.

The model is constructed on the assumption that each distributor has an interest problem; it takes into account 25 different types of distributors and interest rates and arrangements. It is designed to give answers to the question: What will happen if we let distributors delay payment—will they order more lamps?

At one of GE's heavy apparatus operations, a model is producing results that you'd expect only from a ouija board. This division sells on a bid basis, and the computer model is programmed to propose bids on the likelihood of what competitive bids will be. Says a GE man: "They have been amazingly accurate."

ROUTINE. Simulation with computer models also is routine at all of the big package goods companies such as P&G, Pillsbury, General Foods, Libby, McNeill & Libby, and General Mills. Usually, companies such as these test in models the presumed results of price changes and promotions and what the probabilities are of competitive responses.

Producers of consumer durables use models to forecast sales. International Minerals & Chemical Corp. has a model of its complete agricultural chemical business (65% of the company's total volume), which has a strange cycle: Its year begins in July, but no fertilizer sales are made until the following spring.

SURPRISED ADMEN. Models were at the root of all the hoopla in advertising agency circles a year or so ago about using computers to select media. The intention was to simulate a market area, then test the exposure gained by differing combinations of media buys. The problem, to a large extent, was proper data. The agencies didn't have it. Now they are collecting it—and are finding some strange byproducts.

At Leo Burnett Co., Inc., accumulation of demographic and economic data for one account showed a wide open area for a new product. At another agency, the collection of data showed that the agency's principal client should have very high on its magazine schedule one of the "confession" books. The magazine has never made a presentation to the agency—and the client is not yet ready to concede that his customers have such reading tastes.

The agencies are still far from satisfied with the data that can be obtained. The biggest hole is pointed out by Seymour Banks, a vice-president at Burnett: "What happens when people are exposed to an ad?" The agencies, meanwhile, are doing the best they can with what they have.

The top agencies all have simulation models; Norman Sondak, data processing director at J. Walter Thompson Co., says: "We continue to build models closer and closer to reality." And at several agencies, work is beginning on models that simulate test markets.

Bringing Marketing into Management

Advertising practitioners have always presumed that what they do is more art than science. So it may seem strange that all of the larger agencies now have people practicing operations research, which is presumed to be a science—the science of management. In reality it is not strange at all, for part of operations research deals with the weighing of alternatives—and the advertising man may have more numeric alternatives to deal with than anybody.

A media man with one ad and 30 media where he can spot it can be confronted with more than one billion combinations. The computer—that big adding machine—is the only way to run quickly through those combinations and weed out the obviously worthless.

What combinations remain are subject to management decision. The example used is in advertising, but it could just as well be in other marketing functions. Throughout marketing these days you are finding the computer used to weed out the obviously worthless things to do, leaving management with only a few alternatives to consider —sometimes, even, alternatives leading to a go or no-go decision:

What would be the returns now, compared to 60 days from now, on a cents-off promotion? Would it be more efficient to ship to Point A from Plant 1, or build a new distribution location to serve Point A and a potential future Point B? Would it be more economic to double our order for fast-moving baby food and receive shipments every other week rather than every week, even though it ties up more capital? Would it be more profitable to kill immediately Old Product, the life cycle of which is ending, and use the resources to push New Product harder?

TOTAL. Decisions such as these involve determining the proper allocation of a company's total resources—in other words, operations research. Only now are the numbers so necessary for operations research being assembled for the marketing function, for only now is there a way to work with them: the computer. The more EDP sophistication pervades marketing, the closer a company moves toward a total management information system, toward true operations research. Says John Stolle, the OR man at Booz, Allen & Hamilton: "When we add marketing to our collection of trophies, we will be able to build models of total business systems."

It will still be some years before marketing's scalp hangs from the belt of the OR man, but the way marketing data already are being used indicates some changes the future may bring.

III. BIG BROTHER WILL ALWAYS WATCH

What's ahead for marketing because of EDP is summed up pithily by Michael H. Halbert, technical director of the Marketing Science Institute: "A man can no longer get away with the excuse 'We've thought about it, but we don't know how to get it.' "

Today, if "it" exists in numbers, or can be assigned numerical values, "it" can be used in an EDP system. What this means, explains Robert G. Dee, vice-president, marketing, at RCA Electronic Data Processing Div., is that in the future "marketing staffs are going to get a greater amount of direction, and get a better hit value for the money spent."

One of the first groups to feel the effects of this will be the salesmen —no matter what they sell.

Bobbie Brooks, Inc., Cleveland-based manufacturer of ladies' sportswear, presents a fairly common example of what is on the way. Each week, the salesman gets a report showing the current orders and past activity of the stores in his area. This tells him where he should be spending his time.

Bobbie Brooks also prints out a report of each salesman's results by style, color, and frequency of order. "By looking at the report," says Burton L. Kamberg, vice-president, "our supervisors can tell if a man has perhaps prejudged a garment and left it in his car rather than taking it into the stores." If he's taking Thursdays off, or avoiding certain stores, that shows up, too.

"The salesman gets used to living in a goldfish bowl," Kamberg says, "and we don't stress the Big Brother side of the computer, but the helpful side. It gives the salesman an excellent selling tool. He can, for example, tell his customers what styles are going best across the country, and help them in their purchasing."

Death of a Salesman, Birth of a Consultant

The computer not only is changing the selling function: it is going to change the salesman. He will have to know far more about merchandising that he does now; he will have to know far more about his customer's business and how it fits into an EDP system—already, some food companies report that their salesmen have had to show distributors how to fit new products into the IBM Impact system, which began with food distributors. In short, the salesman will have to be more of a consultant than ever.

SALESMEN'S WEEK. Herbert M. Cleaves, senior vice-president of General Foods Corp., describes the week of a food salesman in the computer age—but it could just as well be any salesman:

Monday, the salesman calls on a major food chain, passes right by the buyer and goes to the chain's home economist to ask her support for a new recipe that will be used in a regional promotion. Next, he discusses details of the promotion's advertising program with the chain's advertising manager, and of store displays with the merchandising manager.

Tuesday, the salesman goes from store to store explaining the promotion to the managers and making suggestions for tie-ins and displays. Wednesday, he is in the chain's warehouse to learn how his company can pack a product differently to save the customer money.

Thursday, the salesman is back in the stores, to explain a new shelving arrangement his own company's market planners had worked out to solve a particular problem. The salesman spends all day Friday in his home office working with his direct sales analyst on a presentation to a chain that does not carry his products.

The week has passed, Cleaves emphasizes, and the salesman "hasn't personally made a traditional sales pitch or taken an order." The orders have been transmitted electronically, "and his supervisor knows before he does how well his various marketing efforts are being translated into orders."

EYES AND EARS. Data transmission devices cast a long shadow, blotting out the routine calls that salesmen have been accustomed to make. So in the future the salesman who now spends a good part of his time writing orders is going to have to spend more time digging out new accounts, and ideas for new products.

He will have one other, potentially enormously valuable function. He will be his company's eyes and ears, its intelligence agent, in his territory, compiling information on market growth and development, competitive efforts, and everything his company needs to know.

Lots of Products and Plans for Retailers

In perhaps no area of marketing is EDP going to make as many changes as in retailing—which lags not only in use of EDP, but frequently in modern business thinking.

In a study of department store control systems, Douglas J. Dalrymple, assistant professor of business administration at the University of California at Los Angeles, found

that a small minority of the merchandising executives . . . believed that stock turnover was an important control factor, but to most executives it was only a vague concept of secondary importance.

Yet, fast stock turnover was the weapon the discounters turned loose on department stores 15 years ago. The higher the turnover, the higher the profit on a constant amount of money used in the business.

But the computer is forcing retailers to become aware of the importance of stock turnover.

THE EDP WAY. Stock turnover is usually about four times a year for general merchandise and about twenty times for dry groceries.

There's a traditional way to turn it faster: Simply sell more without carrying a higher inventory. But it's a rare merchant who can do that.

The EDP way to get a higher turnover is by keeping such fresh data on sales that you know what's moving fast and what isn't, and by having a data hookup that will give you automatic replenishment of the fast-moving or high-profit items. In food retailing, one estimate is that a 24-hour replenishment cycle will reduce inventory by 30%, without creating out-of-stock situations that hurt sales.

In general merchandising, Seymour Helfant, head of the Small Stores Div. of the National Retail Merchants Assn., says he has reports of stores using EDP that lower their inventory by 25% and increase profits by 25%. And a specialty store that formerly turned its stock six times a year has added one full turn.

Analysis of information handled by a store's EDP system can also guide store executives in when, what, and how to promote.

BIG AND SMALL. The benefits of EDP are not reserved for the big stores and chains. "Any retailer, regardless of size, will be able to be on-line to a big processing center," says James Hotchkiss, assistant director of product planning of National Cash Register Co., which probably has more experience than any other computer manufacturer with the problems of small retailers. NCR, of course, has data processing centers throughout the country [BW, Aug. 8, '64, p. 66], as do GE, IBM, and other computer manufacturers. NRMA is sponsoring a cooperative processing center for small retailers.

An example of what a data processing center can do for small retailers is found at Santoro Management Consultants, Inc., in Houston. Santoro has 60 clients—whose volumes range from $50,000 to $500,000—for whom it provides a full package: budgets, advertising, merchandising, sales analysis and projection, inventory records. Says Mrs. Daisy Strother, of Fort Worth: "The service took the butterflies out of my stomach. We know which department is making money . . . our buying is controlled, dead merchandise eliminated and we have reorder money."

At present, most of the small stores mail or deliver tapes to the processing centers. But when Hotchkiss says small stores can be "on-line," he means a direct data link to some establishment using a computer. Once such a link is created, it will drive right through a barrier that (excepting, again, only the automobile business) still separates a manufacturer from sure knowledge of what's happening on the retail level.

A few months ago, B. S. Durant, president of RCA Sales Corp., did

a little dreaming for a group of marketing executives. RCA, in common with other consumer electronics producers, is always in doubt as to how much of its product is in distributors' warehouses and how much is moving out of retailers' doors.

Durant began by conceding that a small retailer will probably never be able to afford a computer, "but he could afford a low-cost transactor of some type. . . . Before the dealer goes home at night, he would put the transactor device on standby. Somewhere along about a quarter after two, a central computer would interrogate the transactor and take from it the data covering the dealer's daily business transactions." Durant offered a new, and provocative thought: The independent distributor might have that central computer and be the retailer's data processing center.

If the distributor's computer could interrogate the retailer's transactor, then each night the manufacturer's computer could interrogate the distributor's computer. The next morning, the manufacturer's executives would have—for the first time in their experience—actual records of their product sales at retail the day before.

GLEAMING VISTAS. This opens vistas that gleam so brightly that any marketing man has to shield his eyes to avoid snow blindness. New product performance could be gauged day-by-day and promotion money deployed for maximum effectiveness. A product that isn't going to make it could be withdrawn from the market before it hurt either profits or reputation significantly. When you know precisely what is selling where, and when, you can identify your customers, plan future promotions intelligently, simulate all sorts of situations.

You would even know enough to advertise in Indianapolis.

A Simple Marketing Game[1]

Simon Broadbent

Business games help to train management, simulate complex competitive situations, and are even used in personnel selection. Good general descriptions have recently been published (McRaith and Goeldner, 1962; Eilon, 1963). Most games cover general company activities, including production and finance as well as marketing. Perhaps because they attempt to cover so much, the realism of their marketing problems is sometimes less than striking. The purpose of this paper is to describe and discuss a particular type of game which, while simple, can be adequately realistic.

Why bother to make a game a more realistic and accurate model? To make it indistinguishable from real life is certainly impossible. And a game which claims to be realistic, but is not, could be dangerously misleading. Operating rules which are satisfactory in the game might be transferred uncritically to the board room; a good performance in the game might become the only criterion used in management selection. Such outcomes would certainly be disasters.

Nevertheless, I think a marketing game should be as realistic as it is economic to make it. A player who does badly in the game should always feel that the fault is his, not that of the game's designer. Every player should finish with a better understanding of the critical factors in his own company's operation. And as with all true education, the game should leave behind an attitude of inquiry and analysis, not a ready-made system learned by rote.

Reprinted with permission from the *Journal of Advertising Research,* vol. 4, no. 4 (December, 1964), pp. 29–33. © Advertising Research Foundation, Inc. (1964).

[1] I would like to acknowledge the permission of Courtaulds Ltd., to give some details of this game, and to thank Mr. G. F. Nuttall for the encouragement and advice I have received in preparing marketing games and this paper.

MODEL

The game described here is simple in that it does not use a computer. The mathematical model has been chosen to combine realism with rapid calculation. Two clerks can work out a year's results for six companies in five to ten minutes. Versions of this game have been used in training courses in Great Britain for middle management executives.

The model used is realistic in that its structure and parameters can be chosen to reproduce the essential nature of most given markets. If the market is particularly sensitive to price, or consumer advertising, or product quality, or any other factor, then the model is flexible enough to reproduce these factors.

Basically, the model is the division of a period's overall sales into several independent parts. One part is affected only by brand loyalty, another by competitors' promotions, and so on. Each part is further divided among the competing companies in some relation to the resources each has allocated to the relevant factor. The companies know only the total sales they have achieved, not the way in which these are made up. An example will help to make this clear. We start with a stripped-down version of the game. Later the optional extras can be added.

A Simple Example

In this example the companies (teams) sell a single product in a single static market. Each year, in this simplified version, the companies make only two decisions: the size of the advertising budget and the selling price.

Here is how each company's sales are determined. Suppose that three companies sell a total of 5,000 units of a product each year. Further suppose that only three factors determine each company's market share, as set out in Table 1.

Thus we suppose that three-fifths of all sales (or 3,000 units) are determined by consumers' loyalty, by their saying "we'll buy what we bought last year." The choice of three-fifths (and of every other parameter in the model) is made so that the behavior of the model is similar to that of the market simulated.

One-fifth of the sales are influenced by advertising. In this particular example, advertising does not increase the total market, since total sales are fixed at 5,000 units.

TABLE 1   Effect of Three Factors on Sales

SALES FACTORS	SALES ACCOUNTED FOR BY FACTOR	RULES FOR ALLOCATING AMONG FIRMS
Brand loyalty	3,000	Allocate in same proportion as previous year's total shares
Advertising	1,000	Allocate in same proportion as this year's advertising shares
Price	1,000	Allocate in inverse proportion to price ranking

One-fifth of the sales are determined by the relative prices set by each company, The lowest price gets the largest share of the 1,000 units allotted by this factor, the next price half as much, and so on. Tied prices win equal shares. The size of the shares depends on the number of different prices: the highest-priced company gets none of this part of the total sales.

TABLE 2   Advertising and Price Decisions

COMPANY	ADVERTISING BUDGETS		PRICE
	UNITS	%	
A	50	25	3¢ off
B	90	45	1¢ off
C	60	30	standard
	200	100	

Suppose the companies had equal shares of the market in Year 1, and that they make the advertising and price decisions shown in Table 2. Then by following the rules set out above we determine the companies' sales for Year 2, as shown in Table 3.

TABLE 3   Sales Determined by Three Factors

COMPANY	LOYALTY	ADVERTISING	PRICE	TOTAL SALES IN YEAR 2
A	1,000	250	667	1,917
B	1,000	450	633	1,783
C	1,000	300	—	1,300
	3,000	1,000	1,000	5,000

Argument behind the Model

This crude version of the game may seem far from realistic. The number of influences on sales is small, and they are assumed to act linearly and be additive. How serious are these criticisms?

The number of variables was deliberately restricted in this example; the additions mentioned below can be handled easily. For exposition only, it is convenient to have just three factors.

The linear assumption is in relation to *share* of advertising rather than to actual advertising expenditures. This not only tallies with some actual cases and with common sense, but contains a built-in method of allowing for saturation or diminishing response. Suppose my competitors are spending 150 units, and I am considering spending 50, 100, or 150 units. My share of total advertising does not increase linearly with these amounts, but would be 25 percent (50/200), 40 percent (100/250), or 50 percent (150/300) respectively.

Criticism of the independence or additive assumption has more justification. It is likely that in real situations a price reduction *with* increased advertising has more effect than the sum of each separately. This could be built into the model by adding a term for interaction. The calculation of market shares would, however, then lose the simplicity which makes this game so easy and inexpensive to run.

But perhaps the most interesting comment on this model is that it is exactly equivalent to some of the regression models already in use. To see this, we translate the game just described into the more usual mathematical formulation. Write $m(1)$ for company's market share in Year 1, $a(2)$ for its advertising share in Year 2, and $p(2)$ for its price share (i.e., inverse to price rank) in Year 2. Then the company's market share in Year 2 is given by

$$m(2) = 0.6\,m(1) + 0.2\,a(2) + 0.2\,p(2)$$

The coefficients (0.6, etc.) must add to one, as we can see by adding up the market shares in Year 2 for all the companies. Since these as well as each individual share $m(1)$, $a(2)$, and $p(2)$ add to one (or 100 percent), so must the coefficients.

To consider a more general case, write these coefficients c, d, and e, and suppose also that other terms besides these enter into the division of the market. Our general equation is then

$$m(2) = cm(1) + da(2) + ep(2) + \cdots$$

Since the coefficients must add to one, we can substitute for $cm(1)$ in this equation

$$(1 - d - e - \cdots) \, m(1) = cm(1).$$

We then rewrite the equation, in which $c \, [m(1) - m(1)]$ is cancelled out:

$$[m(2) - m(1)] = d \, [a(2) - m(1)] + e \, [p(2) - m(1)] + \cdots$$

This form has been published before (see Bradford, 1960; Longton and Warner, 1962, who call $a(2) - m(1)$ the dynamic difference). It states that the change in market share from Year 1 to Year 2 is linearly dependent on expressions like $a(2) - m(1)$, i.e., the amount by which advertising share is above or below market share.

We can now also see how the all-important parameters or elasticities d, e, etc., can be estimated. After five or six periods have passed, a company can calculate the regression of its changes in market share on expressions like $a(2) - m(1)$. A company which knows the coefficients in this regression (these estimate the effects of the required parameters) is better able to allocate its resources.

The game is not completely "solved" even when the parameters are accurately estimated. For a company still has to guess how its competitors will react to tactical changes. A price cut may seem a good short-term move, but what would be its long-term effect? Such considerations make the choice of strategies enter the area of mathematical game theory, which, even for a comparatively simple situation as described, as yet gives us little guidance.

Who Wins the Game?

Agreeing on what criterion a company must strive to satisfy is just as important as building an appropriate model. The game may be run as a competition or by some device (such as starting the companies in different situations) in which straight comparisons may be impossible. But in either case the participants must be set a target.

Undoubtedly profit should be made the criterion. But this leaves the question of how to define profit. If each company starts with fixed and equal capital, then overall profit after a reasonable length of time (five years or more) seems a sensible definition. But if companies start from different points, or if money may be borrowed, then the cumulative rate of return on outlay seems a better definition.

Additions and Refinements

We may refine and add as much as we please to the basic model. For each alteration we should ask, "Does this increase clerks' computation time so much that it exceeds the time teams can usefully spend in discussion while waiting for the year's results?," and "Does this add a useful lesson for the players?" Here are the additions and refinements we have found useful:

1. Market. The market may be split into two or more regions. Sales volume in each region may be predetermined, or may vary with the total amount of advertising. The total market size may therefore grow or, in the case of a slump or obsolete product, shrink. In each case the volume of sales determined by the various factors must be listed before calculations by the clerks can begin. Having two or more regions makes the allocation problems more interesting. The information that can be extracted from market research (see below) becomes more valuable. It would also be possible to have two or more products to further complicate the allocation and research problems.

2. Product Quality. By allocating part of their budgets to research and development, companies may increase their chances of "discovering" an improved product. A sales allocation determined by product quality may be made in the same way as for price, or price and quality may be combined as a single factor. Discovery of improved products can easily be regulated by preparing an appropriate deterministic or random number table.

3. Promotion. Rather than a single advertising budget decision, the companies may have to allocate a promotion budget over several alternatives—newspapers, TV, other media, point of purchase, and so on. The effectiveness of each factor must be predetermined; the weighted total of a company's allocation replaces the advertising figure in the simple example.

With care, realism may be increased here without great additional complexity. For example, advertisement production expenditure may be required for each medium, but disregarded in calculating market shares. Other "entry-fee" models may be used. Salesmen may require training and may resign (with random frequency). Space and time charges may be varied from time to time. But if the expenditure is suitably coded, the calculations remain simple.

4. Accounting, Production Planning, Market Research. The following additions do not change the model, and are unimportant as far as

the clerks allocating sales are concerned. But they enhance both the realism of the game and the lessons to be drawn from it.

Since profits should be the criterion of company performance and the effect of price on sales must be gauged, an accounting procedure should be drawn up. This business could become interesting, but for a non-computer game is time consuming. Taxation, calling-in accounts early, divided payments could all be elaborated. But in a marketing game, this should be as simple as possible.

Production and production line planning could also be elaborated, but again simplicity is desirable. At the most, sales forecasting may be required, with penalties (lost sales if out of stock; higher interest and warehousing charges if overstocked) for error in forecasting.

Since one lesson of the game should be the intelligent use of market information, companies should be allowed to buy market research data. This may be on actual or potential sales, by region. They should also be able to acquire analyses of competitors' promotion expenditures. But facts generally known, such as selling prices, retail terms, etc., should be generally announced.

Courtaulds Game

As a relatively simple example, here is a game designed for a management development course at Courtaulds Ltd. The course was attended by middle-level executives, most of whom were engaged on the technical side of the firm's activities. The course was aimed at illustrating the interrelation of all aspects of the company's operations, especially areas with which the executives were not normally concerned. The executives generally agreed that the game met these objectives. One player said: "This game claimed involvement by its realism. Decisions by the teams were speedily reflected in results. Not only did it teach a great deal about various aspects of marketing and their effect on profits, but I found the greatest contribution was the demonstration of the overriding effect of competition (from other teams). The game demonstrated fully that marketing is not the making of logical decisions in a static environment, but trying to make logical decisions in a fast-moving competitive environment."

Table 4 is the Decision Form which Company C (of six companies) completed in "1965," being allowed 20 minutes to do so.

The decisions to be made were:

1. Selling price. Any multiple of two shillings below or above a manufacturers' list or ex-works price of three pounds per unit.

2. Salesmen. Salesmen took a year to train, stayed with a company

**TABLE 4   Decision Form: Courtaulds Game
Company C, Year 1965**

	NORTH	SOUTH	COST	COST INCLUDES THESE EXTRAS
Salesmen in field	12	6	£ 36,000	(2 salesmen in training)
TV advertising units	30	20	106,000	(£6,000 for production)
Newspaper advertising units	25	25	104,000	(£4,000 for production)
			5,000	(Market research)
Total			£251,000	

10 years on the average (they resigned with Poissonian frequency), could be dismissed on a year's notice, and cost £2,000 per year. They could be allotted to either of two regions.

3. TV advertising. A unit of TV time cost £2,000, and £6,000 production charges were to be paid if any TV was used.

4. Newspaper advertising. A unit of newspaper space also cost £2,000, but the production charges were £4,000. Unlike TV, the same number of units had to be bought in each region.

5. Research. Data could be bought on sales breakdowns by region and by company for the previous year, and on competitors' advertising and promotional expenditures.

From the decision forms for all six companies, two clerks were able to allocate sales and salesmen's resignations in less than ten minutes. The same clerks provided the research data. Companies worked out their accounts, on a basis not described in detail here, but which gave cumulative profit as a percent of cumulative outlay. It was the objective to maximize this figure.

CONCLUSIONS

Some lessons learned by players in a marketing game are specific. For example, that being slow to see the effect of price cuts leads to disastrously low turnover, that the market leader can temporarily earn very high profits despite high prices, that for a particular market TV and newspapers have such-and-such sales effectiveness, and that when consumer loyalty is high it pays to win market share as quickly as pos-

sible, and so on. Players likely should apply such deductions from the game to real life, but should be discouraged from assuming they always hold true.

More valuable are the general lessons. For example, that companies should deliberately experiment to estimate the effectiveness of different courses of action; that market research data must be obtained if informed estimates are to be made; that policies on profit should determine sales aims, promotion budgets, etc., and not vice versa; that large market shares are not necessarily profitable; and that large profits are not necessarily a good return on outlay.

REFERENCES

Bradford, G. A. "What General Electric Is Doing to Evaluate the Effect on Sales of Its Industrial and Consumer Advertising." *Supplement to Volume 7 of Association of National Advertisers' Advertising Management Guidebook Series,* 1960.

Elion, Samuel. "Management Games." *Operational Research Quarterly,* vol. 14, no. 2, June 1963, pp. 137–149.

McRaith, J. F., and Charles R. Goeldner. "A Survey of Marketing Games." *Journal of Marketing,* vol. 26, no. 3, July 1962, pp. 69–72.

Longton, Peter A., and Bernard T. Warner. "A Mathematical Model for Marketing." *Metra,* vol. 1, no. 3, September 1962, pp. 297–310.

Index